Sweden

ACS | COBHAM
INTERNATIONAL SCHOOL

Please return or renew this book on or
before the last date stamped below

Becky Ohlsen
Cristian Bonetto

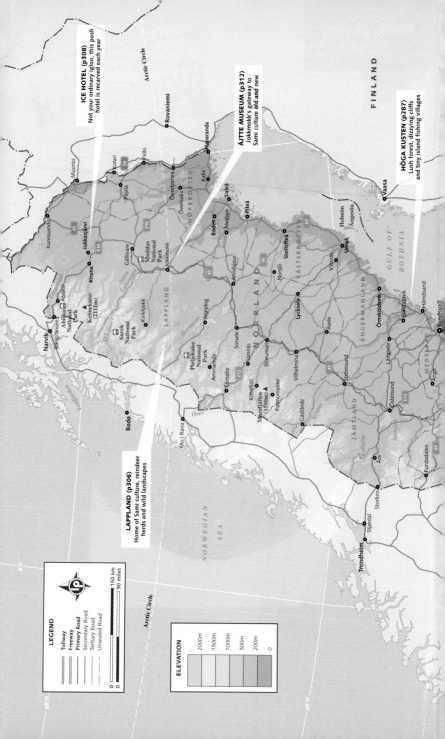

ICE HOTEL (p308)
Not your ordinary igloo, this posh hotel is recarved each year

ÁJTTE MUSEUM (p312)
Jokkmokk's gateway to Sami culture old and new

HÖGA KUSTEN (p287)
Lush forest, dizzying cliffs and tiny island fishing villages

LAPPLAND (p306)
Home of Sami culture, reindeer herds and wild landscapes

FINLAND

NORWEGIAN SEA

GULF OF BOTHNIA

NORRBOTTEN

VÄSTERBOTTEN

ANGERMANLAND

JÄMTLAND

MEDELPAD

LAPPLAND

NORRLAND

Arctic Circle

66°N

64°N

LEGEND
Tollway
Freeway
Primary Road
Secondary Road
Tertiary Road
Unsealed Road

0   150 km
0   90 miles

ELEVATION
2000m
1500m
1000m
500m
200m
0

Rovaniemi
Muonio
Kolari
Pajala
Pello
Övertorneå
Överkalix
Haparanda
Kalix
Luleå
Piteå
Boden
Älvsbyn
Jokkmokk
Muddus National Park
Gällivare
Kiruna
Jukkasjärvi
Karesuando
Abisko National Park
Abisko National Park
Björkliden
Narvik
Kebnekaise (2111m)
Sarek National Park
Kvikkjokk
Padjelanta National Park
Arjeplog
Arvidsjaur
Norsjö
Skellefteå
Byske
Vännäs
Umeå
Holmön
Angesön
Vaasa
Lycksele
Åsele
Örnsköldsvik
Gideåbacka
Härnösand
Sundsvall
Ånge
Stöde
Örnsköldsvik
Ånge
Östersund
Krokom
Ström
Storlien
Storuman
Sorsele
Ammarnäs
Tärnaby
Kittelfjäll
Marsfjället (1590m)
Fatmomakke
Gäddede
Vilhelmina
Dorotea
Strömsund
Åre
Storlien
Funäsdalen
Stjørdal
Trondheim
Mo i Rana
Bodø

Arctic Circle

E8
E10
E10
E10
E45
E45
E4
E4
E12
E14
E14
E45
E75
45
95

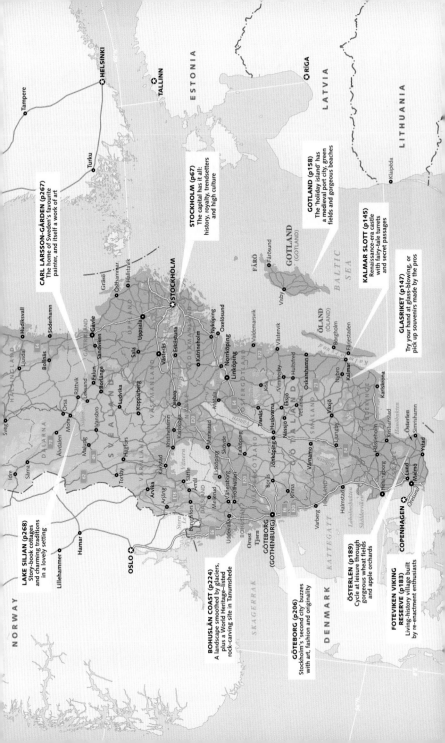

CARL LARSSON-GÅRDEN (p267)
The home of Sweden's favourite painter, and itself a work of art

STOCKHOLM (p67)
The capital has it all: history, royalty, trendsetters and high culture

GOTLAND (p158)
The 'holiday island' has a medieval port city, green fields and gorgeous beaches

KALMAR SLOTT (p145)
Renaissance-era castle with fairy-tale turrets and secret passages

GLASRIKET (p147)
Try your hand at glass-blowing, or pick up souvenirs made by the pros

LAKE SILJAN (p268)
Story-book cottages and charming traditions in a lovely setting

BOHUSLÄN COAST (p224)
A landscape smoothed by glaciers, plus a World Heritage–listed rock-carving site in Tanumshede

GÖTEBORG (p206)
Stockholm's 'second city' buzzes with art, fashion and originality

ÖSTERLEN (p189)
Cycle at leisure through gorgeous wheat fields and apple orchards

FOTEVIKEN VIKING RESERVE (p183)
Living-history village built by re-enactment enthusiasts

On the Road

BECKY OHLSEN
Coordinating Author

I took this photo of my trusty steed while researching the itineraries. I'd decided to cycle around Gotland (p158), despite not having ridden a bike in decades. I recommend the trip wholeheartedly, even for cycling newbies. I camped out on beaches along the way, enjoying the late summer sunsets and incredible evening light.

CRISTIAN BONETTO All good road trips lead to Djurgården (p78), or so they should. Back in Stockholm after seven weeks of cross-country research, the best spot to do absolutely nothing is this rambling garden island, home to one of Europe's finest forests of giant oaks and Scandinavia's densest population of tawny owls.

For author biographies see p352.

Sweden Highlights

Vibrant cities where cutting-edge design, ground-breaking new restaurants and flash clubs will thrill you; vast landscapes of wilderness where dense forests, clear lakes and picturesque wooden cottages will delight you; gripping Norse legends and rich Sami culture will fascinate you – Sweden's highlights are many and varied. Here's what our readers, staff and authors love most about this multifaceted country.

ANDERS BLOMQVIST

1 MIDSUMMER'S DAY

Midsommardag (p19) is *the* festival of the year and there's much revelry to be found all over Sweden: singing, dancing, beer-drinking, strawberries and cream, *snaps,* pickled herring and, of course, folk costumes and the traditional Midsummer pole.

Sally Schafer, Lonely Planet staff, London

HOLG

② STOCKHOLM'S ARCHIPELAGO

Seeming to go on forever, Stockholm's archipelago (p119) is a geographic wonder. Its 24,000 islands and islets stretch 80km east of the city into the Baltic Sea. It is very special to take a ferry on a balmy July evening, wending its way through all the small leisure boats, to one of the beautiful island restaurants and there try all – maybe not all! – the flavours of *aquavit* with your appetiser of pickled or smoked fish. In this one experience you feel very close to the Swedish love of the sea and the outdoor life, and their pride in the beauty of their country.

Ian Christie, traveller, UK

ANDERS BL

③ DJURGÅRDEN

This is the island that time forgot in the middle of Stockholm, where you can visit Sweden as it was through the centuries at the Skansen museum (p78); from Royal Game Park to farms and shops that take you back hundreds of years, there are stunningly beautiful grounds where children can cut timber with the woodcutter and help run the local hardware store. History has never been so alive!

Saras Seth, Lonely Planet staff, London

SLEEPING ON THE AF CHAPMAN SHIP

It might be a bit cramped, but the floating youth hostel that is the *af Chapman* (p90) is probably the most atmospheric place to sleep in Stockholm. I managed to bag the captain's cabin and, squeezed into my bunk, had a fantastic view across the harbour to Gamla Stan and the Royal Palace – all for the price of a meal.

Clifton Wilkinson, Lonely Planet staff, London

4

CHRISTER FREDRIKSSON

SOFO DISTRICT, SÖDERMALM, STOCKHOLM

Södermalm (p81) remains Stockholm's hippest 'hood and the streets south of Folkungagatan (dubbed 'SoFo') are its heart and soul. Home to the retro-chic brigade, it's the place for emerging local fashion, trippy op-shop finds, and buzzing bars and restaurants. The last Thursday of the month is SoFo Night, when many shops open till late and in-store gigs range from DJ sets to fashion shows.

Cristian Bonetto, Lonely Planet author

5

CHRISTIAN ÅSLUND

GRAEME CORNWA

6 FÅRÖ

There's probably no better location on Earth to foster your inner recluse than Fårö (p165) in the months after summer. Creaking pine forests, windswept sheep houses and a paucity of people inspire reflection; the limestone raukar that populate the coast make it monumental. Fine-tune your senses and feel contentedly cast adrift on this island off an island in the middle of the Baltic Sea. It's re-nowned for being Ingmar Bergman's favourite haunt; his spirit may come to linger here still.

Debra Herrmann, Lonely Planet staff, Melbourne

ANDERS BLOM

7 BOHUSLÄN COAST

The Bohuslän Coast (p224) is a minimalist marvel, stretching from north of Göteborg to the Norwe-gian border. Wooden villages cling to spartan granite islands, themselves rising out of the sea like giant whalebacks. Inland, the palate changes from blue and grey to chocolate and green, with velvety valleys framed by chiselled cliffs and splashes of pine.

Cristian Bonetto, Lonely Planet author

Like a kibbutz crossed with a medieval role-playing convention, Vikingareservatet vid Foteviken (p183) is as absorbing as it is eccentric. Just south of Malmö, this Viking reserve is where modern folk ditch mod-cons to eat, work and play like the ancient Norse. Skinned foxes hang from wooden huts, young men duel in Viking garb and the scent of smoke lingers in the air. Despite the novelty factor, it is a real community, so always ask before taking shots of the locals; after all, who dares to irk a Viking?

Cristian Bonetto, Lonely Planet author

8

ANDERS BLOMQVIST

JASON LINDSEY

9 ICE HOTEL & THE AURORA BOREALIS

Although much vaunted, a stay at Jukkasjärvi's Ice Hotel (p308) in the very depths of winter did not appeal until I found out that instead of sleeping in an igloo you can lay your head down in a cosy, heated wooden cabin. Even better, the snug cabins have skylights through which we were lucky enough to view the aurora borealis one night – an unforgettable, magical experience and certainly my Sweden highlight.

Fiona Buchan, Lonely Planet staff, London

JOHN NORMA

10 DOGSLEDDING IN LAPPLAND

A dogsled excursion (p306) has to be the only way to experience Lappland – the exhilaration of the ride itself, the relationships you build with the incredible dogs and the stunning scenery experienced without the racket of a snowmobile. Magic.

Kate Davie, traveller, UK

CRAYFISH PARTY

As summer draws to a close but evenings are still (sometimes) balmy Swedes celebrate with crayfish parties (see p47) – if you're lucky enough to be invited to one, here's what to expect: tradition dictates that the party takes place outdoors, coloured lanterns are strung round the table, guests wear bibs and paper hats, and the crayfish is enjoyed cold with beer and/or *snaps*.

Åsa Sonden, traveller, Sweden

CHRISTIAN ASLUND

11

ABISKO NATIONAL PARK

Anyone even remotely interested in hiking will find this national park (p309) hard to resist. The same goes for landscape photographers, dogsled fans, students of Sami culture and travellers looking to leave all evidence of city life behind. There's very little in this bleak, arid territory to interfere with your view of Lapporten, the swaybacked mountain silhouette that looks like a gateway into Lappland. You can walk to it if you want, or better yet climb up to an ancient Sami sacrificial site for a panoramic view of the whole valley. Even those who are *really* on holiday have an option: a chairlift will carry you up a steep hill near the hostel for views of the midnight sun.

Becky Ohlsen, Lonely Planet author

MEDIACOLOR'S/ALAMY

12

CHRISTER FREDRIK

13 GASTRONOMIC SWEDEN

Having spent a wonderful week driving through the stunning Swedish scenery, it might be slightly controversial but the highlight of my stay was the food! Going there with no preconceptions of a culinary heritage (p45) I was wowed by local meats and fishes, simply done with a tasty twist and always packed with flavours. Pearl barley sausages, reindeer salad and the more widely known meatballs or gravadlax were particularly good, but you still couldn't beat pickled herring served in three ways with local cheese and fresh new potatoes.

James Clifton, traveller, UK

LUCKY LOOK/A

14 INLANDSBANAN HISTORIC TRAIN LINE

Travelling by train is by far the best way to enjoy any country's scenery and the Inland Railway (p278), running through the heart of Sweden, offers some particularly spectacular views. Our highlights along the way included Lake Siljan where we stopped off for a peaceful paddle in a canoe (a big contrast we imagine to the moment it was created by a meteorite 350 million years ago) and the wildlife reserve at Orsa, where bears, lynxes, wolves, wolverines, elk and beavers all roam.

Jo Potts, Lonely Planet staff, London

Handwritten: 7/3/11   914 .85 OHL

Contents

14 CONTENTS

Regional Map Contents

Lappland &
the Far North
p297

Northern Sweden
p277

Central
Sweden
p241

Stockholm
pp70-1

Southwest
Sweden
p205

Southeast
Sweden
p127

Southern
Sweden
p169

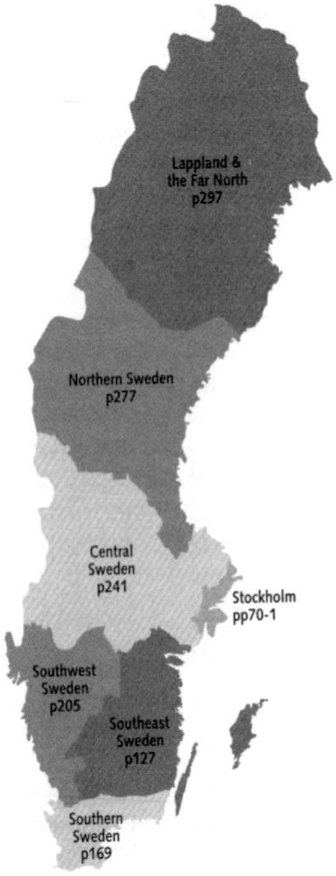

Destination Sweden

There's something almost otherworldly about Sweden – and we mean that in the most flattering way possible. It's just a bit skewed, a bit removed from the norm, and one gets the sense that Sweden likes being that way. For travellers, too, it's a delight to visit somewhere that, while it may not *look* terribly outlandish, still feels distinctly and wonderfully foreign.

This sense of strangeness is partly a result of Sweden's out-there position on the map. But there's more at work than geographical isolation. Sweden's literature and cinema favour a weighty, Gothic sense of drama blended with gallows humor and stark aesthetics – all of which, in some form, at some point, will confront the visitor. For instance, it's hard not to see something faintly hilarious, yet also quite lonely and sad, in the image of a single reindeer wandering crookedly along an all-but-abandoned Lappland highway in the murk of a winter afternoon. There's also something poignant about a capital city that's so far from the middle of anything, yet is so determined to be the centre of everything. Regardless of how it presents itself, the visitor will notice a particular tone in Sweden that hints at many things: depth of feeling, awareness of doom, absence of sentimentality, strength of principle, avoidance of conflict, a somber conviction that certain things simply matter. Of course, such intangibles won't likely make it into your post-trip slide show, but nevertheless the mysterious Swedish sensibility enhances every aspect of a traveller's experience.

It's an exciting time to visit Sweden, too – the small country with its long history of consistent moderation just happens to be in the middle of a whirlwind of change. Swedish music, fashion, film, art and food couldn't be more vibrant, and it's even shaking things up in the often rather stolid world of politics. Don't miss the chance to get in while it's hot.

FAST FACTS

Population: 9.1 million

GDP (2007 estimate): US$300.2 billion; per capita US$41,100

Inflation: 0.9%

Unemployment: 2.5%

Labour force (2008 estimate): 4.4 million

Literacy rate: 99%

Getting Started

Travel in Sweden is extremely easy, and a bit of advance planning can help smooth over any rough patches. Historically an expensive place to travel, it's now more or less in line with the UK in terms of cost. Still, booking ahead for accommodation and transport within the country will help save money, and look into discount travel cards for the major cities before you leave (see p322). Once you arrive, you will find the cities easy to get around and well serviced by public transport, with almost everywhere wheelchair-accessible.

WHEN TO GO

See Climate Charts (p320) for more information.

Despite its north European location, Sweden isn't as cold as you might expect. The south has a year-round temperate climate and summer can be quite warm in the north. Sweden is at its best during summer and autumn (late May to September), but hikers and campers may wish to avoid the peak of the mosquito season (June and July). Due to the country's high latitude, daylight hours are long in summer. Malmö gets 17½ hours of daylight at midsummer, and Sundsvall has constant light during the second half of June, but you have to travel north of the Arctic Circle to experience the true 'midnight sun': in Kiruna, the sun remains above the horizon for 45 days (31 May to 14 July).

Swedes are big on holidays, and even Stockholm shuts down for two or three days around Christmas and Midsummer, so plan accordingly. Most Swedes take their holidays from late June to mid-August, so hostels are crowded, but this is also when most hotels offer discounts of up to 50%. Loners and misanthropes should travel between seasons, in May or early June, when everything is closed and no one's about.

Travel in winter is somewhat restricted and requires some planning as well as serious winter clothing, but there are good opportunities for activities like skiing, dogsledding and snowmobiling. The big cities are in full swing all year, but the smaller towns almost go into hibernation when the temperatures begin to drop. The notable exceptions are the popular ski resort towns like Åre and Jukkasjärvi (home to the Ice Hotel).

COSTS & MONEY

HOW MUCH?

0.7L bottle of Swedish *brännvin* (vodka) Skr225

Coffee and saffron pancake Skr45

Souvenir *Dalahäst* (wooden horse) Skr70-3000

Cinema ticket Skr90

Nightclub admission Skr150

Sweden has a very good standard of living, which means the travel experience is generally high quality but doesn't come cheap. Careful planning can help reduce costs.

During the low-price summer period (June to August), if you stay in a mid-range hotel (which usually includes a huge buffet breakfast), eat a daily special for lunch and have an evening meal at a moderately priced restaurant, you can expect to spend Skr1000 per person per day if you're doubling up, and Skr1500 if you're travelling alone. Staying in hostels, making your own breakfast, eating the daily special for lunch, and picking up supermarket items for dinner will probably cost you Skr450 per day. The cheapest way to visit Sweden is to camp in the woods for free, eat supermarket food, hitchhike or cycle to get around, and visit only the attractions that have free admission – this will cost less than Skr200 per day, depending on your supermarket choices. If you stay in commercial camping grounds and prepare your own meals you can squeak by on around Skr300 per person per day. If there are a few of you, sharing car rental for a weekend in order to see some out-of-the-way places is worth considering (some petrol stations offer small cars for as little as Skr300 per day). Self-service pumps that take banknotes or credit cards are slightly cheaper, though many won't accept foreign credit cards without a PIN code.

DON'T LEAVE HOME WITHOUT...

- Your ID, passport and visa (if applicable)
- Industrial-strength mosquito repellent in summer
- Good walking shoes
- Layers of warm clothing, just in case
- A swimsuit – again, just in case
- Sunglasses – when the sun does shine, it's bright
- A map of Stockholm's tunnelbana (metro)
- A taste for pickled fish
- A fast-acting liver for *snaps* (Swedish liquor)

TRAVELLING RESPONSIBLY

Sweden makes it easy to be a responsible traveller: recycling, for example, is practically effortless, as bins and sorting instructions are everywhere, from inside hotel rooms to near highway rest stops. There's a high level of general environmental consciousness in the country. Two organisations that set standards for labelling products as ecologically sound are the food-focused **KRAV** (www.krav.se), a member of the International Federation of Organic Agriculture Movements, and **Swan** (www.svanen.nu), which has a wider scope and certifies entire hotels and hostels.

Aside from environmental concerns, one of Sweden's biggest challenges is protecting the cultural heritage of the Sami people. The two issues are closely linked: the harnessing of rivers for hydroelectric power can have massive (negative) impact on what has historically been Sami territory, whether by flooding reindeer feeding grounds or by diverting water and drying up river valleys.

In general, the mining, forestry and space industries have wreaked havoc on Sami homelands. Travellers interested in learning more and experiencing Sami culture are encouraged to look for the 'Naturens Bäst' logo, which indicates that an excursion or organisation has been approved by **Svenska Ekoturismföreningen** (www.ekoturism.org, in Swedish), the country's first ecotourism regulating body.

TRAVEL LITERATURE

Good books on travelling or living in Sweden are few and far between. Mary Wollstonecraft's *A Short Residence in Sweden, Norway and Denmark* records the pioneering feminist author's journey to Scandinavia in 1795 in search of happiness. It's a classic of early English Romanticism and well worth a read.

The always hilarious Bill Bryson had an entertainingly difficult time of it in Sweden, as described in two chapters of his European travel book *Neither Here Nor There*.

There are also a couple of good views of Sweden from within, including Selma Lagerlöf's *The Wonderful Adventures of Nils*. This creative account of the country's history and geography is still taught in Swedish classrooms.

Get a taste of a thematic journey in the remotest parts of northern Sweden in Torgny Lindgren's wonderful novel *Hash*. Two odd characters set off on a motorcycle in search of the perfect, life-altering pot of hash *(pölsan)*, a sort of potted-meat dish traditionally prepared in the rural north.

TOP 10

SWEDEN

MUST-READ BOOKS BY SWEDISH AUTHORS

One of the best ways to get inside the collective mind of a country is to read its top authors. Following is a selection of some of the greatest and most popular works by Swedish authors.

- *The Long Ships* (1954) by Frans Gunnar Bengtsson
- *The Wonderful Adventures of Nils* (1906–07) by Selma Lagerlöf
- *Pippi Longstocking* (1945) by Astrid Lindgren
- *Merab's Beauty* (1982) by Torgny Lindgren
- *The Emigrants* series (1949–59) by Wilhelm Moberg
- *Faceless Killers* (1989) by Henning Mankell
- *Marking* (1963–64) by Dag Hammarskjöld
- *Röda Rummet* (1879) by August Strindberg
- *The Evil* (1981) by Jan Guillou
- *Hash* (2004) by Torgny Lindgren

FEEL-BAD FILMS

The Swedish film industry is active and varied (see p41), but most people associate it with the godfather of gloom, Ingmar Bergman. Many filmmakers have followed in his grim footsteps, including these:

- *Songs from the Second Floor* (2000), Roy Andersson – a post-apocalyptic urban nightmare in surreal slow motion; it's not for everyone.
- *Lilya 4-ever* (2002), Lukas Moodysson – a grim tale of human trafficking.
- *Ondskan* (Evil; 2003), Mikael Håfström – violence at a boys' boarding school.
- *Zozo* (2005), Josef Fares – a Lebanese orphan makes his way to Sweden alone, then has culture shock.
- *Darling* (2007), Johan Kling – harsh economic realities bring together a shallow, privileged party girl and a sweet old man in an unlikely friendship.
- *Let the Right One In* (2008), Tomas Alfredson – an excellent, stylish, restrained take on the horror-film genre that gets at what it's like to be a lonely preteen in a cold, hostile world.

INTERNET RESOURCES

Many Swedish towns and organisations have websites in both Swedish and English (although the English pages are often less detailed). Hotels, restaurants and museums throughout the country can also frequently be found online. The following websites are useful for pre-planning:

An introduction to the Sami people (www.itv.se/boreale/samieng.htm) A good place to start learning about the indigenous people of northern Sweden and the issues they face, including racism and habitat destruction.

Smorgasbord (www.sverigeturism.se/smorgasbord/index.html) A comprehensive website devoted to Swedish culture, industry, history, sports, tourism, environment and more, produced by the nonprofit FÖRST Föreningen Sverigeturism (Swedish Tourism Trade Association).

Sweden.se (www.sweden.se) All kinds of useful information about the country, in a variety of languages.

Swedish Film Institute (www.sfi.se) Loads of information on Swedish films and their significance within and outside the country.

Swedish Institute (www.si.se) The Swedish Institute publishes the best academic information on Sweden in English and offers scholarships for study in Sweden.

Visit Sweden (www.visitsweden.com) The official website for tourism in Sweden.

Events Calendar

Swedes love their holidays. Most towns and cities have frequent summer festivals and concerts (usually May to September). Books on festivals include Monica Rabe's *Sweden (Festivals of the World)* and Jan-Öjvind Swahn's *Maypoles, Crayfish and Lucia – Swedish Holidays and Traditions.* Visit www.musik festivaler.se for many more music festivals. Towns hosting large rock concerts include Sundsvall, Östersund and Skellefteå; see town websites for details. For a list of public holidays, see p323.

JANUARY

KIRUNA SNOW FESTIVAL   last week of Jan
Based around a snow-sculpting competition, this annual fest (www.kiruna.com/snowfestival) began in 1985 to celebrate a rocket launch and now draws artists from all over to carve ever-more elaborate and beautiful shapes out of the snow. It also features reindeer-sled racing, with Sami traditions also emphasised.

FEBRUARY

JOKKMOKK WINTER MARKET   1st Thu-Sat in Feb
A large annual gathering of Sami people from across Scandinavia, this festival (www.jokkmokks marknad.se) includes a market, meetings, craft shows, performances and more.

HOUSE OF METAL   early Feb
An annual hardcore music festival (www.house ofmetal.se, in Swedish) in Umeå at Folkets Hus, House of Metal features big-name artists as well as local bands.

MARCH

VASALOPPET   1st Sun in Mar
This huge annual ski race (www.vasaloppet.se) between Sälen and Mora, started in 1922, commemorates Gustav Vasa's history-making flight on skis in 1521; it has grown into a week-long ski fest and celebration with several different races: short, gruelling or just for fun.

APRIL

VALBORGSMÄSSOAFTON (WALPURGIS NIGHT)   30 Apr
This public holiday, a pagan holdover that's partly to celebrate the arrival of spring, involves lighting huge bonfires, singing songs and forming parades; parties are biggest in the student towns.

MAY

FÖRSTA MAJ (MAY DAY)   1 May
Traditionally a workers' marching day in industrial towns and cities, it's observed with labour-movement events, brass bands and marches.

JUNE

SWEDEN ROCK FESTIVAL   early Jun
This large annual three-day summer rock festival is held in Sölvesborg (www.swedenrock.com) and features huge metal and hard-rock bands like AC/DC, In Flames and Dragonforce, with camping available on site.

SWEDISH NATIONAL DAY   6 Jun
Known merely as Swedish Flag Day until 1983, this public holiday commemorates the crowning in 1523 of King Gustav Vasa and Sweden's independence from the Danish-led Kalmar Union.

SMAKA PÅ STOCKHOLM   1st week of Jun
Taste samples from some of Stockholm's top kitchens in manageable quantities, and watch cooking duels at this week-long annual fest in Kungsträdgården (www.smakapastockholm.se).

MIDSUMMER'S EVE & MIDSUMMER DAY   1st Fri-Sat after 21 Jun
Arguably the most important Swedish holiday, Midsummer starts on Friday afternoon/evening with the raising of the maypole, followed by lots of singing and dancing, drinking and the massive consumption of pickled herring with potatoes and sour cream.

HULTSFRED FESTIVAL   mid-Jun
This is a large annual three-day summer rock festival (www.rockparty.se) at Hultsfred, a small southeastern village reachable by train from Stockholm-Arlanda Airport. Artists have included Regina Spektor, Dropkick Murphys and Timbuktu.

ÖJEBY CHURCH MARKET   last weekend in Jun
This market near Piteå attracts some 20,000 visitors each year.

JULY

PITEÅ DANSAR & LER   late Jul
One of Sweden's biggest street festivals (www.pdol.se), the PDOR draws 120,000 visitors for music, dance, crafts, food and a carnival.

STOCKHOLM JAZZ FESTIVAL   19-23 Jul
Held on the island of Skeppsholmen, this internationally known jazz fest (www.stockholmjazz.com) brings artists from all over, including big names like Van Morrison and Mary J Blige; evening jam sessions at famed Stockholm jazz club Fasching are a highlight.

MUSIC VID SILJAN   early Jul
A midsummer music festival (www.musikvidsiljan.se), it takes place in the towns around Lake Siljan, and includes chamber, jazz and folk music; local tourist offices will have up-to-date schedules.

ARVIKA FESTIVALS   mid-Jul
This large annual three-day summer rock festival (www.arvikafestivalen.se, in Swedish) is held in western Värmland near Glafsfjorden, and features mostly Scandinavian rock bands.

FALUN FOLKMUSIK FESTIVAL   mid-Jul
Falun has a popular folk and world-music festival (www.falufolk.com), but funding has been troublesome in recent years and the festival's future is uncertain; check online for the latest news.

RÄTTVIK FOLKLORE FESTIVAL   late Jul
An annual celebration of international folk dance (www.folklore.se) on the shores of Lake Siljan.

CLASSIC CAR WEEK   late Jul-early Aug
Rättvik hosts this gathering of motorheads and the objects of their devotion (www.classiccarweek.com, in Swedish); there are monster truck battles, drive-in movies, laid-back cruising and lots of chrome.

STORSJÖYRAN   late Jul-early Aug
Östersjön hosts this annual three-day music festival (www.storsjoyran.se), which features international artists and crowds of up to 55,000 people.

AUGUST

MEDIEVAL WEEK, VISBY   early Aug
Find yourself an actual knight in shining armour at this immensely popular annual fest (www.medeltidsveckan.se), which puts Gotland's medieval city to great use with a market, games, costumes and a huge banquet.

DALHALLA   early Aug
The stunning Dalhalla venue in Rättvik hosts an opera festival (www.dalhalla.se), with the awesome acoustics of the venue allowing for mostly unamplified performances.

STOCKHOLM PRIDE   1st week in Aug
This annual parade and festival (www.stockholmpride.org/en/) is dedicated to creating an atmosphere of freedom and support for gay, lesbian, bisexual and transgender people.

WAY OUT WEST   mid-Aug
Göteborg hosts this music fest (www.wayoutwest.se) that features the likes of Broder Daniel, Sigur Rós, Grinderman and Franz Ferdinand.

TJEJMILEN   31 Aug
Sweden's biggest sporting event for women (www.tjejmilen.se) features 24,000 runners of all ages in a race that begins from Gärdet in Stockholm.

KRÄFTSKIVOR
(CRAYFISH PARTIES)   late Aug
Swedes celebrate the end of summer by wearing bibs and party hats while eating lots of crayfish and drinking *snaps* (usually aquavit). In the north similar parties take place but with *surströmming* (strong-smelling fermented Baltic herring), while in the south similar gatherings in September feast on eels and *snaps*.

SEPTEMBER

GÖTEBORG INTERNATIONAL
BOOK FAIR   late Sep
Scandinavia's biggest book fair, this event (www.bok-bibliotek.se) brings together authors, readers, publishers, agents, teachers, librarians and the media.

ÖLAND'S HARVEST
FESTIVAL   late Sep
This celebration of the local harvest (www.skor defest.nu) takes place each autumn in Borgholm, Öland.

LIDINGÖLOPPET   late Sep
Enshrined in the *Guinness World Records* as the world's largest terrain race, this annual event (www.lidingoloppet.se) takes place on Lidingö, just northeast of Stockholm.

OCTOBER

STOCKHOLM OPEN   early Oct
A huge event among the international tennis crowd, this annual tournament (www.ifstockholm open.se) draws its share of top-100 male players from all over the world.

HOME: INTERIOR
DESIGN FAIR   early Oct
'Hem' in Swedish, this is the country's largest interior decor and design fair, drawing more than 60,000 visitors eager to check out new furniture trends, textiles, lighting schemes, and arts and crafts. The event (www.hemmassan.se), held in Stockholm, includes displays, lectures and of course shopping.

UPPSALA SHORT FILM FESTIVAL   late Oct
Approaching its 30th anniversary, this annual film festival (www.shortfilmfestival.com) screens more than 300 short films at four cinemas in central Uppsala.

UMEÅ INTERNATIONAL
JAZZ FESTIVAL   late Oct
International jazz musicians have filled Umeå's stages for this annual event (www.umeajazzfes tival.se) 40 years running.

NOVEMBER

STOCKHOLM INTERNATIONAL FILM
FESTIVAL   mid-late Nov
Screenings of new international and independent films, director talks and discussion panels draw cinephiles to this important annual festival (www .stockholmfilmfestival.se); tickets go quickly, so book early if you're interested.

STOCKHOLM INTERNATIONAL
HORSE SHOW   late Nov
This annual horse show (www.stockholmhorse show.com) advertises itself as the largest indoor equestrian event in the world. It takes place in the Globe in southern Stockholm.

DECEMBER

LUCIADAGEN (ST LUCIA DAY)   13 Dec
Wearing a crown of lit candles, Lucia leads a white-clad choir in traditional singing in a celebration that seems to merge the folk tradition of the longest night and the story of St Lucia of Syracuse.

JULAFTON (CHRISTMAS EVE)   24 Dec
The night of the smörgåsbord and the arrival of *jultomten*, the Christmas gnome, carrying a sack of gifts, this is the biggest celebration at Christmas time.

Itineraries
CLASSIC ROUTES

AROUND THE CAPITAL & BEYOND   One Week / Start & End in Stockholm
Start in **Stockholm** (p67), where mandatory attractions include the **Kungliga Slottet** (p74), **Gamla Stan** (p74) and **Skansen** (p78). You can cover those in a couple of days, which leaves an evening for enjoying some of the capital city's nightlife in **Södermalm** (p81) – try the clubs around Medborgarplatsen, and bars in the SoFo district. On day three, take a boat tour to the ancient settlement on **Birka** (p117); it's an all-day affair. The next day, check out the spectacular cathedral and palace at **Uppsala** (p242) and delve into early Swedish history via the burial mounds and museum at **Gamla Uppsala** (p244). Spend the rest of the day exploring the adorable village of **Sigtuna** (p123), with its old-fashioned buildings, cute cafes and atmospheric church ruins. If you fancy a drive, head over to **Göteborg** (p206) and explore the **Bohuslän Coast** (p224) for the last couple of days. Alternatively, you could stay put and sample further from the cultural smörgåsbord that is Stockholm.

This trip takes you through some of Sweden's most accessible highlights in and around the capital city.

THE MIDDLE WAY
Two Weeks / Stockholm to Göteborg

Spend the first week as outlined above, exploring the sights around **Stockholm** (p67). Then head north toward **Lake Siljan** (p268) to take in the surrounding villages, which are famous for being postcard-pretty and steeped in history. Don't miss the family home of noted Swedish painter Anders Zorn in **Mora** (p272), the town where the world's biggest cross-country ski race, **Vasaloppet** (p19), ends. Tour a copper mine in Falun, home of the World Heritage–listed **Falu Kopparbergsgruva** (p266). Stop at **Örebro** (p258) to see the fine castle and to wander through one of Sweden's most beautiful parks before continuing down through the heart of Sweden to **Göteborg** (p206). Spend a day or two in Sweden's engaging second city, making sure you visit its theme park and take time to enjoy the city's hip cafes and bars, as well as its eclectic museums. Spend the rest of your trip exploring the craggy coastline and picturesque fishing villages of the **Bohuslän Coast** (p224).

This journey cuts a swath through the belly of the beast, touching on two of the country's best cities and taking in some archetypal Swedish villages.

TIP TO TAIL
One Month / Kiruna to Malmö

This trip is takes you from the northernmost city in Sweden to just shy of Denmark in the south. Fly in to **Kiruna** (p306), stopping to check out the Ice Hotel if the season is right. Take the train toward Narvik and stop at **Abisko National Park** (p309), a hiker's paradise. Spend a day or so exploring the wilderness, either along the **Kungsleden** (p60) or via any of the shorter nearby trails in the area. Expert hikers may opt instead to spend their mountaineering time in the more challenging **Sarek National Park** (p313). From here, head to **Gällivare** (p311) and catch the historic Inlandsbanan railway to **Jokkmokk** (p312), home of the world's best museum of Sami culture, the **Ájtte** (p312). Continue on the railway through some of the most spectacular scenery in the country, stopping, if your schedule allows, at **Sorsele** (p314), **Storuman** (p316) and **Östersund** (p290). From here, rent a car and cruise over to explore the breathtaking scenery of **Höga Kusten** (High Coast; p287). Continue southward toward **Lake Siljan** (p268) and the surrounding villages. Stop to see the pre-Viking burial mounds **Gamla Uppsala** (p244) with a detour to stroll Sweden's oldest main street in cute **Sigtuna** (p123) on your way to **Stockholm** (p67). The wonderful capital city will hold your attention for as many days as you can devote to it. When it's time to move on, head towards dynamic **Göteborg** (p206), and **Kalmar** (p144) with its fantastic Renaissance-era castle. Visit the island town of **Karlskrona** (p199), which is on the Unesco World Heritage List. Stop and take a deep breath in the beautiful **Österlen area** (p189). Wrap things up by exploring the vibrant southern towns of **Lund** (p179) and **Malmö** (p170), from where it's a cinch to cross the **Öresund bridge** (p171) into Copenhagen.

There's a lot of territory to cover in Sweden, but in a full month you can see most of its highlights by following this top-to-bottom route.

ROADS LESS TRAVELLED

REINDEER GAMES
Five to Seven Days / Luleå to Luleå

From **Luleå** (p302), cruise up to the historic military outpost of **Boden** (p303). Continue heading northwards and cross the Arctic Circle around **Jokkmokk** (p312), which is a Sami cultural centre and home to the excellent **Ájtte Museum** (p312). If the weather's in your favour, branch off to **Kvikkjokk** (p312), next-door neighbour to the rugged **Sarek National Park** (p313). Then push on toward **Gällivare** (p311) and up to **Kiruna** (p306). Sweden's northernmost city is worth some exploring on its own, but it also has a charming neighbour in **Jukkasjärvi** (see boxed text, p308), home to the famous Ice Hotel. From here, you could dash over to **Abisko National Park** (p309) for some spectacular and easily accessible hiking, or go straight north to the remote village of **Karesuando** (p306), on the Finnish border. Make your way along the Sweden-Finland border toward **Pajala** (p305), keeping an eye out for stray Rudolphs – for entertainment, keep a log of the number of reindeer you have to follow at casual trotting speed along a major highway. Stop in **Haparanda** (p305) for some serious shopping, then follow the curve of the coastline back to Luleå.

Dodge herds of reindeer on this journey, where the domesticated critters outnumber cars on the highway.

VICIOUS CYCLING
One to Two Weeks / Visby to Visby

This journey starts directly behind the ferry station in Visby, where you can rent a bicycle and camping equipment from various outlets. Once you've sorted your equipment, head north along the waterfront to catch **Gotlandsleden**, the bicycle trail that circumnavigates the island. Follow it to the grotto at **Lummelunda** (p166), then continue northward past Stenkyrka and around to the inlet at Kappelshamn. From here it's an easy morning's ride to Fårösund, where you can stock up on picnic items and catch the free ferry to the islet of **Fårö** (p166), home of Ingmar Bergman. There's a tourist information centre in Fårö town, near another grocery store and cafe. Take your time circling the islet, stopping at the gravesite of British troops who fought in the Crimean war at **Ryssnäs** (p166) and at any of the beaches or harbours that strike your fancy. Your goal is to reach **Langhammarshammaren** (p166) in time to watch the sunset over the eerie rock formations. Afterwards, head back to Fårösund and follow the Gotlandsleden signs southward, stopping for a peek at **Bungemuseet** (p165). At Slite you can choose to stick to the coastline or head inland through the Kallgateburgs Nature Reserve; the coastal route is lined with pretty beaches, while the inland option passes through pastoral countryside. (The less ambitious can easily loop back to Visby and wrap up their tour at this point.) The paths converge further south to follow along the coast – don't miss the detour to the Bronze Age cairns at **Uggarderojr** (p167) – and go through **Öja** (p167), where there's a fine church. Then loop around to return through **Burgsvik** (p167). Around Sandön you'll have fine views of Lilla Karlsö and **Stora Karlsö** (p164). Continue along the bike path northward until you're back in **Visby** (p158). Make sure you leave time at the end of your trip to enjoy the beautiful medieval city itself.

Cycling the Gotlandsleden is an ideal way to see the best of this idyllic island, from sandy beaches to medieval churches.

TAILORED TRIPS

WORLD HERITAGE SITES

Culture hounds might enjoy a quest to see the best of Sweden as defined by Unesco. To start there's the vast **Laponia area** (p312) in the north, an entire journey's worth of territory on its own. Working your way down, there's **Gammelstad church village** (p302) in Luleå. **Höga Kusten** (High Coast; p287) decorates the coastline from Härnosand to Örnsköldsvik. In Falun there's the **Falu Kopparbergsgruva** (p266), and the nearby picnic-friendly **Engelsberg Bruk** (p257). In the suburbs of Stockholm you'll find the royal palace and grounds of **Drottningholm** (p115), plus the unlikely beauty of the **Skogskyrkogården cemetery** (p85). Also near the capital is the ancient Viking settlement of **Birka** (p117). Moving south, there's **Tanumshede rock carvings** (p224) and the well-preserved naval port of **Karlskrona** (p199). Off the coast are the Hanseatic town of **Visby** (p158) on Gotland and the agricultural landscape of **southern Öland** (p157). There's also the historic **Varberg Radio Station** (p238) in Grimeton.

ACTIVITIES

Outdoorsy types are spoilt for choice in Sweden. There's excellent hiking and camping many of the country's national parks, especially **Abisko** (p309), as well as the more challenging territory of **Sarek National Park** (p313), and the intermediate **Padjelantaleden** (p62) and **Skuleskogen** (p288). Closer to Stockholm is the very accessible wilderness of **Tyresta** (p123).

Cycling is another popular activity, and Sweden is well set up for it. The best areas are found in **Skåne** (p170) and **Gotland** (p158); see the cycle tour of Gotlandsleden (opposite) for one suggestion.

For diving, rock climbing and caving, head south to **Kullaberg Nature Reserve** (p197).

Wintertime brings another batch of activities to the sporting crowd, most notably alpine skiing in resorts such as **Åre** (p293), **Sälen** (p274), **Hemavan** (p315) and **Riksgränsen** (p310). Cross-country skiing is popular along the hiking trail **Kungsleden** (p60) and other long-distance tracks.

Ice skating is a popular activity for kids and adults alike, and it's easy to do on the frozen winter surfaces of **Kungsträdgården** (p86) and other public areas in Stockholm.

Golf is huge in Sweden – there are more than 400 courses to choose from. The most popular options are in the south, but the quirkier choices are up north, including **Björkliden** (p310), near Abisko – home to the country's northernmost course, 240km above the Arctic Circle – and the **Green Line Golf Course** (p305) at Haparanda, where playing a round means repeatedly crossing the Sweden–Finland border.

Both canoeing and kayaking are popular in a number of rivers and the canals that honeycomb **Stockholm** (p85).

History

EARLY HISTORY

Sweden's human history began around 10,000 years ago at the end of the last ice age, once the Scandinavian ice sheet had melted. Tribes from central Europe migrated into the south of Sweden, and ancestors of the Sami people hunted reindeer from Siberia into the northern regions.

These nomadic Stone Age hunter-gatherers gradually made more permanent settlements, keeping animals, catching fish and growing crops. A typical relic of this period (3000 BC to 1800 BC) is the *gångrift*: a dolmen or rectangular passage-tomb covered with capstones, then a mound of earth. Pottery, amber beads and valuable flint tools were buried with the dead. The island of Öland, in southeast Sweden, is a good place to see clusters of Stone Age barrows.

> The Roman historian Tacitus (AD 56-120) first mentions the Svea, a 'militant Germanic race' strong in men, ships and war gear.

As the climate improved between 1800 BC and 500 BC, Bronze Age cultures blossomed. Their *hällristningar* (rock carvings) are found in many parts of Sweden – Dalsland and Bohuslän are particularly rich areas (see p224). The carvings provide tantalising glimpses of forgotten beliefs, with the sun, hunting scenes and ships being favourite themes. Huge Bronze Age burial mounds, such as Kiviksgraven (p190) in Österlen, suggest that powerful chieftains had control over spiritual and temporal matters. Relatively few bronze artefacts are found in Sweden: the metals had to be imported from central Europe in exchange for furs, amber and other northern treasures.

After 500 BC, the Iron Age brought about technological advances, demonstrated by archaeological finds of agricultural tools, graves and primitive furnaces. During this period, the runic alphabet arrived, probably from the Germanic region. It was used to carve inscriptions onto monumental rune stones (there are around 3000 in Sweden) well into medieval times.

> *The Vikings*, by Magnus Magnusson, is an extremely readable history book, covering their achievements in Scandinavia (including Sweden), as well as their wild-natured doings around the world.

By the 7th century AD, the Svea people of the Mälaren valley (just west of Stockholm) had gained supremacy, and their kingdom, Svea Rike (or Sverige), gave the country of Sweden its name. Birka, founded around 760 on Björkö (an island in Mälaren lake), was a powerful Svea centre for around 200 years. Large numbers of Byzantine and Arab coins have been found there, and stones with runic inscriptions are scattered across the area; see p117 for more details.

VIKINGS & THE ARRIVAL OF CHRISTIANITY

Scandinavia's greatest impact on world history probably occurred during the Viking Age (around 800 to 1100), when hardy pagan Norsemen set sail for other shores. In Sweden it's generally thought that population pressures were to blame for the sudden exodus: a polygamous society led to an excess

TIMELINE

c 10,000 BC	c 1700–500 BC	1008
Ice sheets melt and hunters follow reindeer into a newly uncovered Sweden.	Petroglyphs, including 'The Lovers', are carved into the rocks at Vitlycke, Tanum.	Sweden's first Christian king, Olof Skötkonung, is baptised at St Sigfrid's Well in Husaby.

of male heirs and ever-smaller plots of land. Combined with the prospects of military adventure and foreign trade abroad, the result was the Viking phenomenon (the word 'viking' is derived from *vik*, meaning 'bay' or 'cove', and is probably a reference to their anchorages during raids).

The Vikings sailed a new type of boat that was fast and highly manoeuvrable but sturdy enough for ocean crossings, with a heavy keel, up to 16 pairs of oars and a large square sail (the Äskekärr ship, Sweden's only original Viking vessel, is in Göteborg's Stadsmuseum, p210). Initial hit-and-run raids along the European coast (often on monasteries and their terrified monks) were followed by major military expeditions, settlement and trade. The well-travelled Vikings penetrated the Russian heartland and beyond, venturing as far as America, Constantinople (modern-day Istanbul) and Baghdad.

In Sweden the Vikings generally cremated their dead and their possessions, then buried the remains under a mound. There are also several impressive stone ship-settings, made from upright stones arranged in the shape of a ship. If you're interested in Viking culture, Foteviken Viking Reserve (p183) on the southwestern Falsterbo Peninsula is a 'living' reconstruction of a Viking village.

Early in the 9th century, the missionary St Ansgar established a church at Birka. Sweden's first Christian king, Olof Skötkonung (c 968–1020) is said to have been baptised at St Sigfrid's Well in Husaby (p234) in 1008 – the well is now a sort of place of pilgrimage for Swedes – but worship continued in Uppsala's pagan temple until at least 1090. By 1160, King Erik Jedvarsson (Sweden's patron saint, St Erik) had virtually destroyed the last remnants of paganism.

RISE OF THE SWEDISH STATE

Olof Skötkonung was the first king to rule over both the Sveas and the Gauts, creating the kernel of the Swedish state. During the 12th and 13th centuries, these united peoples mounted a series of crusades to Finland, Christianising the country and steadily absorbing it into Sweden.

Royal power disintegrated over succession squabbles in the 13th century. The medieval statesman Birger Jarl (1210–66) rose to fill the gap, acting as prince regent for 16 years, and founding the city of Stockholm in 1252.

King Magnus Ladulås (1240–90) introduced a form of feudalism in 1280, but managed to avoid its worst excesses. In fact, the aristocracy were held in check by the king, who forbade them from living off the peasantry when moving from estate to estate.

Magnus' eldest son Birger (1280–1321) assumed power in 1302. After long feuds with his younger brothers, he tricked them into coming to Nyköping castle (p250), where he threw them into the dungeon and starved them to death. After this fratricidal act, the nobility drove Birger into exile. They then chose their own king of Sweden, the infant grandson of King Haakon

You can see Erik XIV's bedroom at Kalmar Slott (p145) complete with a secret passage to escape from his brother Johan.

King Gustav III wrote his own plays and frequently arrived at formal dinners in fancy dress, to the horror of his more conservative courtiers.

In his private diaries from May to October 1785, when he was 37 years old, King Karl XIII apparently doodled a number of small illustrations of the male reproductive organ.

1050s	1160	1252
An unknown Viking scratches runic graffiti onto a statue in Athens.	King Erik Jedvarsson destroys the last remnants of paganism in Sweden.	Birger Jarl founds the city of Stockholm.

V of Norway. When Haakon died without leaving a male heir, the kingdoms of Norway and Sweden were united (1319).

The increasingly wealthy church began to show its might in the 13th and 14th centuries, commissioning monumental buildings such as the *domkyrka* (cathedral) in Linköping (founded 1250; see p133), and Scandinavia's largest Gothic cathedral in Uppsala (founded 1285; see p245).

However, in 1350 the rise of state and church endured a horrific setback when the Black Death swept through the country, carrying off around a third of the Swedish population. In the wake of the horror, St Birgitta (1303–73) reinvigorated the church with her visions and revelations, and founded a nunnery and cathedral in Vadstena, which became Sweden's most important pilgrimage site.

HANSEATIC LEAGUE & THE UNION OF KALMAR

On his death, it was discovered that Frenchman Jean-Baptiste Bernadotte (king of Sweden for 26 years) had a tattoo that read 'Death to kings!'

A strange phenomenon of the time was the German-run Hanseatic League, a group of well-organised merchants who established walled trading towns in Germany and along the Baltic coast. In Sweden they built Visby (p158) and maintained a strong presence in the young city of Stockholm. Their rapid growth caused great concern around the Baltic in the 14th century: an allied Scandinavian front was vital. Negotiated by the Danish regent Margrethe, the Union of Kalmar (1397) united Denmark, Norway and Sweden under one crown.

Erik of Pomerania, Margrethe's nephew, held that crown until 1439. High taxation to fund wars against the Hanseatic League made him deeply unpopular and he was eventually deposed. His replacement was short-lived and succession struggles began again: two powerful Swedish families, the unionist Oxenstiernas and the nationalist Stures, fought for supremacy.

Out of the chaos, Sten Sture the Elder (1440–1503) eventually emerged as 'Guardian of Sweden' in 1470, going on to fight and defeat an army of unionist Danes at the Battle of Brunkenberg (1471) in Stockholm.

The failing Union's death-blow came in 1520: Christian II of Denmark invaded Sweden and killed the regent Sten Sture the Younger (1493–1520). After granting a full amnesty to Sture's followers, Christian went back on his word: 82 of them were arrested, tried and massacred in Stockholm's main square, Stortorget in Gamla Stan (p85), which 'ran with rivers of blood'.

The brutal 'Stockholm Bloodbath' sparked off a major rebellion under the leadership of the young nobleman Gustav Ericsson Vasa (1496–1560). It was a revolution that almost never happened: having failed to raise enough support, Gustav was fleeing for the Norwegian border when two exhausted skiers caught him up to tell him that the people had changed their minds. This legendary ski journey is celebrated every year in the Vasaloppet race (p273) between Sälen and Mora.

1350s	1397	1477
The Black Death kills a third of the population.	Danish regent Margrethe unites Denmark, Norway and Sweden under the Union of Kalmar.	Scandinavia's oldest university is founded at Uppsala.

GAMMELSTAD

During the 13th century the pope increased the number of fast days, during which only fish could be eaten. This resulted in the rich Gulf of Bothnia fishing grounds becoming of great interest to the rest of Europe, and meant profit for whoever controlled the area.

With the northern border between Sweden and Russia insecure after the Treaty of Nöteborg in 1323, the Swedish crown secured control of northern Bothnia by handing over its river valleys as fiefs to noblemen from central Sweden. In 1327 Luleå was named for the first time in connection with such an enfeoffment and, in the 1340s the region became a parish of its own, with separate chapels in Piteå and Torneå.

By the end of the 14th century, Luleå Old Town (today's Gammelstad) was the centre of a parish stretching from the coast to the mountains along the Lule and Råne rivers. The Luleå farmers prospered during the economic boom of the Middle Ages and a stone church was built in the 15th century.

In 1621 Luleå was granted a town charter, but its development progressed very slowly. This proved to be rather fortunate because by 1649 the previously navigable channel from the archipelago had become too shallow and it was necessary to move the whole city to a better harbour, the present northern harbour of the current Luleå City. The church, the church village and the surrounding buildings became Luleå Old Town (Gammelstad).

Gammelstad church is the largest medieval church in Norrland and the only one with a reredos worthy of a cathedral and choir stalls for a whole consistory.

The church village developed because parishioners had to travel considerable distances to attend church, and required overnight accommodation. Today, Gammelstad is the largest church village in Sweden.

There are two historical walks around Gammelstad: the church walk and the town walk, which can each be done in approximately one hour. See the section on Luleå, p302, for details.

In 1523, Sweden seceded from the union and installed Gustav as the first Vasa king: he was crowned on 6 June, now the country's national day.

VASA DYNASTY

Gustav I ruled for 37 years, leaving behind a powerful, centralised nation-state. He introduced the Reformation to Sweden (principally as a fundraising exercise): ecclesiastical property became the king's, and the Lutheran Protestant Church was placed under the crown's direct control.

After Gustav Vasa's death in 1560, bitter rivalry broke out among his sons. His eldest child, Erik XIV (1533–77), held the throne for eight years in a state of increasing paranoia. After committing a trio of injudicious murders at Uppsala Slott (p244), Erik was deposed by his half-brother Johan III (1537–92) and poisoned with pea soup at Örbyhus Slott (p249). During the brothers' reigns, the Danes tried and failed to reassert sovereignty over Sweden in the Northern Seven Years' War (1563–70).

1523	**1628**	**1700**
Gustav I becomes the first Vasa king.	The royal warship *Vasa* sinks on her maiden voyage.	Peak of the Swedish empire.

Gustav's youngest son, Karl IX (1550–1611), finally had a chance at the throne in 1607, but was unsuccessful militarily and ruled for a mere four years. He was succeeded by his 17-year-old son. Despite his youth, Gustav II Adolf (1594–1632) proved to be a military genius, recapturing southern parts of the country from Denmark and consolidating Sweden's control over the eastern Baltic – the copper mine at Falun financed many of his campaigns (see p266). A devout Lutheran, Gustav II supported the German Protestants during the Thirty Years' War (1618–48). He invaded Catholic Poland and defeated his cousin King Sigismund III, later meeting his own end in battle in 1632.

> The Swedish Parliament was reformed in 1866 to be a bicameral system, which lasted until 1971 when it was reformed yet again and became unicameral.

Gustav II's daughter, Kristina, was still a child in 1632, and her regent continued her father's warlike policies. In 1654 Kristina abdicated in favour of Karl X Gustav, ending the Vasa dynasty.

For an incredible glimpse into this period, track down Sweden's 17th-century royal warship *Vasa* (commissioned by Gustav II in 1625), now in Stockholm's Vasamuseet (p79).

PEAK & DECLINE OF THE SWEDISH EMPIRE

The zenith and collapse of the Swedish empire happened remarkably quickly. During the harsh winter of 1657, Swedish troops invaded Denmark across the frozen Kattegatt, a strait between Sweden and Denmark, and the last remaining parts of southern Sweden still in Danish hands were handed over at the Peace of Roskilde. Bohuslän, Härjedalen and Jämtland were seized from Norway, and the empire reached its maximum size when Sweden established a short-lived American colony in what is now Delaware.

> Although not history textbooks, Vilhelm Moberg's four novels about 19th-century Swedish emigration are based on real people, and bring this period to life. They're translated into English as *The Emigrants*, *Unto A Good Land*, *The Settlers* and *The Last Letter Home*.

The end of the 17th century saw a developing period of enlightenment in Sweden; Olof Rudbeck achieved widespread fame for his medical work, which included the discovery of the lymphatic system.

Inheritor of this huge and increasingly sophisticated country was King Karl XII (1681–1718), an overenthusiastic military adventurer who spent almost all of his reign at war: he managed to lose Latvia, Estonia and Poland, and the Swedish coast sustained damaging attacks from Russia. Karl XII also fought the Great Nordic War against Norway throughout the early 18th century. A winter siege of Trondheim took its toll on his battle-weary army, and Karl XII was mysteriously shot dead while inspecting his troops – a single event that sealed the fate of Sweden's military might.

LIBERALISATION OF SWEDEN

During the next 50 years, parliament's power increased and the monarchs became little more than heads of state. Despite the country's decline, intellectual enlightenment streaked ahead and Sweden produced some celebrated writers, philosophers and scientists, including Anders Celsius, whose tem-

1766	1832	1930s
Swedish parliament passes the world's first *Freedom of the Press Act*.	The Göta Canal opens, linking Sweden's west and east coasts.	The worldwide Depression sparks off plans for the Swedish welfare state.

QUEEN KRISTINA

Queen Kristina (1626–89) lived an eccentric and eventful life. Her father, Gustav II, instructed that the girl be brought up as though she were a prince, then promptly went off and died in battle, leaving his six-year-old successor and his country in the hands of the powerful Chancellor Oxenstierna.

Kristina did indeed receive a boy's education, becoming fluent in six languages and skilled in the art of war. Childish spats with Oxenstierna increased as she grew older; after being crowned queen in 1644, she delighted in testing her power, defying him even when he had the country's best interests at heart.

Envious of the elegant European courts, Kristina attempted to modernise old-fashioned Sweden. One of her plans was to gather leading intellectuals for philosophical conversation. She's often blamed for the death of Descartes, who reluctantly obeyed her summons only to die of pneumonia in the icy north.

Kristina's ever-erratic behaviour culminated in her abdication in 1654. After handing over the crown to her beloved cousin Karl X Gustav, she threw on men's clothing and scarpered southwards on horseback. Kristina finished up in Rome, where she converted to Catholicism.

Contrary, curious and spoilt, and accused of murder and an affair with one of the Pope's cardinals, bisexual, rule-bending Kristina was a fascinating and frustrating character who was too huge and colourful to do justice to here. If you want to know more, an excellent biography is *Christina, Queen of Sweden* by Veronica Buckley.

---

perature scale bears his name; Carl Scheele, the discoverer of chlorine; and Carl von Linné (Linnaeus), the great botanist who developed theories about plant reproduction (see p246).

Gustav III (1746–92) curtailed parliamentary powers and reintroduced absolute rule in 1789. He was a popular and cultivated king who inaugurated the Royal Opera House in Stockholm (1782) and opened the Swedish Academy of Literature (1786), which is now known for awarding the annual Nobel Prize for literature. His foreign policy was less auspicious and he was considered exceptionally lucky to lead Sweden intact through a two-year war with Russia (1788–90). Enemies in the aristocracy conspired against the king, hiring an assassin to shoot him at a masked ball in 1792.

Gustav IV Adolf (1778–1837), Gustav III's son, assumed the throne and was drawn into the Napoleonic Wars, permanently losing Finland (onethird of Sweden's territory) to Russia. Gustav IV was forced to abdicate and his uncle Karl XIII took the Swedish throne under a new constitution that ended unrestricted royal power.

Out of the blue, Napoleon's marshal Jean-Baptiste Bernadotte (1763–1844) was invited by a nobleman, Baron Mörner, to succeed the childless Karl XIII to the Swedish throne. The rest of the nobility adjusted to the idea and Bernadotte took up the offer, along with the name Karl Johan. Karl Johan

1986	**1991**	**1992**
Prime Minister Olof Palme is assassinated while walking home from the cinema.	Sweden applies for membership in the European Community.	The 50-kronor bill is discontinued and the 20-kronor bill is introduced.

judiciously changed sides in the war, and led Sweden, allied with Britain, Prussia and Russia, against France and Denmark.

After Napoleon's defeat, Sweden forced Denmark to swap Norway for Swedish Pomerania (1814). The Norwegians objected, defiantly choosing king and constitution, and Swedish troops occupied most of the country. This forced union with Norway was Sweden's last military action.

INDUSTRIALISATION

Industry arrived late in Sweden (during the second half of the 19th century), but when it did come it transformed the country from one of Western Europe's poorest to one of its richest.

The Göta Canal (p140) opened in 1832, providing a valuable transport link between the east and west coasts, and development accelerated when the main railway across Sweden was completed in 1862. Significant Swedish inventions, including dynamite (Alfred Nobel) and the safety match (patented by Johan Edvard Lundstrom; see p137), were carefully exploited by government and industrialists; coupled with efficient steel-making and timber exports, they added to a growing economy and the rise of the new middle class.

However, when small-scale peasant farms were replaced with larger concerns, there was widespread discontent, exacerbated by famine, in the countryside. Some agricultural workers joined the population drift from rural areas to towns. Others abandoned Sweden altogether: around one million people (an astonishing quarter of the population!) emigrated over just a few decades, mainly to America.

Historically about 30% of the Swedish economy is in the public sector: health care, education, services for the elderly, hospitals and unemployment etc.

TRACING YOUR ANCESTORS   *Fran Parnell*

Around a million people emigrated from Sweden to the USA and Canada between 1850 and 1930. Many of their 12 million descendants are now returning to find their roots.

Luckily, detailed parish records of births, deaths and marriages have been kept since 1686 and there are *landsarkivet* (regional archives) around the country. The national archive is **Riksarkivet** (☎ 010-476 70 00; www.ra.se).

SVAR Forskarcentrum (☎ 0623-725 00; www.svar.ra.se) holds most records from the late 17th century until 1928. You can pay the staff here to research for you or look for yourself.

Utvandrarnas Hus (Emigrant House; p143) in Växjö is a very good museum dedicated to the mass departure. Attached is **Svenska Emigrantinstitutet** (Swedish Emigrant Institute; ☎ 0470-201 20; www.swemi.se), with an extensive research centre that you can use (Skr400 per search).

Also worth a look is *Tracing Your Swedish Ancestry*, by Nils William Olsson, a free do-it-yourself genealogical guide (40 pages). Get a copy by emailing your name and address to ancestry@ swedennewyork.com, or download it from the New York Consulate-General of Sweden's website: www.swedenabroad.com (under Visit Sweden in the menu).

1994	1995	1996
In a storm on the Baltic Sea, the ferry *Estonia* sinks, killing 852 passengers, including 551 Swedes.	Sweden joins the European Union.	The 50-kronor bill is re-introduced, featuring a portrait of singer Jenny Lind.

The transformation to an industrial society brought with it trade unions and the Social Democratic Labour Party (Social Democrats for short), founded in 1889 to support workers. The party grew quickly and obtained parliamentary representation in 1896 when Hjalmar Branting was elected.

In 1905 King Oscar II (1829–1907) was forced to recognise Norwegian independence and the two countries went their separate ways.

WORLD WARS & THE WELFARE STATE

Sweden declared itself neutral in 1912, and remained so throughout the bloodshed of WWI.

In the interwar period, a Social Democrat–Liberal coalition government took control (1921). Reforms followed quickly, including an eight-hour working day and suffrage for all adults aged over 23.

Swedish neutrality during WWII was ambiguous: letting German troops march through to occupy Norway certainly tarnished Sweden's image. On the other hand, Sweden was a haven for refugees from Finland, Norway, Denmark and the Baltic states; downed allied aircrew who escaped the Gestapo; and many thousands of Jews who escaped persecution and death.

After the war and throughout the 1950s and '60s the Social Democrats continued with the creation of *folkhemmet* (the welfare state). The standard of living for ordinary Swedes rose rapidly and real poverty was virtually eradicated.

MODERN SWEDEN

After a confident few decades, the late 20th century saw some unpleasant surprises for Sweden, as economic pressures clouded Sweden's social goals and various sacks of dirty laundry fell out of the cupboard.

In 1986 Prime Minister Olof Palme (1927–86) was assassinated as he walked home from the cinema. The murder and bungled police inquiry shook ordinary Swedes' confidence in their country, institutions and leaders. The killing remains unsolved, but it seems most likely that external destabilisation lay behind this appalling act. Afterwards, the fortunes of the Social Democrats took a turn for the worse as various scandals came to light, including illegal arms trading in the Middle East by the Bofors company.

By late 1992, during the world recession, the country's budgetary problems culminated in frenzied speculation against the Swedish krona. In November of that year the central bank (Sveriges Riksbank) was forced to abandon fixed exchange rates and let the krona float freely. The currency immediately devalued by 20%, interest rates shot up by a world record–breaking 500% and unemployment flew to 14%; the government fought back with tax hikes, punishing cuts to the welfare budget and the scrapping of previously relaxed immigration rules.

Only the US, Switzerland and Denmark rank ahead of Sweden on the World Economic Forum's list of the world's most competitive and prosperous countries.

The Olof Palme International Center (www.palmecenter.org) has taken up the former prime minister's baton, working for cross-border cooperation.

Sweden's presidency of the EU during 2001 was marred by demonstrations that turned to riots in Göteborg.

1999	2000	2001
Volvo announces the sale of its Volvo car division to Ford Motor Company, for Skr50 billion.	The Öresund Bridge links Sweden and Denmark.	Parliament votes 260 to 48 against abolishment of the monarchy.

Sweden joined the League of Nations in 1920 and the UN in 1946, and participates in international peacekeeping efforts through these organisations.

With both the economy and national confidence severely shaken, Swedes narrowly voted in favour of joining the European Union (EU), effective from 1 January 1995. Since then there have been further major reforms and the economy has improved considerably, with falling unemployment and inflation.

Another shocking political murder, of Foreign Minister Anna Lindh (1957–2003), again rocked Sweden to the core. Far-right involvement was suspected – Lindh was a vocal supporter of the Euro and an outspoken critic of both the war in Iraq and Italy's Silvio Berlusconi – but it appears that her attacker had psychiatric problems. Lindh's death occurred just before the Swedish referendum on whether to adopt the single European currency, but didn't affect the eventual outcome: a 'No' vote.

In recent years, rapid changes had begun to affect the make-up of the country. In October 2006, partly as a result of the general sense that Sweden had been relying too heavily on unemployment benefits and had become a nation of 'bystanders', the long-entrenched Social Democrats lost their leadership position in the Swedish Parliament. The centre-right Alliance Party won the election, with new Prime Minister Fredrik Reinfeldt campaigning on a 'work first' platform.

The Southeast Asian tsunami on Boxing Day 2004 killed more people from Sweden than from any other nation outside Asia, with almost 600 Swedes still unaccounted for.

Toward the end of 2008, in response to the global economic crisis, Sweden's central banks cut interest rates by half a point, announcing plans to drop them again within six months. The slump was also beginning to make itself felt in housing prices and slowed construction. The Swedish krona had dropped to its weakest level since 2002. And, as ever, economic tensions were reflected in social anxieties. An annual survey of attitudes toward ethnic diversity, conducted by Uppsala University researchers, indicated twice as many Swedes had an 'extremely negative' attitude toward racial diversity now than in 2005. (Researchers added, however, that Sweden is still well ahead of the rest of Europe in terms of encouraging and tolerating diversity.) An October 2008 study showed that one in three Swedes, particularly the young and single, would like to live in a 'gated community' protected by fences and door codes.

2003	2005	2006
In a national referendum, Sweden votes against adopting the single currency of the European Union.	Swedish Flag Day becomes a national holiday.	Total immigration into Sweden is 95,750, up nearly 50% from previous year.

The Culture

THE NATIONAL PSYCHE

Blonde, blue-eyed, cold and reserved: while these four elements may make up the prevailing stereotype of Swedes, the reality is much more complex and contradictory. Dark hair, impish stature and random acts of generosity are not as uncommon as you may think, while a widespread passion for travel and trends can make for curious locals and clued-up conversations.

Two vital concepts in the typical Swede's mindset are *lagom* and *ordning och reda*. Lagom means 'just right' – not too little, not too much. A good example is *mellanöl* (medium ale) – it's not strong, but not as weak as a light ale. An exception to *lagom* is the smörgåsbord.

Ordning och reda connotes tidiness and order: everything in its proper place in the world. A good example is the queuing system; almost every transaction in Sweden requires participants to take a number and stand in line, which everyone does with the utmost patience. An exception to *ordning och reda* is Stockholm traffic.

LIFESTYLE

Swedes are a friendly sort. *Var så god* is a common phrase and carries all sorts of expressions of goodwill: 'Welcome', 'Please', 'Pleased to meet you', 'I'm happy to serve you', 'Thanks' and 'You're welcome'. Swedes are so generous with their use of 'thank you' *(tack)* that language texts make jokes about it.

It wasn't until the 1930s that urban Swedes surpassed the number of rural Swedes, and even the most seasoned urbanites commonly retain a strong affinity with nature. The rural *sommarstuga* (summer cottage) is almost de rigueur, with 600,000 second homes in the country. Indeed, Sweden boasts the highest number of holiday cottages per capita in the world.

Another common sight is dishy dads pushing baby strollers. Gender equality has advanced further in Sweden than in most countries. The government has a Minister for Integration and Gender Equality, as well as the Office of the Equal Opportunities Ombudsman, the latter ensuring that all employers and institutions of learning actively promote gender equality and prevent sexual discrimination. Women make up around 47% of parliament members in the Riksdag and enjoy enviable childcare services.

Almost 70% of Swedish fathers take parental leave, compared to the EU average of only one in three.

On the flipside, a Swedish study released in 2001 found that 46% of females over the age of 15 who were interviewed had been subjected to violence. In 2006, around 25,500 cases of male violence against women were reported, with many experts believing that the real number is around five times higher.

POPULATION

Sweden's population is relatively small given the size of the country – it has one of the lowest population densities in Europe. Most of the population is concentrated in the large cities of Stockholm, Göteborg, Malmö and Uppsala. Conversely, the interior of Norrland is sparsely populated.

The majority of Sweden's population is considered to be of Nordic stock, thought to have descended from central and northern European tribes that migrated north after the end of the last ice age, around 10,000 years ago.

About 30,000 Finnish speakers form a substantial minority in the northeast, near Torneälven (Torne River). More than 160,000 citizens of other Nordic countries live in Sweden.

About 15% of Sweden's population are either foreign-born or have at least one non-Swedish parent. Most immigrants have come from other European countries, including Russia, the former Yugoslavia, Poland and Greece. The largest non-European ethnic group is made up of Middle Eastern citizens, primarily from Iraq, Turkey and Iran. Other countries with a sizeable presence include Chile and Somalia. There are also around 45,000 Roma.

Sami

With around 15,000 people, the indigenous Sami people (sometimes inappropriately termed 'Lapps') are a significant ethnic minority. For centuries they've roamed northern Scandinavia and northwest Russia, living mainly from large herds of domestic reindeer. These days, around 10% of Sami live from reindeer husbandry, with many more having migrated to Sweden's industrialised south in search of work. The total Sami population (around 60,000) forms an ethnic minority in four countries: Norway, Sweden, Finland and Russia. In Sweden, they're mainly found in the mountain areas along the Norwegian border, north of mid-Dalarna. The Sami people refer to their country as Sápmi.

Listen to Swedish radio via the internet at www.sr.se.

The history of relations between the Sami and Nordic peoples is often a dark one. Since at least the 1600s, the Sami religious practice of shamanism was denigrated, and *noaidi* (Sami spiritual leaders) were persecuted. Use of the Sami language was discouraged, and Sami children were coerced into school to learn Swedish. Generally speaking, the Sami in Sweden still do not enjoy the same rights as Sami people in Norway and Finland; this is partly due to the fact that hydroelectric developments and mining activities, which are of great importance to the Swedish economy, have been established on traditional Sami land. Despite improved mainstream attitudes, many Sami still encounter prejudiced attitudes, which paint them as 'welfare reliant' and as 'having it good'. At an international Sami youth conference held in

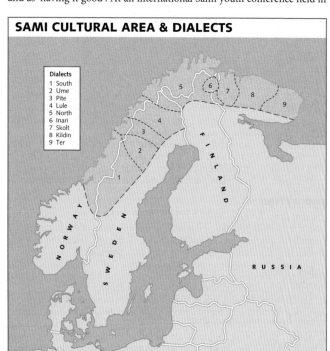

SAMI CULTURAL AREA & DIALECTS

Dialects
1 South
2 Ume
3 Pite
4 Lule
5 North
6 Inari
7 Skolt
8 Kildin
9 Ter

NORWAY

SWEDEN

FINLAND

RUSSIA

October 2008, participants demanded that more be done to address the high level of youth suicide in the Sami community.

Nature plays a crucial role in Sami religious traditions, as does the singing of the emotion-laden storytelling called *yoik* (also spelt *joik*) or 'song of the plains'. Briefly banned as part of the religion's suppression, it's now enjoying a resurgence in popularity. Equally positive is the fact that Sami education is available in government-run Sami schools or compulsory nine-year municipal schools, which provide identical schooling to that received by Swedish children but take into account the Sami cultural and linguistic heritage. Of the 6000 or so Sami who still speak their native tongue, 5000 speak the North Sami dialect.

The booklet *The Saami – People of the Sun & Wind,* published by Ájtte, the Swedish Mountain and Saami Museum in Jokkmokk, does a good job of describing Sami traditions in all four countries of the Sápmi region and is available at tourist shops around the area.

SPORT
Football
Football is the most popular sporting activity in Sweden and there are 3320 clubs with over one million members. The domestic season runs from April to early November. The national arena, Råsunda Stadium in Solna, a suburb in Stockholm's northwest, can hold up to 37,000 roaring spectators.

Now the manager of Mexico's national football team, Sven Göran Eriksson achieved fame and notoriety as the head coach of England's national team, when rumours of scandalous affairs and an excessive salary made fodder for the UK press. Two of Sweden's best-known Swedish football players are Gunnar Nordahl (1921–95), who helped Sweden win gold at the 1948 Olympics and went on to be the all-time top scorer at AC Milan, and Malmö-born Zlatan Ibrahimović (1981–), currently signed to Inter-Milan.

Ice Hockey
There are amateur ice-hockey teams in most Swedish communities. The national premier league, Elitserien, has 12 professional teams; there are also several lower divisions. Matches take place from autumn to late spring, up to four times a week in Stockholm, primarily at Globen arena (see p109).

Skiing
Alpine skiing competitions are held annually, particularly in Åre (Jämtland; p293), where events include Skutskjutet, the world's greatest downhill ski race (with up to 3000 competitors) in late April or early May.

Vasaloppet (www.vasaloppet.se), the world's biggest nordic (cross-country) ski race, takes place on the first Sunday in March, when over 15,000 competitors follow a 90km route. For further details, see the sections on Sälen (p274) and Mora (Dalarna; p273) or check out the Vasaloppet website.

Swedish skiing stars include four-time Olympic gold-medal winner Gunde Svan and giant slalom icon Ingemar Stenmark, who won a total of 86 races in the Alpine Skiing World Cup.

Other Sports
Swedish men have excelled at tennis, including Björn Borg, Mats Wilander and Stefan Edberg (all three have now retired). Borg won the Wimbledon Championships in England five times in a row.

Golf is a similarly popular sport in Sweden with more than 400 courses throughout the country. Annika Sörenstam, ranked as one of the game's leading female players, hails from Sweden.

'Nature plays a crucial role in Sami religious traditions, as does thesinging of emotion-laden story-telling called *yoik* or "song of the plains"'

Bandy, though similar to ice hockey, is played on an outdoor pitch the size of a football field and teams are also the same size as in football.

Sailing is very popular, around Stockholm in particular, where almost half the population owns a yacht.

For more on participating in sports in Sweden, see Outdoor Activities, p58.

MULTICULTURALISM

Swedish music stars José González and Salem Al Fakir and film director Josef Fares are testament to Sweden's increasingly multicultural make-up. In 2007 the small town of Södertälje, 30km south of Stockholm, welcomed 1268 Iraqi refugees alone; the US and Canada combined accepted a paltry 1027. Some 200 languages are now spoken in the country, as well as variations on the standard – the hip-hop crowd, for example, speak a vivid mishmash of slang, Swedish and foreign phrases that's been dubbed 'Rinkeby Swedish' after an immigrant-heavy Stockholm suburb.

Sweden first opened its borders to mass immigration during WWII. At the time it was a closed society, and new arrivals were initially expected to assimilate and essentially 'become Swedish'. In 1975 Parliament adopted a new set of policies that emphasised the freedom to preserve and celebrate traditional native cultures.

Read the news from the underground (mostly in Swedish) at www.sweden.indymedia.org.

Not everyone in Sweden is keen on this idea, with random acts of hate crimes – including the burning down of a Malmö mosque in 2004 – blemishing the country's reputation for tolerance. As hip-hop artist Timbuktu (himself the Swedish-born son of a mixed-race American couple) told the *Washington Post*, 'Sweden still has a very clear picture of what a Swede is. That no longer exists – the blond, blue-eyed physical traits. That's changing. But it still exists in the minds of some people.'

MEDIA

Domestic newspapers are published only in Swedish, but a wide variety of English-language imports are available at major transport terminals and newsstands – often even in small towns.

Nearly 90% of Swedish adults read at least one daily newspaper and most people subscribe for home delivery. *Dagens Nyheter* is a politically independent paper with a liberal bent, while *Svenska Dagbladet* is the more conservative daily; both are distributed across the country though based in Stockholm. The evening papers (*Aftonbladet* and *Expressen*, the Social Democrat and liberal papers respectively) also have national coverage.

ARTS
Literature

The best known of Sweden's artistic greats have been writers, chiefly the poet Carl Michael Bellman (1740–95), influential dramatist and author August Strindberg (1849–1912), and children's writer Astrid Lindgren (1907–2002).

During WWII some Swedish writers took a stand against the Nazis, including Eyvind Johnson (1900–76) with his *Krilon* trilogy, completed in 1943, and the famous poet and novelist Karin Boye (1900–41), whose novel *Kallocain* was published in 1940. Vilhelm Moberg (1898–1973), a representative of 20th-century proletarian literature and controversial social critic, won international acclaim with *Utvandrarna* (The Emigrants; 1949) and *Nybyggarna* (The Settlers; 1956).

Contemporary literary stars include playwright and novelist Per Olov Enquis (1934–), who achieved international acclaim with his novel *Livläkarens besök* (The Visit of the Royal Physician; 2003), in which King Christian VII's physician conspires with the queen to seize power. Left-wing activist and journalist Stieg Larsson (1954–2004) completed three crime novels before his death: the first, *Män som hatar kvinnor* (Men who Hate Women; 2005) was retitled *The Girl with the Dragon Tattoo* for its 2008 English-language release. English translations of his other two works should hit the shelves in 2009 and 2010. Sweden's most famous crime fiction writer, however, remains Henning Mankell (1948–), whose novels feature moody detective Kurt Wallander.

Mikael Niemi's (1959–) novel *Populärmusik från Vittula* (Popular Music; 2003), a coming-of-age story of a wannabe rock star in Sweden's remote north, became an international cult hit, as well as a 2004 film directed by Iranian-born Swedish director Reza Bagher. Nonfiction meister Sven Lindqvist (1932–) is famous for his hard-hitting, sometimes controversial titles. His most famous offering is arguably *Utrota varenda jävel* (Exterminate All the Brutes; 1992), exploring the holocaust-like devastation European colonists wrought on Africa. More recently, his book *Terra Nullius* (2005, translated into English in 2007) is a powerful, moving history of colonial Australia and the attempted destruction of Aboriginal culture.

Cinema & TV

Sweden led the way in the silent-film era of the 1920s with such masterpieces as *Körkarlen* (The Phantom Carriage), adapted from a novel by Selma Lagerlöf and directed by Mauritz Stiller. In 1967 came Vilgot Sjöman's notorious *I Am Curious – Yellow*, a political film that got more attention outside Sweden for its X rating. With a few exceptions, one man has largely defined modern Swedish cinema to the world: Ingmar Bergman. With deeply contemplative films like *The Seventh Seal, Through a Glass Darkly* and *Persona*, the beret-topped director explores human alienation, the absence of god, the meaning of life, the certainty of death and other light-hearted themes.

More recently, the towns of Trollhättan and Ystad have become filmmaking centres, the former drawing the likes of wunderkind director Lukas Moodysson, whose *Lilja 4-Ever, Fucking Åmål* and *Tillsammans* have all been both popular and critical hits. Lebanese-born Josef Fares (*Jalla! Jalla!, Kopps, Zozo, Leo*) is part of a new guard of 'second generation immigrant directors'. Alongside Iranian-born directors Reza Bagher (*Wings of Glass*) and Reza Parsa (*Before the Storm*), Fares has flung the spotlight on the immigrant experience in Sweden. His latest feature, the uncharacteristically dark *Leo*, also marks Fares' on-screen debut.

Another Swedish award-winner is director Roy Andersson, once dubbed a 'slapstick Ingmar Bergman'. His film *Du levande* (You, the Living) scooped up three prizes (including best picture) at Sweden's prestigious Gulbagge (Golden Beetle) Awards in 2008.

Music

Not only is Sweden the third-largest exporter of music in the world, but Swedes also buy more recorded music per capita than any other nationality.

Swedish songwriters and producers are sought-after commodities: Denniz Pop and Max Martin have penned hits for pop divas like Britney Spears and Jennifer Lopez, while Anders Bagge and Bloodshy & Avant (aka Christian Karlsson and Pontus Winnberg) co-created Madonna's 2005 album *Confessions on a Dance Floor.*

Most local pop bands sing in English, which often masks their Swedish identity: who knew the Caesars ('Jerk It Out') were Swedish? Or September, Alcazar and one-hit wonder Emilia ('Big Big World')?

Riding the current wave of Swedish successes are pop icon Robyn, indie melody-makers Peter, Björn & John and the exquisitely mellow José

The trademark red used to paint so many Swedish summer houses and barns is called *Falu Rödfärg* (Falun red paint). The pigment is actually a waste product of the now-defunct Falun copper mine, first referred to in 1570 and originally deployed by the upper classes to mimic the red bricks used on the continent.

THE STORYBOOK WARRIOR

Long before the Spice Girls cashed in on 'girl power', a Vimmerby-born, Stockholm-based secretary was psyching up little girls with tales of the red-headed, pigtailed strongest girl in the world. The secretary was Astrid Lindgren (1907–2002) and her fictional rebel the infamous Pippi Longstocking. In a postwar world of silenced children and rigid gender roles, Pippi was bold, subversive and deliciously empowering. She didn't care for beauty creams, she was financially independent and she could even outlift the strongest man in the world, Mighty Adolf.

The character herself first found life in 1941 when Lindgren's pneumonia-struck daughter, Karin, asked her mother for a story about 'Pippi Longstocking'. The curious name inspired Lindgren to spin a stream of tales about the original wild child, which became an instant hit with Karin and her friends.

While recovering from a sprained ankle in 1944, Lindgren finally put her tales to paper and sent them to a publisher. Rejected but undefeated, she sent a second story to another publisher and scooped second prize in a girls' story competition. The following year, a revamped Pippi manuscript grabbed top honours in another competition, while her story *Bill Bergson Master Detective* shared first prize in 1946.

This was just the beginning of a prolific, award-winning career that would include picture books, plays and songs translated into over 50 languages, as well work in radio, TV and film.

Arguably, Lindgren's greatest legacy to Sweden has been her influence on the rights and protection of society's most vulnerable, from children and the poor to animals. In 1976 Swedish newspaper *Expressen* published an allegorical opinion piece she wrote on an unjust tax-system loophole that saw self-employed writers paying 102% tax on their earnings. Not only did it lead to an amendment in the taxation law, but it also influenced the fall of the Social Democrats, who had been in power for 44 years. In 1978 Lindgren used her acceptance speech for the Peace Prize of the German Book Trade to express her views on the issue of violence against children, rousing intense debate. The following year, Sweden became the world's first nation to ban the smacking of children.

González, whose cover of The Knives' track 'Heartbeats' (famously used in a Sony Bravia ad) catapulted the Göteborg native to international stardom.

Other home-grown stalwarts include the Hives, the Cardigans, Sahara Hotnights, the Shout Out Louds and Håkan Hellström, who is much lauded for his original renditions of classic Swedish melodies.

On the house music front, DJs Axwell, Steve Angello, Sebastian Ingrosso and Eric Prydz (dubbed the 'Swedish House Mafia') have firmly cemented Sweden's cred on the dance floor.

Jazz has been another Swedish musical forte, especially between the 1930s and 1960s. Icons include the Sonora Swing Swingers (think 'Lady Be Good'), trumpeter Rolf Ericson (1922–97) and saxophonist Carl-Henrik Norin (1920–67). Baritone sax Lars Gullin (1928–67) dominated the scene in the 1950s, followed by tenor saxophonist Bernt Rosengren (1937–96) a decade later. Another star of the time was pianist Jan Johansson (1931–68), renowned for blending jazz and folk in a distinctly Swedish fashion. Both Stockholm and Umeå host popular annual jazz festivals.

Although Sweden has never produced a classical composer to match Norway's Edvard Grieg, there has been no shortage of contenders. One of the earliest was Emil Sjögren (1853–1918). He was followed by the Wagnerian Wilhelm Peterson-Berger (1867–1942) and Hugo Alfvén (1872–1960).

And what would a piece on Swedish music be without mentioning the nation's most successful, iconic and dubiously dressed music group? Winners of the 1974 Eurovision Song Contest with 'Waterloo', ABBA's greatest album success to date is the 1992 *Abba Gold* compilation, released 10 years after the group disbanded.

Architecture

Apart from elaborate gravesites, little survives of Bronze Age buildings in Sweden. Several Iron Age relics remain on Öland, including Ismantorp, a fortified village with limestone walls and nine gates.

Excellent examples of Romanesque church architecture dot the country. One of the finest is Domkyrkan (Cathedral) in Lund, consecrated in 1145 and still dominating the city centre with its two imposing square towers.

Gothic styles from the 13th and 14th centuries mainly used brick rather than stone. Some fine examples can be seen at the Mariakyrkan in Sigtuna (completed in 1237) and Uppsala's Domkyrkan, consecrated in 1435.

Gotland is your best bet in Sweden for ecclesiastical Gothic architecture, with around 100 medieval churches gracing the island.

During and after the Reformation, monasteries and churches were plundered by the crown in favour of lavish royal palaces and castles like Gustav Vasa's Kalmar Slott and Gripsholm Slott, which boasts one of Sweden's finest Renaissance interiors.

Magnificently ornate baroque architecture arrived in Sweden (mainly from Italy) during the 1640s while Queen Kristina held the throne. Kalmar Cathedral, designed in 1660, the adjacent Kalmar Rådhus and Drottningholm Slott (1662), just outside Stockholm, were all designed by the court architect Nicodemus Tessin the Elder. Tessin the Younger designed the vast 'new' Royal Palace in Stockholm after the original palace was gutted by fire in 1697.

The late 19th century and early 20th century saw a rise in national romanticism, a particularly Swedish style using wood and brick that produced such wonders as the Stockholm Rådhus (1916) and Stadshus (City Hall; completed in 1923). Another popular style in early-20th-century Sweden was neoclassicism, best exemplified by Stockholm's curvaceous Stadsbiblioteket (City Library; 1924). The building's creator, Erik Gunnar Asplund (1885–1940), remains Sweden's most internationally acclaimed architect.

From the 1930s to the '80s, functionalism and the so-called international style stole the limelight, with their emphasis on steel, concrete and glass. One of the latter's most controversial legacies is the Hötorgscity complex (built 1952–56) in central Stockholm, its five cookie-cutter office blocks blemishing the city skyline.

The subsequent postmodern wave witnessed the mash-up of styles and historical influences, and the rise of contemporary starchitect Gert Wingårdh. Describing his style as 'high organic', the Göteborg local's most prolific projects to date include the visionary, ecofriendly Bo01 housing project at Malmö's Western Harbour redevelopment, Universeum (2001) in Göteborg, and the award-winning House of Sweden (2006) in Washington DC.

Design & Fashion

From Jonas Bohlin 'Tutu lamps' to Tom Hedquist Mellanmjölk milk cartons, Sweden is a living gallery of inspired design. While simplicity still defines the Nordic aesthetic, new designers are challenging Scandi functionalism with bold, witty work. A claw-legged 'Bird Table' by Broberg Ridderstråle and a table made entirely of ping pong balls by Don't Feed the Swedes are two of a plethora of playful creations from design collectives like Folkform, DessertDesign, and Defyra. One of the hottest is Front, an all-female quartet famed for animated creations including a bin that bloats when full.

The source of much of this ingenuity is Sweden's leading design schools, namely Stockholm's Konstfack, University College of Arts, Craft and Design, and Göteborg's School for Design and Crafts (HDK).

Held in February, Stockholm Design Week is one of the world's prolific annual design events.

For the low-down on Sweden's street art scene, check out the brilliant book *Playground Sweden*, published by Dokument and featuring the work and thoughts of Sweden's top street artists. Good online blogs include www.streetartstockholm .se and www.gatukonst .se (both in Swedish).

Aesthetic prowess also fuels Sweden's thriving fashion scene. Since the late 1990s local fashion designers have roused global admiration: Madonna dons Patrik Söderstam trousers and Acne Jeans sell like hot cakes at LA's hip Fred Segal. In fact, Sweden now exports more fashion than pop. Amid industry stalwarts like uberchic Filippa K and skater-cool WESC, rising labels include deconstructionist Fifth Avenue Shoe Repair, ecohip Camilla Norrback and the feminine House of Dagmar, the latter created by three sisters inspired by their needle-savvy grandmother.

Painting, Sculpture & Street Art

Sweden's 19th-century artistic highlights include the warm art nouveau oil paintings of Carl Larsson (1853–1919), the nudes and portraits of Anders Zorn (1860–1920), August Strindberg's violently moody seascapes and the nature paintings of Bruno Liljefors (1860–1939).

Despite an initial caution towards Cubism, some artists embraced the concepts of surrealist and abstract art, albeit with their own Swedish style, such as the bizarre 'dreamland' paintings of Stellan Mörner (1896–1979). Otto Carlsund (1897–1948) was the driving force behind early abstract art in Sweden.

More radical art movements in the 1960s and '70s were influenced by diverse sources, including far-left politics, pop culture and minimalism, while the 1980s and '90s saw the rise of feminist-oriented art from the likes of Lotta Antonsson (1963–) and Ingrid Orfali (1952–).

Post-9/11, an increasingly international Swedish art scene has focused on globalisation, as well as the relationship between the individual and socio-political power structures, as seen in the films of Loulou Cherinet (1970–) and the protest art of Fia-Stina Sandlund (1973–).

Also often political is Sweden's kicking street-art scene, which includes tagging, stencilling, poster art and site-specific installations. Prominent artists include Stockholm's left-wing Hop Louie, famous for using images of Christer Petterson (suspected assassin of former Prime Minister Olof Palme), and Prao, best known for assembling white cabinets in random urban locations filled with goods for the homeless. On the west coast, the spray-can creations of artist Blue are a prominent fixture on Göteborg's urban landscape, her themes ranging from ethereal creatures to explicit sexuality.

Carl Milles (1875–1955) is Sweden's greatest sculptor and was once employed as Rodin's assistant. Millesgården, his home in Lidingö, on Stockholm's outskirts, is one of the city's most whimsical museums (p84).

Theatre & Dance

When King Gustav III founded the Royal Dramatic Theatre (dubbed Dramaten) in Stockholm in 1773, interest in theatre and opera blossomed. Greta Garbo attended the Royal Dramatic Theatre drama school in 1922, and Ingmar Bergman made his directorial debut here in 1951.

In 1773, the arts-loving ruler also founded the Royal Swedish Ballet in Stockholm, the world's fourth-oldest ballet company. The capital's contemporary dance offerings include Moderna Dansteatern (renowned for promoting emerging choreographers and dancers) and Dansens Hus. Stockholm is also home to the Cullberg Ballet, Sweden's most internationally renowned contemporary dance company.

Both Sweden's national and regional theatres are obliged to produce theatre for children. Top writers in the field include Lucas Svensson, Sofia Fredén and Matthias Andersson.

Food & Drink

In less than two decades, Sweden has transformed itself from a dining dowager to a confident gourmet. Epicureans around the world are smitten with the country's new-gen chefs and their often bold, inventive creations. Current luminaries include Bocuse d'Or–recipient Mathias Dahlgren, TV chef Niklas Ekstedt and New York–based Marcus Samuelsson. And while Stockholm takes the cake with its arsenal of Michelin-starred restaurants, culinary enlightenment beckons across the country. Some smaller towns aside, the days of meatballs, mash and not much else are well and truly over.

CONTEMPORARY TENDENCIES

Essentially, contemporary Swedish cuisine melds global influences with local produce and innovation: think baked wood-pigeon with potato-and-apple hash or cauliflower 'cornet' with white chocolate and caviar. Once obsessed with foreign products, locals have discovered the virtues of their own pantry. The result is an intense passion for home-grown ingredients, whether it's apples from Kivik or bleak roe from Kalix. Equally important is the seasonality of food; expect succulent berries in spring, artichokes and crayfish in summer, and hearty truffles and root vegetables in the colder months.

Another growing obsession is a predilection for sustainable farming, small-scale producers and organic produce. Increasingly, restaurants and cafes pride themselves on serving clean, chemical-free grub, as well as actively supporting ethical, eco-friendly agricultural practices. Malmö's award-winning Slow Food restaurant Salt och Brygga (p177) goes one step further, cladding its staff in pure, organic threads.

Click onto www
.scandinaviancooking
.com for articles about
Swedish cuisine and
recipes for Scandi dishes,
savoury and sweet. More
recipes and epicurean
enlightenment await
at the savvy www
.foodfromsweden.com.

TWO MINUTES WITH MATHIAS DAHLGREN

How does your latest dining venture differ from your last restaurant, Bon Lloc? In my new restaurant I create my cuisine from a Swedish and local platform. While I believe that people and ideas should travel, I think fresh ingredients should travel as little as possible. What remains the same is my own curiosity about, and attitude to, the ingredients and ideas I encounter.

Where does Swedish cuisine stand at the moment? After some years of influences outside our own borders, we're now focusing more on our roots. Swedish chefs are increasingly confident about their own abilities to innovate and impress. I think one of the driving forces in the evolution of modern Swedish cuisine is a longing for our own identity.

Some people argue that Sweden offers either expensive fine dining or lousy budget options, with too few good-quality, midpriced eateries. Your thoughts? We have a relatively short history of restaurant culture in Sweden. For a long time, going to a restaurant was associated with luxury for the common Swede. Here, luxury equates with high taxes, in turn creating a high-cost dining experience compared to countries like Spain and Italy. Thankfully, this is changing a bit. Swedish diners have also become more discerning and expectant of good-quality food across the board.

Three foodie experiences visitors to Stockholm shouldn't miss? Aside from my own food bar at Mathias Dahlgren, head to Café Saturnus in Engelbrektsgatan (p103) for their huge and tasty cinnamon scrolls, and don't miss Nystekt Strömming (p104) at Slussen for cheap, tasty Swedish take-away. Another destination is the weekend farmers' markets around town in season. They seem to pop up here and there so it's difficult to recommend any one in particular. Your best bet is to ask at the tourist office, at your hotel, or search online.

Mathias Dahlgren is an award-winning chef at his namesake Stockholm restaurant (p103).

Not surprisingly, this newfound culinary savvy has impacted the tourist trade. Gastro-themed itineraries and activities are on the rise, with everything from Gotland truffle hunts to west-coast lobster safaris, while numerous tourist boards stock culinary guides to their respective region. In Skåne, look out for the free **Culinary Skåne** (www.culinaryskane.com) booklet, produced by an association of local restaurateurs and providores focused on promoting the region's produce, cuisine and epicurean events.

CLASSIC STAPLES & SPECIALITIES

While new-school Swedish nosh thrives on experimentation, it retains firm roots in Sweden's culinary heritage. Even the most avant-garde chefs admire simple, old-school *husmanskost* (everyman cuisine) like *toast skagen* (toast with bleak roe, crème fraiche and chopped red onion), *köttbullar och potatis* (meatballs and potatoes, usually served with lingonberry jam, known as *lingonsylt*), *nässelsoppa* (nettle soup, traditionally served with hard-boiled eggs) and *pytt i panna* (equivalent to hash: a mix of diced sausage, beef or pork fried with onion and potato and served with sliced beetroot and an egg). Seafood staples include caviar, gravadlax or gravlax (cured salmon) and the ubiquitous *sill* (herring), eaten smoked, fried or pickled and often accompanied by Scandi trimmings like capers, mustard and onion.

> Swedes buy more cookbooks per capita than any other nation, and guzzle more coffee than anywhere bar Finland.

The prevalence of preserved grub harks back to a time when Swedes had little choice but to store their spring and summer harvests for the long, icy winter. Arguably, the most contentious of these long-lasting staples is the incredibly pungent, *surströmming* (fermented Baltic herring), traditionally eaten in August and September and served in a slice of *tunnbröd* (thin, unleavened bread) with boiled potato and onions and ample amounts of *snaps* (a distilled alcoholic beverage). It may be an acquired taste, but it has a legion of hardcore fans, mostly in northern Sweden. It even boasts its own festival in the village of Alfta.

Less divisive are Sweden's sweet treats, the most ubiquitous being the *kanelbullar* (cinnamon bun). Several gourmet *konditori* (old-fashioned bakery-cafes) and cafes offer slight variations on the bun, lacing it with anything from chocolate to crushed pistachios. Soft and doughy (at their best), they're a popular staple for *fika,* the Swedes' much-loved afternoon ritual of 'coffee and cake'.

FESTIVE FLAVOURS

Christmas cranks out the *julbord,* a particularly gluttonous version of Sweden's world-famous smörgåsbord buffet. Among the usual delicacies of herring, gravlax, meatballs, short ribs and *blodpudding* (blood pudding)

FOODIE GEMS

The following are five foodie gems you really shouldn't miss, for both atmosphere and flavour:

- Edsbacka Krog (see boxed text, p115) is Sweden's only two-starred Michelin restaurant, with a cheaper spin-off across the road.
- Mathias Dahlgren (p103) does obscenely fine things to local produce at what has become Stockholm's new epicurean mecca.
- Krakas Krog (p165) blends simplicity and elegance with tremendous gourmet creations made with brilliant Gotland produce.
- Da Aldo (p183) is arguably Sweden's finest spot for Roman-style gelato.
- Publik (p217) peddles tasty, honest grub with a side serve of indie cool.

DOS & DON'TS

On formal occasions, do wait for the host or hostess to welcome you to the table before eating or drinking. Aside from formal 'skåls', don't clink glasses (it's considered vulgar) and never sip until the host or hostess says, 'Now everyone may drink when he or she likes.' Don some decent socks when dining in someone's home, as you'll generally be expected to take off your shoes in the foyer. And don't go empty handed; a bottle of wine or flowers will make the right impression.

---

are seasonal gems like baked ham with mustard sauce, and *Janssons frestelse,* a hearty casserole of sweet cream, potato, onion and anchovy. *Julmust,* a sweet dark-brown soft drink that foams like a beer when poured, and *glögg,* warm spiced wine, are also Yuletide staples. The best accompaniment to a warm cup of *glögg,* available at kiosks everywhere in winter, is a *pepparkaka* (gingerbread biscuit).

Sweden's short, intense summers see many hit the countryside for lazy holidays and alfresco noshing. Summer lunch favourites include various *inlagd sill* (pickled herring) with *knäckebröd* (crispbread), strong cheese like the crumbly *Västerbottens ost,* boiled potatoes, diced chives and cream, strawberries, plus a finger or two of *snaps* and some light beer 'to help the fish swim down to the stomach'. Towards the end of summer, Swedes celebrate (or commiserate) its passing with *Kräftskivor* (crayfish parties) where people wearing bibs and party hats get together to eat *kräftor* boiled with dill, drink *snaps* and sing *snapsvisor* (drinking songs).

For sweet tooths, the lead-up to Lent means one thing: the *semla* bun. A wickedly decadent concoction of a wheat-flour bun crammed with whipped cream and almond paste, it was traditionally eaten on *fettisdagen* (Fat Tuesday). These days, it undermines diets as early as January.

> Conscientious food shoppers should look out for the KRAV label, which denotes that the produce in question is certified organic, non-GMO and ethically grown or raised. For more information visit www.krav.se.

SWEDISH SIPPING

Coffee is Sweden's unofficial national drink, with an ever-increasing number of cafes ditching the percolated stuff for Italian-style espresso. Tea is also readily available. *Saft* is cordial commonly made from lingonberries, blueberries and elderflowers.

While the number of wine buffs is increasing, Sweden remains a predominantly beer-drinking nation. *Öl* (beer) is ranked by alcohol content; the stronger the beer, the higher its price and, generally speaking, the more flavour it has. Light beers (*lättöl;* less than 2.25%) and 'folk' beers (*folköl;* 2.25% to 3.5%) account for about two-thirds of all beer sold in Sweden; these can be bought in supermarkets. Medium-strength beer (*mellanöl;* 3.5% to 4.5%) and strong beer (*starköl;* over 4.5%) can be bought only at outlets of the state-owned alcohol store, Systembolaget, or in bars and restaurants.

Swedes generally drink strong beer on special occasions – partly because the everyday beer produced by mass breweries like Falcon, Åbro, Pripps and Spendrups is entirely unremarkable. There are a few good microbrews available in taverns (look for Jämtlands brewery's very good Fallen Angel bitter; Tärnö's Nils Oscar range is good, too), and the major producers also tend to bring out decent speciality beers on a limited scale. The large breweries also produce a wide range of drinks from cider to light and dark lagers, porter and stout. Pear and apple ciders are also common, frequently in light-alcohol or alcohol-free versions. Local megabrew lagers, such as Spendrups, Pripps or Falcon, cost anywhere from Skr40 to Skr58 a pint, and imported beer or mixed drinks can be twice that.

Wines and spirits can be bought only at Systembolaget. Sweden's trademark spirit, *brännvin,* also called aquavit and drunk as *snaps,* is a fiery

> Pick up the gorgeous cookbook *Längtans Mat quavit* (Very Swedish), by Annica Triberg, for a brilliant introduction to Swedish classics, not to mention photos that look good enough to eat.

and strongly flavoured drink that's usually distilled from potatoes and spiced with herbs.

As for the bottom line: the legal drinking age in Sweden is 18 years, although many bars and restaurants impose significantly higher age limits.

THE EATING LOW-DOWN

Most Swedes start the day with coffee and a *frukost* (breakfast) of corn-flakes or muesli with *filmjölk* (cultured milk) or fruit-flavoured yoghurt. Hotels and hostels offer breakfast buffets of several types of bread, pastries, crispbread and/or rolls, with *pålägg* (toppings) including butter, sliced cheese, boiled eggs, sliced meat, liver pâté, Kalles caviar (an iconic caviar spread), pickled herring, sliced cucumber and marmalade.

A hearty lunch has long been a mainstay of the workforce, with cafes and restaurants usually serving a weekday lunch special (or a choice of several) called *dagens rätt* at a fixed price (typically Skr65 to Skr95) between 11.30am and 2pm Monday to Friday. It's a practice originally supported and subsidised by the Swedish government with the goal of keeping workers happy and efficient, and it's still one of the most economical ways to sample top-quality Swedish cooking. The *dagens rätt* usually includes a main course, salad, beverage, bread and butter, and coffee.

Swedish icon Ikea sells a whopping 150 million meatballs a year worldwide.

For a lighter lunch yet, head to a *konditori*, where staples include pastries and the delectable *smörgås* (open sandwich), an artfully arranged creation usually filled with greens, shrimp or salmon, roe, boiled egg and mustard-dill sauce.

Street snacks are the cheapest, quickest way to fill up in Sweden, particularly in cities but also on beaches, along motorways and in many camping areas. A snack kiosk with a grill is known as a *gatukök* – literally, street kitchen. In the world of Swedish street food, hot dogs reign supreme – the basic model is called a *grillad korv med bröd,* grilled sausage with bread (hot dog in a bun), although you can also ask for it boiled *(kokt korv).* Adventurous souls can do a mind-boggling variety of things to the *korv,* chiefly involving rolling it up with any number of accompaniments, from shrimp salad, mashed potatoes or coleslaw to fried onions.

Kebab stands and fast-food windows run a close second on the munch-on-the-go scene.

Opening Times & Tipping

Sweden's official Waffle Day is 25 March.

Restaurants generally open from 11.30am to 2pm for lunch, and from 5pm until 10pm for dinner. Cafes, bakeries and coffee shops are likely to be open all day, from 7am or 8am in the morning until at least 6pm.

Tipping is not common in Sweden. A service cost is figured into the bill. If you've had excellent service, a 10% to 15% tip is a suitable compliment.

Self-Catering

Supermarkets across Sweden have pre-prepared foods for quick snacks, but making your own meals is easy enough too if you're hostelling or staying in camping grounds with good facilities.

Easily found in Swedish towns and villages, the main supermarket chains are ICA, Konsum and Hemköp (the last often found inside Åhléns department stores).

By law, both the item price and the comparative price per kilogram have to be labelled. Plastic carrier bags usually cost Skr2 at the cashier.

The ideal way to buy produce is through small, rural farm shops or roadside stands.

Vegetarians & Vegans

Vegetarian and vegan restaurants are common; they're easy to find in the major cities, and even in rural areas restaurants generally have one or two herbivorous main-course options on the menu. For this reason we haven't created a separate category for vegetarian listings in this book.

EAT YOUR WORDS

Despite the fact that most Swedes speak excellent English (and often several other languages), it's handy, and polite, to be able to order from a Swedish menu. For key phrases and pronunciation guidelines, see p343.

Useful Phrases

Could I see the menu, please?
Kan jag får se menyn?   kan ya for·*se*·a me·*newn*?

Is service included in the bill?
Är serveringsavgiften inräknad?   air ser·*ve*·a·rings aav·yif·*ten* in·*rek*·nad?

I'm a vegetarian.
Jag är vegetarian.   ya air ve·ge·*ta*·ri·an

I don't eat meat.
Jag äter inte kött.   ya *air*·ter *in*·te shert

breakfast	*frukost*	*froo*·kost
lunch	*lunch*	lunfh
dinner	*middag*	*mid*·daa
menu	*meny*	me·*newn*
children's menu	*barnmeny*	baan me·*newn*
wine list	*vinlista*	veen·lis·ta
first course/entrée	*förrätt*	fer·ret
main course	*huvudrätt/varmrätt*	hu·vu·dret/vaam·*ret*
daily special	*dagens rätt*	*daa*·gens ret
	(usually only at lunchtime)	

Food Glossary

BASICS

bröd	brrerd	bread
knäckebröd	knehk·ke·brrerd	crispbread
ost	ost	cheese
senap	*sen*·nap	mustard
smör	smer·rr	butter
smörgås	smer·gors	sandwich
socker	sok·kehrr	sugar
soppa	sop·puh	soup
sylt/marmelad	silt/muhrr·meh·*laad*	jam/marmalade
ägg	ehg	eggs

VEGETABLES & SPICES (GRÖNSAKER & KRYDDOR)

kryddor	krrewd·der	spices
lök	lerk	onion
majs	*ma*·ees	corn
morot	moo·rroot	carrot
paprika	pahp·rri·kuh	capsicum
svamp/champinjoner	svuhmp/fham·pin·*yoo*·nehrr	mushrooms
vitlök	veet·lerk	garlic

FRUIT (FRUKT)

blåbär	blor·baer	blueberries
hallon	hal·lon	raspberries

hjortron	yoor·tron	cloudberries
jordgubbar	yoord·gub·bar	strawberries
lingon	ling·on	lingonberries
smultron	smult·ron	wild strawberries

MEAT (KÖTT)

anka	an·ka	duck
biff/entrecote	bif/uhn·trreh·kor	steak
bröst	brerst	breast
filé	fil·lea	fillet
fläsk griskött/kotlett	flehsk gris·shert/kot·leht	pork chop/cutlet
köttbullar	chert·bul·luhrr	meatballs
kyckling	sheek·ling	chicken
lammkotletter	luhm·kot·leht·tehrr	lamb chops
leverpastej	lea·vehrr·puhs·tehy	liver pâté
oxfilé	ooks·fil·lea	fillet of beef
rådjur	rord·yur	venison
renstek	ren·stek	reindeer
skinka	shing·ka	ham
älg	el·ye	elk

FISH & SEAFOOD (FISK & SKALDJUR)

abborre	uhb·bor·rreh	perch
forell	fo·rrehl	trout
gädda	yed·da	pike
hälleflundra/helgeflundra	hehl·leh/flund·rruh	halibut
hummer	hum·mehrr	lobster
krabba	krruhb·buh	crab
kräftor	kref·tor	crayfish
lax	luhks	salmon
makrill	muhk·rril	mackerel
musslor	mus·ler	mussels
ostron	oost·rron	oysters
räkor	rrair·ker	shrimps/prawns
sill	sil	herring
strömming	strrer·ming	Baltic herring
tonfisk	toon·fisk	tuna
vitling	vit·ling	whiting
ål	orl	eel

DESSERTS (DESSERTER/EFTERRÄTTER)

äppelpaj	ehp·pehl·puhy	apple pie
glass	gluhs	ice cream
kaka	kah·kuh	cake
pannkakor/plättar	puhn·kah·ker/pleht·tuhrr	pancakes
småkakor	smor·kah·ker	sweet biscuits/cookies
våffla	vor·fla	waffle

COOKING STYLES

bakad	baa·kad	roasted/baked
friterad	free·te·rad	deep fried
gravad	graa·vad	cured
grillad	gril·lad	grilled
halstrad	hal·strad	grilled
kokt	kokt	boiled
marinerad	ma·reen·nair·rad	marinated
rökt	rerkt	smoked
stekt	stekt	fried

Environment

THE LAND
Geography

Sweden occupies the eastern side of the Scandinavian peninsula, sharing borders with Norway, Finland and Denmark (the latter a mere 4km to the southwest of Sweden and joined to it by a spectacular bridge and tunnel).

Sweden's surface area (449,964 sq km) is stretched long and thin. Around one-sixth of the country lies within the Arctic Circle, yet Sweden is surprisingly warm thanks to the Gulf Stream: minimum northern temperatures are around -20°C (compared with -45°C in Alaska).

Sweden is a long, drawn-out 1574km from north to south, but averages only about 300km in width.

The country has a 7000km-long coastline, with myriad islands – the Stockholm archipelago alone has up to 24,000. The largest and most notable islands are Gotland and Öland on the southeast coast, and the best sandy beaches are down the west coast, south of Göteborg.

Forests make up an amazing 57% of Sweden's landscape. It's not short of inland lakes, either, with around 100,000 in all. Vänern is Western Europe's largest lake at 5585 sq km. Kebnekaise (2111m), part of the glaciated Kjölen Mountains on the Norwegian border, is Sweden's highest mountain.

Population

Most Swedes live in the flat south of the country, which has an average population density of 35 people per sq km. The capital, Stockholm, has 266 people per sq km, but in the empty north that figure drops to nine.

ARCTIC PHENOMENA

Aurora Borealis

There are few sights as mesmerising as an undulating aurora. Although these appear in many forms – pillars, streaks, wisps and haloes of vibrating light – they're most memorable when they take the form of pale curtains, apparently wafting on a gentle breeze. Most often, the Arctic aurora appears faint green, light yellow or rose-coloured, but in periods of extreme activity it can change to bright yellow or crimson.

The visible aurora borealis, also called northern lights (norrsken), are caused by streams of charged particles from the sun and the solar winds, which are diverted by the Earth's magnetic field towards the polar regions.

Because the field curves downward in a halo surrounding the magnetic poles, the charged particles are drawn earthward here. Their interaction with atoms in the upper atmosphere (about 160km above the surface) releases the energy creating the visible aurora (in the southern hemisphere, the corresponding phenomenon is called the aurora australis). During periods of high activity, a single auroral storm can produce a trillion watts of electricity with a current of one million amps.

The best time of year to catch the northern lights in Sweden is from October to March, although you may see them as early as August in the far north.

Midnight Sun & Polar Night

Because the earth is tilted on its axis, the polar regions are constantly facing the sun at their respective summer solstices, and are tilted away from it in the winter. The Arctic and Antarctic Circles, at latitudes 66°32'N and 66°32'S respectively, are the southern and northern limits of constant daylight on the longest day of the year.

The northern one-seventh of Sweden lies north of the Arctic Circle, but even in central Sweden the summer sun is never far below the horizon. Between late May and mid-July, nowhere north of Stockholm experiences true darkness; in Umeå, for example, the first stars aren't visible until mid-July. Although many visitors initially find it difficult to sleep while the sun is shining brightly outside, most people get used to it.

Conversely, winters in the far north are dark and bitterly cold, with only a few hours of twilight to break the long polar nights. During this period, some people suffer from seasonal affective disorder (SAD), which occurs when they're deprived of the vitamin D provided by sunlight. Its effects may be minimised by taking supplements of vitamin D (as found in cod liver oil) or with special solar spectrum light bulbs.

The 25 historical regions (landskap) are denominators for people's identity and a basis for regional tourist promotion, and are used throughout this book. The 21 counties (län) in Sweden form the basis of local government, and these county administrations are responsible for things like regional public transport (länstrafik) and regional museums (länsmuseum).

Geology

Between 500 and 370 million years ago, the European and North American continental plates collided, throwing up an impressive range of peaks called the Caledonian Mountains, which were as tall as today's Himalayas. Their worn-down stubs form the 800km-long Kjölen Mountains along the border with Norway.

Parts of Skåne and the islands of Öland and Gotland consist of flat limestone and sandstone deposits, probably laid down in a shallow sea east of the Caledonian Mountains during the same period.

Lake Siljan, in the central south, marks the site of Europe's largest meteoric impact: the 3km-wide fireball hurtled into Sweden 360 million years ago, obliterating all life and creating a 75km ring-shaped crater.

WILDLIFE

Thanks to Sweden's geographical diversity, it has a great variety of European animals, birds and plants.

LARGE PREDATORS

Sweden's big carnivores – the bear, wolf, wolverine, lynx and golden eagle – are all endangered species. Illegal hunting carries a maximum prison sentence of four years. Most conflict between human and beast occurs in the Sami reindeer areas: compensation is paid to the Sami whenever predator populations in their lands increase.

Wolves and wolverines top Sweden's most endangered list. Wolf numbers are slowly increasing, however: between 70 and 80 of these beautiful creatures now live in Sweden, mainly in Värmland and Dalarna.

The more solitary wolverine, a larger cousin of the weasel, inhabits high forests and alpine areas along the Norwegian border. Most are in Norrbotten and Västerbotten.

Brown bears were persecuted for centuries, but recent conservation measures have seen numbers increase to around 2000. Bears mostly live in forests in the northern half of the country, but are spreading southwards.

Another fascinating forest dweller is the solitary lynx, which belongs to the panther family and is Europe's only large cat. Sweden's 1000 lynx are notoriously difficult to spot because of their nocturnal habits.

If you have no luck with wildlife in the wild, Grönklitt Björnpark (see p274) has an endangered-animal breeding program with large and natural-looking enclosures.

> The lemming is the smallest but most important mammal in the Arctic regions – its numbers set the population limits for everything that preys on it.

OTHER MAMMALS

The the symbol of Sweden, more than any other animal, is the elk (moose in the USA), a gentle, knobby-kneed creature that grows up to 2m tall. Elk are a serious traffic hazard, particularly at night: they can dart out in front of your car at up to 50km/h. For elk-spotting (and sausages), visit Sweden's biggest elk park Grönåsens Älgpark (p149).

Around 260,000 domesticated reindeer roam the northern areas, under the watchful eyes of Sami herders. They, too, are a major traffic hazard.

Hikers encountering lemmings in the mountains may be surprised when these frantic little creatures become enraged and launch bold attacks. The mouselike lemmings are famous for their extraordinary reproductive capacity. Every 10 years or so, the population explodes, resulting in denuded landscapes and thousands of dead lemmings in rivers and lakes, and on roads.

Musk ox were reintroduced into Norway in the late 1940s, and herds have wandered into Sweden, notably in Härjedalen county. Angry adults have a habit of charging anything that annoys them.

Forests, lakes and rivers support beavers, otters, mink, badgers and pine martens. Weasels and stoats are endemic in all counties; northern varieties turn white in the winter and are trapped for their fur (ermine).

Grey and common seals swim in Swedish waters, although overfishing has caused a serious decline in numbers. In 1988 and 2002, thousands of seals were wiped out by the phocine distemper virus (PDV) after pollution weakened their immune systems. Common dolphins may also be observed from time to time.

> Swedish elk are slightly smaller than their closely related American relatives.

> The fearsome-looking brown bear's favourite food is…blueberries!

BIRDS

Sweden attracts hundreds of nesting species and permanent residents. Some of the best birdwatching sites are the Falsterbo peninsula (p182); Öland, including the nature reserve at its southernmost tip (p157); Getterön Nature

Reserve (p238); Tåkern (p137); Hornborgasjön, between Skara and Falköping in Västergötland; and the national parks Färnebofjärden (p282), Muddus and Abisko (p309).

The golden eagle is one of Sweden's most endangered species. It's found in the mountains, and is easily identified by its immense wing span. Another dramatic bird of prey is the white-tailed sea eagle.

Coastal species include common, little and Arctic terns, various gulls, oystercatchers, cormorants, guillemots and razorbills. Territorial Arctic skuas can be seen in a few places, notably the Stockholm archipelago and the coast north of Göteborg.

Look for goldcrests in coniferous forests. A few spectacular waxwings breed in Lappland, but in winter they arrive from Russia in large numbers and are found throughout Sweden. Grouse or capercaillie strut the forest floor, while ptarmigan and snow buntings hang out above the tree line along the Norwegian border.

Sweden has a wide range of wading and water birds, including the unusual and beautiful red-necked phalaropes, which only breed in the northern mountains. Other waders you're likely to encounter are majestic grey herons (southern Sweden), noisy bitterns (south-central Sweden), plovers (including dotterel, in the mountains) and turnstones.

See p66 for information about local ornithological groups.

FISH & CRUSTACEANS

Many marine species have been badly affected by ecological problems in the Baltic (see p56).

Sprats and herring are economically important food sources. Among other marine species, haddock, sea trout, whiting, flounder and plaice are reasonably abundant, particularly in the salty waters of the Kattegatt and Skagerrak, but the cod is heading for extinction due to overfishing.

Indigenous crayfish were once netted or trapped in Sweden's lakes, but overfishing and disease has driven them to extinction.

Plants

Swedish flora is typical of that in temperate climates, and includes around 250 species of flowering plants.

In the mountains along the border with Norway, alpine and Arctic flowers predominate, including mountain avens (with large white eight-petalled flowers), long-stalked mountain sorrel (an unusual source of vitamin C), glacier crowfoot, alpine aster and various saxifrages.

The limey soils of Öland and Gotland produce rare flowering plants including orchids, all of them protected.

Southern Sweden originally had well-mixed woodland, but much of this has been replaced by farmland or conifer plantations. Northern forests are dominated by Scots pine, Norway spruce and various firs.

Hikers will find a profusion of edible berries, mostly ripe between mid-July and early September. The most popular are blueberries (huckleberries), which grow on open uplands, blue swamp-loving bilberries, red cranberries, muskeg crowberries and amber-coloured cloudberries. The latter, known as *hjortron,* grow one per stalk on open swampy ground and are a delicacy.

NATIONAL PARKS

Sweden was the first country in Europe to set up a national park (1909). There are now 28, along with around 2600 smaller nature reserves; together they cover about 9% of Sweden. The organisation Naturvårdsverket oversees and produces pamphlets about the parks in Swedish and English, along with

---

For proof we aren't making up these crazy bird names, read *Where to Watch Birds in Scandinavia* by Johann Stenlund.

Four of the national parks in Lappland – Muddus, Padjelanta, Sarek and Stora Sjöfallet – are Unesco World Heritage sites.

the excellent book *Nationalparkerna i Sverige* (National Parks in Sweden).

Four of Sweden's large rivers (Kalixälven, Piteälven, Vindelälven and Torneälven) have been declared National Heritage Rivers in order to protect them from hydroelectric development.

The right of public access to the countryside *(allemansrätten)* includes national parks and nature reserves; see p59 for details.

Northern Sweden

Abisko Numerous hiking routes and good accessibility. Northern gateway to the famed Kungsleden hiking track (p60).

Haparanda Skärgård A group of several islands in the far north of the Gulf of Bothnia, with sandy beaches, striking dunes and migrant bird life. Reached by boat from Haparanda.

Muddus Ancient forests and muskeg bogs, plus several deep and impressive gorges, and superb birdwatching opportunities.

Padjelanta High moorland surrounds the lakes Vastenjaure and Virihaure, favoured by a range of Swedish wildlife. The renowned hiking trail, Padjelantaleden, is here (p62).

Pieljekaise Just south of the Arctic Circle, with moorlands, birch forests, flowering meadows and lakes rich in Arctic char.

Sarek Sweden's best-loved national park, with wild mountain ranges, glaciers, deep valleys, impressive rivers and vast tracts of birch and willow forest. There's no road access, but experienced hikers can reach the park from the Kungsleden route.

Stora Sjöfallet This park's famous waterfall has been throttled by hydroelectric development, and the wildlife and vegetation have suffered as a result.

Vadvetjåkka Sweden's northernmost national park. Protects a large river delta containing bogs, lakes, limestone caves and numerous bird species. Access on foot from Abisko.

Central Sweden

Björnlandet In the far south of Lappland and well off the beaten track. Natural forest, cliffs and boulder fields.

Färnebofjärden Noted for its abundant bird life, forests, rare lichens and mosses. Good road access to the eastern side.

Fulufjället Sweden's newest national park (2002) contains Njupeskär, the country's highest waterfall at 93m.

Garphyttan A tiny 111-hectare park easily reached from Örebro. Previously cultivated areas have fantastic springtime flower displays.

Hamra Measuring only 800m by 400m, this is a protected area of virgin coniferous forest. Access from a minor road off the E45.

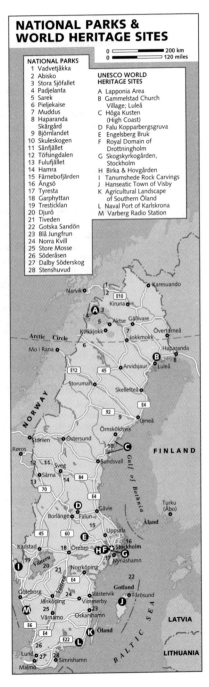

NATIONAL PARKS & WORLD HERITAGE SITES

0 ——— 200 km
0 ——— 120 miles

NATIONAL PARKS
1 Vadvetjåkka
2 Abisko
3 Stora Sjöfallet
4 Padjelanta
5 Sarek
6 Pieljekaise
7 Muddus
8 Haparanda Skärgård
9 Björnlandet
10 Skuleskogen
11 Sånfjället
12 Töfsingdalen
13 Fulufjället
14 Hamra
15 Färnebofjärden
16 Ängsö
17 Tyresta
18 Garphyttan
19 Tresticklan
20 Djurö
21 Tiveden
22 Gotska Sandön
23 Blå Jungfrun
24 Norra Kvill
25 Store Mosse
26 Söderåsen
27 Dalby Söderskog
28 Stenshuvud

UNESCO WORLD HERITAGE SITES
A Lapponia Area
B Gammelstad Church Village; Luleå
C Höga Kusten (High Coast)
D Falu Kopparbergsgruva
E Engelsberg Bruk
F Royal Domain of Drottningholm
G Skogskyrkogården, Stockholm
H Birka & Hovgården
I Tanumshede Rock Carvings
J Hanseatic Town of Visby
K Agricultural Landscape of Southern Öland
L Naval Port of Karlskrona
M Varberg Radio Station

Sånfjället Natural mountain moorland with extensive views. Road and foot access possible from several sides.

Skuleskogen A hilly coastal area with untouched forest, deep valleys, Bronze Age graves, good hiking trails and great sea views. Access from the nearby E4 motorway.

Tresticklan An area of natural coniferous forest, with small rift valleys and fine bird life. Access by road from Dals-Ed, in Dalsland.

Tyresta Stockholm's own national park: an extensive forest area with huge 300-year-old pines and interesting rock formations. Easy access by car or bus.

Töfsingdalen Exceptionally wild and remote, with virtually impenetrable boulder fields and pine forest. Must be approached on foot.

Ängsö A tiny island in the northern Stockholm archipelago noted for wonderful meadows, deciduous forest, bird life and spring flowers. Boat access from Furusund.

Southern Sweden

Blå Jungfrun A wonderful island with smooth granite slabs, caves, a labyrinth and great views. Boat access from Oskarshamn.

Dalby Söderskog A forested haven of peace for people and wildlife. Bus access from Lund.

Djurö Bird life and deer on an archipelago of 30 islands in Lake Vänern. Access by private boat only.

Gotska Sandön A beautiful sandy isle featuring dunes, dying pine forest and varied flora and fauna, including unusual beetles. Boats from Nynäshamn and Fårösund.

Norra Kvill A tiny 114-hectare park noted for its ancient coniferous forest, excellent flora and gigantic boulders.

Söderåsen A new park easily reached by road. Contains deep fissure valleys, lush forests and flowing watercourses. Pleasant hiking trails and cycling paths.

Stenshuvud A small coastal park with a great combination of beaches, forest and moorland. Easily reached by road; buses from Simrishamn.

Store Mosse Dominated by bogs with sand dunes, and noted for its bird life and great views. A road runs through the park.

Tiveden Wild hills, forests and lakes, plus extensive boulder fields, beaches and excellent viewpoints. Minor roads and trails pass through it; access from Rd 49.

ENVIRONMENTAL ISSUES

Ecological consciousness among Swedes is high, and reflected in concern for native animals, clean water and renewable resources. Sweden has a good record when it comes to environmental policies. Industrial and agricultural waste is highly regulated, sewage disposal advanced, greenhouse gas emissions low, and recycling extremely popular.

The North and, particularly, the Baltic Seas are suffering severe pollution, eutrophication and vast algae blooms, caused partly by nitrogen run-off from Swedish farms. As a result, herring, sprats and Baltic salmon contain much higher than average levels of cancer-causing dioxins; they're still being sold in Sweden at the time of writing, but with a health warning attached.

Overfishing of these waters is also a huge cause for concern, with cod and Norwegian lobster on the verge of extinction. Fishing quotas are determined by the EU as a whole, and there's been a constant struggle to achieve balance between sustainable fish stocks and consumer demand, according to the website of the Swedish Government Offices. The current Swedish government has moved to reduce cod-fishing quotas as well as increase the amount of funding for fishing controls.

Some 47% of Sweden's electricity generation comes from hydroelectric sources, mainly dams on large northern rivers. However, there are associated problems, including the displacement of Sami people, landscape scarring, dried-up rivers and waterfalls 'downstream' of the dams, high-voltage power lines sweeping across remote regions, and the depletion of fish stocks, particularly Baltic salmon, which cannot return up-

You can swim, and fish for trout and salmon, in the waters by Stockholm's city centre.

river to their spawning grounds. In 1993 several large rivers were named National Heritage Rivers, a status that protects them from any further hydroelectric development.

Nuclear power generation has always been a contentious issue in Sweden. At a referendum held in March 1980, the electorate narrowly voted for the phasing-out of the nuclear program by 2010. In March 2007, however, even the formerly antinuclear Christian Democrat party abandoned the idea of a phase-out. According to the World Nuclear Association, Sweden has 10 nuclear reactors (as of August 2008), with plans for four more to be built after 2010.

Environmental Organisations

Naturvårdsverket (Swedish Environmental Protection Agency; ☎ 08-698 10 00; www.environ .se) Government-run central environmental authority, with an extensive and informative website.

Svenska Ekoturismföreningen (Swedish Society of Ecotourism; ☎ 063-12 12 44; www .ekoturism.org, in Swedish) Promotes environmentally friendly tourism.

Svenska Naturskyddsföreningen (Swedish Society for Nature Conservation; ☎ 08-702 65 00; www.snf.se/english.cfm) Excellent website on current environmental issues.

Outdoor Activities

Sweden has thousands of square kilometres of forest with hiking and cycling tracks, vast numbers of lakes connected by mighty rivers, and a range of alpine mountains – it's ideal for outdoor activities. Much of the information available on the internet is in Swedish. If you can't read the language, contact the national organisations (listed under individual activities in this section) for the sport you're interested in. Regional and local tourist offices and staff at outdoor stores can also point you in the right direction.

For organised activity holidays, see p339, and also check individual destinations in this book.

HIKING

Swedes love their hiking, and there are many thousands of kilometres of marked trails. European Long Distance Footpaths E1 and E6 run from Varberg to Grövelsjön (1200km) and from Malmö to Norrtälje (1400km), respectively.

Nordkalottleden runs for 450km from Sulitjelma to Kautokeino (both in Norway), but passes through Sweden for most of its route. Finnskogleden is a 240km-long route along the border between Norway and the Värmland region in Sweden.

The Arctic Trail (800km) is a joint development of Sweden, Norway and Finland and is entirely above the Arctic Circle; it begins near Kautokeino in Norway and ends in Abisko, Sweden. The most popular route is Kungsleden, in Lappland. Overnight huts and lodges are maintained by Svenska Turistföreningen (STF; opposite).

The best hiking time is between late June and mid-September, when trails are mostly snow-free. After early August the mosquitoes have gone.

Mountain trails in Sweden are marked with cairns, wooden signposts or paint on rocks and trees. Marked trails have bridges across all but the smallest streams, and wet or fragile areas are crossed on duckboards. Avoid following winter routes (marked by poles with red crosses) since they often cross lakes or marshes.

Safety Guidelines

Before embarking on a walking trip, consider the following points to ensure a safe and enjoyable experience:

- Be sure you are healthy and feel comfortable walking for a sustained period.
- Obtain reliable, up-to-date information about physical and environmental conditions along your intended route, and stock up on good maps.
- Be aware of laws, regulations and etiquette regarding wildlife and the environment, including Sweden's *allemansrätten* (right of public access to the countryside; see opposite).
- Walk only in regions and on trails within your realm of experience.
- Be aware that weather conditions can change quickly in northern Sweden: even in summer, prepare for both cold and warm conditions.
- Before you set out, ask about the environmental characteristics that can affect your walk and how local, experienced walkers deal with these considerations.

English-language coverage of hiking and climbing in the Swedish mountains is scarce; see *Scandinavian Mountains* by Peter Lennon, and ask at tourist offices locally for regional guides.

True North: The Grand Landscapes of Sweden, by Per Wästberg and Tommy Hammarström, contains stunning images by some of Sweden's top nature photographers.

THE RIGHT OF PUBLIC ACCESS

Allemansrätten, the right of public access to the countryside, is not a legal right but a common-law privilege. It includes national parks and nature reserves, although special rules may apply. Full details in English can be found on the website www.allemansratten.se.

You're allowed to walk, ski, boat or swim on private land as long as you stay at least 70m from houses and keep out of gardens, fenced areas and cultivated land. You can pick berries and mushrooms, provided they're not protected species. Generally you should move on after one or two nights' camping.

Don't leave rubbish or take live wood, bark, leaves, bushes or nuts. Fires fuelled with fallen wood are allowed where safe, but not on bare rocks (which can crack from the heat). Use a bucket of water to douse a campfire even if you think that it's completely out. Cars and motorcycles may not be driven across open land or on private roads; look out for the sign *ej motorfordon* (no motor vehicles). Dogs must be kept on leads between 1 March and 20 August. Close all farm gates and don't disturb farm animals or reindeer. Off-limit areas where birds are nesting are marked with a yellow or red-and-yellow sign containing the words *fågelskydd – tillträde förbjudet.*

If you have a car or bicycle, look for free camping sites around unsealed forest tracks leading from secondary country roads. Make sure your spot is at least 50m from the track and not visible from any house, building or sealed road. Bring drinking water and food, and don't pollute any water sources with soap or food waste.

Above all, remember the mantra: 'Do not disturb, do not destroy.'

Equipment

Hikers should be well equipped and prepared for snow in the mountains, even in summer. Prolonged bad weather in the northwest isn't uncommon – Sarek and Sylarna are the most notorious areas. In summer you'll need good boots, waterproof jacket and trousers, several layers of warm clothing (including spare dry clothes), warm hat, sun hat, mosquito repellent (a mosquito head-net is also highly advisable), water bottle, maps, compass and sleeping bag. Basic supplies are often available at huts, and most lodges serve meals (but check first, especially outside of high season). If you're going off the main routes you should obviously take full camping equipment.

Equipment can usually be hired from the STF, but don't rely on this. If you need to replace gear, try the small STF lodge shops or the nationwide chain **Naturkompaniet** (www.naturkompaniet.se). It's a Swedish-only website, but click on 'butiker' and you'll find a list of stores.

Information

Information in English is scarce – the best source is the youth-hostel organisation **Svenska Turistföreningen** (STF; Swedish Touring Association; ☎ 08-463 21 00; www.svenskaturistforeningen.se), one of Sweden's largest tour operators. Most of its publications are Swedish-only, but STF staff will answer questions and provide information in English by phone or email.

For nonmountain walking, address enquiries to **Svenska Gång-och Vandrarförbundet** (SGVF; Swedish Walking Association; ☎ 031-726 61 10; svenskgang@vsif.o.se).

MAPS

STF lodges sell up-to-date maps, but it's a good idea to buy them in advance. Try local and regional tourist offices, or buy online or in person at outdoor-equipment shops or **Kartbutiken** (Map p82; ☎ 08-20 23 03; www.kartbutiken .se; Kungsgatan 74, Stockholm). Maps cost around Skr120 each.

Kungsleden

Kungsleden, meaning 'The King's Trail', is Sweden's most important way-marked hiking and skiing route, running for 450km from Abisko (in the north of Lappland) to Hemavan. The route is normally split into five mostly easy or moderate sections. The fifth section has a gap of 188km in STF's hut network, between Kvikkjokk and Ammarnäs. The most popular section is the northern one, from Abisko to Nikkaluokta; Sweden's highest mountain Kebnekaise (2111m) is a glorious extra for this section.

ABISKO TO NIKKALUOKTA

From Abisko it's 72km to Singi, 86km to Kebnekaise Fjällstation and 105km to Nikkaluokta (seven to eight days; Fjällkartan BD6). This section of Kungsleden passes through spectacular alpine scenery and is usually followed from north to south. It includes a 33km-long trail from Singi to Nikkaluokta, which isn't part of Kungsleden, but allows an easy exit from the area. An alternative (and much more challenging) start is from Riksgränsen on the Norway-Sweden border; the 30km route from there to STF's Unna Allakas is very rocky in places and you'll need to camp en route.

The STF has mountain lodges at Abisko and Kebnekaise, and there are also five STF huts. Many people stop at STF's Kebnekaise Fjällstation for a couple of nights, and some attempt the ascent of Kebnekaise (Sweden's highest mountain) from there – see below.

Public transport is available at Abisko, with rail connections to Narvik (Norway), or east to Kiruna (Skr91, 1½ hours) and beyond. There are two buses that run daily between Abisko and Kiruna (Skr85 to Skr103, 1½ hours), and also a twice-daily bus service that runs between Nikkaluokta and Kiruna (Skr76, one hour).

KEBNEKAISE

The (optional) hike to the top of Sweden's highest mountain is one of the best in the country and the views of the surrounding peaks and glaciers are incredible on a clear day. In July and August, the marked trail up the southern flanks is usually snow-free and no technical equipment is required to reach the southern top (2111m). To get to the northern top (2097m) from the southern top involves an airy traverse of a knife-edge ice ridge with a rope, an ice axe and crampons. Fjällkartan BD6 (Abisko–Kebnekaise) covers the route at 1:100,000, but there's also the very detailed 1:20,000 Fjällkartan Kebnekaise.

The trip involves 1900m of ascent and descent. Allow 12 hours, and an extra 1½ hours if you want to include the northern top.

NIKKALUOKTA TO SALTOLUOKTA

This section is 71km from Nikkaluokta to Vakkotavare, and 38km from Singi to Saltoluokta (five days; Fjällkartan BD8). The scenery south of Singi is more rounded and less dramatic than the landscape around Kebnekaise. STF has mountain lodges at Kebnekaise and Saltoluokta, and regular huts along the trail. You may have to row yourself 1km across lake Teusajaure (there's an STF boat service in peak season). Everyone takes the bus along the road from Vakkotavare to Kebnats (Skr70 to Skr100), where there's an STF ferry across the lake to Saltoluokta Fjällstation. There's a twice-daily bus service from Ritsem to Gällivare via Vakkotavare and Kebnats.

SALTOLUOKTA TO KVIKKJOKK

This section is 73km (four days; Fjällkartan BD10). Excellent side trips can be taken from Aktse into Sarek National Park, the wildest part of Sweden.

'The hike to the top of Kebnekaise is one of the best in the country and the views of the surrounding peaks and glaciers are incredible on a clear day'

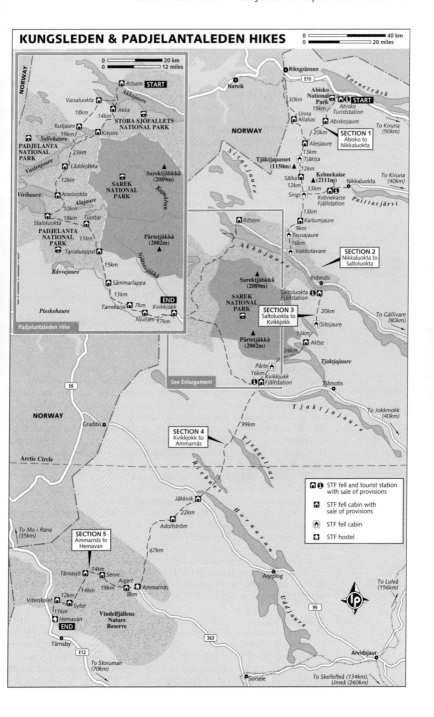

KUNGSLEDEN & PADJELANTALEDEN HIKES

Saltoluokta to Kvikkjokk can be completed in four days, but allow six days to include trips into Sarek.

STF has a lodge at Saltoluokta, huts at Sitojaure, Aktse and Pårte, and another lodge in Kvikkjokk.

Sami families run private boat services across the lakes at Sitojaure and Aktse, which can be arranged through the STF lodges. Kvikkjokk has a twice-daily bus service in summer to Jokkmokk (Skr134) train station.

KVIKKJOKK TO AMMARNÄS

This section is 188km (two weeks; Fjällkartan BD14 for the north section, Fjällkartan BD16 for south). There are only a few locally run huts on this section, so you'll need a tent. The more interesting northern part, Kvikkjokk to Jäkkvik (99km), can be completed in five or six days.

Boat services for lake crossings are available at Kvikkjokk, Vuonatjviken (Lake Riebnes) and Saudal (Hornavan). Buses run six days per week (not Saturday) from Skellefteå to Bodø (Norway) via Jäkkvik, and one to four times daily from Sorsele to Ammarnäs.

AMMARNÄS TO HEMAVAN

This section is 78km (four to five days; Fjällkartan AC2). Most of the south-ernmost section of Kungsleden runs through Vindelfjällens Nature Reserve. The trail is mostly easy, but with a long initial climb.

The STF has hostels at Ammarnäs and Hemavan and five huts en route, which all sell provisions.

The Umeå–Hemavan bus runs three or four times daily (Skr233, six hours, only once on Sunday), and continues to Mo i Rana (Norway; eight hours, once daily).

Padjelantaleden

'The mountainous part of western Jämtland is one of Sweden's most popular hiking areas'

The entire 139km Padjelantaleden can be hiked in eight to 14 days (Fjällkartan BD10 and Fjällkartan BD7). It's generally an easy route, with long sections of duckboards, and all rivers are bridged. The southern section, from Kvikkjokk to Staloluokta (four or five days), is the most popular. At the northern end (by lake Akkajaure), you can start at either STF hut, Vaisaluokta or Akka (the latter is easier). Most of the trail lies in Padjelanta National Park, and all huts in the park are owned by **Naturvårdsverket** (Swedish Environmental Protection Agency; ☎ 08-698 10 00; www.environ.se).

STF runs the Såmmarlappa, Tarrekaise and Njunjes huts at the southern end of the trail, and the hostel at Kvikkjokk. You can buy provisions at Staloluokta, Såmmarlappa, Tarrekaise and Kvikkjokk.

To reach the northern end of the trail, take the bus from Gällivare to Ritsem (twice daily) and connect there with the STF ferry to Vaisaluokta and Änonjálmme (1.5km north of the Akka STF hut), which runs from Midsummer to early September, one to three times daily. For details of boats from the end of Padjelantaleden to Kvikkjokk (up to three times daily from July to mid-September), call ☎ 0971-210 12. **Helicopters** (☎ 0971-210 40, 0971-210 68) serve Staloluokta from Ritsem or Kvikkjokk daily from Midsummer up until early August (adult/child Skr850/600).

Jämtland

The mountainous part of western Jämtland is one of Sweden's most popular hiking areas. There's a good network of easy to moderate hiking trails served by STF lodges and huts. The most popular route is the 'Jämtland Triangle' (47km), which takes a minimum of three days; allow an extra day for an ascent of the magnificent mountain Sylarna (1743m), easily climbed from

STF's Sylarna lodge – the route is clearly marked with cairns. The hike runs between STF's Storulvån, Sylarna and Blåhammaren lodges. Sylarna and Blåhammaren don't have road access and Sylarna only has self-catering; Blåhammaren serves full meals. The section from Sylarna to Blåhammaren is very marshy and can be quite difficult in wet conditions. *Fjällkartan Z6* covers the area.

See p294 for public transport details.

MOUNTAINEERING & ROCK CLIMBING

Mountaineers head for Sylarna, Helagsfjället, Sarek National Park and the Kebnekaise region.

The complete traverse of Sylarna involves rock climbing up to grade 3. The ridge traverse of Sarektjåhkkå (2089m) in Sarek, the second-highest mountain in Sweden, is about grade 4. There are lots of other glacier and rock routes in Sarek. The Kebnekaise area has many fine climbing routes (grades 2 to 6), including the north wall of Kaskasapakte (2043m), and the steep ridges of Knivkammen (1878m) and Vaktposten (1852m). Ice climbing in the northern regions is excellent, if you can put up with the darkness and the cold.

For qualified guides, contact **Svenska Bergsguideorganisation** (Swedish Mountain Guide Association; ☎ 098-01 26 56; www3.utsidan.se/sbo). The website is in Swedish, but under *'medlemmar'* there's a list of guides and their contact details.

Rock climbers can practise on the cliffs around Stockholm and Göteborg – there are 34 climbing areas with 1000 routes around Göteborg, and some 200 cliffs around the capital. Other popular spots are Bohuslän, the Kulla Peninsula (north of Helsingborg) and a newly developed bouldering area, Kjugekull, a few kilometres northeast of Kristianstad. You'll find good climbing walls in Stockholm, Göteborg, Uppsala, Skellefteå and Linköping.

For further information, try the helpful **Svenska Klätterförbundet** (Swedish Climbing Federation; ☎ 08-618 82 70; kansliet@klatterforbundet.com).

CYCLING

Sweden is ideal for cycling, particularly in Skåne and Gotland. It's an excellent way to look for prehistoric sites, rune stones and quiet spots for free camping. The cycling season is from May to September in the south, and July and August in the north.

You can cycle on all roads except motorways (green sign with two lanes and a bridge on it) and roads for motor vehicles only (green sign with a car symbol). Highways often have a hard shoulder, which keeps cyclists well clear of motor vehicles. Secondary roads are mostly quiet and safe by European standards.

You can take a bicycle on some *länstrafik* (public transport) trains and most regional buses (free, or up to Skr60). On the Skåne region's Pågatågen trains, a bike costs the price of a child's ticket. On the Öresund trains (which serve routes between Göteborg and Copenhagen, and Kalmar, Alvesta and Copenhagen) you can book a space for your bike on ☎ 0771-75 75 75. Long-distance buses usually don't accept bicycles; Sveriges Järnväg (SJ) allows them on some trains June through August (Skr112). Bikes are transported free on some ferries, including Vägverket routes.

You can hire bicycles from some campsites, hostels, bike workshops and sports shops for about Skr100 a day, or around Skr500 per week.

Some country areas, towns and cities have special cycle routes – contact local tourist offices for information and maps. Kustlinjen (591km) runs from Öregrund (Uppland) southwards along the Baltic coast to Västervik, and Skånespåret (800km) is a fine network of cycle routes. The well-signposted 2600km-long Sverigeleden extends from Helsingborg in the south

'Cycling is an excellent way to look for prehistoric sites, rune stones and quiet spots for free camping'

ADRENALINE JUNKIES ONLY

One of the fastest-growing summer-season activities in Sweden is downhill mountain biking. The sport takes over ski resorts after the snow melts; fully armoured, riders carry their sturdy little bikes up the hill on chair lifts, then barrel down along rough mountain trails at dizzying speeds. **Åre Bike Park** (www.arebikepark.com; lift day-pass Skr210, bike rentals per day from Skr650; ⏱ mid-Jun–Oct) is the mother lode, with 35km of slopes, 17 trails and a potential vertical drop of almost 900m. Multiday packages are available.

---

to Karesuando in the north, and links points of interest with suitable roads (mostly with an asphalt surface) and bicycle paths.

Brochures and Swedish-text guidebooks with decent maps are available from **Svenska Cykelsällskapet** (Swedish Cycling Association; ☎ 08-751 6204; www.svenska -cykelsallskapet.se).

An unusual and very popular cycling activity is *dressin* – also advertised as 'rail pedal trolley', 'cycle trolley' or 'inspection trolley' rides – where you pedal a wheeled contraption along a disused railway line. Trips cost around Skr550 per day. The best area in the country to try out this novel experience is Värmland, which has miles of old track: phone ☎ 054 148041 or check out 'Activities' on the website www.varmland.org for a list of operators.

Around 6% of Swedes play golf, the highest percentage in the world; the nation of 9 million people has 450 golf courses.

GOLF

Sweden has over 400 golf courses, open to everyone, and many hotel chains offer golf packages. Björkliden, near Abisko, is a golf course 240km above the Arctic Circle, and at the Green Line golf course at Haparanda, playing a round means crossing the Swedish-Finnish border four times. Green fees are around Skr400 (higher near metro areas); for more information, contact **Svenska Golfförbundet** (Swedish Golf Federation; ☎ 08-622 15 00; sgf.golf.se).

CANOEING & KAYAKING

Sweden is a real paradise for canoeists and kayakers (canoes are more common). The national canoeing body is **Svenska Kanotförbundet** (Swedish Canoe Federation; ☎ 0155-20 90 80; www.kanot.com). It provides general advice and produces *Kanotväg*, a free, annual brochure listing 75 approved canoe centres that hire out canoes (for around Skr300/1500 per day/week).

According to the right of common access, canoeists may paddle or moor virtually anywhere provided they respect the privacy of others and avoid sensitive nesting areas. More information is available on the internet at www.kanotguiden.com.

SKIING

Large ski resorts cater mainly to downhill (alpine and telemark) skiing and snowboarding, but there's also scope for cross-country skiing. For resort reviews in English, visit www.goski.com and www.thealps.com. **SkiStar** (www .skistar.com) manages two of the largest places, Sälen and Åre, and has good information on its website.

The ski resort of Åre hosts loads of cool events; check www.skistar.com for the latest.

Cross-country (nordic) skiing opportunities vary, but the northwest usually has plenty of snow from December to April (but not much daylight in December and January). Kungsleden and other long-distance tracks provide great skiing. Practically all town areas (except those in the far south) have marked and often illuminated skiing tracks.

The southernmost large resort in Sweden, Sälen (Dalarna), appeals particularly to families, as does Idre, a little further north. Åre, in Jämtland, is great for long downhill runs (over 1000m descent) and cross-country routes, and is the main party place for young skiers. Nearby ski areas at Duved and Storlien are also good and less crowded. In Lappland, Hemavan gets fairly busy with spring skiers, and there are plans to expand the small ski hill next door at Tärnaby. Riksgränsen (at the border with Norway on the E10 Kiruna–Narvik road) is the world's northernmost ski resort, and offers interesting options – including heli-skiing and alpine ski touring – from mid-February until late June. Downhill runs at Riksgränsen aren't suitable for beginners.

Take the usual precautions: don't leave marked routes without emergency food, a good map, local advice and proper equipment including a bivouac bag. Temperatures of -30°C or lower (including wind-chill factor) are possible, so check the daily forecasts. Police and tourist offices have information on local warnings. In mountain ski resorts, where there's a risk of avalanche (*lavin*), susceptible areas are marked by yellow, multilingual signs and buried-skier symbols. Make sure your travel insurance covers skiing.

> Even if you're visiting in winter, bring a good pair of sunglasses to protect your eyes from glare of snowy surfaces.

BOATING & SAILING

Boating and sailing are hugely popular in Sweden. The 7000km-long coastline, with its 60,000 islands, is a sailor's paradise, but look out for the few restricted military areas off the east coast.

Inland, lakes and canals offer pleasant sailing in spring and summer (the canals are generally open for limited seasons). The main canals are the Göta Canal (see boxed text, p140), the Kinda Canal and the Dalsland Canal. Various companies offer short canal cruises; contact local tourist offices for details. Steamboats and cruisers ply the shores of lakes Vättern and Vänern: see individual town sections for details.

Those with private boats will have to pay lock fees and guest harbour fees (around Skr150 per night, although some small places are free). A useful guide is the free, annual *Gästhamnsguiden*, which is published in Swedish by **Svenska Kryssarklubben** (Swedish Cruising Club; ☎ 08-448 28 80; info@sxk.se). It contains comprehensive details of 500 guest harbours throughout the country. It's also available from larger tourist offices and most of the harbours listed.

Svenska Sjöfartsverket (Swedish Maritime Administration; ☎ 011-19 10 00; www.sjofartsverket .se) can send you information on harbour handbooks and sea charts. For charts you can also try **Kartbutiken** (Map p82; ☎ 08-20 23 03; www.kartbutiken.se).

SKATING

Whenever the ice is thick enough, skating enthusiasts take to Stockholm's lake and canal system seeking the longest possible 'run'. When the Baltic Sea freezes (once or twice every 10 years), fantastic tours of Stockholm's

---

IN THE DRINK

Like the human body, Sweden seems to be mostly water, and its inhabitants take full advantage. Swedes need no encouragement to go leaping into lakes, rivers and the sea, whether to swim, surf or dive. Swimming and fishing are popular within the waterways of Stockholm itself, and equally so in the rest of the country.

The white-sand beaches on the west coast south of Göteborg are some of Sweden's finest. Many campsites have outdoor swimming pools. There are numerous family water parks and, for winter, indoor municipal swimming pools.

Also on the west coast, the area around Varberg (p238) is the premier spot for windsurfing.

There are around 10,000 wrecks lying off Sweden's coastline; those in the Baltic Sea are often in a miraculous state of preservation, thanks to the low salinity of the water. The Kulla Peninsula (p196) also has good diving. Sweden's national diving body **Svenska Sportdykarförbundet** (☎ 08-605 60 00; sportdykning@ssdf.se) can help with queries.

archipelago are possible. The skating season usually lasts from December to March. **Stockholms Skridskoseglarklubb** (Stockholm's Ice Skate Sailing Club; www.sssk .se) has some information in English on its website, but its services are for members only.

DOGSLEDDING & SNOWMOBILE SAFARIS

Organised tours with huskies pulling your sledge are increasingly popular in Lappland, as are snowmobile excursions. For details see destinations in Lappland & the Far North, p296.

BIRDWATCHING

There are many keen ornithologists in Sweden, and there are birdwatchers' towers and nature reserves everywhere; see p53 for details of the best birdwatching sites. For further information, contact **Sveriges Ornitologiska Förening** (Swedish Ornithological Society; ☎ 08-612 25 30; www.sofnet.org, in Swedish).

Sweden has two indigenous horse breeds: the north Swedish horse and the Gotland pony.

HORSE RIDING

Sweden's multitude of tracks, trails, forests, shorelines and mountains make for some fantastically varied riding. Everything from short hacks to full-on treks are on offer (around Skr350/550/850 per two hours/half day/full day) on Swedish or Icelandic horses. Trips can be arranged through local tourist offices or online through www.inatur.se (in Swedish).

FISHING

There are national and local restrictions on fishing in many of Sweden's inland waters, especially for salmon, trout and eel. Before dropping a line, check with local tourist offices or councils. You generally need a permit, but free fishing is allowed on parts of Vänern, Vättern, Mälaren, Hjälmaren and Storsjön lakes and most of the coastline.

Local permits for the waters of a *kommun* (municipality) can be bought from tourist offices, sports or camping shops, and some boat or canoe-hire outfits, and typically cost Skr60 to Skr120 per day, depending on season and location.

Summer is the best fishing time with bait or flies for most species, but trout and pike fishing in southern Sweden is better in spring or autumn and salmon fishing is best in late summer. Ice fishing is popular in winter.

An excellent web resource for fishing in Sweden is www.cinclusc.com /spfguide (in Swedish), or contact **Sportfiskeförbundet** (Angling Federation; ☎ 08-704 44 80; info@sportfiskarna.se).

Stockholm

Sweden's capital is the kind of place other cities love to loathe. Not only is she impossibly beautiful, but she's also fabulous with fashion, deft with design and a music meister. And if that's not galling enough, she's clean, green and civil.

Straddling 14 islands connected by 57 bridges, Scandinavia's urban high achiever will keep you keen with her distinctly different neighbourhoods. The old town, Gamla Stan, is one of Europe's most arresting historic hubs: a near-faultless concoction of richly coloured story-book buildings, regal riches and razor-thin cobblestone streets.

To the south, lofty Södermalm is the city's creative engine room, sprinkled with experimental art, edgy local threads and street-smart bars and clubs. To the north, downtown Norrmalm and ostentatious Östermalm go glam with A-list designer retail, champagne-sipping Prada slaves and Michelin-star nosh spots.

Only minutes away, pristine forests are always on call for the frazzled. A further ferry ride away lies the city's enchanting archipelago *(skärgård)*, with its countless string of islands and bucolic bliss.

Just don't go thinking this Nordic star is a predictable combo of blonde hair, blue eyes, and meatballs on Ikea forks. Around 16% of greater Stockholm's 1.2 million denizens are immigrants, lending the place a dynamic, textured edge.

HIGHLIGHTS

- Get lost in the maze of medieval lanes in head-turning **Gamla Stan** (p74)
- Shop for local threads and groove to indie tunes on the soulful island of **Södermalm** (p81)
- Muse over cutting-edge art at **Moderna Museet** (p80)
- Treat your tastebuds to Scandi flavours at vintage food market **Östermalms Saluhall** (p105)
- Escape the city buzz with some soothing island hopping in the striking **archipelago** (p119)

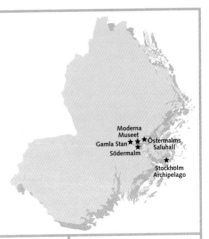

- TELEPHONE CODE: 08 (INNER CITY)
- POPULATION: 802,600
- AREA: 216 SQ KM

HISTORY

Rising land was the driving force behind Stockholm's destiny, as Swedish Viking political power was forced to move from northern Lake Mälaren to the lake's outlet for easier sea-lake trade. In 1250 a town charter was granted and a trade treaty was signed with the Hanseatic port of Lübeck.

Stockholm's official founder, Birger Jarl, commissioned the Tre Kronor castle in 1252 and locks were built on either side of Stadsholmen using timber stocks, apparently inspiring the name Stockholm (tree-trunk islet).

After the Black Death of 1350 wiped out around a third of Sweden's population, Danish Queen Margareta Valdemarsdotter added insult to injury by besieging Stockholm from 1391 to 1395, amalgamating the crowns of Sweden, Norway and Denmark under the highly unpopular Union of Kalmar in 1397. The Danes' popularity wasn't helped by the Stockholm Bloodbath of 1520, in which Danish King Christian II tricked, trapped and beheaded 82 Swedish burghers, bishops and nobles on Stortorget in Gamla Stan for opposing his domination.

One of the 82 victims was the father of Gustav Eriksson Vasa, who managed to stir up a successful rebellion against Danish rule and become Sweden's first king on 6 June 1523, now Sweden's national day.

Vasa's sons, King Erik XIV, King Johan III and King Karl IX, continued their father's nation building, transforming Stockholm into a major military hub during the Thirty Years' War and gaining Sweden an impressive property portfolio, including German and Norwegian territories.

By the end of the 16th century, Stockholm's population was 9000, and the city had spread onto Norrmalm and Södermalm. Officially proclaimed the capital of Sweden in 1634, by 1650 the city boasted a thriving artistic and intellectual culture and a grand new look courtesy of father-and-son architectural maestros the Tessins, creators of Drottningholms Slott.

The following decades weren't as kind to the capital. Starving hordes descended on the city after the devastating famine of 1696–97 and the beloved Tre Kronor went up in flames in 1697. Russian military victories shrunk the Swedish empire, another plague engulfed the city in 1711, and King Karl XII was assassinated in Norway in 1718.

A fragile Stockholm swapped expansion for personal growth. During this time, botanist Carl von Linné (1707–78) developed the template for the classification of plants and animals, Anders Celsius (1701–44) came up with the centigrade temperature scale, and royal palace Kungliga Slottet rose from the ashes of the Tre Kronar. While the reign of Francophile King Gustav III (1771–92) saw Swedish science, architecture and arts blossom, the theatre buff's tyrannical tendencies saw him assassinated by parliament member Jacob Johan Anckarström at a masked ball in the Opera House in 1792. The murder formed the basis of Giuseppe Verdi's opera, *A Masked Ball.*

When Sweden's northern and southern train lines were connected via Stockholm's Centralstationen and Riddarholmen in 1871, an industrial boom kicked in. The city's population reached 245,000 in 1890 (an increase of 77,000 in 10 years) and new districts like Östermalm expanded the city limits.

The elation of hosting the 1912 summer Olympics quickly dissipated when Sweden's refusal to uphold a blockade against Germany during WWI saw Britain attack the country's supply lines and cause starving Stockholmers to riot in Gustav Adolfs torg. Sweden's repeated official neutrality in WWII made it a hot spot for Jewish, Scandinavian and Baltic refugees, the first of many successive waves of migrants, most recently from the Middle East and Africa.

While the city's postwar economic boom saw the advent of Eastern Bloc–style suburban expansion, its shock value paled when compared to the still-unresolved murder of Prime Minister Olof Palme on Sveavägen in 1986, and the stabbing death of foreign minister Anna Lindh at the NK department store in 2003.

The worldwide collapse of the IT economy during the 1990s hit tech-dependent Stockholm particularly hard, although the industry has since picked up. These days, the capital is part of a major European biotechnology region, not to mention an ever-rising star on the world fashion and culinary stage.

ORIENTATION

Stockholm is built on islands, except for the downtown district (Norrmalm), a modernist business and shopping hub. At its heart sits the bustling square Sergels Torg and hulking arts centre Kulturhuset. Sergels Torg is connected to Centralstationen (the central train

STOCKHOLM IN...

Two Days

Beat the crowds to the labyrinthine streets of **Gamla Stan** (p74). Watch St George wrestle the dragon inside **Storkyrkan** (p76) and join a tour of the royal palace, **Kungliga Slottet** (p74), or simply watch the midday changing of the guard. From Slussen, catch the ferry across to Skeppsholmen for lunch and Lichtenstein at **Moderna Museet** (p80), before trekking across to Södermalm for dizzying views atop **Katarinahissen** (p84) and partying at **Mosebacke Etablissement** (p108) or **Debaser** (p108). Spend the next day exploring **Skansen** (p78), before dinner and drinks at **Sturehof** (p104).

Four Days

Follow the two-day plan, then hop on a guided boat tour of **Stockholm's waterways** (p87) for a refreshing perspective. Lunch at **Blå Porten** (p104) before eyeing up a 17th-century giant at **Vasamuseet** (p79) or five centuries of Swedish collectables at nearby **Nordiska Museet** (p80). The next day, head out to beautiful **Millesgården** (p84) for a whimsical cultural jaunt, before a Nordic fashion fix at **PUB** (p110). Up for more? Glam up and party till dawn at **Spy Bar** (p107) or chill with the indie-cool crew at **Pet Sounds** (p106) or **Marie Laveau** (p106).

station), which is also where all three underground metro (tunnelbana or T) lines meet. The busy tourist office, Sweden House, is in the eastern part of Norrmalm, facing the popular park Kungsträdgården. Directly north of Norrmalm is up-and-coming neighbourhood of Vasastaden. Bridges connect both districts to the island of Kungsholmen to the west.

Directly south of Norrmalm, the narrow channels of Norrström separate the downtown from the small island Stadsholmen, which, alongside its neighbouring islets, accommodates Gamla Stan (Old Town). Bridges connect these districts.

On the south side of Gamla Stan, Centralbron (Central Bridge) and the Slussen interchange connect the Old Town to the thriving island of Södermalm, and its spine Götgatan.

To the east of Gamla Stan sits the museum-lined island of Skeppsholmen and its tinier neighbour, Kastellholmen. East of Norrmalm lies the exclusive Östermalm district, the pleasure-boat berths at Nybroviken and the grand waterside boulevard Strandvägen. From Strandvägen, a bridge cross to leafy Djurgården and its mix of nature, museums and fun park.

Mälaren, the lake west of Gamla Stan, contains many other islands. Also in the city's west, the E4 motorway crosses Stora Essingen, Lilla Essingen (and Kungsholmen) on its way north. Yet another series of bridges connects bathing hot spot Långholmen with the western tip of Södermalm and the southern edge of Kungsholmen.

Maps

The free *What's On Stockholm* tourist booklet has good maps, but the folded *Stockholms officiella turistkarta* (Skr25) covers a larger area; both are usually available from tourist offices and hotels.

If you're heading into suburbia, detailed maps of outlying areas can be purchased from tourist offices or map shops. The best available street atlas, *Atlas över Stor-Stockholm* (Kartförlaget; Skr255, in Swedish), covers greater Stockholm.

INFORMATION
Bookshops

Hedengrens (Map p82; ☎ 611 51 28; Sturegallerian) An excellent selection of new books in English.

Kartbutiken (Map p82; ☎ 20 23 03; Kungsgatan 74) The city's widest range of maps and guidebooks.

Kartcentrum (Map p82; ☎ 411 16 97; Vasagatan 16) Also a good selection of maps and guidebooks.

Konst-ig (Map pp70-1; ☎ 20 45 20; Åsögatan 124) A savvy selection of lush books on international and Swedish art, architecture and design, as well as a sip-tastic cafe.

Press Stop Slussen (Map p82; Götgatan 31); Kungsgatan (Map p82; Kungsgatan 14) Found at a few locations around town, and good for both special-interest and international magazines.

Pressbyrån (Map p82; Centralstationen) For English-language newspapers and paperbacks.

Sweden Bookshop (Map p82; ☎ 789 21 31; Slottsbacken 10) A broad selection of high-quality books in English about Sweden and Swedish themes.

The English Bookshop (Map p82; ☎ 790 55 10; Lilla Nygatan 11) Another good choice for Anglophones.

STOCKHOLM

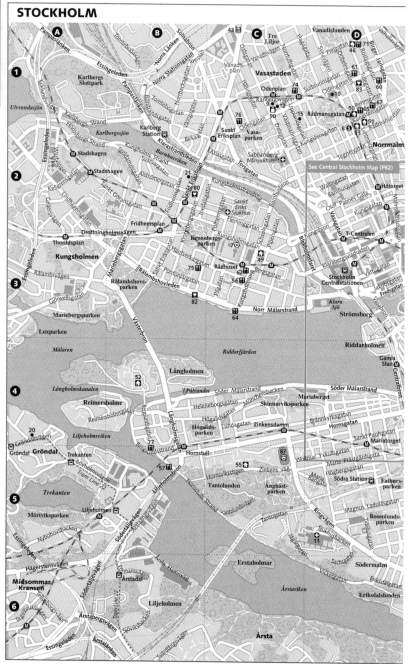

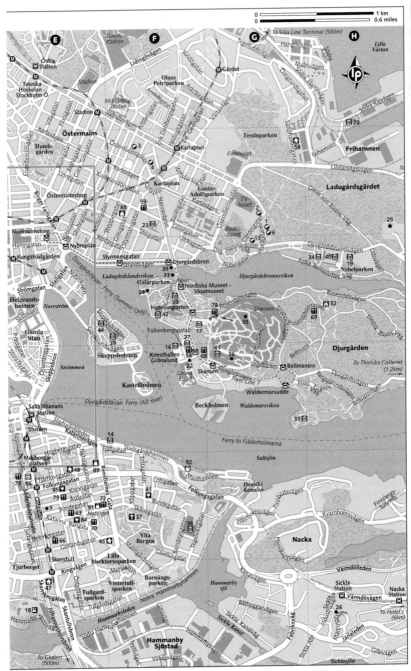

Emergency

24-hour medical advice (☎ 32 01 00)
24-hour police stations Kungsholmen (Map pp70-1; ☎ 401 00 00; Kungsholmsgatan 37, Kungsholmen); Södermalm (Map p82; ☎ 401 03 00; Torkel Knutssonsgatan 20, Södermalm)
AutoAssistans (☎ 020-53 65 36) Roadside assistance for vehicle breakdowns.
Emergency (☎ 112) Toll-free access to the fire service, police and ambulance.

Internet Access

Nearly all hostels have a computer or two with internet access for guests, and most hotels offer wi-fi access in rooms. There are also wi-fi hubs in Centralstationen. Those without their own computer have a number of options around town.

Sidewalk Express (www.sidewalkexpress.se; per hr Skr19) Cityterminalen (Map p82; City Bus Terminalen); Kungsgatan (Map p82; Kungsgatan 44); Slussen (Map p82; Götgatan 25); Vasastaden (Map pp70-1; Odenplan 22) Rows of computer monitors and tall red ticket machines mark

out these self-service internet stations, which are scattered across the city.

Internet Resources

www.alltomstockholm.se Features loads of information on events, restaurants, sports etc; in Swedish.
www.stockholmtown.com With excellent tourist information in English (and many other languages).
www.visit-stockholm.com A newly updated source for travellers, with nearly 500 pages of information on sights, food, accommodation, shopping and getting out of town.

Laundry

Laundry options are limited – it's best to find a hotel or hostel with facilities. A handy, central laundrette is **Tvättomat** (Map pp70-1; ☎ 34 64 80; www.tvattomaten.se; Västmannagatan 61; per load from Skr90; ⏱ 8.30am-6.30pm Mon-Fri, 9.30am-3pm Sat), near metro T-Odenplan.

Left Luggage

There are three sizes of **left-luggage boxes** (per 24hr Skr40-90) at Centralstationen. Similar facilities exist at the neighbouring bus station and at major ferry terminals.

If you have a lost-property inquiry, ask for *tillvaratagna effekter*.

Libraries

Kulturhuset (Map p82; ☎ 50 83 15 08; www.kulturhuset.stockholm.se; Sergels Torg; ⏲ Tue-Sun) Has a reading room with international periodicals, newspapers and books, as well as internet access.

Stadsbiblioteket (Map pp70-1; ☎ 50 83 10 60; Sveavägen 73; ⏲ 9am-9pm Mon-Thu, 9am-7pm Fri, noon-4pm Sat & Sun, shorter hours in summer) The main city library is just north of the city centre. Designed by luminary architect Erik Gunnar Asplund and sporting a curvaceous, technicolour reading room, it's the finest example of Stockholm's 1920s neoclassicist style.

Media

The best overall guide for visitors is the monthly *What's On Stockholm*, available free from tourist offices and online at www.stockholmtown.com.

Tourist offices also carry two separate accommodation guides in English – one for camping, the other for hotels and hostels – and both are free. If you can manage to navigate event listings in Swedish, look for *På Stan*, the excellent weekly arts and culture supplement to the daily *Dagens Nyheter* newspaper.

Similarly, the free monthly newspaper *Nöjes-guiden* has listings in Swedish, focusing on youth culture, live music and nightclubbing.

Medical Services

Apoteket CW Scheele (Map p82; ☎ 454 81 30; Klarabergsgatan 64) Twenty-four-hour pharmacy.

CityAkuten (Map p82; ☎ 412 29 00; Apelbergsgatan 48; ⏲ 8am-8pm) Emergency health and dental care.

Södersjukhuset (Map pp70-1; ☎ 616 10 00; Ringvägen 52) The most central hospital.

Money

ATMs are plentiful, with several at Centralstationen; expect queues.

The exchange company Forex has over a dozen branches in the capital and charges Skr15 per travellers cheque; the following are two handy locations:

Stockholm-Arlanda Airport (Terminal 2; ⏲ 5.30am-10pm Sun-Fri, to 6pm Sat)

Sweden House (Map p82; ☎ 820 03 89; Hamngatan 27; ⏲ 10am-6pm Mon-Fri, 10am-5pm Sat, noon-4pm Sun)

Post

You can buy stamps and send letters at a number of city locations, including newsagents and supermarkets – keep an eye out for the Swedish postal symbol (yellow on a blue background). There's a convenient outlet next to the Hemköp supermarket in the basement of central department store **Åhléns** (Map p82; Klarabergsgatan 50).

Telephone

Coin-operated phones are virtually nonexistent and pay phones are operated with phonecards purchased from any Pressbyrån location (or with a credit card, although this is ludicrously expensive). Ask for a *telefonkort* for Skr50 or Skr120, which roughly equate to 50 minutes and 120 minutes of local talk time, respectively. International calls are charged at a higher rate; for calls abroad, you're better off buying a long-distance calling card, available at many Pressbyrån outlets. For mobile phones, check with your service provider to ensure your network is compatible with Sweden's (see p327).

Toilets

Most public toilets charge Skr5 or Skr10, and most only take Skr5 or Skr10 coins, so keep a few handy. (If you're desperate, head for the toilets in one of the city's free museums, or ask nicely at a cafe or restaurant.)

Tourist Information

Sweden House (Map p82; ☎ 50 82 85 08, www.stockholmtown.se; Hamngatan 27; ⏲ 9am-7pm Mon-Fri, 10am-5pm Sat, 10am-4pm Sun May-Sep; 9am-6pm Mon-Fri, 10am-5pm Sat, 10am-4pm Sun Oct-Apr) The capital's main tourist office is just off Kungsträdgården across from the NK department store. It has loads of good brochures and can help book hotel rooms, theatre and concert tickets, and packages such as boat trips to the archipelago. There's a Forex currency-exchange counter in the same building.

Travel Agencies

STA Travel (Map p82; ☎ 0771-47 48 50; Kungsgatan 30) and the nearby **Kilroy Travels** (Map p82; ☎ 0771-54 57 69; Kungsgatan 4) both specialise in discount youth and student flights.

DANGERS & ANNOYANCES

Late at night, remain vigilant on Sergels Torg, Medborgarplatsen (in Södermalm) and Fridhemsplan (on Kungsholmen) when the bars empty around 1am. Steer clear of night buses at weekends and opt for a taxi instead.

STOCKHOLM

PENNY-PINCHING PACKAGES

Getting your money's worth out of a visit to Stockholm is a lot easier with one or more of the discount packages on offer. The **Stockholm Card** is available from tourist offices, Storstockholms Lokaltrafik (SL) information centres, some museums and some hotels and hostels, or online at www.stockholmtown.com. It gives you entry to 75 museums and attractions, travel on public transport (including Katarinahissen, but excluding some local ferries, some city buses and airport buses), sightseeing by boat, and parking in selected areas. It is valid for 24, 48 or 72 hours and costs Skr330/460/580 (or Skr165/230/290 for accompanying children under 18, maximum two children per adult). To get maximum value, use two 24-hour cards over three days (with a rest day in between) and be sure to note opening hours; for example, Skansen remains open until late, whereas royal palaces are only open until 3pm or 4pm.

Students and seniors get discounted admission to most museums and sights without the card, so you'll need to work out if it's cheaper for you to just get a transport pass and pay admission charges separately.

Stockholm à la Carte (from Skr399) is a cut-price package that includes a hotel room. Available weekends year-round and throughout the summer (mid-June to mid-August), its cost depends on the standard of accommodation (prices for central hotels start at around Skr735 per person). Travel agents in other Scandinavian capitals or major Swedish cities can help with arrangements; otherwise contact **Destination Stockholm** (☎ 663 00 80; www.destination-stockholm.com). The website has lots of good information and lists details of the 33-odd hotels involved in the scheme.

SIGHTS

Stockholm is mad for museums. Around 70 dot the city, with collections spanning everything from Viking boats and bling to swish Swedish design. Many are creatively curated, most brim with atmosphere and the majority offer free audioguides and brochures to enhance your exploration.

Castle and palace fans are equally spoilt: Stockholm boasts 10 royal pads in and around the city, including the largest palace in the world still in use, and the Unesco World Heritage–listed Drottningholm.

Although the Old Town, Gamla Stan, houses the Royal Palace, numerous regally themed museums and some marvellous churches, the city centre (Norrmalm) lays claim to the bulk of the museums. To the east, leafy Djurgården livens up the scene with its famous alfresco museum Skansen, epic Vasa ship museum and historic amusement park. Indeed, sterling sights are scattered across the city, though none are too far-flung and all are easily reached on public transport.

Gamla Stan

The Old Town is Stockholm's historic and geographic heart. Here, cobbled streets wriggle past Renaissance churches, baroque palaces and medieval squares. Sorbet-coloured merchants' houses sag like wizened old men, and svelte laneways harbour anything from dusty toy shops to candlelit cafes and restaurants. Västerlånggatan is the quarter's nerve centre, a bustling thoroughfare lined with galleries, eateries and souvenir shops. Less crowded and more understated, Osterlånggatan delivers a tasteful mix of art galleries, idiosyncratic boutiques and chart-topping restaurants. For the ultimate thrill, however, dive into the tiny alleys… You never know what you might find.

KUNGLIGA SLOTTET

The not-to-be-missed 'new' **Kungliga Slottet** (Royal Palace; Map p82; ☎ 402 61 30; www.royalcourt.se; Slottsbacken; adult/child per attraction Skr90/35, combined ticket Skr130/65; ⏰ most attractions 10am–4pm mid-May– late May & early Sep–mid-Sep; 10am–5pm Jun–Aug; noon–3pm Tue–Sun mid-Sep–mid-May) was built on the ruins of the 'old' royal castle, Tre Kronor, which burned to a crisp in 1697. The north wing survived and was incorporated into the new palace, but its medieval designs are now concealed by a baroque exterior. The new palace, designed by the court architect Nicodemus Tessin the Younger, took 57 years to complete. With 608 rooms, it's the world's largest royal castle still used for its original purpose.

The sumptuous **state apartments**, including the Hall of State and the Apartments of the Royal Orders of Chivalry, are both open to the public (except during state functions, most of which happen in September), with two floors of royal pomp, 18th- and 19th-century furnishings, and portraits of pale princes and princesses. Look for Queen Kristina's silver throne in the Hall of State and for the decadent Karl XI Gallery, inspired by Versailles' Hall of Mirrors and considered the finest example of Swedish late baroque.

The Swedish regalia, crowns, sceptres, orbs and keys are displayed at **Skattkammaren** (Royal Treasury), by the southern entrance to the palace near **Slottskyrkan** (Royal Chapel). **Gustav III's Antikmuseum** displays the Mediterranean treasures, particularly sculpture, acquired by the eccentric monarch. Descend into the basement **Museum Tre Kronor** to eye the foundations of 13th-century defensive walls and exhibits rescued from the medieval castle during the fire of 1697.

The **Changing of the Guard** (☎ 402 63 17) takes place in the outer courtyard at 12.15pm Monday to Saturday and 1.15pm Sunday and public holidays from June to August, and 12.15pm Wednesday and Saturday and 1.15pm Sunday and public holidays from September to May.

HELGEANDSHOLMEN

Though technically separated from Gamla Stan, this little island in the middle of Norrström is home to a couple of fascinating sights. The **Riksdaghuset** (Swedish Parliament; Map p82; ☎ 786 48 62; www.riksdagen.se; Mynttorget 2; admission free; ☾ 1hr tours noon, 1pm, 2pm & 3pm Mon-Fri late Jun-Aug, noon & 1.30pm Sat & Sun rest of year) consists of two parts: the older front section (facing downstream) dates from the early 20th century, but the other more modern part contains the current debating chamber. Tours of the building are surprisingly compelling and serve as a primer on the Swedish system of consensus-building government.

Reopening in early 2010, the atmospheric **Medeltidsmuseet** (Medieval Museum; Map p82; ☎ 50 83 17 90; www.medeltidsmuseet.stockholm.se; Strömparterren) lies at the other end of the island. While preparing to build a Riksdag car park here in the late 1970s, construction workers unearthed foundations dating from the 1530s. The ancient walls were preserved as found and a museum was built around them. Faithful reconstructions of typical abodes, sheds and workshops transport visitors to medieval Stockholm (albeit with a better lighting and sound system).

Also in the museum is the well-preserved, 1520s-era ship, *Riddarsholm*. While the main museum remains closed, a temporary (and very modest) outpost has been set up inside **Kulturhuset** (Sergels Torg; admission free; ☾ 11am-7pm Tue-Fri, 11am-5pm Sat & Sun).

ABBA-SOLUTELY FABULOUS!

Despite the indefinite postponement of its opening (expect a 2010 opening due to construction setbacks; check the website for updates on opening date, hours and prices), Stockholm's eagerly anticipated, epically hyped **ABBA: The Museum** (Map pp70-1; ☎ 650 00 80; www.abbamuseum.com; Stora Tullhuset, Stadsgården) is set to become one of Sweden's major crowd-pullers, with an estimated half-million visitors annually.

Housed in a converted customs building on Södermalm, the museum's three floors will trace the supergroup's rise to pop immortality in what promises to be an interactive, multimedia extravaganza. A series of linear, interactive 'scenes' will have you hanging out in the recreated Polar recording studio, shaking your booty on stage and even creating your own chart topper. Then there's the glittering memorabilia, spanning everything from the group's awards, photographs and instruments to those criminally outrageous costumes. Online tickets are date- and time-specific, and subject to availability, meaning you choose a specific timeslot to visit.

Love them or loathe them, it's impossible not to admire Sweden's most successful musical export, their sales of over 370 million records upstaged only by Elvis and the Beatles. Benny and Björn penned many an ABBA hit on the archipelago island of Viggsö, and the group's final three albums were recorded at No 58 St Eriksgatan on Kungsholmen (Map pp70–1), former home of Polar Studios. In fact, the studio interiors feature in the music clip for their 1979 hit 'Gimme! Gimme! Gimme! (A Man After Midnight)'. Other ABBA sites around Stockholm include the rustic Julius Kronberg's Atelje at Skansen (p78), backdrop for *The Visitors* album cover, and the royal gardens at Drottningholms Slott (p115), backdrop for the 'What's The Name Of The Game?' single sleeve.

OTHER SIGHTS

Livrustkammaren (Royal Armoury; Map p82; ☎ 51 95 55 44; www.livrustkammaren.se; adult/under 19yr Skr60/free; ☉ 10am-5pm Jun-Aug, 11am-5pm Tue-Sun, to 8pm Thu Sep-May) is part of the palace complex, but can be visited separately. It's a royal attic of sorts, crammed with engrossing memorabilia spanning over 500 years of royal childhoods, coronations, weddings and murders. Meet Gustav II Adolf's stuffed battle steed, Streiff; see the masquerade costume worn by Gustav III's on the night he was shot; or go ga-ga over Carl XVI's baby booties. There's a fairy-tale collection of coronation coaches in the basement, including the outrageously rococo number used for the crowning of Adolf Fredrik and Ulrika Eleonora in 1751. The audioguide (Skr20) is a worthy companion.

Across the plaza from the Royal Palace, **Kungliga Myntkabinettet** (Royal Coin Cabinet; Map p82; ☎ 51 95 53 04; Slottsbacken 6; adult/child Skr50/free, Mon admission free; ☉ 10am-4pm) gleams with a priceless collection of currency spanning 2600 years. Treasures include Viking silver, the world's oldest coin (from 625 BC), the world's largest coin (a Swedish copper plate weighing 19.7kg) and the planet's first banknote (issued in Sweden in 1661).

The one-time venue for royal weddings and coronations, **Storkyrkan** (Map p82; ☎ 723 30 09; adult/under 17yr Skr25/free; ☉ 9am-6pm mid-May–Oct, 9am-4pm rest of year) is both Stockholm's oldest building (consecrated in 1306) and its cathedral. Behind a baroque facade, the Gothic-cum-baroque interior includes extravagant royal-box pews designed by Nicodemus Tessin the Younger, as well as German Berndt Notke's dramatic sculpture St George and the Dragon, commissioned by Sten Sture the Elder to commemorate his victory over the Danes in 1471. Keep an eye out for posters and handbills advertising music performances here.

Riddarholmskyrkan (Map p82; ☎ 402 61 30; adult/child Skr30/10; ☉ 10am-4pm mid-May–late May & early Sep–mid-Sep, 10am-5pm Jun-Aug), on the nearby island Riddarholmen, was built by Franciscan monks in the late 13th century. It no longer functions as a church but has been the royal necropolis since the burial of Magnus Ladulås in 1290, and is home to the armourial glory of the Seraphim knightly order. Look for the marble sarcophagus of Gustav II, Sweden's mightiest monarch, and the massed wall plates displaying the coats-of-arms of the knights. There's a guided tour in English at 2pm and 4pm.

Examining almost four centuries of Swedish postal history, the **Postmuseum** (Map p82; ☎ 781 17 55; Lilla Nygatan 6; adult/under 19yr Skr50/free; ☉ 11am-4pm Tue-Sun May-Aug, 11am-4pm Tue-Sun & 11am-7pm Wed Sep-Apr) is not as mind-numbing as it sounds. It's actually rather evocative, featuring old mail carriages, kitsch postcards and a cute children's post office for budding postal workers. There's also a great cafe and a philatelic library with 51,000 books on stamps and postal history.

Nobelmuseet (Map p82; ☎ 53 48 18 00; Stortorget; adult/7-18yr Skr60/20; ☉ 10am-5pm Wed-Mon, to 8pm Tue mid-May–mid-Sep; 11am-5pm Wed-Sun, to 8pm Tue mid-Sep–mid-May; to 8pm Tue year-round), in the Börsen building (the old Stock Exchange), presents the history of the both the Nobel Prizes and their recipients. It is a slick space with some fascinating short films on the theme of 'creativity', an audio archive of acceptance speeches, interviews with and readings from laureates like Ernest Hemingway and Martin Luther King, and cafe chairs signed by the visiting prize winners (flip them over to see!). To get the most out of the museum, join a free guided tour (in English at 11.15am and 3pm daily).

Central Stockholm
NATIONALMUSEUM

Sweden's largest art museum, the **Nationalmuseum** (Map p82; ☎ 51 95 44 10; www.nationalmuseum.se; Södra Blasieholmshamnen; adult/under 19yr Skr100/free; ☉ 11am-5pm Wed-Sun, to 8pm Tue Jun-Aug; 11am-5pm Wed-Sun, to 8pm Tue & Thu Sep-May) houses the national collection of painting, sculpture, drawings, decorative arts and graphics, from the Middle Ages to the present. Some of the art became state property on the death of Gustav III in 1792, making this one of the earliest public museums in the world. Around 16,000 items of painting and sculpture are on display, including magnificent works by the likes of Rembrandt, Rubens and Cézanne, as well as masterpieces by local greats like Andres Zorn, CG Pilo and Carl Larsson. Around 30,000 items make up the decorative arts collection, including porcelain, furniture, glassware, silverware and late-medieval tapestries. Design aficionados will drool over the Den moderna formen 19002000 exhibition, which follows the evolution of Scandi design and features iconic pieces like Gösta

Thames' Cobra telephone and Jonas Bohlin's Concrete Chair. There's also an excellent museum shop and a light-filled terrace cafe.

HISTORISKA MUSEET

The national historical collection awaits at this enthralling **museum** (Map pp70-1; ☎ 51 95 56 00; www.historiska.se; Narvavägen 13; adult/under 19yr Skr60/free; ⊙ 11am-5pm, 11am-8pm Thu Oct-Apr, 10am-5pm May-Sep). From Iron Age skates and a Viking boat to medieval textiles and Renaissance triptychs, it spans over 10,000 years of Swedish history and culture. The undisputed highlight is the subterranean **Gold Room**, a brooding chamber gleaming with Viking bling and rare treasures, including the jewel-encrusted, millennium-old Reliquary for St Elisabeth. The most astonishing artefact, however, is the 5th-century seven-ringed gold collar with 458 carved figures, weighing 823g. Discovered in Västergötland in the 19th century, it was likely used by pagan priests in ritualistic ceremonies. Bring ID to use the museum's free audioguides.

STADSHUSET

A mighty mass of brown bricks (eight million in total), **Stadshuset** (Town Hall; Map p82; ☎ 50 82 90 58; Hantverkargatan 1; entrance by tour only, adult/child Skr60/30; ⊙ tours in English 10am, 11am, noon, 2pm, 3pm & 4pm Jun-Aug; 10am, noon & 2pm Sep-May) is Stockholm's architectural 'alpha male'. Topping its hulking square tower is a golden spire and the symbol of Swedish power, the three royal crowns. (It's no coincidence that the tower is one whole metre taller than Copenhagen's equivalent.) Punctured by two courtyards, the building's interior includes the glittering, mosaic-lined **Gyllene salen** (Golden Hall), Prins Eugen's own fresco recreation of the lake view from the gallery, and the very hall used for the annual Nobel Prize banquet. Part of the tour involves walking down the same stairs you'd use if you'd won the big prize. Entry is by daily tour only, and these may be interrupted from time to time by preparations for special events. The **tower** (adult/child Skr20/free; ⊙ 9am-5pm Jun-Aug, 9am-4pm May & Sep) offers stellar views and a great thigh workout.

OTHER SIGHTS

Delve into the darker side of human nature at **Armémuseum** (Map p82; ☎ 788 95 60; Riddargatan 13; adult/under 19yr Skr50/free; ⊙ 11am-8pm Tue, 11am-5pm Wed-Sun), where three levels of engrossing exhibitions explore the horrors of war through art, weaponry and life-size reconstructions of charging horsemen, forlorn barracks and starving civilians. You can even hop on a replica 'saw horse' for a taste of medieval torture.

A private palace completed in 1898, **Hallwylska Museet** (The Hallwyl Collection; Map p82; ☎ 51 95 55 99; Hamngatan 4; adult/under 19yr Skr50/free, admission & guided tour adult/under 19yr Skr70/free; ⊙ 11.45am-4pm Tue & Thu-Sun, 11.45am-4pm & 5.45-7pm Wed) was once home to compulsive hoarder Wilhelmina von Hallwyl, who collected items as diverse as kitchen utensils, Chinese pottery, 17th-century paintings, silverware, sculpture and her children's teeth! In 1920 she and her husband donated their Cluedo-style pad (including contents) to the nation. The faux-baroque great drawing room is particularly impressive, complete with a rare, playable grand piano. Guided tours in English take place at 1pm daily from late June to mid-August; the rest of the year they're only at 1pm on Sunday (although you can join one of the more regular tours in Swedish).

Vin & Sprithistoriska Museet (Wine & Spirits Museum; Map pp70-1; ☎ 744 70 70; Dalagatan 100; adult/under 18yr Skr50/free; ⊙ 10am-7pm Tue, 10am-4pm Wed-Fri, noon-4pm Sat & Sun) looks at history through a *snaps* glass, exploring the often turbulent relationship between Swedes and their beloved *brännvin* (aquavit) and *punsch*, a Swedish alcoholic beverage made with arrack liqueur. Step inside a recreated 19th-century wine merchant's distillery, get the low-down on Sweden's notoriously conservative alcohol policy, and merrily sniff your way through 57 *akvavit* (aquavit) spices at the smelling organ. The wine bar hosts regular wine-tasting evenings in Swedish (Skr400; book two weeks ahead). Take bus 65 from Centralstationen or walk from T-Odenplan.

Housed in an elegant Italianate building, **Medelhavsmuseet** (Museum of Mediterranean Antiquities; Map p82; ☎ 51 95 53 80; Fredsgatan 2; admission Skr80, with Stockholm Card Skr40; ⊙ noon-8pm Tue-Fri, noon-5pm Sat & Sun, to 5pm Fri Jun-Aug) lures history buffs with its Egyptian, Greek, Cypriot, Roman and Etruscan artefacts. Swoon over sumptuous Islamic art and check out the gleaming gold room, home to a 4th-century BC olive wreath made of gold.

The small but evocative **Strindbergsmuseet** (Map p82; ☎ 411 53 54; Drottninggatan 85; adult/under 19yr Skr50/free; ⊙ noon-7pm Tue, noon-4pm Wed-Sun Mar-Oct;

STOCKHOLM

ALEXANDRA PASCALIDOU

Stockholm perfection on a sunny day? Start with breakfast and great coffee at the Rival (p92) cafe before taking the ferry across from Slussen to Djurgården. It's only a 10-minute trip but it's beautiful and invigorating. On Djurgården, walk along the sea, passing Gröna Lund Tivoli (opposite) and the Vasamuseet (opposite), and have lunch at the classic Ulla Winbladh (p104) where you must try the famous Swedish meatballs. For evening drinks, don't miss Sturehof (p104) or Gondolen (p105).

And when the rain pours? Head to Östermalms Saluhall (p105) for Swedish delicacies and beautiful architecture, then do a little shopping at department store NK (p111) and the surrounding boutiques. Spend the afternoon at Moderna Museet (p80) or visit Kungliga Slottet (p74), before dinner and drinks at Le Rouge (p106); you can choose the bar if you want a less expensive alternative or the restaurant if you fancy a gourmet feed and have some money to spend. It's probably the most romantic place in Stockholm right now.

What do you miss most about Stockholm when you're away? The silence and beauty, the food, the architecture and the order of the place. I also miss the public transport system, which is nice and easy and always on time. I don't miss the dark winter days.

Stockholm is increasingly multicultural. Do you feel 'native' Swedes genuinely accept new-arrivals and second-generation immigrants as equals? Swedes are very friendly and polite, but we still have problems with the integration and acceptance of different immigrants. A lot of immigrants live segregated lives in suburbs like Rinkeby, Tensta and Hjulsta. On the other hand, luxurious neighbourhoods like Östermalm and Gärdet are inhabited mostly by native, wealthy Swedes. There's still a divide between Swedes and the others, but the new generation is generally more open-minded. Generally speaking, it's easy to live in Sweden but it's hard to become a Swede, unless you married to the King or become the King of football, like Zlatan Ibrahimovic.

Stockholm resident Alexandra Pascalidou is a Greek–Swedish journalist, author and media personality.

noon-4pm Tue-Sun Nov-Feb), in the Blue Tower, is the well-preserved apartment where writer and painter August Strindberg (1849–1912) spent his final four years. Peep into his closet, scan his study and library (containing some 3000 volumes), do a round of the dining room, and take in the often absorbing temporary exhibits.

The **Dansmuseet** (Map p82; ☎ 441 76 50; www.dansmuseet.nu; Gustav Adolfs Torg 22-24; admission free, special exhibitions adult/under 19yr Skr40/free; ☺ 11am-4pm Tue, Wed & Fri, 11am-8pm Thu, noon-4pm Sat & Sun, also 11am-4pm Mon May-Sep) focuses on the intersections between dance, art and theatre. Collection highlights include traditional dance masks from Africa, India and Tibet, avant-garde costumes from the Russian ballet, Chinese and Japanese theatre puppets and one of the finest collections of early-20th-century Ballets Ruses costumes.

Djurgården

A whirl of dreamy woods, snug cafes and top-rate museums and galleries, the royal park of Djurgården is unmissable.

Take bus 47 from Centralstationen, the Djurgården ferry services from Nybroplan or Slussen (frequent in summer), or hop aboard the vintage tram from Norrmalmstorg. You can rent bikes by the bridge (see p112), which is by far the best way to explore the area. Parking is limited during the week and prohibited on summer weekends when Djurgårdsvägen becomes a traffic-free thoroughfare.

SKANSEN

The world's first open-air museum, **Skansen** (Map pp70-1; ☎ 442 80 00; www.skansen.se; adult Skr60-145, child Skr20-60; ☺ 10am-8pm May-late Jun; 10am-10pm late Jun-Aug; 10am-8pm Sep; 10am-4pm Mar, Apr & Oct; 10am-3pm Nov-Feb; 10am-4pm Christmas market weekends) was founded in 1891 by Artur Hazelius to give visitors an insight into how Swedes lived once upon a time. You could easily spend a day here and still not see it all (note that prices vary according to the time of year). Around 150 traditional houses and other exhibits from across the country dot the hilltop – it's meant to be 'Sweden in miniature', complete with villages, nature, commerce and industry. The glass-blowers' cottage is a popular stop; watching the intricate forms emerge from glowing blobs of liquid glass is transfixing. The Nordic Zoo, with elk, reindeer, wolverines and other native wildlife, is a highlight, especially in spring when baby critters scamper around. There's also a petting zoo for tactile tots.

Buildings in the open-air museum represent various trades and areas of the country. Most are inhabited by staff in period costume, often creating handicrafts, playing music or churning butter while cheerfully answering questions about the folk whose lives they're recreating. Part of the pharmacy was moved here from Drottningholm castle; two little garden huts came from Tantolunden in Södermalm.

There's a bakery (still operational, serving coffee and lunch), a bank/post office, a machine shop, botanical gardens and Hazelius' mansion. There are also 46 buildings from rural areas around Sweden, including a Sami camp, farmsteads representing several regions, a manor house and a school. A map and an excellent booklet in English are available at Skansen to guide you around. It's also worth noting that the closing times for each workshop can vary, so check times online to avoid disappointment.

Skansen also incorporates a few other museums, including the recently renovated **Tobaks & Tändsticksmuseum** (Tobacco & Matchstick Museum; Map pp70-1; ☎ 442 80 26; 11am-5pm May-Sep, 11am-3pm Tue-Sun Oct-Apr), which traces the history of smoking, and the more salubrious **Skogens Hus** (Forestry Information Centre).

The **Skansen Aquarium** (Map pp70-1; ☎ 442 8039; www.skansen-akvariet.se; adult/6-15yr Skr75/45, 10am-8pm late Jun-early Aug; 10am-6pm Mon-Fri, 10am-7pm Sat & Sun rest of Jun & Aug; 10am-5pm Mon-Fri, 10am-6pm Sat & Sun May; 10am-4pm Mon-Fri, 10am-5pm Sat & Sun Sep-Apr) is also worth a wander, its residents including piranhas, lemurs and pygmy marmosets (the smallest monkeys in the world).

There is a number of cafes, restaurants and hot-dog stands throughout the park. Carrying water isn't a bad idea in summer, and it's not cheating to take the escalator to the top of the hill and meander down from there.

Daily activities take place on Skansen's stages, including folk dancing in summer and an enormous public festival at Midsummer's Eve. If you're in Stockholm for any of the country's major celebrations (such as Walpurgis Night, Midsummer's Eve, Lucia Festival and Christmas), it's a great place to watch Swedes celebrate.

Flip to p19 for more information on these events.

VASAMUSEET
A good-humoured glorification of some dodgy calculations, **Vasamuseet** (Map pp70-1; ☎ 51 95 48 00; www.vasamuseet.se; Galärvarvsvägen 14; adult/under 19yr Skr95/free, 5-8pm Wed Sep-May Skr75; 8.30am-6pm Jun-Aug;, 10am-5pm Thu-Tue & 10am-8pm Wed Sep-May) is the custom-built home of the massive warship *Vasa*. A whopping 69m long and 48.8m tall, the pride of the Swedish crown set off on its maiden voyage on 10 August 1628. Within minutes, the top-heavy vessel and its 100-member crew capsized tragicomically to the bottom of Saltsjön. Tour guides explain the extraordinary and controversial 300-year story of its death and resurrection, which saw the ship painstakingly raised in 1961 and reassembled like a giant 14,000-piece jigsaw. Almost all of what you see today is original.

On the entrance level is a model of the ship at scale 1:10 and a cinema screening a 25-minute film covering topics not included in the exhibitions (in English at 9.30am and 1.30pm daily in summer). There are four other levels of exhibits, covering artefacts salvaged from *Vasa*, life onboard, naval warfare and 17th-century sailing and navigation, plus sculpture and temporary exhibitions. The bottom floor exhibition is particularly fascinating, using modern forensic science to recreate the faces and life stories of several of the ill-fated passengers.

The bookshop is worth a browse and there's a restaurant for a well-earned pit stop. Guided tours are in English every 30 minutes in summer, and at least twice daily the rest of the year.

Give yourself a couple of hours to really absorb the place.

GRÖNA LUND TIVOLI
Crowded fun park **Gröna Lund Tivoli** (Map pp70-1; ☎ 58 75 01 00; www.gronalund.com; 7-64yr/under 7yr Skr70/free; noon-10pm Mon-Sat, to 8pm Sun Jun; 11am-10pm Sun-Thu, to 11pm Fri & Sat Jul-early Aug; hours vary May & early Aug–mid-Sep) has more than 30 rides, ranging from a softcore circus carousel to the terrifying Free Fall, where you drop from a height of 80m in six seconds (there's a lovely, if brief, view over Stockholm at the top). There are countless places to eat and drink in the park, but whether you'll keep it down is another matter entirely. The *Åkband* day pass (Skr280) gives unlimited rides, or individual rides range from Skr20 to Skr60. Big-name concerts are often staged here in summer. Admission is free with the Stockholm Card.

STOCKHOLM

OTHER SIGHTS

The epic **Nordiska Museet** (National Museum of Cultural History; Map pp70-1; ☎ 51 95 60 00; www.nordiskamuseet .se; Djurgårdsvägen 6-16; adult/under 19yr Skr60/free, free admission from 4pm Wed Sep-May; ☑ 10am-5pm Jun-Aug, 10am-4pm Mon-Fri, to 8pm Wed, 11am-5pm Sat & Sun Sep-May) is Sweden's largest cultural history museum and its second-largest indoor space. The building itself is an eclectic, Renaissance-style castle designed by Isak Gustav Clason, who also drew up Östermalms Saluhall (p105). Inside you'll find a sprawling collection of all things Swedish, from sacred Sami objects to fashion, shoes, home interiors and even table settings. The museum boasts the world's largest collection of paintings by August Strindberg, as well as a number of his personal possessions. In all, there are over 1.5 million items from 1520 to the present day. Topping it off are the often dynamic temporary exhibitions. The insightful audioguide (Skr20) offers several hours of English commentary.

Junibacken (Map pp70-1; ☎ 58 72 30 00; adult/3-15yr Skr110/95; ☑ 9am-6pm Jul, 10am-5pm Jun & Aug, 10am-5pm Tue-Sun Sep-May) whimsically recreates the fantasy scenes of Astrid Lindgren's books for children. Catch the flying Story Train over Stockholm, shrink to the size of a sugar cube, and end up at Villekulla cottage where kids can shout, squeal and dress up like Pippi Longstocking. The bookshop is a treasure trove of children's books, as well as a great place to pick up anything from cheeky Karlsson dolls to cute little art cards with story-book themes.

Prins Eugens Waldemarsudde (Map pp70-1; ☎ 54 58 37 00; www.waldemarsudde.com; Prins Eugens väg 6; adult/under 19yr Skr90/free; ☑ 11am-5pm Tue-Sun, to 8pm Thu), at the southern tip of Djurgården, is a soul-perking combo of water views and art. The palace once belonged to the painter prince, who favoured art over typical royal pleasures. In addition to Eugen's own work, it holds his impressive collection of Nordic paintings and sculpture, including works by Anders Zorn and Carl Larsson. The buildings and galleries, connected by tunnels, are surrounded by soothing gardens and an old windmill.

On the northern side of Djurgården, **Rosendals Slott** (Map pp70-1; ☎ 402 61 30; Rosendalsvägen; adult/7-18yr Skr60/25, combination ticket incl entry to Gustav III's Paviljong & Ulriksdal Slott Skr100/40; ☑ tours hourly noon-3pm Tue-Sun Jun-Aug) was built as a palace for Karl XIV Johan in the 1820s. One of Sweden's finest examples of the Empire style, it sparkles with sumptuous royal furnishings. Admission is by guided tour only. While you're out this way, don't miss the wonderful cafe, set among lush gardens and greenhouses and serving tasty organic grub.

Thielska Galleriet (off Map pp70-1; ☎ 662 58 84; Sjötullsbacken; adult/under 16yr Skr50/free; ☑ noon-4pm Mon-Sat, 1-4pm Sun), found at the east end of Djurgården, is a must for Nordic art buffs, with a savvy collection of late 19th- and early 20th-century works from greats like Edvard Munch, Anders Zorn and Bruno Liljefors. Take bus 69 from Centralstationen.

Liljevalchs Konsthall (Map pp70-1; ☎ 50 83 13 30; Djurgårdsvägen 60; adult/child Skr50/free; ☑ 11am-5pm Tue-Sun, to 8pm Tue & Thu Sep-May) has four exhibitions a year of contemporary Swedish and international art, including the popular Spring Salon.

Other minor museums around Djurgården include the charmingly creaky, 1893 **Biologiska-museet** (Museum of Biology; Map pp70-1; ☎ 442 82 15; Hazeliusporten; adult/6-15yr Skr30/10; ☑ 11am-4pm Apr-Sep, noon-3pm Tue-Sun Oct-Mar) and **Aquaria Vattenmuseum** (Map pp70-1; ☎ 660 90 89; Falkenbergsgatan 2; adult/6-15yr Skr80/40; ☑ 10am-6pm mid-Jun–Aug, 10am-4.30pm Tue-Sun rest of year), a conservation-themed aquarium complete with steamy tropical jungle, sharks and electric-blue surgeon fish.

Skeppsholmen

Moderna Museet (Modern Museum; Map pp70-1; ☎ 51 95 52 00; www.modernamuseet.se; Exercisplan 4; adult/under 19yr Skr80/free; ☑ 10am-8pm Tue, 10am-6pm Wed-Sun) is Stockholm's modern-art maverick, its booty ranging from painting and sculpture to photography, video art and installations. Permanent fixtures include work by Pablo Picasso, Salvador Dalí, Robert Rauschenberg, Yinka Shonibare and Paul McCarthy, complemented by top-notch temporary shows. Andy Warhol's first international retrospective was held here in 1968 and it was here that the world first heard his famously misquoted line: 'In the future everybody will be world famous for 15 minutes.' Ponder the quote at the slinky foyer espresso bar, or take in the water views from the fabulous 1st-floor restaurant-cum-cafe. Bibliophiles and design fans will adore the well-stocked gift shop.

The adjoining **Arkitekturmuseet** (Museum of Architecture; ☎ 58 72 70 02; Exercisplan 4; www.arkitektur museet.se; adult/under 19yr Skr50/free, admission free 4-6pm Fri; ☑ 10am-8pm Tue, 10am-6pm Wed-Sun), housed in a converted navy drill hall, focuses on the built environment, with a permanent exhibition spanning 1000 years of Swedish architecture and an archive of 2.5 million documents, photographs, plans, drawings and models. Temporary exhibitions also cover international names and work. The museum organises occasional themed architectural tours of Stockholm; check the website or ask at the information desk.

Across the bridge from Nationalmuseum, **Östasiatiska Museet** (Museum of Far Eastern Antiquities; Map pp70-1; ☎ 51 95 57 50; adult/under 20yr Skr60/free; ☯ 11am-8pm Tue, 11am-5pm Wed-Sun) houses Asian decorative arts, including one of the world's finest collections of Chinese stoneware and porcelain from the Sing, Ming and Qing dynasties. The often refreshing temporary exhibitions cover a wide range of themes, with past shows including comic-book manga and Chinese video art.

Ladugårdsgärdet

The vast parkland of Ladugårdsgärdet is part of the 27-sq-km **Ekoparken** (www.ekoparken.com), the world's first national park within a city. An impressive 14km long, its combo of forest and open fields stretches far into the capital's northern suburbs. This section of it, reached by bus 69 from Centralstationen or Sergels Torg, boasts three fine museums and one of Stockholm's loftiest views.

Sjöhistoriska Museet (National Maritime Museum; Map pp70-1; ☎ 51 95 49 00; Djurgårdsbrunnsvägen 24; adult/under 18yr Skr50/free; ☯ 10am-5pm Mon-Sun) is a must for fans of model ships (there are over 1500 mini vessels in the collection). The museum's exhibits also explore Swedish shipbuilding, sailors and life on deck.

Just around from the maritime museum, **Tekniska Museet** (Museum of Science & Technology; Map pp70-1; ☎ 450 56 00; www.tekniskamuseet.se; Museivägen 7; adult/6-19yr Skr70/40, admission free from 5pm Wed; ☯ 10am-5pm Mon-Fri, to 8pm Wed, 11am-5pm Sat & Sun) is a sprawling wonderland of interactive science and technology exhibits. One of its biggest drawcards is **Cino4** (adult/4-19yr Skr60/30), Sweden's first 4-D, multisensory cinema.

Etnografiska Museet (National Museum of Ethnography; Map pp70-1; ☎ 51 95 50 00; Djurgårdsbrunnsvägen 34; adult/under 20yr Skr60/free; ☯ 10am-5pm Tue-Fri, 10am-8pm Wed, 11am-5pm Sat & Sun) has evocative displays on various aspects of non-European cultures, including dynamic temporary exhibitions. The cafe is a treat, with great music,

imported sweets and beverages, and authentic global dishes.

About 500m from the museums is the 155m **Kaknästornet** (Kaknäs TV tower; Map pp70-1; ☎ 667 21 80; adult/child Skr35/15; ☯ 9am-10pm Jun-Aug; 10am-9pm Sep-Dec; 10am-9pm Mon-Sat, 10am-6pm Sun Jan-May), the automatic operations centre for radio and TV broadcasting in Sweden. Opened in 1967, it's still the city's tallest building. There's a small visitor centre on the ground floor and an **observation deck** and restaurant near the top, both providing stellar city and archipelago views.

One kilometre further northwest, **Magasin 3** (Map pp70-1; ☎ 54 56 80 40; www.magasin3.com; Elevator 4, Magasin 3 Bldg, Frihamnen; adult/under 20yr Skr40/free; ☯ noon-7pm Thu, noon-5pm Fri-Sun, closed Jun-Aug & during Christmas holidays), is one of Stockholm's best contemporary art galleries. Located in a dockside warehouse, its six to eight annual shows often feature specially commissioned, site-specific work from the likes of American provocateur Paul McCarthy. Take bus 1 or 76 from the city centre.

Södermalm

Once-working-class 'Söder' is Stockholm's coolest 'hood, jammed with up-and-coming boutiques and galleries, effortlessly hip cafes and bars, and a fistful of decent museums. SoFo (the area south of Folkungagatan) is the trendiest district, while Hornstull (at the island's western edge) melds indie cool with old-school Söder shab.

Stockholms Stadsmuseum (City museum; Map p82; ☎ 50 83 16 59; Slussen; admission free; ☯ 11am-5pm Tue-Sun, 11am-8pm Thu) is housed in the late-17th-century palace designed by Nicodemus Tessin the Elder, in Ryssgården. Evocative exhibits cover Stockholm's development from fortified port to modern metropolis, via plague, fire and good old-fashioned scandal. The temporary exhibitions are often fresh and eclectic.

In a former bus depot near the Viking Line terminal, **Spårvägsmuseet** (Transport Museum; Map pp70-1; ☎ 462 55 31; Tegelviksgatan 22; adult/under 19yr incl Leksaksmuseet Skr30/15; ☯ 10am-5pm Mon-Fri, 11am-4pm Sat & Sun) is Stockholm's transport museum and an atmospheric spot to spend a rainy afternoon. An impressive collection of around 40 vehicles includes horse-drawn carriages, vintage trams and buses, and a retro metro carriage (complete with original advertisements). Take bus 2 or 66.

CENTRAL STOCKHOLM

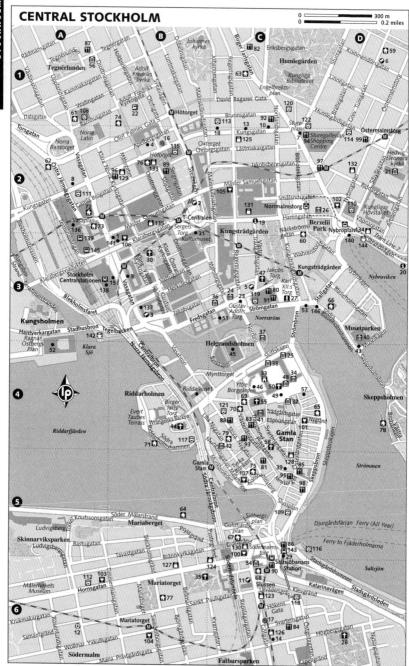

Sharing an entrance with Spårvägsmuseet, **Leksaksmuseet** (Toy Museum; Map pp70-1; ☎ 641 61 00; Tegelviksgatan 22; admission with Spårvägsmuseet ticket; 🕙 10am-5pm Mon-Fri, 11am-4pm Sat & Sun) is packed with everything you probably ever wanted as a child (and may still be hankering for as an adult). Get nostalgic over lovingly worn teddy bears, vintage Barbies, model railways, planes and cars, or battle it out with a video game.

Make your way to the northern cliffs of Södermalm for romantic vistas and evening walks among the vintage wooden houses. Some interesting neighbourhoods await around the **Katarina kyrka** (Map p82), in the park near **Sofia kyrka** (Map pp70–1), around the **Puckeln Shop District** (Hornsgatan) and on Lotsgatan and Fjällgatan, not too far from the Viking Line terminal.

You'll also get great views from the balcony of **Katarinahissen** (Map p82; ☎ 743 13 95; Slussen; adult/7-15yr Skr10/5; ⏱ 8am-10pm mid-May–Aug, 10am-6pm Sep–mid-May), a lift that dates from the 1930s and which takes you up 38m to the heights of Slussen. If you prefer, zigzagging wooden stairs also lead up the cliffs to the balcony. At the top is one of the city's finest restaurants, Gondolen (p105).

Northern Suburbs

The areas just north of central Stockholm breathe easy with their lush, green spaces. Several sprawling parks, from Djurgården in the south, form Ekoparken (see p81), the first such protected city area in the world. Hagaparken (see opposite) is another prime spot for lazy ambling, bike riding and catching some offbeat attractions.

MILLESGÅRDEN

Well worth the effort to reach it, beautiful **Millesgården** (Map p116; ☎ 446 75 94; Carl Milles väg 2, Lidingö; adult/child Skr80/free; ⏱ 11am-5pm mid-May–Sep, noon-5pm Tue-Sun Oct–mid-May) was the home and studio of sculptor Carl Milles, whose delicate water sprites and other whimsical sculptures dot the city landscape. The grounds include a crisp modern gallery for changing exhibitions of contemporary art, Milles' elaborately Pompeiian house, and an exquisite outdoor sculpture garden, where items from ancient Greece, Rome, medieval times and the Renaissance intermingle with Milles' own creations. There's also a museum shop and a cafe. Take the metro to Ropsten, then bus 207.

NATURHISTORISKA RIKSMUSEET & COSMONOVA

Sweden's largest museum, **Naturhistoriska Riksmuseet** (National Museum of Natural History; Map p116; ☎ 51 95 40 40; www.nrm.se; Frescativägen 40; adult/under 19yr Skr70/free; ⏱ 10am-7pm Tue, Wed & Fri, 10am-8pm Thu, 11am-7pm Sat & Sun) was founded by Carl von Linné in 1739. There are hands-on displays about nature and the human body, as well as whole forests' worth of taxidermied wildlife, dinosaurs, marine life and the hardy fauna of the polar regions. The museum is located 300m north of T-Universitetet metro stop.

Adjoining Naturhistoriska Riksmuseet is **Cosmonova** (Map p116; ☎ 51 95 51 30; adult/5-18yr Skr85/50, no children under 5yr admitted), a combined planetarium and Imax theatre with themes ranging from mummies and dinosaurs to the deep sea and prehistoric sea 'monsters'. Films are screened on the hour, and reservations are recommended.

HAGAPARKEN

Crowning a hilltop at **Haga park** (Map p116) is the peculiar **Koppartälten** (Copper Tent; ⏱ dawn-dusk), built in 1787 as a stable and barracks for Gustav III's personal guard. It now contains a cafe, a restaurant and **Haga Parkmuseum** (admission free), with displays about the park, its pavilions and the royal palace, Haga slott (not open to the public).

Gustav III's Paviljong (Gustav III's Pavilion; ☎ 402 61 30; adult/7-18yr Skr60/25 by guided tour only; ⏱ tours hourly noon-3pm Tue-Sun Jun-Aug) is a superb example of late neoclassical style; the furnishings and decor reflect Gustav III's interest in all things Roman after his Italian tour in 1782.

The steamy **Fjärilshuset** (Butterfly House; ☎ 730 39 81; adult/4-15yr Skr80/40; ⏱ 10am-5pm Mon-Fri, 11am-6pm Sat & Sun Apr-Sep; 10am-4pm Mon-Fri, 11am-5pm Sat & Sun Oct-Mar) recreates a tropical environment, complete with free-flying birds and butterflies, and some very friendly fish.

To reach Hagaparken, take bus 515 from Odenplan to Haga Norra.

ULRIKSDALS SLOTT

Further north, 17th-century royal pad **Ulriksdal Slott** (Map p116; ☎ 402 61 30; Ulriksdals Park; guided tours adult/7-18yr Skr60/25; tours ⏱ hourly noon-3pm Tue-Sun Jun-Aug) was home to King Gustaf VI Adolf and his family until 1973. Several of their exquisite apartments, including the drawing room, dating from 1923, are open to the public. The stables house Queen Kristina's magnificent 17th-century coronation carriage (call ahead for access), while the **Orangery** (⏱ noon-4pm Tue-Sun Jun-Aug) contains Swedish sculpture and Mediterranean flora. Head to T-Bergshamra metro stop, then take bus 503.

Southern Suburbs

One of Stockholm's more unusual attractions, **Skogskyrkogården** (Map p116; Söckenvagen; admission free) is an arrestingly beautiful cemetery set in soothing pine woodland. Designed by the great Erik Gunnar Asplund and Sigurd Lewerentz, it's on the Unesco World Heritage list and famed for its functionalist buildings. Famous residents include Stockholm screen goddess Greta Garbo. To get there, take the metro to T-Skogskyrkogården.

Fjäderholmarna

Located on the eastern side of Djurgården, these tiny, delightful islands, known as Feather Islands, offer an easy escape from the city. They're just 25 minutes away by boat and a favourite swimming spot for locals. **Boats** (adult/child return Skr95/45) to the islands depart hourly from either Nybroplan or Slussen between May and early September. There are a couple of craft shops and restaurants here, though the main activity is low-key chilling. The last boats leave the islands at around midnight, making them a perfect spot to soak up the long daylight hours.

ACTIVITIES

A number of activities are available in and around Stockholm, many of them water-based. Popular outdoor destinations include the archipelago islands (packed with good swimming spots) and the plethora of picnic-friendly parks and gardens. Summer sees punters embrace the long daylight hours to swim, sail, hike, walk or cycle. In winter, snowy days bring out the cross-country skiers. Hit the tourist office for details.

Swimming

If you insist on both indoor and outdoor pools (with all the trimmings), try sprawling **Eriksdalsbadet** (Map pp70-1; ☎ 50 84 02 58; Hammarby Slussväg 8; adult/4-19yr Skr75/35) in Södermalm's south. For more atmospheric splashing about there's art nouveau **Centralbadet** (Map p82; ☎ 54 52 13 15; www.centralbadet.se; Drottninggatan 88; adult Skr120, after 3pm Fri & Sat Skr170; ⊗ 6am-9pm Mon-Fri, 8am-9pm Sat, 8am-6pm Sun), where entry includes pool, sauna and gym access. Treatments, including massage, facials and body wraps, are available for an additional fee; these are best booked two weeks ahead. You can also hire bathers (Skr35), towels (Skr30) and robes (Skr50).

Swimming is also permitted just about anywhere people can scramble their way to the water. Popular spots include the rocks around Riddarfjärden and the leafy island of Långholmen, the latter also sporting a popular gay beach.

Sailing & Boating

From **Sjöcafé** (Map pp70-1; ☎ 660 57 57; canoes per 1st hr/next hr/day Skr75/65/300; ⊗ 9am-9pm Apr-Sep), by the bridge leading to Djurgården, you can rent bikes, in-line skates, kayaks, canoes, row boats and pedal boats. Opposite, floating resto-bar **Strandbryggan** (Map pp70-1; ☎ 660 37 14; www.strandbryggan.se, in Swedish; Strandvägskajen 27, Strandvägen) rents out sailing and motor boats in various sizes from April to September. Sailing boats cost around Skr495 per hour, and all boats can be rented for a day, weekend or week.

Cycling

Cycling is best in the parks and away from the busy central streets and arterial roads, but some streets have special cycle lanes (often shared with pedestrians). **Stockholm City Bikes** (☎ 077-444 24 24; www.stockholmcitybikes.se) has 67 self-service bicycle hire stands across the city. To use, you'll need to purchase a bike card (three-day/season card Skr125/250) from the tourist office (see p73) or Storstockholms Lokaltrafik (SL) centres. Rechargeable season cards are valid from April to the end of October. Bicycles can also be rented from **Sjöcafé** (Map pp70-1; ☎ 660 57 57; bicycles per hr/day Skr65/250). Tourist offices can supply maps of cycle routes; see p336 for further information.

Hiking & Climbing

Serious hiking trips in town are limited, but the parks offer some good walks, especially on Djurgården. Climbers have better options, with around 150 cliffs within 40 minutes' drive of the city. There's also one of Sweden's largest indoor climbing centres, **Klätterverket** (Map pp70-1; ☎ 641 10 48; Marcusplatsen 17, Nacka; member/nonmember Skr60/80) next to the J-train Sickla stop, with around 1000 sq metres of artificial climbing.

WALKING TOUR

Stockholm is a compact city, and many of its top historical sights can be visited in a couple of hours on a walking tour.

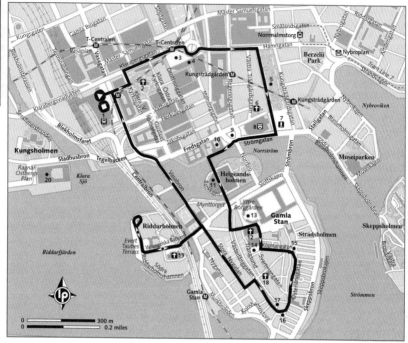

Start Centralstationen	
Finish Centralstationen	
Distance 3.5km	
Duration two to three hours	

Starting in the middle at **Centralstationen (1)**, cross Vasagatan and enter the side street Klara Vattugränd. Turn left onto Klara V Kyrkogatan, past the church **Klara kyrka (2)**, then turn right onto Klarabergsgatan. This is one of Stockholm's main shopping strips, lined with big-name retailers and department stores.

Follow Klarabergsgatan to **Sergels Torg (3)**, home to frenzied commuters, casual shoppers, and the odd demonstration and shady deal. Pop into arts hub **Kulturhuset (4)**, with its exhibitions, theatres, cafes, a comic-book library and creative spaces for youth. Until early 2010, it's also housing the Medeltidsmuseet (see p75).

Continue a short way along Hamngatan before turning right at the tourist office (Sweden House) into the grand **Kungsträdgården (5)**.

This park, originally the kitchen garden for the Royal Palace, is now a popular spot for sun-soaking in the warmer months, and ice-skating in the colder ones. The 17th-century church **Sankt Jakobs kyrka (6)** has an ornate pulpit that's worth a quick look.

Walk through the park to its southern end at **Karl XII's Torg (7)**, where there's a statue of the warmongering King Karl XII. On your right is **Operan (8)**, the Royal Opera House (opened in 1896) and across the road you'll see the narrow strait Norrström, the freshwater outflow from Mälaren lake. Continue along the waterfront, past Operan and **Gustav Adolfs Torg (9)**, to the grandiose **Sophia Albertina Palace (10)**, which houses the Foreign Ministry, then turn left and cross the Riksbron bridge. Continue across the islet **Helgeandsholmen (11;** Island of the Holy Spirit), between the two parts of Sweden's parliament building, Riksdagshuset. After crossing over the short Stallbron bridge, you'll arrive on Stadsholmen, Stockholm's medieval core.

Cross Mynttorget and follow Väster-långgatan for one block, then turn left (east) into Storkyrkobrinken to reach **Storkyrkan (12)**, the city's cathedral and oldest building. Facing the cathedral across the cobbled square is **Kungliga Slottet (13**; p74), the 'new' Royal Palace. Källargränd leads southward to **Stortorget (14)**, where the Stockholm Bloodbath took place in 1520. Three sides of the square are formed by quaint tenements painted in varying earthy tones; on the fourth side of the square there's Börsen, the Stock Exchange and Swedish Academy building, now home to an inspiring museum about the Nobel Prizes and their recipients.

The narrow streets of the eastern half of Gamla Stan still wind along their medieval 14th-century lines and are linked by a fantasy of lanes, arches and stairways. Head east along Köpmangatan to small square **Köpmantorget (15)** and the oft-photographed statue of *St George and the Dragon*. Turn right into Österlånggatan and follow it past antique shops, art galleries, handicraft outlets and Den Gyldene Freden, which has been serving food since 1722, until you reach **Järntorget (16)**, where metals were bought and sold in days long past. From there, keep right and turn into Västerlånggatan, looking out for **Mårten Trotzigs Gränd (17)** by No 81: this is Stockholm's narrowest lane, at less than 1m wide. Follow Prästgatan to the lavishly decorated German church, **Tyska kyrkan (18)**.

Crowded Västerlånggatan is lined with shops, cafes and tacky souvenirs; unless you're desperate for a Viking key ring, follow the quieter parallel street, Stora Nygatan, instead. At Riddarhustorget, turn left (southwest) and cross the short Riddarholmsbron to **Riddarholmen** (Knights Island). The large church **Riddarholmskyrkan (19)** has an iron spire and a basement full of royal corpses.

Beyond Riddarholmskyrkan, you'll come to the far side of the island, which features great views across the lake to the impressive **Stadshuset (20**; Town Hall) and the eastern end of **Kungsholmen** (King's Island).

Retrace your steps to Riddarhustorget and then turn left (northwest), before crossing over Vasabron and making your way along Vasagatan back to Centralstationen.

STOCKHOLM FOR CHILDREN

Stockholm spoils kids: the miniature crowd is welcome in restaurants and many museums have thoughtful play areas. One of the top attractions for kids is **Skansen** (p78), with its open-air format, petting zoo and glass-blowers' workshop. Another winner is **Junibacken** (p80), which sees tykes and their parents 'fly' through the strange and fantastical world of Pippi Longstocking. Also on Djurgården, **Gröna Lund Tivoli** (p79) has enough carnival rides, games and sticky treats to keep the little ones smitten. **Leksaksmuseet** (p83) is crammed with toys, both to look at and to play with, while **Kulturhuset** (p73) is a parent's dream – you can drop off the smallest kids at Rum för Barn (4th floor), and keep teens entertained with do-it-yourself art projects in the workshop at Lava. **Stadsteatern** (p109) and **Dramaten** (p109) both run children's plays regularly.

TOURS

Stockholm Sightseeing (Map p82; ☎ 12 00 40 00; www.stockholmsightseeing.com) operates frequent cruises from early April to mid-December around the central bridges and canals from Strömkajen (near the Grand Hotel), Nybroplan or Stadshusbron; you'll find ticket booths at these departure points. Some of the one-hour tours are free for Stockholm Card holders, but the two-hour tour, Under the Bridges of Stockholm (Skr180), covers more territory and passes under 15 bridges and through two locks, with a recorded commentary in several languages to fill in the history of the areas you pass by.

City Sightseeing (Map p82; ☎ 12 00 40 00; www.citysightseeing.com; Gustav Adolfs Torg) is the land-based sister operation, and runs daily 1½-hour coach tours of the city (Skr240) departing from Gustav Adolfs Torg. Both the 2½-hour tour (Skr330, April to mid-December) and 3½-hour tour (Skr395, including light lunch, early May to mid-September) combine the coach tour with a boat tour around Djurgården and the city's closest archipelago islands (Skr395, 2½ hours). One-hour walking tours around Gamla Stan (Skr100, late June to August) are also available.

There's a fact-packed, one-hour **English-language guided walk** (per person Skr75; ⏱ 7.30pm Mon, Tue & Thu May-Aug, 1.30pm Sat & Sun Sep-Nov, Mar & Apr) through Gamla Stan with an authorised guide. Meet at the Obelisk at Slottsbacken, outside the royal palace; reservations are not required.

For an adrenalin-pumping introduction, **RIB Sightseeing** (Map pp70-1; ☎ 20 22 60;

STOCKHOLM

www.ribsightseeing.se; Museikajen 1; adult/child Skr345/195) runs high-speed, high-thrill cruises through Stockholm and the archipelago on rigid, inflatable speedboats. Departing by the National Museum, tours last 1½ hours and run from mid-May to late September. Book ahead.

Stockholm is one of the few cities that allows hot-air balloons to fly over it. Book a tour with **Far & Flyg** (Map pp70-1; ☎ 645 77 00; www .farochflyg.se; per person Skr1995; ☻ May-Sep) for an unforgettable perspective on the city.

FESTIVALS & EVENTS

There's a bounty of festivals, concerts and other happenings on Sergels Torg and Kungsträdgården throughout the summer, and the major museums exhibit temporary exhibitions on a grand scale. *What's On Stockholm* lists daily events.

The biggest events in Stockholm are those celebrated throughout the country, such as Midsummer, Walpurgis Night, Lucia Festival, Christmas and New Year's Eve. See p19 for more information, and if you're in Stockholm at the right time, head to Skansen to party Swedish-style.

Lidingöloppet (www.lidingoloppet.se) The world's largest cross-country foot race, with 30,000 participants, is held in late September in Lidingö, on Stockholm's outskirts.

Smaka På Stockholm A six day celebration of Stockholm's food scene in late May/early June, which includes gourmet food stalls and entertainment on central Kungsträdgården.

Stockholm International Film Festival (www.film festivalen.se) In November, a major celebration of local and foreign cinema with guest speakers who are often top directors.

Stockholm Jazz Festival (www.stockholmjazz.com) One of Europe's premier jazz festivals, held in mid-July.

Stockholms Kulturfestival (www.kulturfestivalen .stockholm.se) In August, one week of everything (and anything) from sidewalk opera to street theatre and dance gigs, with most of the 400-odd cultural events free.

Stockholm Marathon (www.stockholmmarathon.se) Run in June.

Stockholm Open (www.stockholmopen.se) Nine days of international tennis and courtside celebrity-spotting, held in October.

Stockholm Pride (www.stockholmpride.org) In late July/ early August Stockholm goes pink with five brilliant days of queer parties and cultural events plus a pride parade.

SLEEPING

Whether you slumber in youth hostels, B&Bs, boutique digs or big-name chains, you can expect high quality accommodation

in Stockholm. The trade-off is that it can be an expensive city to sleep in, but deals do exist! Major hotel chains are invariably cheaper booked online and in advance, and most hotels offer discounted rates on weekends (Friday, Saturday and often Sunday night) and in summer (from Midsummer to mid-August), sometimes up to 50% off the listed price.

The handy booklet *Hotels and Youth Hostels in Stockholm*, available free from tourist offices, lists most hotels and their regular and discount rates.

A number of agencies, including **Bed & Breakfast Service** (☎ 660 55 65; www.bedbreakfast.se) and **Bed & Breakfast Agency** (☎ 643 80 28; www.bba .nu), can arrange apartment or B&B accommodation from around Skr400 per person per night.

Stockholm has HI-affiliated STF hostels (where a membership card yields a Skr50 discount), as well as SVIF hostels and independent hostels (no membership cards required). Many have options for single, double or family rooms. Generally, you'll pay extra to use the hostel's linen; bring your own sleeping sheet to save around Skr50 per night. Many hostels have breakfast available, usually for an additional Skr50 to Skr70.

Hostels tend to fill up during the late afternoon in peak summer season, so arrive early or book in advance. They can also be busy in May, when Swedish school groups typically visit the capital.

The following options are organised by neighbourhood and price range. Room prices are for peak season, unless otherwise stated. For hotels operating a flexible pricing system, both the lowest and highest prices are given. The price you'll pay will depend on several variables, including demand at time of booking.

Gamla Stan

Ideal for romantics, though admittedly pricier than other parts of the city, Stockholm's medieval nexus has several atmospheric slumber spots that put you in easy reach of other thriving city neighbourhoods.

MIDRANGE

Rica Hotel Gamla Stan (Map p82; ☎ 723 72 50; www .rica.se; Lilla Nygatan 25; s Skr895-2245, d Skr995-2595; ☐) If you fancy classic Swedish interiors, rush to Rica, where the smallish rooms feature anything from powder-blue wallpaper and dainty furniture to vintage chandeliers. The revamped bathrooms add a modern edge to the 17th-century building, and the location is perfect for soaking up Gamla Stan's history.

Lord Nelson Hotel (Map p82; ☎ 50 64 01 20; www .lordnelsonhotel.se; Västerlånggatan 22; s Skr990-1990, d Skr1790-2390, summer & weekend s/d Skr990/1790; 🖳) Yo-ho-ho, me scurvy barnacles! It's a tight squeeze but this pink-painted, glass-fronted building feels like a creaky old ship loaded with character. At just 5m wide, the 17th-century building is Sweden's narrowest hotel. Its nautical theme extends to brass and mahogany furnishings, antique sea-captain trappings and a model ship in each of the small rooms. Some are in need of a little TLC, but all are comfy and clean, and we adore the little rooftop sundeck.

ourpick Mälardrottningen (Map p82; ☎ 54 51 87 80; www.malardrottningen.se; Riddarholmen; cabin s/d from Skr1180/1300) At one time the world's largest motor yacht, this stylish, cosy option features well-appointed cabins, each with a bathroom. The vessel was launched in 1924 and once owned by American heiress Barbara Hutton (a modest gift from her father for her 18th birthday). Upper-deck, seaside rooms offer the best views, and three rooms come with queen-sized beds for spacious slumber.

Lady Hamilton Hotel (Map p82; ☎ 50 64 01 00; www .ladyhamiltonhotel.se; Storkyrkobrinken 5; s Skr1490-2290, summer & weekends Skr1290-1850, d Skr2190-3290, summer & weekends Skr2090-2490) Expect old-style luxury (with more modern touches where it counts; for example, in the bathrooms). The building dates back to the 1470s, and is packed with antiques and portraits of Lady Hamilton herself. If you're not a fan of church bells, request a room away from Storkyrkobrinken.

TOP END
First Hotel Reisen (Map p82; ☎ 22 32 60; www.first hotels.com/reisen; Skeppsbron 12; s Skr1390-2640, d Skr1590-2840, summer s/d from Skr930/1130; 🖳) Stockholm's oldest hotel once hummed with sailors. These days it's pulling a trendier crowd with its sexy black foyer and slinky resto-bar. Cool gives way to classic in the clean, comfortable (though slightly tired-looking) rooms. The real highlight is the candlelit basement plunge pool, complete with 16th-century, barrel-vaulted ceiling.

Victory Hotel (Map p82; ☎ 50 64 00 00; www.vic toryhotel.se; Lilla Nygatan 5; s Skr2650-2850, discounted to Skr1490-2650, d Skr3390-4290, discounted to Skr2450-3890; 🖳) Nautical antiques, art and model ships define the wonderfully quirky Victory. Most rooms are fairly small (though perfectly comfy), while the museum-like suites are larger. There are also four apartments available for long-term rentals.

Central Stockholm
The handiest area for Centralstationen and Cityterminalen, Stockholm's bustling, 'downtown' Norrmalm district is awash with shops and an easy walk to several major sights. Just to the north, trendy Vasastan harbours some top-notch eating and drinking spots.

BUDGET
ourpick City Backpackers (Map p82; ☎ 20 69 20; www.citybackpackers.org; Upplandsgatan 2A; dm from Skr230; 🖳) Head here, the closest hostel to Centralstationen, for clean rooms, friendly staff, free bike hire and excellent facilities, including a sauna, a laundry and a kitchen (with a free stash of pasta). City tours are also offered, from a free weekly neighbourhood walk to themed, payable options like 'Historic Horror'.

Hostel Bed & Breakfast (Map pp70-1; ☎ 15 28 38; info@hostelbedandbreakfast.com; Rehnsgatan 21; dm from Skr270, s/d Skr490/740; 🖳) Near T-Rådmansgatan, north of the city centre, this pleasant, informal basement hostel comes complete with a kitchen and laundry.

MIDRANGE
Queen's Hotel (Map p82; ☎ 24 94 60; info@queenshotel .se; Drottninggatan 71A; s/d Skr1220/1520, summer & weekends Skr1020/1120; 🖳) A marble staircase and antique lift lead you up to this homely hotel, located in an early 20th-century building on a central pedestrian mall. Rooms are simple, white and soothing, with classic furniture, wooden floors and the odd chandelier.

TOP END
Rica Hotel Kungsgatan (Map p82; ☎ 723 72 20; info .kungsgatan@rica.se; Kungsgatan 47; s Skr995-1875, d Skr1295-2125) Shopaholics will appreciate the direct elevator link to fashion hot-spot PUB (p110) at this temptingly central option. When we visited, the hotel was undergoing a major revamp, which will eventually see the addition of a slinky new lobby bar. Refurbished

rooms sport black wallpaper and lacquered wall panels, red lamps and flatscreen TVs, while the ecofriendly bath products are a civilised touch.

Clarion Hotel Sign (p82; ☎ 676 98 10; www .clarionsign.com; Östra Järnvägsgatan 35; r Skr1000-3000; P ⌨ ☎) Stockholm's largest hotel is also its latest design option. Behind the striking granite and glass facade, trendsetters lounge on Arne Jacobsen Egg chairs, nosh at celebrity chef Marcus Samuelsson's ultra-hip grillbar-restaurant Aquavit, and recharge at the rooftop Selma CitySpa+, complete with 35°C plunge pool. The seriously slick rooms showcase design objects from across Scandinavia, with each floor dedicated to a particular Nordic nation's designers.

Rex Hotel (Map pp70-1; ☎ 16 00 40; www.rexhotel .se; Luntmakargatan 73; s Skr1590-1890, summer & weekends Skr990-1190, d Skr1990-2290, summer & weekends Skr1190-1390; ⌨) While a little less luxe than its sibling Hotel Hellsten across the street, Rex's stylish, functional rooms still deliver the same flatscreen TVs and svelte, Greekstone bathrooms. Rooms in the brand-new extension feature urbane concrete walls, walnut furniture and lush velvet textiles. Other positives include a fab glassed-in breakfast space and fascinating travel photography by the affable owner.

our pick Hotel Hellsten (p82; ☎ 661 86 00; www .hellsten.se; Luntmakargatan 68; s Skr1690-1990, discounted to Skr1190-1390, d Skr2090-2390, discounted to Skr1490-1690; ⌨) Hip Hellsten is owned by anthropologist Per Hellsten, whose slick slumber number features objects from his travels and life, including Congan tribal masks and his grandmother's chandelier. Rooms are supremely comfortable and individually styled, with themes ranging from rustic Swedish to Indian exotica; some even feature original tile stoves. The sleek bathrooms sport phones and handcut Greek slate. Hotel extras include a sauna and a small fitness room, as well as live jazz in the ethno-chic lounge on Thursday evening.

Grand Hôtel Stockholm (Map p82; ☎ 679 35 00; www .grandhotel.se; Södra Blasieholmshamnen 8; s Skr1900-4200, d Skr2500-6900; ⌨) This is where the literati, glitterati and nobility call it a night. A waterfront landmark, with several exclusive restaurants and a see-and-be-seen piano bar, it remains Stockholm's most sumptuous lodgings. Room styles span royal Gustavian to contemporary chic. Room 701 has a unique tower with a 360-degree view; room 702 is the astounding Nobel Room, where the literature prize–winner slumbers overnight.

Nordic Sea Hotel (Map p82; ☎ 50 56 30 00; www.nor dicseahotel.com; Vasaplan 4; s Skr1650-3400, weekends & summer Skr890-2050, d Skr2250-3800, weekends & summer Skr1120-2650; ⌨) This sister hotel to the slightly more upmarket and smaller Nordic Light has an impressive 9000L aquarium in the foyer. Its bar is the famous Absolut Icebar (p107), built entirely of ice, where you can throw on a parka and mittens and drink chilled vodka concoctions out of little ice glasses.

Nordic Light Hotel (p82; ☎ 50 56 30 00; www.nordic lighthotel.com; Vasaplan 7; s Skr2250-4300, weekends & summer Skr1530-3250, d Skr2450-4300, weekends & summer Skr1730-3250; ⌨) Another design option, the Nordic Light is a minimalist Scandi statement, with slick, well-equipped rooms. The signature 'mood rooms' ditch conventional artwork for custom-designed light exhibits, which guests can adjust to suit their temperament. Additional hotel perks include a minigym, saunas and a chic lobby bar.

Berns Hotel (Map p82; ☎ 56 63 22 00; www.berns.se; Näckströmsgatan 8; s/d from Skr2650/2950; ⌨) Popular with rock stars, the rooms at forever-hip Berns come equipped with CD players and styles ranging from 19th-century classical to contemporary sleek. Some rooms are more impressive than others (the balcony rooms get our vote); Room 431 was once a dressing room used by the likes of Marlene Dietrich and Ella Fitzgerald. Part of an historical entertainment complex, with buzzing restaurants, bars and live acts, it's a sparkly choice for the party crew.

Skeppsholmen

Connected to the city centre by bridge and to Djurgården by ferry, this leafy island is home to some marvellous museums and views, as well as a sterling hostel.

our pick Vandrarhem af Chapman & Skeppsholmen (Map p82; ☎ 463 22 66; www.svenskaturistfore ningen.se/afchapman; adult/child dm from Skr185/110, s & d from Skr520; ⌨) The legendary *af Chapman* is a storied vessel that has done plenty of travelling of its own. It's now well anchored in a superb, quiet location, swaying gently off Skeppsholmen. Bunks in dorms below decks have a nautical ambience, unsurprisingly. Staff members are friendly and knowledgable about the city and surrounding areas. Apart from showers and toilets, all facilities are on dry land in the Skeppsholmen hostel, where you'll find a good kitchen with a laid-back common room and a separate TV lounge. Laundry facilities and 24-hour internet access are available.

Östermalm

Ostentatious Östermalm melds A-league boutiques, nosh spots and nightclubs with some outstanding museums. There's a good range of accommodation options, too, from friendly hostels to top-of-the-line design hotels.

BUDGET

our pick **STF Vandrarhem Gärdet** (Map pp70-1; ☎ 463 22 99; gardet@stfturist.se; Sandhamnsgatan 59; s/d from Skr450/680, d/tr with kitchenette Skr760/970; 🖳) Located in quiet Gärdet, a quick metro ride from Östermalm, Stockholm's first 'designer hostel' ditches low-cost drab for smart, contemporary rooms featuring red pin chairs, fluffy sheepskins, textured rugs and designer flatscreen TVs. All have their own bathroom, some boast a small kitchenette, and towels and sheets are included in the price. Take bus 1 from Centralstationen to Östhammarsgatan bus stop.

MIDRANGE

A&Be Hotell (Map p82; ☎ 660 21 00; www.abehotel.com; Grev Turegatan 50; s Skr540-840, d Skr690-990) Staying in this intimate, pretty, old-fashioned hotel is like crashing with an elderly aunt – antique rugs and chandeliers, anonymous portraits of the aristocracy, potted plants and lampshades galore. Run by a warm Polish family, its quietest rooms are those facing the garden. Breakfast is an extra Skr50.

Crystal Plaza Hotel (Map p82; ☎ 406 88 00; www.crystalplazahotel.se; Birger Jarlsgatan 35; standard s Skr850-1600, d 1100-1800; 🖳) Flaunting an eight-storey tower and neoclassical columns, this friendly hotel, housed in an 1895 building, offers wonderfully cosy (albeit smallish) rooms, many of which have been recently renovated. Rates are cheapest when booked early.

Birger Jarl Hotel (Map pp70-1; ☎ 674 18 00; www.birgerjarl.se; Tulegatan 8; s Skr890-1950, d Skr1190-2350; 🖳) With slick, black-clad staff looking straight out of a Filippa K fashion catalogue, this is another hit with Scandi design fans. Interiors mix understated chic with subtle nods to the original '70s fit-out. Each room is designed by a different Swedish designer, and there's a gym and sauna to boot.

TOP END

Hotel Stureplan (Map p82; ☎ 440 66 00; www.hotelstureplan.se; Birger Jarlsgatan 24; standard small r Skr1250-4350; 🖳) A new boutique offering, stylish Stureplan offers individually designed rooms with pared-back Gustavian chic (think high ceilings, spangly chandeliers and antique tiled stoves) and high-tech touches like flatscreen TVs. The homely vibe continues with a gorgeous library-cum-lounge and a glam champagne bar that's oh-so-Östermalm. Check the website for packages and early-booking discounts.

Långholmen

BUDGET

Långholmen Hotell & Vandrarhem (Map pp70-1; ☎ 668 05 10; www.langholmen.com; adult/child 3-15yr dm Skr220/105, cell s Skr420, 2-bed cells Skr540, hotel s/d Skr1435/1740; 🖳) Guests at this hotel-hostel, in a former prison on Långholmen island, sleep in bunks in a cell. The friendly, efficient staff members assure you they will not lock you in. The kitchen and laundry facilities are good, the restaurant serves meals all day and weekend and summer discounts are available. Långholmen's popular summertime bathing spots are a towel flick away.

Södermalm

Södermalm, a 15-minute walk or quick subway ride from the Viking Line boats and Centralstationen, is your best bet for interesting budget or midrange accommodation. At the other end of the spectrum, it's also home to the design-literate Clarion.

BUDGET

Zinkensdamm Hotell & Vandrarhem (Map pp70-1; ☎ 616 81 00; www.zinkensdamm.com; Zinkens väg 20; dm Skr220, d with/without bathroom Skr730/530; 🖳) With a foyer that looks like one of those old Main Street facade recreations you find in cheesy museums, the Zinkensdamm STF is unabashedly fun. It's attractive and well equipped – complete with an ubersleek guest kitchen and personal lockers in each room – and caters for families with kids as well as pub-going backpackers. It can be crowded and noisy, but that's the trade-off for an upbeat vibe. While the hostel breakfast buffet isn't spectacular, hostellers can buy the better hotel breakfast.

Den Röda Båten – Mälaren/Ran (Map p82; ☎ 644 43 85; www.theredboat.com; Söder Mälarstrand, Kajplats 6; hostel dm Skr230-260, hostel d Skr590-690, hotel s/d incl bathroom & breakfast Skr700/1200; 🖳) 'The Red Boat' is a hotel and hostel on two vessels, *Mälaren* and *Ran*. The hostel section is the cosiest of Stockholm's floating accommodations, thanks to lots of dark wood, nautical memorabilia and friendly staff. Hotel-standard rooms are also excellent.

our pick **Bed & Breakfast 4 Trappor** (Map pp70–1; ☎ 642 3104, 0735-69 38 64; www.4trappor.se; Gotlandsgatan 78; apt per 1/2 guests Skr650/800, incl breakfast Skr700/900) For elegant slumming, it's hard to beat this sassy, urbane apartment, complete with cosy, floorboarded bedroom (maximum two guests), modern bathroom and well-equipped kitchen (espresso machine included!). Breakfast is served in the wonderful owners' next-door apartment, and the SoFo address means easy access to Stockholm's coolest shops and hangouts. There's a two-night minimum stay and a discounted rate for stays of over five nights. It's a huge hit, so book months ahead.

MIDRANGE

Hotel Anno 1647 (Map p82; ☎ 442 16 80; www.anno1647 .se; Mariagränd 3; budget s Skr895–1065, weekends & summer Skr595–745, d Skr995–1245, weekends & summer Skr795–940, standard s Skr1590–1940, weekends & summer Skr945–1295, d Skr1895–2390, weekends & summer Skr1295–1695; 🖳) Just off buzzing Götgatan, this historical slumber spot has labyrinthine hallways, affable staff, and both budget and standard rooms. The latter are the winners, with old floorboards, rococo wallpaper and the odd chandelier. Economy rooms are simple but clean, with shared bathrooms and more noise from the street at night.

our pick **Rival Hotel** (Map p82; ☎ 54 57 89 00; www .rival.se; Mariatorget 3; s Skr1290–2290, d Skr1390–2490; 🖳) Owned by ABBA's Benny Anderson and overlooking leafy Mariatorget, this ravishing design hotel is a chic retro gem, complete with vintage 1940s movie theatre and over-the-top art deco cocktail bar. The super-comfy rooms feature posters from great Swedish films and a teddy bear to make you feel at home. Both the smoking and nonsmoking rooms boast flatscreen TVs and good-sized bathrooms, and there's a scrumptious designer bakery-cafe beside the foyer.

Columbus Hotell (Map pp70–1; ☎ 50 31 12 00; www .columbus.se; Tjärhovsgatan 11; s Skr1295, discounted to Skr995–1295, d Skr1595, discounted to Skr1295–1595, budget annex s/d/tr Skr725/925/1150; 🖳) Family-owned and highly recommended, Columbus is nestled in a quiet part of Södermalm, near T-Medborgarplatsen,

and set around a cobblestone courtyard by a pretty park. Accompanying the budget rooms (which have TV, telephone and shared bathroom facilities) are wonderfully homely hotel-standard rooms.

TOP END

Clarion Hotel (Map pp70–1; ☎ 462 10 00; www.clarionstock holm.com; Ringvägen 98; s Skr895–2195, d Skr1095–2695; 🖳) This designer darling feels like a modern art museum, its wide ramp leading into the foyer dotted with ubercool furniture and modelled on the Tate Modern. The foyer also features a huge wall mural and sculptures by Kirsten Ortwed, and there's a fetching lounge-bar for a stylish sip. Rooms are an uncluttered combo of sleek lounges, huge beds with designer sheets and massive windows for urban gazing.

Hilton Stockholm Slussen (Map p82; ☎ 51 73 53 00; www.hilton.com; Guldgränd 8; standard r Skr1590–2890, weekends Skr1090–2890, junior ste Skr2590–4590, weekends Skr2090–4590; 🖳) Perched between the chaotic Slussen interchange and Södermalm's underground highway, Stockholm's white-on-white Hilton sports modern comfortable rooms with swirly marble bathrooms. Several boast stunning city views, and there's a hugely popular bar as well.

Kungsholmen

This mostly residential island has one large and high-quality sleeping option, which is well placed for Kungsholmen's cast of first-class restaurants.

First Hotel Amaranten (Map pp70–1; ☎ 692 52 00; www.firsthotels.com/amaranten; Kungsholmsgatan 31; s Skr1000–2050, d Skr1200–2250; summer s/d from Skr655/855; 🖳) Evoking an upmarket furniture showroom, this smooth chain hotel boasts a plunge pool and stylish spa centre. Retox in the swanky bar or retreat to your mod-Scandi room, where the wi-fi is free.

Outlying Areas

BUDGET

If things get desperate in town, there are more than 20 hostels around the county easily reached by SL buses, trains or archipelago boats within an hour or so. There are also numerous summer camping grounds, many offering cheap cabin accommodation. More options are mentioned in the Around Stockholm section (see p115).

(Continued on page 101)

SWEDISH CULTURE

The word 'culture' is an especially large umbrella when it comes to Sweden – it covers everything from club-hopping and furniture shopping to mountain treks and dogsled tours, with plenty of room in between for tracking down ancient rune stones, hanging out with Pippi Longstocking or learning about life as a Sami reindeer herder.

Connecting with Nature

The Swedish reverence for nature runs deep – no surprise, given the country's excess of startling natural beauty. Lakes, mountains, seascapes, haunted forests, bald hills, bleak horizons, rocky isles: Sweden has them all, and the Swedes are happy to share. Getting into nature here is simpler than you may think.

❶ Kullaberg Nature Reserve
At the tip of the Kulla Peninsula, Kullaberg boasts Scandinavia's brightest lighthouse, Kullens fyr, plus steep cliffs and incredible sunsets. It's great for hiking, caving and exploring tide pools (p197).

❷ Abisko National Park
Hike along the Navvy Trail into Norway or up to a Sami sacrificial site, where the stunning mountain silhouette of Lapporten gives you an eyeful (p309). Or ride up the chairlift to view the midnight sun from Nulla hilltop.

❸ Stockholm Archipelago
The capital city's favourite playground, Stockholm's archipelago (p119) consists of about 24,000 widely scattered islands, some mere pebbles and others home to hostels, restaurants or summer cottages. An archipelago cruise of any kind may well end up being your most vivid Stockholm memory.

❹ Höga Kustenleden
Following this trail (p288), even for a half-day trip, leads you through deep forest and pretty farmland one moment and out to the edge of a seaside cliff the next – stay alert! The trail passes through several fishing villages.

❺ Kungsleden
Stretch your legs on an easy day hike or tackle the whole thing, end to end; Sweden's royal trail (p60) is a popular and accessible route. Longer treks let you camp trailside or stay in well-maintained huts and hostels along the way.

❻ Österlen
Cycle through fragrant apple orchards and rest along the sandy beaches in this lovely corner of Skåne, a coastal nature reserve with a mellow vibe (p189).

Swedish Heritage

Seen from a certain perspective, the line from Vikings in longboats to Pippi Longstocking is a pretty clear one. Get a handle on the Sweden of today by exploring the remnants and relics of Sweden's past, from rune stones and rock carvings to wooden villages and iconic cultural figures.

❶ Skansen
Take a tour of Old Sweden in miniature at the much-loved open-air museum Skansen (p78), the best family attraction in the city. It's educational, too – you and the kids can learn to be glass-blowers, bakers or candle-stick-makers.

❷ Ales Stenar
The largest stone-ship setting in Sweden, Ales Stenar (p188) has a similar atmosphere of mystery to England's Stonehenge, and – who knows? – might have served the same function.

❸ Pippi Longstocking
Dress up like the strongest girl in the world at Junibacken (p80), the amusement park that re-creates the home of Astrid Lindgren's heroine. At Vimmerby, snoop around the author's childhood home (p153), or go Pippi-mad at Astrid Lindgrens Värld (p152).

❹ Birka
Ferry out to the old Viking trading centre (p117) on Björkö in Mälaren lake. Founded in AD 760 to expand and control trade in the region, it's sort of an ancient shopping mall, albeit one with fortified walls and ramparts for protection.

❺ Sigtuna
Only 40km northwest of Stockholm, Sigtuna (p123) is one of the cutest, most historically relevant villages in the area. Founded around AD 980, it's the oldest surviving town in Sweden, and its Stora gatan is most likely Sweden's oldest main street.

❻ Gamla Uppsala
One of Sweden's largest and most atmospheric pre-Viking burial sites, Gamla Uppsala (p244) combines a lovely setting with a well-arranged, enlightening museum to make for an excellent day out.

Contemporary Culture

Vikings are one thing, but what's really fierce these days is Swedish design, be it in the realm of furniture and interior spaces, clothing, lighting, sound, restaurants or glassware.

① Glasriket

Learn to blow glass or just decide to blow your whole budget in Sweden's Glasriket, the 'Kingdom of Crystal' (p147), where the line between shops and museums is pleasantly blurred.

② Moderna Museet

Once it shifts from edgy to established – a transformation that can take years or decades – the best contemporary Swedish art and design might be enshrined here (p80). Next door's Architecture Museum is a survey of Stockholm's built history.

③ Göteborg

The so-called 'second city' arguably comes in first for its lively and varied underground scenes, famously elusive but tirelessly sought-after. For fashion clues, try the shops on Magasinsgatan (p219), and for everything else, ask around – half the fun is in the chase.

④ DesignTorget

If you love good design but don't own a Gold Amex, check out this bargain-shopper's dream (p110), which sells the work of emerging designers alongside established names.

⑤ Röda Sten

Occupying a defunct, graffitied power station in a funky corner of Göteborg, Röda Sten (p211) is one of Sweden's coolest art centres, with four floors of gallery space, live music, weekly club nights and aggressively offbeat events.

⑥ Malmö

With its own brand of wild energy, Malmö (p170) is home to – well, many things, including some great clubs, one of Europe's most recognisable silhouettes (Turning Torso) and the Form/Design Center, your one-stop warehouse of Scandi-cool design, art and architecture.

Sami Culture

The indigenous population of northern Sweden is slowly beginning to be recognised as a national treasure. Travellers are increasingly interested in learning about the Sami people, and there are more and more opportunities for them to do so; for more details, see the Culture chapter (p38).

① Lappstaden

The Sami are traditionally a nomadic people. Early efforts to introduce Christianity imposed a certain amount of pew time per person, so to make church visits manageable they built cottages for overnighting. Some 80 of these are preserved in Lappstaden (p314) in Arvidsjaur; there are daily tours and an annual feast and meeting.

② Gárdi

Talk to a Sami reindeer herder about what his work is like while touring the enclosure where the animals are kept. Gárdi (p307) is near the church in Jukkasjärvi, the town near Kiruna that's more famous as the home of the Ice Hotel.

③ Ájtte Museum

For a thorough introduction to Sami culture, including traditional costumes, musical instruments and singing techniques, shaman practices, ecological positions, reindeer herding through the generations, and woodworking and silversmithing, this museum (p312) in Jokkmokk is tops. Jokkmokk is also home to the annual Sami winter fair.

(Continued from page 92)

Klubbensborg (Map p116; ☎ 646 12 55; klubbens borg@telia.com; Klubbensborgsvägen 27; dm from Skr200, s/d Skr450/750; 🖳) Southwest of central Stockholm, this agreeable SVIF hostel boasts a gorgeous lakeside setting. Several buildings date back to the 17th century, and there's a kitchen, laundry, cafe and summer camping area. The downside: it's a meandering 1km walk from the closest metro station (T-Mälarhöjden).

Bredängs Vandrarhem & Camping (Map p116; ☎ 97 62 00; mail@bredangvandrarhem.se; Stora Sällskapsväg 51; sites Skr250, dm Skr200, 4-bed cabins Skr920; 🕐 campsite early Apr–early Oct, hostel early Jan–mid-Dec) Another lakeside option, 10km southwest of central Stockholm. It's well equipped, with a hostel and cabins. Take the metro to T-Bredäng, then walk 700m. If you're driving, it's well signposted from the E4/E20 motorway.

Hotel Formule 1 (Map p116; ☎ 744 20 44; Mikrofonvägen 30; r Skr390) Just about the cheapest hotel option going, with small, uninspiring rooms that accommodate up to three people. Facilities are shared, and it's 4km southwest of town (take the metro to T-Telefonplan), but who can argue at that price?

TOP END

Hotel J (off Map pp70–1; ☎ 601 30 00; www.hotelj.com; Ellensviksvägen 1, Nacka Strand; s Skr1795-2195, d Skr2195-2595, summer & weekend s/d from Skr1275/1575; 🖳) This is a popular weekend getaway for Stockholmers, with a breezy Hamptons vibe. The chic summer house, built in 1912, is named after the boats used in the America's Cup. The scent of nonchalant wealth wafts unmistakably through the air here. Rooms are decorated with furnishings by hip design store R.O.O.M. Take the metro to T-Slussen then bus 404 or 443.

EATING

Stockholmers like to think of themselves as consummate foodies. In a city with seven Michelin-starred restaurants, it's understandable. Here, top chefs are veritable celebrities, and a table at their dining dens a prized possession. But it's not just about the food, it's also about the style. That Thomas Sandell decked out Kungsholmen or that Ilse Crawford designed Mathias Dahlgren is almost as much a drawcard as the fare itself. Admittedly, these epicurean highlights don't come cheap, although a few places offer more kronor-friendly lunch menus or lower-fuss bar grub.

If you're after a cheap, filling lunch, your best bet is one of Stockholm's atmospheric cafes. Aside from the beloved Swedish ritual of coffee and cakes, these bolt holes serve filling grub, from salads, focaccias and classic Swedish sandwiches *(smörgåsar)* to warming soups, quiche and pasta dishes.

Also less likely to break the bank are Stockholm's old-school restaurants, often serving up *husmanskost* (classic Swedish home cooking). Equally affordable is the ever-growing number of ethnic eateries, where flavours span anything from Ethiopian to tongue-teasing Thai.

For a quick, inexpensive snack, it's hard to go past a *grillad korv med bröd* – your basic grilled hot dog on a bun – available for between Skr15 and Skr30 from carts all over town.

For a comprehensive list of vegan restaurants in and around Stockholm, log on to www .veganstockholm.se.

Gamla Stan
BUDGET

Chokladkoppen (Map p82; ☎ 20 31 70; Stortorget; cakes & snacks Skr30-70) Arguably Stockholm's best-loved cafe, hole-in-the-wall Chokladkoppen sits slap bang on the Old Town's enchanting main square. It's a gay-friendly spot, with cute, gym-fit waiters, a look-at-me summer terrace and yummy grub like broccoli and blue-cheese pie and scrumptious cakes.

Sundbergs Konditori (Map p82; ☎ 10 67 35; Järntorget 83; bagels & ciabatta Skr55-60) Dating from 1785, this is Stockholm's oldest bakery-cafe, complete with chintzy chandeliers, regal oil paintings and a copper samovar full of self-serve coffee. Mix and match with gleaming pastries and a soothing selection of bagels, ciabatta, pies and omelettes.

Café Art (Map p82; ☎ 411 76 61; Västerlånggatan 60; lunches Skr69) This atmospheric, barrel-vaulted cellar cranks up the cosy factor with its candlelit tables, snug nooks and art-slung walls. A perfect spot for *fika* (coffee and cake), it also makes a mean baguette and great shrimp salads.

MIDRANGE

Hermitage (Map p82; ☎ 411 95 00; Stora Nygatan 11; lunch/dinner Skr80/95) Don't let the '80s-style coffeeshop decor put you off; herbivores love Hermitage for its simple, tasty, vegetarian nosh. Salad, homemade bread, tea and coffee are included in the price.

Siam Thai (Map p82; ☎ 20 02 33; Stora Nygatan 25; dagens rätt from Skr80, mains Skr165-205; ⏲ lunch Mon-Sat, dinner Mon-Sun) Bamboo-lined Siam channels Bangkok with its real-deal, Southeast Asian flavours. Spice it up with anything from prawns with eggplant in green curry to deep-fried chicken wrapped in pandanus leaves.

Zum Franziskaner (Map p82; ☎ 411 83 30; Skeppsbron 44; dagens rätt Skr80, husmanskost Skr139-298; ⏲ closed Sun) It's only natural that a place founded by German monks in 1421 (it claims to be the oldest restaurant in town) should peddle bottled German and Austrian beers and hearty sausages. Local offerings include the delicious *isterband* (a savoury country sausage) and spruced-up Swedish *husmanskost* like roe deer with lingonberries, fennel, goat's cheese and potato cake. The current building dates from 1906, its interior an atmospheric combo of wooden stalls, ornate cabinets and ceiling artwork.

TOP END

our pick **Leijontornet** (Map p82; ☎ 14 23 55; Lilla Nygatan 5; starters Skr110-135, 3-/5-course menu Skr695/1050; ⏲ dinner Mon-Sat, bar from 5pm Mon-Sat) Leijontornet boasts a Michelin star along with 14th-century defence tower ruins in the dining room. The menu itself is unapologetically contemporary, with organic seasonal produce transformed into show-stoppers like roe deer with baked plums, forest mushrooms, ox marrow, black pudding and woodruff-flavoured gravy. For fab mid-priced fare, opt for the trendy bar, where DJs hit the decks on Friday and Saturday.

our pick **Den Gyldene Freden** (Map p82; ☎ 24 97 60; Österlånggatan 51; lunch mains Skr165-265, dinner mains Skr175-425; ⏲ closed Sun) Simmering since 1722, this venerable barrel-vaulted restaurant is run by the Swedish Academy, where (rumour has it) its members meet to decide the winners of the Nobel Prize. Personally, we think it should go to the chefs, whose sublime offerings include civilised *husmanskost* dishes like quail stuffed with duck liver, celeriac purée, Gotland truffles and rôti jus.

Central Stockholm

BUDGET

Vetekatten (Map p82; ☎ 21 84 54; Kungsgatan 55; tea, coffee & snacks from Skr25; ⏲ 7.30am-8pm Mon-Fri, 9.30am-5pm Sat, noon-5pm Sun) A cardamom-scented labyrinth of cosy nooks, antique furnishings and oil paintings, Vetekatten is not so much a cafe as an institution. Wish back the old days over filling sandwiches, heavenly scrolls and warming cups of tea.

Caffé Nero (Map pp70-1; ☎ 22 19 35; Roslagsgatan 4; coffee & pastries from Skr25; ⏲ 7am-10pm Mon-Fri, 8am-10pm Sat, 8am-6pm Sun) Architect Tadao Ando would approve of the brutal (and brutally hip) concrete interiors at this Vasastan hangout, where local hipsters down mighty caffé, grappa shots, salubrious panini and Italian home cooking, from sublime veal meatballs to a naughty tiramisu.

MIDRANGE

Tranan (Map pp70-1; ☎ 52 72 81 00; Karlbergsvägen 14; starters Skr55-125, mains Skr95-295; ⏲ 11.30am-midnight Mon-Thu, 11.30am-1am Fri, 5pm-1am Sat, 5-11pm Sun, 6pm-midnight Mon-Sun late Jun-Aug) Stockholmers swear by this bistro-style eatery, with technicolour brush strokes pimping up the walls. Food combines Swedish *husmanskost* with savvy Gallic touches. On weekends DJs hit the decks in the pumping, 30-something basement bar (except in summer, when the bar is closed).

Sibiriens Soppkök (Map pp70-1; ☎ 15 00 14; Roslagsgatan 25; meals Skr70-135; ⏲ 10am-10pm Mon-Fri, noon-10pm Sat) Sibiriens makes soup so sexy that tables are hard to come by at this intimate bolt-hole; book ahead or head in early. At the top of the class is the seafood soup, a luscious blend of tomato, saffron, orange, wine, salmon, prawns and mussels. Lavish liquids aside, the ever-changing daily menu includes tapas, pasta and Med-leaning wines.

Republik (Map pp70-1; ☎ 54 59 05 50; www.restaurant-republik.com, in Swedish; Tulegatan 17; lunch Skr79-89, mains Skr135-235; ⏲ lunch Mon-Fri, dinner Tue-Sat) Republik's buzzing bar was voted Stockholm's best a few years ago, yet the ultimate indulgence here is the restaurant. Clued-up staff, a metro-chic vibe and a seriously smooth Euro-fusion menu will leave you glowing.

Lao Wai (Map pp70-1; ☎ 673 78 00; Luntmakargatan 74; lunch Skr80, mains Skr125-185; ⏲ lunch Mon-Fri, dinner Tue-Sat) Tiny, herbivorous Lao Wai does sinfully good things to tofu and vegetable combos, hence the faithful regulars. Nosh virtuously on dishes like Sichuan-style smoked tofu with shitake, chillies, garlic shoots, snow peas and black beans.

ourpick **Bakfickan** (Map p82; ☎ 676 58 08; mains Skr135-275; ⏰ 11.30am-11pm Mon-Fri, noon-10pm Sat) Calling the Opera House home, the 'back pocket' of fine-dining darling Operakällaren (below) is crammed with opera photographs and deco-style lampshades. Dexterous old-school waiters serve comforting Swedish *husmanskost* and the counter seats make it a perfect spot for solo supping. Come late at night and you just might stumble across a bitching soprano.

TOP END

Pontus! (Map p82; ☎ 54 52 73 00; Brunnsgatan 1; bar menu Skr95-270, mains Skr185-420; ⏰ lunch Mon-Fri, dinner Mon-Sat) While we adore the literary-themed, custom-made wallpaper, the real stars here are the mouth-watering nosh, crafty cocktails and glam-hip vibe. Down Thai mojitos and super sushi at the trendy bar, or head one floor down for luxe dining at chi-chi circular booths. French and Swedish cooking collide, with fair-trade, organic and local produce transformed into the likes of boiled lobster with smoked Swedish duck, brioche and preserved plum. From Thursday to Saturday, DJs spin soul, electronica and vintage disco.

Grill (Map p82; ☎ 31 45 30; Drottninggatan 89; starters Skr125-230, mains Skr175-310; ⏰ 11.15am-2pm & 5pm-1am Mon-Fri, 11.15am-2pm & 4pm-1am Sat, 3-10pm Sun, closed early Jul-early Aug) Kick-started by culinary stars Melker Andersson and Danyel Couet, this outrageous restaurant-bar features differently themed spaces, from Miami art deco to AstroTurf garden party. The menu is a global affair, innovatively arranged by grill type. Vegetarians aren't overlooked, service is casual and accommodating, and there's a popular Sunday grill buffet (Skr295).

Operakällaren (Map p82; ☎ 676 58 00; Jakobs Torg 10; starters Skr235-295, mains Skr250-450, tasting menu Skr950; ⏰ 6-10pm Tue-Sat) Inside Stockholm's show-off Opera House, the century-old Operakällaren is another gastronomic event. Decadent chandeliers, golden mirrors and exquisitely carved ceilings set the scene for French-meets-fusion adventures like seared scallops with caramel, cauliflower purée, pata negra ham and brown butter emulsion. Book at least two weeks ahead.

Grands Veranda (Map p82; ☎ 679 35 86; Grand Hôtel Stockholm, Södra Blasieholmshamnen 8; breakfast buffet/smörgåsbord Skr245/425, mains Skr155-365; ⏰ 7-11pm, smörgåsbord 1-4pm & 6-10pm Sat & Sun Feb, 6-10pm Mon-Fri, 1-4pm & 6-10pm Sat & Sun Mar, Apr & Sep-Nov, noon-3pm & 6-10pm Mon-Fri, 1-4pm & 6-10pm Sat & Sun May-Aug; Christmas buffet Dec) Head here, inside the Grand Hôtel, for the famous breakfast buffet or the gluttonous smörgåsbord. Get in early for a window seat and tuck into both hot and cold Swedish staples, including gravadlax with a moreish mustard sauce. It's like a belt-busting crash course in classic Nordic flavours.

ourpick **Mathias Dahlgren** (Map p82; ☎ 679 35 84; Grand Hôtel Stockholm, Södra Blasieholmshamnen 6; matbaren mains Skr245-395, matsalen mains Skr325-455, 6-course tasting menu Skr1300; ⏰ matbaren noon-1.30pm & 6pm-midnight, matsalen one sitting only 7pm-midnight) Chef Matthias Dahlgren is hot property and his namesake newcomer has foodies in a flutter. Set in the Grand Hôtel, it's divided into three spaces: a luxe bar, Matbaren (Food Bar) for casual noshing, and the more formal Matsalen (Dining Room). The latter is where Dahlgren really delivers his tour de force: think organic foie gras terrine with mango, black sesame and black pepper, or fried apple with goat's milk ice-cream, vanilla cream and rye bread, bowling over the critics. Book ahead.

Östermalm

BUDGET

Café Saturnus (Map p82; ☎ 611 77 00; Eriksbergsgatan 6; baguettes/pastries Skr25/55, Skr25; ⏰ 7am-8pm Mon-Fri, 9am-7pm Sat & Sun) For velvety caffé latte, Gallic-inspired baguettes and perfect pastries, saunter into this casually chic bakery-cafe. Sporting a stunning mosaic floor, and a hit with everyone from yummy mummies to Swedish princesses, it's a fabulous spot to flick through the paper while devouring Stockholm's finest cinnamon bun.

MIDRANGE

Brasserie Elverket (Map pp70-1; ☎ 661 25 62; Linnégatan 69; lunch Skr79-145, dinner mains Skr185-285, 2-course theatre menu Skr265; ⏰ 11am-1am Tue-Sat) In an old electricity plant reborn as an experimental theatre, this slick, dimly-lit resto-bar peddles bold, adventurous grub like melon and vanilla consommé served with cardamom pannacotta and a pineapple-sage salsa. Starters are a pick-and-mix tapas-style affair, and the weekend brunch buffet (Skr189) is one of Stockholm's best. Fed, kick back in the slinky lounge with an absinthe-laced Belgian Bastard.

Örtagården (Map p82; ☎ 662 17 28; Nybrogatan 31, 1st fl, Östermalms Saluhall Bldg; lunch/dinner buffet Skr85/135; ⏰ 10.30am-9.30pm Mon-Fri, 11am-9pm Sat &

Sun) Perched above Östermalms Saluhall, this popular, casual restaurant spoils punters with its extensive vegetarian lunch and dinner buffet, which includes fresh fruit and diet-defying sweet treats.

Sturehof (Map p82; ☎ 440 57 30; Stureplan 2; mains Skr155-545; ⏰ 11am-2am Mon-Fri, noon-2am Sat, 1pm-2am Sun) Superb for late-night sipping and supping, this buzzing, convivial brasserie sparkles with gracious staff, celebrity regulars, and fabulous seafood-centric dishes (the bouillabaisse is brilliant). Both the front and back bars are a hit with the eye-candy brigade and perfect for a post-meal flirt.

Djurgården
BUDGET
ourpick Rosendals Trädgårdskafe (Map pp70-1; ☎ 54 58 12 70; Rosendalsterrassen 12; cakes Skr25-35, sandwiches Skr45-65; ⏰ 11am-5pm Mon-Fri, 11am-6pm Sat & Sun May-Sep, 11am-4pm Tue-Sun Oct-Dec, closed Jan) Rosendals is an idyllic spot for heavenly carrot cake and an organic wine in the summer or a warm cup of glögg (mulled wine) and a lussekatte (saffron bun) in winter. Much of the produce is biodynamic and grown on site, and the cafe-shop (closed January and February) sells everything from preserved lemons and freshly baked bread to Rosendals' very own cookbook. Take bus 47, then it's a 15-minute walk from Djurgårdsbron.

Blå Porten (Map pp70-1; ☎ 663 87 59; Djurgårdsvägen 64; pastries from Skr20, mains Skr78-150; ⏰ 11am-7pm, to 9pm Tue & Thu, longer hours in summer) Blissful on sunny days, when you can linger over lunch or fika (coffee and cake) in the Monet-like garden, this cafe next to Liljevalchs Konsthall boasts an obscenely tempting display of baked goods, as well as lip-smacking Scandi and global meals. Mercifully, many of Djurgården's museums are within rolling distance.

TOP END
Wärdshuset Ulla Winbladh (Map pp70-1; ☎ 663 05 71; www.ullawinbladh.se; Rosendalsvägen 8; starters Skr95-185, mains Skr110-395) Named after one of Carl Michael Bellman's lovers, this villa was built as a steam bakery for the Stockholm World's Fair (1897) and now serves fine food in intimate rooms and a blissful garden setting. Sup on skilful dishes like lake Hjälmaren pikeperch fried with mustard, creamy barley and crayfish, or opt for simple Scandi favourites (Skr110 to Skr145), including herring with Kvibille cheese and homemade crispbread.

Roxette fans – ask the staff to point out singer Marie Fredriksson's artwork. Book a week ahead in summer.

Restaurang Hasselbacken (Map pp70-1; ☎ 51 73 43 07; www.restauranghasselbacken.com; Hazeliusbacken 20; mains Skr245-315, 2-/3-course menu Skr385/435; ⏰ lunch Mon-Fri, dinner Mon-Sun) Slip into this vintage, jewel-box dining room for modern Scandi fare like white asparagus with rhubarb glaze, black morel and parmesan foam. In between swoons, take in the superb coffered ceiling. The restaurant is part of Scandic Hotel Hasselbacken.

Södermalm
BUDGET
Nystekt Strömming (Map p82; Södermalmstorg; ⏰ hours vary, generally 10am-6pm Mon-Fri, 11am-4pm Sat & Sun) The best place to get fried (stekt) herring in all of Stockholm is this humble cart outside the metro station at Slussen. Combo plates cost about Skr30 to Skr50.

String (Map pp70-1; ☎ 714 85 14; Nytorgsgatan 38; coffee & pastries around Skr45, salads Skr59-69; ⏰ 9.30am-9pm Mon-Thu, 9.30am-7.30pm Fri, 10.30am-7pm Sat & Sun) This retro-funky SoFo cafe does a bargain weekend brunch buffet (Skr65; 10.30am to 1pm). Load your plate with everything from cereals, yoghurt and fresh fruit to pancakes, toast and amazing homemade hummus. Fancy that '70s chair you're plonked on? Take it home; almost everything you see is for sale.

MIDRANGE
Crêperie Fyra Knop (Map p82; ☎ 640 77 27; Svartensgatan 4; crepes from Skr48, mains Skr80-98; ⏰ dinner Mon-Fri, lunch & dinner weekends) Head here for perfect crêpes in an intimate setting with a hint of shantytown chic – think reggae tunes and old tin billboards for Stella Artois. A good place for a quiet tête-á-tête before you hit the clubs down the street.

ourpick Östgöta Källaren (Map pp70-1; ☎ 643 22 40; Östgötagatan 41; lunch Skr68-98, mains Skr115-189; ⏰ to 1am, kitchen closes 11.30pm) The regulars at this soulful pub-cum-restaurant range from multipierced rockers to blue-rinse grandmas, all smitten with the dimly lit romantic atmosphere, amiable vibe and hearty Swedish, Eastern European and French-Med grub.

Pelikan (Map pp70-1; ☎ 55 60 90 90; Blekingegatan 40; mains Skr75-185; ⏰ dinner daily, lunch Sat & Sun; minimum age 23yr) Lofty ceilings, wood panelling and nononsense waiters in waistcoats set the scene for classic husmanskost at this century-old beer hall. The herring options are particularly good and there's usually a vegetarian special to boot.

Bistro Street (Map pp70-1; ☎ 658 63 50; www .streetinstockholm.se, in Swedish; Hornstulls Strand 4; lunch Skr82-125, dinner mains Skr155-255; ⊗ 11am-11pm Mon & Tue, 11.30am-1am Wed-Sat, 11.30am-6pm Sun) Södermalm's weekend market street is one of Stockholm's coolest hang-outs, and this is its equally popular restaurant-bar-lounge. Grit-chic concrete floors, hot-pink warehouse ceiling and low-slung bulbs mix it with mainly organic, tasty grub spanning Swedish and Mediterranean cuisines. DJs work the wax at the regular Friday and Saturday club nights, and the waterside tables are coveted summertime spots.

ourpick Koh Phangan (Map pp70-1; ☎ 642 50 40; www.kohphangan.nu, in Swedish; Skånegatan 57; mains Skr139-265; ⊗ to 11pm Sun-Fri, to midnight Sat) Best at night, this outrageously kitsch Thai restaurant has to be seen to be believed. Tuck into your *kao pat gai* (chicken fried rice) in a real *tuk-tuk* to the accompanying racket of crickets and tropical thunder, or kick back with beers in a bamboo hut. DJs occasionally hit the decks and it's best to book ahead.

TOP END

Gondolen (Map p82; ☎ 641 70 90; Stadsgården 6; mains Skr130-320, 3-course menu Skr490, degustation menu Skr750; ⊗ lunch Mon-Fri, dinner Mon-Sat) Perched atop the iconic Katarinahissen (the vintage Slussen elevator), Gondolen combines killer city views with contemporary Nordic brilliance from chef Erik Lallerstedt. Play 'spot the landmark' while carving into gems like thyme-roasted halibut with lobster sauce and root-vegetable cake.

Kungsholmen

BUDGET

Vurma (Map pp70-1; ☎ 650 93 50; Polhemsgatan 15; sandwiches Skr27-69, salads Skr73, ⊗ 10am-6pm) Squeeze in among the chattering punters, fluff up the cushions and eavesdrop over a vegan latte at this kitsch-hip cafe-bakery. The scrumptious sandwiches and salads are utterly inspired; try the *chevre*, marinated chicken, tomato, cucumber, walnuts, apple and mustard salad. You'll find other branches in Vasastan (Map pp70–1; Gästrikegatan 2) and Södermalm (Map pp70–1; Bergsunds Strand 31).

Il Caffé (Map pp70-1; ☎ 652 30 04; Bergsgatan 17; focaccia Skr47-95; ⊗ 8am-6pm Mon-Fri, 10am-6pm Sat & Sun)

Low-strung lights, edgy graphic murals and indie-cool regulars load this cafe bolt-hole with boho grit. The authentic focaccias are great, and best washed down with a jumbo-sized caffé latte.

MIDRANGE

Kungsholmen (Map pp70-1; ☎ 50 52 44 50; Norr Mälarstrand, Kajplats 464; soup Skr95-230, sushi 140-325, grill Skr215-325; ⊗ 5pm-1am Mon-Sun) Owned by celebrity chef Melker Andersson, this hip, sexed-up 'food court' features six open kitchens cooking up different specialities, including soups, sushi, bistro grub, bread and ice cream. Add a sleek, cocktail-savvy bar, weekend DJ sessions and a waterside location, and you'll understand why it's best to book.

ourpick Bergamott (Map pp70-1; ☎ 650 30 34; Hantverkargatan 35; mains Skr180-350; ⊗ lunch Mon-Fri, dinner Tue-Sat) The *trés*-cool French chefs in the kitchen don't simply whip up to-die-for French-Italian dishes – they'll probably deliver them to your table, talk you through the produce and suggest the perfect drop. It's never short of a convivial crowd, so book ahead, especially when jazz musicians drop by for a soulful evening jam.

Market Halls

From Kalix roe to robust chorizo, Stockholm's market halls are prime spots to dig into local and global treats.

Östermalms Saluhall (Map p82; Östermalmstorg; ⊗ 9.30am-6pm Mon-Thu, to 6.30pm Fri & 4pm Sat) Stockholm's historic, blue-riband market spoils tastebuds with fresh fish, seafood and meat, as well as fruits, vegetables and hard-to-find cheeses. The building itself is a Stockholm landmark, designed as a Romanesque cathedral of food in 1885. For a quick lunch, belly up to the bar at Sushi Baren; for a real treat, book a table at Lisa Elmqvist (meals Skr140 to Skr310), one of the city's top seafood eateries (trust the staff's recommendations). There's a clean, free, well-hidden toilet in the far corner opposite the market entrance.

Hötorgshallen (Map p82; Hötorget; ⊗ 10am-6pm Mon-Fri, 10am-3pm Sat Jun & Jul; 10am-6pm Mon-Thu, 10am-6.30pm Fri, 10am-4pm Sat rest of year) Located below Filmstaden cinema, Hötorgshallen is Stockholm at its multicultural best, its stalls selling everything from fresh Nordic seafood to fluffy hummus and fragrant teas. Ready-to-eat options include Lebanese spinach parcels, kebabs and vegetarian burgers. For the ultimate feed, squeeze into galley-themed dining nook Kajsas Fiskrestaurang for soulful *fisksoppa* (fish stew) with mussels and aioli (Skr80).

Söderhallarna (Map pp70-1; Medborgarplatsen 3; 10am-6pm Mon-Wed, 10am-7pm Thu & Fri, 10am-4pm Sat) This more modern food hall peddles everything from cheese and smallgoods to decent vegetarian grub.

Self-Catering
The handiest central supermarket is **Hemköp** (Map p82; Klarabergsgatan 50; 7am-9pm Mon-Fri, 10am-9pm Sat & Sun), in the Åhléns department store. Others include:

Coop Konsum (Map p82; Katarinavägen 3-7; 7am-9pm Mon-Fri, 9am-9pm Sat & Sun)

ICA Baronen (Map pp70-1; Odengatan 40; 8am-10pm)

Vivo T-Jarlen (Map p82; inside Östermalmstorg Tunnelbana station; 7am-9pm Mon-Fri, 10am-7pm Sat, 11am-7pm Sun) Enter from Grev Turegatan.

DRINKING
Stockholm's bar scene is as kicking as it is pricey. From grit-chic factory conversions to raucous vintage beer halls, you're bound to find a spot worth a toast. Many of the city's hottest restaurants have bars attached, making for an easy night on the tiles. For beautiful crowds and a glammy vibe, your best bet is Östermalm. Hip spots also stud Norrmalm, Vasastaden and Kungsholmen, although the undisputed bar scene heavyweight is Södermalm, where options offer everything from old-school pubs to alt-cool bar-gallery hybrids.

Marie Laveau (Map p82; 668 85 00; www.marielaveau.se, in Swedish; Hornsgatan 66; 5pm-midnight Tue & Wed, 5pm-3am Thu-Sat) In an old sausage factory, this kicking Söder play-pen draws a boho-chic crowd. The designer-grunge bar (think chequered floor and subway-style tiled columns) serves killer cocktails and contemporary nosh (Skr84 to Skr199), while the sweaty basement hosts thumping club night Bangers 'n' Mash on Saturday.

Pet Sounds Bar (Map pp70-1; 643 82 25; www.petsoundsbar.se, in Swedish; Skånegatan 80; from 5pm Mon-Sat) A SoFo favourite, this jamming bar pulls in music journos, indie culture vultures and the odd Goth rocker. While the restaurant serves decent Italo-French grub, the real fun happens in the basement. Head down for a mixed bag of live bands, release parties and DJ sets.

Soldaten Svejk (Map pp70-1; 641 33 66; Östgötagatan 35) In this crowded, wooden-floored, amber-windowed pub, decorated with heraldic shields, punters pine for Prague with great Czech beer on tap, including the massively popular Staropramen. Line your stomach with simple, solid Czech meals (Skr97 to Skr125); the smoked cheese is sublime. Head in early or prepare to queue for a table.

Berns Salonger (Map p82; 56 63 22 22; www.berns.se; Berzelii Park; bistro 11.30am-midnight Mon-Fri, noon-midnight Sat, 1-11pm Sun, nightclub 11pm-4am Thu-Sat, also Wed & Sun occasionally, midnight-5am Thu-Sat) A Stockholm institution since 1862, this glitzy entertainment palace remains one of Stockholm's hottest party spots. While the gorgeous ballroom hosts some brilliant live music gigs, the best of Berns' bars is the intimate basement bar-club 2.35:1, packed with cool creative types, top-notch DJs and projected art-house images.

Allmänna Galleriet 925 (Map pp70-1; 41 06 81 00; www.ag925.se; Kronobergsgatan 37; from 5pm Tue-Sat, closed mid-Jun–Jul) AG925 has all the 'It kid' prerequisites – an obscure urban location (ex-silver factory and anonymous facade), spot industrial fit-out (steel-plate floors, white-tiled walls, Tom Dixon lights) and edgy art slung on the walls. While the bistro is mostly a hit-and-miss affair, the grit-chic bar never fails to impress with its well-priced, well-mixed liquids.

Le Rouge (Map p82; 50 52 44 30; Österlånggatan 17; 11.30am-2pm & 5pm-1am Mon-Thu, 11.30am-2pm & 4pm-1am Fri, 5pm-1am Sat) Fin-de-siècle Paris is the inspiration for Gamla Stan's latest sip'n'sup darling, a decadent melange of rich red velvet, tasselled lampshades, inspired cocktails and French bistro grub. Run by two of Stockholm's hottest chefs (Danyel Couet and Melker Andersson), the adjoining fine-dining restaurant serves up luxe French and Italian dishes in period-glam surrounds. DJs hit the decks Thursday to Saturday.

Olssons Video (Map pp70-1; 673 38 00; Odengatan 41; 9pm-3am Wed, Thu & Sat, 5pm-3am Fri, earlier openings in summer) While the retro neon signage, tinted mirrors, dancing pole and cucumber cocktail might allude to a kinky disposition, this Vasastan staple was actually once a shoe shop. The 'video' refers to the projected Studio 54–style films, easily upstaged by the hip young crowd, super-cool tunes (from retro to electro) and mighty red mojitos. Head in before 10pm or prepare to queue.

Mälarpaviljongen (Map pp70-1; ☎ 650 87 01; www
.malarpaviljongen.se, in Swedish; Norr Mälarstrand 63;
☽ from 11am summer only) When the sun's out,
few places beat this alfresco waterside resto-
bar for some Nordic *dolce vita*. A hit with both
gay and straight punters, its cosy, glassed-in
gazebo is only upstaged by the ubercool floating pontoon, where sexy crowds and lakeside
views make for a fabulous evening guzzle.
Call ahead for opening times, which are at
the weather's mercy.

El Mundo (Map pp70-1; ☎ 743 03 53; www.matkultur
.nu, in Swedish; Erstagatan 21; ☽ 5pm-midnight Mon-
Sat, from 4pm Fri) Backgammon boards, Mexi-
cana film posters and a bar made from
pressed olive-oil tins give this intimate
hang-out a sultry Latin vibe. Out the back
there's a closet-sized art gallery and out
the front a convivial 30-something crowd.

Lilla Baren at Riche (Map p82; ☎ 54 50 35 60;
Birger Jarlsgatan 4; ☽ 5pm-2am Tue-Sat) A current
darling of Östermalm's hip parade, this
skinny hang-out is a metro-sexy mix of
smooth bar staff, skilled DJs and a packed
crowd of fashion-literate media types; head
in by 9pm to score a seat. The adjoining
restaurant is one of Stockholm's best for
Scandi-meets-French-Med cuisine.

Akkurat (Map p82; ☎ 644 00 15; www.akkurat.se, in
Swedish; Hornsgatan 18; ☽ to midnight Mon, to 1am Tue-
Sun) Valhalla for beer fiends, heaving Akkurat
boasts a huge selection of Belgian ales as
well as a good range of Swedish-made microbrews, notably the semidivine Jämtlands
Bryggeri trio: Heaven, Hell and Fallen Angel.
Extras include a vast wall of whiskey, and
mussels on the menu.

Absolut Icebar (Map p82; ☎ 50 56 31 24; www.nordic
hotels.se; Nordic Sea Hotel, Vasaplan 4; admission prebooked
Skr180, drop-in Skr195; ☽ drop-in 9.45pm-1am Fri & Sat, also
Thu Jun–mid-Sep, reservations recommended all other times)
It's touristy. Downright gimmicky! And you're
utterly intrigued, admit it: a bar built entirely
out of ice, where you drink from glasses carved
of ice on tables made of ice. The admission
price gets you warm booties, mittens, a parka
and one drink. Refill drinks cost Skr95.

Systembolaget

The state-owned alcohol monopoly is the
only place to buy real booze to take away.
A complete listing is given online; the following are some handy central branches:

Systembolaget (www.systembolaget.se) Klarabergsgatan
(Map p82; ☎ 21 47 44; Klarabergsgatan 62; ☽ 10am-

8pm Mon-Fri, 10am-3pm Sat); Lilla Nygatan (Map p82;
☎ 411 65 06; Lilla Nygatan 11; ☽ 10am-6pm Mon-Wed,
to 7pm Thu & Fri, 10am-3pm Sat); Regeringsgatan (Map
p82; ☎ 796 98 10; Regeringsgatan 44; ☽ 10am-7pm
Mon-Fri, 10am-3pm Sat)

ENTERTAINMENT

Scan the local papers (see p73) for up-to-date
listings of entertainment events, particularly
the Friday 'På Stan' section of *Dagens Nyheter*
newspaper. The monthly *What's On Stockholm*
brochure, available free from the tourist office,
is another guide.

Nightclubs

Stockholm is home to some mighty clubs, with
DJ royalty regularly on the decks. You'll find
the slickest spots in cash-flash Östermalm,
especially on and around Stureplan. Expect an
entry charge of Skr100 to Skr200 at the trendiest venues, not to mention notoriously picky
door bitches (style up or opt out!). Södermalm
offers a more varied scene, with club nights
spanning local indie to salsa.

Spy Bar (Map p82; ☎ 54 50 37 01; www.thespybar
.com, in Swedish; Birger Jarlsgatan 20; admission Skr160;
☽ 10pm-5am Wed-Sat) Set in a turn-of-the-century flat (spot the tiled stoves), this party
stalwart pulls in a 20- and 30-something
media crowd, as well as the odd American
heiress (yes, Paris partied here). Expect
three bars, electro, rock and hip-hop beats
and no entry after 2am (unless you're well
connected, darling).

Sturecompagniet (Map p82 ☎ 611 78 00; www
.sturecompagniet.se; Sturegatan 4; admission Skr120, after
midnight Skr140; ☽ 10pm-3am Thu-Sat) Swedish
soap stars, flowing champagne and look-
at-me attitude set a decadent scene at this
glitzy, multilevel play-pen. Dress to impress and flaunt your wares to commercial house. Guest DJs have included Roger
Sanchez.

Café Opera (Map p82; ☎ 676 58 07; www.cafeopera
.se; Operahuset, Karl XXI's Torg; admission Skr180; ☽ 10pm-
3am Wed-Sun) Rock stars and wannabe playboys
need a suitably excessive place to schmooze,
booze and groove, one with bulbous chandeliers, haughty ceiling frescoes and a jet-
set vibe. This bar-club combo fits the bill.
The adjoining Veranden bar is a crisp white
creation by architect trio Claesson Koivisto
Rune and a choice hang-out for bartenders,
meaning a mediocre martini is strictly out of
the question.

STOCKHOLM

GAY & LESBIAN STOCKHOLM

Still glowing from EuroPride 2008, Stockholm is a dazzling spot for queer travellers. Sweden's legendary open-mindedness makes homophobic attitudes rare and party-goers of all persuasions are welcome in any bar or club. As a result, Stockholm doesn't do a 'gay ghetto', although you'll find most of the queer-centric venues in Södermalm and Gamla Stan. For club listings and events, pick up a free copy of street-press magazine *QX*, found at many clubs, shops and cafes around town. Its website (www.qx.se) is more frequently updated. *QX* also produces a free, handy *Gay Stockholm Map*.

Good bars and clubs include the following:

Lady Patricia (Map p82; ☎ 743 05 70; Stadsgårdskajen 152; ☽ Sun) This is a perennial Sunday-night favourite with its superb seafood restaurant, two crowded dance floors, drag shows and Schlager-loving crowd. It's all aboard a docked old royal yacht.

Lino Club Sthlm (Map p82; ☎ 411 69 76; www.linoclub.se; Södra Riddarholmshamnen 19; ☽ Sat) Stockholm's hottest Saturday night gay club, it has four bars, three dance floors and a mingle-friendly outdoor terrace.

RFSL (Map pp70-1; ☎ 50 16 29 50; www.rfsl.se/stockholm, in Swedish; Sveavägen 57-59) The national organisation for gay and lesbian rights is a good source of information, with a library and cafe to boot.

Roxy (Map pp70-1; ☎ 640 96 55; www.roxysofo.se; Nytorget 6; ☽ closed Mon) A chic resto-bar in Södermalm, it's popular with lipstick lesbians, publishing types and SoFo's creative set, all of whom nibble on brilliant mod-Med nosh to sultry tango tunes.

Side Track (Map p82; ☎ 641 16 88; www.sidetrack.nu; Wollmar Yxkullsgatan 7; ☽ Wed-Sat) This establishment is particular hit with down-to-earth guys, with a low-key, pub-like ambience and decent grub for peckish punters on the prowl.

Torget (Map p82; ☎ 20 55 60; www.torgetbaren.com; Mälartorget 13) In Gamla Stan, this is Stockholm's premier gay bar-cum-restaurant, with eye-candy staff, mock-baroque touches and a civilised salon vibe.

Grodan (Map p82; ☎ 679 61 00; www.grodan nattklubb.se, in Swedish; Grev Turegatan 16; admission Skr120; ☽ 10pm-3am Fri & Sat) At street level there's a packed bar and mock-baroque restaurant serving great mod-nosh. In the cellar, A-list DJ talent from Stockholm, London and beyond (think Axwell, Özgur Can and Ben Watt) spin the vinyl, pumping out house and electro tracks for sweat-soaked clubbers.

Live Music

Stockholm's music scene is alive and varied. On any night you can catch anything from emerging indie acts to edgy rock, blues and Balkan pop. Jazz and blues have a particularly strong presence, with several legendary venues saxing it up and an annual jazz festival held in mid-July.

All the following clubs have admission charges that vary depending on what's on that night.

Debaser (Map p82; ☎ 462 98 60; www.debaser.se, in Swedish; Karl Johanstorg 1, Slussen; ☽ 7pm-1am, to 3am club nights Sun-Thu, 8pm-3am Fri & Sat) The king of rock clubs hides away under the Slussen interchange. Emerging or bigger-name acts play most nights, while the killer club nights

span anything from rock-steady to punk and electronica.

Debaser Medis (Map p82; Medborgarplatsen 8; ☽ 7pm-1am Sun-Thu, 7pm-3am Fri & Sat) One metro stop further south is Debaser's sprawling sister venue, with three floors rocking to live acts and DJ-spun tunes.

Mosebacke Etablissement (Map p82; ☎ 55 60 98 90; www.mosebacke.se, in Swedish; Mosebacketorg 3; tickets free-Skr250; ☽ to 11pm Mon & Tue, to 1am Wed & Sun, to 2am Thu-Sat) Eclectic theatre and club nights aside, this historic culture palace hosts a mixed line-up of live music. Tunes span anything from home-grown pop to antipodean rock. The outdoor terrace (featured in the opening scene of August Strindberg's novel *The Red Room*) combines dazzling city views with a thumping summertime bar.

Glenn Miller Café (Map p82; ☎ 10 03 22; Brunnsgatan 21A; ☽ 5pm-1am Mon-Thu, 5pm-2am Fri & Sat) Simply loaded with character, this tiny jazz and blues bar draws a faithful, fun-loving crowd. It also serves excellent, affordable French-style classics like mussels with white wine sauce.

Fasching (Map p82; ☎ 53 48 29 60; www.fasching.se, in Swedish; Kungsgatan 63; tickets Skr100-300; ☽ to midnight Mon-Thu, 4am Fri & Sat) Music club Fasching peddles kick-arse jazz, swing and tango jams. DJs take over with either Afrobeat, Latin, neo-soul or R'n'B on Friday nights and retro-soul, disco and rare grooves on Saturdays.

Stampen (Map p82; ☎ 20 57 93; www.stampen.se; Stora Nygatan 5; admission free Mon-Thu, Skr120 Fri & Sat; ⏰ 8pm-1am Mon-Wed, to 2am Thu-Sat) Once a pawn shop, Stampen is better known as one of Stockholm's music club stalwarts, swinging to live jazz and blues every night. The free blues jam, at 2pm on Saturday, pulls everyone from local musos to the odd music legend.

Concerts, Theatre & Dance

Stockholm is a theatre city, with outstanding dance, opera and music performances; for an overview, pick up the free *What's On Stockholm* guide from the tourist office. Ticket sales are handled by the tourist office at Sweden House. Alternatively, you can buy tickets direct from **Ticnet** (☎ 0771-70 70 70; www.ticnet.se).

Tickets generally aren't cheap and often sell out, especially for Saturday shows, but you can occasionally get good-value last-minute deals. Operas are usually performed in their original language, while theatre performances are invariably in Swedish.

Konserthuset (Map p82; ☎ 50 66 77 88; www.konserthuset.se; Hötorget; tickets Skr80-325) Head here for classical concerts and other musical marvels, including the Royal Philharmonic Orchestra.

Operan (Map p82; ☎ 791 44 00; www.operan.se; Operahuset, Gustav Adolfs Torg; tickets Skr40-790) The Royal Opera is the place to go for thunderous tenors, sparkling sopranos and classical ballet. It also has some bargain tickets in seats with poor views for as little as Skr40, and occasional lunchtime concerts for Skr180 (including light lunch).

Folkoperan (Map p82; ☎ 616 07 50; www.folkoperan.se; Hornsgatan 72; tickets Skr260-420) Folkoperan gives opera a thoroughly modern overhaul with its intimate, cutting-edge and sometimes controversial productions. The under-26s enjoy half-price tickets.

Dramaten (Map p82; ☎ 667 06 80; www.dramaten.se; Nybroplan; tickets Skr190-320) The Royal Theatre stages a range of plays in a sublime art nouveau environment. Dramaten's experimental stage Elverket (Map pp70–1) at Linnégatan 69 (same contact details), pushes the boundaries with edgier offerings performed in a converted power station.

Stockholms Stadsteatern (Map p82; ☎ 50 62 02 00; Kulturhuset, Sergels Torg; tickets around Skr250, under 26yr around Skr100) Regular performances are staged here, plus guest appearances by foreign theatre companies.

Dansens Hus (Map p82; ☎ 50 89 90 90; www.dansenshus.se; Barnhusgatan 12-14; tickets free-Skr300) The stomping ground of Mats Ek's Cullberg Ballet, this place is an absolute must for contemporary dance fans. Guest artists have included everyone from British choreographer Akram Khan to Canadian innovator Daniel Léveillé.

Globen (off Map pp70-1; ☎ 0771-31 00 00; www.globen.se; Globentorget 2) This huge white spherical building (it looks like a giant golf ball) just south of Södermalm hosts regular big-name pop and rock concerts, as well as sporting events and trade fairs. Take the metro to T-Globen.

Sport

Bandy matches, a uniquely Scandinavian phenomenon, take place all winter at Stockholm's ice arenas.

Head over to **Zinkensdamms Idrottsplats** (Map pp70-1; ☎ 668 93 31; Ringvägen 16), where watching a bandy match is great fun. The sport, a precursor to ice hockey but with more players (11 to a side) and less fighting, has grown massively popular since the rise of the Hammarby team in the late '90s. There's a round vinyl ball instead of a puck, and the rules are similar to football, except that you hit the ball with a stick instead of kicking it. The season lasts from November to March, so make sure you bring your own thermos of *kaffekask* – a warming mix of coffee and booze. For the low-down on upcoming matches, check out www.svenskbandy.se/stockholm (in Swedish). Tickets (Skr120) can be purchased at the arena gate.

For the ultimate Scandi sport experience, head to an ice hockey game. Contact **Globen** (☎ 50 83 53 00; www.globen.se; Arenavägen, Johanneshov; tickets Skr150-200) for details; matches take place here up to three times a week from October to April. There are regular football fixtures here, too. Purchase tickets through **Ticnet** (☎ 0771-31 00 00; www.ticnet.se). The nearest metro station is T-Globen.

Impromptu public skating areas spring up during the winter at Kungsträdgården in Norrmalm and at Medborgarplatsen in Södermalm. Skate-rental booths next to the

STOCKHOLM

rinks hire out equipment (Skr40/20 per adult/child per hour).

SHOPPING

A progressive design and fashion hub, Stockholm is bliss for retail revellers. Good local buys include edgy streetwear, designer objects and furnishings (see boxed text, below), and edible treats like cloudberry jam, pickled herring in *brännvin* (aquavit) sauce and bottles of Yule-time Blossa *glögg* (spiced wine). Södermalm's SoFo district (the streets south of Folkungagatan) is your best bet for new-school, home-grown fashion.

Non-EU residents are entitled to a duty-free refund of up to 17.5% on single purchases of more than Skr200 bought from tax-free shopping outlets (look for the 'Tax Free' sticker).

PUB (Map p82; ☎ 402 16 11; Drottninggatan 72-6; ☺ 10am-7pm Mon-Fri, 10am-6pm Sat, 11am-5pm Sun) Until recently, historic department store PUB was best known as the former workplace of Greta Garbo. A major revamp has since turned it into Stockholm's hottest new fashion and lifestyle hub. Bag yourself fresh Nordic labels like Stray Boys, House of Dagmar and Baum & Pferdgarten, refuel at the slinky cafe-bar or check out the edgy art space.

Ekovaruhuset (Map p82; ☎ 22 98 45; Österlånggatan 28) With a sister shop in Manhattan, this enlightened concept store stocks fair-trade organic products, from cosmetics and chocolates to trendy threads and too-cute babywear. Expect anything from Edun T-shirts from Peru to in-the-know labels like Zion and Misericordia.

Chokladfabriken (Map pp70-1; ☎ 640 05 68; Renstiernas Gata 12; ☺ closed Sun) For an edible souvenir, head straight to this savvy chocolate peddler, where seasonal Nordic ingredients are used to make heavenly cocoa treats. There's a cafe for an on-the-spot fix, and smaller branches in Norrmalm (Map p82; Regeringsgatan 58) and Östermalm (Map pp70-1; Grevgatan 37).

DesignTorget Götgatan (Map p82; ☎ 462 35 20; Götgatan 31, Södermalm); Sergels Torg (Map p82; ☎ 50 83 15 20; Basement, Kulturhuset, Sergels Torg) If you love good design but don't own a Gold Amex, head to this clued-up chain, which sells the work of emerging designers alongside established denizens.

Tjallamalla (Map pp70-1; ☎ 640 78 47; www.tjallamalla.com; Bondegatan 46; ☺ noon-6pm Mon-Fri, noon-4pm Sat) Raid the racks at this fashion icon for rookie designers like Hot Sissy, Papagaio

---

DESIGN & THE CITY

From cult fabrics to starchitect bars, Stockholm is a design buff's dream. Most of Sweden's creative big guns are based here and its league of design shops, studios and galleries are the perfect crash course in crisp, clean Nordic aesthetics. A good place to start is at the permanent design exhibition at **Nationalmuseum** (p76). Once you're clued-up, pay homage at stalwart design retailer, **Svenskt Tenn** (Map p82; ☎ 670 16 00; Strandvägen 5), home to rich, floral fabrics by design legend Josef Frank. Nearby, both **Nordiska Galleriet** (Map p82; ☎ 442 83 60; Nybrogatan 11) and **Modernity** (Map p82; ☎ 20 80 25; Sibyllegatan 6) stock cult furniture, as well collectable lighting and glassware.

Further west in Vasastan, **Upplansgatan** (Map p82) is a street famous for its antique shops, packed with retro oddities. Close by, gallery-cum-shop **Platina** (Map pp70-1; ☎ 30 02 80; Odengatan 68) showcases contemporary and cutting-edge jewellery design from Sweden and beyond. For conscientious handicrafts, don't miss **Iris Hantverk** (Map p82; ☎ 21 47 26; Kungsgatan 55), where much of the stuff is made by (and to raise money for) the vision impaired.

Across town, Södermalm is home to some superb craft collectives, including ubercool **Konsthantverkana** (Map p82; ☎ 611 03 70; Södermalmstorg 4) and **Blås & Knåda** (Map p82; ☎ 642 77 67; Hornsgatan 26), the latter run by around 45 Swedish potters and glass-blowers. On the same street, former model-singer **Efva Attling** (Map p82; ☎ 642 99 49; Hornsgatan 44) is one of Stockholm's foremost silversmiths, creating stunning, clean-cut designs with names like Make Love Not War and Homo Sapiens. Södermalm's main drag Götgatan is also a design mecca, and home to democratically priced **DesignTorget** (above) and the iconic **10 Swedish Designers** (Map p82; ☎ 643 25 04; Götgatan 25). Known in Swedish as Tiogruppen, 10 Swedish Designers hit the scene in 1970 when emerging textile designers (including the famous Tom Hedqvist) decided to spike the Swedish design scene with unapologetically bold, geometric patterns. These days, their eye-catching graphics plaster everything from tote bags and wallets to cushions, plates and napkins.

and organic Malmö streetwear label, Kärleksgatan. Graduates from Stockholm's prestigious Beckmans College of Design School sometimes sell their collections here on commission.

For your all-in-one retail therapy, scour department-store giant **Åhléns** (Map p82; ☎ 676 60 00; Klarabergsgatan 50) or its upmarket rival **NK** (Map p82; ☎ 762 80 00; Hamngatan 12-18).

GETTING THERE & AWAY
Air
Stockholm's main airport, **Stockholm-Arlanda** (☎ 797 60 00; www.arlanda.se, www.lfv.se), is 45km north of the city centre and can be reached from central Stockholm by both bus and express train (see p112).

Bromma Airport (☎ 797 68 00) is 8km west of Stockholm and is used for some domestic flights. **Skavsta Airport** (☎ 0155-28 04 00), 100km south of Stockholm, near Nyköping, is mostly used by low-cost carriers like Ryanair and Wizz Air.

The **SAS** (☎ 0770-72 77 27; www.sas.se) network serves 28 Swedish destinations from Arlanda, and has international services to Copenhagen, Oslo, Helsinki and a host of other European cities including Amsterdam, Barcelona, Brussels, Berlin, Dublin, Frankfurt, Geneva, Hamburg, London, Manchester, Milan, Moscow, Paris, Rome, St Petersburg and Zagreb. It also flies direct to Chicago, New York, Bangkok and Beijing.

Finnair (☎ 0771-78 11 00; www.finnair.com) flies several times daily to Helsinki. **Blue1** (☎ 0900-102 58 31; www.blue1.com) also has direct flights to Helsinki, as well as to Tampere, Turku/Åbo and Vaasa.

Boat
Both **Silja Line** (Map p82; ☎ 22 21 40; www.tallinksilja .com; Silja & Tallink Customer Service Office, Cityterminalen) and **Viking Line** (Map p82; ☎ 452 40 00; www .vikingline.fi; Cityterminalen) run ferries to Turku and Helsinki. **Tallink** (Map p82; ☎ 22 21 40; www .tallinksilja.com; Silja & Tallink Customer Service Office, Cityterminalen) ferries head to Tallinn (Estonia) and Riga (Latvia).

Bus
Most long-distance buses arrive and depart from **Cityterminalen** (Map p82; www.cityterminalen .com), which is connected to Centralstationen. The **main counter** (⏰ 7am-6pm) sells tickets for several bus companies, including Flybussarna

(airport coaches), Swebus Express, Svenska Buss, Eurolines and Y-Buss.

Swebus Express (Map p241; ☎ 0771-21 82 18; www .swebusexpress.com; 2nd level, Cityterminalen) runs daily to Malmö (9¼ hours), Göteborg (seven hours), Norrköping (two hours), Kalmar (six hours), Mora (4¼ hours), Örebro (three hours) and Oslo (eight hours). There are also direct runs to Gävle (2½ hours), Uppsala (one hour) and Västerås (1¾ hours).

Ybuss (☎ 020-033 44 44; www.ybuss.se, in Swedish; Cityterminalen) runs services to the northern towns of Sundsvall, Östersund and Umeå. You'll also find a number of companies running buses from many provincial towns directly to Stockholm. See the relevant destination chapters for details.

Car & Motorcycle
The E4 motorway passes through the city, just west of the centre, on its way from Helsingborg to Haparanda. The E20 motorway from Stockholm to Göteborg via Örebro follows the E4 as far as Södertälje. The E18 from Kapellskär to Oslo runs from east to west and passes just north of central Stockholm.

For car hire close to Centralstationen head to **Avis** (Map p82; ☎ 20 20 60; Vasagatan 10B) or **Hertz** (Map p82; ☎ 454 62 50; Vasagatan 26).

Train
Stockholm is the hub for national train services run by **Sveriges Järnväg** (SJ; ☎ 0771-75 75 75; www.sj.se). and **Tågkompaniet** (☎ 0771-44 41 11; www .tagkompaniet.se, in Swedish).

Centralstationen (Stockholm C; ⏰ 5am-midnight) is the central train station. In the main hall you'll find the **SJ ticket office** (⏰ domestic tickets 7.30am-7.45pm Mon-Fri, 8.30am-6pm Sat, 9.30am-7pm Sun; international tickets 10am-6pm Mon-Fri; general customer service 6am-11pm Mon-Fri, 6.30am-11pm Sat, 7am-11pm Sun). You'll also find **automated ticket machines** (⏰ 5am-11.50pm Mon-Sun).

Direct SJ trains to/from Copenhagen, Oslo and Storlien (for Trondheim) arrive and depart from Centralstationen, as do the overnight services from Göteborg (via Stockholm and Boden) to Kiruna and Narvik; the Arlanda Express; and the SL *pendeltåg* (local train) commuter services that run to/from Nynäshamn, Södertälje and Märsta. Other SL local rail lines (Roslagsbanan and Saltsjöbanan) run from Stockholm Östra (T-Tekniska Högskolan) and Slussen, respectively.

In the basement at Centralstationen, you'll find lockers costing Skr40 to Skr90 (depending on size) for 24 hours, toilets for Skr5 and showers (next to the toilets) for Skr30. These facilities are open 5am to 12.30am daily. There's also a left-luggage office, open daily, and a **lost property office** (☎ 50 12 55 90; sj.lostproperty@bagport.se; ⊗ 9am-7pm Mon-Fri); look for the 'Hittegods' sign.

Follow the signs to find your way to the local metro (T-bana) network; the underground station here is called T-Centralen.

GETTING AROUND
To/From the Airports

The **Arlanda Express** (☎ 020-22 22 24; www.arlandaexpress.com; adult tickets from Skr220) train service from Centralstationen takes 20 minutes to reach Arlanda; trains run every 10 to 15 minutes from about 5am to 12.30am. The same trip in a taxi costs around Skr495, but agree on the fare first and don't use taxis without a contact telephone number displayed. **Taxi Stockholm** (☎ 15 00 00) is one reputable operator.

The cheaper option is the **Flygbuss** (www.flygbussarna.se) service between Arlanda airport and Cityterminalen. Buses leave every 10 or 15 minutes (Skr110, 40 minutes). Tickets can be purchased online, at Cityterminalen or on arrival at the Flygbuss counter at Arlanda airport's main terminal.

Bicycle

Stockholm boasts a wide network of bicycle paths, and in summer you won't regret bringing a bicycle with you or hiring one to get around. The tourist offices have maps for sale, but they're not usually necessary if you have a basic city map.

Top day trips include Djurgården; Drottningholm (return by steamer); Haga Park or the adjoining Ulriksdal Park, and a loop from Gamla Stan to Södermalm, Långholmen and Kungsholmen (on lakeside paths). Trails and bike lanes are clearly marked with traffic signs.

Some long-distance routes are marked all the way from central Stockholm: Nynäsleden to Nynäshamn joins Sommarleden near Västerhaninge and swings west to Södertälje. Roslagsleden leads to Norrtälje (linking Blåleden and Vaxholm). Upplandsleden leads to Märsta north of Stockholm, and you can ride to Uppsala via Sigtuna. Sörmlandsleden leads to Södertälje.

Bicycles can be carried free on SL local trains, except during peak hour (6am to 9am and 3pm to 6pm weekdays). They're not allowed in Centralstationen or on the metro, although you'll occasionally see some daring souls.

Stockholm City Bikes (☎ 077-444 24 24; www.stockholmcitybikes.se) has 67 self-service bicycle hire stands across the city. You'll need to purchase a bike card (three-day/season card Skr125/250) from the tourist office (p73) or from SL information centres. Rechargeable season cards are valid from April to the end of October.

Sjöcafé (☎ 660 57 57; ⊗ 9am-9pm Apr-Sep), by the bridge across to Djurgården, rents out bikes for Skr65/250 per hour/day (with options for longer rentals). For about the same price they also rent in-line skates, another nifty way to get around.

Boat

Djurgårdsfärjan city ferry services connect Gröna Lund Tivoli on Djurgården Nybroplan (summer only) and Slussen (year-round) as frequently as every 10 minutes in summer (and less frequently at other times); a single trip costs Skr30 (free with the SL transport passes).

Car & Motorcycle

Driving in central Stockholm is not recommended. Skinny one-way streets, congested bridges and limited parking all present problems; note that Djurgårdsvägen is closed near Skansen at night, on summer weekends and some holidays. Don't attempt driving through the narrow streets of Gamla Stan.

Parking is a major problem, but there are *P-hus* (parking stations) throughout the city; they charge up to Skr60 per hour, though the fixed evening rate is usually more reasonable. If you do have a car, one of the best options is to stay on the outskirts of town and catch public transport into the centre.

Public Transport

Storstockholms Lokaltrafik (SL; www.sl.se) runs all tunnelbana (T or T-bana) metro trains, local trains and buses within the entire Stockholm county. There is an SL information office at **Centralstationen** (basement concourse; ⊗ 6.30am-11.15pm Mon-Sat, 7am-11.15pm Sun) and another near the **Sergels Torg entrance** (⊗ to 6.30pm Mon-Fri, to 5pm Sat & Sun), which issues timetables and sells the SL Tourist Card and Stockholm Card. You can also call ☎ 600 10 00. for schedule and travel information.

The Stockholm Card (see boxed text, p74) covers travel on all SL trains and buses in greater Stockholm and costs Skr330/460/580 per 24/48/72 hours (seven to 17 years Skr165/230/290). The 24-hour (Skr100) and 72-hour (Skr200) SL Tourist Cards are primarily for transport and only give free entry to a few attractions. The 72-hour SL Tourist Card (Skr260) is good value, especially if you use the third afternoon for transport to either end of the county – you can reach the ferry terminals in Grisslehamn, Kapellskär or Nynäshamn, as well as all of the archipelago harbours. If you want to explore the county in more detail, bring a passport photo and get yourself a 30-day SL pass (Skr690, or Skr420 for children age seven to 18 years and seniors).

On Stockholm's public transport system the minimum fare costs two coupons, and each additional zone costs another coupon (up to five coupons for four or five zones). Coupons cost Skr20 each (Skr15 from ticket machines at Tunnelbana stations), but it's much better to buy strips of tickets for Skr180. Coupons are stamped at the start of a journey. Travelling without a valid ticket can lead to a fine of Skr600 or more. Coupons, tickets and passes can be bought at metro stations, Pressbyrån kiosks, SL railway stations and SL information offices. Tickets cannot be bought on buses.

International rail passes (eg Scanrail, Interrail) aren't valid on SL trains.

BUS
While the bus timetables and route maps are complicated, they're worth studying as there are some useful connections to suburban attractions. Ask **SL** (☎ 600 10 00) or any tourist office for the handy inner-city route map *Innerstadsbussar*.

Inner-city buses radiate from Sergels Torg, Odenplan, Fridhemsplan (on Kungsholmen) and Slussen. Bus 47 runs from Sergels Torg to Djurgården, and bus 69 from Centralstationen and Sergels Torg to the Ladugårdsgärdet museums and Kaknästornet. Useful buses for hostellers include bus 65 (Centralstationen to Skeppsholmen) and bus 43 (Regeringsgatan to Södermalm).

Inner-city night buses run from 1am to 5pm on a few routes. Most leave from Centralstationen, Sergels Torg, Slussen, Odenplan and Fridhemsplan to the suburbs.

Check where the regional bus hub is for each outlying area. Islands of the Ekerö municipality (including Drottningholm palace) are served by buses with numbers 301 to 323 from T-Brommaplan. Buses to Vaxholm (the 670) and the Åland ferries (the 637 to Grisslehamn and 631 to Kapellskär) depart from T-Tekniska Högskolan. Odenplan is the hub for buses to the northern suburbs, including Hagaparken.

METRO
The most useful mode of transport in Stockholm is the tunnelbana, run by SL. Its lines converge on T-Centralen, connected by an underground walkway to Centralstationen. There are three main lines with branches. See the Stockholm Metro Map (p114) for route details. The blue line has a comprehensive collection of modern art decorating the underground stations, and several stations along other lines are decorated as well, often by famous artists.

TRAIN
Local trains *(pendeltåg)* are most useful for connections to Nynäshamn (for ferries to Gotland), to Märsta (for buses to Sigtuna and the short hop to Arlanda Airport) and to Södertälje. There are also services to Nockeby from T-Alvik; Lidingö from T-Ropsten; Kårsta, Österskär and Näsbypark from T-Tekniska Högskolan; and to Saltsjöbaden from T-Slussen. SL coupons and SL travel passes are valid on all of these trains, and should be bought before boarding.

TRAM
The historic **No 7 tram** (☎ 660 77 00) runs between Norrmalmstorg and Skansen, passing most attractions on Djurgården. Both the Stockholm Card and SL Tourist Card are valid onboard.

Taxi
Taxis are readily available but expensive, so check for a meter or arrange the fare first. The flag fall is Skr38, then about Skr13 per kilometre. At night, women travelling alone should ask about *tjejtaxa*, a discount rate offered by some operators. Only use one of the main, reputable firms, such as **Taxi Stockholm** (☎ 15 00 00), **Taxi 020** (☎ 020-93 93 93) and **Taxi Kurir** (☎ 30 00 00).

STOCKHOLM TRANSPORT MAP

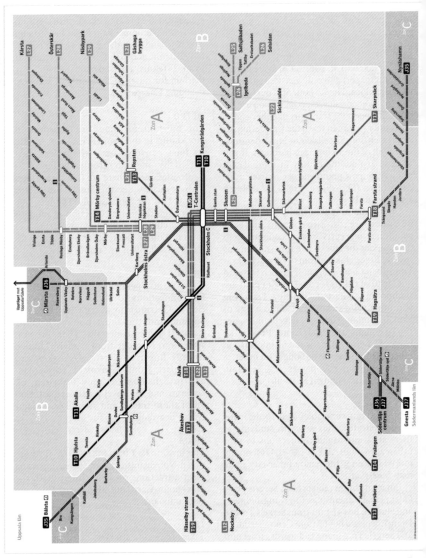

AROUND STOCKHOLM

With royal palaces, vintage villages and Viking traces, the greater Stockholm county is certainly worth a venture or three. Handily, the SL Tourist Card or travel passes allow unlimited travel on all buses and local trains in the area. Free timetables are available from the SL office in Centralstationen, the SL terminals at Slussen or Östrastationen and the SL website.

Just to the east of Stockholm, the magical islands of the Stockholm archipelago have inspired the likes of writer August Strindberg and artist Andres Zorn. Ferry services aren't expensive and there's a travel pass available if you fancy a fix of island hopping.

EKERÖ DISTRICT

The pastoral Ekerö district, 20km west of Stockholm, is home to the romantic Drottningholm castle as well as several large islands in Mälaren lake, a dozen medieval churches and the Unesco World Heritage site at Birka.

Drottningholm

The royal residence and parks of Drottningholm on Lovön are justifiably popular attractions and easy to visit from the capital. If you're not short of time you can cycle out to the palace. Otherwise, take the metro to T-Brommaplan and change to any bus numbered between 301 and 323. If you're driving, there are few road signs for Drottningholm, so get hold of a decent map. The car park is second on the left after crossing Drottningholmsbron.

Strömma Kanalbolaget (Map p82; ☎ 1200 40 00; www.strommakanalbolaget.com) will take you to the palace by boat. Frequent services depart from Stadshusbron (Stockholm) daily between May and mid-September, with less frequent daily departures mid- to late-September, and weekend-only services in October (one way/return Skr105/140). A *kombibiljett* (combined ticket, Skr270) includes return travel and admission to the palace and Chinese Pavilion.

It's a good idea to use the Stockholm Card here, as otherwise seeing everything on the grounds can get expensive.

DROTTNINGHOLMS SLOTT

Still the royal family pad for part of the year, the Renaissance-inspired main **palace** (☎ 402 62 80; www.royalcourt.se; adult/child Skr70/35, combined ticket incl Chinese Pavilion Skr110/55; ☼ 10am-4.30pm May-Aug, noon-3.30pm Sep, noon-3.30pm Sat & Sun Oct-Apr, closed mid-Dec–early Jan), with its geometric baroque gardens, was designed by architectural great Nicodemius Tessin the Elder and begun in 1662, about the same time as Versailles. You can either walk around the wings open to the public on your own or take a one-hour guided tour (no additional charge; English tours at 10am, noon, 2pm and 4pm daily from June to August, reduced schedule rest of the year). Tours are recommended, especially for an insight into the cultural milieu that influenced some of the decorations.

The **Lower North Corps de Garde** was originally a guard room, but it's now replete with gilt-leather wall hangings, which used to feature in many palace rooms during the 17th century. The **Karl X Gustav Gallery**, in baroque

---

TWICE THE STAR

Sweden's only Michelin two-star restaurant, **Edsbacka Krog** (Map p116; ☎ 96 33 00; www.edsback akrog.se; Sollentunavägen 220, Sollentuna; mains from Skr420, 4-/8-course menu Skr870/1300; ☼ 5.30pm-midnight Mon-Fri, 2pm-midnight Sat) is the ultimate dining indulgence and a mecca for fussy epicureans. Set snugly in an inn dating back to 1626 and headed by revered Swedish chef Christer Lingström, its seasonal Swedish-French menu is indescribably sublime – think crab with lemon sole accompanied by almonds, carrots and Swedish caviar, or cottage-cheese sorbet with a taste of herbs, flowers and champagne. (Inspired condiments may include whipped butter with apricot and rosemary.) The set menus are the best value, with 'unofficial' extras like caramelised foie gras with baked apple popping up unannounced.

Across the street, the more casual **Edsbacka Bistro** (Map p116; ☎ 631 00 34; www.edsbackakrog .se; Sollentunavägen 223; meals Skr95-285, 3-course menus from Skr410; ☼ 11.30am-11pm Mon-Fri, 2-11pm Sat, 2-9pm Sun) serves up simpler, cheaper grub with the same Lingström finesse.

Take suburban J-train to Sollentuna Centrum, then hop on bus 525, 527 or 607.

STOCKHOLM

AROUND STOCKHOLM

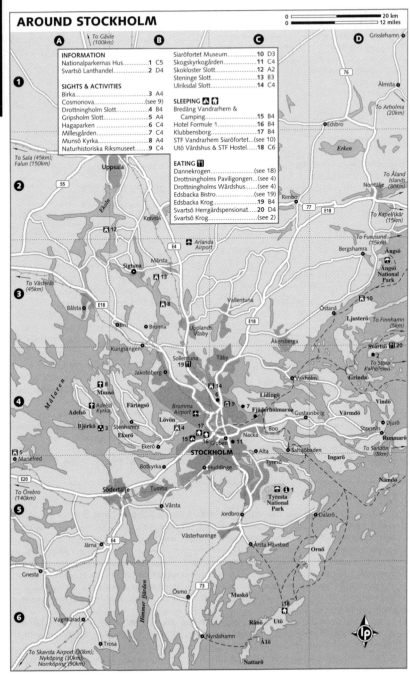

0 — 20 km
0 — 12 miles

INFORMATION
Nationalparkernas Hus...............**1** C5
Svartsö Lanthandel..................**2** D4

SIGHTS & ACTIVITIES
Birka..**3** A4
Cosmonova...............................(see 9)
Drottningholm Slott.................**4** B4
Gripsholm Slott........................**5** A4
Hagaparken **6** C4
Millesgården............................**7** C4
Munsö Kyrka.............................**8** A4
Naturhistoriska Riksmuseet.......**9** C4

Siaröfortet Museum................**10** D3
Skogskyrkogården...................**11** C4
Skokloster Slott......................**12** A2
Steninge Slott........................**13** B3
Ulriksdal Slott........................**14** C4

SLEEPING
Bredäng Vandrarhem &
Camping...............................**15** B4
Hotel Formule 1......................**16** B4
Klubbensborg.........................**17** B4
STF Vandrarhem Siaröfortet...(see 10)
Utö Värdshus & STF Hostel......**18** C6

EATING
Dannekrogen........................(see 18)
Drottningholms Paviligongen...(see 4)
Drottningholms Wärdshus.......(see 4)
Edsbacka Bistro....................(see 19)
Edsbacka Krog........................**19** B4
Svartsö Herrgärdspensionat...**20** D4
Svartsö Krog...........................(see 2)

style, depicts this monarch's militaristic exploits, though the ceiling shows classical battle scenes. The highly ornamented **State Bedchamber of Hedvig Eleonora** is Sweden's most expensive baroque interior, decorated with paintings that feature the childhood of Karl XI. The painted ceiling shows Karl X and his queen, Hedvig Eleonora. Although Lovisa Ulrika's collection of more than 2000 books has been moved to the Royal Library in Stockholm, her library here is still a bright and impressive room, complete with most of its original 18th-century fittings. The elaborate staircase, with statues at every turn, was the work of both Nicodemius Tessin the Elder and the Younger. Circular **Drottningholms Slottskyrka** (admission free), the palace chapel, wasn't completed until the late 1720s.

DROTTNINGHOLMS SLOTTSTEATER & TEATERMUSEUM

Slottsteater (Court Theatre; ☎ 759 04 06; www.dtm .se; admission by tour adult/child Skr60/40; ☺ tours hourly noon-4pm May, 11am-4pm Jun-Aug, 1-3pm Sep) was completed in 1766 on the instructions of Queen Lovisa Ulrika. Remarkably untouched from the time of Gustav III's death (1792) until 1922, it's now the oldest theatre in the world still in its original state; performances are held here in summer (see right) using 18th-century machinery, including ropes, pulleys, wagons and wind machines. Scenes can be changed in less than seven seconds!

Illusion was the order of the day here, and accordingly the theatre makes use of fake marble, fake curtains and papier-mâché viewing boxes. Even the stage was designed to create illusions regarding size.

The fascinating guided tour takes you into other rooms in the building, where highlights include hand-painted 18th-century wallpaper and an Italianate room *(salon de déjeuner)* with fake three-dimensional wall effects and a ceiling that looks like the sky.

KINA SLOTT

At the far end of the gardens is **Kina Slott** (☎ 402 62 70; adult/child Skr60/30, combined ticket incl royal palace Skr110/55; ☺ 11am-4.30pm May-Aug, noon-3.30pm Sep), a lavishly decorated Chinese pavilion built by King Adolf Fredrik as a birthday surprise for Queen Lovisa Ulrika (1753). Restored between 1989 and 1996, it boasts one of the finest rococo chinoiserie interiors in Europe. There's a cafe on the premises serving good waffles, and the admission price includes guided tours, which run at 11am, 1pm and 3pm daily from June to August (the schedule is reduced in May and September).

On the slope below Kina Slott, the carnivalesque **Guards' Tent** (admission free; ☺ 11am-4.30pm mid-Jun–mid-Aug) was erected in 1781 as quarters for the dragoons of Gustav III, but it's not really a tent at all. The building now has displays about the gardens and Drottningholm's Royal Guard.

EATING

Bring a picnic with you and nibble in the gardens, or munch away at one of the two restaurants by the palace. There's also a small kiosk by the driveway entrance.

Drottningholms Paviljongen (☎ 759 04 25; light meals Skr45-100, mains Skr155-225) Close to the boat dock, this cafe peddles light meals like sandwiches and heartier mains, as well as coffee and cakes. Outdoor seating lends the place a garden-party vibe.

Drottningholms Wärdshus (☎ 759 03 08; mains Skr150-260) Opposite the palace grounds, this more upmarket option has a predilection for meaty mains, from roast lamb to seared cod.

ENTERTAINMENT

Drottningholms Slottsteater (☎ 660 82 25; www.dtm .se; Drottningholm; tickets Skr165-410) The royal palace's whimsical 18th-century theatre stages mostly opera productions in summer that are well worth an encore.

Ekerö & Munsö

These long and narrow islands in Mälaren lake are joined together and have a main road running most of their length. The free car ferry to Adelsö departs from the northern end of Munsö.

The two churches of Ekerö and Munsö both date from the 12th century. **Munsö kyrka** is a particularly fetching structure with a round tower and narrow steeple.

Buses 311 and 312 frequently run out here from T-Brommaplan in Stockholm.

Birka

The Viking trading centre of **Birka** (☎ 12 00 40 00; www.vikingastaden.se; ☺ 11am-6.30pm late Jun–mid-Aug, 11am-3pm May-late Jun & mid-Aug–early Sep), on

STOCKHOLM

IDIOSYNCRATIC ISLANDS

If you're after an offbeat island jaunt, consider catching a boat across **Åland**, which is popular with local day-trippers. Technically Finnish but officially autonomous, the Åland islands (population 25,400) sport their own flag and culture. It all goes back to a League of Nations decision made in 1921 to quash a Swedish-Finnish spat over sovereignty. Åland took its own flag in 1954, and has been issuing its own stamps (prized by collectors) since 1984. Both the euro and Swedish krona are legal tender here. A number of Swedish dialects are spoken, while a few Ålanders speak Finnish.

Although Åland joined the EU along with Finland in 1995, it was granted a number of exemptions, including duty-free tax laws, which allowed the essential ferry services between the islands and mainland Finland and Sweden to continue operating profitably.

The islands are a hit for summer cycling and camping holidays; there are medieval churches, ruins and fishing villages to explore. The capital (and only town) of Åland is **Mariehamn**. In summer it heaves with tourists, but still manages to retain its village flavour and the marinas at the harbours are a picture-perfect sight when loaded up with gleaming sailing boats. The main pedestrian street, Torggatan, is a colourful and crowded hive of activity, and there are some fine museums – enough to allow a leisurely day's exploration. Åland's most striking attraction is the medieval castle, **Kastelholm**, in Sund 20km northeast of Mariehamn. You can only visit on guided tours, which run frequently (in English) from June to August.

For more information, click onto www.visitaland.com or contact the main companies operating between Sweden and Åland. Of these, **Viking Line** (www.vikingline.aland.fi) and **Silja Line** (www.silja.com) continue on to Finland, while **Eckerö Linjen** (www.eckerolinjen.fi), **Ånedin Linjen** (www.anedinlinjen.com) and **Birka Cruises** (www.birkacruises.com) operate only between the islands and Sweden. Once on the islands, you can happily pedal almost anywhere thanks to the bridges and handy network ferries.

Björkö in Mälaren lake, is now a Unesco World Heritage site. It was founded around AD 760 with the intention of expanding and controlling trade in the region. The village attracted merchants and craft workers, and the population grew to about 700. A large defensive fort with thick dry-stone ramparts was constructed next to the village. In 830 the Benedictine monk Ansgar was sent to Birka by the Holy Roman Emperor to convert the heathen Vikings to Christianity, hanging around for 18 months. Birka was abandoned in the late 10th century when Sigtuna took over the role of commercial centre.

The village site is surrounded by the largest Viking age cemetery in Scandinavia, with around 3000 graves. Most people were cremated, then mounds of earth were piled over the remains, but some Christian coffins and chambered tombs have been found. The fort and harbour have also been excavated. A cross to the memory of St Ansgar can be seen on top of a nearby hill.

Exhibits at the brilliant **Birka Museum** (🕑 11am-6.30pm late Jun–mid-Aug, 11am-3pm May-late Jun & mid-Aug–early Sep) include finds from the excavations, copies of some of the most magnificent objects, and an interesting model of the village in Viking times.

Daily cruises to Birka run from early May to early September; the round-trip on Strömma Kanalbolaget's *Victoria* from Stadshusbron, Stockholm, is a full day's outing (Skr270). The cruise price includes a visit to the museum and a guided tour in English of the settlement's burial mounds and fortifications. Call ☎ 12 00 40 00 for details; boats leave around 9.30am. Ferries do not run during the Midsummer holidays.

Boats also leave from Adelsö (Hovgården) to Birka (Skr100, including museum entry); call ☎ 12 00 40 00 for details. Summer cruises to Birka depart from many other places around Mälaren, including Härjarö, Södertälje, Strängnäs and Västerås.

VAXHOLM

Despite the summer hordes, Vaxholm redeems itself with its easy accessibility, charming side streets and story-book summerhouses. The latter were a hit with fashionable 19th-century urbanites, who flocked here for some seaside R&R. An easy 35km northeast of the city, the settlement itself was founded in 1647, with the oldest buildings in Norrhamn, a few minutes' walk north of the town hall. Equally photogenic is Hamngatan, awash with interesting architecture, galleries, boutiques and souvenir shops. Vaxholm's most famous local, however, is its hulking fortress. It's also the gateway to the archipelago's central and northern reaches.

Information

The **tourist office** (☎ 54 13 14 80; www.vaxholm.se; ⏰ 10am-6pm Mon-Fri, 10am-4pm Sat & Sun Jun-Aug; 10am-3pm Mon-Fri, 10am-2pm Sat & Sun Sep-May) inside the *rådhus* (town hall) is off Hamngatan; look for the onion dome, a product of the *rådhus* rebuilding in 1925. Also on Hamngatan are a bank, supermarkets and other services.

Sights

The construction of **Vaxholm Kastell** (Citadel; ☎ 54 17 21 57; adult/under 19yr Skr50/free; ⏰ 11am-4pm Jun, 11am-5pm Jul & Aug, 11am-5pm 1st & 2nd weekends Sep), a fortress on an islet just east of the town, was originally ordered by Gustav Vasa in 1544, but most of the current structure dates from 1863. The fortress was attacked by the Danes in 1612 and the Russian navy in 1719. Nowadays, it's home to the National Museum of Coastal Defence and a restaurant and conference centre. The ferry across to the island departs regularly from Söderhamn (the bustling harbour) and costs Skr40 return.

The **Hembygdsgård** (☎ 54 13 17 20; Trädgårdsgatan 19; admission free; ⏰ 11am-4pm Sat & Sun May-Aug) preserves the finest old houses in Norrhamn. The **fiskarebostad** is an excellent example of a late-19th-century fisherman's house, complete with typical Swedish fireplace. The cafe here is open daily from May to mid-September.

Sleeping & Eating

Vaxholm/Bogesunds Slottsvandrarhem (☎ 54 17 50 60; info@bogesundsslottsvandrarhem.se; dm from Skr185; Ⓟ 🖥) By a castle 5km southwest of Vaxholm, this is a pleasant, well-equipped STF hostel, complete with summertime cafe and a blissfully bucolic setting. Bus 681 stops on the main road about 500m from the hostel.

Waxholms Hotell (☎ 54 13 01 50; info@waxholms hotell.se; Hamngatan 2; s/d from Skr1100/1125; 🖥) Just opposite the harbour front, Waxholms combines art nouveau and modern detailing. Discounted rooms are available here in July, and on weekends year-round. This grand place is in the centre of the action, and there are restaurants on the premises,

including Kabyssen with meals (Skr100 to Skr325) and a popular outdoor terrace.

Melanders Fisk (☎ 54 13 34 66; Hamngatan 2; ⏰ 10am-6pm Fri, 10am-2pm Sat, longer hours in summer) On the waterfront, Melanders Fisk is a sound bet for quality grub. Predictably, it's the venerable fish and seafood dishes that keep the punters rolling in.

Getting There & Away

Bus 670 from the metro station T-Tekniska Högskolan runs regularly to the town.

Waxholmsbolaget (Map p82; ☎ 679 58 30; www.waxholmsbolaget.se) boats sail frequently between Vaxholm and Strömkajen in Stockholm (about 40 minutes). **Strömma Kanalbolaget** (Map p82; ☎ 12 00 40 00; www.strommakanalbolaget.com) sails between Strandvägen and Vaxholm three times daily from mid-June to mid-August (one way/return Skr125/200); once daily Tuesday to Sunday from early May to mid-June and mid-August to early October; once daily Thursday to Sunday early February to early May and early October to late November; and once daily Saturday and Sunday late November to late December and mid-January to early February (no services late December to mid-January).

STOCKHOLM ARCHIPELAGO

Mention the archipelago to Stockholmers and prepare for gushing adulation. Buffering the city from the open Baltic Sea, it's a mesmerising wonderland of buffed isles studded with deep forests and fields of wild flowers. Exactly how many islands there are is debatable, with headcounts ranging from 14,000 to 100,000 (the general consensus is 24,000). Whatever the number, it's an unmissable area and much closer to the city than many visitors imagine, with regular ferry services and a number of organised tours for easy island hopping. Hostels, camping grounds and more upmarket slumber options make longer stays an inviting option, as does the growing number of smashing restaurants. And while the archipelago is an obvious summer playground, don't underestimate its wintertime appeal, when silent, snow-laced landscapes make for a soothing sojourn.

Information

Destination Stockholms Skärgård (☎ 54 24 81 00; www.dess.se; Lillström, 18497 Ljusterö) For information on cabin and chalet rental in the archipelago.

Visit Skärgården (Map p82; ☎ 10 02 22; www
.visitskargarden.se, in Swedish; Kajplats 18, Strandvägen;
☺ 9am-5pm Mon-Fri, 10am-4pm Sat, 11am-4pm Sun)
This new waterside information centre can advise on (and
book) various types of archipelago accommodation and
tours, as well as give you ideas on what to see and do.
www.skargardsstiftelsen.se For excellent archipelago
information in English and other languages.

Activities

The biggest boat operator in the archipelago
is **Waxholmsbolaget** (Map p82; ☎ 679 58 30; www
.waxholmsbolaget.se). Timetables and information
are available from its offices outside the Grand
Hotel on Strömkajen in Stockholm, at the
harbour in Vaxholm, and online. The company divides the archipelago into three areas:
Norra Skärgården is the northern section
(north from Ljusterö to Arholma); Mellersta
Skärgården is the middle section, taking
in Vaxholm, Ingmarsö, Stora Kalholmen,
Finnhamn, Möja and Sandhamn; and Södra
Skärgården is the southern section, with boats
south to Nämdö, Ornö and Utö.

Waxholmsbolaget's Båtluffarkortet (Boat
Hiking Pass) gives unlimited rides on its services (Skr420 for five days) plus a handy archipelago map with suggested itineraries.

If time is short, consider taking the
Thousand Island Cruise offered by **Stromma
Kanalbolaget** (Map p82; ☎ 12 00 40 00; www.strom
makanalbolaget.com; Nybrokajen), running daily between late June and early August. The full-day
tour departs from Stockholm's Nybrokajen
at 9.30am and returns at 8.30pm; the cost of
Skr995 includes lunch, dinner, drinks and
guided tours ashore. The tour includes three
island stops and swimming opportunities.

Islands

ARHOLMA

Arholma is one of the most interesting islands
in the archipelago's far north. Everything
was burnt down during a Russian invasion
in 1719; the landmark lighthouse was rebuilt
in the 19th century. A popular resort in the
early 20th century, it's noted for its traditional
village and chapel, as well as its fine sandy
beaches and rocky bathing spots.

Arholma has a summer cafe, a shop, a
simple camping ground and bike and kayak
rental. **Vandrarhem Arholma** (☎ 0176-560 18; beds
Skr140; ☺ year-round) is a pleasant STF hostel in a renovated barn; advance booking
is essential.

You can take bus 676 from Stockholm
Tekniska Högskolan to Norrtälje, then 636 to
Simpnäs (three to six daily), followed by a 20-
minute ferry crossing to the island (Skr30).

SIARÖFORTET

The tiny island of Kyrkogårdsön, in the important sea lane just north of Ljusterö (40km
due northeast of Stockholm), may be only
400m long but it's one of the archipelago's
most fascinating islands.

After the outbreak of WWI, military au-
thorities decided that the Vaxholm Kastell
just didn't cut it, so construction of a new
fort began on Kyrkogårdsön in 1916. Dubbed
Siaröfortet, it's now a fascinating **museum**
(Skr50), where you can check out the officers'
mess, kitchen, sleeping quarters and tunnels,
plus two impressive 15.2cm cannons (they're
trained on passing Viking Line ferries!). There
are no fixed opening times; contact the STF
hostel to arrange a tour.

STF Vandrarhem Siaröfortet (☎ 24 30 90; beds
Skr180; ☺ late Apr–mid-Oct) is an excellent STF
hostel in the old soldiers' barracks. Canoe hire
and breakfast are available; advance booking
is recommended.

Blidösundsbolaget (☎ 24 30 90; www.blidosunds
bolaget.se, in Swedish) ferries to Siaröfortet depart
from Strömkajen in Stockholm and sail to
Siaröfortet via Vaxholm around three times
daily in the peak summer season (mid-
June to mid-August), with greatly reduced
services the rest of the year. The journey takes one hour and 45 minutes from
Stockholm (Skr85) and 50 minutes from
Vaxholm (Skr55).

FINNHAMN

This 900m-long island, northeast of
Stockholm, combines lush woods and
meadows with sheltered coves, rocky cliffs
and visiting eagle owls. While it's a popular
summertime spot, there are enough quiet
corners to indulge your inner hermit.

Vandrarhem Finnhamn (☎ 54 24 62 12; info@
finnhamn.nu; dm Skr260; ☺ year-round; 🖳) is an STF
hostel in a large wooden villa, with boat hire
available. It's the largest hostel in the archipelago; advance booking is essential. The
Finnhamns Café & Krog (☎ 54 24 64 04) boasts
good meals and a sterling view.

Waxholmsbolaget (Map p82; ☎ 679 58 30) sails
from Strömkajen (Stockholm) to Finnhamn,
via Vaxholm, around twice daily (Skr130,

2½ hours). **Cinderella Båtarna** (Map p82; ☎ 12 00 40 00) also sails here daily from early May to mid-September, with reduced services mid-April to early May. Boats depart from Strandvägen in Stockholm (Skr140, one hour and 10 minutes).

SANDÖN

A manageable 2.5km long, Sandön is the archipelago's summertime party hot spot. Stockholm status slaves sail in on 12-footers for Midsummer schmoozing and boozing, while serious sailors flock here for regattas like the Gotland Rund each July. So the place is rather expensive and best visited as a day trip. Camping is prohibited. Sandön's hub is the northern settlement of Sandhamn. Here, narrow alleys, rust-red cottages and the Royal Swedish Yacht Club's Hamptons-style clubhouse keep the cameras clicking. For the best beaches, head to Trovill, near the island's southern tip.

Dykarbaren (☎ 57 15 35 54; lunch meals Skr90-250, dinner mains Skr165-275) is a popular restaurant-bar just 50m from the quay, with lunch specials from Skr75.

The historic **Sandhamns Värdshus** (☎ 57 15 30 51; mains Skr110-223; s/d from Skr740/990) serves a lip-smacking fish and shellfish casserole.

Leader of the island's culinary pack is **Seglarrestaurangen** (☎ 57 45 04 21; mains Skr170-300), considered one of the archipelago's best restaurants. You'll find it inside the upmarket **Seglarhotellet** (☎ 57 45 04 00; www.sandhamn.com; d Skr2090-2290), whose **spa centre** (adult/child Skr100/50, hotel guests free) combo of indoor pool, Jacuzzi, sauna and gym is open to nonguests.

Waxholmsbolaget (☎ 679 58 30) sails from Strömkajen to Sandhamn, via Vaxholm, once daily (Skr140, three hours). **Cinderella Båtarna** (☎ 12 00 40 00) does the same run from mid-April to mid-September; boats leave from Strandvägen (Skr140).

A quicker option is to take bus 433 or 434 from Slussen to Stavsnäs (50 minutes) and catch a ferry from there (Skr75, 40 to 60 minutes). Check ferry times at www.waxholms bolaget.se before catching the bus to avoid a long wait at Stavsnäs.

Strömma Kanalbolaget (☎ 12 00 40 00) runs tours from Nybroplan to Sandhamn daily between early June and mid-August (one way/return Skr205/275), departing at 9.45am and returning at 5.45pm (with two hours at Sandhamn). The price includes a one-hour guided walk.

SVARTSÖ

Rugged Svartsö (Black Island) is another 'mid archipelago' gem. At just over 5km wide and 2km long, its resident population of 77 booms to 2500 in the summer, when fans step ashore for low-fuss rural bliss. Thick with tall trees, old farmers' fields and five lakes, its relatively flat landscape makes it perfect for a day's lazy cycling. It's also a good spot for birdwatching in the spring and autumn.

At its southernmost point sits tiny Alsvik, one of two ferry stops on Svartsö (the other is at Skälvik). Here you'll find a waterside **cafe** in the summer, as well as five tiny, basic **cabins** (☎ 54 24 71 10; Skr450) for rent. Accommodation is of the bunk-bed variety, with a handy cooker in each cabin. There are no bathroom facilities; there's a bathing spot 100m away for back-to-nature grooming.

Also at the harbour, handy **Svartsö Lanthandel** (☎ 54 24 73 25; www.svartsolanthandel.se, in Swedish; ☽ year-round) is a grocery store, pharmacy and post office in one (check website for current opening hours). You can order alcohol (delivered to the island twice a week), withdraw money and hire bicycles (Skr50/125 per hour/day). Nearby, restaurant-bar **Svartsö Krog** (☎ 54 24 72 55; mains Skr169-250; ☽ lunch & dinner Apr-Dec) serves tasty Swedish grub in a rustic-chic setting. The bar mural honours old locals.

Svartsö Herrgårdspensionat (☎ 54 24 70 17; www .svartsoherrgardspensionat.se, in Swedish; ☽ May-Oct) offers more upmarket accommodation in a summerhouse built by famous theatre director Gustaf Collijn in 1906. The cosy rooms ooze vintage charm (think wooden floorboards, pale hues and ceramic tile stoves), although all share an outdoor toilet and shower. Downstairs, the vintage-chic **restaurant** comes with a crackling fire and fabulous seasonal menus using local produce. Other perks include both a lakeside and seaside sauna. From Alsvik, the *pension* is located 3km away by road or 1km via walking track through forest. An easier option is to disembark the ferry at Svartsös second port, Skälvik, located a few hundred metres from the *pension*.

Waxholmsbolaget (☎ 679 58 30) sails from Strömkajen in Stockholm to Alsvik and Skälvik, via Vaxholm, twice daily (Skr110 one way, approximately two hours). Around four daily ferries head to Svartsö from Boda.

To reach Boda, take bus 438 from Slussen in Stockholm, but check the ferry schedule

STOCKHOLM

at www.waxholmsbolaget.se beforehand to avoid long connection times.

From early May to mid-September, **Cinderella Båtarna** (☎ 12 00 40 00) runs several times daily in peak season to Svartsö (Skr135, 1½ hours), via Vaxholm, from Strandvägen. Reduced services operate between mid-April and early May.

UTÖ

Star of the archipelago's southern section, Utö has it all: sublime sandy beaches, lush fairytale forests, sleepy farms, abundant birdlife and a scandalously good restaurant. Thirteen kilometres long and up to 4km wide, its network of roads and tracks make for heavenly cycling sessions.

You can get a reasonable sketch map of the island from the **tourist office** (☎ 50 15 74 10; ⏱ 10am-4pm May-Sep), found in a small cabin by the guest harbour at Gruvbryggan, also known as Gruvbyn (the northernmost village). When the tourist office is closed, ask at the *värdshus*, just up the hill.

Sights & Activities

Most of the sights are at the northern end of the island, near Gruvbryggan. The most unusual is Sweden's oldest iron mine, which opened in 1150 but closed in 1879. The three pits are now flooded – the deepest is Nyköp ingsgruvan (215m). The **mining museum** (opposite the *värdshus*) keeps variable hours, so check locally. The well-preserved, 18th-century **miners' houses** on Lurgatan are worth a peek, while the Dutch-style **windmill** (⏱ 11am-3pm mid-Jun–mid-Aug) peddles beautiful coastal views. The best sandy beach is **Stora Sand** on the south coast; it's a gorgeous 40-minute bike ride from the *värdshus*. Routes to the beach are occasionally closed due to military training exercises; ask at the tourist office for updates. To eye up the **glaciated rock slabs** on the east coast, walk for about 20 minutes through the forest towards Rävstavik.

Sleeping & Eating

STF hostel (☎ 50 42 03 15; receptionen@utovardshus .se; Gruvbyggan; dm Skr330) Open from May to September, this hostel, associated with the nearby *värdshus*, is in a former summer house. Reception and meals are at the *värdshus*.

Utö Värdshus (☎ 50 42 03 00; receptionen@uto vardshus.se; d chalets incl breakfast per person from Skr995)

This is the only hotel on the island, with good facilities and a sterling gourmet restaurant (closed January; lunches Skr89 to Skr119, mains around Skr200).

Dannekrogen (☎ 50 15 70 79; mains Skr150-200) Near the Gruvbryggan harbour, Dannekrogen has a younger, more casual vibe, with grub ranging from hearty fish stew to trendy polenta. The adjoining bakery peddles scrumptious treats, including some delicious carrot cake cupcakes.

There's a handy little supermarket across the street.

Getting There & Around

From Stockholm, Waxholmsbolaget sails once daily to Utö (Skr130, 3½ hours). A quicker way to reach the island is to take the *pendeltåg* from Stockholm Centralstationen to Västerhaninge, then bus 846 to Årsta brygga. From there, Waxholmsbolaget ferries leave up to eight times a day in summer (less frequently the rest of the year) for Utö (Skr75, 45 minutes), but make sure you know whether your boat stops at Spränga or Gruvbryggan first. Ask at the **guest harbour** (☎ 50 15 74 10) about bike hire (from Skr85 per day).

KAPELLSKÄR

Kapellskär is so tiny it can't really even be described as a village – there's little to it except for a camping ground, hostel and large ferry terminal. The coastline, however, is spectacular, dotted with small, still-working fishing villages, and the surrounding countryside is delightfully pastoral. Most people come here for ferry connections to Finland and Estonia; see p334 for details.

There's also a small memorial for the 852 passengers killed in the Estonia ferry disaster of September 1994; it's up the hill across the main road from the ferry terminal.

An **STF hostel** (☎ 0176-441 69; Riddersholm; beds 180; ⏱ year-round) sits off the E18, 2km west of the ferry terminal; book in advance outside of the peak summer season (mid-June to mid-August). There's no restaurant, so bring provisions.

Viking Line's direct bus from Stockholm Cityterminalen to meet the ferries costs Skr55, but if you have an SL pass, take bus 676 from T-Tekniska Högskolan to Norrtälje and change to bus 631, which runs every two hours or so weekdays (three times Saturday and once Sunday).

TYRESTA NATIONAL PARK

Some of the best hiking and wilderness scenery can be found in the 4900-hectare Tyresta National Park, only 20km southeast of Stockholm. Established in 1993, the park is noted for its two-billion-year-old rocks and virgin forest, which includes 300-year-old pine trees. It's a beautiful area, with rocky outcrops, small lakes, marshes and a wide variety of birdlife.

At the southwestern edge of the park is **Nationalparkernas Hus** (National Parks Visitors Centre; ☎ 08-745 33 94; admission free; ♥ 9am-4pm Tue-Fri, 10am-5pm Sat & Sun Mar-Oct, to 4pm Sat & Sun Nov-Feb). Here you can discover all of Sweden's national parks (28 at the time of research) through exhibitions and slide shows, but be sure to check out the centre itself – it's built in the shape of Sweden, complete with all 41 corners! There are even 'lakes' on the floor, indicated by different stones.

Ask for the national park leaflet in English and the *Tyresta Nationalpark och Naturreservat* leaflet in Swedish, which includes an excellent topographical map at 1:25,000 scale. From the visitors centre there are various trails into the park. *Sörmlandsleden* track cuts across 6km of the park on its way to central Stockholm.

Access to the park is easy. Take the *pendeltåg* to Haninge centrum (also called Handen station) on the Nynäshamn line, then change to bus 834. Some buses run all the way to the park, while others stop at Svartbäcken (2km west of Tyresta village).

SIGTUNA

A mere 40km northwest of Stockholm, Sigtuna is one of the cutest, most historically relevant villages in the area. Founded around AD 980, it's the oldest surviving town in Sweden, and the main drag, Stora gatan, is most likely Sweden's oldest main street.

Around the year 1000, Olof Skötkonung ordered the minting of Sweden's first coins in the town, and ancient church ruins and rune stones are scattered everywhere. Indeed, there are about 150 runic inscriptions in the area, most dating from the early 11th century and typically flanking ancient roads.

Most of Sigtuna's original buildings went up in flames in devastating late-medieval fires, but the main church survived and many of the quaint streets and wooden abodes still follow the medieval town plan.

Information

The **tourist office** (☎ 59 48 06 50; info@sigtunaturism.se; Storagatan 33; ♥ 10am-6pm Mon-Sat, 11am-5pm Sun Jun-Aug, 10am-5pm Mon-Fri, 11am-4pm Sat & Sun Sep, 10am-5pm Mon-Fri, 11am-4pm Sat, noon-4pm Sun Oct-May) inhabits an 18th-century wooden house, Drakegården. Stora gatan is also home to banks and supermarkets.

Sights

During medieval times, Sigtuna boasted seven stone-built churches, though most have since crumbled. The ruins of **St Per** and **St Lars** can be seen off Prästgatan. **St Olof church** was built in the early 12th century, but by the 17th century it was a ruin. The adjacent **Mariakyrkan** (♥ 9am-4pm Sep-May, 9am-8pm Jun-Aug) is the oldest brick building in the area – it was a Dominican monastery church from around 1250, but became the parish church in 1529 after the monastery was demolished by Gustav Vasa. Pop in for restored medieval paintings and free weekly concerts in the summer.

Sigtuna Museum (☎ 59 12 66 70; Stora gatan 55; adult/under 20yr Skr20/free; ♥ noon-4pm Tue-Sun Sep-May, noon-4pm Jun-Aug) looks after several attractions in the town, all of them on Stora gatan and near the tourist office. **Lundströmska gården** (adult/child Skr10/5; ♥ noon-4pm mid-Jun–mid-Aug, noon-4pm Sat & Sun Sep) is an early-20th-century, middle-class home and general store, complete with period furnishings and goods. **Sigtuna rådhus** (admission free; ♥ noon-4pm Jun-Aug, noon-4pm Sat & Sun Sep), the smallest town hall in Scandinavia, dates from 1744 and was designed by the mayor himself. It's on the town square opposite the tourist office. The main museum building has displays of gold jewellery, runes, coins and loot brought home from abroad.

The magnificent private palace **Steninge Slott** (☎ 59 25 95 00), 7km east of Sigtuna, dates from 1705 and was designed by Nicodemus Tessin the Younger. On the **guided palace tour** (tours Skr70; ♥ 1pm, 2.30pm & 4pm early Jul–mid-Aug; 1pm, 2.30pm & 4pm Sat & Sun early May-early Jul; 2pm Sat & Sun mid-Aug–early May; in Swedish, prebook English tour), you'll see luxuriously ornate interiors. In the beautiful grounds there is also the excellent **Cultural Centre** (gallery tours Skr80, ♥ gallery tour early May–mid-Sep; cultural centre 11am-7pm Mon-Fri, 10am-5pm Sat & Sun early May–mid-Aug; 11am-5pm Mon-Fri, 10am-5pm Sat & Sun mid-Aug–early May), complete with an art gallery, a glassworks, a candle-making area, a cafe and a restaurant.

Another palace, **Rosersbergs Slott** (☎ 59 03 50 39; guided tours adult/child Skr60/30; ☺ tours hourly 11am-4pm Jun-Aug), is on Mälaren lake about 9km southeast of Sigtuna. Built in the 1630s it was used as a royal residence from 1762 to 1860; the interior boasts exquisite furnishings from the Empire period (1790–1820). Highlights include the lavishly draped State Bedchamber and Queen Hedvig Elisabeth Charlotta's conversation room. The palace cafe serves delicious light meals and cakes in regal surrounds.

Rosersbergs Hotell & Konferens (☎ 12 20 20 00; www.rosersbergsslott.se; s/d Skr425/850; P ☐) is housed in a palace wing once used to accommodate royal family guests. Rooms are simple yet impeccably stylish, with old wooden floorboards, Gustavian-style furnishings, the odd tile stove and views of either the palace courtyard or gardens. All rooms have basins, though facilities are shared. A restaurant is planned for the opposite wing in 2009.

Best in a light snow, **Skokloster Slott** (☎ 402 30 60; skokloster@lsh.se; adult/under 19yr Skr75/free; ☺ 11.30am-4.30pm Sat & Sun Apr & Oct; 11.30am-4.30pm Tue-Sun May; 11.30am-5.30pm Tue-Sun Jun; 10.30am-5.30pm daily Jul & Aug; 12.30-4.30pm Tue-Fri, 11.30am-4.30pm Sat & Sun Sep), around 11km due northwest of Sigtuna (26km by road), is a whitewashed baroque palace with a fragile beauty unusual in Sweden. It was built between 1654 and 1671 and has impressive stucco ceilings and collections of furniture, textiles, art and arms. There's also a small cafe. Guided tours run daily from April to October; it's a good idea to call in advance to check times, as the schedule can change.

Sleeping & Eating

Stora Brännbo (☎ 59 25 75 00; Stora Brännbovägen 2-6; s/d from Skr1100/1600, summer Skr550/800; P ☐) Just north of central Sigtuna, this large hotel and conference centre offers small, contemporary rooms in soothing neutral hue, with flatscreen TVs and fluffy bathrobes. There's a sauna, Jacuzzi and gym (Skr150 per day) for guests and the bountiful breakfast includes waffles and freshly squeezed OJ.

Sigtunastiftelsens Gästhem (☎ 59 25 89 00; Manfred Björkquists allé 2-4; s/d from Skr1995/3500) This attractive, imposing place is run by a Christian foundation. It might look like a cross between a cloister and a medieval fortress, but rooms are much cosier than that this would imply.

Sigtuna Stadshotell (☎ 59 25 01 00; info@sigtuna stadshotell.se; Stora Nygatan 3; s/d Skr2090/2490, discounted to Skr1890/2190; ☐) The pick of Sigtuna's lodgings, this recently renovated number features pale, sleek and uberstylish interiors, spa treatments and a clued-up restaurant that has critics hailing it 'a rising star'.

Tant Brunn Kaffestuga (☎ 59 25 09 34; Laurentii gränd) In a small alley off Storagatan, this delightful 17th-century cafe is set around a pretty courtyard. It's well worth seeking out for its home-baked bread and pastries (the apple pie is divine); just watch your head as you walk in, as the roof beams sag precariously.

Farbror Blå Café & Kök (☎ 59 25 60 50; Stora torget 14; mains Skr195-215) Adjacent to the town hall, this cosy nosh spot is the 'uncle' *(farbror)* to the 'aunt' of Tant Brunn; both names are taken from a popular children's story. Head in for bistro-style meals like veal cutlet with honey-roasted potatoes, tomato-basil cream cheese and black pepper sauce.

Getting There & Around

Travel connections are easy from Stockholm. Take a local train to Märsta, from where there are frequent buses to Sigtuna (570 or 575). To get to Rosersbergs Slott, take the SL *pendeltåg* train to Rosersberg, then walk the final 2km to the palace (signposted). For Skokloster, take a half-hourly SJ train to Bålsta, then bus 311 (ask the driver to let you off at the stop for Skokloster).

MARIEFRED
☎ 0159

Tiny, lakeside Mariefred is a pretty little village that pulls in the crowds with its grand castle, Gripsholm Slott.

Information

The **tourist office** (☎ 297 90; www.mariefred.se; ☺ 10am-6pm Mon-Fri, 11am-5pm Sat Jun-Aug; also 11am-5pm Sun Jul & early–mid-Sep; 10am-3pm Mon-Sat early–mid-Sep; 11am-3pm Sat mid-Apr–May) offers a map and notes (in English) for a self-guided walking tour of the idyllic village centre, with cobblestone streets and 18th-century buildings.

Sights

Gripsholm Slott (☎ 101 94; adult/child Skr70/35; ☺ 10am-4pm mid-May–mid-Sep) is the epitome of castles, with its round towers, spires, drawbridge and creaky wooden halls. It contains some of the state portrait collection, which dates from the 16th century.

Originally built in the 1370s, it passed into crown hands by the early 15th century. In 1526 Gustav Vasa took over and ordered the demolition of the adjacent monastery. A new castle with walls up to 5m thick was built using materials from the monastery, but extensions, conversions and repairs continued for years. The oldest 'untouched' room is Karl IX's bedchamber, dating from the 1570s. The castle was abandoned in 1715, but renovated and extended during the reign of Gustav III (especially between 1773 and 1785). The moat was filled in and, in 1730 and later in 1827, two 11th-century rune stones were found. These stones stand by the access road and are well worth a look; one has a Christian cross, while the other describes an expedition against the Saracens. Gripsholm Slott was restored again in the 1890s, the moat was cleared and the drawbridge rebuilt.

Another worthy pit stop is nearby **Grafikens Hus** (☎ 231 60; adult/under 19yr Skr70/free; ☯ 11am-5pm May-Sep, 11am-5pm Sat & Sun Oct-Apr), a centre for contemporary graphic art and printmaking.

Sleeping & Eating

Gripsholmsviken Hotell & Konferens (☎ 367 00; www .gripsholmsviken.se; s with/without bathroom Skr1140/495, d Skr1840/660, s/d with bathroom discounted to Skr660/990; ☯ mid-Jun–mid-Aug) Once a hostel, this revamped option now offers hostel and hotel lodgings in what was once a royal distillery commissioned by Gustav III in the late 18th century. The in-house restaurant is a slinky affair, there's a cafe on the leafy grounds, and the castle is a mere 500m to the east.

Gripsholms Värdshus & Hotell (☎ 347 50; info@ gripshols-vardshus.se; Kyrkogatan 1; s/d from Skr1700/2290,

summer Skr1290/1690; ☐) Opened in 1609, Gripsholms is Sweden's oldest inn and Mariefred's slumber darling. Charming and elegant, its 45 individually furnished rooms are full of antiques, many also having great views of the castle. There's also a beautiful, highly regarded restaurant (mains Skr175 to Skr300) on site.

Broccoli (☎ 132 00; meals Skr69-155; ☯ 11am-5pm May-Aug, noon-4pm Thu-Sun Sep-Apr) Sharing an entrance with Grafikens Hus (see left), this tasty cafe is a better option than the overpriced, underwhelming Gripsholms Slottcafé near the castle. There's an emphasis on local produce, with edibles ranging from focaccias and salads to ditch-the-diet cakes.

Getting There & Away

Mariefred isn't on the main railway line – the nearest station is at Läggesta, 3km to the west, with trains from Stockholm every two hours in the summer. A **museum railway** (☎ 210 06; www .oslj.nu; one way/return from Skr50/70) from Läggesta to Mariefred runs on weekends from early May to late September (daily from Midsummer to mid-August), roughly every hour during the day; call to check the schedule. Bus 303 runs hourly from Läggesta to Mariefred.

The steamship **S/S Mariefred** (☎ 08-669 88 50) departs from Stadshusbron (Stockholm) for Mariefred from Tuesday to Sunday mid-June to mid-August, and weekends only from late May to mid-June and from mid-August to early September (Skr220 return). A ticket from Stockholm, including an SJ train, the museum railway and S/S *Mariefred*, costs around Skr275 one way and is available at the tourist office in Stockholm.

Southeast Sweden

Stoic castles, story-book towns and magical islands – Sweden's southeast is a veritable treasure trove.

Carved by the epic Göta Canal, Östergötland is home to the small but perky industrial cities of Norrköping and Linköping. This is where you'll also find lovable, lakeside Vadstena: St Birgitta's terrestrial stomping ground and home to a hulking Renaissance castle.

Further south, Småland sparkles with its ethereal forests, preserved pastel towns and show-off Kalmar castle. Snoop through Astrid Lindgren's childhood home in Vimmerby, pig out on peppermint rock in sweet-smelling Gränna or blow glass (or your budget) in the world-renowned Glasriket (Kingdom of Crystal).

Offshore Öland is one of Sweden's favourite chill-out spots, with a beguiling mix of dazzling beaches, windswept fields, ring forts and Iron Age burial sites. Not surprisingly, much of the island sits on the Unesco World Heritage list.

Yet the real ace of spades is the island of Gotland. One of Sweden's historical heavyweights, it's a mesmerising spectacle of rune-stone scattered landscapes, hauntingly beautiful medieval churches and the walled, Hanseatic town of Visby (another Unesco favourite).

HIGHLIGHTS

- Lazily cruise the lock-laced **Göta Canal** (p140)
- Snoop around Astrid Lindgren's childhood home at **Astrid Lindgrens Näs** (p153) or go Pippi-mad at **Astrid Lindgrens Värld** (p152), both in Vimmerby
- Blow your own glass vase, or bag one from a master in **Glasriket** (p147)
- Watch the sun set in silence from the haunting, southernmost point of **Öland** (p153)
- Prowl medieval walls, hunt for truffles or succumb to a culinary adventure on the cultured island of **Gotland** (p158)

| ■ POPULATION: 1,226,162 | ■ AREA: 46,807 SQ KM | ■ HIGHEST POINT: STENABOHÖJDEN (327M) |

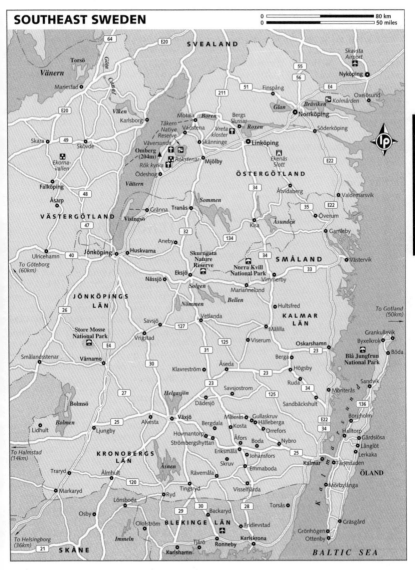

Orientation

Southeast Sweden stretches south along the coast from Stockholm to Blekinge and inland as far as Lake Vättern. It incorporates the following *landskap* areas: Östergötland, the eastern part of Gotland, which is split off from the western half by the massive Lake Vättern; Småland (including Jönköpings

län, Kronobergs län and Kalmar län); and the islands of Gotland and Öland, both off the east coast.

Information
REGIONAL TOURIST OFFICES

Visitors can contact the following for more detailed information on the area:

Gotlands Turistförening (☎ 0498-20 17 00; www
.gotland.info; Skeppsbron 4-6, 62125, Visby)
Kalmar Turistbyrå (☎ 0480-41 77 00; www.kalmar.se,
in Swedish; Box 23, 39120 Kalmar)
Smålands Turism (☎ 036-35 12 70; www.visit-sma
land.com; Lantmätargränd 2, Box 1027, 55111 Jönköping)
Turism i Kronoberg (☎ 0470-74 25 70; turism
.kronoberg@kommun.vaxjo.se; Stationen, Norra
Järnvägsgatan, 35230 Växjö)
Ölands Turist (☎ 0485-56 06 00; www.olandsturist.se;
Träffpunkt Öland, Box 74, 38621 Färjestaden)
Östsvenska Turistrådet (☎ 011-15 51 20; www
.ostgotaporten.com; 60181 Norrköping)

Getting Around

Small airports are scattered through the region, usually with daily direct flights to/from
Stockholm and Copenhagen; see destination
sections for details.

Year-round ferry services connect
Visby on Gotland to both Oskarshamn
and Nynäshamn.

Express buses mainly travel along the coast
(to Västervik, Oskarshamn, Kalmar and
Karlskrona), follow the E4 via Jönköping,
or cruise along Rd 33 from Jönköping to
Västervik (via Eksjö and Vimmerby). A few
express services go through the region's
interior; these are operated by **Svenska Buss**
(☎ 0771-67 67 67; www.svenskabuss.se, in Swedish)
and **Swebus Express** (☎ 0771-21 82 18; www.swebus
express.com).

The main Malmö–Stockholm railway runs
through the region, but you'll have to change
to local trains to reach most places of interest. **Sveriges Järnväg** (SJ; www.sj.se) trains run
north from Karlskrona to Kalmar.

There are also SJ services from Kalmar
to Linköping, and an inland route from
Kalmar to Göteborg. Although the Nässjö–
Jönköping and Nässjö–Falköping trains
are run by Vättertåg, tickets are purchased
through **SJ** (☎ 0771-75 75 75) or **Tågkompaniet**
(☎ 0771-44 41 11).

FOR FOODIES

■ **Krakas Krog** (p165)

■ **Smakrike Krog & Logi** (p165)

■ **Bakfickan** (p163)

■ **Stångs Magasin** (p134)

■ **Choklad Companiet** (p131)

The following companies provide regional
transport links. If you're planning to spend
some time here, enquire about monthly passes
or a *sommarkort*, offering discount travel from
Midsummer to mid-August. Check also the
respective websites for routes, schedules, fares
and passes; these sites don't always have information in English, but you'll usually reach
someone who speaks English if you call.
Jönköpings Länstrafik (☎ 0771-44 43 33; www.jlt.se)
Kalmar Läns Trafik (☎ 0491-76 12 00; www.klt.se)
Kollektiv Trafiken (☎ 0491-21 41 12)
Länstrafiken Kronoberg (☎ 0771-76 70 76; www
.lanstrafikenkron.se)
ÖstgötaTrafiken (☎ 0771-21 10 10; www.ostgotat
rafiken.se)

ÖSTERGÖTLAND

Östergötland harbours gems on both sides
of the Göta Canal, which threads diagonally
across the region. Along its banks, the region's main towns are mostly 19th-century
industrial heartlands, laced with some impressive postindustrial conversions. The region's west, bordered by the mighty Lake
Vättern, is a lo-fi treat of flat lush countryside steeped in ancient history. This is
where you'll find Sweden's rune stone su-
perstar and the unmissable medieval town
of Vadstena.

NORRKÖPING

☎ 011 / pop 126,680

The envy of industrial has-beens all across
Europe, Norrköping has cleverly regenerated
its defunct mills and canals into a posse of
cultural and gastronomic hang-outs fringing
waterfalls and locks. Retro trams rattle down
streets lined with eclectic architecture, while
some 30km to the northeast, the animal park
at Kolmården swaps urban regeneration for
majestic Siberian tigers.

Norrköping's industrial identity began
in the 17th century, but took off in the late
19th century when textile mills and factories
sprang up alongside the swift-flowing Motala
ström. Seventy per cent of Sweden's textiles
were once made here, the last mill shutting
shop in the 1970s.

Information

Banks and ATMs line Drottninggatan.
Forex (☎ 16 80 32; www.forex.se; Drottninggatan 46;
🕑 9am-7pm Mon-Fri, 9am-4pm Sat) Money exchange.

NORRKÖPING

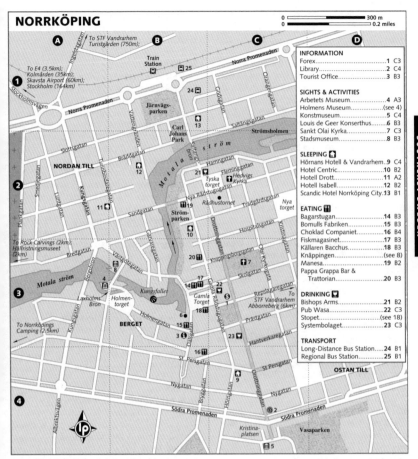

0 _____ 300 m
0 _____ 0.2 miles

SOUTHEAST SWEDEN

Library (Stadsbiblioteket; Södra Promenaden 105; 8am-8pm Mon-Thu, 8am-6pm Fri, 11am-4pm Sat & Sun) Free internet access.

Tourist office (☎ 15 50 00; www.destination.norr koping.se; Dalsgatan 16; 10am-5pm Mon-Fri, 10am-2pm Sat & Sun Jul–mid-Aug, shorter hours rest of year) Free internet access.

Sights & Activities

Industrilandskapet, Norrköping's star turn, is the impeccably preserved industrial area near the river. Pedestrian walkways and bridges lead past magnificent former factory buildings and around the ingenious system of locks and canals. The most thunderous waterfall is **Kungsfallet**, near the islet Laxholmen.

Within the area are several interesting museums, all with free admission. The innovative **Arbetets Museum** (☎ 18 98 00; Laxholmen; 11am-5pm) documents working life. There's one permanent display about Alva Carlsson, a typical worker in the former cotton mill, and temporary exhibitions focusing mainly on gender issues, human rights or multiculturalism. The seven-sided building, completed in 1917 and dubbed the 'flatiron', is a work of art in itself.

Holmens Museum (☎ 12 89 92; 9am-12.30pm Tue & Thu) describes the history of Louis de Geer's paper factory, which was founded in the early 17th century.

Over the bridge, **Stadsmuseum** (☎ 15 26 20; Holmbrogränd; 10am-5pm Tue, Wed & Fri, to 4pm

Jun-Aug, 10am-8pm Thu, 11am-4pm Sat & Sun) delves into the town's industrial past, complete with still-functioning machinery, a great cafe and dynamic temporary exhibitions.

A modern addition to the riverside scenery is the extraordinary 1300-seat **Louis de Geer Konserthus** (☎ 15 50 30; www.louisdegeer.com; Dalsgatan 15), in a former paper mill. Still containing the original balconies, it's a superb setting for orchestral, jazz and pop concerts.

Over near Vasaparken, **Konstmuseum** (☎ 15 26 00; Kristinaplatsen; admission free; 🕒 noon-4pm Tue & Thu-Sun, noon-8pm Wed Jun-Aug, 11am-5pm Wed & Fri-Sun, 11am-8pm Tue & Thu Sep-May) is Norrköping's impressive art museum. Its collection boasts important early-20th-century works, including modernist and cubist gems, as well as Carl Larsson's dreamy *Frukost i det gröna*.

Two kilometres west of the city centre, near the river, await fine examples of **Bronze Age rock carvings**, with an adjacent museum, **Hällristningsmuseet** (☎ 16 55 45; www.ffin.se; Himmelstalund; admission free, guided tours adult/under 18yr Skr30/free; 🕒 10am-3pm Tue-Fri, 9.30am-3pm Sat & Sun May-Aug). Guided tours of the carvings must be booked in advance. The site is a 30-minute walk along the river.

From July to mid-August, **vintage tram 1** operates a short guided tour through central Norrköping. It leaves from Söder Tull at 6pm and 6.30pm on Tuesdays and Thursdays (Skr40).

KOLMÅRDEN

This **zoo** (☎ 24 90 00; www.kolmarden.com; 🕒 10am-6pm Jul–mid-Aug, 10am-5pm May, Jun & rest of Aug, Sat & Sun Sep-early Oct) is Scandinavia's largest, with some 750 residents from all climates and continents. It's divided into two areas: the main **Djurparken** (zoo; adult/3-12yr Skr245/145) with a dolphin show and **Safariparken** (adult/3-12yr Skr140/100), complete with a safari park **bus tour** (Skr30) for the carless. A combined ticket for the zoo and safari park costs Skr295/185. The cable car (Skr80/40) around the park gives a better view of the forest than of the animals.

A separate **Tropicarium** (☎ 39 52 50; adult/4-15yr Skr90/60; 🕒 9.30am-7pm late Jun-early Aug; 10am-6pm early–mid-Aug; 10am-4pm Mon-Fri, 10am-5pm Sat & Sun mid-Aug–late Sep; 10am-3pm late Sep-Apr; 10am-5pm Mon-Fri, 10am-5.30pm Sat & Sun May & Jun) opposite the entrance titillates with its motley crew of spiders, sharks, alligators and snakes.

You'll need a whole day to fully appreciate the zoo. Kolmården lies 35km north of Norrköping, on the north shore of Bråviken. Take regular bus 432 or 433 from Norrköping (Skr60, 40 minutes).

Sleeping

CAMPING & HOSTELS

Norrköpings Camping (☎ 17 11 90; info@norrkopingscamping.com; Campingvägen; sites Skr120, 2-/4-bed cabins Skr400/550) This little campsite sits on the south bank of Motala ström, approximately 2.5km from the city. It's short on bells and whistles, but there's a small cafe on site. Public transport is nonexistent.

STF Vandrarhem Turistgården (☎ 10 11 60; info@turistgarden.se; Ingelstagatan 31; dm/s/d from Skr195/290/405; P 💻) A pleasing little hostel about 800m north of the train station.

STF Vandrarhem Abborreberg (☎ 31 93 44; abborreberg@telia.com; dm Skr220; 🕒 Apr–mid-Oct; P) Stunningly situated in a coastal pine wood 6km east of town, this sterling hostel offers accommodation in huts scattered through the surrounding park. The associated ice-cream parlour is a hit with gluttons. Take bus 116 to Lindö.

Hörnans Hotell & Vandrarhem (☎ 16 58 90; www.hotellhornan.com; cnr Hörngatan & Sankt Persgatan; dm/s/d Skr270/405/740) The only central budget option, with comfy rooms above a busy pub-restaurant. All come with cable TV.

HOTELS

Hotell Isabell (☎ 16 90 82; www.hotelisabell.se; Vattengränden 7; s Skr475, d with/without bathroom Skr675/575; 💻) A cheapish, satisfactory option. Reception hours are limited, so phone ahead.

Hotell Drott (☎ 18 00 60; info@hotelldrott.com; Tunnbindaregatan 19; s/d Skr710/860, discounted to Skr495/710; P 💻) Peaceful Hotell Drott serves up old-fashioned but comfy rooms, as well as a kitchen for self-caterers. Breakfast includes meatballs and light evening meals are an option.

Hotel Centric (☎ 12 90 30; info@centrichotel.se; Gamla Rådstugugatan 18; s/d Skr710/860, discounted to Skr495/710; P 💻) Spacious rooms and solid wooden furniture are the trademark at Norrköping's oldest hotel.

Scandic Hotel Norrköping City (☎ 495 52 00; norrkopingcity@scandic-hotels.com; Slottsgatan 99; s Skr1250-1650, discounted to Skr790-990, d Skr1350-1750, discounted to Skr890-1090; P 💻) Near the train station, the Scandic City makes up for its dowdy foyer with crisp, modern rooms featuring retro-cool wallpaper and flatscreen TVs. Hotel perks include a sauna and Jacuzzi.

Eating & Drinking

our pick **Choklad Companiet** (☎ 12 61 61; Prästgatan 3; ❧ closed Sun) Head to this chocolate shop-cum-cafe for exquisite homemade gelato (try the white chocolate, lime and chilli), desserts, pralines and truffles. As for the espresso, it could make an Italian barista weep.

Manesa (☎ 450 14 38; Gamla Rådstugugatan 10; tapas dishes Skr29-99; ❧ 2pm-1am Mon-Sat Jun-Aug, from 4pm Sep-May) Polished punters adore this sassy tapas-cocktail lounge. Join them on leather lounges for global finger food like Japanese tempura and moreish tuna-and-guacamole seafood spoons. Rum rules the cocktail list, with over 30 types of the tropical drop on offer.

Bagarstugan (☎ 470 20 20; Skolgatan 1A; sandwiches Skr40-49, salads Skr59-65; ❧ 10am-6pm Mon-Fri, 10am-4pm Sat, noon-4pm Sun) This stylish, floor-boarded bakery-cafe peddles freshly-baked cookies, cinnamon buns, muffins and scones, as well as salubrious salads, sandwiches and take-away homemade marmalades. There's a courtyard for alfresco noshing.

Källaren Bacchus (☎ 10 07 40; Gamla Torget 4; lunch Skr68, mains Skr182-295) A perennially popular restaurant-pub with a great summer garden courtyard and snug vaulted cellar. Steak is a speciality, while tasty fish dishes may include fried pike perch with chilli-lime butter and potato pastry.

Fiskmagasinet (☎ 13 45 60; Skolgatan 1; lunch Skr73, mains Skr195-315; ❧ lunch & dinner Mon-Sat) Housed in a recently converted 19th-century *snus* (snuff) factory, urbane Fiskmagasinet combines an intimate bar with a casually chic dining room serving savvy seafood dishes like grilled scampi with mashed potato, truffle and port wine reduction, as well as cheaper Swedish classics.

Bomulls Fabriken (☎ 13 44 00; Dalsgatan 13; lunch Skr89, mains Skr139-289; ❧ Tue-Sat from 5pm, plus lunch Mon-Fri winter) Wedged between the tourist office and Louis de Geer Konserthus, this trendy warehouse bistro serves crossover grub like asparagus risotto with orange-marinated fennel, carrot salad and grilled bread. It turns into a nightclub on Friday and Saturday, with two dance floors serving up R&B, old-school rock and Schlager to revellers 25 years and over.

Knäppingen (☎ 10 74 45; Västgötegatan 21; lunch Skr89; ❧ closed Mon) The Stadsmuseum's cafe makes a refreshing change, offering focaccias, tacos, crêpes and better veggie options than boring pasta. In summer, you can munch away in a sunny courtyard tucked between stately old mills.

Pappa Grappa Bar & Trattorian (☎ 18 00 14; Gamla Rådstugugatan 26-28; mains Skr120-255; ❧ 6pm-late Mon-Sat, pizzeria also open Sun) Gobble up a brilliant wood-fired pizza in the pizzeria, or slip into the vaulted restaurant for scrumptious antipasto and meat and fish mains. Established by an Italian ballroom dancing champion, there's also an on-site deli for take-home treats.

Favourite post-work drinking spots include cellar pub **Stopet** (☎ 10 07 40; Gamla Torget) and nearby **Pub Wasa** (☎ 18 26 05; Gamla Rådstugugatan). The **Bishop's Arms** (☎ 36 41 20; Tyska Torget 2), at the Grand Hotel, is a good English-style pub with a great river view.

The blocks between Drottninggatan and Olai Kyrkogata contain shopping centres that are packed with chain stores and supermarkets.

For an alcohol fix, drop into **Systembolaget** (Drottninggatan 50B).

Getting There & Away

Sweden's third-largest airport, **Stockholm Skavsta** (www.skavsta-air.se) is 60km away. To get there take the train to Nyköping, then catch a local bus. **Norrköping Airport** (www.norrkopingfly |gplats.se) has direct flights from Copenhagen, Munich and Helsinki.

The regional bus station is next to the train station, and long-distance buses leave from a terminal across the road. **Swebus Express** (☎ 0771-21 82 18; www.swebusexpress.com) has very frequent services to Stockholm (Skr170, 2¼ hours) and Jönköping (Skr215, 2½ hours), and several services daily to Göteborg (Skr330, five hours) and Kalmar (Skr265, four hours). **Svenska Buss** (☎ 0771-67 67 67; www .svenskabuss.se, in Swedish) runs similar, though less frequent, routes.

Norrköping is on the main north–south railway line, and SJ trains depart every one to two hours for Stockholm (Skr95 to Skr400, 1½ hours) and Malmö (Skr554 to Skr906, 3¼ hours). Trains run roughly every hour north to Nyköping (Skr60 to Skr72, one hour) and every 20 minutes south to Linköping (Skr80, 25 minutes).

Getting Around

The minimum fare on Norrköping's urban transport is Skr20. Trams cover the city and are the quickest option for short hops, especially along Drottninggatan from the train station.

For a taxi, ring **Norrköpings Taxi** (☎ 10 01 00).

LINKÖPING

☎ 013 / pop 140,370

Most famous for its mighty medieval cathedral, Linköping fancies itself as Norrköping's more upmarket rival. Its most infamous claim to fame is the 'bloodbath of Linköping'. Following the Battle of Stångebro (1598), many of King Sigismund's defeated Catholic army were executed here, leaving Duke Karl and his Protestant forces in full control of Sweden.

While quite the modern, industrial city today (manufacturer Saab is the major employer), pockets of its past survive in its churches, castle, museums and the picture-perfect streets around Hunnebergsgatan and Storgatan.

Information

There are banks and other services around Stora Torget.

Gaming 9 (Drottninggatan 36; per hr Skr30; 🕙 10am-1am Mon-Thu & Sat, 10am-11pm Fri, noon-1am Sun) Internet access.

Library (Stadsbiblioteket; ☎ 20 66 03; Östgötagatan 5; 🕙 10am-7pm Mon-Thu, 10am-6pm Fri, 11am-3pm Sat May-Aug; 8am-8pm Mon-Thu, 8am-6pm Fri, 11am-4pm Sat & Sun Sep-Apr) A striking building, with free internet access (bring ID) and an excellent cafe.

Tourist office (☎ 20 68 35; www.linkoping.se; Östgötagatan 5) In the library. Open during library hours, but staffed only between 10am and 5pm Monday to Friday.

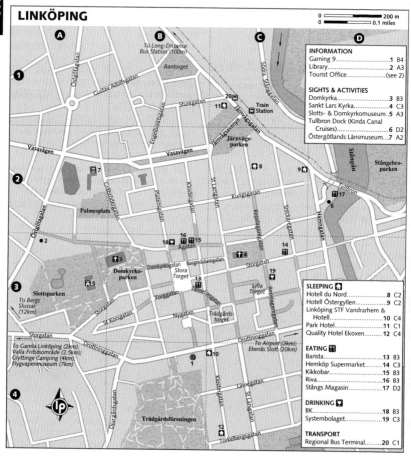

LINKÖPING

INFORMATION	
Gaming 9	1 B4
Library	2 A3
Tourist Office	(see 2)

SIGHTS & ACTIVITIES	
Domkyrka	3 B3
Sankt Lars Kyrka	4 C3
Slotts- & Domkyrkomuseum	5 A3
Tullbron Dock (Kinda Canal Cruises)	6 D2
Östergötlands Länsmuseum	7 A2

SLEEPING	
Hotell du Nord	8 C2
Hotell Östergyllen	9 C2
Linköping STF Vandrarhem & Hotell	10 C4
Park Hotel	11 C1
Quality Hotel Ekoxen	12 C4

EATING	
Barista	13 B3
Hemköp Supermarket	14 C3
Kikkobar	15 B3
Riva	16 B3
Stångs Magasin	17 D2

DRINKING	
BK	18 B3
Systembolaget	19 C3

TRANSPORT	
Regional Bus Terminal	20 C1

Sights
GAMLA LINKÖPING & VALLA FRITIDSOMRÅDE
The town's best attractions lie just outside the centre. **Gamla Linköping** (☎ 12 11 10; admission free), 2km west of the city, is one of the biggest living-museum villages in Sweden. It's a gorgeous combo of cobbled streets, picket-fenced gardens and around 90 19th-century houses. There are about a dozen themed museums (all free, with various opening times), artisan shops and a small chocolate factory. Take bus 202 or 214 (Skr20).

Just 300m through the forest is **Valla Fritidsområde**, a recreation area with domestic animals, a children's playground, minigolf, small museums and vintage abodes.

KINDA CANAL
While upstaged by the Göta Canal, Linköping boasts its own canal system, the 90km **Kinda Canal**. Opened in 1871, it has 15 locks, including Sweden's deepest. Cruises include evening sailings, musical outings and wine-tasting trips. For a simple day excursion, from late June to early August the **M/S Kind** (☎ 0141-23 33 70; adult/6-15yr Skr370/110) leaves Tullbron dock at 10am on Tuesday, Thursday and Saturday, and travels to Rimforsa (return by bus or train included).

OTHER SIGHTS
Made from blocks of handcarved limestone, the enormous **Domkyrka** (☉ 9am-6pm) was the country's largest and most expensive church in the Middle Ages. Its foundations were laid around 1250 and its 107m spire and vast interior still impress. Inside sits a vivid 16th-century triptych by Dutchman Marten van Heemskerck.

The struggle between church and state is explored in the nearby castle's **Slotts- & Domkyrkomuseum** (☎ 12 23 80; adult/under 7yr Skr40/free; ☉ 11am-4pm Tue-Fri, noon-4pm Sat & Sun Apr-Sep, noon-4pm Tue-Sun Oct-Mar), where the bolshy King Gustav Vasa and the last Catholic bishop, Hans Brask, made friends, ate, drank and fell out again. Archaeological finds include two mummified black rats from the bishop's privy.

Just north of the cathedral, **Östergötlands Länsmuseum** (☎ 23 03 00; Vasavägen; adult/child Skr20/10; ☉ 10am-4pm Tue-Sun, til 8pm Tue & Thu Sep-mid Dec & mid-Jan–May) has a decent European art collection (Cranach's painting of Eden, *Original Sin*, is wonderful, with a smiling Eve

twiddling her toes), and Swedish art dating from the Middle Ages.

The concrete floor of **Sankt Lars Kyrka** (Storgatan; ☉ 11am-5pm Mon-Fri, 11am-1pm Sat, 3-8pm Sun) was built in 1802 above the previous medieval church crypt. Ask the rector to lead you downstairs, where fascinating finds include 11th-century gravestones, a teen skeleton (complete with fatal blow to the skull) and fragments of the medieval church's painted roof tiles.

Approximately 7km west of the centre is **Flygvapenmuseum** (☎ 28 35 67; Carl Cederströms gatan; adult/under 18yr Skr40/free; ☉ 10am-5pm Jun-Aug, noon-4pm Tue-Sun Sep-May), with exhibits on airforce history and 60 aircraft fit for a *Top Gun* remake. To get there, take bus 213.

Ekenäs Slott (☎ 771 46; tours adult/10-15yr Skr60/25; ☉ guided tours on the hour 1-3pm Tue-Sun Jul; Sat & Sun Jun & Aug), built between 1630 and 1644, is one of the best-preserved Renaissance castles in Sweden. Features include three spectacular towers, a moat, and furnishings from the 17th to 19th centuries. Located 20km east of Linköping, you'll need your own transport to get there.

Sleeping
Glyttinge Camping (☎ 17 49 28; glyttinge@nordiccamp ing.se; Berggårdsvägen 6; sites from Skr165; ☉ year-round) This huge campsite, with minigolf and cycle hire, lies 4km west of the city centre.

Linköping STF Vandrarhem & Hotell (☎ 35 90 00; www.lvh.se; Klostergatan 52A; dm from Skr210, hotel s/d Skr765/840, weekends Skr496/596; ☐) This swish central hostel has hotel-style accommodation too, mostly with kitchenettes. All rooms have private bathrooms and TVs. Book ahead.

Hotell Östergyllen (☎ 10 20 75; www.hotelloster gyllen.se; Hamngatan 2B; s/d from Skr425/620) Despite the forlorn ambience (think lino floors and anonymous corridors), this budget hotel offers cheap, comfy-enough rooms not far from the train station. You can pay up to Skr200 extra for a private bathroom.

Hotell du Nord (☎ 12 98 95; www.hotelldunord .se; Repslagaregatan 5; s/d from Skr720/900, discounted to Skr530/690; ☐P) Plonked in parkland, with its main 19th-century building looking like a doll's house, Hotell du Nord boasts friendly staff, light and pleasant rooms (those in the aesthetically challenged rear building are freshly renovated and larger), as well as a patio for outdoor summer breakfasts.

Park Hotel (☎ 12 90 05; www.fawltytowers.se; Järnvägsgatan; s/d Skr890/1090, discounted to Skr650/850;

THE SWEET STENCH OF SUCCESS

Take some slaughterhouse innards, add a splash of seized alcohol, mix them together with human waste and heat the lot to 70°C. Pour the slush into an anaerobic digester, allow 30 days of decomposition and presto: ecofriendly biogas. This cleaner, greener energy source is increasingly powering everything from Sweden's buses, trucks and cars to the world's first biogas train, running between Linköping and Västervik. Carbon neutral and renewable, its other benefit is that it's locally produced.

One of the largest producers of biogas is SvenskBiogas, whose Linköping plant turns a whopping 50,000 tons of waste each year into fossil-free fuel. Tullverket (Swedish Customs) supplies most of the alcohol, which is seized from citizens re-entering the country with more than is permitted under the 'personal use' rule.

The good news for both SvenskBiogas and the environment is that the biogas market is booming. Vehicles running on alternative fuels made up about 20% of new car sales in Sweden last year and the figures are expected to soar. Enlightened local councils make 'switching to green' a tempting option: ecofriendlier cars are exempt from road tolls in Stockholm and enjoy free parking in most large Swedish cities.

In small-town Växjö, where biogas is produced at the local sewerage works, residents and businesses are entitled to subsidies to buy greener cars. The town's main taxi company runs a hybrid biogas- and ethanol-run fleet, with its drivers put through an 'eco-driving' course to get them driving in more fuel-efficient ways. Not surprisingly, Växjö itself won a Sustainable Energy Europe Award in 2007 for its green ambitions, which includes slashing carbon dioxide emissions per capita by 70% by 2025. Impressively, over 50% of Växjö's total energy is currently derived from renewable sources.

$\boxed{P}$ $\boxed{\square}$) Disturbingly billed as Sweden's 'Fawlty Towers', this hotel resembles that madhouse in appearance only (yes, there's an elk head at reception). A smart family-run establishment close to the train station, it's peppered with chandeliers, oil paintings and clean, parquet-floored rooms.

Quality Hotel Ekoxen (☎ 25 26 00; www.ekoxen .se; Klostergatan 68; s Skr1295-1495, discounted to Skr795-1095, d Skr71495-1695, discounted to Skr760-1295; $\boxed{P}$ $\boxed{\square}$) The large Ekoxen has stylish, modern, newly renovated rooms. There's a spa and massage centre (including flotation tanks) and an acclaimed restaurant.

Eating & Drinking

Most places to eat (and drink) are found around the main square or nearby streets, especially along buzzing Ågatan.

BK (☎ 10 01 11; Ågatan 47; tapas around Skr35, mains Skr145-249) Particularly heaving on Friday nights, BK peddles exotic tapas and mod mains like grilled elderflower-cured salmon with dill polenta and blanched summer vegetables. Food aside, BK is a winner with thirsty locals.

Barista (☎ 10 10 90; Tanneforsgatan 11; sandwiches Skr56-72; 9am-8pm Mon-Fri, 10am-5pm Sat, 11am-4pm Sun) This hip cafe chain (attached to the equally hip store DesignTorget) peddles decent fair-trade coffee and other trendy perishables like chai tea, organic focaccias and pick-me-up chocolate bars under fashionable low-slung lamps.

Stångs Magasin (☎ 31 21 00; Södra Stånggatan 1; lunch around Skr90, mains Skr245-295; lunch Mon-Fri, from 6pm Mon-Fri & from 4pm Sat Sep-Jun, from 2.30pm Tue-Sat Jul & Aug) In a 200-year-old warehouse down near the Kinda Canal docks, this elegant award-winner fuses classic Swedish cuisine with continental influences – think glazed duck breast with almond potato puree and artichoke ragout in a wine balsamic sauce. The lunch buffet is good value.

Kikkobar (☎ 13 13 10; Klostergatan 26; mains Skr135-280) Head here for Zen designer details with Japanese classics like tempura, spicier Southeast Asian numbers like tom yum soup, and the odd Western staple.

Riva (☎ 12 95 15; Ågatan 43; mains Skr149-256; from 5pm Tue-Fri, from 6pm Sat) Trendy Riva serves Italian-with-twist bistro grub like buttered *taglierini* pasta with chilli-sautéed scampi, prawns, mussels, shallots, white wine, cherry- and sun-dried tomatoes.

The Hemköp supermarket on Storgatan is open until 10pm daily. The **Systembolaget** (☎ 12 25 81; Repslagaregatan 25-27) is a short walk away.

Getting There & Away

The **airport** (☎ 18 10 30) is only 2km east of town. **Skyways** (☎ 0771-95 95 00; www.skyways.se) flies direct to Stockholm Arlanda on weekdays. **KLM** (☎ 08-58 79 97 57; www.klm.com) flies daily to Amsterdam. There's no airport bus, but taxi company **Taxibil** (☎ 14 60 00) charges around Skr150 for the ride.

Regional and local buses, run by **Östgöta Trafiken** (☎ 0771-21 10 10; www.ostgotatrafiken.se), leave from the terminal next to the train station; route maps and timetables are available at the information office.

Journeys cost from Skr20; the 24-hour *dygnskort* (travel card; adult/under 26 years Skr140/110) is valid on all buses and local trains within the region. Tickets can be purchased at Pressbyrån outlets or at the train station. Tickets purchased on-board vehicles cost an extra Skr20.

Up to five express buses per day go to Vadstena; otherwise change at Motala.

Long-distance buses depart from a terminal 500m northwest of the train station. Swebus Express runs 10 to 12 times daily to Jönköping (Skr158, 1½ hours) and seven to eight times daily to Göteborg (Skr269, four hours), and north to Norrköping (Skr67, 45 minutes) and Stockholm (Skr231, three hours).

Linköping is on the main north–south railway line. Regional and express trains run to Stockholm roughly every hour; express trains go to Malmö. Frequent regional trains run north to Norrköping (Skr80, 25 minutes). Kustpilen SJ trains run every few hours to Norrköping, Nyköping and Kalmar.

Getting Around

Most city buses depart from Centralstationen. For a taxi, ring **Taxibil** (☎ 14 60 00). Bicycle hire is available at **Bertil Anderssons Cykel & Motor** (☎ 31 46 46; Plantensgatan 27).

BERGS SLUSSAR
☎ 013

Bergs Slussar, 12km northwest of Linköping, is one of the most scenic sections of the Göta Canal: there are seven locks with a height gain of 19m – very impressive in canal terms! The nearby ruin **Vreta kloster**, Sweden's oldest monastery, was founded by Benedictine monks in 1120. While it's worth a look, the adjacent 13th-century **abbey church** is admittedly more interesting.

There's a beautifully located **STF Vandrarhem** (☎ 603 30; bergsslussar@sverige.nu; dm Skr195; May-Aug) near the locks, with a cafe, minigolf and bike hire. You'll find a couple of cafes and restaurants out this way, including **Kanalkrogen** (☎ 600 76; meals Skr220-245), with a great range of meals.

Buses 521 and 522 run regularly from Linköping.

VADSTENA
☎ 0143 / pop 7540

On Vättern lake, Vadstena is a legacy of both church and state power, and today St Birgitta's abbey and Gustav Vasa's castle compete with each other for admiration. The atmosphere in the old town (between Storgatan and the abbey), with its wonderful cobbled lanes, evocative street names and wooden buildings, makes the place a satisfying pit stop.

Information

The **tourist office** (☎ 315 70; www.vadstena.com; 10am-6pm Jul, 10am-6pm Jun & early Aug, 10am-2pm Mon-Fri rest of year) planned to relocate to Rödtornet (Sånggatan) in 2009. Head in for details about town walks and local boat tours. You'll find banks and other services east of the castle, on Storgatan and around Stora Torget.

ALL HAIL HULTSFRED

Like a Glastonbury with spruce, the annual **Hultsfredsfestivalen** (Hultsfred Festival; ☎ 0495-695 00, ticket sales 0771-70 70 70; www.rockparty.se; 4-day pass from Skr1390) is one of Sweden's music fest heavyweights, boasting five stages and acts spanning rock, pop and indie. Past line-ups have included Rage Against The Machine, Baby Shambles and Swedish band The Hives. It's held over three or four days in mid-June, in small-town Hultsfred, around 20km south of Vimmerby. Most ticket types include access to the festival's camping area (check website for updates on one-, two- and three-day passes). Trains connect Hultsfred to Linköping (and major cities beyond). For further information, check the festival website.

Sights

Overlooking the lake, the mighty Renaissance castle **Vadstena Slott** (☎ 315 70; Slottsvägen; adult/7-15yr Skr55/10; ⊙ 11am-6pm Jul-mid-Aug; 11am-4pm Jun & mid-late Aug; tours 1pm Mon-Fri, 1pm & 3pm Sat & Sun Jun; 1pm Mon-Fri, noon, 2pm & 4pm Sat & Sun Jul–late-Aug; 1pm daily late Aug–mid-Sep) was the family project of the early Vasa kings. The lower floors contain a small historical display. The furnished upper floors are more interesting, but only open during guided tours (in English mid-May to mid-September; call ahead for times); it's worth going on one if only to visit the chapel, with its incredible 17-second echo!

The **Sancta Birgitta Klostermuseet** (☎ 100 31; Lasarettsgatan; adult/8-18yr Sk50/20; ⊙ 10.30am-5pm Jul-early Aug; 11am-4pm Jun & rest of Aug; 11am-4pm Sat & Sun May, Sep & Oct) is in Bjälboättens Palats (a royal residence that became a convent in 1384), and tells the story of St Birgitta's roller-coaster life and those of all her saint-and-sinner children. Artefacts include the coffin that was brought back from Rome in.

'Of plain construction, humble and strong', **Klosterkyrkan** (abbey church; admission free; ⊙ 9am-8pm Jul, 9am-7pm Jun & Aug, 9am-5pm May & Sep) was built in response to one of St Birgitta's visions. After the church's consecration in 1430, Vadstena became *the* top pilgrimage site in Sweden. Step inside for medieval sculptures and carved floor slabs.

Both the old courthouse **rådhus**, on the town square, and **Rödtornet** (Sånggatan) are late medieval constructions.

Sleeping

Chain hotels don't get a look-in here; pretty and personal is the rule. Book accommodation well in advance.

STF Vandrarhem Vadstena (☎ 103 02; Skän ningegatan 20; dm Skr180; Ⓟ) A short walk from the town centre sits this big hostel, with affable staff, sunny dorms and a large underground kitchen decorated with cheery Dala horses. Book ahead from late August to early June.

Vätterviksbadet (☎ 127 30; sites Skr195, r & cabins from Skr350; ⊙ May–mid-Sep; ⚄) A quality campsite near the lake, 2km north of town, it has family-friendly amenities including a beach with shallow waters, minigolf, boules, a sauna, a water slide, a kiosk, a cafe and a pub.

27:ans Nattlogi (☎ 765 64; 27ans@va-bostaelle .se; Storgatan 27; s/d from Skr500/850; Ⓟ) Wooden floors give a homely vibe to the six rooms (some with views of Klosterkyrkan). More

expensive rooms have private bathrooms. All include breakfast.

Pensionat Solgården (☎ 143 50; www.pension atsolgarden.se, in Swedish; Strågatan 3; s/d from Skr540/690; ⊙ May-Sep) Set in an utterly adorable wooden villa, this family-run hotel boasts lovingly decorated rooms; some have private bathrooms and all have an art/artist connection. They're all *very* different – check the photos on the website to choose your favourite.

Vadstena Klosterhotel (☎ 315 30; hotel@klosterhotel .se; s/d from Skr1095/1395; Ⓟ 🖥) History and luxury merge at this wonderfully atmospheric hotel in St Birgitta's old convent. The bathrooms are a wee bit dated, but the medieval-style rooms are great, with chandeliers, high wooden beds and heaven-sent coffee-makers. Most boast lake views.

Eating & Drinking

Hamnpaviljongen (☎ 310 95), in the park facing the castle, is an alfresco cafe with decent sandwiches, light meals and a refreshing verdant vibe.

Restaurant Munkklostret (☎ 130 00; lunch Skr85, mains Skr200-324; ⊙ from noon in summer, shorter hours in winter) The Klosterhotel's ravishing restaurant is the best nosh spot in town. Seasonal, succulent steak, lamb, game and fish dishes are flavoured with herbs from the monastery garden, and served in the monks' old dorms.

Rådhuskällaren (☎ 121 70; Rådhustorget; mains Skr119-195) Under the old courthouse, this affable 15th-century cellar restaurant dishes out simple but filling burger, pasta and fish meals. Its outdoor area is a favourite afternoon drinking spot in summer.

There's a central supermarket, **CoopKonsum** (Rådhustorget; ⊙ to 11pm) and a nearby **Systembolaget** (☎ 100 36; Hovsgatan 4).

Getting There & Around

See Linköping (p135) for regional transport information. Only buses run to Vadstena – take bus 610 to Motala (for trains to Örebro), or bus 661 to Mjölby (for trains to Linköping and Stockholm). **Swebus Express** runs on Friday and Sunday to/from Stockholm (Skr277, 4¼ hours). **Blåklints Buss** (☎ 0142-121 50; www.blaklints buss.se, in Swedish) runs one to three services daily from the Viking Line Terminal in Stockholm to Vadstena (Skr170).

Sport Hörnan (☎ 103 62; Storgatan 14; ⊙ 9.30am-6.30pm Mon-Fri, 9.30am-2pm Sat) has bikes for rent (Skr140/400 per day/week).

AROUND VADSTENA
Rök
Sweden's most famous rune stone, the 9th-century **Rökstenen**, is near the church at Rök (just off the E4 on the road to Heda and Alvastra). It's a monumental memorial stone raised to commemorate a dead son, and features the longest runic inscription in the world. It's an ancient, intricate verse so cryptic that scholars constantly scrap over its interpretation. The outdoor exhibition and stone are always open.

Buses are virtually nonexistent, though the scenic flatlands around Vättern make for perfect cycling.

Väversunda
The Romanesque 12th-century limestone **Väversunda kyrka**, situated 15km southwest of Vadstena, is a bizarre-looking church, and contains restored 13th-century wall paintings. The adjacent **Tåkern Nature Reserve** pulls in a diverse cast of birds; there's a birdwatcher's tower near the church.

Again, buses are hopeless; peddling is your best option.

SMÅLAND
The region of Småland is one of dense forests, glinting lakes and bare marshlands. Historically it served as a buffer zone between the Swedes and Danes; the eastern and southern coasts in particular witnessed territorial tussles. Today it's better known for the Glasriket (Kingdom of Glass), a sparsely populated area in the central southeast dotted with crystal workshops. Småland is broken up into smaller counties *(län)*: Jönköpings in the northwest, Kronobergs in the southwest and Kalmar in the east.

JÖNKÖPING & HUSKVARNA
☎ 036 / pop 123,710
Whenever you hear the scratching of matches on sandpaper, spare a thought for Jönköping – birthplace of the safety match. You can visit the restored production area here to learn more about this vital, but undervalued, necessity.

Fairy-tale illustrator John Bauer was inspired by the deep green forests around Jönköping, and the town museum shows off his superb otherworldly drawings of trolls, knights and princesses. Other famous exports include ABBA's Agnetha Fältskog, and indie band The Cardigans.

From Jönköping, at Vättern's south end, an urban strip stretches 7km eastwards, sucking in Huskvarna, which is famous for its sewing machines, chainsaws and motorbikes.

Information
You'll find banks along Östra Storgatan.
Library (Dag Hammarskjölds plats) Has internet access and a cafe, and is adjacent to the Länsmuseum.
Tourist office (☎ 10 50 50; www.jonkoping.se; ☻ 9.30am-7pm Mon-Fri, 9.30am-3pm Sat & Sun mid-Jun–mid-Aug; to 6pm Mon-Fri & to 2pm Sat & Sun mid-Aug–mid-Sep; to 6pm Mon-Fri & 2pm Sat rest of year) In the Juneporten complex at the train station.

Sights & Activities
JÖNKÖPING
Apparently 'the only match museum in the world', **Tändsticksmuseet** (☎ 10 55 43; Tändsticksgränd 27; adult/under 19yr Skr40/free; ☻ 10am-5pm Mon-Fri, 10am-3pm Sat & Sun Jun-Aug, 11am-3pm Tue-Sat Sep-May), in an old match factory, deals with this practical Swedish invention. It's quite an eye-opener: the industry was initially based on cheap child labour, workers frequently suffered from repulsive 'phossy jaw', and it was common knowledge that phosphorus matches were good for 'speeding up inheritance and inducing abortions'.

Near the Tändsticksmuseet, the **Radio Museum** (☎ 71 39 59; Tändsticksgränd 16; admission Skr20; ☻ 10am-5pm Mon-Fri, 10am-2pm Sat, 11am-3pm Sun Jun–mid-Aug; closed Sun & Mon mid-Aug–May) boasts over 1000 radio sets and related memorabilia.

Jönköpings Länsmuseum (☎ 30 18 00; www.jkpglm.se; Dag Hammarskjölds Plats 2; adult/under 18yr Skr40/free; ☻ 11am-5pm Mon, Tue & Thu-Sun, 11am-8pm Wed Jul & Aug, closed Mon Sep-Jun) covers local history and contemporary culture, but the real reason for coming here is to see the haunting fantasy works of artist John Bauer (1882–1918).

West of town is the expanse of **Stadsparken**. Its curiosities include the 1458 ornithological taxidermic masterpieces of **Fågelmuseet** (☎ 12 99 83; admission free; ☻ 11am-5pm May-Aug), and the **Friluftsmuseet** (☎ 30 18 00; admission free; ☻ 11am-4pm Jun-Aug) with a photogenic crew of old buildings.

From May to October, you can choose various **cruises** (☎ 070-637 17 00; www.rederiabkind.se) on Lake Vättern, aboard the M/S *Nya Skärgården*. There's a Friday evening buffet trip (Skr405), while several other trips combine dinner

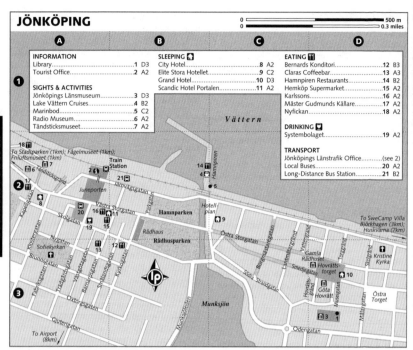

JÖNKÖPING

0 ————— 500 m
0 ————— 0.3 miles

INFORMATION
Library..1 D3
Tourist Office...............................2 A2

SIGHTS & ACTIVITIES
Jönköpings Länsmuseum.................3 D3
Lake Vättern Cruises.......................4 B2
Marinbod.......................................5 C2
Radio Museum................................6 A2
Tändsticksmuseet...........................7 A2

SLEEPING
City Hotel......................................8 A2
Elite Stora Hotellet........................9 C2
Grand Hotel.................................10 D3
Scandic Hotel Portalen.................11 A2

EATING
Bernards Konditori........................12 B3
Claras Coffeebar...........................13 A3
Hamnpiren Restaurants..................14 B2
Hemköp Supermarket.....................15 A2
Karlssons......................................16 A2
Mäster Gudmunds Källare...............17 A2
Nyfickan.......................................18 A2

DRINKING
Systembolaget...............................19 A2

TRANSPORT
Jönköpings Länstrafik Office............(see 2)
Local Buses..................................20 A2
Long-Distance Bus Station..............21 B2

Vättern

and live music, costing around Skr445. The boat departs from Hamnpiren; book at the tourist office.

For waterskiing or boat hire, contact **Marinbod** (☎ 12 04 87; Hamnpiren; ⊙ May-early Sep). Waterskiing, wakeboarding and kneeboarding all cost Skr800 per hour; small motor boats cost Skr150 per three hours or Skr250 per day.

HUSKVARNA

Square-jawed men going hunting while their wives snuggle up to their sewing machines: the **Husqvarna fabriksmuseum** (☎ 14 61 62; www.husq varna-museum.nu; Hakarpsvägen 1; adult/12-18yr Skr40/20; ⊙ 10am-5pm Mon-Fri, noon-4pm Sat & Sun May-Sep; 10am-3pm Mon-Fri, noon-4pm Sat & Sun Oct-Apr) conjures up a vivid 1950s world. The factory began as an arms manufacturer, before diverting into motorbikes, chainsaws, cooking ranges and microwave ovens. The atmospheric museum charts the company's rise.

For powerful drama, catch Huskvarna's **Fallens Dag** (Waterfall Day) in late August. When darkness falls the floodgates open and a torrential illuminated waterfall is released; contact the tourist office for details.

From Jönköping, take bus 1 to Huskvarna (Skr20), 7km away.

Sleeping

JÖNKÖPING

SweCamp Villa Björkhagen (☎ 12 28 63; villa bjorkhagen@swipnet.se; Friggagatan 31; sites Skr185-235, r/cabins Skr350/775) About 3km east of town, this large lakeside campsite offers various accommodation options, plus playgrounds, pedal cars and minigolf for kids.

Elite Stora Hotellet (☎ 10 00 00; info@jonkoping.elite .se; Hotellplan; s Skr550-1800, d Skr800-2200, s/d discounted to Skr750/950; P ▣) The Elite is Jönköping's harbourside show-stopper. Rooms are chic, with either Carl Larsson–inspired undertones or a more contemporary combo of black-and-white photographs and natural hues. There's a sauna, pool table and slinky restaurant, as well as a banqueting hall fit for royalty.

City Hotel (☎ 71 92 80; hotel@cityhotel.nu; Västra Storgatan 25; s/d from Skr795/895, discounted to Skr545/595; ▣) Midrange, family-run City is a step up in quality from the Grand. A slinky lobby and a batch of new, pricier rooms (think flat-screen TVs, giant black-and-white photos of

Jönköping and oak-toned functionalist furniture) counterbalance the dated-yet-comfy older rooms. Extras include a Jacuzzi and three saunas.

Grand Hotel (☎ 71 96 00; info@grandhotel-jonkoping .se; Hovrättstorget; s from Skr890-1240, d Skr1080-1440, s/d discounted to Skr550/720; ☐) In a stately early 20th-century building, this homely central choice offers budget, standard and superior rooms. All are clean and comfy, many are spacious, and several look out over the square.

Scandic Hotel Portalen (☎ 585 42 00; www.scan dichotels.com; Barnarpsgatan 6; s Skr890-1490, d Skr990-1590; P ☐) One of Scandic's two Jönköping hotels, the Portalen is a mash-up of minimalist Scandi cool and 1980s drab. The rooms themselves are simple yet stylish, and the superiors have private fridges and coffee-makers. The hotel also boasts a large spa with beauty treatments.

HUSKVARNA
STF Vandrarhem Huskvarna (☎ 14 88 70; www.hhv .se; Odengatan 10; hostel s/d Skr330/380, hotel s/d Skr595/780; ☐) Standards are high at this sizeable year-round hostel. Twinkling rooms feature TV and private toilets (except room 37, which is correspondingly cheaper), and breakfast is available (Skr60).

Eating & Drinking
For bobbing boats and tasty seafood, head straight for Hamnpiren (the harbour pier), where you'll find a row of restaurants with good lunch specials (around Skr75) and merry dinner crowds. For cheaper alternatives, try inside the Juneporten transport and shopping complex.

Nyfickan (☎ 19 06 86; lunch Skr60) In a quirky brick building that once belonged to the match-making empire, Nyfickan is part of the town's cultural centre. Chill out boho-style with good coffee, cakes, tacos, falafel and sandwiches. There's a decent veggie selection, and gluten- and sugar-free options.

Karlssons (☎ 71 21 60; Västra Storgatan 9; meals Skr99-239; ☐ from 5pm Sun-Fri, from 6pm Sat) Beside the Scandic Hotel Portalen, Karlssons is Jönköping's hottest new resto-bar. Slip into the slick interior (or onto the buzzing roof terrace) for well-mixed cocktails and bistro-style brilliance like pan-fried salmon with potato salad and lime yoghurt.

Mäster Gudmunds Källare (☎ 10 06 40; Kapellgatan 2; lunch Skr70, dinner mains Skr139-199; ☐ closed Sun summer) This much-loved restaurant sits in a 17th-century cellar, with beautiful vaulted ceilings and good-value lunches. Evening mains are mainly meaty and fishy local dishes, with a few nods to French fare.

Other worthy cafes include **Claras Coffeebar** (☎ 30 01 15; Barnarpsgatan 18) and **Bernards Konditori** (☎ 71 11 21; Kyrkogatan 12).

Just around the corner from Scandic Hotel Portalen is a **Hemköp supermarket** (Barnarpsgatan; ☐ 8am-8pm). Nearby is the **Systembolaget** (cnr Skolgatan & Trädgårdsgatan).

Getting There & Around
Jönköping airport (☎ 31 11 00) is located about 8km southwest of the town centre. **Skyways** (☎ 0771-95 95 00) has daily flights to/from Stockholm Arlanda, and **SAS** (☎ 0770-72 77 27) operates six flights weekly to/from Copenhagen. Bus 18 serves the airport, or else a taxi costs around Skr180.

Most local buses leave from opposite Juneporten on Västra Storgatan. Local transport is run by **Jönköpings Länstrafik** (☎ 0771-44 43 33; www.jlt.se, in Swedish; Juneporten; ☐ 7.30am-6pm Mon-Fri); there's an office with information, tickets and passes in Juneporten.

The long-distance bus station is next to the train station. There are at least eight daily **Swebus Express** (☎ 0771-21 82 18; www.swebusexpress .com) services to Göteborg (Skr134, two hours) and Stockholm (Skr312, 4½ hours); at least three to Helsingborg (Skr263, three hours) and Malmö (Skr293, 4½ hours); and two to Karlstad (Skr250, four hours). **Bus4You** (☎ 0771-44 40 00; www.bus4u.se, in Swedish) runs its Stockholm–Göteborg route via Jönköping several times daily. **Svenska Buss** (☎ 0771-67 67 67; www.svenskabuss.se, in Swedish) also operates a daily service each way between Göteborg and Stockholm.

Jönköping is on a regional train line; you'll need to change trains in either Nässjö or Falköping to get to or from larger towns.

Taxi Jönköping (☎ 34 40 00) is the local taxi company. You can hire bicycles from **Marinbod** (☎ 12 04 87; Hamnpiren; per day Skr150; ☐ May-early Sep).

GRÄNNA & VISINGSÖ
☎ 0390
All that's missing from Gränna are Oompa-Loompas. The scent of sugar hangs over the village, and shops overflow with the village's trademark red-and-white peppermint rock

SOUTHEAST SWEDEN

THE GÖTA CANAL

Not only is the Göta Canal Sweden's greatest civil engineering feat, idling along it on a boat or cycling the towpaths is one of the best ways to soak up Gotland's gorgeous countryside.

The canal connects the North Sea with the Baltic Sea, and links the great lakes Vättern and Vänern. Its total length is 190km, although only around 87km is human-made – the rest is rivers and lakes. It was built between 1802 and 1832 by a burly team of some 60,000 soldiers, and provided a hugely valuable transport and trade link between Sweden's east and west coasts.

The canal has two sections: the eastern section from Mem (southeast of Norrköping) to Motala, (north of Vadstena on Vättern); and the western section from Karlsborg (on Vättern) to Sjötorp (on the shores of Vänern). The system is then linked to the sea by the Trollhätte Canal, in Västergötland. Along these stretches of the canal are towpaths, used in earlier times by horses and oxen pulling barges. Nowadays they're the domain of walkers and cyclists, with the occasional canalside youth hostel breaking the journey.

Boat trips are obviously a favourite way to experience the canal. You can go on a four- or six-day cruise of its entire length, travelling from Stockholm to Göteborg (or vice versa) and stopping to enjoy the wayside attractions; see p337 for more information. Shorter, cheaper boat trips along sections of the canal are also available – any tourist office in the area should be able to give you the low-down. Staff can also fill you in on the range of canoeing, cycling or even horse-riding possibilities along certain parts.

A good website for ideas and inspiration formation is www.gotakanal.se.

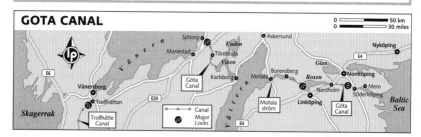

GOTA CANAL

(polkagris). It's a touristy spot, but the steep streets, lakeside location and excellent polar exhibition redeem the place.

Across the water and 6km west is peaceful Visingsö. Connected by frequent ferries and home to Sweden's largest oak forest, it's a great place to cycle or chill.

Information

There's a **tourist office** (☎ 410 10; www.grm.se; Grenna Kulturgård, Brahegatan 38; ☼ 10am-6pm mid-May–Aug, 10am-4pm mid-May) in central Gränna, and another **tourist office** (☎ 401 93; www.visingso.net; ☼ 10am-5pm May-Aug, to 7pm late-Jun–mid-Aug, 11am-6pm Mon, 8am-2pm Tue-Fri Sep-Apr) at the harbour in Visingsö. The latter offers **bicycle hire** (per 3hr/day Skr50/70).

There's free internet (bring ID) at Gränna **library** (☎ 410 15; ☼ 10am-7pm Mon-Thu, 10am-1pm Fri), upstairs from the tourist office.

Brahegatan, the main street of Gränna, has a bank and an ATM.

Sights

In the same building as the tourist office, **Gränna Museum: Andréexpedition Polarcenter** (adult/child Skr50/20; ☼ 10am-6pm mid-May–Aug, 10am-4pm Sep–mid-May) describes the disastrous attempt of Salomon August Andrée to reach the North Pole by balloon in 1897. It's riveting stuff, particularly the poignant remnants of the expedition: cracked leather boots, monogrammed handkerchiefs, lucky amulets, and mustard paper to ward off those polar winds.

Don't be put off by Andrée's ballooning tragedy; for Skr1895 per person you can take a one-hour scenic **hot-air balloon trip** (☎ 305 25; bengt@flyg-ballong.nu) over the area.

Several sweet-makers have kitchens where you can watch the town's trademark sweets being made. One is **Grenna Polkagriskokeri** (☎ 100 39; Brahegatan 39), directly opposite the tourist office, which uses an authentic 19th-century recipe. You can also catch crispbread in the making at **Gränna Knäcke** (☎ 100 57; Brahegatan 43).

Visingsö has a 17th-century **church, castle** and **aromatic herb garden**. An extensive network of footpaths and bicycle trails lead through tranquil woods.

The beautiful lakes of Bunn and Ören, and their dark forests, inspired local artist John Bauer to paint his trolls and magical pools (see p137). From mid-June to late August, you can take a **boat tour** (☎ 510 50; adult/under 12yr Skr150/75; ✆ 12.30pm Sat & Sun Jun, 12.30pm Jul & Aug) to the lakes, departing from Bunnströms badplats, 2.5km from Gränna.

Sleeping & Eating

GRÄNNA

The tourist office arranges private rooms from Skr140 to Skr250 per person per night (plus Skr100 booking fee). For a choice of food in a great waterside setting, head down to the harbour (1.5km) where restaurants peddle everything from Greek, French and Italian fare to Swedish dishes (most are open summer only).

Grännastrandens Camping (☎ 107 06; info@gran nacamping.se; Hamnen; sites from Skr160, 4-bed cabins from Skr500; ✆ May-Sep) A hit with families, this bustling harbourside campsite features a cafe, a shop and minigolf.

Strandterrassens Vandrarhem (☎ 418 40; www .strandterrassen.se; Hamnen; dm Skr200; P) Right beside Grännastrandens Camping (above), this hostel offers simple, bright, clean rooms in long wooden cabins, as well as a cafe.

Gyllene Uttern (☎ 108 00; info@gylleneuttern.se; s/d from Skr1255/1470, discounted to Skr940/1255; P 🖥) South of town is imposing Gyllene Uttern, an elegant hotel off the E4. Rooms are simple but masterful, and there are good-value packages including a 'Romantic' weekend option.

ourpick Hotell Västanå Slott (☎ 107 00; info@ vastanaslott.se; d from Skr1490; ✆ May-Dec; P) This stately manor house, about 6km south of town, is perfect for regal relaxation. Per Brahe owned it in the 17th century, although today it's decorated according to its 18th-century past, with chandeliers, brooding oil paintings and suits of armour.

Fiket (☎ 100 57; Brahegatan 57) The pick of Gränna's eateries is this time-warp bakery-cafe, complete with retro jukebox, chequered floor and record-clad walls. Tackle tasty grilled baguettes, quiches, salads and drool-worthy pastries, either indoors or on the breezy balcony.

You'll find two supermarkets on nearby Hamnvägen, just off Brahegatan.

VISINGSÖ

STF Vandrarhem Visingsö (☎ 401 91; stfkontakt@ visingso-vandrarhem.se; hostel dm/s/d from Skr170/ 250/400; ✆ May-Oct) This hostel lies in an oak wood around 3km from the ferry pier. The *vandrarhem* (hostel) is scattered across three buildings, with a separate kitchen-shower block.

Visingsö Värdshus (☎ 404 96; mains Skr79-165; ✆ May-Aug) Expect simple meals like grilled chicken, salads, burgers and baked potatoes at this rustic place in the woods. The speciality is fish from Vättern lake.

Restaurant Solbacken (☎ 400 29; lunch Skr72, mains Skr90-150; ✆ May-Aug) Local fish also find themselves on the menu at this lively restaurant, pub and pizzeria at Visingsö harbour. The fish is smoked at the owners' own farm and the kitchen uses mostly organic vegetables.

Getting There & Around

Local bus 121 runs hourly from Jönköping to Gränna (Skr55, one hour). Bus 120 runs several times Monday to Friday from Gränna to the mainline train station in Tranås (Skr55, one hour). Daily Swebus Express destinations include Göteborg, Jönköping, Linköping, Norrköping and Stockholm. Swebus Express services stop 3km outside Gränna. Catch bus 121 into town or walk (30 minutes).

The Gränna–Visingsö **ferry** (☎ 410 25) runs half-hourly in summer (less frequently the rest of the year). Return tickets for foot passengers are Skr50 per adult, and Skr25 for those aged between six and 15 years; a bicycle is Skr30 and a car with up to five people is Skr230.

EKSJÖ

☎ 0381 / pop 16,440

Eskjö is one of the most exquisitely preserved wooden towns in Sweden. The area south of Stora Torget was razed to the ground in a blaze in 1856, paving the way for beautiful neoclassical buildings. To the north of the square, buildings date back to the 17th century. Both sides will have you swooning over the jumble of candy-coloured houses and flower-filled courtyards.

Information

The **tourist office** (☎ 361 70; www.eksjo.se; Norra Storgatan 29; ✆ 8am-8pm Jul–mid-Aug, 10am-6pm Mon-Fri, 10am-2pm Sat rest of year) can arrange English-language guided town **tours** (per person Skr40; ✆ Mon-Sat late Jun-early Aug). The hire of bicycles

(Skr60/225 per day/week) and two-person tandems (Skr90/250) is also available.

Sights

Stroll through the town's delightful streets and yards, especially those north of Stora Torget. Check out the buildings at **Fornminnesgårdens Museum** (☎ 148 39; Arendt Byggmästares gatan 22; admission Skr10; ⌚ 11am-5pm Mon-Sat mid-Jun–mid-Aug); some were built in the 1620s. Exhibits chart the history of the area from the Stone Age to modern times.

Award-winning **Eksjö Museum** (☎ 361 60; Österlånggatan 31; admission Skr40; ⌚ 11am-6pm Mon-Fri, 11am-3pm Sat & Sun Jul & Aug, 1-5pm Tue-Fri, 11am-3pm Sat & Sun Sep-Jun) tells the town's story from the 15th century onwards. The top floor is devoted to local Albert Engström (1869–1940), renowned for his burlesque, satirical cartoons. Eksjö was once known as the 'Hussar Town', and the region's long-standing military connections are also explored at the museum.

Aschanska gården (☎ 361 65; Norra Storgatan 18) is an evocative, 19th-century bourgeois house with guided tours at 1pm and 4pm daily July and August (Skr50), as well as Christmas tours in December.

The **Skurugata Nature Reserve**, 13km northeast of Eksjö, is based around a peculiar 800m-long fissure in the rocks. Its sides tower to 56m, yet in places the fissure is only 7m wide. In times past, the ravine was believed to harbour trolls and thieves. The nearby hill of **Skuruhatt** (337m) offers impressive forest views. You'll need your own transport to get here.

The **Höglandsleden** passes through the reserve; ask the tourist office for details of this walking trail and of the **Höglandstrampen cycle route** (booklets cost Skr40).

Sleeping

Eksjö Camping (☎ 395 00; info@eksjocamping.nu; sites Skr140, 2-/4-bed cabins from Skr300/450) This friendly nook by picturesque Husnäsen lake, about a kilometre east of town, has a restaurant and cafe, plus minigolf and good swimming. There's also a hostel (dorm beds Skr250).

STF Vandrarhem Eksjö (☎ 361 70; vandrarhem@eksjo.se; Österlånggatan 31; dm/s/d from Skr200/300/470) In the heart of the old town, this *vandrarhem* is based in a supremely quaint wooden building, with a gallery running round the upper floor. Reception is at the tourist office.

Stadshotell (☎ 130 20; info@eksjostadshotell.se; Stora Torget; s/d Skr995/1350, discounted all summer to Skr745/990, nonsummer weekends Skr595/890; 💻) The flouncy-looking Stadshotell dominates one edge of the huge 19th-century main square. Bland decor aside, rooms are comfy and roomy, with flatscreen TVs and good-sized bathrooms. There's an elegant restaurant-bar to boot.

our pick **Hotell Vaxblekaregården** (☎ 140 40; www.vaxblekaregarden.com; Arendt Byggmästares gata 8; s/d Skr950/1350, discounted to Skr650/950; 💻) Set in a converted 17th-century wax-bleaching workshop, this boutique number features stylish, pared-back rooms with wooden floorboards, Carl Larsson–inspired wallpaper and wrought-iron bedheads. The lounge-laced backyard hosts barbecues and live music gigs on Saturday evenings from mid-June to mid-August.

Eating & Drinking

Lennarts Konditori (☎ 61 13 90; Stora Torget) With an outdoor terrace and views of dramatic Stora Torget, the place to go for cakes, crêpes and quiche is this old-school *konditori* (bakery-cafe).

Amasian Taste (☎ 100 20; Norra Storgatan 23; lunch Skr75, pizzas Skr69-85, à la carte dishes Skr79-189) 'Amasian' might be pushing it, but this modest East-meets-West joint does a decent, well-priced lunch buffet for those sick of meatballs and mash.

There's both a central **Hemköp supermarket** (Österlånggatan) and a **Systembolaget** (Södra Storgatan 4).

Getting There & Around

The bus and train stations are in the southern part of town. The tiny *länståg* (regional train) runs up to seven times daily to/from Jönköping. Local buses run to Nässjö (Skr42, hourly to 6pm, then less frequently Monday to Friday, three to four at weekends). Swebus Express runs two buses on the Göteborg–Jönköping–Eksjö–Vimmerby–Västervik route on Friday and Sunday.

VÄXJÖ

☎ 0470 / pop 79,560

A venerable old market town, Växjö (pronounced *vak*-choo, with the 'ch' sound as in the Scottish 'loch'), in Kronobergs län, is an important stop for Americans seeking their Swedish roots. In mid-August, **Karl Oscar Days** commemorates the mass 19th-

SOUTHEAST SWEDEN

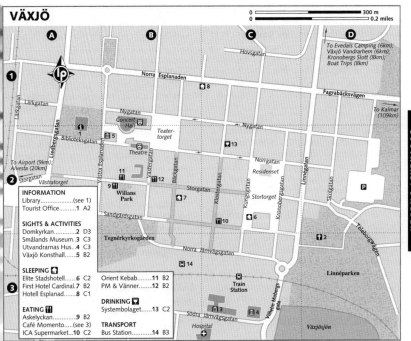

century emigration from the area, and the Swedish-American of the year is chosen. Another town highlight is a fantastic glass collection.

Information

Pedestrianised Storgatan has banks and other services.

Tourist office (☎ 414 10; www.turism.vaxjo.se; Västra Esplanaden 7; ☒ 9.30am-6pm Mon-Fri, 10am-2pm Sat Jun-Aug, 9.30am-4.30pm Mon-Fri rest of year) Shares a building with the library, which offers free internet access.

Sights

Utvandrarnas Hus (Emigrant House; ☎ 201 20; www .utvandrarnashus.se; Vilhelm Mobergs gata 4; adult/under 19yr Skr40/free; ☒ 9am-5pm Tue-Fri, 11am-4pm Sat & Sun May-Aug, 9am-4pm Tue-Fri, 11am-4pm Sat Sep-Apr) boasts engrossing displays on the emigration of over one million Swedes to America (1850–1930). It also includes a replica of Vilhelm Moberg's office and original manuscripts of his famous emigration novels. The centre also houses an excellent research facility (open Tuesday to Friday only, reservations advised) for those

tracing their Swedish ancestors (see boxed text, p34).

Next door, **Smålands Museum** (☎ 70 42 00; www .smalandsmuseum.se; Södra Järnvägsgatan 2; adult/under 19yr Skr40/free; ☒ 10am-5pm Mon-Fri, 11am-5pm Sat & Sun Jun-Aug, closed Mon Sep-May) has a superb exhibition about Sweden's 500-year-old glass industry, with objects spanning medieval goblets to cutting-edge contemporary sculptures. There's also a great cafe.

Opposite the library, **Växjö Konsthall** (☎ 414 75; Västra Esplanaden 10; admission free; ☒ noon-6pm Tue-Fri, noon-4pm Sat & Sun) showcases contemporary work by local and national artists; expect anything from minimalist ceramics to mixed-media installations.

Looking like an ode to Pippi Longstocking, the bizarre **Domkyrkan** (Cathedral; ☒ 9am-5pm) has been struck by lightning and repeatedly ravaged by fire – the latest renovation was in 1995. Waiting inside is a fine 15th-century altar and a whimsical contemporary sculpture by Erik Höglund. Don't miss the Viking rune stone in the eastern wall.

In 1542, Småland rebel Nils Dacke spent Christmas in **Kronobergs Slott**, now a ruin.

The 14th-century castle is on a small island (reached by footbridge) in Helgasjön lake, about 8km north of the town. **Boat trips** (☎ 70 42 00; adult/5-12yr Skr125/50; ⏱ Wed, Sat & Sun Jun-early Sep) on Sweden's oldest steamship, *Thor*, leave from below the ruins. Take bus 1B from town. Inquire at the tourist office about guided summer **walking tours** (⏱ 5.30pm Tue & Thu) of town.

Sleeping

Evedals Camping (☎ 630 34; evedals.camping@telia .com; Evedalsvägen; sites Skr190, 4-/5-bed cabins Skr750/900) Evedal is a huge lakeside recreation area, 6km north of the centre. Perks include beaches, swimming, canoeing and boating (Skr175/250 per half-/full day) on Helga lake. In addition, there are two restaurants nearby: Restaurang Brunnen and the more upmarket Evedals Värdshus.

Växjö Vandrarhem (☎ 630 70; www.vaxjovandrarhem .nu; dm from Skr200; ℗ ▣) Also at Evedal, this former spa hotel dates from the late 18th century. All rooms have washbasins, and there's a big kitchen, a laundry and a wonderful lounge in the attic. It's well loved, so book early. Take bus 1C from town.

Elite Stadshotellet (☎ 134 00; info@vaxjo.elite.se; Kungsgatan 6; s Skr550-1450, d Skr650-1850; ℗ ▣) At the time of research, new rooms were being built and bathrooms were getting a make-over at this look-at-me 19th-century building. Single rooms aren't particularly roomy but all are smart and comfortable, and there's a slinky glassed-in restaurant-bar for urbane sipping and supping.

Hotell Esplanad (☎ 225 80; www.hotellesplanad .com; Norra Esplanaden 21A; s/d Skr850/950, discounted to Skr550/720; ℗ ▣) One of the cheapest central options is the Esplanad, it has unfussy yet bright and adequate rooms. There are a few even cheaper rooms with corridor bathrooms.

First Hotel Cardinal (☎ 72 28 00; cardinal@first hotels.se; Bäckgatan 10; s Skr956-1296, d Skr1396-1696, s/ d discounted to Skr696/896; ℗ ▣) A jump up in quality, the central Cardinal offers simple, stylish rooms with Persian rugs and the odd antique touch. There's also a small fitness centre, a bar and a restaurant serving modern Nordic nosh.

Eating & Drinking

Askelyckan (☎ 123 11; Storgatan 25; ⏱ closed Sun) This this too-cute bakery-cafe is a top lunch spot, with sandwiches, baguettes, great pastries and a large shady courtyard.

Orient Kebab (☎ 120 32; Storgatan 28; meals around Skr55-75; ⏱ to 9pm) Don't let the lurid plastic Arabian Nights exterior put you off; this no-frills joint serves satisfying kebabs, falafel, burgers and pizzas to take away.

Café Momento (☎ 391 29; meals around Skr70) Smålands Museum's in-house cafe serves brilliant hot and cold gourmet sandwiches, pies, salads, soup, spuds and cakes. In summer, nibble blissfully in the cute courtyard.

PM & Vänner (☎ 70 04 44; Storgatan 24; mains Skr159-259; ⏱ closed Sun) Stylish and sexy, PM & Vänner serves up new-school Swedish flavours with global twists. Local produce sparkles in dishes like lumpsucker roe with yoghurt jelly, apple-and citrus foam, oatmeal crunch and potatoes, while the occasional DJ sets keep fashionable foodies humming.

There's an **ICA supermarket** (cnr Klostergatan & Sandgärdsgatan; ⏱ to 8pm Mon-Fri, to 5pm Sat & Sun) and **Systembolaget** (Klostergatan 14).

Getting There & Away

Småland Airport (☎ 75 85 00; www.smalandairport.se) is 9km northwest of Växjö. **SAS** (☎ 0770-72 77 27; www.flysas.com) has direct flights to Stockholm-Arlanda; **Fly Smaland** (☎ 0771-71 72 00; www.fly smaland.com) to Stockholm Bromma, Berlin and Vilnius; and **Ryanair** (☎ 0900-202 02 40; www.ryan air.com) to Düsseldorf Weeze. An airport bus (Flygbussen) connects with flights (Skr20), otherwise take a **taxi** (☎ 135 00).

Länstrafiken Kronoberg (☎ 0771-76 70 76; www .lanstrafikenkron.se, in Swedish) runs the regional bus network, with daily buses to Halmstad, Jönköping and Kosta. Long-distance buses depart beside the train station. **Svenska Buss** (☎ 0771-67 67 67; www.svenskabuss.se, in Swedish) runs one or two services daily to Eksjö (Skr210, 1½ hours), Linköping (Skr290, 3¼ hours) and Stockholm (Skr390, 6½ hours).

Växjö is served by SJ trains running roughly hourly between Alvesta (on the main north–south line; Skr37 to Skr55, 15 minutes) and Kalmar (Skr118, 1¼ hours). A few trains run daily directly to Karlskrona (Skr118, 1½ hours), Malmö (Skr214, two hours) and Göteborg (Skr240, 3¼ hours).

KALMAR

☎ 0480 / pop 61,530

Not only is Kalmar dashing, it claims one of Sweden's most spectacular castles, with an interior even more perfect than its turreted outside. Other local assets include Sweden's

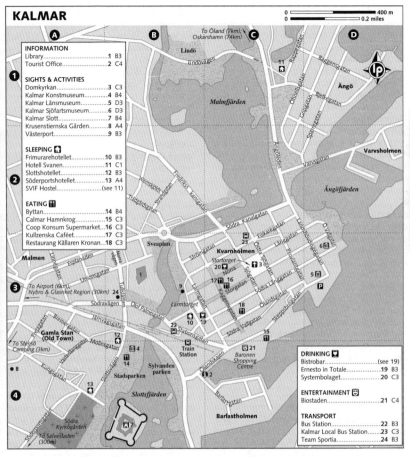

KALMAR

INFORMATION
Library...............................1 B3
Tourist Office......................2 C4

SIGHTS & ACTIVITIES
Domkyrkan.........................3 C3
Kalmar Konstmuseum............4 B4
Kalmar Länsmuseum.............5 D3
Kalmar Sjöfartsmuseum.........6 D3
Kalmar Slott........................7 B4
Krusenstiernska Gården.........8 A4
Västerport..........................9 B3

SLEEPING
Frimurarehotellet................10 B3
Hotell Svanen.....................11 C1
Slottshotellet......................12 B3
Söderportshotellet...............13 A4
SVIF Hostel.....................(see 11)

EATING
Byttan...............................14 B4
Calmar Hamnkrog...............15 C3
Coop Konsum Supermarket...16 C3
Kullzenska Caféet................17 C3
Restaurang Källaren Kronan..18 C3

DRINKING
Bistrobar.......................(see 19)
Ernesto in Totale.................19 B3
Systembolaget....................20 C3

ENTERTAINMENT
Biostaden...........................21 C4

TRANSPORT
Bus Station.........................22 B3
Kalmar Local Bus Station.......23 C3
Team Sportia......................24 B3

largest gold hoard, from the 17th-century ship *Kronan* and the story-book cobbled streets of Gamla Stan (Old Town) to the west of Slottshotellet.

The short-lived Kalmar Union of 1397, when the crowns of Sweden, Denmark and Norway became one, was agreed to at the castle.

Information
You'll find banks and other services on Storgatan.

Library (☎ 45 06 30; Tullslätten 4; closed Sun May-Aug) Offers free internet access. Bring ID.

Tourist office (☎ 41 77 00; www.kalmar.se/turism; Ölandskajen 9; 9am-9pm Mon-Fri, 10am-5pm Sat & Sun late Jun-mid-Aug; 9am-7pm Mon-Fri, 10am-4pm

Sat rest of Jun & Aug; 9am-5pm Mon-Fri, 10am-4pm Sat, 10am-1pm Sun early-mid-Sep; 9am-5pm Mon-Fri, 10am-1pm May & rest of Sep; 9am-5pm Mon-Fri Oct-Apr) Handy for information on the region.

Sights
KALMAR SLOTT
Fairy-tale turrets, a drawbridge, a foul dungeon and secret passages…yes, **Kalmar Slott** (☎ 45 14 90; adult/5-16yr Skr80/20; 10am-6pm Jul; 10am-5pm Aug;10am-4pm May, Jun & Sep; 11am-3.30pm Sat & Sun Apr & Oct; 11am-3.30pm 2nd weekend of month Nov-Mar) has everything that a proper castle should. This powerful Renaissance building was once the most important in Sweden, and it's fortified accordingly. It also boasts one of the best-preserved interiors from the period.

King Erik's chamber is a real scene-stealer. Erik's rivalry with his brother Johan caused him to install a secret passage in the loo! There's also a superb suspended ceiling in the **Golden Hall**; eye-boggling wall-to-wall and floor-to-ceiling marquetry in the **Chequered Hall**; an elaborate **bed**, stolen as war booty then carefully vandalised so that no Danish ghosts could haunt it; and a delightful **chapel**, one of Sweden's Most Wanted for weddings.

For more information, join one of the **guided tours** (in English at 2.30pm late Jun, also 11.30am & 1.30pm Jul–mid-Aug, 11.30am only mid-Aug–early Sep), included in the admission price. There are also children's activities here in summer.

KALMAR LÄNSMUSEUM

The highlight of this fine **museum** (☎ 45 13 00; www.kalmarlansmuseum.se; Skeppsbrogatan; adult/under 18yr Skr50/free; 🕑 10am-6pm mid-Jun–mid-Aug, 10am-4pm Mon-Fri, 11am-4pm Sat & Sun mid-Aug–mid-Jun), in an old steam mill by the harbour, are finds from the 17th-century flagship *Kronan*. The ship exploded and sank just before a battle in 1676, with the loss of almost 800 men. It was rediscovered in 1980, and over 22,000 wonderfully preserved items have been excavated so far, including a spectacular gold hoard, clothing and musical instruments.

OTHER SIGHTS

Aft and slightly to port of the county museum, **Kalmar Sjöfartsmuseum** (☎ 158 75; Södra Långgatan 81; adult/7-12yr Skr30/10; 🕑 11am-4pm mid-Jun–mid-Sep, noon-4pm Sun mid-Sep–mid-Jun) houses an eccentric maritime collection, with bottled ships, foghorns and things made out of knots and armadillos.

Home to a spectacular pulpit, the baroque **Domkyrkan** (Cathedral; Stortorget) was designed by Tessin, King Karl X Gustav's favourite architect. For the low-down, plug into one of the audiophones by the main door.

Krusenstiernska Gården (☎ 41 15 52; Stora Dammgatan 11; adult/child Skr25/7; 🕑 house tours hourly 1-3pm Mon-Fri Jun-Aug; garden 11am-6pm Mon-Fri, noon-5pm Sat & Sun Jun & Aug, 11am-6pm Mon-Fri, noon-5pm Sun Jul, 11am-5pm Mon-Fri, noon-5pm May, 11am-5pm Mon-Fri Sep) is a stuck-in-time 19th-century middle-class home, around 500m from the castle's entrance. Tours of the house are on the hour, but entry to the beautiful gardens and cafe is free.

The striking **Kalmar Konstmuseum** (☎ 42 62 82; www.kalmarkonstmuseum.se; Stadsparken; adult/under 20yr Skr40/free; 🕑 11am-5pm, to 8pm Wed), in the park near the castle, dishes out brilliant temporary exhibitions featuring local and global art-scene 'It' kids.

Västerport was the original point of entry into the city. Nowadays you can watch glass-blowing and pottery-making at the studios here, and buy the results.

Sleeping

Stensö Camping (☎ 888 03; www.stensocamping.se; Stensövägen; sites/cabins Skr170/500; 🕑 mid-Mar–Sep; 🖳) There are family-friendly facilities galore at this campsite, 3km southwest of town, including swimming; boat, canoe and bicycle rental; a restaurant; and minigolf. Buses 401 and 411 stop around 600m away.

Hotell Svanen (☎ 255 60; www.hotellsvanen.se; Rappegatan 1; dm Skr195, s/d from Skr540/680; 🅿 🖳) This 'low-price hotel' is an excellent choice, with simple, pleasing rooms with cable TV and private toilets. The SVIF hostel (see p319) is part of the hotel, sharing the all-day reception, kitchen, drinks machines and sauna. Svanen is on the island of Ängö, about 1km north of town; walk, or take bus 402.

Söderportshotellet (☎ 125 01; Slottsvägen 1; s/d Skr550/735; 🕑 mid-Jun–mid-Aug) Right outside the castle, Söderportshotellet offers summertime accommodation in student digs. Rooms are modest yellow-washed affairs; some on the upper floor have castle views. There's a super cafe-restaurant downstairs with regular blues and jazz gigs.

ourpick Slottshotellet (☎ 882 60; www.slottshotellet.se; Slottsvägen 7; s Skr1190-1390, discounted to Skr1090-1190, d Skr1590-1790, discounted to Skr1390-1590; 🅿 🖳) Kalmar's top pick is this wonderfully romantic, cosy hotel, based in four buildings in a gorgeous green setting near the castle. Most rooms have antique furnishings and some even feature vintage Swedish tile stoves. Staff are wonderful and there's an on-site summer restaurant.

Frimurarehotellet (☎ 152 30; www.frimurare hotellet.com; Larmtorget 2; s/d Skr1240/1460, discounted to Skr820/995; 🖳) In the heart of the action, this 19th-century building contains spacious, personable rooms with polished wooden floors. The plant-filled lounge comes with complimentary tea, coffee and biscuits, while one cheaper room (about Skr200 less) has a hallway shower.

Eating & Drinking

A good area for upmarket dining is the harbour; the view of huge timber yards and cranes is industrial, but you don't want showy sailing boats *all* the time…

Kullzenska Caféet (☎ 288 82; 1st fl, Kaggensgatan 26; snacks from Skr30) The pick of the town's cafes, this gorgeous maze of genteel 19th-century rooms features original tiled stoves and furniture. There's a range of sandwiches and cakes (try the yummy fruit crumbles).

Bistrobar (☎ 200 50; Larmtorget 4; pizzas Skr94-99, mains Skr169-189) The glam new kid in town, this restaurant-bar combo has an enviable location on a fountain-studded square. While the chocolate wicker lounges and Café del Mar tunes make for a perfect vino session, ditch the overpriced, underwhelming mains for the more satisfying pizzas.

Byttan (☎ 163 60; Stadsparken; lunch buffet Skr95, dinner mains Skr89-189) Set in the park by the castle, sassy resto-bar Byttan combines a chi-chi terrace with velour lounges and a crackling fire inside. The bistro-style menu ranges from grilled meats to salads, with a competent cocktail list to sex things up.

Calmar Hamnkrog (☎ 41 10 20; Skeppsbrogatan 30; mains Skr130-245; ⏱ lunch Mon-Fri, dinner Mon-Sat) Harbourside Hamnkrog serves the best food in town, its small but well-formed menu combining Swedish favourites and continental innovation.

Restaurang Källaren Kronan (☎ 41 14 00; Ölandsgatan 7; mains Skr135-275; ⏱ closed Mon) Six cellars have been transformed into a high-calibre experience, where a select evening menu is served under a cosy vaulted ceiling. There's even a 17th century–inspired menu, with mains like wild boar fillet with apple and plum compote.

Ernesto in Totale (☎ 200 50; Larmtorget 4; mains Skr148-248; ⏱ lunch Sat & Sun, dinner Mon-Sun) Run by a real-deal Neapolitan, this Italian cafe, restaurant and bar also attracts scores of people with its baristi, extensive menu (including Neapolitan-style pizzas), and well-mixed drinks.

Both the **Coop Konsum supermarket** (Storgatan 24) and **Systembolaget** (Norra Långgatan 23) are centrally located.

Entertainment

The **Biostaden** (☎ 122 44; tickets Skr90) cinema is in the Baronen shopping centre on Skeppsbrogatan.

Getting There & Around

The **airport** (☎ 45 90 00; www.kalmarairport.se) is 6km west of town. **SAS** (☎ 0770-72 77 27) flies several times daily to Stockholm Arlanda, while **Kalmarflyg** (www.kalmarflyg.se, in Swedish) flies to Stockholm Bromma. The Flygbuss airport bus (Skr40) provides connections to central Kalmar.

All regional and long-distance buses depart from the train station; local town buses have their own station on Östra Sjögatan. Regional buses are run by **Kalmar Länstrafik** (☎ 0491-76 12 00; www.klt.se, in Swedish), including buses to Öland.

Roughly three **Swebus Express** (☎ 0771-21 82 18; www.swebusexpress.com) services daily run north to Västervik (Skr185, two hours), Norrköping (Skr224, four hours) and Stockholm (Skr224, 6½ hours); and one to three services daily run south to Karlskrona (Skr82, 1¼ hours), Karlshamn (Skr110, two hours), Kristianstad (Skr182, three hours), Lund (Skr247, four hours) and Malmö (Skr247, 4½ hours).

Svenska Buss (☎ 0771-67 67 67; www.svenskabuss.se, in Swedish) has four services per week on the same route; journey times and prices are similar. **Silverlinjen** (☎ 0485-261 11; www.silverlinjen.se, in Swedish) runs one to three daily direct buses from Öland to Stockholm (Skr280), calling at Kalmar; reservations are essential.

SJ trains run every hour or two between Kalmar and Alvesta (Skr151 to Skr164, 1¼ hours), where you can connect with the main Stockholm–Malmö line and with trains to Göteborg. Trains run to Linköping up to nine times daily (Skr238, three hours), also with connections to Stockholm.

For bicycle hire (summer only), contact **Team Sportia** (☎ 212 44; Södravägen 2; per day/week Skr100/400; ⏱ Mon-Sat). **Taxi Kalmar** (☎ 44 44 44) can help you get around town.

GLASRIKET

With its hypnotic glassblowing workshops, the **'Kingdom of Crystal'** (www.glasriket.se) is Sweden's third-biggest drawcard after Stockholm and Göteborg. There are at least 11 glass factories (look for *glasbruk* signs), most with long histories: Kosta, for example, was founded in 1742. The region is also immensely popular with Americans tracing their ancestors, many of whom emigrated from this area at the end of the 19th century.

The glassworks have similar opening hours, usually 10am to 6pm Monday to

---

HERRING À LA GLASSWORKS

Glassworks were once more than just a workplace – they were a community hub and an after-hours gathering spot for workers, hunters and vagrants. They were the place to go to keep warm on long winter evenings, tell stories, make music and enjoy the company of others. Naturally, good grub and drink were a vital part of these gatherings – strong *aquavit* (a potent, vodka-like spirit) was shared and food was cooked using the furnaces and cooling ovens. Today visitors to Glasriket can partake in *hyttsill* parties, schmoozing at long tables and munching on trad-style dishes like salted herring, smoked sausage and the regional speciality *ostkaka* (cheesecake).

Parties cost Skr325 (under 10s are free), and include beer, soft drinks and coffee (*aquavit* costs extra). They're held almost daily from June to August at the larger glassworks of Kosta, Målerås and Orrefors. Contact the regional tourist offices or the glassworks themselves to book a spot.

Friday, 10am to 4pm Saturday and noon to 4pm Sunday. Expert glass designers produce some extraordinary avant-garde pieces, often with a good dollop of Swedish wit involved. Factory outlets have substantial discounts on seconds (around 30% to 40% off), and larger places can arrange shipping to your home country.

There's a **Glasriket Pass** (Skr95), allowing free admission into 'hot shops' and museums, and discounts on purchases and *hyttsill* parties (see boxed text, above); but unless you're intending to go completely glass crazy, it doesn't really add up.

Most of Glasriket is in Kalmar län, with some in Kronobergs län; all parts are covered in this section.

Getting There & Around

Apart from the main routes, bus services around the area are practically nonexistent. The easiest way to explore is with your own transport (beware of elk). Bicycle tours on the unsurfaced country roads are excellent; there are plenty of hostels, and you can camp almost anywhere except near the military area on the Kosta–Orrefors road.

Kalmar Länstrafik's bus 139 runs from mid-June to mid-August only and calls at a few of the glass factories. The service operates four times per day on weekdays, once on Saturday, and runs from Nybro to Orrefors and Målerås. Year-round bus services connect Nybro and Orrefors (up to nine weekdays), and Kosta is served by regular bus 218 from Växjö (two or three daily).

Buses and trains run from Emmaboda to Nybro and Kalmar (roughly hourly); trains also run to Karlskrona, Växjö and Alvesta, from where there are direct services to Göteborg and Stockholm.

Nybro

☎ 0481 / pop 19,640

The biggest town in Glasriket, Nybro makes a good base for exploration. It was once a centre for hand-blown light bulbs(!), and still has two glassworks on its doorstep. Nybro's **tourist office** (☎ 450 85; www.nybro.se, in Swedish; Stadshusplan; 10am-6pm Mon-Fri, 10am-4pm Sat mid-Jun–Aug, 10am-5pm Mon-Fri Sep–mid-Jun) is inside the town hall.

Of the two glassworks, 130-year-old **Pukeberg** (☎ 800 29; www.pukeberg.se; Pukebergarnas väg), just southeast of the centre, is perhaps more interesting for its quaint setting. **Nybro** (☎ 428 81; Herkulesgatan; www.nybro-glasbruk.se) is smaller and laced with quirky items (think Elvis Presley glass platters).

There's a superior homestead museum **Madesjö Hembygdsgård** (☎ 179 35; adult/child Skr30/10; 10am-5pm Mon-Fri, 11am-5pm Sat & Sun mid-May–mid-Sep), about 2.5km west of town. Housed inside the 200m-long *kyrkstallarna* (former church stables), it contains an admirable collection, with cannonballs, clothing, coffins, carpenters tools, a classroom and a fantastic (ice-)cycle – and they're just the things beginning with 'C'.

Joelskogens Camping (☎ 450 86; www.joelskogens camping.se; Grönvägen 51; site Skr130; May–mid-Sep) Campers should head for this little lakeside ground just out of the centre, with basic facilities (a kitchen, laundry and shop) and a small beach.

The local STF hostel, **Nybro Lågprishotell & Vandrarhem** (☎ 109 32; Vasagatan 22; dm Skr225, hotel s/d Skr490/790; P), near Pukeberg, is clean and comfortable, with a kitchen on each floor as well as a sauna. More expensive 'hotel' rooms have cable TV, nonbunk beds and private showers and toilets. You can also rent bicycles.

The town's other option, **Stora Hotellet** (☎ 519 38; info@storahotellet.se; Mellangatan 11; s/d Skr1090/1350, discounted to Skr795/990), is this chintzy yet agreeable central hotel, by the tourist office. It contains Scandinavia's largest work of art, an impressive 70-sq-metre fresco of Nybro's industrial history. The restaurant is the best choice in town for a feed (meals Skr95 to Skr245).

SJ trains between Alvesta and Kalmar stop here every hour or two. Regional bus 131 runs to/from Kalmar.

Orrefors
☎ 0481

Established in 1898, **Orrefors** (☎ 341 95; www .orrefors.se; ☉ year-round) is arguably the most famous of Sweden's glassworks. The huge site is home to a factory with glass-blowing demonstrations, plus a large shop with a shipping service. The ubersleek museum-gallery showcases a range of stunning glassworks spanning 1910 to the present day, as well housing a stylish bar-cum-cafe **Kristallbaren** (sandwiches Skr60).

If you need a lie-down after all the glass-buying, **Vandrarhem Orrefors** (☎ 300 20; Silversparregatan 14; dm/s/d from Skr170/320/390; ☉ May-Sep) is an excellent hostel located conveniently near the factory. Quaint red houses surround a grassy garden, and the peaceful rooms have proper beds. Breakfast is available on request.

In a recently renovated 19th-century cottage opposite the hostel, **Orrefors Bed & Breakfast** (☎ 301 30, www.bnb.nu; Silversparregatan 17; s/d Skr520/590, small/large apt with bathroom Skr920/1620; ☉ Jun-Aug) has simple yet comfortable rooms with shared facilities. The friendly owners run short summer courses in glass-blowing (three hours, Skr300) at the nearby **Riksglasskolan** (National School of Glass; ☎ 302 64; www.riksglasskolan.se; Simon Gates väg).

In the factory grounds, **Orrefors Värdshus** (☎ 300 59; meals around Skr95; ☉ 10.30am-4pm Mon-Fri, noon-4pm Sat & Sun) is an inn that serves good lunches.

Gullaskruv & Målerås
☎ 0481

Don't miss the glassworks at Gullaskruv, about 6km northwest of Orrefors. Here, Uruguayan-born artist **Carlos R Pebaqué** (☎ 321 17; www.carlosartglass.com) creates extraordinary vases in his one glass oven.

The large and popular **Mats Jonasson factory** (☎ 314 00; www.matsjonasson.com), 8km further northwest in Målerås, sells somewhat kitsch engraved glass-animal designs from around Skr159. There's also a restaurant for a post-shopping refuel.

A kilometre or so southeast of Gullaskruv, **Hälleberga Bed & Breakfast** (☎ 320 21; www.halle berga.se, in Swedish; Hälleberga 108; per adult/7-12yr/under 7yr Skr350/250/100; ℗), a youth hostel-turned-B&B, boasts a tranquil rustic setting. Rooms all have washbasins, and linen and breakfast are included in the price.

Handy for the Mats Jonasson glassworks, **Malerås Vandrarhem** (☎ 311 75; frank.fender@telia.com; Lindvägen 5, Målerås; hostel beds per person Skr150; ℗), an SVIF hostel, is another cheap, simple option.

For coffee and buns, try **Café Konditori** (☎ 310 44; Lindvägen 1, Målerås; ☉ closed Sun) attached to Målerås' bakery.

Kosta
☎ 0478

Kosta is where Glasriket started in 1742. Today the **Kosta Boda** (☎ 503 00; www.kostaboda.se) complex pulls in coach-loads of visitors, who raid the vast discount outlets (there's even discounted designer threads these days). Funnily Sweden even manages to make its tourist traps pleasant places. The Kosta Boda exhibition gallery (Skr30) contains some inspired creations. There are plenty of glass-blowing demos in the old factory quarters, and some great cafes and restaurants, too.

For a close encounter with a beautiful bandy-legged elk, head for **Grönåsens Älgpark** (☎ /fax 507 70; www.moosepark.net; ☉ 10am-6pm Apr–mid-Sep, 10am-5pm mid-Sep–Oct), Sweden's biggest elk park, located 3km west of town towards Orrefors. You can admire these

---

A CULTURAL BLOW-OUT

Feel inspired by Glasriket's top designers? If so, have a go at **glass-blowing** (Skr150; ☉ mid-Jun–mid-Aug) yourself. Several hotshots – Orrefors, Kosta, Pukeberg and Johansfors – risk litigation by allowing you to blow, shape and 'open out' the treacly molten glass. It's great fun, and the endearingly misshapen result will be a source of pride for years to come. Your masterpiece has to cool for two hours before you can take it away.

gentle creatures on a 1.3km walk in the forested enclosure (Skr40). Ironically, you can also buy elk sausages to roast on the outdoor barbecue or purchase an elk-skin baseball cap. And, talking of horror, don't miss the display in the building behind the shop: you'll drive 50% slower after you've seen the crumpled metal and lolling tongue…

There are great facilities at **Kosta Bad & Camping** (☎ 505 17; info@glasriketkosta.se; sites Skr145, cabins from Skr425; ☼ Apr–Oct; ☒), on the edge of Kosta village, including a sauna, kids' pool and a shop.

Across from the Kosta Boda factory, sleek **Kosta Boda Art Hotel** (☎ 500 06; www.kostahotell.se; Stora vägen 75; s/d from Skr1095/1695; ℗ ☐) is set to open in 2009. Made with 100 tons of glass, in-house assets will include a designer glass bar and pool, a restaurant and spa treatments. The 105 rooms themselves will feature glasswork and textiles by Kosta Boda artists.

Peckish punters should head for the buzzing **Café Kosta** (☎ 502 60) inside the factory's outlet store, with tasty quiches and grilled panini for around Skr55.

OSKARSHAMN
☎ 0491 / pop 26,300

Oskarshamn is useful for its regular boat connections with Gotland, with a few sights to help kill time.

The **tourist office** (☎ 881 88; www.oskarshamn.se; Hantverksgatan 18; ☼ 9am-6pm Mon-Fri, 10am-3pm Sat & Sun Jun-late Aug, 9.30am-4.30pm Mon-Fri late Aug-May) is in Kulturhuset, along with the library, which has free internet access. There are ATM machines at the Flanaden shopping centre.

Sights
Upstairs in Kulturhuset, **Döderhultarmuseet** (☎ 880 40; ☼ 10am-6pm Mon-Fri & 11am-4pm Sat & Sun Jun–mid-Aug, noon-4pm Tue-Fri, 10am-2pm Sat mid-Aug–May) features around 200 works by homegrown artist Axel Petersson 'Döderhultarn' (1868–1925), who captured local characters and occasions in vigorous and funny wood carvings. Also upstairs, with the same opening hours, **Sjöfartsmuséet** (☎ 880 45) showcases local maritime exhibits.

One admission price (adult/under 20 years Skr40/free) covers entry to both museums.

BLÅ JUNGFRUN NATIONAL PARK
Blå Jungfrun (Blue Maiden), a 1km-long granite island, is known as the 'Witches'

Mountain' because, according to tradition, this is where they gather every Easter to meet the devil. The island is a nature reserve with fantastic scenery, gnarled trees, blue hares and bird life, and the curious stone maze, **Trojeborg**.

Between mid-June and August a local **launch** (adult/7-15yr Skr200/100) departs up to five times weekly (usually *not* Monday and Tuesday) from Brädholmskajen, the quay at the head of the harbour in Oskarshamn, allowing passengers 3½ hours to explore the island. Contact the tourist office for bookings.

Sleeping & Eating
Gunnarsö Camping (☎ 882 00; Östersjövägen; sites low/high season Skr140/160; ☼ May–mid-Sep; ☒) Located 3km southeast of town, this has seaside sites, a heated pool, a restaurant and other family campsite necessaries. However, public transport connections are poor.

Vandrarhemmet Oscar (☎ 158 00; info@forum oskarshamn.com; Södra Långgatan 15-17; hostel dm/s/d Skr205/305/410, hotel s/d Skr780/1050, discounted to Skr650/800; ℗ ☐) This shiny hotel-hostel hybrid is a brilliant budget option. Rooms have TV, fans and bathrooms – only the kitchen for self-caterers gives it away as a hostel. It's conveniently placed for travellers, just opposite the bus station.

There are no outstanding eateries, but there are a couple of pleasant ones.

Coffeehouse Kronan (☎ 143 80; Flanaden 6; snacks from Skr45) A great lunch stop, with filled baguettes and panini, plus tasty cakes, good coffee and outdoor summer seating.

Cecil Kinesiska Restaurang (☎ 187 50; Lilla Torget; dishes Skr98-169) Peddles Chinese chow and the odd Swedish and French dish.

Steakhouse Oscar (☎ 772 28; Lilla Torget; lunch Skr75, mains Skr109-189) Across the square, this place serves steaks and Swedish fare, with a couple of vegetarian options.

There's a Hemköp supermarket nearby at the Flanaden shopping centre.

Getting There & Away
Oskarshamn Airport (☎ 332 00) is 12km north of town and **Skyways** (☎ 0771-95 95 00; www .skyways.se) flies direct to Stockholm Arlanda three times daily Monday to Wednesday, and twice daily Thursday and Friday. An extra flight each weekday flies to Stockholm Arlanda via Linköping.

Long-distance bus services stop at the very central bus station. Regional bus services run up to six times daily from Oskarshamn to Kalmar (Skr75, 1½ hours) and Västervik (Skr67, one hour).

Swebus Express has three daily buses between Stockholm and Kalmar, calling in at Oskarshamn. The closest train station is in Berga, 25km west of town. Here, regional trains run from Linköping and Nässjö. Local buses connect Berga and Oskarshamn.

Boats to Visby depart from the Gotland Ferry Terminal near the now-disused train station, daily in winter and twice daily in summer. Boats to Öland depart from the ferry terminal off Skeppsbron; see p147 for more information.

VÄSTERVIK
☎ 0490 / pop 36,460

Västervik is a popular coastal summer resort, with cute cobbled streets, buzzing nightlife, sandy beaches just east of town, and 5000 islands on the doorstep. Harried by the Danes in its early years, it bloomed into a major shipbuilding centre between the 17th and

19th centuries. Famous sons include former tennis player Stefan Edberg and ABBA's Björn Ulvaeus. Björn often returns in mid-July for **VisFestivalen**, Västervik's famous folk-song festival.

In a striking old art nouveau bathhouse, the **tourist office** (☎ 889 00; www.vastervik.se/turist; Strömsholmen; ☻ 10am-6pm Mon-Fri, 10am-2pm Sat May-late Jun, 10am-7pm Mon-Fri, 10am-5pm Sat & Sun late Jun-Aug, 10am-5pm Mon-Fri Sep-Apr) is located on an islet linked by road to the town centre. The **library** (☎ 887 77; Spötorget; ☻ Mon-Fri summer, also Sat winter) has free internet access.

Sights & Activities

Ask the tourist office for its town-walking brochure, which leads you round the best of Västervik's beautiful old buildings. **St Petri Kyrka** is a dramatic mass of spires and buttresses, while the older, calmer **St Gertruds Kyrkan** (Västra Kyrkogatan) dates from 1433 and has taken lightning strikes and riots in its stride.

Nearby, **Aspagården** (Västra Kyrkogatan 9), dating from the 17th century, is the oldest wooden house in town. Other abodes from the 1740s can be seen at picture-perfect **Båtmansstugorna** (Båtmansgatan) – former ferrymen's cottages.

Displays at **Västerviks Museum** (☎ 211 77; admission Skr20; ⌚ 11am-4pm Mon-Fri, 1-4pm Sat & Sun Jun-Aug, 11am-4pm Tue-Fri, 1-4pm Sun Sep-May), just north of the tourist office, cover the town's history. You'll also find **Unos Torn** here, an 18m-high lookout tower with archipelago views.

Various **archipelago tours** (adult Skr100-150) depart from Skeppsbron daily from mid-June to the end of August. Contact the tourist office for information and tickets, or buy tickets directly at the Skärgårdsterminalen pier kiosk.

Sleeping

The town bursts at the seams in summer, so book your accommodation ahead.

Lysingsbadets (☎ 889 20; lysingsbadet@vastervik .se; sites low/high season Skr150/270, hostel beds per person Skr135/170, cabins from Skr195/405; P ⬛) This huge, five-star 'holiday village' by the sea (2.5km southeast of town) features a restaurant, golf, a swimming pool, beaches, and boat, bicycle and kayak hire, as well as extra activities like pony trekking. The hostel opens June to August, but cabins and hotel rooms are available year-round. Take local bus 5 (Skr15).

Båtmansstugor (☎ 317 67, 194 03; Strömsgatan 42; cottages per person Skr300) This delightful collection of 18th-century fishermen's cottages sits in an atmospheric old part of town. Most sleep four and have their own kitchen, though bathrooms are shared.

Västerviks Stadshotell (☎ 820 00; info@stadshotellet .nu; Storgatan 3; s/d Skr1340/1820, discounted to Skr880/1180; P ⬛) Central Stadshotell flaunts modern, comfortable rooms, a sauna, Jacuzzi and gym, private parking (Skr90 per day), a swanky restaurant-bar and a nightclub that seriously kicks on Saturday night.

Eating & Drinking

Restaurang Smugglaren (☎ 213 22; Smugglaregränd 1; mains Skr190-255; ⌚ from 6pm Mon-Sat) In a cosy wooden building tucked down an alley off Strandvägen, Smugglaren serves up fine hearty grub like nettle soup with quail eggs and wild boar fillet with mushroom risotto. Model ships, paraffin lamps and the odd elk head crank up the eccentricity.

Waterside Fiskaretorget is a hive of activity, studded with several restaurant-bars that have popular summer terraces. **Harry's** (☎ 173 00) and the **Brig** (☎ 342 00) are on the square; both open noon to late daily (until 2am or 3am Friday

and Saturday) in summer, shorter hours during winter. They offer low-fuss bar grub, plus à la carte options for finer dining.

Västervik's fast-food speciality is French fries, mashed potato and shrimp salad (Skr25); look out for it at stands along the waterside. The Systembolaget is on Kvarngatan.

Getting There & Away

Long-distance buses stop outside the train station, at the eastern edge of the town centre. Trains run between Västervik and Linköping up to 10 times daily (Skr147, 1¾ hours). Daily bus services run roughly every hour to 90 minutes to Vimmerby (Skr58, one hour), and every two hours to Oskarshamn (Skr67, one hour) and Kalmar (Skr115, 2¾ hours).

Svenska Buss runs to Stockholm, Kalmar, Karlskrona and Malmö four times per week. On Friday and Sunday, Swebus Express runs one bus each way on its Västervik–Vimmerby–Eksjö–Jönköping–Göteborg route.

VIMMERBY

☎ 0492 / pop 15,600

Vimmerby is the birthplace of Astrid Lindgren, and home to one of Sweden's favourite drawcards – a theme park based on the Pippi Longstocking books. Almost everything in town revolves around the strongest girl in the world – there's little escape!

Facing Stora Torget is Vimmerby's helpful **tourist office** (☎ 310 10; www.vimmerbyturistbyra.se; Rådhuset 1, Stångågatan 29; ⌚ 9am-5.30pm Mon-Fri, 9am-2pm Sat mid-May–early Jun; 9am-6pm Mon-Fri, 9am-2pm Sat & Sun to late Jun & mid-Aug–late Aug; 9am-8pm late Jun-early Aug; 9am-5pm Mon-Fri Sep–mid-May). If you don't know whether Mr Nilsson is a horse or a monkey, **Vimmerby Bokhandeln** (☎ 123 10; Stora Torget 8) sells Pippi books in English.

Sights & Activities

Young children and Pippi Longstocking aficionados shouldn't miss **Astrid Lindgrens Värld** (☎ 798 00; www.alv.se; mid-May–early Jun adult/3-12yr/family Skr165/125/520, early Jun-Aug Skr275/165/795; ⌚ 10am-5pm mid-May–early Jun, to 6pm early Jun-Aug), on the northern edge of town. Actresses dressed as Pippi (complete with gravity-defying pigtails) sing and dance their way around the 100 buildings and settings from the books. Prices drop outside peak season, as there are fewer activities and theatre performances. Cars are charged a cheeky Skr30. The theme park is a 15-minute walk from central Vimmerby.

There's a reasonably priced restaurant, a fast-food joint and coffee shops in the park. Dedicated fans can crash at the on-site camping ground (see below).

Nearby you'll find **Astrid Lindgrens Näs** (☎ 76 94 00; www.astridlindgrensnas.se; Prästgården 24; combination ticket adult/6-14yr Skr80/35, tours adult/under 15yr Skr95/75; 🕑 10am-6pm May-Aug), a fascinating cultural centre set on the farm on which Lindgren grew up. There's a permanent exhibition about the writer's life, as well as temporary exhibitions inspired by Lindgren's stories and legacy. The true highlight, however, is the 30-minute **guided tour** (🕑 daily summer, by appointment only rest of year) of Lindgren's childhood home, which she faithfully restored in the 1960s. Guides bring the place to life with entertaining anecdotes, which you can ponder over a decent coffee and a book at the centre's mod-chic cafe and gift shop. Call ahead for tour times.

When you've reached ginger-plait overload, wander down Storgatan for a fix of quaint 18th- and 19th-century wooden abodes. Another option is **Museet Näktergalen** (☎ 76 94 59; Sevedegatan 43; adult/child Skr20/10; 🕑 noon-5pm Mon-Fri, 10am-2pm Sat mid-Jun–mid-Aug), a petite 18th-century house with traditionally painted walls and ceilings.

Sleeping & Eating

There's a **camping ground** (sites low/high season Skr155/295, 4-bed cabins from Skr495/995; 🕑 mid-May–Aug) at the theme park, and lots of accommodation in town, much of it offering theme-park packages; ask the tourist office for details.

Vimmerby Vandrarhem (☎ 100 20; info@vimmerby vandrarhem.nu; Järnvägsallén 2; r from Skr450; P 🖥) This cheerful hostel, based in a fine wooden building, is right near the train station. There are more expensive doubles available, with proper (nonbunk) beds, plus a garden with barbecue.

Vimmerby Stadshotell (☎ 121 00; www.vimmerby stadshotell.se; Stora Torget 9; s/d Skr1250/1450, weekends rest of year Skr695/795; P 🖥) You can't miss this dashing pink building on the town square. Rooms aren't as grand as the exterior implies, but they're comfortable, with cable TV and minibars. Staff are friendly and there's a decent in-house restaurant.

Konditori Brödstugan (☎ 104 21; Storgatan 42; meals around Skr65) One very busy lunch spot is this bakery-cafe, with a wide choice of quiches, salads, baked potatoes and hot dishes.

Getting There & Away

All bus and train services depart from the Resecentrum, downhill past the church from Stora Torget. Swebus Express runs once daily on Friday and Sunday to Eksjö, Jönköping and Göteborg, and in the other direction to Västervik (Skr58, 1¼ hours). Svenska Buss operates daily between Stockholm, Linköping and Vimmerby.

After Vimmerby, services continue on to either Oskarshamn, Åseda, or Kalmar and Nybro.

Trains run several times daily south to Kalmar and north to Linköping.

ÖLAND

☎ 0485 / pop 25,000

Like a deranged vision of Don Quixote, Öland is *covered* in old wooden windmills. Symbols of power and wealth in the mid-18th century, they were a must-have for every aspiring man-about-town and the death knell for many of Öland's oak forests. Today 400 or so remain, many lovingly restored by local windmill associations.

At 137km long and 16km wide, the island is Sweden's smallest province. Once a regal hunting ground, it's now a hugely popular summer destination for Swedes – the royal family still has a summer pad here. The island gets around two million visitors annually, mostly in July.

Around 90% of them flock to the golden shores fringing the northern half of the island to bask and bathe.

Behind the beaches, fairy-tale forests make for soulful wanders.

South of Färjestade, the entire island is a Unesco World Heritage site, lauded for its unique agricultural landscape, in continuous use from the Stone Age to today, and peppered with runic stones and ancient burial cairns.

There are surprisingly few hotels, but you can stay in innumerable private rooms (booked through the tourist offices), more than 25 campsites and at least a dozen hostels (book ahead). Camping between Midsummer and mid-August can cost up to Skr300 per site.

Ölands Skördefest (www.skordefest.nu), the island's three-day harvest festival in late September, is Sweden's biggest.

SOUTHEAST SWEDEN

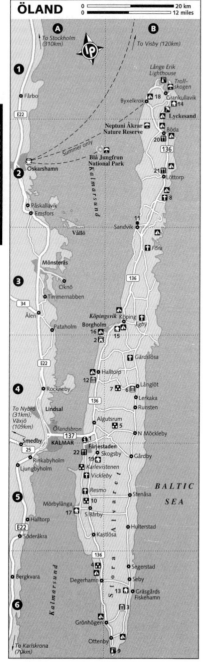

SOUTHEAST SWEDEN

Information

The bridge from Kalmar lands you on the island just north of Färjestaden, where there's a well-stocked **tourist office** (☎ 56 06 00; www.olands turist.se; ☉ 9am-6pm Mon-Fri, 9am-5pm Sat, 9am-3pm Sun May & Jun; 9am-7pm Mon-Fri, 9am-6pm Sat, 9am-5pm Sun Jul–mid-Aug; 9am-5pm Mon-Fri, 9am-4pm Sat, 9am-3pm Sun rest of Aug; 9am-5pm Mon-Fri, 9am-3pm Sat Sep, 9am-5pm Mon-Fri rest of year; closed late Dec-early Jan) at the Träffpunkt Öland centre. Staff can book island accommodation (for a Skr195 booking fee), as well as organise themed packages, including cycling, spa and gourmet getaways. Model monks and ring forts illustrate the island's history in the **Historium** inside the tourist office, and there's a **Naturum** (in Swedish) for wildlife spotters.

There's a smaller tourist office in Borgholm (see right).

Getting There & Around

BICYCLE

There are no bicycle lanes on the bridge between Öland and Kalmar, so cyclists should exercise caution! Bicycles aren't allowed on the bridge in summer – instead there's a free *Cykelbuss* service to get you across (roughly hourly; enquire at the tourist office in Kalmar). If you fancy peddling your way across Öland, check www.cyklapaoland.se for cycling routes and other handy information.

The following shops hire out bicycles in summer for around Skr100 per day, or about Skr400 a week:

Byxelkroks Cykeluthyrning (☎ 070-579 61 00; Hamnkontoret, Byxelkrok)
Färjestadens Cykelaffär (☎ 300 74; Storgatan 67, Färjestaden)
Hallbergs Hojjar (☎ 109 40; Köpmangatan 19, Borgholm)

BOAT

From mid-June to mid-August, **M/S Solsund** (☎ 070-621 42 60) sails daily from Byxelkrok (northwest Öland) and Oskarshamn (on the mainland 60km north of Kalmar). One-way tickets cost Skr150 per adult and Skr100 for those aged between seven and 16 years. A car and up to five people costs Skr550, and a bicycle is free.

BUS

Silverlinjen (☎ 0485-261 11; www.silverlinjen.se, in Swedish) runs one to two daily direct buses from Öland to Stockholm (Skr280, 6½ hours), calling at Kalmar – reservations are essential.

Buses connect all the main towns on the island from Kalmar, and run every hour or two to Borgholm (Skr50, one hour) and Mörbylånga (Skr34, one hour). A few buses per day run to Byxelkrok and Grankullavik (both Skr91, around 2¼ hours), in the far north of the island. Services to the south are poor, with some improvement May to August.

BORGHOLM & AROUND

Öland's 'capital' and busiest town, Borgholm seeps a vaguely tacky air with its discount shops and summer hordes of teens on the pull. The most dramatic (and satisfying) sight is the enormous ruined castle on its outskirts.

The **tourist office** (☎ 890 00; Sandgatan 25; ⊙ 9am-6pm Mon-Fri, 10am-4pm Sat late May-Jun; 9am-6pm Mon-Fri, 9am-5pm Sat, 10am-4pm Sun Jul-early Aug; 9am-5.30pm Mon-Fri, 10am-4pm Sat early Aug–mid-Aug; 9am-5.30pm rest of year) is at the bus station. Banks and other services are on Storgatan.

Sights

Northern Europe's largest ruined castle, **Borgholms Slott** (☎ 123 33; www.borgholmsslott.se; adult/12-17yr Skr50/20; ⊙ 10am-6pm May-Aug, 10am-4pm Apr & Sep), looms just south of town. This epic limestone structure was burnt and abandoned early in the 18th century, after life as a dye works. There's a great museum inside and a nature reserve nearby, as well as summer concerts and children's activities.

Sweden's most famous 'summer house', **Solliden Palace** (☎ 153 55; adult/7-17yr Skr65/35; ⊙ 11am-6pm mid-May–mid-Sep), 2.5km south of the town centre, is still used by the Swedish royals. Its exceptional gardens are open to the public and are well worth a wander.

VIDA Museum & Konsthall (☎ 774 40; www.vidamuseum.com; adult/under 15yr Skr40/free; ⊙ 10am-6pm Jul-early Aug, 10am-5pm May, Jun & early Aug-Sep, 10am-5pm Sat & Sun only Apr & Oct-Dec) is a strikingly modern museum and art gallery in Halltorp, about 9km south of Borgholm. Its finest halls are devoted to two of Sweden's top glass designers.

On the east coast, about 13km southeast of Borgholm, is **Gärdslösa kyrka** (⊙ 11am-5pm mid-May–mid-Sep), the best-preserved medieval church (1138) on Öland, with reasonably intact wall and ceiling paintings.

Sleeping

The tourist office can help you find rooms round town.

Kapelludden Camping & Stugor (☎ 56 07 70; Sandgatan 27; info@kapelludden.se; sites low/high season Skr170/280, 6-bed cabins Skr1220, weekly rental only in high season; ▣ 🏊) Just near the tourist office this beachside campsite is the handiest. It's a huge place (some 450 sites) and has five-star, family-oriented facilities, though it can get rowdy in summer.

Ebbas Vandrarhem & Trädgårdscafé (☎ 103 73; rum@ebbas.se; Storgatan 12; s/d Skr325/580, lunch Skr85; ⊙ May-Sep) Right in the thick of things, Ebbas cafe has a small STF hostel above it. Five of the cosy lemon-yellow rooms overlook the gorgeous rose-laced garden, and four the bustling pedestrianised main street. There's a kitchen for self-caterers…or just pop downstairs

SOUTHEAST SWEDEN

for decent hot and cold grub (lunch Skr85), served until 9pm in the summer (earlier at other times). Book ahead in summer.

Villa Sol (☎ 56 25 52; www.villasol.nu; Slottsgatan 30; s/d low season from Skr350/500, high season from Skr500/700) Villa Sol has a super garden and small but thoughtfully decorated rooms. Each has a different colour scheme – we like the Yellow Room best, for its sunny disposition and private balcony. Prices exclude breakfast, but there is a guest kitchen. Rooms with private bathrooms cost around Skr250 extra.

Guntorps Herrgård (☎ 130 00; www.guntorpsherr gard.se; Guntorpsgatan; s/d from Skr995/1195) This is a delightful old farmhouse east of town. The accommodation is excellent and unintentionally camp, with peachy tones and chandeliers above the beds. There's the added drawcard of a huge smörgåsbord (Skr195 per person; from 6pm daily in summer) offering superb samples of local dishes.

Hotell Borgholm (☎ 770 60; www.hotellborgholm .com; Trädgårdsgatan 15; d Skr1095-1755; ✗ ▢) Cool grey hues, bold feature walls, and smart functionalist furniture make for stylish slumber at this urbane hotel. Rooms are spacious, with the recently opened top-floor options especially slick. Owner Karin Fransson is one of Sweden's top chefs, so a table at the restaurant here is best booked ahead.

Eating & Drinking

Nya Conditoriet (☎ 100 11; Storgatan 28) This busy old-fashioned bakery-cafe serves yummy sandwiches and pastries.

Pubben (☎ 124 15; Storgatan 18) There are snacks and light meals here, but punters mainly come to this English-style pub for the beer and hefty selection of whiskeys. Complete with a summery terrace, it's the most heaving bar in town.

There are supermarkets on Storgatan, and a central **Systembolaget** (Östra Kyrkogatan 19).

NORTHERN ÖLAND

At Sandvik on the west coast, about 30km north of Borgholm, **Sandvikskvarn** (☎ 261 72; www.sandvikskvarn.com; pizzas from Skr78; ❤ noon-8pm May-Sep, to 10pm mid-Jun–mid-Aug) is a Dutch-style windmill and one of the largest in the world. In summer, you can climb its seven storeys for good views across to the mainland. The rustic restaurant serves the local speciality, *lufsa* (baked pork and potato; Skr69); and there's an adjacent pizzeria.

Atmospheric **Källa kyrka**, at a little harbour about 36km northeast of Borgholm, off Rd 136, is a fine example of Öland's medieval fortified churches. The broken **rune stone** inside shows the Christian Cross growing from the pagan tree of life.

Grankullavik, in the far north, has sandy beaches and summer crowds; **Lyckesand** is one of the island's best beaches and the strangely twisted trees and ancient barrows at the nearby **Trollskogen** (Trolls' Forest) nature reserve are well worth a visit. On the far north's western edge is the beautiful **Neptuni åkrar** nature reserve, famed for its spread of blue viper's bugoss flowers in early summer.

Neptuni Camping (☎ 284 95; www.neptunicamp ing.se; Småskogsvägen; sites Skr165, cabins from Skr370), a wild and grassy place, is handy for people jumping off the ferry in Byxelkrok, and has good amenities.

Kaffestugan (☎ 221 27; Boda; sandwiches Skr45-50, salads Skr60-80; ❤ 7am-6pm Jun-Aug, 7am-6pm Sat & Sun only April, May & Sep), on the main road in tiny Boda, is a clued-up cafe that micro-roasts its own fair-trade coffee and bakes everything from luscious berry tarts and cakes to organic breads and moreish lavender-and-chocolate biscotti.

Lammet & Grisen (☎ 203 50; Löttorp; ❤ from 5pm), 10km south of Böda, is popular for its all-you-can-eat evenings (adult Skr395), with whole spit-roasted lamb and pork on the menu, plus live entertainment. The restaurant is particularly family-friendly.

Bus 106 runs a route to the north from Borgholm.

CENTRAL ÖLAND

Fortresses, a zoo and a charming farm village are central Öland's star attractions. The largest settlement is Färjestaden (Ferry Town), where you'll find banks, services and a Systembolaget. The town lost its purpose in life after the bridge was built, although an effort has been made to rejuvenate the old jetty.

Ölands Djurpark (☎ 392 22; admission Skr240; ❤ 10am-6pm late May–mid-Jun & mid–late Aug, to 7pm mid-Jun–mid-Aug, 11am-4pm early–late May & Sep) is a zoo, amusement park and water park favoured by families, just north of the bridge near the tourist office. Kids under 1m tall get in free.

The largest Iron Age ring fort in Sweden, **Gråborg** was built as the Roman Empire was crumbling. Its impressively monumental walls measure 640m around, even though much of the stonework was plundered for later housing. After falling into disuse, the fort sprang back to life around 1200, when the adjacent **St Knut's chapel** (now a ruin) was built. The Gråborg complex is about 8km east of Färjestaden, just off the Norra Möckleby road; you need your own transport to get there.

The vast **Ismantorp fortress**, with the remains of 88 houses and nine mysterious gates, is deep in the woods, 5km west of the Himmelsberga museum. It's an undisturbed fortress ruin, illustrating how the village's tiny huts were encircled by the outer wall – Eketorp (right) is an imaginative reconstruction of similar remains. The area, just south of the Ekerum–Långlöt road, can be visited at any time.

A 17km **hiking trail** leads from Gråborg to Ismantorp fortress.

The best open-air museum on Öland is **Himmelsberga** (☎ 56 10 22; adult/under 15yr Skr55/free; ⏱ 10am-5.30pm mid-May–Aug), a farm village on the east coast at Långlöt. Its quaint cottages are fully furnished. There's hay in the mangers and slippers by the door; it's so convincing you'd swear the inhabitants just popped out for a minute. Extras include a dinky cafe and modern art gallery.

STF Vandrarhem Ölands Skogsby (☎ 383 95; info@vandrarhskogsby.se; dm/s/d Skr200/250/400; ⏱ mid-Apr–Sep; **P**), a charming, low-fuss STF hostel, claims to be Sweden's oldest (it dates from 1934). It's based in a flowery old wooden house, 3km southeast of Färjestaden. The Färjestaden–Mörbylånga bus 103 (Skr25) runs past at least five times daily.

There are a few good eateries at the old jetty in Färjestaden, including **På Kaj4** (☎ 310 37; mains Skr95-145; ⏱ from 11.30am Jun-Aug, shorter hours rest of year), where you can sample fresh seafood dishes, steaks and Med-style nibbles. Best of all, there's a large sunny terrace with appetising views over Kalmarsund.

SOUTHERN ÖLAND

The southern half of the island has made it onto Unesco's World Heritage List. Its treeless, limestone landscape is hauntingly beautiful and littered with the relics of human settlement and conflict. Besides linear villages, Iron Age fortresses and tombs, this area is also a natural haven for plants and wildlife.

Birds, insects and flowers populate the striking limestone plain of **Stora Alvaret**. Bird-spotting is best in May and June, which is also

when the Alvar's rock roses and rare orchids burst into bloom. The plain occupies most of the inland area of southern Öland, and can be crossed by road from Mörbylånga or Degerhamn.

The ancient grave fields of **Mysinge** and **Gettlinge**, stretching for kilometres on the ridge alongside the main Mörbylånga–Degerhamn road, include burial sites and standing stones from the Stone Age to the late Iron Age. The biggest single monument is the Bronze Age tomb **Mysinge hög**, 4km east of Mörbylånga, from where there are views of almost the whole World Heritage site.

If you can't picture how the ring forts looked in their prime, take a trip to **Eketorp** (☎ 66 20 00; www.eketorp.se; adult/6-14yr Skr95/45; ⏱ 11am-5pm May-early Sep, to 6pm Jul–mid-Aug). The site has been partly reconstructed to show what the fortified villages, which went in and out of use over the centuries, were like in medieval times. Children will love the scampering pigs, and the fort is particularly fun when there are re-enactment days – phone for details. Excavations at the site have revealed over 26,000 artefacts, including three tonnes of human bones; some of the finds are on display at the little **museum** inside. There's a free daily **tour** in English from late June to the end of August (call for times). The fort is 6km northeast of Grönhögen; there are several buses (summer only) from Mörbylånga.

On the east coast, about 5km north of Eketorp, **Gräsgårds Fiskehamn** is a delightful little fishing harbour. A little further north, there's an 11th-century rune stone at **Seby**, and in **Segerstad** there are standing stones, stone circles and over 200 graves.

Öland's southernmost point is a stark, striking spectacle of epic sky, sea, and rock-strewn pastures. A nature reserve, almost surrounded by sea, it's justifiably popular with bird-spotters. There's a free **Naturum** (☎ 66 12 00; ⏱ 10am-6pm Jul–mid-Aug, 11am-5pm May & Jun, 11am-4pm late Mar-Apr & mid-Aug–Sep, 11am-3pm Oct-Nov, noon-4pm Fri-Sun early-late Mar), a great cafe-restaurant and, at 42m, Scandinavia's tallest lighthouse, **Långe Jan** (adult/7-15yr Skr30/10) to climb.

Sleeping & Eating
Mörby Vandrarhem & Lågprishotell (☎ 493 93; morby@hotelskansen.com; Bruksgatan; hostel 1-/2-/4-/6-bed r Skr300/500/700/900, hotel s/d from Skr500/700; ⏱ May-Aug; **P** ⏺ ⏺) In the small village of Mörbylånga, this place has a mixture of

hostel- and hotel-style accommodation. It's great for families, with nearby park and beaches, and bikes for hire. There's a pool and restaurant on-site.

Kajutan Hotell & Vandrarhem (☎ 408 10; noren _per@yahoo.se; 1-/2-/3-/4-bed r Skr300/500/600/700, hotel s/d Skr890/1050) Kajutan is down by Mörbylånga harbour. Rooms were revamped in 2006 and there's a busy bar-restaurant for handy munching (pizza Skr85 to Skr95, mains Skr139 to Skr225). Summer lunches, served in a sunny courtyard, are a particular hit.

Gammalsbygårdens Gästgiveri (☎ 66 30 51; info@ gammalsbygarden.se; s/d Skr700/900; ☒ closed Christmas-Easter; Ⓟ ☐) Criminally cosy, this country farmhouse sits on the hauntingly beautiful southeast coast, 5km north of Eketorp. The picture-perfect lounge is complemented by individually decorated rooms (all doubles except one), with neat whitewashed walls and nifty floor-heating. A couple have private balconies. The food (mains around Skr160), mostly fish and venison, is also wonderful – reservations are a must.

Restaurang Fågel Blå (☎ 66 12 01; meals Skr79-175; ☒ 10am-4pm early–mid-Jul & mid–late Aug; 10am-6pm mid-Jul–mid-Aug; 11am-3pm Mon-Fri, 11am-4pm Sat & Sun Apr, Jun & Sep; 8.30am-2pm Mon-Fri, 8.30am-4pm Sat & Sun early–mid-Oct; 11am-3pm, 11am-3pm Mon-Fri, 7.30am-4pm Sat & Sun May) Head to this renowned cafe-restaurant, evocatively set by the lighthouse in the far south, for local favourites like Ottenby lamb, roast deer with potato and turnip gratin, or baked Baltic salmon, all served with a side of sea views.

You'll find supermarkets in Mörbylånga.

GOTLAND

Gorgeous Gotland has much to brag about: a Unesco-lauded capital, truffle-sprinkled woods, A-list dining hot spots, talented artisans and more hours of sunshine than anywhere else in Sweden. It's also one of the country's richest historical regions, with around 100 medieval churches and countless prehistoric sites, from stone ship settings and burial mounds to hilltop fortress remains. Information boards indicate sites along roadsides.

The island lies nearly halfway between Sweden and Latvia, in the middle of the Baltic Sea, roughly equidistant from

the mainland ports of Nynäshamn and Oskarshamn. Gotland is both a region (landskap) and a county (län). Just off its northeast tip lies the island of Fårö, most famous as the home of Sweden's directing great, the late Ingmar Bergman (see p166). The island national park of Gotska Sandön lies 38km further north, while the petite islets of Stora Karlsö and Lilla Karlsö sit just off the western coast.

Information on the island abounds, with both www.gotland.net and www.guteinfo.com (in Swedish) good places to start.

VISBY

☎ 0498 / pop 22,240

The port town of Visby is medieval eye-candy and enough in itself to warrant a trip to Gotland. Inside its thick city walls await twisting cobbled streets, fairy-tale wooden cottages, evocative ruins and steep hills with impromptu Baltic views. The city wall, with its 40-plus towers and the spectacular church ruins within, attest to the town's former Hanseatic glories.

A Unesco World Heritage site, Visby swarms with holidaymakers in the summer, and from mid-June to mid-August cars are banned in the old town. For many, the highlight of the season is the costumes, performances, crafts, markets and re-enactments of **Medeltidsveckan** (Medieval Week; www.medeltidsveckan .com), held during the first or second week of August. Finding accommodation during this time is almost impossible unless you've booked ahead.

Information

Bank (Adelsgatan) With ATM.

ICA supermarket (Stora Torget) Sells stamps, as does the tourist office.

Library (☎ 29 90 00; Cramergatan; ☒ 10am-7pm Mon-Fri, noon-4pm Sat & Sun) Free internet access (Skr20 mid-June to mid-August).

Tourist Information Centre (☎ 20 17 00; www .gotland.info; Skeppsbron 4-6; ☒ summer 8am-7pm, shorter hours rest of year) The tourist office is at the harbour.

Sights & Activities

The town is a noble sight, with its 13th-century wall of 40 towers – savour it for a few hours while walking around the perimeter (3.5km). Also take time to stroll around the Botanic Gardens and the narrow roads

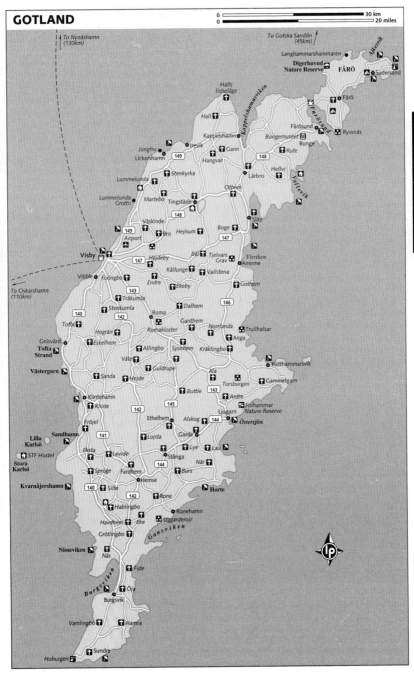

GOTLAND

and scandalously cute lanes just south of the gardens. Pick up a copy of the booklet *Visby on Your Own* (Skr40, available at the tourist office), which will guide you around the town and give you interesting snippets of local history.

In summer the tourist office also organises two-hour guided walking tours of the town (Skr80), with English-language walks up to four times a week.

The ruins of 10 medieval churches, all located within the town walls, include **St Nicolai Kyrka**, built in 1230 by Dominican monks. The monastery was burned down when Lübeckers attacked Visby in 1525. The **Helge And Kyrka** ruin is the only stone-built octagonal church in Sweden, built in 1200, possibly after the Bishop of Riga; the roof collapsed after a fire in 1611. On Stora Torget, **St Karins Kyrka** has a beautiful Gothic interior and was founded by Franciscans in 1233. The church was extended in the early 14th century, but the monastery was closed by the Reformation and the church fell into disrepair.

The ruins contrast with the stoic **Sankta Maria kykra** (Cathedral of St Maria; ☺ 8am-9pm Sun-Fri, to 7pm Sat late Jun-early Aug; 8am-7pm early–late Jun & early Aug-late Sep; 8am-5pm Mon-Wed & Fri, 8am-6pm Sat, 9am-8pm Sun late Sep-early Jun). Built in the late 12th and early 13th centuries and heavily touched up over the centuries, its whimsical towers are topped by baroque cupolas. Soak up the beautiful stained-glass windows, carved floor slabs and the ornate carved reredos. Alongside several of the ruins, the cathedral is used for intimate **music concerts** (tickets Skr200-300) in summer. Check the tourist office website for details.

Gotlands Fornsal (☎ 29 27 00; www.lansmuseet gotland.se; Strandgatan 14; adult/under 19yr Skr75/free; ☺ 10am-6pm Fri-Wed, to 7pm Thu Jun–mid-Sep, noon-4pm Tue-Sun mid-Sep–May) is one of the mightiest regional museums in Sweden. While highlights include amazing 8th-century pre-Viking picture stones, human skeletons from chambered tombs and medieval wooden sculptures, the star turn is the legendary Spillings horde. At 70kg it's the world's largest booty of preserved silver treasure. Included in the ticket price is entry to the nearby **Konstmuseum** (☎ 29 27 75; Sankt Hansgatan 21; adult/under 19yr Skr50/free; ☺ 11am-5pm mid-Jun–mid-Aug, noon-4pm Tue-Sun mid-Aug–mid-Jun), which has a small permanent collection that primarily focuses on Gotland-inspired 19th- and 20th-century art. More exciting are the temporary exhibitions, which often showcase contemporary local artists.

Sleeping

STF Vandrarhem Visby/Rävhagen (☎ 24 04 50; info@ resestugan.se; dm from Skr175, s/d from Skr350/400; ☺ year-round) This leafy hostel is 3km southeast of the town centre, just off Rd 143.

Fängelse Vandrarhem (☎ 20 60 50; Skeppsbron 1; dm from Skr180, d from Skr240) As hard to get into as it once was to get out of, this hostel offers beds year-round in the small converted cells of an old prison. It's in a handy location, between the ferry dock and the harbour restaurants, and there's a cute terrace bar in summer. Reserve well in advance and always call ahead before arriving to ensure someone can let you in.

Visby Strandby (☎ 20 33 00; www.gtsab.se; Rd 149, Snäck; sites high season Skr200, 4–6-bed cabins high season

---

THE ISLAND OF CHURCHES

Gotland boasts the highest concentration of medieval churches in northern Europe. A God-pleasing 92 inhabit villages outside Visby; more than 70 still harbour medieval frescos and a few also contain extremely rare medieval stained glass. Visby alone has a dozen church ruins and a fairy-tale cathedral.

A church was built in most villages between the early 12th century and the mid-14th century, Gotland's golden age of trading. After 1350 war and struggle saw the money run out and the tradition end. Ironically, it was the lack of funds that helped keep the island in an ecclesiastical time warp; the old churches weren't demolished, and new ones weren't constructed until 1960. Each church is still in use, and the posse of medieval villages still exist as entities.

Most churches are open 9am to 6pm daily from mid-May to late August. Some churches have the old key in the door even before 15 May, or sometimes the key is hidden above the door.

The Churches in the Diocese of Visby is a particularly useful English-language brochure, available free from tourist offices or online at www.gotland.info.

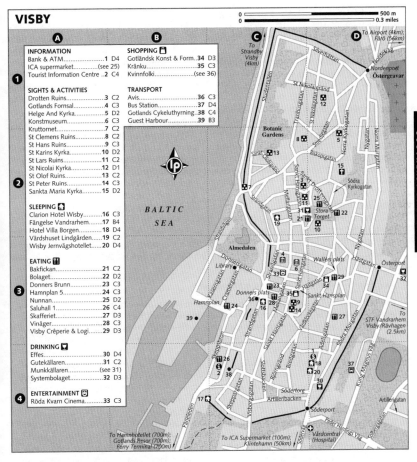

VISBY

INFORMATION
Bank & ATM....................**1** D4
ICA supermarket.............(see 25)
Tourist Information Centre .**2** C4

SIGHTS & ACTIVITIES
Drotten Ruins....................**3** C2
Gotlands Fornsal................**4** C3
Helge And Kyrka................**5** D2
Konstmuseum....................**6** C3
Kruttornet.........................**7** C2
St Clemens Ruins...............**8** C3
St Hans Ruins....................**9** C3
St Karins Kyrka.................**10** D2
St Lars Ruins....................**11** C2
St Nicolai Kyrka................**12** D1
St Olof Ruins....................**13** C2
St Peter Ruins...................**14** C3
Sankta Maria Kyrka..........**15** D2

SLEEPING
Clarion Hotel Wisby..........**16** C3
Fängelse Vandrarhem......**17** B4
Hotel Villa Borgen...........**18** D4
Värdshuset Lindgården.....**19** C2
Wisby Jernvägshotellet....**20** D4

EATING
Bakfickan.......................**21** C2
Bolaget..........................**22** D2
Donners Brunn.................**23** C3
Hamnplan 5.....................**24** C3
Nunnan..........................**25** D2
Saluhall 1.......................**26** C4
Skafferiet.......................**27** D3
Vinäger..........................**28** C3
Visby Crêperie & Logi......**29** D3

DRINKING
Effes..............................**30** D4
Gutekällaren...................**31** C2
Munkkällaren..................(see 31)
Systembolaget.................**32** D3

ENTERTAINMENT
Röda Kvarn Cinema..........**33** C3

SHOPPING
Gotländsk Konst & Form..**34** D3
Kränku..........................**35** C3
Kvinnfolki.....................(see 36)

TRANSPORT
Avis..............................**36** C3
Bus Station.....................**37** D4
Gotlands Cykeluthyrning..**38** C4
Guest Harbour................**39** B3

*BALTIC
SEA*

SOUTHEAST SWEDEN

Skr6365; 🖳) This recommended campsite lies 4km north of Visby and within walking distance of a small but popular sandy beach. Facilities include a small shop, a restaurant, a swimming pool and minigolf, with wi-fi available in the cabins. A bus service connects the site to Visby.

Wisby Jernvägshotellet (☎ 20 33 00; www.gtsab .se; Adelsgatan 9; 2-/4-bed r low season from Skr300/650, high season from Skr650/1095; ☽ year-round) Call ahead to book at this small, comfortable and very central hostel with spotless modern facilities.

Hamnhotellet (☎ 20 12 50; Färjeleden 3; s/d low season Skr560/600, hotel s/d high season Skr1095/1340, annexe s/d high season Skr785/995; 🅿 🖳) Close to the ferry terminal, Hamnhotellet offers clean, comfortable rooms and a decent buffet breakfast.

Opt for the cheaper annexe rooms, which are perfectly adequate with private bathroom and TV.

Gotlands Resor (☎ 20 12 60; info@gotlandsresor.se; Färjeleden 3) This travel agency, in Hamnhotellet, books stylish, fully equipped cottages (from Skr670 per night) in eastern and northern Gotland. Bookings for the summer should be made six months ahead. The agency also organises bike hire and rents camping equipment.

Hotel Villa Borgen (☎ 20 33 00; www.gtsab.se; Adelsgatan 11; s/d low season from Skr695/795, high season Skr1095/1395; 🖳) This place has satisfying rooms set around a pretty, quiet courtyard, and an intimate breakfast room with French doors and stained glass for that boutique feeling.

Clarion Hotel Wisby (☎ 25 75 00; cl.wisby@choice.se; Strandgatan 6; s Skr995-1795, d Skr1420-2190; 🖳) Top of the heap in Visby is the luxurious, landmark Wisby. Medieval vaulted ceilings and look-at-me candelabra contrast with funky contemporary furnishings. The gorgeous pool (complete with medieval pillar) occupies a converted merchant warehouse.

Värdshuset Lindgården (☎ 21 87 00; lindgarden .vardshuset@telia.com; Strandgatan 26; s/d mid-May–Sep Skr1195/1395, Oct–mid-May Skr750/950; 🖳) This is a sound central option, with rooms set facing a soothing central garden beside a popular restaurant. Dine outdoors and listen to music in the romantic courtyard in summer.

Eating & Drinking

There are more restaurants per capita in Visby than in any other Swedish city. Most are clustered around the old town squares, on Adelsgatan or at the harbour. Wherever you choose, do not pass up a chance to try *saffranspankaka* (a saffron pancake with berries and cream), the island's speciality. You'll find it at many cafes in Visby and around the island, usually for around Skr60.

Skafferiet (☎ 21 45 97; Adelsgatan 38; sandwiches from Skr35) Shamelessly charming, this casual lunch spot offers salubrious sandwiches and lip-smacking cakes and pastries.

Visby Crêperie & Logi (☎ 28 46 22; crêpes Skr39-126, 🕓 11am-11pm May-Aug, 11am-2pm & 4-11pm Tue-Sun Sep-Apr) Cheapish, cheerful and a hit with arty types, this lovable bolt hole serves scrumptious crêpes, from a moreish lamb, *chevre*, honey, rocket and almond combo to a wicked chocolate composition sexed-up with white chocolate chunks and ice cream.

Vinäger (☎ 21 11 60; Hästgatan 3; sandwiches Skr49-68, salads Skr85-95; 🕓 cafe 9am-9pm Jun-Aug, 9am-10pm Mon-Fri, 10am-6pm Sat, 10am-10pm Sun Sep-May, outdoor restaurant 9am-10pm summer only) Sporting a slick,

---

RAGNAR OLOFSSON & CAMILLA BÄCKMAN

Truffle harvesters Ragnar Olofsson and Camilla Bäckman are Gotland natives.

What sparked your passion for truffles? A newspaper article back in 2001 about an Uppsala University researcher, studying the island's truffles. At the time, most Gotland locals had no idea what they were picking up, even though the island was covered in them. Ragnar quickly saw a business opportunity, thinking back to the 1940s when rape harvesting turned many Gotland farmers into instant millionaires. Many of the cashed-up farmers then bought yellow Mercedes, hence the high number of old yellow cars on Gotland's roads today. Sadly, few locals shared Ragnar's enthusiasm to begin with. Many who did have truffles growing on their property were concerned about going public and having complete strangers on their land hunting for them.

What changed people's minds? A journalist found out that we were harvesting truffles and wrote about it. As the media interest grew, so did the public's curiosity. We were even asked to examine the Swedish Royal Family's Öland property for truffles; we found some, on the spot where they store their garbage. It took a couple of years to convince Swedish chefs, who traditionally imported French truffles. An increased interest in local produce helped change their minds and we're now supplying some of Sweden's top restaurants. We even sell to Copenhagen's current dining hot spot. In short, the business potential became clearer. Much to the dismay of the French, our Burgundy truffles are exactly the same as theirs.

How has the truffle industry affected Gotland? Ironically, truffles often grow on culturally significant land, so in a roundabout way they're helping to maintain and protect these heritage areas. Increasing demand has helped boost the local economy in the past four years, too. In 2007 between 100kg and 200kg of truffles were harvested here, with a value of Skr5 per gram (or Skr5000 per kilogram). We usually collect truffles from the farmers' land ourselves, giving the farmers a share of the profit and turning otherwise unusable land into a money-maker for them. From a tourism perspective, Gotland is no longer just a summer destination, with growing numbers heading over for the truffle harvesting season in October and November.

So visitors can get involved in the harvest? Sure. We offer truffle safari packages, which include a truffle hunt with Lizzie and Java (our fluffy, truffle-sniffing Lagotto Romagnolo dogs). As you can see, we've come a long way since the days when locals thought we were harvesting chocolate.

ethno-chic interior, this hip cafe-bar puts the emphasis on fresh food, whether it's a fetta and hummus wrap, lingonberry and cardamom muffins or sinfully good carrot cake. Directly across the street, Vinäger's outdoor resto-bar cranks up the X-factor with a glam alfresco lounge, smooth cocktails and a dinner menu featuring Gotland's only sushi option.

Effes (☎ 21 06 22; snacks & meals Skr70-145) Check out this pub-bar, just off Adelsgatan. Gloriously grungy and packed with characters (rockers and Goths love the place), Effes is built into the town wall and is a good place for a meal or drink. There's an outdoor courtyard, pool tables and live music in summer.

Nunnan (☎ 21 28 94; meals Skr88-195; ⊙ lunch & dinner summer, dinner only winter) A slice of Mykonos on Visby's main square, Nunnan peddles good Greek grub, including decent vegetarian options, to an often eclectic crowd.

ourpick Bakfickan (☎ 27 18 07; mains Skr128-258; ⊙ lunch & dinner) White tiled walls, merrily strung lights and boisterous crowds define this foodie-loved bolt-hole, where enlightened seafood gems might include Pollock with lobster risotto and wild garlic.

Bolaget (☎ 21 50 80; Stora Torget 16; mains Skr179-205; ⊙ to 2am, closed Mon in winter) Take a defunct Systembolaget shop, chip the 'System' off the signage, and reinvent the space as a buzzing, bistro-inspired hot-spot. Top-notch seasonal flavours shine through in French-inspired dishes like duck with cherry sauce, cocoa beans and walnut-roasted potatoes. Staff are amiable and the summertime square-side bar seating is the place for serious people watching.

Donners Brunn (☎ 27 10 90; Donners plats; mains Skr195-285) If you're craving a luxe feed, book a table at classic Donners Brun. Seasonal menus blend Swedish and global flavours (think grilled pata negra with chorizo, fennel slaw and deep-fried potatoes), while the alfresco summer bar is a fine spot to savour a cheeky John Holmes cocktail.

Hamnplan 5 (☎ 21 07 10; Hamnplan 5) Down by the water, Hamnplan 5 is an upmarket restaurant by day and a nightclub by night.

Other hang-outs around the harbour are a hit on warm summer days and evenings, including the cheap stalls selling ice cream, sandwiches and pizza inside Saluhall 1.

A pair of neighbouring restaurant-bars with seemingly infinite levels of seating,

from cellars to balconies, **Gutekällaren** (☎ 21 00 43) and **Munkkällaren** (☎ 227 14 00) are both home to nightclubs loved by summer crowds.

There's a tiny **ICA supermarket** (Stora Torget) for self-caterers and a larger one on Söderväg, south of Söderport. **Systembolaget** (Österväg 3C) lies just outside the Österport city gate.

Entertainment

For rainy days, there's the retro **Röda Kvarn cinema** (☎ 21 01 81; Mellangatan 17; tickets Skr85; ⊙ from 5pm).

Shopping

Gotländsk Konst & Form (☎ 21 03 49; Wallérs plats 5; ⊙ closed Sun) Cool local art and handicrafts are the focus at this artisans' cooperative, with stock ranging from textiles and threads to ceramics, pottery, jewellery, glassware and painting. You can bag anything from mauve-hued local-wool cushions to loft-worthy bowls.

Kvinnfolki (☎ 21 00 51; Donners plats) This is another great place for idiosyncratic local handicrafts, whether it's funky bags with a folk twist, ceramic colanders or downright quirky mugs.

Kränku (☎ 21 74 81; Sankt Hansplan 4) Tea fiends head here for local blends, which make for soothing, civilised souvenirs.

Getting There & Away

AIR

There are regular **Skyways** (☎ 0771-95 95 00; www.skyways.se) flights between Visby and Stockholm's Arlanda and Bromma airports (up to three times a day for each airport). Flights between Stockholm and Visby generally cost from Skr517; click on the 'Low fare calendar' link on the website to check for the best prices.

The cheaper local airline is **Gotlands Flyg** (☎ 22 22 22; www.gotlandsflyg.se), with regular flights between Visby and Stockholm Bromma (one to 10 times daily). Prices start at Skr321 one way; book early for discounts, and inquire about stand-by fares (adult/under 26 years Skr621/321). Popular summer-only routes include Göteborg, Hamburg, Oslo and Helsingfors.

The island's **airport** (☎ 26 31 00) is 4km northeast of Visby. No buses serve the airport directly; you're best bet is to catch a taxi into/from town (around Skr145).

BOAT

Year-round car ferries between Visby and both Nynäshamn and Oskarshamn are operated by **Destination Gotland** (☎ 0771-22 33 00; www.destinationgotland.se). There are departures from Nynäshamn one to five times daily (about three hours). From Oskarshamn, there are one or two daily departures in either direction (three to four hours).

Regular one-way adult tickets for the ferry start at Skr180, but from mid-June to mid-August there is a far more complicated fare system; some overnight, evening and early-morning sailings in the middle of the week have cheaper fares.

Transporting a bicycle costs Skr45; a car usually starts at Skr298, although again in the peak summer season a tiered price system operates. Booking a nonrefundable ticket, three weeks in advance, will save you money. If you're thinking of taking a car on the ferry between mid-June and mid-August, reserve a place well in advance.

Getting Around

There are over 1200km of roads in Gotland, typically running from village to village through picture-perfect landscapes. Cycling on the quiet roads is heavenly, and bikes can be hired from a number of places in Visby. The forested belt south and east of Visby is useful if you bring a tent and want to take advantage of the liberal camping laws.

Many travel agents and bike-rental places on the island also rent out camping equipment. In Visby, hire bikes from Skr75 per 24 hours at **Gotlands Cykeluthyrning** (☎ 21 41 33), behind the tourist office on the harbour. They also rent tents (Skr100/500 per day/week), or for Skr250 per day (Skr1250 per week) you can hire the 'camping package' – two bikes (or one tandem bike), a tent, a camping stove and two sleeping mats. **Gotlands Resor** (☎ 20 12 60; info@gotlandsresor.se; Färjeleden 3) offers similar packages.

A few companies and service stations offer car hire. In Visby, **Avis** (☎ 21 98 10; god man@gotlandica.se; Donners plats 2), rents small cars from Skr585/3240 per day/week. At the **guest harbour** (☎ 21 51 90) you can also hire cars, motorbikes and mopeds.

Kollektiv Trafiken (☎ 21 41 12) runs buses via most villages to all corners of the island. The most useful routes, which have connections up to seven times daily, operate between Visby and Burgsvik in the far south, Visby and Fårösund in the north (also with bus connections on Fårö), and Visby and Klintehamn. A one-way ticket will not cost you more than Skr68 (although if you take a bike on board it will cost an additional Skr40), but enthusiasts will find a monthly ticket good value at Skr675.

AROUND VISBY

There's not much but forest and farmland until you're at least 10km from Visby. If you're heading northeast, visit the remarkable Bro church, which has several 5th-century picture stones in the south wall of the oratory, beautiful sculptures and interior lime paintings.

Heading southeast on Rd 143, on your way to Ljugarn, pull over to check out the 12th-century Cistercian monastery ruin **Romakloster** (☎ 501 23; admission free, guided tour adult/child Skr50/free; ⌚ 10am-6pm May-Sep, 10am-4pm rest of year), a kilometre from the main road. Summer theatre performances here cost around Skr350 (tickets from Visby tourist office). The 18th-century manor house is also impressive.

Dalhem, 6km northeast of the Cistercian monastery, has a large church with some 14th-century stained glass (the oldest in Gotland) and magnificent (albeit restored) wall and ceiling paintings; take note of the scales of good and evil. There's also a historic **steam railway** (☎ 380 43; adult/4-12yr Skr50/30; ⌚ 11.15am-3.30pm Wed, Thu, Sat & Sun Jul-early Aug, Sun only Jun & rest of Aug) and museum in Dalhem.

The town of Klintehamn has a good range of services. From here, you can catch a passenger-only boat to the island nature reserve **Stora Karlsö** (www.storakarlso.com) one to three times daily from May to early September (adult/child return Skr225/110, 30 minutes). You can visit the island as a day trip (with 4½ hours ashore) or stay overnight at the hostel (see below).

Fairly remote, the island is home to extensive birdlife including thousands of guillemots and razorbills.

Sleeping & Eating

Pensionat Warfsholm (☎ 24 00 10; warfsholm@telia .com; sites Skr100, dm/s/d from Skr170/495/750) In Klintehamn, this hotel/hostel/campground combo sports a beautiful waterside location and restaurant.

STF hostel (☎ 24 04 50; boka@storakarlso.com; dm Skr240) If you want to get away from it all, Stora

Karlsö's simple STF hostel is a sound choice. Visitors can also opt to stay in the old lighthouse or in the lighthouse-keeper's former living quarters (singles/doubles Skr590/780), where linen and room service is included in the price. There's also a nature exhibit, restaurant and cafe on the island. Book ahead.

EASTERN GOTLAND

Ancient monuments include the Bronze Age ship setting, **Tjelvars grav**, 1.5km west of Rd 146 (level with Visby), and its surrounding landscape of standing stones, almost all linked with the Gutasaga legends. **Gothem church** is one of the most impressive in Gotland; the nave is decorated with friezes dating from 1300. **Torsburgen**, 9km north of Ljugarn, is a partly walled hill fort (the largest in Scandinavia) measuring 5km around its irregular perimeter.

Ljugarn is a small seaside resort, and there are impressive *raukar* (column) formations at **Folhammar Nature Reserve**, 2km north. Southwest of Ljugarn and the village of Alskog, the impressive **Garde church** has four extraordinary medieval lych gates and an upside-down medieval key in the door; the original 12th-century roof is still visible.

Around 20km north of Ljugarn, in the tiny hamlet of Kräklingbo, **Leonettes Konst & Keramik** (☎ 532 40; www.leonette.com; Hajdeby, Kräklingbo; 🕑 10am-6pm Mon-Fri, 10am-4pm Sat & Sun in summer, call ahead rest of year) is home to Californian expat Dan Leonette and his highly regarded, idiosyncratic ceramics and art, created using techniques like raku and sawdust firing. Between 1pm and 3pm on most Thursdays in the summer, you can watch the master fire his wares (call ahead to ensure it's on).

Truffle-hunting safaris (www.gotlandstryffel.se) in the area are a unique way for foodies to discover more about this delicacy and local produce in general. Check the websites for package prices, which include a five-star dinner (featuring truffles, of course) and an accommodation option.

Sleeping & Eating

There's a Konsum supermarket in Ljugarn, and some fine dining options in the area.

STF hostel Ljugarn (☎ 49 31 84; ljugarn@gotland sturist.se; dm from Skr130; 🕑 mid-May–Aug) This place has a fine spot at the eastern end of the Ljugarn village (down by the water).

Frejs Magasin (☎ 49 30 11; info@ljugarn.com; s/d Skr600/750, with private facilities Skr800/900) Sprinkled with antiques, this large, central, wooden-built pension is framed by Ljugarn's green countryside. It also offers three- and four-bed rooms, and has apartments and cabins available by the week, if you're in a group.

Bruna Dörren (☎ 49 32 89; Strandvägen 5; pizzas Skr60-95, mains Skr95-189) A casual restaurant and pizzeria, with a spacious outdoor courtyard and beachside location.

Smakrike Krog & Logi (☎ 49 33 71; www.smakrike .se; Claudelins väg 1; s/d/ste Skr1450/1995/3150, discounted to Skr750/1050/1795; restaurant mains Skr179-265; 🕑 restaurant 5-11pm Jun-Aug, 5-9pm Fri & Sat only Sep-Dec & Mar-May; [P] [🖳]) Just up the street, this fine-dining restaurant turns superlative local produce into revelations like halibut sashimi with blood orange and ginger vinaigrette. The restaurant's affable owners also operate a stylish bed and breakfast upstairs, where original wooden beams and walls mix it with designer wallpaper, recess lighting and slick bathrooms (some with giant bathtubs).

our pick **Krakas Krog** (☎ 530 62; mains Skr195-280; 🕑 4-10pm Wed-Sun early Jun-Aug) Kräklingbo is home to this intimate, fine-dining restaurant, co-owned by Ulrika Karlsson (one of Sweden's top sommeliers and food critics). Here, seasonal island produce is transformed into sublime dishes like organic duck liver and goose blood pudding with apple and white raisins. The adventurous five-course tasting menu (Skr600) is great value and booking is a must.

NORTHERN GOTLAND & FÅRÖ

It's hard to imagine a better way to absorb the area than by cycling up to Fårö and following the bike trails around the beautiful, windswept little island. There's an **information centre** (☎ 0498-22 40 22; 🕑 10am-5pm Jul & Aug, 10am-5pm Mon, Tue & Fri-Sun May & Jun) with internet access in Fårö town.

On your way, step back in time at the **Bungemuseet** (☎ 22 10 18; adult/child Skr70/free, adult Jul–mid-Aug Skr80; 🕑 11am-5pm mid-May–Aug, 11am-6.30pm Jul–mid-Aug), an open-air museum with 17th- to 19th-century houses, picture stones dating from 800 and a historic playground. It's near the northeastern tip, about 1km south of where the ferry connects to Fårö. Across the road is a cute cafe with superlative saffron pancakes.

The **grotto** (☎ 27 30 50; adult/4-15yr Skr100/70; ☼ May–mid-Sep) south of Lummelunda is the island's largest.

The temperature here is a cool 8°C, so rug up. The impressive *raukar* formations at nearby **Lickershamn** are up to 12m high; look out for **Jungfru** (signposted), with its haunting legend. Near the Jungfru trailhead at Lickershamn there's a campground and friendly **cafe/bar** (☼ noon-10pm mid-Jun–Aug, noon-2pm & 6-9pm Mon-Fri, noon-10pm Sat & Sun late May–mid-Jun) serving both local and Med-style dishes and tapas (from Skr80), as well as a hut selling smoked fish (11am to 7pm in summer).

The frequent ferry to **Fårö** is free for cars, passengers and cyclists. This island, once home to Ingmar Bergman, has magnificent *raukar* formations; watch the sunset

at **Langhammarshammaren** if you can. At the island's eastern tip, the rocks by Fårö lighthouse are laced with fossils. British troops who fought in the Crimean war are buried at **Ryssnäs** in the extreme south; obey signs posted along roads here, as this area is still used for military exercises.

Sleeping & Eating

There's a good STF hostel in **Lärbro** (☎ 22 50 33; dm/s Skr190/290; ☼ reception 8-11am & 5-10pm), on Rd 148 between Visby and Fårösund, open from mid-May to the end of August. It has a gym open to hostel guests for Skr85.

Nearby, the solitary island of Furillen is home to uberchic boutique hotel **Fabriken Furillen** (☎ 22 30 40; fabriken@furillen.com; d Skr1950-2800; P 🖳). Surreally set in a disused quarry,

---

BERGMAN WEEK

The wild, mysterious landscape of Fårö is not easily forgotten, as anyone who has visited can testify. The tiny island just off the northern tip of Gotland particularly haunted Ingmar Bergman (14 July 1918–30 July 2007), the legendary Swedish director, who first visited Fårö in 1960 while scouting locations for *Through a Glass Darkly*. Bergman went on to shoot seven films on the island and is now buried there.

Since 2004 Fårö has been home to **Bergman Week** (www.bergmanveckan.se), a six-day celebration of Bergman's life and work. The event consists of a film series, guest speakers (recently including fellow filmmaker Jan Troell), seminars and tours of film locations around the island. Event organisers hope to establish a Bergman Centre in the late director's house and a vacant school building.

Jannike Åhlund, one of the people behind Bergman Week, has been a summer resident of Fårö for 10 years. Åhlund kindly spoke to us about the event, the director and the remote landscape that inspired him.

How long have you been involved in Bergman Week? This summer will be the sixth BW, and I've been involved in all, save the first, which was organised by longtime collaborator and Fårö resident Arne Carlsson. I added ideas, basically making the Bergman Week into a miniature festival, centred around Bergman topics in all shapes and forms, with the help of bright actors, guests and lecturers, and hopefully adding ever-new perspectives on Bergman's work.

What are your favourite Bergman films? *Autumn Sonata* and *Wild Strawberries*.

Did you meet the man himself, and if so, what was he like? We met quite a bit. I interviewed him on four occasions, spoke to him on the phone regularly and also on Fårö, where I have a summer house, and during his participation in BW. What was he like? Curious, a quick intellect and a great sense of humour. Also childish, vengeful and a lover of gossip.

How will the festival change in the wake of Bergman's death? Will it continue? Contentwise it will be the same high spirits. No memorials – that's just the point with Bergman Week. It is not a statue we erect over our titan – we do it out of love and lust for his work. And yes, it will continue.

What do you like best about Fårö? The wild and untamed nature, the climate, the isolation.

What one thing should visitors to Sweden not miss? The archipelago, taking a boat ride in the archipelago.

Are there other sites one should add to the itinerary for a Bergman pilgrimage? Well, Dalarna is Bergman childhood (summer) territory. And you can of course see a play at Dramaten (p109) anytime and feel the presence of his demons…

its 16 severely sleek rooms (think concrete walls and floors softened with luxe Swedish furnishings) are masterfully set in a soaring machinery storehouse.

The restaurant serves customised three-course meals for guests, while cashed-up hermits can rent Mats Theselius–designed cabins costing Skr5500 the first night, Skr500 the second, Skr50 the third and Skr5 the fourth.

There's a beachside **SVIF hostel** (☎ 27 30 43; dm from Skr175; ☺ May-Sep) in Lummelunda, signposted from the main road; call ahead if you'll be arriving after 5pm.

There's an ICA supermarket (with an ATM) on the main street near the ferry terminal in Fårösund, and another on Fårö near the tourist office.

GOTSKA SANDÖN NATIONAL PARK

Isolated **Gotska Sandön** (www.gotskasandon.se), with an area of 37 sq km, is an unusual island with lighthouses at its three corners, 30km of beaches, sand dunes, pine forest and a church. There's a fantastic network of trails right around the island.

Camping (sites per person Skr70, beds in basic huts Skr140, cabins from Skr500) near the northern tip is possible; there are basic facilities but you must bring all supplies with you.

Boats (☎ 24 04 50; ☺ mid-May–early Sep) run from Fårösund and Nynäshamn three to four times weekly when operating (Skr795/995 return from Fårösund/Nynäshamn, Skr100 for bikes).

SOUTHERN GOTLAND

Hemse is a commercial centre, with good services (such as supermarkets, banks and a bakery). The smaller village of **Burgsvik**, further south, is similar.

Öja church dates from 1232 and has Gotland's highest church tower (67m). It has a magnificent cross, and the wall and ceiling paintings are remarkably detailed. Look for the inscribed stone slabs under the covered shelter just outside the churchyard. Seven kilometres south of Burgsvik, in the old Vamlingbo prästgård (vicarage) on Rd 142, **Museum Lars Jonsson** (☎ 20 26 91; www.larsjonsson.se; adult/under 18yr Skr40/free; ☺ 11am-5pm May–mid-Sep, 11am-5pm Sat & Sun rest of Sep, Easter-Apr & Dec), showcases delicate paintings and watercolours by local artist Lars Jonsson, famed for his depictions of Gotland's birdlife and coastal landscapes. There's also a cinnamon-scented cafe, Naturum and soothing garden.

Hablingbo church boasts three lavishly carved doorways, a votive ship, carved floor slabs and rune stones.

Lojsta has the deepest lakes in Gotland, remains of an early medieval fortress and a fine church. On the eastern coast near Ronehamn, **Uggarderojr** is a huge, late–Bronze Age cairn with nearby traces of settlement. The cairn, probably a navigation marker, is now a long way inland due to postglacial uplift.

Sleeping & Eating

The Hablingbo **STF hostel** (☎ 48 71 61; vand rarhem@gutevin.se; dm Skr280; ☺ May-Sep; ☐) is next to Gute Vin – a good restaurant and commercial vineyard.

In Björklunda, 2km north of Burgsvik, **Gunnels B&B Björklunda** (☎ 49 71 90; www.gunnels bjorklunda.se; hostel dm/s Skr200/250, B&B s/d Skr550/700; ℗) vaguely recalls a Greek villa with its whitewashed buildings. Both the hostel and B&B rooms are clean and comfy (albeit dated), with some boasting private kitchenettes.

Southern Sweden

Artists adore southern Sweden. Down here the light is softer, the foliage brighter and the shoreline more dazzling and white.

Sweden's southernmost county, Skåne (Scania) was Danish property until 1658 and still flaunts its differences. You can detect them in the strong dialect *(skånska)*, the half-timbered houses and Skåne's hybrid flag: a Swedish yellow cross on a red Danish background. After all, Copenhagen is a mere bridge away from vibrant Malmö, Skåne's biggest city and Sweden's most continental.

A quick trip south of Malmö is a bona fide Viking settlement and some of the country's finest birdwatching opportunities. Just to the north, picture-perfect, erudite Lund is Sweden's answer to Cambridge.

Pottery studios, cultured manors and dramatic cliffs dot Skåne's northwest coast, while its southern shore is home to medieval showpiece Ystad, mysterious Bronze Age remains and the seductive apple-orchard landscapes of Österlen.

Northeast of Skåne lies the upstaged county of Blekinge, splashed with deep forests and fish-filled lakes and once seat of Sweden's 17th-century sea power. Topping its crown is the naval city of Karlskrona, a Unesco World Heritage–listed pairing of brutal fortresses and grandiloquent design.

HIGHLIGHTS

- Hit the pavement in multicultural **Malmö** (p170) for a spicier slice of Swedish life
- Hang out with verified Vikings at the **Foteviken Viking Reserve** (p183)
- Walk in the footsteps of fictional crime-fighter Inspector Wallander (p187) in medieval **Ystad** (p185)
- Explore the exotic **Kulla Peninsula** (p196) on an Icelandic horse
- Cycle past sweet-smelling orchards or hike through the coastal nature reserve in mellow **Österlen** (p189)

- AREA: 13,968 SQ KM
- POPULATION: 1,351,257
- HIGHEST ELEVATION: SÖDERÅSEN 212M

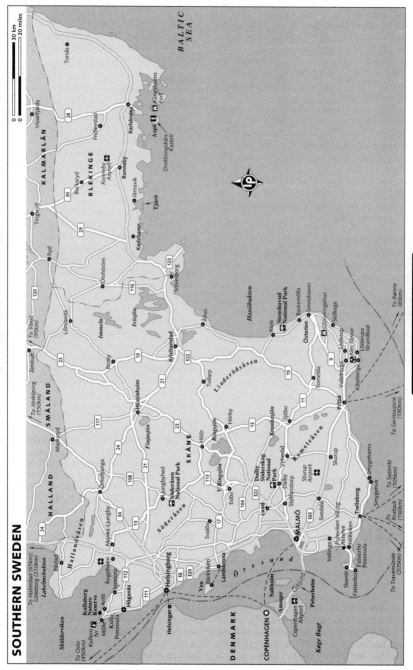

Information

There are tourist offices in all major towns. **Tourism in Skåne** (☎ 040-20 96 00; www.skane.com; Stortorget 9, 21122 Malmö) is great for information, brochures and maps on Skåne. **Blekinge Turism** (☎ 0455-30 50 20; www.blekingeturism.com; Ronnebygatan 2, 37132 Karlskrona) provides information on the Blekinge region.

If you enter Skåne from Denmark via the Öresund bridge, there's a tourist office just off the motorway a few kilometres into the country. Called **Skånegården** (☎ 040-34 12 00; Skånegårdsvägen 5), it's open Monday to Saturday from October to the end of May (see p172) and supplies information on Malmö, Skåne and the rest of Sweden. Many of the tourist offices in Skåne also stock information for Copenhagen and Denmark.

Getting Around

Skånetrafiken (☎ 0771-77 77 77; www.skanetrafiken .skane.se) operates Skåne's efficient local bus and train networks (the latter known as Pågatågen). Regular connections to Denmark are via the Öresund bridge (see boxed text, opposite) or the Helsingborg–Helsingør ferry (p196).

An integrated Öresundregionen transport system links trains from Helsingborg via Malmö and Copenhagen to Helsingør. For a round-trip tour of the Öresund or a visit to Copenhagen, the 'Around the Sound' card (Skr249) gives 48 hours' unlimited travel on ferries and local trains in Skåne and along the coast north of Copenhagen.

If you're staying in Skåne for some time, enquire about monthly passes or a *sommarkort,* offering discount travel from late June to mid-August – see the Skånetrafiken website for details. **Blekingetrafiken** (☎ 0455-569 00; www.blekinge trafiken.se) runs public transport in the Blekinge region.

SKÅNE

Skåne (Scania) is Sweden at its most continental. Connected to Denmark by bridge, its trademark mix of manors, gingerbread-style abodes and delicate, deciduous forests are a constant reminder that central Europe is just beyond the horizon. Dominating the scene is metropolitan Malmö, defined by its melting-pot tendencies and striking, twisting tower. Further out, velvety fields, sandy coastlines

and stoic castles create one of Sweden's finest cycling backdrops. Add to this the fact that Skåne is often dubbed Sweden's 'larder' and you have yourself one scrumptious Scandi treat.

MALMÖ

☎ 040 / pop 280,800

Once dismissed as crime-prone and tatty, Sweden's third-largest city has rebranded itself as progressive and downright cool. It's no coincidence that two of Stockholm's hippest icons – rock club Debaser and fashion-forward boutique Tjallamalla – have come to town.

Malmö's second wind blew in with the opening of the mammoth Öresund bridge and tunnel in 2000 (see boxed text, opposite), connecting the city to bigger, cooler Copenhagen and creating a dynamic new urban conglomeration. Such a cosmopolitan outcome seems only natural for what is Sweden's most multicultural metropolis – 150 nationalities make up Malmö's headcount. Here, Nordic reserve is countered by hotted-up cars with doof-doof stereos and exotic Middle Eastern street stalls.

Even the city's lively historic core echoes its multicultural past. The showpiece square of Stortorget evokes Hamburg more than it does Stockholm, while nearby Lilla Torg is a chattering mass of alfresco supping and half-timbered houses that give away the Danish connection.

History

Malmö really took off in the 14th century with the arrival of the Hanseatic traders, when grand merchants' houses went up, followed by churches and a castle. The greatest medieval expansion occurred under Jörgen Kock, who became the city's mayor in 1524. The town square, Stortorget, was laid out at that time, and many of the finest 16th-century buildings still stand. After the city capitulated to the Swedes in 1658, Malmö found its groove as an important commercial centre and its castle was bolstered to protect trade.

New-millennium Malmö has traded in its 20th-century heavy industries (car and aircraft manufacture, and shipbuilding) for cleaner, greener companies, particularly in the service, financial and IT sectors. The launch of a new university campus in the late 1990s also helped redefine the city, creating a thriving

SOUTHERN SWEDEN

BRIDGING THE GAP

Opened in 2000, the **Öresund bridge** (www.oresundsbron.com) is the planet's longest cable-tied road and rail bridge, measuring 7.8km from Lernacken (on the Swedish side, near Malmö) to the artificial island of Peberholm (Pepper Island), south of Saltholm (Salt Island). From the island, a further 3km of undersea tunnel finally emerges just north of Copenhagen airport.

Local commuters pay via an electronic transmitter, while tolls for everyone else are payable by credit card, debit card or in Danish and Swedish currency at the Lernacken toll booths. The crossing isn't cheap – for a motorcycle the price is Skr190, private vehicles (up to 6m) pay Skr345 and private vehicles with trailers, vans or minibuses cost Skr690. Discounts are available with the Malmökortet (below). An alternative option is to catch a commuter train to Copenhagen (Skr95), an easy 35-minute trip from Malmö and a good excuse to explore Denmark's so-hip capital.

If you're travelling between Sweden and Denmark with your own transport, you may want to consider other options (such as ferries between Helsingborg and Helsingør; see p196).

---

student population (currently around 21,000). The next chapter in Malmö's development is the ambitious Citytunnel project, which will connect Centralstationen to the Öresund bridge, giving the city two handy new train stations in the process.

Orientation

Gamla Staden (Old Town) is Malmö's heart, encircled by a canal. There are three principal squares here: Stortorget, Lilla Torg and Gustav Adolfs Torg. The castle, Malmöhus Slott, in its park setting, guards the western end of Gamla Staden. Across the canal on the northern side you'll find the bus and train stations as well as the redeveloped harbour precinct. South of the city centre is a complex network of up-and-coming streets with most interest focused on the square Möllevångstorget. The Öresund bridge is about 8km west of the city centre and is served by a motorway that passes south and east of the city.

Information

BOOKSHOPS

Akademibokhandeln (☎ 664 29 90; Södra Tullgatan 3; ☺ Mon-Sat) Good selection of general books and guidebooks.
Hamrelius (☎ 12 02 88; Södergatan 28) Wide variety of English-language books.
Pressbyrån (Centralstationen; ☺ to 11pm) Newspapers and international magazines.

DISCOUNT CARDS

The discount card Malmökortet offers free bus transport and street parking, entry to several museums, and discounts at other attractions and on sightseeing tours. It's good value at Skr130/160/190 for one/two/three days –

the price includes one adult and up to two children under 16. Buy it at the tourist office.

EMERGENCY

Akutklinik (☎ 33 10 00; entrance 36, Södra Förstads gatan 101) Emergency ward at the general hospital.
Police station (☎ 20 10 00; Porslinsgatan 6)

INTERNET ACCESS

Malmö Stadsbibliotek (☎ 660 85 00; Regements gatan; ☺ 10am-7pm Mon-Thu, 10am-6pm Fri, 11am-3pm Sat Jun-Aug; 10am-8pm Mon-Thu, 10am-6pm Fri, 11am-4pm Sat & Sun Sep-May) Free internet access at the library.
Sidewalk Express (Centralstationen; per hr Skr19)

LAUNDRY

Most hotels, hostels and camping grounds have laundries.
Tvätt-Tjänst i Malmö (☎ 611 70 70; St Knuts Torg 5; ☺ 8am-5pm Mon-Fri Aug-Jun)

LEFT LUGGAGE

There are small/large lockers in Central sta-tionen for Skr25/40 per 24 hours.

MEDICAL SERVICES

You can call the dentist and doctor on duty on ☎ 1177.
Apotek Gripen (☎ 19 21 13; Bergsgatan 48; ☺ 8am-10pm) After-hours pharmacy.

MONEY

Banks and ATMs are found on Södergatan.
Forex (☎ 30 40 31; Centralstationen; ☺ 7am-9pm) Money exchange, with another branch opposite Central-stationen on Skeppsbron, one on Gustav Adolfs Torg and another at Davidshallsgatan 27.
X-Change (☎ 788 88; Hamngatan 1; ☺ 8.30am-7pm Mon-Fri, 9am-4pm Sat) Money exchange.

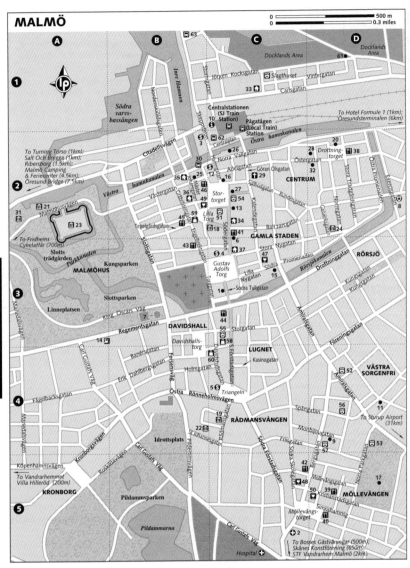

MALMÖ

SOUTHERN SWEDEN

POST

You can buy stamps and post letters from numerous shops and kiosks.

TOURIST OFFICES

For excellent online information, log onto www.malmo.com.
Skånegården (☎ 040-34 12 00; www.skane.com;

Skånegårdsvägen 5; 🕑 9am-8pm Mon-Fri, 9am-4pm Sat & Sun mid-Jun–mid-Aug; 9am-6pm Mon-Fri & 9am-4pm Sat & Sun early–mid-Jun & mid–late Aug; 9am-5pm Mon-Fri, 10am-3pm Sat & Sun Sep; 9am-5pm Mon-Fri, 10am-3pm Sat Oct-May) On the E20, 800m from the Öresund bridge tollgate, a tourist office designed purely to give information on the region and Sweden to motorists entering the country from Denmark.

Tourist office (☎ 34 12 00; www.malmo.se; ☺ 9am-7pm Mon-Fri, 10am-4pm Sat & Sun mid-Jun–early Sep; 9am-6pm Mon-Fri, 10am-3pm Sat & Sun late May–mid-Jun; 9am-5pm Mon-Fri, 10am-3pm Sat & Sun early Sep–late May) Inside Centralstationen; has free online hotel-booking service. Bookings made at the tourist office incur a Skr70 booking fee.

Sights
MALMÖHUS SLOTT
The addition of red-brick, Functionalist buildings in the 1930s might make it look a bit like a factory, but Malmöhus Slott has an intriguing history and houses some of the marvellous Malmö Museer (right).

Erik of Pomerania built the first fortress here in 1436 to control the growing medieval town and Öresund shipping. This castle was destroyed between 1534 and 1536 during a popular uprising in Skåne. Immediately after the rebellion, King Christian III of Denmark had the castle rebuilt in forbidding late-Gothic and early-Renaissance styles.

Malmöhus Slott's most famous prisoner (from 1567 to 1573) was the Earl of Bothwell. Bothwell married Mary, Queen of Scots, but was forced to flee from Scotland after she was deposed. On reaching Europe, he was detained by the Danes until his death in 1578.

After the Swedish takeover of Skåne in 1648, the Danes made a futile attempt to recapture the castle in 1677. When peace was restored, interest in the castle waned and most of it became derelict by the 19th century. A devastating fire in 1870 left only the main building and two gun towers intact; these sections were revamped in 1930.

MALMÖ MUSEER
Various museums in and around Malmöhus Slott make up the **Malmö Museer** (☎ 34 44 37; www.malmo.se/museer; Malmöhusvägen; combined entry adult/7-15yr Skr40/10, free with Malmökortet; ☺ 10am-4pm Jun-Aug, noon-4pm Sep-May). There are cafe-restaurants inside all the museums.

Inside the Castle
The intriguing **aquarium** has a nocturnal hall wriggling with everything from bats to electric eels, and local swimmers like cod and pike. It's associated with the **Naturmuseum** (Natural History Museum).

The unmissable **Malmö Konstmuseum** boasts a fabulous collection of Swedish furniture and handicrafts as well as Scandinavia's largest collection of 20th-century Nordic art, while the **Stadsmuseum** (City Museum) combines exhibitions on the region's cultural history with more international themes. Ask for the English-language information sheets at reception. The **Knight's Hall** contains various late-medieval and Renaissance exhibits, such as the regalia of the order of St Knut. The northwest **cannon tower** is an atmospheric mix of cannons, shiny armour and the skeleton of a 17th-century prisoner…still in shackles!

On Malmöhusvägen

A short distance to the west, the technology and maritime museum **Teknikens och Sjöfartens Hus** is home to aircraft, vehicles, a horse-drawn tram, steam engines, and the amazing 'U3' walk-in submarine, outside the main building. The submarine was launched in Karlskrona in 1943 and decommissioned in 1967. Upstairs, a superb hands-on experiment room will keep kids (as well as you!) engrossed for ages.

Next door, **Fiskehoddorna** (☎ 12 83 40; 6.30am-1pm Tue-Sat) is a row of former fishermen's huts selling fresh fish.

The old **Kommendanthuset** (Commandant's House) arsenal, opposite the castle, hosts photography exhibitions.

SANKT PETRI KYRKA

This red-brick Gothic beast is Malmö's oldest **church** (Göran Olsgatan; 10am-6pm), built in the early 14th century. Protestant zealots whitewashed the medieval frescoes in 1555, but the original wall-paintings in the **Krämarekapellet** (inside at the rear of Sankt Petri Kyrka) have been successfully restored. There's a magnificent altarpiece dating from 1611 and a votive ship in the south aisle, dedicated to all who died at sea in WWII. Much of the church has been rebuilt; the 96m tower went up in 1890.

ART & DESIGN

At the time of research, the extraordinary **Rooseum** (Gasverksgatan 22), a turbine hall turned contemporary art gallery, was shut indefinitely. Contact the tourist office for updates.

Malmö Konsthall (☎ 34 12 94; www.konsthall.malmo .se; St Johannesgatan 7; admission free; 11am-5pm, to 9pm Wed during exhibitions only), south of central Malmö, is one of Europe's largest contemporary art spaces, with exhibitions spanning both Swedish and foreign talent.

Form/Design Center (☎ 664 51 50; Lilla Torg 9; admission free; 11am-5pm Tue, Wed & Fri, 11am-6pm Thu, 11am-4pm Sat & Sun) showcases cutting-edge design, architecture and art against the 16th-century **Hedmanska Gården**. Pore over design magazines in the cafe or bag Scandi-cool design, fabrics and toys in the gallery shop.

The surrounding cobbled streets are restored pockets of the late-medieval town; the half-timbered houses now house galleries and boutiques selling some brilliant arts and crafts.

For emerging, lesser-known and Scanian artists, check out **Galleri PingPong** (☎ 12 10 59; www.galleripingpong.se; Rådmansgatan 7; 3-6pm Thu & Fri, noon-4pm Sat during exhibitions) and **Skånes Konstförening** (☎ 10 33 80; www.skaneskonst.se; Bragegatan 15/Ystadvägen 22; 1-5pm Wed-Fri, 1-4pm Sat during exhibitions).

UNUSUAL BUILDINGS

The northwest harbour redevelopment is home to the **Turning Torso**, a striking skyscraper that twists through 90 degrees from bottom to top. Designed by Spaniard Santiago Calatrava and inaugurated in 2005, it's now Sweden's tallest building (190m).

For vintage veneers, head for the statue of King Karl X Gustav in the centre of **Stortorget** and spin around (clockwise from the northwestern corner) to see the following buildings. **Kockska Huset** (1524) is a stately pile that mayor Jörgen Kock had built for himself; it's where Gustav Vasa stayed when he dropped into town. There's a top-notch restaurant (Årstiderna; p177) in the vaults beneath. The **County Governor's Residence** is a grand, stuccoed masterpiece built in the 19th century but with a deceptively Renaissance style. Next door **Rådhuset** (the city hall) was originally built in 1546, but has since been altered. At the southeastern corner of the square, the city's oldest pharmacy, **Apoteket Lejonet**, flaunts an exquisite art-nouveau interior, with carved wooden shelves, antique medicinal bottles and a glass-plated ceiling. Founded in 1571, the business originally occupied **Rosenvingeskahuset** on Västergatan.

Just off Östergatan, **St Gertrud Quarter** is a cute cluster of 19 buildings from the 16th to 19th centuries, with the mandatory mix of cobbled walkways, restaurants and bars. Across the road, **Thottska Huset** is Malmö's oldest half-timbered house (1558). It's now a restaurant, so peek inside!

OTHER SIGHTS

Koggmuseet (☎ 33 08 00; www.koggmuseet.se, in Swedish; Skeppsbron 10; adult/6-15yr Skr40/20; ☺ 11am-4pm Jun-Aug, 11am-4pm Tue-Sun Sep-May) is a small museum about cogs (14th-century trading vessels), with two beautiful reconstructed **medieval ships** moored outside. Weather permitting, you can enjoy a sailing on the **small cog** (adult/child Skr30/20; ☺ noon & 2pm Tue-Fri Apr-Sep).

Run by the Red Cross, **Humanitetens Hus** (☎ 32 65 40; Drottningtorget 8; admission free; ☺ noon-8pm Tue, noon-4pm Wed-Fri) has poignant exhibitions on the theme of courage and responsibility. Among the permanent fixtures is one of 36 famous 'white buses' used by the Swedish Red Cross in WWII to save 20,000 people from concentration camps.

Family-friendly **Folkets Park** (Amiralsgatan 37; ☺ park 7am-8pm year-round, attractions noon-7pm May–mid-Aug) boasts a fairground, pony rides and **reptile house** (☎ 30 52 37; adult/5-14yr Skr60/30; ☺ 10am-5pm Mon-Fri, noon-6pm Sat & Sun May & Jun; 10am-7pm Mon-Fri, noon-7pm Sat & Sun Jul & Aug; 10am-5pm Mon-Fri, noon-5pm Sat & Sun Sep-Apr).

Activities

Ask the tourist office for the free cycling map *Cykla i Malmö*. See p179 for bike rental information.

Partly reopened in late 2008, and due to fully reopen in summer 2009, the restored **Aq-va-kul** (☎ 30 05 40; www.aq-va-kul.com, in Swedish; Regementsgatan 24; adult/2-6yr/7-17yr/family Skr75/30/50/185) is a water park with heated indoor and outdoor pools, and a waterslide, wave machine, sauna, solarium and Turkish bath. Check out the website for updates to opening hours.

Ribersborg is a fetching sandy beach backed by parkland, about 2km west of the town centre. Off the beach, at the end of a 200m-long pier, is the adorable, wooden **Ribersborgs Kallbadhus** (☎ 26 03 66; adult/7-17yr Skr55/30; ☺ 8.30am-7pm Mon-Fri, 8.30am-4pm Sat & Sun early May–Aug; noon-7pm Mon-Fri, 9am-4pm Sat & Sun Sep–early May), an open-air naturist saltwater pool, with separate sections for men and women, and a wood-fired **sauna** (☺ 11am-7pm Mon-Fri, 9am-4pm Sat & Sun early May–Aug; noon-7pm Mon-Fri, 9am-4pm Sat & Sun Sep–early May) dating from 1898.

To scoot round Malmö's canals in a pedal boat, head to **City Boats Malmö** (☎ 0704-71 00 67; www.cityboats.se; Amiralsbron, Södra Promenaden; per 30/60min Skr80/130; ☺ daily May-Aug, Sat & Sun Sep), just east of Gustav Adolfs Torg.

Tours

To experience Malmö by water, visit **Rundan** (☎ 611 74 88; www.rundan.se; adult/5-15yr/family Skr85/50/240), opposite Centralstationen. Fifty-minute boat tours of the canals run regularly from May to September (11am to 7pm late June to late August, less frequently at other times), weather depending.

The 1½-hour **sightseeing bus tours** (☎ 18 83 75; adult/6-16yr Skr150/75, free with Malmökortet) are great for getting your bearings. Tours run at 10am, 11.30am and 1.30pm daily (from early June to late August), with reduced services in May and September. A 2½-hour **tour** (adult/6-16yr Skr220/110) also includes a boat trip along Malmö's canals, running daily from 11.30am and 1.30pm, with weekend-only services in May and September. Pick up your ticket at the tourist office, and the staff will show you where to catch the bus on Norra Vallgatan.

Festivals & Events

Malmö's premier annual event – with 1.5 million visitors – is the week-long **Malmö Festival** (www.malmofestivalen.se) in mid-August. The mostly free events include theatre, dance, live music, fireworks and sizzling food stalls.

The week-long **Regnbågsfestivalen** (Rainbow Festival) is Malmö's queer celebration, held in late September and packed with exhibitions, films, parties and a pride parade. Contact **RFSL-Malmö** (☎ 611 99 62; malmo@rfsl.se; Monbijougatan 15), Malmö's gay and lesbian centre, for details.

Sleeping
CAMPING, HOSTELS & PRIVATE ROOMS

Private rooms or apartments from about Skr375 per person are available through **City Room** (☎ 795 94; www.cityroom.se); bed sheets and towels cost an additional Skr100 per set. The agency has no office address but is staffed on weekdays from 9am to noon. Otherwise, contact the tourist office.

STF Vandrarhem Malmö (☎ 822 20; www.malmohostel.se; Backavägen 18; dm Skr150-190, s/d from Skr315/410; P ▣) Well-equipped, if rather large and impersonal, the STF hostel sits 3.5km south of the city centre, overlooking the E6 (take bus 2 from Centralstationen).

Vandrarhemmet Villa Hilleröd (☎ 26 56 26; info@villahillerod.se; Ängdalavägen 38; dm Skr190-240; ▣) This newish hostel sits in a delightful little detached house in the city's west. Little touches such as house plants keep things homely. If you need to cancel your reservation, do so before

6pm on the expected day of arrival or you'll be charged for the night.

Malmö Camping & Feriecenter (☎ 15 51 65; malmo camping@malmo.se; Strandgatan 101; sites Skr200, 2-bed cabins Skr550) By the beach, this campsite has a great view of the Öresund bridge. It's about 5km southwest of the centre of town: take bus 4 from Gustav Adolfs Torg (Skr16).

ourpick Bosses Gästvåningar (☎ 32 62 50; info @bosses.nu; Södra Förstadsgatan 110B; s/d/tr/q from Skr350/495/595/750; ▯) The quiet, clean rooms in this central SVIF hostel are like those of a budget hotel, with proper beds, TVs and shared bathrooms. Service is helpful and the hostel is close to Möllevångstorget and opposite the hospital (follow the signs for 'Sjukhuset' if arriving by car).

HOTELS

The tourist office has a free online hotel booking service: follow the website's links (www .malmo.se).

Hotel Formule 1 (☎ 93 05 80; www.hotelformule1.com; Lundavägen 28; r Skr390) Bargain-basement Formule 1 is 1.5km east of Stortorget, with smallish, functional rooms sleeping up to three people for a flat rate.

Comfort Hotel Malmö (☎ 33 04 40; malmo@comfort .choicehotels.se; Carlsgatan 10C; s Skr500-1545, d Skr800-2045; ▯ ▯) This modern hotel (handy the for train and ferry) has friendly staff and clean, modern (albeit plain-looking) rooms. There's a good-value Skr70 evening buffet Monday to Thursday.

Scandic Hotel St Jörgen (☎ 693 46 00; stjorgen@ scandic-hotels.com; Stora Nygatan 35; s Skr740-1490, d Skr940-1890; ▯ ▯) A sleek, minimalist foyer contrasts with more classically styled rooms at this friendly, upmarket chain. Most rooms have bathtub/shower combos and many look out onto Gustav Adolfs Torg. There are a few windowless 'cabin' rooms, and it's a good idea to book online for the best rates.

Hotel Baltzar (☎ 665 57 00; www.baltzarhotel .se; Södergatan 20; s Skr1180-1550, discounted to Skr800, d Skr1600-1900, discounted to Skr950-1200; ▯) Smack in the heart of town (though it's remarkably quiet), this imposing listed building boasts spacious, flouncy rooms with elegant curtains, armchairs and antique furniture.

ourpick Hotel Duxiana (☎ 607 70 00; bokning@ malmo.hotelduxiana.com; Mäster Johansgatan 1; s/d/junior ste Skr1190/2090/2590, discounted to Skr890/1490/1995; ▯) Close to Centralstationen, ubersleek Hotel Duxiana is one for the style crew. In a palate

of white, black and gunmetal grey, design features include Bruno Mattheson sofas and the same heavenly beds supplied to the world's first seven-star hotel in Dubai. Single rooms are small but comfy, while the decadent junior suites feature a claw-foot bathtub facing the bed.

Mäster Johan Hotel (☎ 664 64 00; www.masterjo han.se; Mäster Johansgatan 13; s Skr1970-2375, discounted to Skr1150-1350, d Skr2220-2625, discounted to Skr1400-1600; ▯ ▯) Just off Lilla Torg is one of Malmö's finest slumber spots, with spacious, elegantly understated rooms featuring beautiful oak floors and snowy-white fabrics. Bathrooms flaunt Paloma Picasso–designed tiles, there's a sauna and gym, and the immaculate breakfast buffet is served in a glass-roofed courtyard.

Eating

Malmö isn't short on dining experiences, whether its vegan grub chowed down in a grungy left-wing hang-out or designer supping on contemporary Nordic flavours. For sheer atmosphere, head to the restaurant-bars on Lilla Torg. Top-notch foodie hot spots dot the city and are your best bet for revamped Scanian classics.

Malmö Chokladfabrik (☎ 45 95 05; Möllevångsgatan 36; ⏲ noon-6pm Mon-Fri, 10am-2pm Sat) Not only does Malmö's 'chocolate factory' peddle heavenly cocoa concoctions (pear and cognac praline, anyone?), you can watch them being made and devour them at the chocolate-scented cafe.

Dolce Sicilia (☎ 611 31 10; Drottningtorget 6; gelato from Skr25; ⏲ 11am-9pm Mar-Oct, 11am-6pm Nov-Feb) Head to Dolce Sicilia, run by certified Sicilians, for fresh, organic Italian-style gelato (the chilli chocolate and fig flavours are divine). Savoury edibles include ciabatta (Skr55) and salads (Skr65).

ourpick Solde (☎ 692 80 87; Regementsgatan 3; panini Skr40; ⏲ Mon-Sat) Malmö's coolest cafe is a grit-chic combo of concrete bar, white-tiled walls, art exhibitions and indie-hip regulars. The owner is an award-winning barista; watch him in action over lip-smacking Italian panini, biscotti and *cornetti* (croissants).

Glassfabriken (☎ 23 81 01; Kristianstadsgatan 16; meals around Skr50; ⏲ Tue-Sun) Easy to miss, this grungy, alcohol-free cafe/cultural bolt hole cranks out cheap, salubrious grub such as vegan salads, ciabatta and freshly baked cakes. Play board games over mango milkshakes, check out the local art on display or catch the occasional music or theatre gig.

Krua Thai (☎ 12 22 87; Möllevångstorget 14; mains Skr80-95; ⏰ 11am-3pm Mon, 11am-3pm & 5-10pm Tue-Fri, 1-10pm Sat, 2-10pm Sun) Down the southern end of town is this authentic, long-standing Thai joint. The family also run a central takeaway (Södergatan 22) for spicy meals on the move.

Rådhuskällaren (☎ 790 20; Stortorget 1; mains Skr105-195; ⏰ lunch Mon-Fri, dinner Mon-Sat, 1-7pm Sun) Tucked away in the city hall's 16th-century barrel-vaulted cellar, Rådhuskällaren balances digestible prices with fusion fare like Cajun-blackened salmon with sautéed *pak choi*, mango and creamy potato cake.

our pick Salt och Brygga (☎ 611 59 40; Sundspromenaden 7, Västra Hamnen; mains Skr195-250; ⏰ 11.30am-4pm & 5-10pm Mon-Fri, noon-10pm Sat & Sun May-Aug; Mon-Fri 11.30am-2.30pm & 6-9pm Mon-Fri, 12.30-9pm Sat Sep-Apr) Overlooking the Öresund bridge, this stylish, contemporary Slow Food restaurant presents updated Swedish cuisine with a clear conscience. Everything is organic (including the staff's uniforms), waste is turned into biogas, and the interior is allergy-free. Flavours are clean and strictly seasonal – think rhubarb soup with lemon verbena, Tahitian vanilla ice cream and Tonka beans. You'll need to book ahead.

our pick Årstiderna (☎ 23 09 10; Frans Suellsgatan 3; mains Skr235-375; ⏰ lunch Mon-Fri, dinner Mon-Sat) If you're out to impress, book a candle-lit table at A-list Årstiderna. Located in the vaulted cellar of Kockska Huset (p174), its soft, elegant atmosphere is seamlessly paired with luxe creations like cognac-infused lobster soup with shellfish spring roll.

Trappaner (☎ 57 97 50; Tegelgårdsgatan 5; mains around Skr295; ⏰ lunch Tue-Fri, dinner Tue-Sat) Tiny, fine-dining Trappaner melds seasonal produce and bold creativity to create sublime dishes like tempered scallops with chamomile, apple must and ground elder. Wines are mostly biodynamic and the tasting menus are perfect for an epicurean adventure.

Self-caterers should head to **Mästerlivs supermarket** (Engelbrektsgatan 15; ⏰ 9am-9pm). The best produce market is on Möllevångstorget, from Monday to Saturday.

Drinking

Bars in Malmö generally stay open until around 1am, although some bars close later on Friday and Saturday evenings.

On Lilla Torg, hit **Victors** (☎ 12 76 70), **Moosehead** (☎ 12 04 23) and **Mello Yello** (☎ 30 45 25); they're great spots, with affable service,

alfresco summer seating (you may have to wait for a table), tasty meals and everything from Chilean whites to outrageous cocktails.

The heaving bars around Möllevångstorget tend to pull a more student, indie crowd, including pared-back DJ-bar **Volym** (☎ 12 45 20; Kristianstadsgatan 7) and the equally hip **Tempo Bar & Kök** (☎ 12 60 21; Södra Skolegatan 30). Both serve great grub.

Systembolaget (Malmborgsgatan 6) sells beers, wines and spirits.

Entertainment

Pick up local newspaper *Sydsvenskan* on a Friday, when it contains the listings mag *Dygnet Runt* (which covers Lund as well as Malmö). Also, scan the weekly street press *Nöjesguiden*. They're both in Swedish but the club and film information is decipherable. Alternatively, take the regular train to Copenhagen for a huge array of options.

NIGHTCLUBS

Clubs generally stay open until around 1am, and clubs to 3am, 4am or 5am on Friday and Saturday. The minimum age requirements (20 to 25) vary from venue to venue and from night to night, so bring ID. Entry usually costs between Skr100 and Skr200.

Debaser (☎ 23 98 80; www.debaser.se, in Swedish; Norra Parkgatan 2; ⏰ 7pm-3am Wed-Sun) Stockholm's music club heavyweight has opened shop in Malmö, with live gigs and club nights spanning anything from indie, pop and hip-hop to soul, electronica and rock. There's a buzzing outdoor bar-lounge overlooking Folkets Park and decent grub until 10pm for a pre-party feed.

Jeriko (☎ 611 84 29; www.jeriko.nu, in Swedish; Spångatan 38) Regular live jazz, folk and world music gigs, with club nights on the weekend.

Kulturbolaget (☎ 30 20 11; www.kulturbolaget.se, in Swedish; Bergsgatan 18) Big-name rock, pop and blues acts perform here, but even if there's no one playing, 'KB' has a kicking bar, nightclub (usually Friday and Saturday) and a well-priced, diner-style restaurant-bar.

Inkonst (☎ 30 65 97; www.inkonst.com, in Swedish; Bergsgatan 29; ⏰ 11pm-3am) This multifunction cultural hang-out serves up some brilliant club nights, pumping out anything from underground UK grime and garage to hip hop and R'n'B. Guest DJs have included the likes of Wiley and Ghetto. Check the website for club-night themes and dates.

Étage (☎ 23 20 60; Stortorget 6; ⏰ 11pm–4am Mon & Thu, 11pm–5am Fri & Sat) Central and mainstream, Étage boasts five bars, glammed-up party crowds and two crowded dance floors (one playing retro, the other the latest house tunes).

Club Wonk (☎ 23 93 03; Amiralsgatan 20; ⏰ 10am–5pm Sat) Malmö's best bet for queer clubbers, Wonk works up the crowd with three bars, lusty video projections and two dance floors (one playing techno, the other playing Schlager).

CINEMAS

Malmö's numerous cinemas include the following:

Biograf Spegeln (☎ 12 59 78; Stortorget 29) Alternative selections.

Filmstaden Malmö (☎ 660 20 90; Storgatan 22) Hollywood releases.

Shopping

The current hot spot for up-and-coming designers and vintage threads is the streets around Davidshallstorg, south of Gamla Staden.

Tjallamalla (☎ 791 90; Davidshallsgatan 15; ⏰ Mon-Sat) Stockholm's legendary purveyor of new and emerging designers now feeds local trendsetters on cult labels like Whyszeck, Merde! and Lund+Berg.

Chique (☎ 0733-39 21 71; Kärleksgatan 3; ⏰ Mon-Sat) In a district famed for vintage stores, this is one of the best. Its candy-store interior heaves with impeccable retro gems, from '70s Christian Dior handbags to dazzling '80s knits and studly cowboy boots.

Formargruppen (☎ 780 60; www.formargrupp .se; Engelbrektsgatan 8; ⏰ Mon-Sat) Representing a dynamic collective of Swedish artists, artisans and designers, this central shop-gallery stocks striking wares, from ceramics and pottery to jewellery and textiles.

Getting There & Away
TO/FROM THE AIRPORT

Flygbuss (☎ 0771-77 77 77; www.flygbussarna.com) runs from Centralstationen to **Sturup airport** (adult/16-25yr/under 16yr with an adult Skr99/79/free, 40 minutes) roughly every 40 minutes on weekdays, with six services on Saturday and seven on Sunday; a taxi shouldn't cost more than Skr400.

AIR

Sturup airport (☎ 613 10 00; www.malmoairport.se) is 33km southeast of Malmö. **SAS** (☎ 0770-72 77 27; www.sas.se) has up to 11 nonstop flights to Stockholm Arlanda daily.

Malmö Aviation (☎ 0771-55 00 10; www.malmoavia tion.se) flies several times daily to Stockholm Bromma airport. International destinations include Antalya (Turkey), Budapest (Hungary), Gran Canaria (Canary Islands) and Heraklion (Crete).

Trains run directly from Malmö to Copenhagen's main airport (Skr95, 35 minutes, every 20 minutes), which has a much wider flight selection.

BUS
Local & Regional

The *länstrafik* (public transport network) operates in zones, with a single journey ranging from Skr16 within the city of Malmö to a maximum of Skr84 within the county. Local trains are your best bet for travel to/from the major towns in Skåne; buses are a good option for towns and out-of-the-way areas not on the train lines.

Local city buses depart from Centralplan, in front of the train station. Tickets can be purchased onboard the bus. Most long-distance regional buses leave from the bus station on Spårvägsgatan, while a few go from the section of Norra Vallgatan in front of Centralplan.

Bus 146 is a useful service to the ferries departing from Trelleborg (Skr51, 40 minutes); this service runs once or twice an hour. Bus 100 to Falsterbo (Skr51, one hour) is equally useful.

Long-Distance

There are two bus terminals with daily departures to Swedish and European destinations. **Travelshop** (Malmö Buss & Resecenter; ☎ 33 05 70; www.travelshop.se; Skeppsbron 10), north of the train station, by the harbour, services (and sells tickets for) several companies, including **Swebus Express** (☎ 0771-21 82 18; www.swebusexpress .com), which runs two to four times daily to Stockholm (Skr400 to Skr600, 8½ hours), four times to Jönköping (Skr293, 4½ hours) and up to 10 times daily to Göteborg (Skr270, three to four hours); five continue to Oslo (Skr442, eight hours).

Säfflebussen (☎ 0771-15 15 15; www.safflebus sen.se) has six buses on the Copenhagen–Malmö–Göteborg route per day, with a couple originating from Berlin and continuing on to Oslo.

The second long-distance bus terminal, **Öresundsterminalen** (☎ 59 09 00; www.oresundster minalen.se; Terminalgatan 10) is reached via bus 35 from Centralstationen towards Flansbjer (Skr16, 30 minutes). From here **Svenska Buss** (☎ 0771-67 67 67; www.svenskabuss.se) runs a service to Stockholm (Skr400, 11 hours) via Karlskrona, four times weekly.

Eurolines also runs services from here to several European destinations – see p331 for details.

Trains are your best option for journeys to Copenhagen and beyond.

CAR & MOTORCYCLE

The E6 motorway runs north–south through Malmö's eastern and southern suburbs on its way from Göteborg to Trelleborg. The E65 motorway runs east to Ystad, the E22 runs northeast to Lund and Kristianstad, and the E20 heads west across the Öresund bridge (p171) to Copenhagen and north (with the E6) to Göteborg.

Several of the larger car-hire companies, such as **Avis** (☎ airport 50 05 15, Centralstationen 778 30; Skeppsbron 13), are represented at Sturup airport and directly opposite Centralstationen. **Hertz** (☎ 33 07 70; Jörgen Kocksgatan 1B) offers a discount to Malmökortet holders.

TRAIN

Pågatågen (local trains) run regularly to Helsingborg (Skr94, one hour), Landskrona (Skr81, 40 minutes), Lund (Skr44, 15 minutes), Simrishamn (Skr84, 1½ hours), Ystad (Skr72, 50 minutes) and other towns in Skåne. Bicycles are half-fare, but are not allowed during peak times except from mid-June to mid-August. The platform is at the end of Centralstationen and you buy tickets from the machine. International rail passes are accepted.

The integrated Öresundregionen transport system operates trains from Helsingborg via Malmö and Copenhagen to Helsingør. The Malmö to Copenhagen Kastrup airport or Copenhagen central station trips take 20 and 35 minutes, respectively (both journeys Skr95); trains leave every 20 minutes.

X2000 (Skr281, 2½ hours) and regional (Skr294, 3¼ hours) trains run several times daily to/from Göteborg. X2000 (Skr422 to Skr1000, 4½ hours, hourly) and Intercity (Skr642, 6½ hours, infrequently) trains run between Stockholm and Malmö.

Getting Around

The customer desks in Centralstationen, Gustav Adolfs Torg and Värnhemstorget (at the east end of Kungsgatan) offer bus information and tickets. Local tickets cost Skr16 for an hour's travel. The bus hubs are Centralplan (in front of Centralstationen), Gustav Adolfs Torg, Värnhemstorget and Triangeln. Malmökortet includes free city bus travel.

Parking in the city is expensive: typical charges are around Skr15 per hour or Skr90 per day (24 hours). Most hotels also charge for parking. Parking in municipal spaces ('Gatukontoret'; ask the tourist office which symbol to look for) is free with Malmökortet.

Malmö's taxis are notorious for ripping people off – avoid them or at least agree on the fare with the driver before hopping in. The tourist office recommends **Taxi Skåne** (☎ 33 03 30) and **Taxi 97** (☎ 97 97 97).

Rent-A-Bike (☎ 0707-49 94 22; www.rent-a-bike.se; Skeppsbron 10; per 24hr Skr120) is located 450m from the Centralstationen tourist office. Otherwise, try **Fridhems Cykelaffär** (☎ 26 03 35; Tessins väg 13; per day Skr75) west of the castle. Both offer discounts to Malmökortet holders.

LUND

☎ 046 / pop 105,300

Centred on a striking cathedral (complete with a giant in the crypt and a magical clock), learned Lund is a soulful blend of leafy parks, medieval abodes and coffee-sipping bookworms. Like most university hubs, however, it loses some of its buzz during the summer, when students head home for the holidays.

Lund is Sweden's second-oldest town, founded by the Danes around 1000 and once the seat of the largest archbishopric in Europe. It's also the birthplace of the inkjet printer!

Information

Banks, ATMs and other services line the main street (Stora Södergatan, changing to Kyrkogatan).

Read about the **university** (www.lu.se) online, and check out www.lund.se for information about the town.

Akademibokhandeln (☎ 19 60 00; Stortorget 2; ⊙ 10am-7pm Mon-Fri, 10am-4pm Sat) Fantastic university bookshop with a huge selection of foreign-language books.

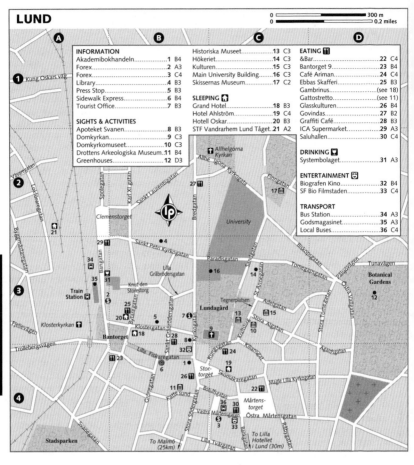

LUND

INFORMATION
Akademibokhandeln................1 B4
Forex....................................2 A3
Forex....................................3 C4
Library..................................4 B3
Press Stop.............................5 B3
Sidewalk Express....................6 B4
Tourist Office.........................7 B3

SIGHTS & ACTIVITIES
Apoteket Svanen.....................8 B3
Domkyrkan.............................9 C3
Domkyrkomuseet....................10 C3
Drottens Arkeologiska Museum..11 B4
Greenhouses..........................12 D3

Historiska Museet..................13 C3
Hökeriet...............................14 C3
Kulturen...............................15 C3
Main University Building.........16 C3
Skissernas Museum................17 C2

SLEEPING
Grand Hotel...........................18 B3
Hotel Ahlström.......................19 C4
Hotell Oskar..........................20 B3
STF Vandrarhem Lund Tåget....21 A2

EATING
&Bar.....................................22 C4
Bantorget 9............................23 B4
Café Ariman..........................24 C4
Ebbas Skafferi.......................25 B3
Gambrinus..........................(see 18)
Gattostretto.........................(see 11)
Glasskulturen........................26 B4
Govindas...............................27 B2
Graffiti Café..........................28 B3
ICA Supermarket....................29 A3
Saluhallen.............................30 C4

DRINKING
Systembolaget.......................31 A3

ENTERTAINMENT
Biografen Kino.......................32 B4
SF Bio Filmstaden..................33 C4

TRANSPORT
Bus Station...........................34 A3
Godsmagasinet......................35 A3
Local Buses..........................36 C4

Forex Bangatan (☎ 32 34 10; Bangatan 8; ⊗ 8am-7pm Mon-Fri, 8am-4pm Sat); Västra Mårtensgatan (☎ 14 07 80; Västra Mårtensgatan 6; ⊗ 9am-7pm Mon-Fri, 10am-3pm Sat) Two central money-exchange offices.

Library (Sankt Petri Kyrkogatan 6; ⊗ 10am-8pm Mon-Thu, 10am-7pm Fri, 10am-4pm Sat, 1-5pm Sun) Free internet access.

Press Stop (Klostergatan 8; ⊗ 10am-6pm Mon-Fri, 10am-1pm Sat) Good choice of foreign magazines and newspapers.

Sidewalk Express (www.sidewalkexpress.se; per hr Skr19) Sidewalk Express internet terminals are found inside the 7-Eleven shop on Lilla Fiskaregatan.

Tourist office (☎ 35 50 40; www.lund.se; Kyrkogatan 11; ⊗ 10am-7pm Mon-Fri, 10am-3pm Sat, 11am-3pm Sun mid-Jun–Aug; 10am-5pm Mon-Fri, 10am-3pm

Sat May–mid-Jun & Sep, 10am-5pm Mon-Fri Oct-Apr) Opposite the cathedral.

Sights

DOMKYRKAN

Lund's twin-towered Romanesque cathedral, **Domkyrkan** (☎ 35 87 00; ⊗ 8am-6pm Mon-Fri, 9.30am-5pm Sat, 9.30am-6pm Sun), is magnificent. Try to pop in at noon or 3pm (1pm and 3pm on Sunday and holidays) when the marvellous astronomical clock strikes up *In Dulci Jubilo* and the wooden figures at the top whirr into action. Within the crypt, you'll find Finn, the mythological giant who helped construct the cathedral, and a 16th-century well carved with comical scenes.

MUSEUMS

Kulturen (☎ 35 04 00; www.kulturen.com; Tegnerplatsen; adult/child Skr70/free; ◷ 11am-5pm mid-Apr–Sep, noon-4pm Tue-Sun Oct–mid-Apr), opened in 1892, is a huge open-air museum filling two whole blocks. Its 30-odd buildings include everything from the meanest birch-bark hovel to grand 17th-century houses. Permanent displays encompass Lund in the Middle Ages, vintage toys, ceramics, silver and glass (among many others); ask about guided tours in English. The popular outdoor cafe flanks several **rune stones**.

Behind the cathedral, **Historiska Museet** (☎ 222 79 44; Kraftstorg; adult/under 18yr Skr30/free; ◷ 11am-4pm Tue-Fri, noon-4pm Sun) has a large collection of pre–Viking Age finds, including a 7000-year-old skeleton. It's joined with **Domkyrkomuseet**, which explores the history of the church in the area; the rooms filled with countless statues of the crucified Christ are supremely creepy.

The wonderful **Skissernas Museum** (Sketch Museum; ☎ 222 72 83; Finngatan 2; adult/under 18yr Skr50/free; ◷ noon-5pm Tue-Sun, to 9pm Wed) has the world's largest collection of sketches and designs for public artworks, from both Swedish and foreign artists, including Henri Matisse, Fernand Léger and Diego Rivera.

Subterranean **Drottens Arkeologiska Museum** (☎ 14 13 28; Kattesund 6A; admission free; ◷ 9am-6pm Mon-Sat) contains the foundations of an 11th-century church, as well as a grisly collection of skeletons that build a picture of the Middle Ages through their diseases and amputations. Entrance is through the Gattostretto (p182) restaurant.

Numerous galleries and small, special-interest museums and archives are dotted around town, many attached to university departments – enquire at the tourist office.

OTHER SIGHTS

The main **university building**, topped by four sphinxes representing the original faculties, is worth a peek.

The 8-hectare **Botanical Gardens** (☎ 222 73 20; Östra Vallgatan 20; admission free; ◷ 6am-9.30pm mid-May–mid-Sep, 6am-8pm mid-Sep–mid-May), east of the town centre, feature around 7000 species. Also on site are tropical **greenhouses** (admission free; ◷ noon-3pm).

Check out the recently restored pharmacy, **Apoteket Svanen** (Kyrkogatan 5), close to the tourist office. Across the park, **Hökeriet** (☎ 35 04 04; cnr St Annegatan & Tomegapsgatan; ◷ noon-5pm Tue-Sun) is a vintage general store.

Sleeping

The tourist office can arrange a private room from Skr300 per person plus a Skr50 booking fee.

STF Vandrarhem Lund Tåget (☎ 14 28 20; www .trainhostel.com; Vävaregatan 22; dm Skr150) This quirky hostel is based in old railway carriages in parkland behind the station. The triple bunks and tiny rooms are okay if you're cosying up with loved ones, but a little claustrophobic with strangers. Less novel are the hot-water vending machines in the showers (have a few Skr1 coins handy).

Hotel Ahlström (☎ 211 01 74; www.hotellahlstrom .se, in Swedish; Skomakaregatan 3; s/d with shared bathroom Skr730/900, discounted to Skr550/700, d with shared bathroom Skr1100, discounted to Skr900) Lund's oldest hotel is friendly and affordable, and on a quiet, central street. Rooms have parquet floors, cool white walls and washbasins (most bathrooms are shared). Breakfast (included in room prices) is brought to your door.

Lilla Hotellet i Lund (☎ 32 88 88; lillahotellet@ telia.com; Bankgatan 7; s/d Skr1280/1480, discounted to Skr780/980; ◷ mid-Aug–mid-Jul; P ⌨) Partly housed in an old shoe factory, this homely spot peddles cosy rooms (think patchwork quilts and DVD players), as well as a sunny courtyard and guest lounge.

Hotell Oskar (☎ 18 80 85; www.hotelloskar.com; Bytaregatan 3; s/d Skr1395/1595, discounted to Skr895/1095; ⌨) This dinky place in a 19th-century townhouse has smashing rooms filled with sleek Scandi design. It's also well equipped, with DVD players, kettles and stereos.

Grand Hotel (☎ 280 61 00; hotel@grandilund.se; Bantorget 1; s Skr1525-1975, discounted to Skr795-1275, d Skr2175-2375, discounted to Skr1675-1775; ⌨) Lund's most luxurious establishment is the Grand, which opened in 1899 and is resplendent with gilt and chandeliers. Rooms are smallish, but decorated in grand style with heavy wooden beds, Persian carpets and cherub wallpaper. Extras include a sauna and upmarket dining at Gambrinus (p182).

Eating & Drinking

Saluhallen (Mårtenstorget; ◷ Mon-Sat) A mouthwatering market hall, it peddles reasonably priced grub, from fresh fish and piping-hot pasta to Thai, kebabs and croissants.

Glasskulturen (☎ 211 00 14; Stortorget 8) On the main square, join the queues for delectable gourmet ice cream.

Café Ariman (☎ 13 12 63; Kungsgatan 2B; snacks around Skr40; ⏰ 11am-midnight Mon, 11am-1am Tue-Thu, 11am-3am Fri & Sat, 3-11pm Sun, closed Sun in summer) Head to this hip, grungy hang-out for cathedral views, strong coffee and fine cafe fare such as ciabatta, salads and burritos. It's popular with left-wing students: think nose-rings, dreads and leisurely chess games. From September to May, DJs hit the decks on Friday and Saturday nights.

Gattostretto (☎ 32 07 77; Kattesund 6A; salads Skr60; mains Skr170-210 ⏰ 9am-6pm Mon-Sat) Located over medieval ruins and co-run by an affable Roman chef, this breezy cafe-restaurant serves a tasty slice of *dolce vita*. Guzzle down proper Italian espresso and a slice of *torta rustica*, or long for Rome over hearty ragú, zesty artichoke salad or a warming *pollo alla cacciatore* (chicken cacciatore).

Ebbas Skafferi (☎ 13 41 56; Bytaregatan 5; lunch Skr65; ⏰ 9am-7pm Mon-Fri, 9am-6pm Sat & Sun) Ebbas is the perfect cafe: think warm wooden tables, green plants and flowers, odd bits of artwork, a laid-back courtyard, and scrumptious coffee, tea and tasty grub such as hearty risotto and moreish cheesecake.

Govindas (☎ 12 04 13; Bredgatan 28; lunch Skr70; ⏰ lunch Mon-Sat) In a quiet, leafy cobbled courtyard, vegetarian Govindas is a hit with kronor-conscious students.

&Bar (☎ 211 22 88; Mårtenstorget 9; lunch Skr70-80, dinner mains Skr145-225) Chic &Bar is relaxed enough to attract a range of people for its lunchtime bagels, salads and specials, while à la carte dinner mains traverse Swedish and international influences. From 10pm, head in for cocktails and smooth lounge tunes.

Gambrinus (☎ 280 61 00; Bantorget 1; lunch around Skr170, dinner mains Skr235-295, Lund menu Skr360) The star turn at the Grand Hotel's gourmet nosh spot is the Lund menu, featuring creative interpretations of regional classics using seasonal local produce. While the speciality is sweetbreads, there's a vegetarian menu for herbivorous guests.

Bantorget 9 (☎ 32 02 00; Bantorget 9; mains Skr245-315; ⏰ from 6pm Mon-Sat) This is another gourmet darling, where you can snuggle down in cosy candlelight and feast on the likes of spring chicken with foie gras, almonds and pears. There's a worldly wine list to further oil the evening.

Self-caterers should head to the **ICA supermarket** (Bangatan; ⏰ 8am-10pm) opposite the train station. For alcohol, **Systembolaget** (Bangatan 10) is near the supermarket.

Entertainment

Pick up the brochure *i Lund* from the tourist office for the entertainment run-down.

Cinemas in Lund include the following:

Biografen Kino (☎ 30 30 80; Kyrkogatan 3) Art-house films.

SF Bio Filmstaden (☎ 0856-26 00 00; Västra Mårtensgatan 12) Mainstream flicks.

Getting There & Away

Flygbuss (☎ 0771-77 77 77) runs regularly to Malmö's Sturup airport (Skr99); see p178.

It's 15 minutes from Lund to Malmö by train, with frequent Pågatågen departures (Skr39). Some trains continue to Copenhagen (Skr125, one hour). Other direct services run from Malmö to Kristianstad and Karlskrona via Lund. All long-distance trains from Stockholm or Göteborg to Malmö stop in Lund.

Long-distance buses leave from outside the train station. Most buses to/from Malmö (except buses to Trelleborg and Falsterbo) run via Lund. See p178 for details.

Getting Around

Stadsbussarna (☎ 0771-77 77 77) local town buses cost Skr15 per ride; the terminal is on Botulfsplatsen, west of Mårtenstorget. Phone **Taxi Skåne** (☎ 33 03 30) for a taxi. For bike hire, head to **Godsmagasinet** (☎ 35 57 42; Bangatan; per day/week Skr20/130; ⏰ 6.30am-9.30pm Mon-Fri), a bicycle lock-up in the northernmost train-station building.

FALSTERBO PENINSULA

☎ 040

This laid-back peninsula 30km south of Malmö lures sun-lovers with its sandy beaches and ornithologists with its impressive posse of feathered creatures. Eclectic extras include the unmissable Foteviken Viking Reserve and the offbeat amber museum.

The area's major **tourist office** (☎ 42 54 54; www.vellinge.se/turism, in Swedish; Östra Hamnplan 2; ⏰ 10am-6pm Mon-Fri, 10am-2pm Sat & Sun mid-Jun–mid-Aug; 10am-noon & 1-4pm Mon-Fri Apr–mid-Jun & mid-Aug–mid-Oct; 10am-noon & 1-3pm Mon-Fri mid-Oct–mid-Dec & early Jan–Mar) is just outside Höllviken, near the lifting bridge. The town of Höllviken has banks and supermarkets.

Bärnstensmuseum

Trapped in sticky resin 40 million years ago, insects fight, mate and feed in pieces of amber at the **Bärnstensmuseum** (Amber Museum; ☎ 45 45 04; www.brost.se; Södra Mariavägen 4; adult/child Skr20/10; ⏰ 10am-6pm mid-Jun–mid-Aug; 11am-5pm mid-May–mid-Jun & mid-Aug–Sep; 11am-5pm Sat & Sun Oct–mid-May). It's small but interesting; museum staff acted as advisors to the makers of *Jurassic Park*.

The museum is near Höllviken's southern edge, just off the coast road towards Trelleborg.

Foteviken Viking Reserve

If you mourn the passing of big hairy men in longboats, find solace at one of Sweden's most absorbing attractions, about 700m north of Höllviken. **Foteviken Viking Reserve** (Vikingareservatet vid Foteviken; ☎ 33 08 00; www.foteviken .se; adult/6-15yr Skr60/25; ⏰ 10am-4pm Jun-Aug, 10am-4pm Mon-Fri late-April–May & Sep-Oct) is an evocative 'living' reconstruction of a late–Viking Age village. Entry price includes a fantastic one-hour guided tour (Swedish, plus English), departing at 11am, 1pm and 2.30pm.

Around 22 authentic reconstructions of houses with reed or turf roofs have been built on the coast, near the site of the Battle of Foteviken (1134). These belong to various tradespeople, like the town's *jarl* (commander of the armed forces), juror and scribe; and the chieftain, whose home has wooden floorboards, fleeces and a Battle of Foteviken tapestry. There's even a shield-lined great hall (the Thinghöll), a lethally powerful war catapult and nifty Viking-made handicrafts to buy.

Amazingly, the reserve's residents live as the Vikings did, eschewing most modern conveniences and adhering to old traditions, laws and religions – even after the last tourist has left.

Viking Week is usually held in late June, and culminates in a Viking market, complete with agile warriors in training.

There's a reasonable **hostel** (☎ 040-33 08 06; cottages per night/week Skr630/3600) just outside the reserve for visitors.

Falsterbo & Skanör

Little **Falsterbo Museum** (☎ 47 05 13; bengt.04472242@ telia.com; Sjögatan; adult/7-16yr Skr20/10; ⏰ 10am-7pm mid-Jun–mid-Aug), at the southern tip of the peninsula, is a pleasing jumble: a small Naturum, old shops and smithies, WWII mines and the remains of a 13th-century boat.

Falsterbo's long sandy **beach** is popular with locals and Malmö leisure-seekers. The sandy hook-shaped island of **Måkläppen** is a nature reserve, off-limits to the public from March to October. Residents include seals and over 50 species of birds, including little terns, Kentish plovers (rare in Sweden) and avocets; in the autumn, between one and three million migrating birds rest their wings here. Near the museum is **Falsterbo Fågelstation** (☎ 47 06 88; falsterbo@skof.se; Sjögatan; guided tours per person Skr30, minimum Skr300 for groups of less than 10; ⏰ Apr, May & Aug-Oct, advanced booking required), a bird observatory studying these feathery visitors.

The super-friendly **Ljungens Camping** (☎ 47 11 32; ljungenscamping@telia.com; Strandbadsvägen; sites Skr160-200; ⏰ mid-Apr–Sep) is a couple of kilometres from Falsterbo. Its amenities include minigolf.

ourpick Da Aldo (☎ 47 40 26; Mellangatan 47; gelato from Skr25, piadine Skr49; ⏰ 8.30am-10pm summer, 11am-6pm Wed-Sun rest of year), in the town of Skanör, an easy 1.5km north of Falsterbo, is an outstanding cafe where Calabrian expat Aldo makes sublime gelato using strictly Italian ingredients and no added egg, cream or butter. Lunch options, from frittata and salads to *piadine* (Italian flat-bread sandwiches) and stuffed aubergine, are well priced and equally authentic. As for the coffee…*buonissimo!*

By the harbour, marine-chic **Skanörs Fiskrögeri** (☎ 47 40 50; Skanörs Hamn; mains Skr190-455; ⏰ lunch & dinner Jun-Aug, dinner Thu & Fri, lunch & dinner Sat & Sun Mar-May & Sep) is a must for seafood-lovers. The fish soup is exquisite and there's a gourmet seafood deli to boot.

Bus 100 (Skr51, 55 minutes, every 30 minutes Monday to Saturday, every 30 to 60 minutes Sunday) runs from Malmö to Falsterbo and Skanör.

TRELLEBORG
☎ 0410 / pop 41,000

Trelleborg is the main gateway between Sweden and Germany, with frequent ferry services. It's not really on the tourist trail: if you're entering Sweden from here, consider heading on for Malmö or Ystad.

Information

Banks and ATMs line Algatan.

Forex (CB Friisgatan 3; ⏰ 8am-9.30pm Mon-Fri, 8am-2pm Sat, noon-3pm Sun) Money exchange.

GZ (☎ 413 40; Algatan 66; per hr Skr20; ⏰ noon-midnight Mon-Sun) Internet access.

Library (☎ 531 80; CB Friisgatan 17-19; ⏱ 10am-6pm Mon-Fri, 11am-2pm Sat, closed Sat Jun-Aug) Free internet access.

Tourist office (☎ 73 33 20; www.trelleborg.se/turism; Hamngatan 9; ⏱ 9am-7pm Mon-Fri, 10am-6pm Sat, 10am-5pm Sun Jun-Aug; 9am-5pm Mon-Fri Sep-May) Inside the harbour-side complex, it also sells stamps.

Sights

Trelleborgen (☎ 460 77; admission free; ⏱ 10am-5pm mid-Jun–Aug, 9am-5pm Mon-Fri Sep–mid-Jun) is a 9th-century Viking ring fortress, discovered in 1988 off Bryggaregatan (just west of the town centre). It's built to the same pattern as Danish fortresses of the same era, showing the centralised power of Harald Bluetooth at work. A quarter of the palisaded fort and a wooden gateway have been recreated, as has a Viking farmhouse and a medieval house built within the walls. An on-site **visitors centre** (adult/under 15yr Skr40/free; ⏱ 10am-5pm mid-Jun–Aug, 10am-3pm Mon-Fri Sep–mid-Jun) showcases finds from the archaeological digs, including Viking jewellery, grooming implements and a circa-10th-century skull illustrating the ancient trend of teeth filing.

Just east of the town centre, **Trelleborgs Museum** (☎ 73 30 50; Östergatan 58; adult/under 20yr Skr30/free, includes admission to Axel Ebbe Konsthall; ⏱ 1-5pm Tue-Sun) covers a wide range of themes, including a 7000-year-old settlement discovered nearby.

By the town park, **Axel Ebbe Konsthall** (☎ 530 56; Hesekillegatan 1; adult/under 20yr incl admission to Trelleborgs Museum Skr30/free; ⏱ 1-4pm Tue-Sun summer) features nude sculptures by Scanian Axel Ebbe (1868–1941). For a preview, check out the fountain **Sjöormen**, literally 'the sea monster', in Storatorget.

Sleeping & Eating

The tourist office can book private rooms from Skr300.

Dalabadets Camping (☎ 149 05; Dalabadets Strandväg 2; sites Skr200, 4-bed cabins from Skr450) This is the nearest camping ground, over 3km to the east. It's a well-equipped place between Rd 9 and the beach.

Night Stop (☎ 410 70; Östergatan 59; s/d Skr250/350; ℗) Simple and functional with shared bathrooms, Night Stop has the cheapest beds in town. Open 24 hours, it's about 500m from the ferry (turn right along Hamngatan after disembarking), diagonally opposite the museum. Breakfast is an additional Skr50.

Hotell Horizont (☎ 71 32 39; info@horizont.nu; Hamngatan 9; s/d Skr950/1150, discounted to Skr890/1050; ℗ 🍴 🖥) Crash here for clean, modern rooms, some with harbour views. Featuring a top-floor restaurant, bar and cafe, it's in the same building as the tourist office.

Dannegården (☎ 481 80; office@dannegarden.se; Strandgatan 32; s/d Skr985/1148, discounted to Skr700/952; ℗ 🖥) Trelleborg's most beautiful slumber spot is this old sea captain's villa. Rooms are discreetly luxurious, although those in the newer wing lack the same baronial charm. Extras include a reputable restaurant and gorgeous gardens.

Café Vattentornet (☎ 73 30 70; Stortorget; sandwiches from Skr25; ⏱ Mon-Sat) On the ground floor of the splendid 58m-high water tower (1912), Café Vattentornet sells sandwiches, cakes and other yummy snacks, with fabulous outdoor tables in the summer.

Restaurang & Pizzeria Istanbul (☎ 44 44 44; Algatan 30; mains Skr60-220) This bustling place has a huge menu of pasta, pizza, salad and kebabs, plus pricier local fish and meat dishes.

Getting There & Away

Bus 146 runs roughly every half-hour between Malmö (Skr51, 45 minutes) and Trelleborg's bus station, some 500m inland from the ferry terminals. Bus 165 runs frequently Monday to Friday (five services Saturday and four services Sunday) from Lund (Skr63, one hour and five minutes). See p188 for bus travel from Ystad.

For details of international trains from Malmö to Berlin via Trelleborg, see p332.

Scandlines (☎ 650 00; www.scandlines.se) ferries connect Trelleborg to Sassnitz (five daily) and Rostock (two or three daily). **TT-Line** (☎ 562 00; www.ttline.com) ferries shuttle between Trelleborg and Travemünde three to five times daily, and between Trelleborg and Rostock up to three times daily. Buy tickets inside the building housing the tourist office (Hamngatan 9). See p335 for details.

SMYGEHUK
☎ 0410

Thanks to the power of geography – it's Sweden's most southerly point (latitude 55°20'3") – diminutive Smygehuk has become something of a tourist magnet, despite its modest attractions.

To the east of the harbour, a summer **tourist office** (☎ 240 53; ⏱ 10am-7pm Jul, 10am-6pm Jun

& Aug) and cafe sit inside **Köpmansmagasinet**, a renovated 19th-century warehouse with local exhibitions of fantastic handicrafts and art (for sale). Nearby, a huge 19th-century **lime kiln** recalls the bygone lime industry; it smoked its last in 1954.

West of the harbour, scramble to the top of the now-defunct **lighthouse** (17m), dating from 1883, and visit the tiny maritime museum inside **Captain Brinck's Cabin** (donation appreciated; ☉ summer). Opening hours are erratic; the lighthouse is managed by the hostel warden, and she opens it if/when she feels like it. A soothing **coastal path** features prolific bird life.

STF Vandrarhem Smygehuk (☎ 245 83; info@smygehukhostel.com; dm from Skr150; ☉ Feb-Nov; **P**) is a comfortable, well-equipped hostel in the old lighthouse-keeper's residence, next to the lighthouse. Book ahead outside the high season.

Harbour eating options include a fast-food kiosk and a fish smokehouse.

The Trelleborg to Ystad bus service (see p188) stops in Smygehuk.

YSTAD
☎ 0411 / pop 27,700

Half-timbered houses, rambling cobbled streets and the haunting sound of a nightwatchman's horn give this medieval market town an intoxicating lure. Fans of writer Henning Mankell know it as the setting for his best-selling Inspector Wallander crime thrillers, while fans of drums and uniforms head in for the spectacular three-day **Military Tattoo** in August.

Ystad was Sweden's window to Europe from the 17th to the mid-19th century, with new ideas and inventions – including cars, banks and hotels – arriving here first. Now a terminal for ferries to Bornholm and Poland, the port's transitory feel doesn't spread to the rest of Ystad: settle in for a few days and let the place work its magic.

Information
Banks, and other services line Hamngatan.
Forex (ferry terminal; ☉ 8am-9.30pm Mon-Fri, 10am-9.30pm Sat & Sun) Money exchange.
Library (Surbrunnsvägen 12; ☉ 11am-7pm Mon-Thu, 11am-5pm Fri, 10am-2pm Sat) Free internet access.
Tourist office (☎ 57 76 81; www.ystad.se; St Knuts Torg; ☉ 9am-7pm Mon-Fri, 10am-6pm Sat & Sun mid-Jun–mid-Aug; 9am-5pm Mon-Fri mid-Aug–mid-Jun;, plus 11am-2pm Sat mid-May–mid-Jun & late Aug–late Sep) Just opposite the train station; it also offers free internet access.

Sights
Half-timbered houses are scattered liberally round town, especially on Stora Östergatan. Most date from the latter half of the 18th century, although the facade of beautiful **Änglahuset** on Stora Norregatan originates from around 1630.

Don't miss the **Sankta Maria Kyrka** (Stortorget; ☉ 10am-6pm Jun-Aug, 10am-4pm Sep-May). Ever since 1250, a night watchman has blown his horn through the little window in the church clock tower (every 15 minutes from 9.15pm to 3am). The watchman was traditionally beheaded if he dozed off! Among the highlights are a 17th-century baroque pulpit, along with a line of pews near the entrance for women who had recently given birth and hadn't yet been churched. **Latinskolan**, next to Sankta Maria Kyrka, is a late-15th-century brick building and the oldest preserved school in Scandinavia.

Klostret i Ystad (☎ 57 72 86; St Petri Kyrkoplan; adult/under 16yr Skr50/free; ☉ 10am-5pm Mon-Fri, noon-4pm Sat & Sun Jun-Aug, noon-5pm Tue-Fri, noon-4pm Sat & Sun Sep-May), in the Middle Ages Franciscan monastery of Gråbrödraklostret, features local textiles and silverware. The monastery includes the 13th-century deconsecrated Sankt Petri Kyrkan (now used for art exhibitions), which has around 80 gravestones from the 14th to 18th centuries. Included in the same ticket, and with the same opening hours, is the **Ystads Konstmuseum** (☎ 57 72 85; St Knuts Torg). In the same building as the tourist office, its savvy collection of southern Swedish and Danish art includes work by the great Per Kirkeby.

For fetching interiors, pop into **Charlotte Berlins Museum** (☎ 188 66; Dammgatan 23; adult/under 16yr Skr10/free; ☉ noon-5pm Mon-Fri, noon-4pm Sat & Sun Jun-Aug), which is a late-19th-century middle-class abode.

Sleeping
Travellers with their own wheels can select from the B&B and cabin options along the scenic coastal roads on either side of Ystad. The tourist office can arrange B&B accommodation for around Skr600 to Skr800 per double room.

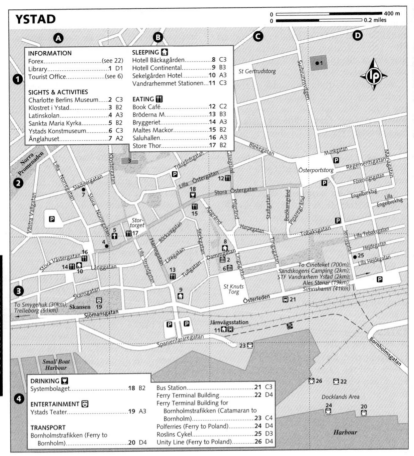

YSTAD

STF Vandrarhem Ystad (☎ 665 66; kantarellen@ turistlogi.se; Fritidsvägen 9; dm Skr170) In a charming sky-blue building, this beachside hostel has good facilities for travellers, including bike rental for covering the 2km into the town centre.

Sandskogens Camping (☎ 192 70; info@sandskogen scamping.se; sites low/high season Skr175/220, cabins from Skr420-520; ☯ May-Sep) This super-friendly (and super-busy) wooded site is 2km east of Ystad on Rd 9 to Simrishamn, across the road from the beach and STF hostel. Bus 572 drives past from town.

Vandrarhemmet Stationen (☎ 0708-57 79 95; ystad.stationen@home.se; dm from Skr200) More convenient is the central SVIF hostel, in the renovated railway building at Ystad train station. Bring cash as credit cards aren't accepted.

Hotell Bäckagården (☎ 198 48; www.backagarden .nu; Dammgatan 36; s/d from Skr620/750; ☐) Exuding a warm and homely feel, this cosy guesthouse occupies a 17th-century home one block behind the tourist office. The lovely walled garden is perfect for sunny breakfasts.

Sekelgården Hotel (☎ 739 00; info@sekelgarden.se; Långgatan 18; s/d from Skr795/995; ☐ ☐) A romantic family-run hotel in a superb half-timbered house (1793), the rooms here take their inspiration from historical styles or people. There's also a sauna and gorgeous courtyard.

Hotell Continental (☎ 137 00; www.hotelcontinen tal-ystad.se; Hamngatan 13; s incl breakfast Skr840-1290, d incl breakfast Skr940-1595; ☐ ☐) On the site of the old customs house, the Continental is reputedly Sweden's oldest hotel, having opened in 1829. Loaded with old-world charm (think grand chandeliered foyer and marble staircase), its rooms are less luxe, although all are clean and feature ultra-comfy beds. There's a bar, a restaurant and a fantastic breakfast buffet.

Eating & Drinking

Book Café (☎ 134 03; Gåsegränd; ⏰ Tue-Sat) Plunge into that Henning Mankell novel at this adorable cafe, complete with book-crammed living room, 18th-century courtyard, and a delicious array of focaccias, pastries and coffee.

Bröderna M (☎ 271 43; Hamngatan 11; pizzas Skr50-115) Relaxed and contemporary, this is your best bet for a decent pizza in Ystad. Upmarket varieties include a lip-licking bresaola, pecorino, rocket and roasted pine-nuts combo.

Bryggeriet (☎ 699 99; Långgatan 20; mains Skr80-190) Unique Bryggeriet is a relaxed meat-leaning restaurant-pub in an old brewery. The courtyard is an excellent spot to linger over a well-cooked meal and Ystad Färsköl, a beer brewed on the premises.

ourpick Store Thor (☎ 185 10; Stortorget; lunch around Skr85, mains Skr120-240; ⏰ closed Sun winter) Ystad's coolest spot to sip'n'sup, Store Thor occupies the arched cellar of the old town hall (1572). Nibble on tapas or tuck into succulent grilled meats and sterling dishes such as cognac raw-spiced salmon with dill-stewed potatoes. The square-side terrace is a hit with trendy summertime night owls.

Most budget eating places are on Stora Östergatan, the main pedestrian street, like busy **Maltes Mackor** (☎ 101 30; ⏰ Mon-Sat) at No 12, with a great range of sandwiches and rolls. The **Saluhallen** (Stora Västergatan; ⏰ 8am-8pm), behind the church, is handy for groceries. For alcohol, there's **Systembolaget** (Stora Östergatan 13).

Entertainment

The extraordinary **Ystads Teater** (☎ 57 71 99; Skansgatan; tickets around Skr300) has remained virtually unchanged since opening in 1894 and its repertoire spans operas, musicals, tango and big-band gigs. Guided tours (usually in Swedish) of the building take place daily from late June to August. Contact the tourist office for details.

SOUTHERN SWEDEN

INSPECTOR WALLANDER'S YSTAD

Fans of crime thrillers most likely know the name of Henning Mankell (1948–), author of the best-selling Inspector Wallander series. The books are set in the small, seemingly peaceful town of Ystad. The gloomy inspector paces its medieval streets, solving gruesome murders through his meticulous police work…but at a cost to his personal life, which is slowly and painfully disintegrating. The first book is *Faceless Killers*, but it's generally agreed that Mankell really hit his stride in number four, *The Man Who Smiled*. Impressively, Mankell's nail-biting stories have been translated into 36 languages.

Between 2005 and 2006, 13 Wallander films were shot in and around Ystad, starring Krister Henriksson in the lead role. The first, an adaptation of the latest Wallander novel, *Before The Frost*, is followed by 12 independent stories by Mankell. In 2008 a further 13 Wallander films were shot here, alongside a BBC-commissioned TV series starring Kenneth Branagh as Wallander.

Interactive film centre **Cineteket** (☎ 0411-57 70 57; www.cineteket.se; Elis Nilssons väg 8; adult/3-18yr/family Skr120/60/300; ⏰ 10am-5pm mid-May–mid-Sep, times vary rest of year) runs guided tours at 11am daily (mid-May to mid-September) of the adjoining Ystad Studios, where sets include forensic detective Leif Nyberg's laboratory and the inspector's own apartment.

The Ystad tourist office provides a free map with featured locations in town. For a quirkier excursion around Wallander's Ystad, the volunteer fire brigade runs tours on a veteran fire engine on Tuesday and Thursday evenings in Swedish and on Monday and Wednesday evenings in German, from late June to mid-August. Contact the tourist office for details, and book a few days in advance.

These days, Mankell spends much of his time in Maputo, Mozambique, where he juggles writing, running a theatre company and his AIDS education work. His wife, Eva Bergman, is the daughter of the late film director Ingmar Bergman.

Getting There & Away

BOAT

Unity Line (☎ 55 69 00; www.unityline.se) and **Polferries** (☎ 040-12 17 00; www.polferries.se) operate daily crossings between Ystad and Swinoujscie; see p335 for details. Ystad's ferry terminal is within walking distance of the train station (drivers follow a more circuitous route).

Bornholmstrafikken (☎ 55 87 00; www.bornholm strafikken.dk) run frequent ferries and catamarans between Ystad and Rønne, on the Danish island of Bornholm: see p335. Catamarans operate from a terminal directly behind the train station.

BUS

Buses depart from outside Ystad train station. Bus 190 runs from Ystad to Trelleborg (Skr63, one hour) via Smygehuk 12 times daily on weekdays, six times on Saturday and twice on Sunday. The direct bus to Simrishamn (Skr45, one hour) via Löderup runs three to nine times daily.

SkåneExpressen bus 6 runs to Lund (Skr81, 1¼ hours, hourly weekdays, infrequently on weekends) and bus 4 runs three to nine times daily to Kristianstad (Skr63, 1¾ hours). Local train is the only way to get to Malmö.

TRAIN

Pågatågen trains run roughly every hour (fewer on weekends) from Malmö (Skr75, 50 minutes). Other local trains run up to 12 times daily to Simrishamn (Skr39, 40 minutes).

Getting Around

There are a handful of local bus services; all depart from outside the tourist office (St Knuts Torg). Try **Taxi Ystad** (☎ 720 00) for a taxi or **Roslins Cykel** (☎ 123 15; Jennygatan 11; per day/week Skr65/295; Mon-Sat) for bike hire.

AROUND YSTAD
Ales Stenar

Ales Stenar has all the mystery of England's Stonehenge, with none of the commercial greed. It's Sweden's largest stone ship setting and an intriguing sight. The 67m-long oval of stones, shaped like a boat, was probably constructed around AD 600 for reasons unknown. Limited excavations at the site have revealed no body; it's possible that this wasn't a grave but a ritual site, with built-in solar calendar (the 'stem' and 'stern' stones point towards the midsummer sunset and midwinter sunrise).

The enigmatic ship is in the middle of a raised field, with an uncannily low and level 360-degree horizon. There's a tiny **shack** at Kåseberga harbour offering information about the stones. Visitors do swamp the place, particularly in summer, and the harbour car park is chaotic – the one off the main road is better. From either place, the setting is a 1km walk.

Free to visit and always open, Ales Stenar lies 19km east of Ystad at Kåseberga. It's badly served by public transport. Bus 322 from Ystad runs three times daily in summer; at other times, take bus 570 from Ystad to Valleberga *kyrka* (church) and then walk 5km south to Kåseberga.

Löderups Strandbad
☎ 0411

With its long, white-sand beaches, the Baltic resort of Löderups Strandbad, 4km east of Ales Stenar, is perfect for lounging, although it can get busy during the school holidays.

Dag Hammarskjölds Backåkra (☎ 52 60 10; Löderup; adult/under 15yr Skr30/free; noon-5pm mid-Jun–mid-Aug, Sat & Sun only rest of Aug), about 1km east of Löderups Strandbad, was a summer house acquired by the secretary-general of the UN in 1957. Hammarskjöld was killed in a mysterious plane crash in Zambia four years later; many of his unusual belongings and souvenirs were moved to this peaceful place to form a memorial museum. The old farmhouse is set in a **nature reserve** of sand dunes, heath and wildflower meadows.

On the edge of the Hagestad Nature Reserve, **Löderups Strandbads Camping** (☎ 52 63 11; sites Skr160, cabins from Skr500; Apr-Sep) is a pleasant spot in a pine forest next to the beach.

Beside the main road, the helpful **STF Vandrarhem Backåkra** (☎ 52 60 80; www.backakra.se; dm Skr180; mid-Jun–mid-Aug;) has simple but cheery rooms, a great garden and bicycles for rent, plus it's within walking distance of the beach. Book ahead in summer.

Near the campsite, the family hotel **Löderups Strandbad Hotell** (☎ 52 62 60; www.loderupsstrandbad .com; s/d Skr670/895, discounted to Skr515/740;) is a popular summer spot, complete with sauna, heated outdoor pool and restaurant. Cheaper rooms (without bathrooms) are available, as are some great cabins, all with sea views (rented by the week only in high season; Skr6995).

See left for bus details from Ystad.

ÖSTERLEN
☎ 0414 / pop 19,400

Softly lit Österlen is an alluring area of waving wheat fields, tiny fishing villages and glorious apple orchards. Everything moves at a slow, seductive speed: cycling is the best way of fitting in with the tempo.

Simrishamn

Summer holidaymakers mill around Simrishamn harbour, idly licking ice creams or waiting for the ferry to the Danish island of Bornholm. The quaint pastel-hued houses on **Lilla Norregatan** are worth a look, as is nearby **Sankt Nikolai Kyrka**. Engine-heads shouldn't miss **Österlens Motor & Teknikmuseum** (☎ 0702-03 94 20; www.osterlensmotormuseum.se, in Swedish; Fabriksgatan 10; adult/7-14yr Skr75/50; �‌ noon-6pm Mon-Fri, 11am-4pm Sat & Sun early Jun–mid-Oct), with its booty of classic cars, bikes and buggies.

The **tourist office** (☎ 81 98 00; www.turistbyra.simrishamn.se; Tullhusgatan 2; ☉ 9am-8pm Mon-Fri, 10am-8pm Sat, 11am-8pm Sun Jun-Aug; 9am-5pm Mon-Fri Sep-May) has information on the whole of Österlen. For internet access, try **Konsol Butiken** (☎ 178 70; Stora Rådmansgatan 7; per 20min Skr10; ☉ noon-9pm Mon-Fri, noon-midnight Sat & Sun), just off Lilla Norregatan. Banks and other services line Storgatan.

SLEEPING & EATING

Tobisviks Camping (☎ 41 27 78; sites/cabins from Skr120/600; ☲) By the beach 2km north of the town centre, this serviceable site neighbours a swimming pool.

STF Vandrarhem Simrishamn (☎ 105 40; info@simrishamnsvandrarhem.se; Christian Barnekowsgatan 10C; dm Skr200; ☉ Mar-Nov; 🖳) Pick up a map before setting off – this place is well hidden, near the town hospital. It's worth seeking out, however, offering spotless, colourful, homely lodgings with bathroom and TV in every room. Outside summer, bookings are essential.

Maritim Krog & Hotell (☎ 41 13 60; info@maritim.nu; Hamngatan 31; s/d from Skr900/1100) The old blue building by the harbour is a wonderful boutique hotel with stylish decor (ask for the superlative Herring Room, with balcony and sea views). It's also home to a fantastic restaurant (lunch Skr80, mains Skr170 to Skr210) specialising in fish dishes.

Kamskogs Krog (☎ 143 48; www.kamskogskrog.se; Storgatan 3; lunch Skr85, dinner mains Skr145-220; ☉ noon-10pm Jul & Aug, shorter hours Sep-Jun) Local ingredients and skilful preparation define this *krog* (restaurant), with dishes like crème brûlée with

apple and nut salad in Kivik Calvados. The outdoor seats are perfect for nosey noshing.

GETTING THERE & AROUND

BornholmExpress (☎ 107 00; www.bornholmexpress.dk; adult/6-14yr return Skr300/150) runs a ferry service between Simrishamn and Allinge (on the Danish island of Bornholm) from mid-June to mid-August.

SkåneExpressen bus 3 runs roughly every hour on weekdays (less frequently on weekends) from Simrishamn train station to Kristianstad via Kivik (not stopping at the Stenshuvud National Park access road). Bus 5 to Lund runs up to 11 times on weekdays (infrequently on weekends). There's a direct bus to Ystad via Löderup three to nine times daily.

Local trains run up to 12 times daily from Simrishamn to Ystad (Skr39, 40 minutes), with connections from Ystad to Malmö and Lund.

Call **Taxi Österlen** (☎ 177 77) for a taxi. For bike hire, try **Österlens Cykel & Motor** (☎ 177 44; Stenbocksgatan; per day from Skr70; ☉ Mon-Sat), in the *godsmagasinet* (goods depot) at the train station.

Glimmingehus & Skillinge

The striking, five-storey **Glimmingehus** (Glimminge castle; ☎ 186 20; adult/under 19yr Skr60/free; ☉ 10am-6pm Jun–late Aug, 11am-4pm mid-Apr–May & late Aug–Sep, 11am-4pm Thu-Sun Oct), about 5km inland, has scarcely been tinkered with since its construction in the early 1500s, making it one of the best-preserved medieval castles around. Features include an all-encompassing moat and 11 resident ghosts! Guided tours in English are at 2pm daily from July to mid-September (at 2pm weekends from mid-April to late June and from mid-September to late October). In summer, there's a cafe and a program of medieval events and activities: contact the castle for details.

ᴏᴜʀ ᴘɪᴄᴋ Sjöbacka (☎ 301 66; info@sjobacka.nu; d from Skr700), a B&B 700m west of Skillinge, the closest settlement to the castle, occupies a super-cosy Scanian farmhouse complete with fireplace, antiques and heaving bookshelves. Skillinge is a reasonably active fishing village with a couple of restaurants and a fish smokehouse

Bus 322 runs three times daily between Skillinge and Ystad from mid-June to mid-August only.

Kivik

Rosy apples and burial cists make for strange bedfellows in sleepy, soothing Kivik (north of Simrishamn).

Believed to be a site of ancient human sacrifice, **Kiviksgraven** (Kungagraven; ☎ 703 37; adult/under 16yr Skr20/free; ⌚ 10am-6pm mid-May–Aug) is Sweden's largest Bronze Age grave, dating from around 1000 BC. It's an extraordinary shield-like cairn, about 75m in diameter, which once contained a burial cist and eight engraved slabs. What you see inside are replicas; the tomb was looted in the 18th century. The on-site cafe hires informative audioguides (Skr15).

Nearby, **Kiviks Musteri** (☎ 719 00; www.kiviks musteri.se; ⌚ Mar-Dec) is an apple orchard open to the public. There you can visit **Äpplets Hus** (adult/under 12yr Skr50/free; ⌚ late Mar-Nov), a museum devoted to the myths, history, cultivation and artistry of apples. Buy apple juice, cider and apple brandy from the well-stocked shop or sample the fairly apple-free menu at the restaurant. Kiviks Musteri is a few (signposted) kilometres out of town.

In Kivik, **STF Vandrarhem Hanöbris** (☎ 700 50; www.osterlen.tv/vandrarhem; Eliselundsvägen 6; dm from Skr200; ⌚ Apr-Oct) offers clean rooms in a 19th-century dancehall given an unfortunate modernist makeover.

our pick **Kivik Strand Logi & Café** (☎ 711 95; info@ kivikstrand.se; Tittutvägen; hostel/hotel d Skr740/1110, discounted to Skr660/1100; ⌚ Easter-Oct; P), down by the beach in a meticulously restored 19th-century schoolhouse, is a superlative hostel-B&B combo that's more chic boutique than backpacker bolt hole (think Gustavian-inspired interiors, rustic floorboards and a savvy sprinkling of antiques). The communal kitchen is seriously slick, and the obscenely cute cafe serves exceptional espresso. Book ahead.

For bus information see p189.

Stenshuvud National Park

Just south of Kivik, this enchanting **national park** (www.stenshuvud.se) features lush woodland, marshes, sandy beaches and a high headland. Among its more unusual residents are orchids, dormice and tree frogs. Several superb walks in the area include the hike up to a 6th-century ruined hill fort. The long-distance path **Skåneleden** (www.skaneleden.org) also runs through the park, along the coast; the best section is from Vik to Kivik (two or three hours).

The **Naturum** (visitor centre; ☎ 708 82; ⌚ 11am-6pm Jun–mid-Aug, 11am-4pm mid-Aug–mid-Dec & mid-Jan–May)

is 2.5km from the main road. Rangers lead 1½-hour guided tours of the park from there at 2pm daily, as well as at 10am Monday to Friday from July to mid-August (Sundays only mid-April to mid-June and September to mid-October). Call ahead to arrange an English-language tour.

Pretty **Kaffestugan Annorlunda** (☎ 242 86), on the road to the Naturum, serves meals and snacks daily from mid-May to August.

KRISTIANSTAD
☎ 044 / pop 77,250

Scruffy undertones aside, Kristianstad (kri-shan-sta) is worth a wander for its exquisite cathedral, quirky street sculptures and sprinkling of handsome 18th- and 19th-century buildings (among the 1970s dross).

Known as the most Danish town in Sweden, its construction was ordered by the Danish king Christian IV in 1614. Its rectangular street network still follows the first town plan, although the original walls and bastions have long gone. Both a major transport hub and gateway to Skåne's southern coast, it's also the region's administrative and political centre.

Information
Lilla Torg has banks and ATMs.

Library (Föreningsgatan 4; ⌚ 10am-7pm Mon-Thu year-round, plus 10am-6pm Fri, 10am-3pm Sat & 10am-2pm Sun Jun-Aug) Free internet access.

Tourist office (☎ 13 53 35; www.kristianstad.se; Stora Torg; ⌚ 10am-7pm Mon-Fri, 10am-3pm Sat, 10am-2pm Sun mid-Jun–mid-Aug, 10am-5pm Mon-Fri, 10am-2pm Sat rest of year)

Sights & Activities
One of the finest Renaissance churches in Scandinavia, **Trefaldighetskyrkan** (Västra Storgatan 6; ⌚ 8am-4pm) was completed in 1628 when Skåne was still under Danish control. The light-filled interior still has many of its original fittings, including wonderfully carved oak pews and an ornate marble and alabaster pulpit.

Riverside **Tivoliparken** is great for a summertime evening stroll or a waffle or two at the much-loved cafe. For a walking tour round 23 of the town's stately **buildings** (including the Renaissance-style town hall and the restored rampart Bastinonen Konungen), pick up the free English brochure *Kristianstad at Your Own Pace* from the tourist office.

The **Regionmuseet & Konsthall** (☎ 13 52 45; Stora Torg; admission free; ⌚ 11am-5pm Jun-Aug, noon-5pm

SOUTHERN SWEDEN

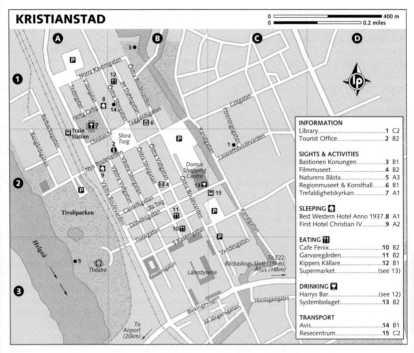

KRISTIANSTAD

INFORMATION
Library...........................1 C2
Tourist Office...................2 B2

SIGHTS & ACTIVITIES
Bastionen Konungen.............3 B1
Filmmuseet.....................4 B2
Naturens Bästa.................5 A3
Regionmuseet & Konsthall.......6 B1
Trefaldighetskyrkan............7 A1

SLEEPING
Best Western Hotel Anno 1937.8 A1
First Hotel Christian IV.........9 A2

EATING
Cafe Fenix....................10 B2
Garvaregården.................11 B2
Kippers Källare...............12 B1
Supermarket................(see 13)

DRINKING
Harrys Bar.................(see 12)
Systembolaget.................13 B2

TRANSPORT
Avis..........................14 B1
Resecentrum...................15 C2

Tue-Sun Sep-May) was originally intended as a palace, but the building ended up being used as an arsenal. It now houses local history exhibits and art, handicrafts and silverware displays. The **Café Miro** here serves great organic lunches, with herbs and flowers picked from the owner's garden.

Swedish film-making began in Kristianstad, so it's appropriate that **Filmmuseet** (☎ 13 57 29; Östra Storgatan 53; admission free; ☷ 1-6pm Thu-Sat late Jun–mid-Aug, noon-5pm Sun mid-Aug–mid-Jun), Sweden's only film museum, is based here.

Naturens Bästa (☎ 61 98 40; www.flodbaten.se) run two-hour boat trips (adult/child/family Skr100/60/260) into Kristianstad's unique wetland area, three times daily between May and early September. However, there are several weeks when the boats *don't* run: contact the company or the tourist office to check departures and book tickets.

Festivals & Events

Held annually in July, **Kristianstadsdagarna** (www .kristianstadsdagarna.nu, in Swedish) is a week-long festival with music, dance, exhibitions and foodie events, mostly held in Tivoliparken.

Sleeping & Eating

Budget accommodation is limited in town.

Bäckaskogs Slott (☎ 530 20; info@backaskogslott.se; Barumsvägen 255, Kiaby; cottage s/d incl breakfast Skr400/600, castle Skr1150/1550, discounted to Skr1000/1400; P ▯) This dreamy castle sits between two lakes 15km northeast of Kristianstad. Built as a monastery in the mid-13th century, it's a stunning spot, with different tiers of accommodation available in various wings and outhouses, and a well-priced restaurant. Bus 558 (Skr20, 20 minutes) runs hourly on weekdays between Kiaby and Kristianstad Resecentrum (less frequently on weekends).

First Hotel Christian IV (☎ 12 63 00; www.firsthotels .com; Västra Boulevarden 15; s Skr648-1348; d Skr848-1548; P ▯) While we adore the parquet floors and high ceilings, some rooms at Kristianstad's finest hotel are due for a makeover (think peeling wallpaper and frosted shower screens). The beautiful turn-of-the-century building was once a bank and one of the vaults now contains a wine cellar. (Just as well there's an in-house restaurant!)

Best Western Hotel Anno 1937 (☎ 12 61 50; info@hotelanno.se; Västra Storgatan 17; s/d Skr1095/1295, discounted to Skr695/895; 🖳) A rustic beam here, a 17th-century wall there: history pops up all over the place at this friendly hotel. Opposite the cathedral, its pale-toned rooms are simple yet tastefully designed with up-to-date touches like flatscreen TVs. There's a sauna, as well as free bike hire and wi-fi.

Café Fenix (☎ 20 90 80; Östra Storgatan 69; sandwiches Skr40-70; ⏰ 9am-6pm Mon-Fri, 10am-2pm Sat) A hit with local hipsters, this sleek new cafe is best for its epic sandwiches and scrumptious pastries, cakes and muffins. Grab a pavement table, slip on some shades, and eye up the passing talent.

Garvaregården (☎ 21 35 00; Tivoligatan 9; lunch Skr60, dinner mains Skr90-240) A half-timbered facade, crooked 17th-century gallery and flower-fringed terrace crank up the charm, while the house speciality lobster-stuffed steak cranks up the luxe factor. Simpler fare includes decent pasta dishes.

Kippers Källare (☎ 10 62 00; Östra Storgatan 9; mains Skr180-260; ⏰ Tue-Sat) Listed in the *White Guide* (Sweden's foodie bible) and sporting a 17th-century arched cellar, this is the most atmospheric restaurant in town. Herbivores are catered for and heaving Harrys Bar is on the same premises.

There's a supermarket and Systembolaget inside the Domus shopping centre on Östra Boulevarden.

Getting There & Around
Skyways (☎ 0771-95 95 00) flies direct most days to Stockholm from Kristianstad's **airport** (☎ 23 88 50), about 20km south of town. **Airport buses** (☎ 0441-230 00; Skr80) depart from the Resecentrum 50 minutes before flight departure times.

Buses depart from the Resecentrum on Östra Boulevarden. Frequent SkåneExpressen buses include: bus 1 to Malmö (Skr87, 1½ hours), bus 2 to Lund (Skr81, 1½ hours), bus 3 to Simrishamn (Skr45, 1¼ hours) and bus 4 to Ystad (Skr63, 1½ hours); the latter two services run infrequently on weekends. **Svenska Buss** (☎ 0771-67 67 67; www.svenskabuss.se) runs to Malmö, Karlskrona, Kalmar and Stockholm four times weekly.

The train station is across town from the Resecentrum. Trains run daily to Lund (Skr94, one hour) and Malmö (Skr94, 1¼ hours); many services continue on to Copenhagen (Skr190, two hours). Regular trains also run to Helsingborg (Skr87, 1½ hours).

Öresundstågen trains run every hour or two to Malmö (with connections at Hässleholm for Stockholm).

Call **Taxi Kristianstad** (☎ 24 62 46) for a taxi and **Avis** (☎ 10 30 20; Östra Storgatan 10) for car hire.

ÅHUS
☎ 044 / pop 8980
The small coastal town of Åhus (about 18km southeast of Kristianstad) is a popular summer spot thanks to its long sandy **beach**. The area is also known for its **eels**: the Eel Coast runs south from Åhus, and this delicacy is served up boiled, fried, smoked, grilled or cooked on a bed of straw at restaurants and at autumn Eel Feasts throughout the region.

There's a well-stocked **tourist office** (☎ 13 47 77; touristinfo.ahus@kristianstad.se; Järnvägsgatan 7; ⏰ 10am-7pm Mon-Fri, 9am-6pm Sat, 10am-2pm Sun Jun-Aug, 10am-5pm Mon-Fri Sep-May), with useful facilities (bank, supermarket etc) nearby.

Åhus is home to the **Absolut Vodka distillery** (☎ 28 80 00; Köpmannagatan 29), where half a million bottles are produced daily. Free tours of the place run six times daily on weekdays from late June to the end of August (call ahead for times). The tour bus departs from outside the factory entrance, 400m southwest of the tourist office. At all other times, tours must be booked in advance.

Naturens Bästa (p191) also runs its two-hour **boat trips** (adult/child/family Skr70/50/190) from Åhus from early June to early August. Contact **Landskapet** (☎ 28 93 95; www.landskapet.se) or the tourist office for more information.

Very close to the harbour is **STF Vandrarhem Åhus** (☎ 24 85 35; info@cigarrkungenshus.se; Stavgatan 3; dm Skr180-240, hostel s/d from Skr250/400, B&B per person from Skr275; 🅿 🖳), an agreeable youth hostel and B&B based in a 19th-century cigar factory.

The harbour has several good dining options.

Bus 551 runs several times an hour (roughly hourly on weekends) between Kristianstad and Åhus (Skr24, 21 minutes); get off at the Glashyttan stop for the tourist office.

HELSINGBORG
☎ 042 / pop 125,000
At its heart, Helsingborg is a sparkly showcase of rejuvenated waterfront, metro-glam restaurants, lively cobbled streets and lofty castle ruins. With Denmark looking on from a mere 4km across the Öresund, its flouncy,

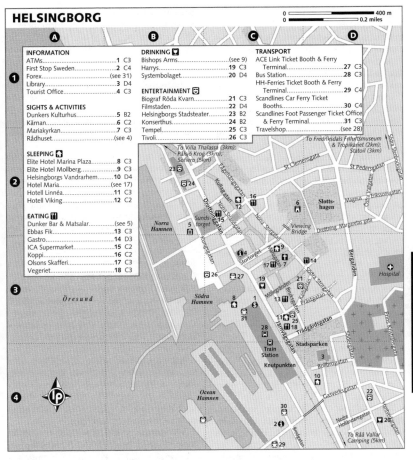

HELSINGBORG

0 ————————— 400 m
0 ————————— 0.2 miles

INFORMATION	
ATMs	1 C3
First Stop Sweden	2 C4
Forex	(see 31)
Library	3 D4
Tourist Office	4 C3

SIGHTS & ACTIVITIES	
Dunkers Kulturhus	5 B2
Kärnan	6 C2
Mariakyrkan	7 C3
Rådhuset	(see 4)

SLEEPING	
Elite Hotel Marina Plaza	8 C3
Elite Hotel Mollberg	9 C3
Helsingborgs Vandrarhem	10 D4
Hotel Maria	(see 17)
Hotell Linnéa	11 C3
Hotell Viking	12 C2

EATING	
Dunker Bar & Matsalar	(see 5)
Ebbas Fik	13 C3
Gastro	14 D3
ICA Supermarket	15 C2
Koppi	16 C2
Olsons Skafferi	17 C3
Vegeriet	18 C3

DRINKING	
Bishops Arms	(see 9)
Harrys	19 C3
Systembolaget	20 D4

ENTERTAINMENT	
Biograf Röda Kvarn	21 C3
Filmstaden	22 D4
Helsingborgs Stadsteater	23 B2
Konserthus	24 B2
Tempel	25 C3
Tivoli	26 C3

TRANSPORT	
ACE Link Ticket Booth & Ferry Terminal	27 C3
Bus Station	28 C3
HH-Ferries Ticket Booth & Ferry Terminal	29 C4
Scandlines Car Ferry Ticket Booths	30 C4
Scandlines Foot Passenger Ticket Office & Ferry Terminal	31 C3
Travelshop	(see 28)

turreted buildings feel like a brazen statement. It's hardly surprising: Helsingborg's strategic position on the sound saw it battled over and battered down with tedious regularity during the many Swedish-Danish wars. In 1709 the Danes invaded Skåne, but were finally defeated the following year in a battle just outside Helsingborg. One wonders what those armies would make of the over 14 million annual passengers who now traverse the sound with seasoned nonchalance.

Information

The Knutpunkten complex on the seafront has currency-exchange facilities and ATMs, as well as left-luggage lockers. For banks, head to Stortorget.

First Stop Sweden (☎ 10 41 30; www.firststop sweden.com; Bredgatan 2; ☺ 9am-8pm Mon-Fri, 9am-5pm Sat & Sun late Jun–mid-Aug; 9am-6pm Mon-Fri, 9am-4pm Sat, 9am-2pm Sun late May–late Jun & mid–late Aug; 8am-5pm Mon-Fri Sep–late May) Near the car-ferry ticket booths, it dispenses tourist information on the whole country and has a currency-exchange counter.

Forex (☎ 042 24 47 00; www.forex.se; Level 1 Knutpunkten, Kungstorget 8; ☺ 7am-9pm Mon-Sun) Foreign exchange office.

Library (Stadsbibliotek; ☎ 042-10 69 00; Stadsparken; ☺ 9am-7pm Mon-Fri & 11am-4pm Sat, also noon-4pm Sun Oct-Mar) Free internet access (bring ID).

Tourist office (☎ 10 43 50; www.helsingborg.se; Rådhuset, Stortorget; ☺ 9am-8pm Mon-Fri, 9am-5pm Sat & 10am-3pm Sun mid-Jun–Aug, 10am-6pm Mon-Fri, 10am-2pm Sat Sep–mid-Jun)

SOUTHERN SWEDEN

Sights

TOWN CENTRE

Dramatic steps and archways lead up from Stortorget to the square tower **Kärnan** (☎ 10 59 91; adult/under 16yr Skr20/10; ✆ 10am-6pm Jun-Aug, closed Mon Sep-May), all that remains of the medieval castle. The castle became Swedish property during the 17th-century Danish-Swedish War, and was mostly demolished once the fighting stopped. The tower was restored from dereliction in 1894, and the view from the top (34m) is regal indeed.

Just north of the transport terminals, the crisp and white **Dunkers Kulturhus** (☎ 10 74 00; www.dunkerskulturhus.se; Kungsgatan 11; exhibitions adult/under 18yr Skr70/free; ✆ 10am-5pm Tue-Sun, to 8pm Thu) houses an interesting town museum and temporary art exhibitions (admission includes entry to both), plus a concert hall, urbane restaurant and cafe (opposite), and design-savvy gift shop. The building's creator, Danish architect Kim Utzon, is the son of Sydney Opera House architect Jørn Utzon.

From here, saunter along **Norra Hamnen** (the North Harbour) where sleek apartments, restaurants and bars meet docked yachts and preened locals in one rather successful harbour-redevelopment project.

In the old town, the 15th-century Gothic brick **Mariakyrkan** (☎ 37 28 30; Mariatorget; ✆ 8am-6pm Mon-Fri, 9am-6pm Sat & Sun) has a magnificent interior, including a triptych dating from 1450 and an ornate Renaissance pulpit. The mighty **Rådhuset** (town hall; Stortorget) was completed in 1897 in neo-Gothic style and contains stained-glass scenes illustrating Helsingborg's history.

Small and specialist museums (about the fire brigade, medical history, sport, schools and military defence) dot the town: contact the tourist office for details.

FREDRIKSDAL & SOFIERO

Just 2km northeast of the centre, the Fredriksdal area is well worth a visit. Take bus 1 or 7 to the Zoégas bus stop.

One of Sweden's best open-air museums, **Fredriksdals Friluftsmuseum** (☎ 10 45 00; www.fredriksdal.helsingborg.se; adult/under 18yr May-Sep Skr70/free, Apr & Oct Skr30/free, Nov-Mar free; ✆ 10am-7pm Jun-Aug, 10am-5pm May & Sep, 11am-4pm Oct-Apr) is based around an 18th-century manor house, with a street of old houses, a children's farm, a graphics museum and blissfully leafy grounds. Local wildflowers grace the beautiful botanic

gardens, and there's a wonderful summer program of activities and performances in the French baroque open-air theatre. The museum entrance, located just off Hävertgatan, is an easy 250m walk south of the Zoégas bus stop on Ängelsholmsvägen.

Tropikariet (☎ 13 00 35; Hävertgatan 21; adult/4-12yr Skr80/40; ✆ 11am-5pm Tue-Sun, last entry at 4pm) is a semi-zoo, with reptile house, aquarium and exotic furry critters housed in faux natural habitats. It's just opposite the entrance to Fredriksdals museum.

About 5km north of the town centre, **Sofiero** (☎ 13 74 00; www.sofiero.helsingborg.se; Sofierovägen; adult/7-18yr Skr80/20; ✆ park 11am-6pm mid-Apr–Sep, palace & orangery 11am-5pm mid-Apr–Sep) is an impressive former royal summer residence and park with wonderful rhododendrons (best seen in full bloom in May and June) and top-notch summer concerts. Bus 219 runs out there.

Sleeping

CAMPING, HOSTELS & PRIVATE ROOMS

Råå Vallar Camping (☎ 18 26 00; raavallar@nordic camping.se; Kustgatan; sites Skr170-250, cabins Skr650-790; 🐾) About 5km south of the city centre, by Öresund, this is a huge, well-equipped camping ground, with a shop, cafe and sandy beach. Take bus 1 from the town hall.

Helsingborgs Vandrarhem (☎ 14 58 50; info@hbg turist.com; Järnvägsgatan 39; dm from Skr195) Despite the rather annoying vibe, Helsingborg's only central hostel offers clean, comfortable rooms about 200m from Knutpunkten. Reception opens between 3pm and 6pm.

Villa Thalassa (☎ 38 06 60; www.villathalassa.com; Dag Hammarskjöldsväg; dm from Skr200, 2-/4-bed r with private bathroom s/d Skr600/800; ℗) This SVIF option is a lovely early-20th-century villa situated in beautiful gardens. Hostel accommodation is in huts, but the hotel-standard rooms (with or without private bathroom) are a cut above. The villa lies 3km north of central Helsingborg in the Pålsjö area. Bus 219 stops 500m short, at the Pålsjöbaden bus stop.

HOTELS

Elite Hotel Mollberg (☎ 37 37 00; mollberg.helsingborg@elite.se; Stortorget 18; s Skr600-900, d Skr900-1450; ℗ 🖥) The main square is dominated by this flouncy 19th-century building. An understated elegance underpins the classic rooms, although the 1980s-era bathrooms could do with a revamp. The restaurant here is one of the best in town.

Hotell Linnéa (☎ 37 24 00; www.hotell-linnea.se; Prästgatan 4; s Skr680-1195, discounted to Skr625-775, d Skr1245-1445, discounted to Skr895-995) Charming, central Linnéa boasts wonderful management and cosy, personalised rooms with wooden floors, antique furniture and loads of character. It also does a decent Danish breakfast.

Elite Hotel Marina Plaza (☎ 19 21 00; reservations.marinaplaza@elite.se; Kungstorget 6; s Skr750-1950, d Skr950-2150; P ⌨) The Mollberg's sister establishment has modern, luxurious rooms right by the harbour (some with sea views), a number of restaurants and bars, and a sauna and gym.

ourpick Hotel Maria (☎ 24 99 40; www.hotelmaria.se; Mariagatan 8A; s/d from Skr950/1250, discounted to Skr800/950; ⌨) Tucked away behind Olsons Skafferi (right), Hotel Maria is utterly inspired, with each room flaunting a different historical style. Themes include National Romantic, art deco and '70s disco. Beds are divinely comfy, the staff friendly and there's a tapas bar downstairs. The hotel closes during the Christmas–New Year break.

Hotell Viking (☎ 14 44 20; hotell.viking@helsingborg.se; Fågelsångsgatan 1; s/d from Skr995/1475, discounted to Skr695/1025; P ⌨) The savvy, idiosyncratic rooms at this sterling number are constantly updated. Styles range from sexy modern to classically romantic, and each features a locally made teddy bear to cuddle (and adopt if you bond). Room 15 (Skr1675) remains the flashiest, with its own computer, leather recliners and whirlpool massage bath.

Eating

Helsingborg boasts an appetising selection of restaurants and cafes, although a fair few close on Sundays.

Ebbas Fik (☎ 28 14 40; Bruksgatan 20; cakes Skr15-35, sandwiches Skr22-75; ☻ 9am-6pm Mon-Fri, 9am-4pm Sat) It's still 1955 at this kitsch-tastic retro cafe, complete with jukebox, retro petrol pump and hamburgers made to Elvis' recipe. The extensive cafe menu also includes (huge) sandwiches, baked potatoes and crazy cakes and buns.

ourpick Koppi (☎ 13 30 33; Norra Storgatan 16; sandwiches/salads Skr60/70; ☻ Mon-Sat) This hip cafe-microroastery is your best bet for top-notch coffee. The savvy young owners sell their own roasted beans, alongside scrumptious edibles like fresh salads and gourmet ciabatta.

Vegeriet (☎ 24 03 03; Järnvägsgatan 25; lunch around Skr75; ☻ Mon-Sat) Vegetarians adore this appealing cafe-restaurant for tasty, flesh-free versions of quiche, lasagne, tortilla and stir-fry, and vegans aren't forgotten either. The place usually shuts for about a month during summer.

Olsons Skafferi (☎ 14 07 80; Mariagatan 6; lunch Skr75-90, dinner mains Skr130-235; ☻ lunch & dinner Mon-Sat) Olsons is a super little spot, with alfresco seating on the pedestrian square right in front of Mariakyrkan. It doubles as an Italian deli and cafe, with rustic good looks, spangly chandeliers and pasta that would make Bologna proud. The dinner menu offers more elaborate Mediterranean flavours.

ourpick Dunker Bar & Matsalar (☎ 32 29 96; Kungsgatan 11; lunch Skr90-145, restaurant mains Skr170-245) At the Kulturhus (opposite), svelte, contemporary, light-filled Dunker combines harbour views with great grub such as homemade pizzas and king crab–stuffed ravioli served with lobster bisque. There's a great weekend brunch (August to June) and live music on Thursdays in July.

Pålsjö Krog (☎ 14 97 30; Drottninggatan 151; mains Skr160-290; ☻ from 11.30am Mon-Sat, from 1pm Sun) Near Villa Thalassa, this is a great old seaside inn revamped into an elegant nosh spot. There's a fabulous veranda and outdoor seating, plus tasty, bistro-style dishes like blue mussel soup.

Gastro (☎ 24 34 70; Södra Storgatan 11-13; mains Skr195-295; ☻ dinner Mon-Sat) While we're not sold on the name, the dishes at this sharp, stylish award-winner will leave you smitten. On leather banquettes, under low-slung lamps, diners swoon over haute gems such as cured Norwegian cod with horseradish, lobster-steamed leeks and crispy cauliflower.

For quick snacks, try the Knutpunkten complex. The **ICA Supermarket** (Drottninggatan 48) is the best centrally located supermarket.

Drinking

There are several good pubs and bars around town, including **Harrys** (☎ 13 91 91; Järnvägsgatan 7) and the **Bishops Arms** (☎ 37 37 77; Södra Storgatan 2), both English-style pubs with a range of beers and comprehensive food menus.

There's a Systembolaget on Södergatan.

Entertainment

Helsingborgs Stadsteater (☎ 10 68 10; Karl Johans gata 1) has regular drama performances, and its neighbour, the **Konserthus** (☎ 10 43 50; Drottninggatan 19), regularly plays host to Helsingborg's

SOUTHERN SWEDEN

Symphony Orchestra. Information and tickets are available from the tourist office.

The **Tivoli** (☎ 18 71 71; Kungsgatan 1) is an enduring nightclub with a younger crowd and occasional live music. Popular restaurant-lounge hybrid **Tempel** (☎ 32 70 20; www.tempel.dj; Bruksgatan 2; ☺ from 6pm Tue-Sat) dishes out decent club nights on Fridays and Saturdays.

Biograf Röda Kvarn (☎ 14 50 90; Karlsgatan 7) is Helsingborg's oldest cinema. It shows mostly independent films, but closes from mid-June to mid-August. For mainstream efforts, try **Filmstaden** (☎ 21 07 47; Södergatan 19).

Getting There & Away

The main transport hub is the waterfront Knutpunkten complex.

BOAT

Knutpunkten is the terminal for the frequent **Scandlines** (☎ 18 61 00; www.scandlines.se) car ferry to Helsingør (one way Skr28, car plus nine people Skr335, free with rail passes). Across the inner harbour, **ACE Link** (☎ 38 58 80) has a terminal with a passenger-only ferry to Helsingør every 20 minutes in summer and every 30 minutes the rest of the year (one way Skr44, free with rail passes). There's also a frequent **HH-Ferries** (☎ 19 80 00; www.hhferries.se) service to Helsingør (adult Skr24, car plus nine people Skr300, rail passes not valid).

BUS

The bus terminal is at ground level in Knutpunkten. Regional Skånetrafiken buses dominate (see respective destinations for details), but long-distance services are offered by **Swebus Express** (☎ 0771-21 82 18; www.swebusexpress.com), **Svenska Buss** (☎ 0771-67 67 67; www.svenskabuss.se) and **Säfflebussen** (☎ 0771-15 15 15; www.safflebussen.se).

All three companies run north to Göteborg (Swebus Express and Säfflebussen services continue to Oslo), and south to Malmö. Swebus Express and Säfflebussen also operate services northeast to Stockholm via Karlstad. Fares to Stockholm cost around Skr500 (7½ hours), to Göteborg Skr250 (three hours), and to Oslo Skr300 (seven hours).

TRAIN

Underground platforms in Knutpunkten serve SJ, Pågatågen and Öresundståg trains, which depart daily for Stockholm (Skr630, five to

seven hours), Göteborg (Skr230, 2½ to three hours) and nearby towns including Lund (Skr75), Malmö (Skr87), Kristianstad (Skr87) and Halmstad (Skr107), as well as Copenhagen (Denmark) and Oslo (Norway).

Getting Around

Town buses cost Skr16 and run from Rådhuset (town hall). **Bike hire** (per 24hr/week Skr120/600) is available at Travelshop, located at the bus station at Knutpunkten. Contact **Taxi Helsingborg** (☎ 18 02 00) for cabs, and **Statoil** (☎ 15 10 80; Garnisonsgatan 2) for car hire.

KULLA PENINSULA
☎ 042

A seductive brew of golden light, artisan studios and sleepy fishing villages, Skåne's northwest coast is a perfect place to spend a few soothing days.

GETTING THERE & AWAY

Bus 220 run at least hourly from Helsingborg to Höganäs (Skr39, 40 minutes). From there, bus 222 runs every hour or two to Mölle (Skr27, 20 minutes), while bus 223 runs to Arild (Skr27, 20 minutes).

Höganäs

Gateway to the Kulla Peninsula, the coal-mining town of Höganäs (21km north of Helsingborg) deceives visitors with its plain-Jane appearance. Yet, not only is it a famous pottery centre but it harbours a few cultural gems.

The small **tourist office** (☎ 33 77 74; turistbyran@ hoganas.se; Centralgatan 20; ☺ noon-4pm Mon-Fri Oct-Mar, 10am-4pm Mon-Fri Apr–mid-Jun & mid-Aug–Sep, 9am-4.30pm Mon-Fri mid–late Jun & early–mid-Aug, 9am-4pm Mon-Fri, 10am-2pm Sat late Jun-early Aug) is a good source of information on the entire Kullabygden area. Pick up the free guide to Höganäs' impressive posse of **public art**, liberally sprinkled around town. Two of the most entertaining works are a family of pigs on Storgatan and a levitating dog on Köpmansgatan.

More art beckons at **Höganäs Museum & Konsthall** (☎ 34 13 35; www.hoganasmuseum.se, in Swedish; Polhemsgatan 1; adult/child Skr50/10; ☺ 1-5pm Tue-Sun Feb–late Dec), whose highlight is a brilliant collection of witty, exquisitely humane sculptures from home-grown artist Åke Holm. The venue also houses Höganäs' most famous four-legged local, Bob the puma (see boxed text, p198).

TIA LINDSTRÖM RÅBERG

Now based in Stockholm, school teacher Tia's fondest memories are of her native Kulla Peninsula.

What does the Kulla Peninsula mean to you? It's my spiritual home. The place is filled with so many memories of my childhood and that of my children. I now live in Stockholm but come down here every summer with my youngest daughter, Tove. It's food for the soul and our place of refuge.

What do you miss most about Skåne? The smell of salt and seaweed, the open sea. There are no islands between the shore and the horizon in Skåne, giving the coast a sense of freedom lacking in the Stockholm archipelago. Then there's the unique Scanian architecture and the beautiful beech forests.

An underrated local attraction? The town of Höganäs (opposite). It's not a smashing place to look at, but it's filled with whimsical sculptures from some famous names, including British artist Antony Gormley. Krapperups Slott (below) is also wonderful. Although the original manor was from the 14th century, the current one dates back to 1570. The gardens are stunning, the cafe bakes wonderful bread and the summer music concerts are impressive.

A definite must see? The Kullaberg Nature Reserve (below). I call the road leading up to it 'The Italian Way' because it reminds me a bit of the Amalfi Coast. A lovely cove for a swim here is Josefinelust: follow the signs from the main road. If you have time, don't miss Lars Vilks' famous sculpture Nimis (below). If you're interested in art and ceramics, a good time to visit the Kulla Peninsula is around Easter for the week-long **Konstrundan** (www.konstrundan.nu), when local artists open up their studios. Ask at the Höganäs tourist office (opposite) for details.

Höganäs Saltglaserat (☎ 21 65 40; www.hoganas saltglaserat.se, in Swedish; Bruksgatan 36B; ☒ 10am-6pm Mon-Fri, to 5pm Sep–mid-Jun, 11am-3pm Sat & Sun) is Sweden's most famous pottery factory, established in 1835. Its trademark brown salt-glazed pottery is a veritable national icon and its famous Höganäskrus (little jug) is mentioned in the opening line of August Strindberg's novel *Natives of Hemsö*. Watch the potters spin their wares (daily in July and August, weekdays at other times) and step inside the original, 170-year old kilns.

Seven kilometres further north on Rd 111, **Krapperups Slott** (☎ 34 41 90; info@krapperup .se; Krapperups Kyrkovägen 13; admission free, gallery Skr30; ☒ garden year-round; cafe 11am-5pm mid-Jun–mid-Aug, 11am-5pm Sat & Sun mid-Aug–mid-Jun, closed Jan; gallery/museum 1-5pm mid-Jun–mid-Aug, 1-5pm Sat & Sun Easter–mid-Jun & 2 weekends in Dec) is one of Sweden's oldest estates and home to an exquisite garden. The manor's exterior is inlaid with giant white stars representing the coat of arms of the Gyllenstierna family, who lived here for centuries. One-hour tours of the building (Skr100; Easter to late June and mid-September to mid-October) can be booked by emailing kul turintendenten@krapperup.se. The grounds also house an art gallery and local museum, a cafe and a gift shop. The converted stables play host to the annual **Musik i Kullabygden** (☎ 34 79

50; www.musikikullabygd.se, in Swedish), a week-long music festival in July spanning folk, jazz, classical and opera.

Bus 222 from Höganäs stops at the estate.

Mölle & Surrounds

The steep, picket-fence-pretty village of Mölle is the area's main tourist centre. It also enjoys a scandalous past. In the 19th century it was one of the first seaside resorts to encourage mixed bathing, much to the horror of the country…and to the delight of racy Berliners, who flocked here on a direct rail link from the German capital.

These days, people head in to enjoy **Kullaberg Nature Reserve** (Skr40 road toll), which occupies the tip of the Kulla Peninsula and houses Scandinavia's brightest lighthouse, **Kullens fyr**.

The reserve offers a dramatic spectacle of plunging cliffs, windswept vegetation and incredible sunsets, and a number of **hiking trails** crisscross the area, leading to ancient caves, tide pools and secluded swimming spots.

Looking like a cubby house gone mad, the driftwood sculpture **Nimis**, and its younger, concrete sibling **Arx**, stand on a beach on the peninsula's northern side. Created without permission by eccentric artist Lars Vilks, their existence has sparked several court cases

---

THE HÖGANÄS PUMA

Small towns are apt at peddling anecdotes about offbeat locals, but few match Höganäs' tale. The story involves the town's general practitioner, Dr Gustaf Alling. Born into poverty in 1878, the cigar-chomping doc had a soft spot for Höganäs' downtrodden coal miners, travelling as far away as South America to study the working conditions in other mines in a bid to improve the workers' health.

His other passion was animals, his quirky collection of pets including turtles and peacocks. Upstaging them all, however, was Bob, an orphaned female puma Alling adopted in Argentina in 1927. In Höganäs, the purring giant was free to roam the doctor's house, starting each day with a 2kg breakfast of raw meat. She also managed the odd escape, much to the horror of locals. To Alling, however, Bob was never a threat, just a good faithful friend and confidant.

Alas, not even the good doctor's love could save poor Bob from the gumboot that choked her to death in 1941. Stuffed for posterity, the ill-fated feline ended up stored and forgotten at Stockholm's Naturhistoriska Riksmuseet until, in 1996, she was finally returned to Höganäs. You'll find her in a glass case at the Höganäs Museum & Konsthall (p196), below a photo of her two-legged soul mate and next door to the house they once called home.

---

between Vilks and the County Council, not to mention the odd fire and chainsaw attack. In 1996 the crafty Vilks founded micronation **Ladonia** (www.ladonia.net) at the site, effectively turning his works into protected 'national monuments'.

The reserve is a veritable wonderland for active types: hit www.kullabergnatur.se for a list of available activities, which include **guided walking tours**. The **diving** here is reputedly the best in Sweden and the helpful crew at **Kullen Dyk** (☎ 34 77 14; www.kullendyk.nu, in Swedish), 2km southeast of Mölle next door to First Camp Möllehässle, can get you flippered and submerged. You can also go on **caving expeditions** (☎ 042-33 77 74; turistbyran@hoganas.se) with experienced guides, brave the primordial cliffs on a **rock-climbing course** (☎ 34 77 05) or try your luck at **fishing**.

A novel way of exploring the area is on an **Icelandic horse** (☎ 34 54 66; www.mollargarden.se, in Swedish), one of the world's gentlest, most peculiar-looking equine breeds. Riders must be over nine years old and weigh less than 95kg, and tours can be tailored to include caving or diving expeditions.

Five kilometres east of Mölle, the fishing village of **Arild** lays on the charm with its petite pastel houses, teeny-tiny harbour and supporting cast of roses, hollyhocks, butterflies and coastal nature reserves.

Accommodation in the area generally isn't cheap and fills up fast.

The friendly **First Camp Möllehässle** (☎ 34 73 84; www.firstcamp.se/molle; sites from Skr190, discounted to Skr120, 2-person cabin from Skr420) is a good bet.

It's 2km southeast of Mölle, and you can rent bikes here for exploring the area (Skr60 per day).

Exuding faded grandeur, the **Grand Hotel Mölle** (☎ 36 22 30; www.grand-molle.se; Bökebollsvägen 11; s/d from Skr1100/1200; P 💻) sits regally above Mölle. Although service can be a bit stroppy, rooms are an agreeable blend of modern Scandi style and nautical undertones (the rooms with balconies and sea views are more expensive). There's also an in-house gourmet restaurant.

Strand Hotell (☎ 34 61 00; www.strand-arild.se; Stora Vägen 42; d from Skr1100; P 💻), a civilised option in picture-perfect Arild, oozes old-world appeal. Four of the elegant rooms in the old building boast balconies with sea views, while the modern annexe features long thin rooms with terraces and sea views for all. There's a fine in-house restaurant here, too.

Ellens Café i Ransvik (☎ 34 76 66; sandwiches Skr55-85; 🕑 Apr-Sep) is a long-standing favourite, overlooking a popular bathing spot about 1km beyond the Kullaberg toll booth. Munch happily on sandwiches, salads and the scrumptious carrot cake, before taking a dip from the rocks.

Just up from the harbour in Mölle, **Mölle Krukmakeri & Café** (☎ 34 79 91; Mölle Hamnallé 9; sandwiches/soup Skr75/85, pasta & salad Skr95; 🕑 daily mid-Jun–late Aug, Sat & Sun late Aug–mid-Jun) is a cosy cafe and ceramics gallery run by potter Lisa Wohlfart. Stock up on their sleek, contemporary wares or simply tuck into fantastic homemade grub like tomato and spinach soup and hazelnut cinnamon scrolls.

Signposted off the main road between Arild and Jonstorp, **Flickorna Lundgren** (☎ 34 60 44; coffee & cookies Skr84; ☺ May–mid-Sep) is a huge, justifiably famous cafe in a gorgeous garden setting. Grab a large plate of pastries and your copper kettle, and lose yourself in a cloud of flowers.

BLEKINGE

With its long coastline and safe harbours, Blekinge's past and present are faithfully fastened to the sea. Sweden and Denmark once squabbled over the area, a trump card in power games over the Baltic. The region's own prized possession is the Unesco-lauded naval town of Karlskrona, famed for its baroque design. The region's second largest town, Karlshamn, was the exit point for thousands of 19th-century emigrants bound for America. Beyond the urban is a low-key landscape of fish-filled rivers and lakes, brooding forests and a stunning archipelago fit for lazy island-hopping.

KARLSKRONA

☎ 0455 / pop 62,340

If you like your Swedes in uniform, you'll appreciate Karlskrona. Marine cadets pepper the streets of what has always been an A-league naval base. In 1998 the entire town was added to the Unesco World Heritage List for its impressive collection of 17th- and 18th-century naval architecture.

It was the failed Danish invasion of Skåne in 1679 that sparked Karlskrona's conception, when King Karl XI decided that a southern naval base was needed for better control over the Baltic Sea. Almost immediately, it became Sweden's third-biggest city. Much of the town is still a military base, so to see certain sights you'll need to book a tour at the tourist office and have ID at the ready.

Information

You'll find ATMs in the Wachtmeister shopping centre on Borgmästeregatan.

Library (☎ 30 34 65; Stortorget 15-17; ☺ 10am-7pm Mon-Fri, 10am-1pm Sat mid-Jun–mid-Aug, longer hours mid-Aug–May) Free internet access.

Tourist office (☎ 30 34 90; www.karlskrona.se/tourism; Stortorget 2; ☺ 9am-8pm Jun-Aug, 9am-6pm Mon-Fri, 10am-4pm Sat Sep-May) Internet access and super-helpful staff.

Sights & Activities

FORTIFICATIONS

Karlskrona's star is the extraordinary off-shore **Kungsholms Fort**, with its curious circular harbour, built in 1680 to defend the town. Four-hour, guided **boat tours** (adult/12-18yr Skr180/80; ☺ 10am mid-Jun–Aug) to the fort depart from Fisktorget; book at the tourist office or Marinmuseum (bring ID). In July there's also a three-hour tour departing from Marinmuseum. Another option is the boat operated by **Skärgårdstrafiken** (☎ 783 30), which runs from Fisktorget and circles the fort five times daily from mid-June to mid-August (adult/child Skr80/40); inform the tourist office of your visit in advance if you choose this second option.

Bristling with cannons, the tower **Drottningskärs Kastell** on the island of Aspö was described by Admiral Nelson of the British Royal Navy as 'impregnable'. You can visit it on a **Skärgårdstrafiken boat** (return adult Skr40-130, child Skr20-70; ☺ Jun-Aug), departing from Fisktorget.

MUSEUMS

The striking **Marinmuseum** (☎ 359 30 02; Stumholmen; adult/under 19yr Skr60/free; ☺ 10am-6pm Jun-Aug, 11am-5pm Tue-Sun Sep-May) is the national naval museum. Dive in for reconstructions of a battle deck in wartime, a hall full of fantastic figureheads, piles of model boats, and even some of the real thing – such as a minesweeper, a sailing ship and the Swedish navy's debut submarine. Temporary exhibitions move beyond the marine (a recent show focused on contemporary Polish art) and the savvy **cafe** (lunch Skr90) boasts generous servings and waterside decking for a satisfying recharge.

The evocative **Blekinge Museum** (☎ 30 49 60; Fisktorget 2; admission free; ☺ 10am-6pm Jun-Aug, 11am-5pm Tue-Sun, to 7pm Wed Sep-May) explores the local fishing, boat-building and quarrying trades. The most captivating part is Grevagården, an impressively preserved 18th-century abode crammed with thousands of vintage objects, from fans and fashion to bizarre wax models of syphilis-plagued faces. Topping it off is a petite baroque garden and a pleasant cafe.

Museum Leonardo da Vinci Ideale (☎ 255 73; Drottninggatan 28; admission Skr20) showcases a private collection of original art. Call ahead to visit.

OTHER SIGHTS & ACTIVITIES

Karlskrona's monumental square, Stortorget, was planned to rival Europe's best. Alas, the

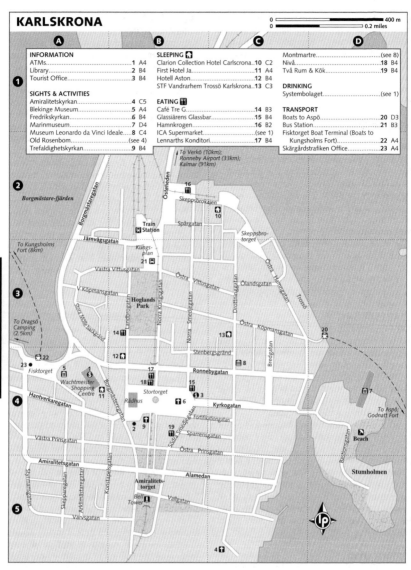

KARLSKRONA

funds ran out, resulting in a somewhat odd mix of grand architectural gestures and humble stand-ins. Dominating the square are the courthouse, along with the baroque church **Fredrikskyrkan** (☼ 11am-4pm Mon-Fri, 9.30am-2pm Sat) and **Trefaldighetskyrkan** (Trinity Church; ☼ 11am-4pm Mon-Fri, 9.30am-2pm Sat), inspired by Rome's Pantheon.

Sweden's oldest wooden church is the stocky **Amiralitetskyrkan** (☎ 103 56; Vallgatan), whose gorgeous pastel interior is worth a peek. Outside, the wooden statue **Old Rosenbom** raises his hat to charitable visitors.

Pick a sunny summer afternoon for a tour around Karlskrona's **archipelago**, made up of almost 1000 islands. A three-hour tour osts Skr130/70 per adult/child. Contact the Skärgårdstrafiken office at Fisktorget or log into www.affarsverken.se for timetables and information.

Enquire at the tourist office about three-hour **guided tours** (adult/12-18yr Skr225/80; ☾ Sat May–mid-Sep) of the city, which consist of a one-hour walk followed by a ferry trip to Godnatt Fort, a curious 19th-century fortress-cum-lighthouse that appears to emerge straight out of the water. Another option is to pick up the free *Object 560* brochure, which maps out a walking tour of architectural and historical highlights in town.

Sleeping

STF Vandrarhem Trossö Karlskrona (☎ 100 20; www karlskronavandrarhem.se; Drottninggatan 39; dm/s/d from kr140/245/320) Modern, clean and friendly, this hostel has a laundry, TV room and backyard for kids to play in; parking on the opposite side of the street is free.

Dragsö Camping (☎ 153 54; info@dragsocamping.nu; Dragsövägen; sites from Skr190, 2-bed cabins Skr750-850, d kr320; ☾ Apr–mid-Oct) This large, good-looking campsite, 2.5km northwest of town, is situated on a scenic bay. Facilities include boat and bicycle hire, as well as a Karlskrona-themed minigolf course. Bus 7 stops about a kilometre short of the camping ground.

First Hotel Ja (☎ 555 60; www.firsthotels.se; Borg-mästaregatan 13; s Skr599-1399, discounted to Skr599-099, d Skr749-1549, discounted to Skr749-1249; ⓟ 💻) Karlskrona's top slumber spot boasts slick, hip, recently renovated rooms in white and charcoal hues, with blissful beds and flatscreen TVs. Hotel perks include a sauna, bar-restaurant and a great breakfast buffet (included in room prices). Book online for the best rates.

Clarion Collection Hotel Carlscrona (☎ 36 15 00; cc.carlscrona@choice.se; Skeppsbrokajen; s Skr890-1900, d kr1110-2120; ⓟ 💻) Handy for the train station, this sassy chain hotel combines original rustic beams and slinky furniture in the bar, and navy blues, greys and handsome wooden furnishings in its stately rooms. Staff are very helpful.

Hotell Aston (☎ 194 70; www.hotellaston.se; Land-srogatan 1; s/d incl breakfast Skr1045/1195, discounted to kr695/895; ⓟ 💻) This 3rd-floor place is a smart, central option. The spacious rooms sport neutral tones, marine-themed photography and art, as well as simple, modern furnishings. There's a sauna and, if you're lucky, you'll get waffles for breakfast.

Eating & Drinking

Glassiärens Glassbar (☎ 170 05; Stortorget 4; ☾ May-Sep) The queues at this legendary ice-cream peddler are matched by the mammoth serves. Piled high in a heavenly waffle cone, the two-flavour option (Skr30) is a virtual meal.

Lennarths Konditori (☎ 31 03 32; Norra Kungsgatan 3; ☾ Mon-Sat) We dig the tubular retro ceiling almost as much as we dig the calorific treats at this old-school bakery; try the delectable *munk* (think doughnut meets apple strudel).

Nivå (☎ 103 71; Norra Kungsgatan 3; light meals Skr40-90, grill Skr150-325; ☾ Mon-Sat) Just off Stortorget, this slinky steakhouse has an excellent menu of light, well-priced dishes (nachos, burgers, salads), plus heartier meals from the grill. It's also a popular evening bar; its doors stay open until at least 1am.

Hamnkrogen (☎ 803 36; Skeppsbrokajen 18; lunch from Skr55, mains Skr90-160) Right on the guest harbour, easy-going Hamnkrogen keeps punters chuffed with pizzas, steaks and grills. If you fancy something spicier, opt for the great tandoori dishes, baltis and biryanis, cooked by the restaurant's Indian chef.

Café Tre G (☎ 31 03 33; Landbrogatan 9; meals around Skr65; ☾ 9am-9pm Mon-Fri, 9am-6pm Sat, 10am-6pm Sun) Run by the team from Lennarths Konditori, this cafe is a hit with everyone from prim pensioners to indie types. Fill up on anything from baked potatoes, quiche and pasta salads to perfect pralines, pastries and muffins.

Montmartre (☎ 31 18 33; Ronnebygatan 18; pizza Skr65-80, mains Skr80-190) Next door to the Museum Leonardo da Vinci Ideale, the atmospheric Montmartre evokes a French bistro with its wine-red drapes, tasselled lampshades and oil paintings. The menu is a worldlier affair, with pizzas, Swedish favourites and zestier fusion numbers such as grilled tuna with wasabi, lime and chilli.

Två Rum & Kök (☎ 104 22; Södra Smedjegatan 3; fondue Skr240, mains Skr200-260; ☺ Mon-Sat) Another good choice for evening dining is this gourmet den, best known for its magnificent fondue (minimum two persons); with flavours spanning Tex-Mex and French to Cajun.

The ICA supermarket and Systembolaget are in the Wachtmeister shopping centre.

Getting There & Around

Ronneby airport (☎ 0457-255 90) is 33km west of Karlskrona; the Flygbuss leaves from Stortorget (Skr80). SAS flies to Stockholm Arlanda daily, and Blekingeflyg flies to Stockholm Bromma Sunday to Friday.

The bus and train stations are just north of central Karlskrona. **Blekingetrafiken** (☎ 0455-569 00; www.blekingetrafiken.se) operates regional buses.

Svenska Buss runs four times a week from Malmö to Stockholm, calling at Kristianstad, Karlshamn and Karlskrona. Swebus Express service 834 runs once to twice daily from Malmö to Kalmar, calling at Kristianstad, Karlshamn and Karlskrona.

Kustbussen runs six times daily on weekdays (twice daily on weekends) each way between Karlskrona and Kalmar (around Skr150, 1½ hours).

Direct trains run at least 13 times daily to Karlshamn (Skr70, one hour) and Kristianstad (Skr117, two hours), at least seven times daily to Emmaboda (Skr54, 40 minutes), and 10 times to Lund (Skr177, two hours and forty minutes) and Malmo (Skr177, three hours). Trains also run at least a couple of times to Göteborg (Skr382, five hours). Change at Emmaboda for Kalmar.

Stena Line (☎ 031-704 0000; www.stenaline.se) ferries to Gdynia (Poland) depart from Verkö, 10km east of Karlskrona (take bus 6).

For a taxi, call **Zon Taxi** (☎ 230 50).

KARLSHAMN

☎ 0454 / pop 31,050

With its quaint cobbled streets, old wooden houses and splash of art-nouveau architecture, you'd never guess that quiet Karslhamn was once so wicked. Alcoholic drinks, tobacco, snuff and playing cards were produced in great quantities here, and it was a major 19th-century smugglers' den. Karlshamn was also the port from where many Swedes left for America. One of Sweden's biggest free festivals, the **Baltic Festival** (Östersjöfestivalen; ☎ 810 00; balticfestival@karlshamn.se) in mid- to late July, sees a quarter of a million people roll in for bands and a carnival parade.

Information

Most services line Drottninggatan. The **tourist office** (☎ 812 03; www.karlshamn.se; Ronnebygatan 1; ☺ 9am-7pm Mon-Fri, 10am-6pm Sat, noon-6pm Sun mid-Jun–early Aug; 9am-5pm Mon-Fri mid-Aug–mid-Jun; also 10am-2pm Sat mid-May–mid-Jun & early–mid-Aug) can help with information and bookings.

Sights

The poignant **utvandrar-monumentet** is in a park by the harbour, commemorating all the America-bound emigrants. The monument's figures are characters from Vilhelm Moberg's classic work *The Emigrants*: Karl Oscar, looking forward to the new country, and Kristina, looking back towards her beloved Duvemåla. Nearby, you can peer through the windows of a 300-year-old **fishing cottage**.

The 'culture quarter' **Karlshamns Kulturkvarter** (☎ 148 68; Vinkelgatan 8; admission Skr20; ☺ noon-5pm Tue-Sun Jun-Aug, 1-4pm Mon-Fri Sep-May) provides interesting information about Karlhamn's tobacco and *punsch*-producing history, mixed in 15with some beautiful 18th-century merchants' houses.

Sleeping & Eating

STF Vandrarhem Karlshamn (☎ 140 40; stfturistkhamn@ hotmail.com; Surbrunnsvägen 1C; dm Skr185; P) On the eastern side of the town grid, near the train station, this hostel offers good rooms, all with private bathrooms. Kids will love the nearby playground, created by children.

First Hotel Carlshamn (☎ 890 00; carlshamn@ firsthotels.se; Varvsgatan 1; s Skr800-1400, d Skr1000-1600; P ⌨) Although the rooms are begging for a revamp (think mission brown furniture and bathrooms straight out of 1985), they are spotlessly clean and comfortable, and some even offer harbour views. Other positives include a sauna, small gym, top-quality restaurant and handy location opposite the tourist office.

Fiskstugan (☎ 190 35; Vägga Fiskhamn; sandwiches Skr45-65, meals Skr70-130; ☺ lunch & dinner mid-Apr–early Sep) A 25-minute stroll southeast of the centre, this smart, casual seafood restaurant sits on a pretty little harbour. Choose your nosh at the deli-style counter (the grilled seafood kebabs are delicious), then soak up the semibucolic views while your food is cooked. Ask the tourist office for directions.

Köpmannagården (☎ 317 87; Drottninggatan 88; pizzas Skr65-90; ✆ Wed-Mon) For a cheapish feed, try this pleasant restaurant and pizzeria with its rustic summer courtyard.

Gourmet Grön (☎ 164 40; Östra Piren, Biblioteksgatan 6; tapas/buffet Skr70-150; ✆ 11.30am-3pm Mon-Fri) Oozing contemporary cafeteria cool, this waterside award-winner serves wonderful buffets with an strong emphasis on vegetarian food. You can nibble on a ciabatta, tapas-style goodies or inventive spreads with Mediterranean influences.

Getting There & Away

The bus and train stations are in the northeastern part of town. For travel information, see opposite.

Lisco Line (☎ 0454-33680; www.lisco.lt) sails once a day between Karlshamn and Klaipėda in Lithuania.

Southwest Sweden

Sweden's southwest has a knack for diversity. One day you're partying hard in a disused power station, the next you're gliding silently across a crisp, clean lake. Heading the cast is Sweden's 'second city' of Göteborg (Gothenburg in English), and its arsenal of kicking bars, cafes, museums and theme-park thrills. Take advantage of the excellent summer pass and explore the city for next to nothing.

The rest of the Västergötland region is low-key and eclectic: don't miss Trollhättan, Sweden's film-production capital; Läckö Slott, fairy-tale castle supreme; and the quiet delights of the Göta Canal, which threads its way across the region.

North of Göteborg lies the arrestingly beautiful Bohuslän coastline, a minimalist marvel of electric blue waters, granite islands and sparkling red-and-white fishing villages. Behind it, cocoa-coloured cliffs frame luridly green valleys, while mysterious Bronze Age rock carvings intensify the region's enigmatic air.

Further inland, Dalsland county evokes a Swedish *Twin Peaks* with its brooding, watery landscape of silent lakes and thick dark forests. Flanked by Europe's third-largest lake, Vänern, it's a canoeists' paradise and a perfect spot to ditch the crowds.

For wilder waves and attitude, hit the Halland coast, home to sandy Blue Flag beaches, Sweden's top windsurfing and a hedonistic summer vibe.

HIGHLIGHTS

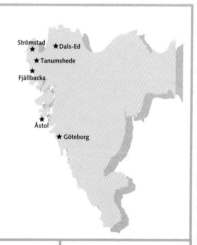

- Wise up on contemporary art and counter-culture cool at converted power station **Röda Sten** (p211) in Göteborg

- Take in coastal perfection and a perfect sunset from high above **Fjällbacka** (p227)

- Peddle (or splash) your way around the dazzling Koster islands, off the coast of **Strömstad** (p229)

- Decode mystic **Bronze Age artwork** (p224) at the Unesco World Heritage site in Tanumshede, Bohuslän

- Feast on herring and archipelago views on the tiny island of **Åstol** (p225)

- Glide across silent lakes and international borders from secretive **Dals-Ed** (p230)

Map labels: Strömstad ★ · ★ Dals-Ed · ★ Tanumshede · Fjällbacka ★ · ★ Åstol · ★ Göteborg

■ AREA: 30,584 SQ KM	■ POPULATION: 1,838,691	■ HIGHEST ELEVATION: GALTÅSEN (362M)

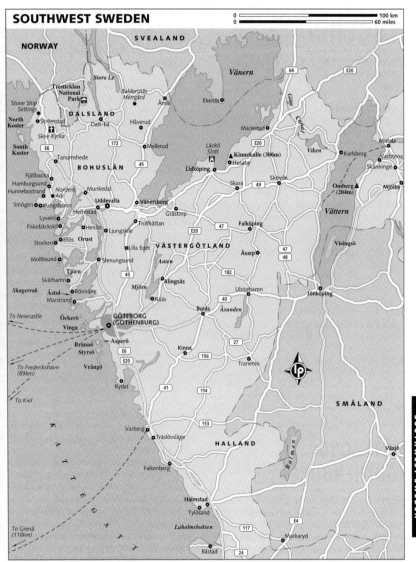

SOUTHWEST SWEDEN

SOUTHWEST SWEDEN

Orientation & Information

Götaland covers a large slice of Sweden, containing five different *landskap* (regions): Bohuslän, Dalsland and Västergötland in the west, Halland in the south, and Östergötland in the east (covered in the Southeast Sweden chapter, p128). These regions are grouped together into the three *län* (counties): Västra Götalands län (taking in Västergötland, Dalsland and Bohuslän), Hallands län and Östergötlands län.

Götaland is also the region containing Sweden's two largest lakes – Vänern and Vättern – connected by the Göta Canal. The latter lake divides Götaland into two distinct parts.

The following agencies offer detailed information on the area:

HallandsTurist (☎ 035-17 98 00; www.hallandsturist .se; Box 538, 30180 Halmstad)

Västsvenska Turistrådet (☎ 031-81 83 00; www .vastsverige.com; Kungsportsavenyn 31-35, 41136 Göteborg)

Getting Around

Västtrafik (☎ 0771-41 43 00; www.vasttrafik.se) and **Hallandstrafiken** (☎ 0771-33 10 30; www.hlt.se) provide regional transport links. If you're planning to spend some time exploring the southwest counties, it's worth enquiring about discount cards, monthly passes or a *sommarkort*, offering cheaper travel in the peak summer period (from late June to mid-August). Also check the respective websites for routes, schedules, fares and passes; the information isn't always in English, but you'll usually reach an English-speaker if you call.

The main railway lines in the west connect Göteborg to Karlstad, Stockholm, Malmö and Oslo. In the east, the main line runs from Stockholm via Norrköping and Linköping to Malmö. Express buses connect major towns on much the same routes.

One of the best ways of seeing the region is by taking the long, unforgettable journey along the Göta Canal (see p140) – from the rolling country of Östergötland, north of Linköping, into the great lake Vättern, continuing into Västergötland on the other side and on to Göteborg.

GÖTEBORG (GOTHENBURG)

☎ 031 / pop 493,500

Often caught in Stockholm's shadow, gregarious Göteborg socks a mighty punch of its own. Some of the country's finest talent hails from its streets, including music icons José González and Soundtrack of Our Lives. Ornate architecture lines its tram-rattled streets, grit-hip cafes hum with bonhomie, and must-sees include Scandinavia's amusement park heavyweight.

East of Kungsportsavenyn boulevard (dubbed the 'Champs Élysées' in brochures and a 'tourist trap' by locals), the Haga and Linné districts both buzz with creativity.

Fashionistas design fair-trade threads, artists collaborate over mean espressos and street artists sex-up forlorn facades. Stockholm may represent the 'big time', but many of the best ideas originate in this grassroots town.

When the sun shines, hop on a boat for a blissful cruise along the Göta älv (Göta river). Alternatively, catch a tram and head out to the nearby archipelago for a mellow spot of island-hopping.

Best of all, Göteborg is comparatively cheaper than its east-coast rival, making it a top introduction to Sweden that shouldn't make your piggy bank turn up its trotters.

HISTORY

Gamla Älvsborg fortress, standing guard over the river 3km downstream of the centre, is Göteborg's oldest significant structure, with portions dating back to medieval times. It was a key strategic point in the 17th-century territorial wars, and was held by Denmark for seven years before being yielded to Sweden in 1619. Two years later, the Swedes founded Göteborg.

The Dutch played an important part in shaping the fledgling city. Still fearful of Danish attack, the Swedes employed Dutch experts to construct a defensive canal system in the centre. The workers lived in what is now the revitalised Haga area: around a fifth of the original buildings are still standing. Most of Göteborg's oldest wooden buildings went up in smoke long ago – the city was devastated by no fewer than nine major fires between 1669 and 1804.

Once Sweden had annexed Skåne in 1658, Göteborg expanded as a trading centre. Boomtime came in the 18th century, when merchant companies like the Swedish East India Company made huge amounts of wealth. Look around and you'll notice the many grandiose buildings built using that period's profits.

From the 19th century, shipbuilding was a major part of the city's economy, until the industry totally collapsed in the 1980s. Volvo's first car wheeled out of Göteborg in 1927. It's now one of Sweden's largest companies (although it was taken over by Ford in 1999), and it's estimated that a quarter of the city relies on the company in some way. Today, Göteborg is Sweden's most important industrial and commercial city and Scandinavia's busiest port.

ORIENTATION

Both Centralstationen and the Nordstan shopping complex sit at the northern end of central Göteborg. From here, shop-lined Östra Hamngatan leads southeast through town. Upon crossing one of the city's few remaining 17th-century canals, it becomes Kungsportsavenyn (known simply as 'Avenyn'), leading up to Götaplatsen. The Avenyn is Göteborg's showpiece boulevard, lined with shops, restaurants, galleries, theatres and street cafes. Directly west is the Vasastan district, with a cooler selection of shops, bars and eateries. Further west is the picture-perfect Haga district, followed by the boho-grunge of the Linné district, west of Jarntorget.

The former shipyards and much of the heavy industry (including Volvo) are on the northern island of Hisingen. Hisingen is reached by road via the monumental bridge Älvsborgsbron, southwest of the city; by Götaälvbron, north of Centralstationen; and by the E6 motorway tunnel, Tingstadstunneln, northeast of the city centre.

The E6 motorway, just east of the city centre, connects Oslo and Malmö.

INFORMATION

Bookshops

Akademibokhandeln Nordstan (☎ 61 70 30; Nordstan shopping complex; ⏱ 10am-7pm Mon-Fri, 10am-6pm Sat, 11am-5pm Sun); Vasagatan (☎ 60 96 80; Vasagatan 26-30; ⏱ 10am-6pm Mon, 10am-5pm Tue-Thu, 10am-4pm Fri) The best selection of English-language books in the city.

Pocketshop (☎ 10 49 40; Centralstationen; ⏱ 6.15am-9.15pm Mon-Fri, 7am-8pm Sat, 8.30am-9pm Sun) English-language books.

Press Stop (☎ 15 84 45; Drottninggatan 58; ⏱ 9.30am-6.30pm Mon-Fri, 10am-4.30pm Sat) English-language newspapers and magazines.

Pressbyrån (☎ 15 37 90; Centralstationen; ⏱ 6am-10pm Mon-Fri, 8am-8pm Sat, 8am-10pm Sun) Similar to Press Stop, with another outlet in Centralstationen open until midnight.

Emergency

Police station (☎ 114 14; Stampgatan 28)

Internet Access

Sidewalk Express (www.sidewalkexpress.se; per hr Skr19) Sidewalk Express computers are found at Centralstationen and the 7-Eleven shop on Vasaplatsen. To log on, buy vouchers from the coin-operated machines and enter the username and password issued.

Left Luggage

Luggage **lockers** (small/large up to 24hr Skr30/40) are available at both Centralstationen and the long-distance bus terminal Nils Ericson Terminalen.

Libraries

Stadsbiblioteket (☎ 61 65 00; Götaplatsen; ⏱ 10am-8pm Mon-Fri, 11am-5pm Sat & Sun, closed Sun Jun-Aug) The city library has imported newspapers and magazines, books in English, a good cafe, an exhibition space and free internet access (bring ID).

Medical Services

For 24-hour medical information, phone ☎ 0771-70 31 50.

Akuttandvården (☎ 80 78 00; Odinsgatan 10) Emergency dental treatment.

Apotek Vasan (☎ 0771-45 04 50; Nordstan shopping complex; ⏱ 8am-10pm) Late-night pharmacy.

Östra Sjukhuset (☎ 343 40 00) Major hospital about 5km northeast of central Göteborg, near the terminus at the end of tram line 1.

Money

Banks with ATMs are readily available, including inside the Nordstan shopping complex and along Kungsportsavenyn.

Forex (☎ 0200-22 22 20; www.forex.se) Central-stationen (⏱ 7am-9pm Mon-Sun); Kungsportsavenyn 22 (⏱ 9am-7pm Mon-Fri, 10am-4pm Sat); Kungsportsplatsen (⏱ 9am-7pm Mon-Fri, 10am-4pm Sat); Landvetter Airport (⏱ 5am- 9pm Mon-Fri, 5am-8pm Sat, 5am-7pm Sun); Norstan shopping complex (⏱ 9am-7pm Mon-Fri, 10am-6pm Sat, 11am-5pm Sun) Foreign-exchange office with numerous branches.

Post

Postal services are now mainly provided by kiosks, newsagents, petrol stations and supermarkets – look for the blue-and-yellow postal symbol.

Post office (Nordstan shopping complex; ⏱ 7am-7pm Mon-Fri)

Tourist Offices

Branch tourist office (Nordstan shopping complex; ⏱ 10am-6pm Mon-Fri, 10am-6pm Sat, noon-5pm Sun)

Main tourist office (☎ 61 25 00; www.goteborg.com; Kungsportsplatsen 2; ⏱ 9.30am-8pm mid-Jun–mid-Aug; 9am-5pm Sep-Apr; 9.30am-6pm Mon-Fri, 10am-2pm Sat & Sun May–mid-Jun & end Aug) Central and busy, it has a good selection of free brochures and maps.

SOUTHWEST SWEDEN

GÖTEBORG (GOTHENBURG)

Keillers
Park

To Volvo Museum (6km);
Lilleby Havsbad Camping (20km)

HISINGEN

Stalhandsgatan

Lundby
Strand

Göta   älv

Lindholm

Rosenlund

102

Eriksberg

Ostindiefararen

To Nya Älvsborgs
Fästning (7km)

103

Oscarsleden

Karl Johansgatan

Amiralitetsgatan

Kabelgatan

Andreegatan

Masthamnsgatan

Förstalånggatan

LINNÉ

Masthuggs-
torget

Stigbergsliden

Stigbergstorget

Storebackegatan

Bangatan

August Kobbsgatan

Slottsskogsparken

Klippan

Chapm
Torg

To Röda Sten (600m);
'The Thing' (600m)

Olivedalsgatan

Särögatan

Vegagatan

Prinsgatan

Andra Långgatan

Tredje Långgatan

Nordhemsgatan

Landsvägsgatan

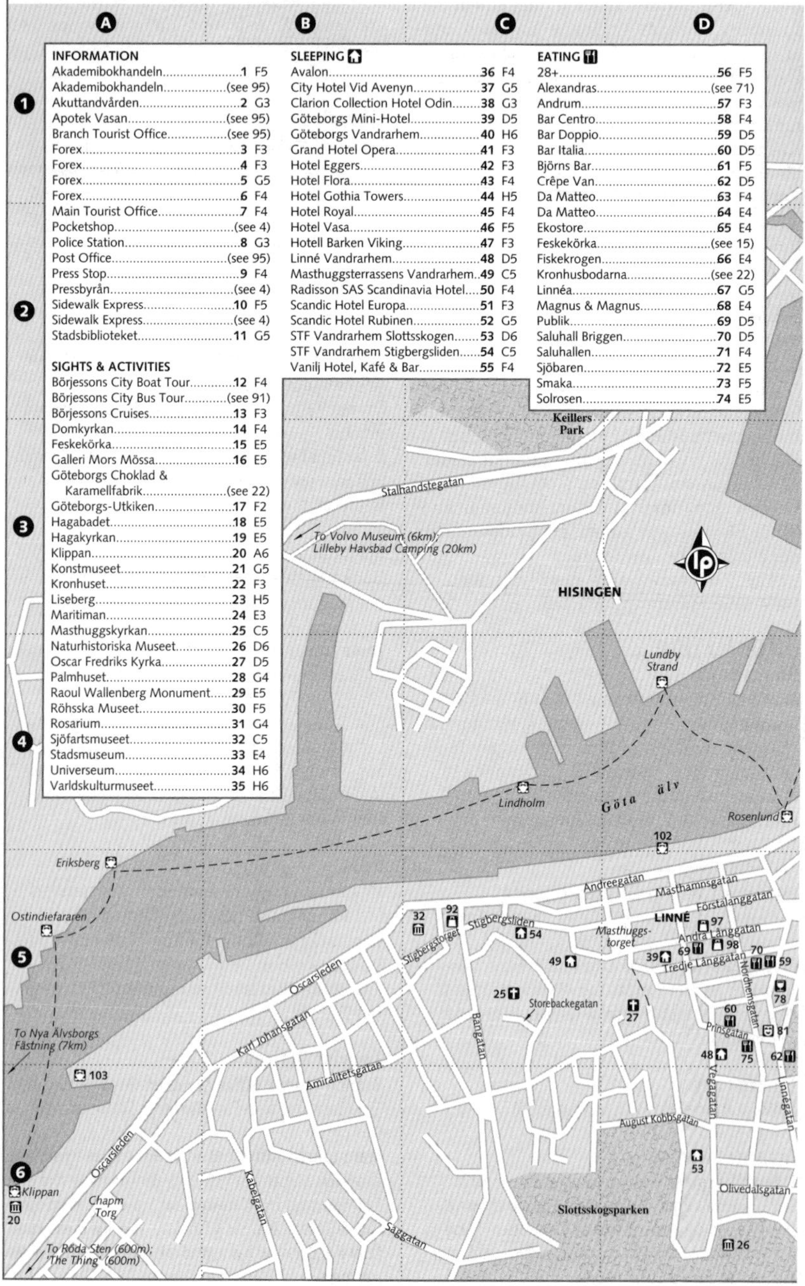

SOUTHWEST SWEDEN

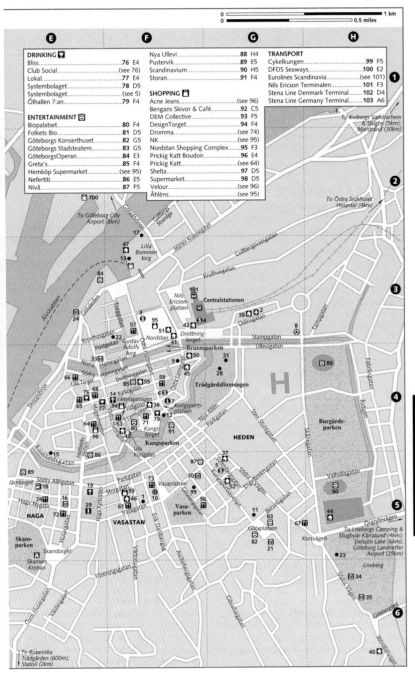

DRINKING
Bliss.....................................**76** E4
Club Social.........................(see 76)
Lokal..................................**77** E4
Systembolaget....................**78** D5
Systembolaget....................(see 5)
Ölhallen 7:an.....................**79** F4

ENTERTAINMENT
Biopalatset.........................**80** F4
Folkets Bio.........................**81** D5
Göteborgs Konserthuset.......**82** G5
Göteborgs Stadsteatern.........**83** G5
GöteborgsOperan................**84** E3
Greta's...............................**85** F4
Hemköp Supermarket..........(see 95)
Nefertiti.............................**86** E5
Nivå..................................**87** F5

Nya Ullevi.........................**88** H4
Pustervik............................**89** E5
Scandinavium......................**90** H5
Storan................................**91** F4

SHOPPING
Acne Jeans.........................(see 96)
Bengans Skivor & Café.........**92** C5
DEM Collective....................**93** F5
DesignTorget.......................**94** F5
Dromma.............................(see 74)
NK....................................(see 95)
Nordstan Shopping Complex...**95** F3
Prickig Katt Boudoir.............**96** E4
Prickig Katt.........................(see 64)
Shelta................................**97** D5
Supermarket........................**98** D5
Velour...............................(see 96)
Åhléns...............................(see 95)

TRANSPORT
Cykelkungen.......................**99** F5
DFDS Seaways.....................**100** E2
Eurolines Scandinavia............(see 101)
Nils Ericson Terminalen.........**101** F3
Stena Line Denmark Terminal...**102** D4
Stena Line Germany Terminal....**103** A6

To Kvibergs Vandrarhem & Stugby (5km); Marstrand (30km)

To Östra Sjukhuset Hospital (4km)

To Göteborg City Airport (8km)

Lilla Bommen torg

Nils Ericson-platsen

Centralstationen

Marten Krakowgatan

Gullbergsvassgatan

Kruthusgatan

Gullbergs Strandgata

Odinsgatan

Drottning-torget

Brunnsparken

Stampgatan

Ullevigatan

Nordstan

Gustav Adolfs torg

Norra Hamngatan

Södra Hamngatan

Lilla Torget

Kronhusgatan

Postgatan

Drottninggatan

Trädgårdsföreningen

H

Kungsports-platsen

Nya Allén

Parkgatan

Steri Sturegatan

Burgårds-parken

Skeppsbron

Lilla Torget

Kungstorget

Kungsparken

HEDEN

Lilla Korsgatan

Rosenlundsgatan

Hvitfeldts-

Järntorget

Södra Allégatan

Parkgatan

Vasaplatsen

Vasa-parken

Södra vägen

Enta Vägen

Valhallagatan

HAGA

Haga Nygata

VASASTAN

Erik Dahlbergsg

Engelbrektsgatan

Berzeliigatan

Orgrytevägen

To Lisebergs Camping & Stugbyar Kärralund (4km); Delsjön Lake (6km); Göteborg Landvetter Airport (25km)

Skans-parken

Skanstorget

Skansen Kronan

Föreningsgatan

Götaplatsen

Korsvägen

Liseberg

Övre Husargatan

Vasagatan

Viktoriagatan

Aschebergsgatan

Södra vägen

Götabergsgatan

Mölndalsån

To Botaniska Trädgården (600m); Statoil (2km)

SOUTHWEST SWEDEN

GÖTEBORG PASS

The brilliant Göteborg Pass discount card is well worth bagging, even if all you're planning to do is park in Göteborg (home to Sweden's priciest street parking and most dedicated traffic wardens). Other perks include free or reduced admission to a bundle of attractions (including Liseberg and the museums), plus free city sightseeing tours and travel by public transport within the region.

The card costs Skr225/160 per adult/child for 24 hours or Skr310/225 for 48 hours. It's available at tourist offices, hotels, Pressbyrån newsagencies and online at www.goteborg.com.

Göteborgspaketet is an accommodation package offered at various hotels with prices starting at Skr540 per person per night in a double room. It includes the Göteborg Pass for the number of nights you stay. You can book the package in advance over the internet or telephone the tourist office on ☎ 61 25 00. More expensive packages include theatre or concert tickets, casino passes, spa visits etc.

DANGERS & ANNOYANCES

Travellers (solo women especially) should take care around the Nordstan shopping complex late at night.

SIGHTS
Lisebeg

Scream yourself silly at this mighty **theme park** (☎ 40 01 00; www.liseberg.se; adult/under 7yr Skr70/free; ⏰ to 10pm or 11pm most days May-Aug, to 9pm or 10pm during Christmas period), southeast of the city centre. Sweden's largest, it draws over three million visitors every year, and sometimes it feels as though they're all visiting at once!

There's a number of blockbuster rides, including the 90km/h wooden roller coaster Balder, and the stomach-churning Kanonen, where you're blasted from 0 to 75km/h in under two seconds. For views of the city without losing your lunch, the ride to the top of the Liseberg Tower, 83m above the ground, climaxes in a slow spinning dance with a breathtaking panorama. Softer options include carousels and fairy-tale castles, as well as summertime shows and concerts.

Each ride costs between one and four coupons (Skr20 each) per go, but it probably makes sense to buy a pass (one/two days Skr290/380). Opening hours are complex – check the website. To get there, take tram 4 or 5, and enter from Örgrytevägen or Getebergsled.

Museums

After Liseberg, museums are Göteborg's strongest asset: admission to most is covered by the Göteborg Pass (above). All have good cafes attached and several have specialist shops.

STADSMUSEUM

You'll find the remains of the Äskekärr Ship, Sweden's only original Viking vessel, at **Stadsmuseum** (☎ 61 27 70; Östindiska huset, Norra Hamngatan 12; adult/under 25yr Skr40/free; ⏰ 10am-5pm May-Aug, 10am-5pm Tue-Sun, to 8pm Wed Sep-Apr), alongside silver treasure troves, weaponry and bling from the same period. Other highlights include exhibits on Göteborg's history and an impressive booty of East Indian porcelain (the museum is located in the 18th-century former HQ of the Swedish East India Company).

UNIVERSEUM

The spectacular **Universeum** (☎ 335 64 50; www.universeum.se; Södra Vägen 50; adult/4-16yr/family low season Skr145/95/440, high season Skr165/135/540; ⏰ 10am-7pm late Jun-Aug, 10am-6pm Sep-late Jun) is a top spot for families and nature fiends. A funicular takes you to the top of an indoor mountain, from where you follow the course of a Scandinavian stream down through rivers and lakes to the sea – shark tunnel ahoy! Things take a tropical turn in the absorbing rainforest: birds and butterflies flitter, while more gruesome denizens dwell in Piranha River, Caiman Creek, Anaconda Swamp and Stingray Lagoon. When you're done, go button crazy with the fantastically fun, hands-on science exhibitions, where themes range from nanotechnology and space travel to mixing music.

RÖHSSKA MUSEET

Refreshing **Röhsska Museet** (☎ 61 38 50; www.designmuseum.se; Vasagatan 37; adult/under 20yr Skr40/free; ⏰ noon-8pm Tue, noon-5pm Wed-Fri, 11am-5pm Sat & Sun) is Sweden's only art and design museum. Exhibitions cleverly contrast the classic and the cutting-edge, whether it's Josef Frank and Bruno Mathsson furniture or 18th-century porcelain and Scandi-cool coat-stands. Eastern treasures include Chinese sculptures and Japanese theatre masks, while the museum's burgeoning fashion collection spans haute couture to '80s politicised T-shirts. Temporary exhibitions often favour the offbeat – think skateboard art and denim.

RÖDA STEN

Occupying a defunct, graffitied power station beside the giant Älvsborgsbron, **Röda Sten** (☎ 12 08 16; www.rodasten.com; Röda Sten 1; adult/under 21yr Skr40/20; ☺ noon-5pm Tue-Sun, to 7pm Wed) is one of Sweden's coolest art centres. Its four gritty floors are home to any number of temporary exhibitions, ranging from edgy Swedish photography to New York sound installations. There's an indie-style cafe with summertime riverside seating, weekly live music and club nights (see p219) and offbeat one-offs like punk bike races, boxing matches and stand-up comedy. To get

there, take tram 3 or 9 to Vagnhallen Majorna, walk towards Klippan (p213), continue under Älvsborgsbron and look for the brown-brick building.

Beside Röda Sten, check out work-in-progress **The Thing**, a communal 'sculpture' in the vein of Lars Vilks' Nimis (p197). On weekends, families head here with hammers and nails to further its evolution.

MARITIMAN

Near the opera house, the world's largest floating **ship museum** (☎ 10 59 50; Packhuskajen; adult/7-15yr Skr80/40; ☺ 10am-6pm Jun-Sep, 10am-4pm Apr, May & Oct, 10am-4pm Fri-Sun Mar & Nov) is made up of 20 historical crafts, including fishing boats, a light vessel and a firefighter, all linked by walkways. Shinny down into the 69m-long submarine *Nordkaparen* for a throat-tightening glimpse into underwater warfare. Another highlight is the labyrinthine 121m-long destroyer *Småland*, which saw service from 1952 to 1979. Inside, hunched figures listen to crackling radio messages, and the bunks look just-slept-in – you half expect to

---

CREATIVE OUTSKIRTS

In 2008, one of the world's A-league travel magazines published an article on four up-and-coming neighbourhoods around the world. One of the 'It kids' was tiny Kvarnbyn, a district of the town of Mölndal (Valley of the Mills), lying 8km south of Göteborg. Here, a brooding landscape of roaring rapids gripped by grain mills and historic factories has been transformed into a dynamic yet low-key hub for architects, designers, artists and artisans, many of whom have escaped the high rents and pressures of big brother Göteborg.

The district's cultural nexus is the smart, interactive **Mölndals Museum** (☎ 031-431 34; www .museum.molndal.se; Kvarnbygatan 12; admission free; ☺ noon-4pm Tue-Sun). Nominated for a European Museum of the Year Award in 2005, it's like a vast warehouse, with its 10,000-strong booty of local nostalgia spanning a 17th-century clog to kitchen kitsch and a recreated 1930s worker's cottage. With a focus on memories and feelings, it's an evocative place where you can plunge into racks of vintage clothes, pull out hidden treasures and learn more about individual items on the digital catalogue. One particular highlight is the eclectic collection of chairs, including beautifully crafted pieces from the nearby village of Lindome, one of Sweden's most historic furniture-making areas. The temporary exhibitions are fresh (anything from computer games to a retrospective on paper) and the in-house cafe boasts summertime seating right by the rapids. The museum also hires out a brilliant, hand-held computer guide (Skr25; in Swedish), which leads you through Kvarnbyn's industrial landscape using a lively mix of historical anecdotes, animation and sound-scapes.

Best of all, Kvarnbyn hosts three vibrant annual cultural events. On a Sunday in mid- to late April, **Öppet hus i Kvarnbyn** (Open House) sees local artists and designers open their studios to the public. In September, **Kulturnatt** (Culture Night; www.kulturnatt.molndal.se, in Swedish) is a star-lit spectacle of open studios and art installations, as well as dance and music performances, while December brings with it a **Christmas market**, with savvy local wares including textiles, art and craft. For more information on the district, visit www.vastsverige.se. To reach Kvarnbyn from Göteborg, catch a Kungsbacka-bound train to Mölndal station, then bus 756 to Mölndals Museum.

meet uniformed sailors in the dim, twisting passages…

Allow a couple of hours to explore.

KONSTMUSEET

Göteborg's premier art collection awaits at **Konstmuseet** (☎ 61 29 80; www.konstmuseum.goteborg .se; Götaplatsen; adult/under 25yr Skr40/free, during special exhibitions adult Skr60; ☷ 11am-6pm Tue & Thu, 11am-9pm Wed, 11am-5pm Fri-Sun), with works by the French impressionists, Rubens, Van Gogh, Rembrandt and Picasso, as well as Scandinavian masters such as Bruno Liljefors, Edvard Munch, Anders Zorn and Carl Larsson.

Other highlights include a superb sculpture hall, the **Hasselblad Center** (☎ 20 35 30) photographic collection, and temporary exhibitions showcasing next-gen Nordic art.

Outside, Götaplatsen is dominated by the bronze **Poseidon fountain**, infamous for scandalising locals upon its unveiling in 1931. This 7m-high colossus originally had private parts most men could only wish for. Alas it was all too much for Göteborg's strait-laced citizens, who forced poor Poseidon to undergo drastic reduction surgery.

VARLDSKULTURMUSEET

In a striking building by London-based architects Cécile Brisac and Edgar Gonzalez, the enlightened **Varldskulturmuseet** (Museum of World Culture; ☎ 63 27 30; www.varldskulturmuseet.se; Södra Vägen 54; adult/under 21yr Skr40/free; ☷ noon-5pm Tue & Fri-Sun, noon-9pm Wed & Thu) sees ethnography, art and global politics collide in immersive multimedia exhibitions. Recent themes have included hip-hop culture and freedom movements across the globe.

SJÖFARTSMUSEET

The main museum of maritime history is **Sjöfartsmuseet** (☎ 368 35 50; www.sjofartsmuseum .goteborg.se; Karl Johansgatan 1-3; adult/under 25yr Skr40/ free; ☷ 10am-5pm Tue-Sun, to 8pm Wed), by Stigbergs-storget about 2km west of the city centre. Tram 3, 9 or 11 will get you there. The collection includes model ships, cannons, a ship's medical room and a large collection of figureheads, such as the vicious-looking Vinthunden from the frigate with the same name. The attached **aquarium** (included in the entry fee) wriggles with Nordic marine life. Outside, the **Sjömanstornet** (Mariner's Tower), topped by a statue of a grieving woman, commemorates Swedish sailors killed in WWI.

NATURHISTORISKA MUSEET

The **Natural History Museum** (☎ 775 24 00; www .gnm.se; Slottsskogsparken; adult/under 25yr Skr40/free; ☷ 11am-5pm Tue-Sun) contains the world's only stuffed blue whale. In the lead-up to Christmas, visitors are occasionally allowed to step inside its mouth for that Jonah feeling. As natural history museums go, this is an impressive one, with an overall collection spanning 10 million specimens of wildlife from around the world. To get there, take tram 1 or 6.

NYA ÄLVSBORGS FÄSTNING

At the mouth of the Göta älv, squat red **Elfsborgs Fortress** has had a gripping history. Built in the 17th century to defend the young city from Danish attack, it saw action again in the early 18th century during the Great Nordic War. Visitors can see the church built for Karl XII's troops, and the dungeons for when they misbehaved.

The fortress lies about 8km downstream from Göteborg. Boat trips and **guided tours** (adult/6-16yr/family Skr140/70/385) are run four times daily from early July to late August by Börjessons (see p214). Tours depart from Lilla Bommen harbour, north of the train station. Several are free for Göteborg Pass holders.

VOLVO MUSEUM

Pay homage to one of Sweden's enduring icons at the **Volvo Museum** (☎ 66 48 14; Hisingen; adult/child Skr30/10; ☷ 10am-5pm Tue-Fri, 11am-4pm Sat & Sun), which contains everything from the company's debut vehicle to the most cutting-edge experimental designs – including the first jet engine used by the Swedish Air Force.

The museum is about 8km west of the city centre at Arendal. Fittingly, it's tricky to get to without a car. Take tram 5 or 10 to Eketrägatan, then bus 32 to Arendal Skans.

Parks & Gardens

Laid out in 1842 and recently restored to better reflect its original plan, the lush **Trädgårdsföreningen** (City Park; ☎ 365 58 58; www .tradgardsforeningen.se; Nya Allén; adult/under 15yr Skr15/ free; ☷ 7am-8pm mid-Apr–late Sep, entrance fee 9am-7pm, 7am-6pm late Sep–mid-Apr, no entrance fee) is a large protected area off Nya Allén. Full of flowers and tiny cafes, it's popular for lunchtime escapes and home to Europe's largest **rosarium**,

SOUTHWEST SWEDEN

with around 2500 varieties. The gracious 19th-century **Palmhuset** (☎ 365 58 58; admission free; ☻ 10am-5pm May-Aug, 10am-4pm Sep-Apr) is a bite-size version of Crystal Palace in London, with five differently heated halls: look out for the impressive camellia collection and the 2m-wide tropical lily pads.

More botanical bliss awaits at the **Botaniska Trädgården** (Carl Skottsbergsgatan 22A; admission free; ☻ gardens 9am-sunset, greenhouses 10am-5pm May-Aug, 10am-4pm Sep-Apr). Sweden's largest botanical garden, it breathes easy with around 16,000 plant species.

Just across Dag Hammarskjöldsleden, **Slottsskogsparken** (admission free; ☻ 24hr) is superb for a stroll. The Naturhistoriska Museet (op-posite) is perched on a hill in the park, with other attractions including **Barnens Zoo** (Children's Zoo; admission free; ☻ daily May-Aug) and **Djurgårdarna** (admission free), an animal park with farm ani-mals, elk, deer and other furry and feathered Swedish creatures. Feeding time at the seal pond is 2pm daily.

The rocky heights of Ramberget (87m) in **Keillers Park** (Hisingen) give the best view of the city. Get there on the city bus tour (see p214) or take a tram to Ramsbergsvallen and walk up.

Churches

Göteborg's churches aren't very old but they are a better reflection of Swedish architecture than Stockholm's Italian imitations.

The elegant **Domkyrkan** (Gustavi Cathedral; Västra Hamngatan; ☻ 9am-6pm Mon-Fri, 11am-5pm Sat, 10am-3pm Sun Jun-Aug; 8am-6pm Mon-Fri, 9am-4pm Sat, 10am-3pm Sun Sep-May) was consecrated in 1815 – the two previous cathedrals having been de-stroyed by town fires. Although many of the cathedral's contents are modern, seasoned features include an 18th-century clock and reredos.

The park behind the beautiful 19th-century **Hagakyrkan** (☎ 731 61 60; Haga Kyrkoplan; ☻ 11am-3pm Mon-Thu & Sat) is home to a simple yet moving **monument** to Swedish hero Raoul Wallenberg. A Nordic Schindler of sorts, Wallenberg is credited with saving the lives of around 15,000 Hungarian Jews during WWII. Wallenberg himself was arrested by the Russian gov-ernment in 1945 and executed two years later.

One of Göteborg's most distinctive build-ings, **Masthuggskyrkan** (Storebackegatan; ☻ 9am-6pm Jun-Aug, 9am-4pm Sep-May) is a welcome landmark for sailors and a smashing viewpoint over the

western half of the city. Completed in 1914, its interior resembles an upturned boat.

Other Sights

The **Haga district** is Göteborg's oldest suburb, dating back to 1648. A hardcore hippy hang-out in the 1960s and '70s, its cobbled streets and vintage buildings are now a gentrified blend of cafes, op shops and boutiques. It's also home to **Galleri Mors Mössa** (☎ 13 22 82; Husargatan 11; ☻ usually noon-4pm Mon-Thu), one of Göteborg's better private art galleries.

A short walk further west, the **Linné district** holds fast to its grungy roots, especially along the Långgatan streets. Here, uberhip cafes, junk shops and street-smart boutiques mix it with seedy sex shops and eclectic locals. It's a magnet for creative types and home to the kicking **Andra Långdagen block party**, a wild, one-day street bash on Andra Långgatan organised by the street's traders and fans. Held annu-ally between April and June (check the Andra Långgatan group on Facebook for dates), it's a thumping concoction of curbside DJ sets, film screenings, barbecues, clothes swaps and back-yard B-boy battles. Looking out over the 'hood is the spindly, neo-Gothic **Oscar Fredriks kyrka** (☎ 731 92 50; Oscar Fredriks Kyrkogatan; ☻ 8am-4pm Mon-Fri), another 19th-century ecclesial creation.

Across town, the red-and-white 'skyscraper' **Göteborgs-Utkiken** (☎ 15 61 47; Lilla Bommen torg 1; adult/child Skr30/15; ☻ 11am-4pm Jul & Aug, 11am-4pm Mon-Fri Sep-Jun), nicknamed 'The Lipstick' for obvious reasons, has killer views of the har-bour from the top.

Once a bustle of industry (with glassworks, foundries, breweries and salting houses) the **Klippan precinct** has been revamped into a rather fetching heritage centre. It includes 18th-century sailor's cottages, the remains of Gamla Älvsborgs fort (ransomed from the Danes in 1619), a brewery opened by the Scot David Carnegie (now a hotel) and St Birgittas kapell. Klippan is just off Oscarsleden, about 400m east of Älvsborgsbron – take tram 3 or 9 to Vagnhallen Majorna.

Kronhuset, lying between Postgatan and Kronhusgatan, is the city's oldest secular building, a former arsenal built in Dutch style between 1642 and 1654. It was here that Karl X held the disastrous *riksdag* (parliament) in 1660 – he died while it was in session. **Kronhusbodarna**, across the courtyard from Kronhuset, houses several workshops mak-ing and selling pottery, silverware, glass and textiles. It's also home to the wicked **Göteborgs Choklad & Karamellfabrik** (☎ 775 90 64; ☯ 11am-5pm Mon, 11am-6pm Tue-Fri, 11am-4pm Sat), a candy factory-cum-shop where the sticky treats include *skumklubba* (marshmallows on a stick, dipped in dark chocolate and desiccated coconut).

Equally tummy-rumbling is **Feskekörka** (Fish Church; ☎ 711 35 09; Rosenlundsgatan; ☯ 9am-5pm Tue-Thu, 9am-6pm Fri, 10am-2pm Sat, also 9am-5pm Mon Jul & Aug), a curious-looking fish market shaped like a church.

ACTIVITIES

Cyclists should ask the tourist office for the free map *Cykelkarta Göteborg*, covering the best routes in and around the city. See p221 for bike hire.

For a vintage splash, head to the magnificent indoor swimming pool **Hagabadet** (☎ 60 06 00; Södra Allégatan 3; ☯ 6.30am-8pm Mon-Thu, 6.30-7pm Fri, 9am-6pm Sat, 3-8pm Sun Jul–mid-Aug; 6.30am-9.30pm Mon-Thu, 6.30am-8.30pm Fri, 9am-7pm Sat, 10am-7pm Sun mid-Aug–Jun). For Skr360 you can swim all day and use the attached sauna, gym and aerobics facilities; between 6.30am and 9am, a dip in the pool costs Skr115. There's also a luxe choice of spa treatments and a bookable Roman bath (Skr498 per person for two hours).

Outdoor swimming is best in **Delsjön lake**, 6km east of the centre (take tram 5 to Töpelsgatan). You can also hire **canoes** (☎ 40 34 88) and **fish** for pike or perch here: ask the tourist office for tackle shop details, as you'll need a permit.

Bohusleden is an easy walking trail that runs for 360km through Bohuslän, from Lindome (south of Göteborg) to Strömstad, passing just east of the city. Purchase guides to the north and south routes from the tourist offices (Skr50).

For perfect **island-hopping**, take tram 11 southwest to Saltholmen and you'll have at least 15 different islands to explore – see p222.

There's some good **rock climbing** around Göteborg. Tram 6, 7 and 11 go to Kviberg, close to some of the best climbing, at Utby. Contact **Göteborgs Klätterklubb** (☎ 43 13 86; www .gbgkk.nu, in Swedish) for information.

TOURS

Börjessons (☎ 60 96 70; www.borjessons.com) run 50-minute city bus and boat tours (some under the name 'Paddan Sightseeing'). They're a great way to get your bearings and are free

with the Göteborg Pass, as are tours to Nya Älvsborgs Fästning (p212). There may be restrictions on the times that you can go; check first.

The **City Bus Tour** (adult/6-16yr Skr130/70) departs Stora Teatern five to six times daily from mid-May to mid-August (once daily at other times).

The **City Boat Tour** (adult/6-16yr Skr130/70) leaves Kungsportsbron daily from late April to late December.

The tour to **Nya Älvsborgs Fästning** (adult/6-16yr Skr150/80) departs Lilla Bommen torg daily from early July through August.

Börjessons also runs tours from Lilla Bommen torg to **Vinga** (p223) and around the island of **Hisingen** (adult/6-16yr from Skr180/90; 6.30pm Tue-Sat late Jun-Aug, 6.30pm Tue & Wed mid-Apr–late Jun & early–mid-Sep), among others. Updated timetables and prices for all tours are available at www.stromma.se.

FESTIVALS & EVENTS

Göteborg International Film Festival (www.filmfestival .org) is one of Scandinavia's major film festivals, with flicks spanning all continents and genres. It's usually held in late January.

A hip-shaking line-up of world music, **Clandestino Festival** (www.bwanaclub.org) is held over two days in June. In early August, **Way Out West** (www.wayoutwest.se) is a mighty three-day music festival pulling in big guns like Kanye West, Sonic Youth, the Hives and José González.

SLEEPING

Göteborg has several high-quality hostels near the city centre. Most hotels offer decent discounts at weekends and in summer. For Skr60, the tourist office can arrange your accommodation for you.

Camping

Lilleby Havsbad Camping (☎ 56 22 40; info@lilleby camping.se; Lillebyvägen; sites low/high season Skr170/220; ☯ Jun-Aug) This agreeable, seaside spot lies 20km west of the city centre in Torslanda. Take bus 25 from near Centralstationen to Lillebyvägen, then change to bus 23.

Lisebergs Camping & Stugbyar Kärralund (☎ 84 02 00; karralund@liseberg.se; Olbergsgatan 1; sites low/high season with car Skr225/375, cabins & chalets from Skr495/595) Liseberg fun park owns and operates a range of accommodation around Göteborg. Located 4km east of central Göteborg, this family-friendly campsite is the closest one to town (tram 5 to Welandergatan), with 35 unreservable tent sites – so turn up early.

Hostels

Most hostels are clustered in the central southwestern area, in apartment buildings that sometimes inspire little confidence from the outside, but inside offer accommodation of a very high standard. All are open year-round.

STF Vandrarhem Stigbergsliden (☎ 24 16 20; www.hostel-gothenburg.com; Stigbergsliden 10; dm/d from Skr150/350; 🖳) In a renovated 19th-century seaman's institute (take tram 3, 9 or 11 to Stigbergstorget), this is a hostel with history. Staff are greatly helpful, and besides the usual stuff (big kitchen, laundry, TV room), perks include a sheltered garden and bike rental (Skr50 per day).

our pick **STF Vandrarhem Slottsskogen** (☎ 42 65 20; www.sov.nu; Vegagatan 21; dm Skr185-210, s/d Skr345/490; 🖳) Unlike many Swedish hostels, big, friendly Slottsskogen is a cracking place for meeting other travellers. For a small extra payment there's access to a laundry, sauna and sun bed, and the buffet breakfast (Skr55) is brilliant. Parking spaces can be booked for a fee and reception is closed between noon and 2pm. Take tram 1 or 6 to Olivedalsgatan.

Masthuggsterrassens Vandrarhem (☎ 42 48 20; www.mastenvandrarhem.com; Masthuggsterrassen 10H; dm/d Skr190/480; 🖳) If you're after a good night's sleep, try this clean, quiet, well-run place. Fine facilities include three lounges, three kitchens and a little library (mostly Swedish books), and it's handy if you're catching an early ferry to Denmark. Take tram 3, 9 or 11 to Masthuggstorget and follow the signs.

Göteborgs Vandrarhem (☎ 40 10 50; www.goteborgsvandrarhem.se; Mölndalsvägen 23; dm/s/d Skr250/550/550) Nifty for those desperate to get to Liseberg as early as possible, extras include a sauna and big sunny terrace. Take tram 4 to Getebergsäng.

Kvibergs Vandrarhem & Stugby (☎ 43 50 55; www.vandrarhem.com; Kvibergsvägen 5; low season 1-/2-/3-/4-bed r Skr270/360/460/560, high season 2-/3-/4-bed r Skr475/580/700; 🖳) This sterling SVIF hostel, a few kilometres northeast of the city centre (tram 6, 7 or 11), boasts super amenities, including flatscreen TVs, wi-fi, sauna, sun beds, laundry, table tennis, two kitchens and two lounges. There are no dorms; you rent out the entire room. Hotel-style rooms and cabins are also available.

Also recommended:

Göteborgs Mini-Hotel (☎ 24 10 23; www.minihotel.se; Tredje Långgatan 31; dm Skr150-190, d Skr400) The spartan rooms might lack warmth, but they're clean, cheap and close to the Linné district's buzzing bars and cafes. Breakfast is available June to August.

Linné Vandrarhem (☎ 12 10 60; www.vandrarhem met-linne.com, in Swedish; Vegagatan 22; dm first night Skr280, subsequent nights Skr220, 2-/3-bed r Skr440/660; 🖳) Down the road from Slottsskogen, this SVIF hostel is another good option with bike hire (Skr50 per day).

Hotels

BUDGET

City Hotel Vid Avenyn (☎ 708 40 00; www.cityhotelgbg.se; Lorensbergsgatan 6; s/d without bathroom from Skr495/595) The City represents excellent value for such a central hotel (within yards of Sweden's 'Champs Élysées'). Staff are friendly, rooms are comfy and for about Skr200 extra you can have a private bathroom. A continental breakfast (included in the room price) is brought to your door, or for Skr25 more you can opt for the breakfast buffet at the new in-house restaurant-pub (which boasts 60 varieties of beer).

MIDRANGE

Grand Hotel Opera (☎ 80 50 80; www.hotelopera.se; Norra Hamngatan 38; s/d budget Skr795/1095, standard Skr1195/1495; 🖳) By the train station and bus terminal, this hotel has budget rooms (in an older part of the hotel) that are small but adequate, while standard rooms are larger, better decorated and have extras like desks. At the time of research the hotel was set to add a restaurant-pub, spa and 130 brand-spanking new rooms (costing Skr500 to Skr700 more than a current standard).

Hotel Vasa (☎ 17 36 30; www.hotelvasa.se; Viktoriagatan 6; s/d from Skr925/1145; 🖳) The attractive, family-run Hotel Vasa lies in trendy, inner-city Vasastan. Hotel perks include a courtyard garden, a Jacuzzi in two of the doubles, and a book about Göteborg in every comfy room.

Vanilj Hotell, Kafé & Bar (☎ 711 62 20; www.hotel vanilj.se; Kyrkogatan 38; s/d incl breakfast from Skr995/1145, weekends from Skr695/795; 🅿 🖳) On a quiet, central street, this petite slumber spot is cosy, homelike and adorable. Individually decorated rooms span country checks to Scandinavian cool, and breakfast is served in the buzzing cafe downstairs. Get there early for one of the five parking spaces.

ourpick Hotel Flora (☎ 13 86 16; www.hotelflora.se; Grönsakstorget 2; s/d Skr1195/1495; 🖳) An extreme makeover has turned Flora from frumpy to fabulous, its uberslick rooms now flaunting black-and-white interiors, designer chairs, flatscreen TVs and sparkling bathrooms. The top-floor rooms have air-con, several rooms offer river views and the chic split-level courtyard is perfect for sophisticated chilling.

Hotel Royal (☎ 700 11 70; www.hotelroyal.nu; Drottninggatan 67; s/d from Skr1295/1495; 🖳) Göteborg's oldest hotel (1852) has aged enviably. The grand entrance has been retained, complete with painted glass ceiling and sweeping staircase, and the elegant, airy rooms make necessary 21st-century concessions like flatscreen TVs and renovated bathrooms. There's also homemade cake for guests. Check the website for special offers.

Hotel Eggers (☎ 333 44 40; www.hoteleggers.se; Drottningtorget; s/d from Skr1495/1835; P 🖳) Elegant Eggers would make a great set for a period drama. Founded as a railway hotel in 1859, its rooms are a Regency-style treat. A good few have private balconies overlooking the bustling square, and nearby parking spots (Skr120 per 24 hours) can be booked at reception.

Hotell Barken Viking (☎ 63 58 00; barken.viking@ liseberg.se; Gullbergskajen; s/d Skr1495/2050; 🖳) Freshly revamped, *Barken Viking* is an elegant four-masted sailing ship, converted into a stylish hotel and restaurant and moored near Lilla Bommen harbour. Rooms are smart and suitably nautical, with handsome blue carpet, Hamptons-style linen and warm wood panelling. The discounted May to September rate includes entry to Liseberg.

TOP END
Clarion Collection Hotel Odin (☎ 745 22 00; www.ho telodin.se; Odinsgatan 6; apt s Skr1095-1995, d Skr1395-2295; 🖳) Spacious and slinky, this modern hotel features fabulous apartments filled with the kind of decor and gadgets you'd kill for at home, and all come equipped with everything you need for a long, civilised stay (including a full kitchen and lounge with TV and stereo).

Radisson SAS Scandinavia Hotel (☎ 758 50 00; Södra Hamngatan 59-65; s/d low season from Skr1290/1390, high season from Skr2040/2140; P 🖳 🕮) Another luxe number, with rooms running around a vast atrium lined with shops, bar and restaurant. Rooms are fresh, spacious and contemporary (beds come with light-up perspex headboards)

and there's a health club (Skr100), complete with pool.

Hotel Gothia Towers (☎ 750 88 10; hotelreservations @gothiatowers.com; Mässans Gata 24; s/d from Skr1645/1895; P 🖳) Sweden's largest hotel is the 23-storey Gothia Towers (take tram 5). Its 704 rooms ooze Nordic cool, especially the 'Design' options: they're all sharp, clean lines and good bathroom windows for a vista-friendly soak. More bird's-eye views await at Sky bar and restaurant Heaven 23, a hit with non-guests and home to Göteborg's best shrimp sandwich.

Avalon (☎ 751 02 00; www.avalonhotel.se; Kungstorget 9; s/d from Skr1890/2190; 🖳 🕮) The new, design-conscious Avalon is steps away from the main tourist office. Rooms are sleek and uncluttered, with flatscreen TVs and heavenly pillows. Some rooms feature a mini-spa (three even have their own gym equipment), and the hip resto-bar is an after-work hot spot. The ultimate highlight is the rooftop pool (open May to September), which leans out over the edge for a dizzying dip. Check the website for packages.

The Scandic chain (which usually offers its best rates online) has several hotels in Göteborg, including the following:

Scandic Hotel Rubinen (☎ 751 54 00; rubinen@ scandichotels.com; Kungsportsavenyn 24; r Skr750-2250; 🖳) In the heart of the Avenyn action, with slick, recently renovated rooms and a restaurant–cocktail bar serving Caribbean-influenced dishes.

Scandic Hotel Europa (☎ 751 65 00; europa@scandi chotels.com; Köpmansgatan 38; s Skr950-2250, d Skr1050-2350; 🖳 🕮) With 6th-floor pool and sauna area.

EATING
Göteborg isn't short on great epicurean experiences, whether it's New Nordic nosh devoured to DJ-spun tunes or late-night curbside crêpes. Stray off Kungsportsavenyn for anything from retro panino bars to champagne-and-lobster dining rooms. Cool cafes, cheap ethnic gems and foodie favourites abound in the Vasastan, Haga and Linné districts, often with lower prices than their tourist-trap Avenyn rivals. Alas, many places close on Sundays.

Restaurants
BUDGET
Andrum (☎ 13 85 04; Östra Hamngatan 19; large plate Skr70; ⏰ 11am-9pm Mon-Fri, noon-8pm Sat & Sun) Vegetarians love this casual, meat-free spot

with its value-for-money all-day lunch buffet. It's simple, tasty, wholesome stuff, and cheerfully recommended.

Solrosen (Kaponjärgatan 4; dinner mains Skr75-80; 11.30am-11pm Mon-Thu, 11.30am-midnight Fri, 11.30am-1am Sat, 2-8pm Sun, closed Sun in summer) A 1970s survivor, this laid-back student favourite is a Haga institution (note the photos of passed-on regulars above the counter). Pay tribute over soulful vegetarian dishes and a bountiful salad buffet. For the best value, choose one of the hot dishes on the menu board, which also include the salad buffet in the price.

MIDRANGE

our pick Publik (☎ 14 65 20; Andra Långgatan 20; lunch Skr65, mains Skr100-130; 11.30am-1am Mon-Sat) Arguably Göteborg's coolest hang-out (think grit-chic interiors, local art exhibitions, DJ-spun tunes and creative indie crowds), this cafe-bar hybrid also serves brilliant, great-value grub like goat's cheese–stuffed aubergines with red pesto potatoes. The well-priced house wine is perfectly drinkable and there's a backyard courtyard for fine-weather lounging.

Sjöbaren (☎ 711 97 80; Haga Nygata 25; mains Skr100-260; 11am-11pm Mon-Thu, 11am-midnight Fri, noon-midnight Sat, 1-10pm Sun, opens 3pm Sun in summer) In the Haga district, cosy Sjöbaren combines nautical interiors with sublime Swedish seafood. If the weather's on your side, chow down classics like gravlax or fish soup in the gorgeous garden courtyard.

our pick Smaka (☎ 13 22 47; Vasaplatsen 3; mains Skr120-205; 5pm-2am Mon-Thu & Sun, 5pm-3am Fri & Sat) This lively, down-to-earth restaurant-bar cooks up brilliant, old-school Swedish *husmanskost* (home cooking) like the specialty meatballs with mashed potato and lingonberries. Mod-Swedish options might include a goat's cheese soup with roasted beetroot and asparagus.

Björns Bar (☎ 701 79 79; Viktoriagatan 12; mains Skr125-145; 6pm-1am Mon-Thu, 5pm-3am Fri & Sat) Serious foodies and night owls swear by this stylish basement bolt hole, serving fabulous hot nosh until midnight, and cheese and antipasto platters until closing. Staff are passionate about the finely tuned food, which spans Swedish and Spanish flavours (think Kalix caviar on toasted brioche or Spanish blood sausage with tomato bread).

Tranquilo (☎ 13 45 55; Kungstorget 14; meals Skr140-235; 11.30am-late Mon-Sat, from 9pm Sun) Complete with

glowing pink-and-blue bar and a giant Rio-style Jesus on the ceiling, this hip, bombastic resto-bar peddles grilled meats and tropic-flavoured brilliance like grilled mango and goat's cheese burger with grilled corn and rhubarb chutney. Done, order a pineapple mojito and flirt to a bossa nova beat at the bar.

TOP END

Linnéa (☎ 16 11 83; Södra Vägen 32; mains Skr225-245, 4-/5-course menu Skr495/650; from 5.30pm Mon-Sat) New Swedish cuisine shines brightly at intimate Linnéa. Treat your taste buds to bold creations like duck breast with black chokeberry gravy and iced beetroot. Book ahead.

Fiskekrogen (☎ 10 10 05; Lilla Torget 1; mains Skr285-375; lunch & dinner Mon-Sat) Another high achiever, Fiskekrogen serves superlative fish and seafood creations in former Swedish East India Company buildings. Slip into the chic circular dining room, Blåskajsa, choose your drop from the 500-plus wine list, and prepare to toast the chefs. Book ahead.

28+ (☎ 20 21 61; Götabergsgatan 28; mains Skr325-375; 6-11pm Mon-Sat) Stylish, award-winning 28+ is another fine-dining darling, wowing palates with intriguing dishes like duck terrine with fresh berries, roasted brioche and sweet-and-sour strawberries. For the ultimate indulgence, succumb to the seven-course degustation menu (Skr975). The restaurant closes in summer.

our pick Magnus & Magnus (☎ 13 30 00; Magasinsgatan 8; 2-/3-/4-/6-course tasting menus Skr445/555/555/785; from 6pm) A big hit with the VIPs, this ever-fashionable restaurant serves inspired Euro-fusion flavours. The summer courtyard (which comes complete with bar, DJs and different club nights from Wednesday to Monday) draws an ubercool crowd.

Cafes

Bar Italia (Prinsgatan 7; panini Skr30-40; 7.30am-6pm) In the Linné district is this cultish espresso bar, complete with Italian baristi and suspended Vespa. In warm weather, watch the hip brigade squeeze onto the pavement banquette for perfect caffeine, *cornetti* (croissants), gourmet calzone and gossip.

Bar Centro (☎ 711 00 27; Kyrkogatan 31; focaccia Skr30-60; 6am-6pm Mon-Fri, 7am-5pm Sat, 8am-5pm Sun) Fans of this iconic, retro espresso bar spill out onto the street, downing smooth espresso and tasty focaccias. The few window seats are perfect for urban voyeurs.

SOUTHWEST SWEDEN

Bar Doppio (☎ 42 56 66; Linnégatan 7; soup Skr40, brunch Skr70; ☻ 8am-6pm Mon-Fri, 9am-5pm Sat & Sun, from 7am Mon-Fri mid-Aug–May) More class-A caffeine awaits at this Scandi-cool cafe, where regulars keep track of their tabs on a giant blackboard. Run by two young Antipodeans, it's a laid-back hang-out with a great neighbourhood vibe and fresh grub like homemade muesli, soup, focaccia and biscotti.

our pick Da Matteo (☎ 13 06 09; Vallgatan 5; pizzas Skr75-90, salads Skr80-95; ☻ 9am-7pm Mon-Fri, 10am-5pm Sat, 11am-4pm Sun) A mecca for coffee snobs, head here for wickedly fine espresso, moreish mini *sfogliatelle* (Neapolitan pastries) and savouries like real-deal pizzas, panini and salads. There's a sun-soaked courtyard and a second branch on Viktoriapassagen.

Quick Eats

For something quick, the Nordstan shopping complex has loads of fast-food outlets.

Super + Sushi (☎ 12 20 90; Prinsgatan 4; ☻ to 9pm) Close to several of the hostels, head here for excellent Japanese lunch deals, including miso soup, green tea and 10 pieces of sushi for Skr65.

Alexandras (☎ 711 23 81; Kungstorget; soups & stews around Skr40) Located in the central Saluhallen, this famous eatery dishes out excellent hearty soups and stews, and is particularly welcoming on a chilly day.

Crêpe Van (crêpes Skr40-60; ☻ 4-9pm Mon-Thu, 4pm-3am Fri & Sat) Sweet tooths should head to this unassuming takeaway van, also a favourite of 'flushed and clumsy' patrons late on Friday and Saturday.

Self-Catering

Saluhallen (Kungstorget; ☻ 9am-6pm Mon-Fri, 9am-3pm Sat) Göteborg's main central market is jammed with tasty budget eateries and food stalls, and the perfect place to stock up that picnic basket.

Saluhall Briggen (Nordhemsgatan 28; ☻ 9am-6pm Mon-Fri, 9am-2pm Sat) It might lack Saluhallen's size and buzz, but this covered market (in an old fire-station) will have you drooling over its bounty of fresh bread, cheeses, quiches, seafood and ethnic treats. It's particularly handy for the hostel district.

Feskekörka (☎ 711 35 09; Rosenlundsgatan; ☻ 9am-5pm Tue-Thu, 9am-6pm Fri, 10am-2pm Sat, also 9am-5pm Mon Jul & Aug) A market devoted to fresh fish and squamous things, the 'Fish Church' is heaven (sorry) for seafood fans. Takeaway treats include fresh fish'n'chips, and yummy shrimp and avocado salads.

Hemköp supermarket (Nordstan shopping complex; ☻ 8am-9pm Mon-Fri, 10am-8pm Sat & Sun) Major supermarket in the thick of things.

Ekostore (☎ 13 60 23; Ekelundsgatan 4; ☻ 10am-7pm Mon-Fri, 10am-2pm Sat Jul & Aug, 10am-8pm Mon-Fri, 10am-4pm Sat Sep-Jun) An eco-chic grocery store selling organic and fair-trade products.

Systembolaget Kungsportsavenyn (☎ 18 65 24; Kungsportsavenyn 18); Linné district (☎ 14 65 21; Linnégatan 28B) Systembolagets are scattered across Göteborg, selling beer, wine and spirits. These are two particularly handy outlets.

DRINKING

Swedish licensing laws mean that bars must have a restaurant section, although in most cases, it's vice versa. While Kungsportsavenyn brims with beer-downing tourists, try the following savvier options.

our pick Lokal (☎ 13 32 00; Kyrkogatan 11; ☻ 4pm-1am Mon-Sat) Awarded Best Bar in Göteborg and run by the team from Publik (p217), this effortlessly cool hang-out pulls everyone from artists and media types to the odd punk rocker. Drinks are inspired (think kiwi and ginger daiquiri), the pick-and-mix menu brims with fusion flavours, and music spans soul, jazz and electro. And staff donate 10% of their tips to a Cambodian orphanage.

Club Social (☎ 13 87 55; Magasinsgatan 3; ☻ 4pm-2am Tue-Sat) A black-and-white leather bar demands classic cocktails, and this glam-cool newbie delivers just that. Join in-the-know locals for smooth Bellinis, a tapas-fuelled catch-up session or the petite selection of foodie-minded mains, which change daily according to what's good at the morning market.

Bliss (☎ 13 85 55; Magasinsgatan 3; ☻ 11.30am-2.30pm Mon-Fri, 6pm-1am or 2am Tue-Thu & Sat, 5pm-1am or 2am Fri) Bliss boasts one of the hippest interiors in Göteborg, with low designer seats and slick contemporary tones. It's a long-standing nocturnal favourite: if you're not up to a main meal (they're usually delicious; lunch Skr80, dinner mains around Skr200), you can nibble on tapas-style snacks and groove to live DJs until late.

Ölhallen 7:an (☎ 13 60 79; Kungstorget 7) For low-fuss, old-school soul, don't miss this little gem – a well-worn Swedish beer hall that hasn't changed in about 100 years. There's no food, wine or pretension, just beer, and plenty of choices.

SOUTHWEST SWEDEN

ENTERTAINMENT
Nightclubs

Clubs have varying minimum-age limits, ranging from 18 to 25, and many may charge admission depending on the night.

Nefertiti (☎ 711 15 33; www.nefertiti.se, in Swedish; Hvitfeldtsplatsen 6; admission Skr90-320) A Göteborg institution, this effortlessly cool venue is famous for its smooth live jazz, blues and world music, usually followed by kicking club nights spanning everything from techno, deep house and soul to hip hop and funk. Times vary, so check the website.

Storan (☎ 60 45 00; www.storan.nu, in Swedish; Kungsparken 1) Another local icon, this old opera house now pumps out everything from live indie tunes to weekly club nights. The frozen margaritas at the in-house resto-bar, Grill El Mundo, enjoy cult status. Check the website for upcoming gigs.

Pustervik (☎ 368 32 77; www.pustervik.gotherborg.se, in Swedish; Järntorgsgatan 12) Culture vultures and party people pack this hybrid venue, with its heaving downstairs bar and upstairs club and stage. Gigs range from independent theatre and live music (anything from emerging singer-songwriters to Neneh Cherry) to regular club nights spanning hip hop, soul and rock.

Röda Sten (☎ 12 08 16; www.rodasten.com; Röda Sten 1; ☺ Fri & Sat) Paging Berlin with its post-industrial look, this power station-turned-art gallery cranks up the party vibe with live bands on Friday nights and club nights on Saturdays. Expect indie pop the first Saturday of the month, followed by '80s tunes (complete with retro-clad punters), reggae, and techno each subsequent Saturday.

Nivå (☎ 701 80 90; Kungsportsavenyn 9; admission free-Skr140; ☺ to 3am Wed, to 4.30am Fri & Sat) This styled-up bar-restaurant metamorphoses into a crowd-pleasing (and crowded) club as the week draws on, with several floors of grinding, dance-floor action.

Greta's (☎ 13 69 49; Drottninggatan 35; ☺ to 4am Fri & Sat) The nearest thing in Göteborg to a gay club, Schlager-happy Greta's is kitsch-a-licious fun on Friday and Saturday nights. The minimum age is 20.

Concerts, Theatre & Cinema

Check the local events listings for movies and shows or with the tourist office for what's on where.

Göteborgs Stadsteatern (City Theatre; ☎ 61 50 50; www.stadsteatern.goteborg.se; Götaplatsen; tickets from Skr220; ☺ closed summer) Stages theatre productions in Swedish.

Göteborgs Konserthuset (Concert Hall; ☎ 726 53 10; www.gso.se; Götaplatsen; tickets Skr80-300; ☺ closed summer) Home to the local symphony orchestra, with top international guests and some sterling performances.

GöteborgsOperan (☎ 13 13 00; www.opera.se, in Swedish; Christina Nilssons Gata; tickets Skr90-565) At Lilla Bommen harbour, this place stages classical and modern ballet and opera and assorted musical performances in a striking contemporary building.

Nya Ullevi (☎ 81 10 20; www.ullevi.se; Skånegatan) The city's outdoor stadium hosts huge pop and rock concerts.

Scandinavium (☎ 81 10 20; www.scandinavium.se; Valhallagatan 1) An indoor concert venue near Nya Ullevi.

If you're craving celluloid, the multiscreen **Biopalatset** (☎ 17 45 00; Kungstorget) is good central option for mainstream films. For independent and art-house offerings, try **Folkets Bio** (☎ 42 88 10; Linnégatan 21).

Sport

Göteborgers are avid sports fans. The city's two biggest stadiums are the outdoor Nya Ullevi (above) for **football** matches, and the indoor Scandinavium (above) for **ice hockey**.

SHOPPING

DesignTorget (☎ 774 00 17; Vallgatan 14) Cool, affordable design objects from both established and up-and-coming Scandi talent.

Prickig Katt (☎ 13 13 50; Magasinsgatan 17; ☺ Mon-Sat) The outrageous 'Spotted Cat' has retro-clad staff and idiosyncratic fashion from Dutch, Danish and home-grown labels, as well as kitschy wares and out-there handmade millinery and bling.

Prickig Katt Boudoir (☎ 13 90 50; Magasinsgatan 19; ☺ Mon-Sat) Nearby, this store panders to trendsetting guys, who come seeking non-conformist labels like Denmark's Humor and Göteborg's Gissy. Unisex extras include anything from hot-pink mock-rococo mirrors to street-art tomes. Sharing the same address, local label **Velour** (☎ 775 38 00; ☺ Mon-Sat) and Stockholm legend **Acne Jeans** (☎ 13 85 80) stock slick, stylish streetwear for guys and girls.

DEM Collective (☎ 12 38 84; Storgatan 11; ☺ Mon-Sat) Head to this bite-size boutique for Scandi-cool fair-trade threads. Completely organic, designs are minimalist, street smart

ANNIKA AXELSSON & KARIN STENMAR

Fair-trade activists and founders of emerging fashion label DEM Collective (p219), Annika Axelsson and Karin Stenmar are also passionate Göteborg locals.

What does Göteborg do better than Stockholm? Stockholmers love to discuss great ideas. In Göteborg, there's less talk, more action. It probably reflects our working-class roots. We've always had a strong student and activist culture here. Göteborg opened its first fair-trade, organic shop in the late 1960s. Stockholm only recently opened its first.

Any shortcomings? Göteborg locals can get a little protective about what they do, especially in the art scene. It's like: 'This is our thing and we don't really care what other places are doing.' It's quite ironic considering how much foreign influence has shaped this city over the centuries.

A perfect day in Göteborg? If it's sunny, take the tram to Saltholmen and catch a ferry to Brännö (p222). It's one of the archipelago's most beautiful islands and a lot of artistic people have moved there. If it's raining, head to Röhsska Museet (p210). The curator is a progressive thinker, expanding the fashion collection to include recycled clothes and not just haute couture. Varldskulturmuseet (p212) is also fantastic.

Favourite places to eat? For lunch, head to Alexandras (p218) for delicious soups. For dinner, don't miss Björns Bar (p217). It's a wine bar with good drops by the glass and fantastic staff who know a lot about food. Another favourite is Publik (p217).

How did DEM Collective come about? We met seven years ago while studying project management. Karin was running a club night at Nefertiti (p219) and asked where she could source T-shirts that were organic, fair-trade and actually fashionable. We realised that there was a gap in the market, so in 2004 we set up a factory in Sri Lanka, specifically outside a free-trade zone so that our employees could return to their families at the end of the day. We've recently started collaborating with an organic textile company in Egypt too. Our aim is to prove that it's possible to be both profitable and make positive, lasting change in the world.

and supremely comfortable. To learn about the founders, see the boxed text, above.

Dromma (☎ 711 33 40; Östra Skansgatan 3C; ◷ noon-6pm Mon-Fri, 11am-4pm Sat) Female fashionistas dig Dromma for its gorgeous new and vintage threads, which include limited-edition gems from up-and-coming Nordic designers.

Shelta (☎ 24 28 56; Andra Långgatan 21) Pimp your style with limited-edition and must-have sneakers and streetwear from big players and lesser-known labels.

Supermarket (☎ 24 28 32; Andra Långgatan 18) Shelta's glam spin-off shop, Supermarket focuses on hard-to-find Nordic and Japanese threads for the male style crew. In fact, it's the sole Scandinavian distributor for several labels.

Bengans Skivor & Café (☎ 14 33 00; www.bengans .se; Stigbergstorget 1) Göteborg's mightiest music store is set in an old cinema, complete with retro signage and indie-cool cafe. Monthly in-store gigs (check the website) take place on a hole-in-the-wall stage. Take tram 3, 9 or 11 to Stigbergstorget.

Sweden's largest mall, **Nordstan shopping complex** (☎ 62 39 76), boasts about 150 shops, including upmarket department store **NK** (☎ 710 10 00; Östra Hamngatan 42) and cheaper **Åhléns** (☎ 333 4000; Östra Hamngatan 18).

GETTING THERE & AWAY
Air
Twenty-five kilometres east of the city, **Göteborg Landvetter Airport** (☎ 94 10 00; www.lfv .se) has up to 22 direct daily flights to/from Stockholm Arlanda and Stockholm Bromma airports (with SAS and Malmö Aviation), as well as daily services to Umeå and several weekly services to Borlänge, Luleå and Sundsvall. It's Sweden's second-biggest international airport.

Direct European routes include Amsterdam (KLM), Brussels (Brussels Airlines), Copenhagen (SAS), Frankfurt (Lufthansa and SAS), Helsinki (Finnair and Blue1), London (SAS), Manchester (City Airline), Munich (Lufthansa), Oslo (Wideroe) and Paris (Air France).

Göteborg City Airport (☎ 92 60 60; www.gote borgairport.se), some 15km north of the city at Säve, is used for budget Ryanair flights to destinations including London Stansted, Glasgow and Frankfurt.

SOUTHWEST SWEDEN

Boat

Göteborg is a major entry point for ferries, with several car/passenger services to Denmark, Germany and Norway: for details see p334.

Nearest to central Göteborg, the **Stena Line** (☎ 704 00 00; www.stenaline.se) Denmark terminal near Masthuggstorget (tram 3, 9 or 11) has around eight daily departures for Frederikshavn in peak season, with a 20% discount for rail-pass holders.

Further west is the Stena Line terminal for the daily car ferry to Kiel (Germany). Take tram 3 or 9 to Chapmans Torg.

Bus

The bus station, Nils Ericson Terminalen, is next to the train station. There's a **Västtrafik information booth** (☎ 0771-41 43 00; ⏱ 6am-10pm Mon-Fri, 9am-10pm Sat, 9am-7pm Sun) here, providing information and selling tickets for all city and regional public transport within the Göteborg, Bohuslän and Västergötland area.

Eurolines (☎ 10 02 40; www.eurolines.com; Nils Ericsonplatsen 5) has its main Swedish office at the bus station in central Göteborg. See p334 for details on international bus services offered by the company.

Swebus Express (☎ 0771-21 82 18; www.swebus express.com) has an office at the bus terminal and operates frequent buses to most major towns and cities. Services to Stockholm (Skr420, seven hours) run five to seven times daily. Other direct destinations include Copenhagen (Skr300, four to five hours), Halmstad (Skr108, 1¾ hours), Helsingborg (Skr200, three hours), Jönköping (Skr140, 1¾ hours), Oslo (Skr220, four hours), Malmö (Skr281, three hours) and Örebro (Skr250, four hours).

Svenska Buss (☎ 0771-67 67 67; www.svenska buss.se) has daily departures for Stockholm (Skr410, 7½ hours) via Jönköping (Skr130, 2¼ hours).

Prices can be considerably lower than those quoted here for advanced bookings, especially for Swebus Express.

Car & Motorcycle

The E6 motorway runs north–south from Oslo to Malmö just east of the city centre and there's also a complex junction where the E20 motorway diverges east for Stockholm.

International car-hire companies Avis, Europcar and Hertz have desks at Göteborg Landvetter and City Airports. For car hire in town, contact one of the petrol stations – for example, **Statoil** (☎ 41 11 62; Marklandsgatan 2) in southwestern Göteborg.

Train

Centralstationen is Sweden's oldest railway station and now a listed building. It serves SJ and regional trains, with direct trains to Copenhagen (Skr387, four hours) and Malmö (Skr329, 3¼ hours), as well as numerous other destinations in the southern half of Sweden.

Intercity trains to Stockholm depart approximately every one to two hours (Skr490, five hours), with quicker but more expensive X2000 trains (Skr1110, three hours) also approximately every one to two hours.

Overnight trains to the far north of Sweden (via Stockholm) are operated by Tågkompaniet, though tickets can be purchased directly at www.sj.se.

GETTING AROUND

To/From the Airport

Göteborg Landvetter Airport, 25km east of the city, has a frequent Flygbuss service to/from Nils Ericson Terminalen (one way Skr75, 30 minutes). A taxi from the city centre to the airport will cost Skr345.

Buses from Göteborg City Airport to Nils Ericson Terminalen leave 50 minutes after flight arrivals. For the return journey, they leave the bus terminal around 2½ hours before flight departures (one way Skr60, 30 minutes). A taxi should cost around Skr305.

Bicycle

For bicycle hire try **Cykelkungen** (☎ 18 43 00; Chalmersgatan 19; per day/week Skr120/500).

Public transport

Buses, trams and ferries run by **Västtrafik** (☎ 0771-41 43 00; www.vasttrafik.se) make up the city's public transport system; there are Västtrafik information booths selling tickets and giving out timetables inside **Nils Ericson Terminalen** (⏱ 6am-10pm Mon-Fri, 9am-10pm Sat, 9am-7pm Sun), in front of the train station on **Drottningtorget** (⏱ 6am-8pm Mon-Fri, 8am-8pm Sat & Sun) and at **Brunnsparken** (⏱ 7am-7pm Mon-Fri, 9am-6pm Sat).

Holders of the Göteborg Pass travel free, including on late-night transport. Otherwise a city transport ticket costs adult/child Skr25/12 (Skr40 on late-night transport). Easy-to-use Maxirabatt 100 'value cards' cost Skr100 (from Västtrafik information booths or Pressbyrån newsagencies) and work out much cheaper than buying tickets each time you travel. A 24-hour Dagkort (day pass) for the whole city area costs Skr65.

The easiest way to cover lengthy distances in Göteborg is by tram. Lines, numbered 1 to 13, converge near Brunnsparken (a block from the train station).

Västtrafik has regional passes for 24 hours/30 days (adult Skr240/1350, under 26 years Skr240/1150) that give unlimited travel on all *länstrafik* (regional) buses, trains and boats within the Göteborg, Bohuslän and Västergötland area.

Taxi

One of the larger companies is **Taxi Göteborg** (☎ 65 00 00). Taxis can be picked up outside Centralstationen, at Kungsportsplatsen and on Kungsportsavenyn. Women travelling alone at night can expect a fare discount.

AROUND GÖTEBORG

SOUTHERN ARCHIPELAGO
☎ 031 / pop 4300

A car-free paradise, the southern archipelago is a short hop from Göteborg's hustle. Despite the summer crowds, you'll always find a quiet bathing spot or serene pocket of green.

There are nine major islands and numerous smaller ones. The largest island, Styrsö, is less than 3km long. Military restrictions saw most of the area closed to foreigners until 1997; it's now a residential hot spot for cashed-up commuters.

Take tram 11 from central Göteborg to Saltholmen, from where an excellent 16-destination passenger-only ferry network runs round the islands. The Göteborg Pass is valid, or you can buy a ticket (one way Skr25) taking you all the way from central Göteborg to Vrångö; bikes (if there's space available) cost an extra Skr10, although they're not allowed on trams.

Boats run frequently to Asperö (nine minutes), Brännö (20 minutes) and Styrsö (30 minutes) from around 5.30am to 1am (less frequently at weekends); services to the other islands are more limited.

The best information about the islands is the English-language booklet *Excursions in the Southern Archipelago*, published by Västtrafik and available from the tourist offices or Västtrafiken information booths (see p221).

Brännö
pop 790

Brännö's beaches and outdoor dance floor are its biggest attractions, although it's hard to take your eyes off the local *lastmoped*: bizarre-looking motorised bikes with large trays attached.

The busiest ferry terminal is Rödsten, in the northeast, but ferries also call at Husvik in the southwest.

From the church in the centre of the island, follow the cycling track through the woods towards the west coast. A 15-minute walk from the end of the track leads to a stone causeway and the island **Galterö** – a strange treeless landscape of rock slabs, ponds, deserted sandy beaches and haunting bird calls. You can watch ships of all sizes and colours heading into or out of Göteborg harbour.

From mid-June to mid-August, **Börjessons** (☎ 60 96 70; www.stromma.se) runs evening cruises (usually on Thursday) from Lilla Bommen harbour to Husvik's **pier dance floor**, where passengers can groove for a couple of hours before returning to Göteborg. The tour costs Skr200 per adult; dinner is available on board at an additional cost. Check the website for the latest prices and timetables.

Get away from it all at **Pensionat Bagge** (☎ 97 38 80; www.baggebranno.se; s/d low season Skr375/675, high season Skr475/795), a simple, friendly place about a kilometre south of the ferry quay, which comes complete with bike hire (Skr85 per day).

With the same owners, **Brännö Värdshus** (☎ 97 04 78; info@brannovardshus.se; Husviksvägen; mains Skr100-210; ⏰ 11am-11pm mid-Jun–mid-Aug; 11am-9pm Tue-Sun May; 11am-7pm Thu-Sun mid-Aug–Apr) houses a cosy restaurant, cafe and bakery and serves excellent meals, including the local speciality *rödspätta* (plaice). It also hosts regular live jazz and folk gigs in the summer. There's a grocery shop near the church.

Other Islands

Just southeast of Brännö, **Köpstadsö** is a small island with a quaint village of pretty painted houses and narrow streets. Transport on the island is even more basic than it is on Brännö: locals use individually named wheelbarrows, parked by the quay.

In the central part of the archipelago, **Styrsö** has two village centres (Bratten and Tången, both with ferry terminals), a mixture of old and modern houses, and a history of smuggling. There's a cafe, pizzeria and supermarket at Tången. A bridge crosses from Styrsö to densely populated neighbouring **Donsö**, with a functioning fishing harbour.

The southern island of **Vrångö** has a good swimming beach on the west coast, about 10 minutes' walk from the ferry. The northern and southern ends of the island are part of an extensive nature reserve.

Tiny **Vinga**, 8km west of Galterö, has impressive rock slabs and decent swimming, and has been home to a lighthouse since the 17th century. The writer, composer and painter Evert Taube was born here in 1890 – his father was the lighthouse-keeper. **Börjessons** (☎ 60 96 70; www.stromma.se) runs exhilarating, three-hour tours on high-speed RIB boats (Skr490) from Lilla Bommen (Göteborg) to Vinga (daily in July, and weekly in May, June, August and September). Check the website for updated times and prices.

MARSTRAND
☎ 0303 / pop 1300

Looking like a Tommy Hilfiger ad (think crisp white summer houses and moneyed eye-candy on gleaming boats), this former spa town and island is a Swedish royal favourite. Boasting the country's most popular *gästhamn* (guest harbour), it's *the* weekend destination for yachting types and a see-and-be-seen summer magnet. If you can tolerate the hiked-up prices, it's a spot worth soaking up.

Opposite the ferry terminal is the **tourist office** (☎ 600 87; tk.marstrand@kungalv.se; Hamngatan 33; 11am-5pm Mon-Sat, noon-4pm Sun early–late Jun; 11am-6pm Mon-Fri, 11am-5pm Sat & Sun late Jun–Aug; 8am-noon Mon-Fri Sep-May). There's no ATM or Systembolaget, so bring wealth and wine with you.

Looming over the town is doughty **Carlstens Fästning** (☎ 602 65; www.carlsten.se; adult/7-15yr Skr70/25; 11am-6pm Jun–mid-Aug; 11am-4pm mid-late Aug; 11am-4pm Sat & Sat Sep-May), a fortress constructed in the 1660s after the Swedish takeover of Bohuslän; later building work was completed by convicts sentenced to hard labour. Its impressive round tower reaches 96m above sea

level, and there are smashing archipelago views from the top. Admission includes a guided tour (call ahead for English-language tour times), although you can explore by yourself with an audio guide.

Pick up the English-language *Discover Marstrand* brochure from the tourist office and set off for an hour's walk round the island. Sterling structures include the **town hall**, which is the oldest stone building in the county, and the 13th-century **Maria Kyrka**.

Budget accommodation is not Marstrand's forte. The most reasonably priced option is **Marstrands Varmbadhus Båtellet** (☎ 600 10; marstrandsvarmbadhus@telia.com; Kungsplan; d/tr/q from Skr675/885/1180;), a private hostel with associated pool and sauna. Turn right after disembarking from the ferry and follow the waterfront for 400m. Only dormitory accommodation is available in the summer.

Located at the northern end of the harbour, the **Hotell Nautic** (☎ 610 30; www.hotellnautic.com; Långgatan 6; B&B s/d Skr880/1150;) has bright, simple rooms decked out in blues and creams. A couple have balconies with great sea views.

Marstrand's numerous eating options include fast-food stalls along the harbour. Follow your nose to **Bergs Konditori** (☎ 600 96; Hamngatan 9; snacks Skr20-70; May-Aug), a dockside *konditori* (bakery-patisserie) selling fresh bread, cakes, quiches and sandwiches.

For fresh seafood, head to **Marstrands Wärdshus** (☎ 603 69; Hamngatan 23; noon-late Easter-Sep), a harbourside crustacean restaurant. Yacht-spot on the alfresco terrace with a speciality Seabreeze cocktail in hand.

From Göteborg you can take bus 312 to Arvidsvik (on Koön) then cross to Marstrand by frequent passenger-only ferry. The complete journey takes about an hour. Buy a Maxirabbat 100 ticket (Skr100) from the Västtrafik information booth at Nils Ericson Terminalen in Göteborg and validate it on the bus.

BOHUS FÄSTNING
☎ 0303

Survivor of no fewer than 14 sieges, the hulking ruins of **Bohus Fästning** (☎ 992 00; adult/7-16yr Skr45/25, cash only; 10am-7pm May-Aug, 11am-3pm Sep, 11am-3pm Sat & Sun Oct, 11am-5pm Sat & Sun Apr) stand on an island in the Nordre älv, near Kungälv. Construction of the fortress was ordered in 1308 by the Norwegian king to protect Norway's southern border. The building was

---

ROCK CARVINGS 101

Bohuslän's Bronze Age rock carvings *(hällristningar)* are a prolific sight, a phenomenal 3000-year-old artistic record of religious beliefs, rites and everyday living. Under open skies, the carvings are free to view. The enlightening book, *The Rock Carving Tour* (Skr50), available only from Bohusläns Museum (p228), contains thoughtful interpretations and detailed maps showing you how to find the best Bohuslän sites.

The **Tanum plain** is particularly rich in carvings, and the entire 45-sq-km area has been placed on the Unesco World Heritage List. Start your odyssey at **Vitlycke**, within the Tanum area, where you'll find ships, animals, humans and tiny footsteps scattered through the woods. The splendid 22m **Vitlycke Rock** forms a huge canvas for 500 carvings of 'love, power and magic'. These range from simple cup marks to some of Sweden's most famous rock-art images, including the *Lovers*, showing a sacred marriage.

If you're bewildered by the long-armed men, sexual imagery and goat-drawn chariots, cross the road to **Vitlycke Museum** (☎ 0525-209 50; www.vitlyckemuseum.se; admission free; ⏰ 10am-6pm May-Aug, times vary rest of year, closed Nov-Mar), which has a determined go at explaining them. Digital handheld guides can be hired for Skr40, but it's much better to catch the English tour, complete with clued-up human being. Call ahead for tour times.

You'll need your own transport to get to Vitlycke. By public transport, the nearest you can get is to Tanumshede, 2.5km north: regional buses on the Göteborg–Uddevalla–Strömstad route stop here. Tanumshede train station is further away still.

---

enlarged over the centuries, becoming one of Sweden's toys at the Peace of Roskilde in 1658. Its substantial remains include a remarkable **round tower**. Tourist information for the area is available at the fortress.

Complete with cafe, **STF Vandrarhem & Camping Kungälv** (☎ 189 00; info@kungalvsvandrarhem.se; Färjevägen 2, Kungälv; sites/dm Skr130/200, 4-bed cabins Skr595; ⏰ campsite May–mid-Sep; 🖳) boasts a riverside setting directly across the road from the fortress.

Nearby on the river, **Kungälvs Båtuthyrning** (☎ 579 00; www.kbu.se, in Swedish; Filaregatan 11) rents small boats (Skr150/775 per hour/day).

Grön Express bus runs at least every 30 minutes from Göteborg to Kungälv; get off at the Eriksdal stop and walk the remaining 500m. Journey time is 30 minutes.

BOHUSLÄN

BOHUSLÄN COAST

Dramatic, stark and irrepressibly beautiful, the Bohuslän coast is one of Sweden's natural treasures, its landscape of craggy islands and rickety fishing villages washed in a strangely ethereal light.

If you're heading north from Göteborg, stop at the **tourist office** (☎ 0303-833 27; www.bastkusten.se; Kulturhuset Fregattan; ⏰ 10am-6pm Mon-Sat, 11am-3pm Sun mid-Jun–mid-Aug; 9am-5pm Mon-Fri mid-Aug–mid-Jun) in Stenungsund to pick up brochures and maps of the surrounding area.

Transport connections are good – the E6 motorway runs north from Göteborg to Oslo via the larger towns of Stenungsund, Ljungskile, Herrestad, Munkedal and Tanumshede, passing close to Strömstad before crossing the Norwegian border. Local trains run frequently from Göteborg to Strömstad, via much the same towns as the E6 route. Bus connections from these towns to the outlying islands exist, although some aren't terribly regular.

It's an area suited for independent exploration – consider hiring a car or bike in Göteborg and take it in at your own pace.

Tjörn & Around
☎ 0304 / pop 14,940

A large bridge swoops from Stenungsund (on the Swedish mainland) to the island of Tjörn (www.sodrabohuslan.com), a magnet for artists thanks to its striking landscapes and stunning watercolour museum. Sailors are equally smitten, with one of Sweden's biggest sailing competitions, the **Tjörn Runt**, taking place here in August.

Skärhamn and **Rönnäng**, in the southwest, are the island's main settlements. Their few facilities include a small **tourist office** (☎ 60 10 16; turistbyran@tjorn.se; Södra Hamnen; ⏰ 10am-6pm Jun-Aug, noon-5pm Tue-Sat Sep-May) at Skärhamn. At the time of research, the office's future location was undecided so it's best to call ahead.

Skärhamn is also home to the superb **Nordiska Akvarellmuseet** (Nordic Watercolour Museum; ☎ 60 00 80; www.akvarellmuseet.org; Södra Hamnen 6; adult/under 25yr Skr75/free; ☺ 11am-6pm late May–mid-Sep, noon-5pm Tue-Sun mid-Sep–late May), a sleek waterside building housing world-class exhibits. Attached is award-winning gourmet cafe-restaurant **Vatten** (☎ 67 00 87), whose legendary fish dishes are perfectly matched by the archipelago backdrop.

Up the hill is a working smithy, **Smedja Volund** (☎ 67 17 55; info.volund@swipnet.se; Gråskärsvägen 9; ☺ 11am-6pm mid-Jun–mid-Aug, noon-5pm Tue-Sun mid-Aug–mid-Jun), with a cafe and a studio displaying Berth the blacksmith's idiosyncratic ironwork; Berth himself is often at work in the forge.

The Tjörnexpressen bus runs up to 10 times weekdays (twice Saturday and Sunday) from Göteborg's bus terminal to Tjörn, calling at Skärhamn, Klädesholmen and Rönnäng. Bus 350 from Stenungsund crosses the island to Rönnäng.

KLÄDESHOLMEN

The 'herring island' of Klädesholmen, to the far south of Tjörn, is one of the west coast's most flawless spots. A mash-up of red and white wooden cottages, its activity is fairly subdued due to the departure of the herring (there were once 30 processing factories here, today reduced to a handful). Find out more at the tiny **herring museum** (☎ 67 33 08; kladesholmens-museum@swipnet.se; Sillgränd 8; adult/child Skr10/5; ☺ 3-7pm Jul-early Aug, 3-7pm Sat & Sat rest of Aug).

Salt & Sill (☎ 67 34 80; www.saltosill.se; mains Skr175-345; ☺ May-Sep & Dec, call ahead other times) is a stylish waterside restaurant with an emphasis on local seafood and produce. The herring board is legendary, with herring prepared in six different ways with all the Scandi trimmings. In 2008 the owners opened Sweden's first **floating hotel** (s/d Skr1490/1990, discounted to Skr1290/1590; ▣). A row of slick cubic buildings will house 22 contemporary rooms (and a suite), each featuring the hues of its namesake herb or spice.

ÅSTOL & RÖNNÄNG

Nearby **Åstol** looks straight out of a curious dream – think a tiny, barren chunk of rock dotted with rows of gleaming white houses that seem perched on top of each other from the sea. There's not much to do, but it's utterly loveable. Amble round the car-free streets, soak up the views of the other islands, and feast on fish at **Åstols Rökeri** (☎ 67 72 60; ☺ noon-midnight mid-Jun–mid-Aug), a fish smokery with summer restaurant attached.

You can reach Åstol by ferry from **Rönnäng** (Skr30, roughly hourly between 5.30am and 11.30pm).

Rönnängs Vandrarhem (☎ 67 71 98; Nyponvägen 5; dm from Skr250; ▣ ▣), an SVIF hostel in Rönnäng, about 1km from the ferry, is good and spacious, with one sizeable kitchen and a rambling, country home feel. There's a leafy terrace for lazy summer barbecues.

Orust

☎ 0304 / pop 15,370

Sweden's third-biggest island, **Orust** (www.orust.se) boasts lush woodlands and some breathtakingly pretty fishing villages. It also has a thriving boat-building industry, with over half of Sweden's sailing craft made here. A bridge connects Orust to Tjörn, its southern neighbour.

Orust's **tourist office** (☎ 33 44 94; turistbyran@orust.se; Norra Strandvägen 3; ☺ noon-4pm Mon-Sat, 10am-2pm Sun mid-Jun–mid-Aug, noon-4pm Mon-Fri, 10am-2pm Sat mid-Aug–mid-Jun) is in the town of Henån.

There's an outstanding STF hostel, **Tofta gård** (☎ 503 80; www.toftagard.se; dm/s/d Skr230/330/460), near Stocken in the island's west, about 5km from the larger village of Ellös. It's located in an old farmhouse and outbuildings in a blissfully bucolic setting, with good walking, swimming and canoeing nearby. There's also a cafe and restaurant here in peak season. Book ahead between October and May.

MOLLÖSUND

Super-cute Mollösund, in the island's southwest, is the oldest fishing village on the Bohuslän coast. There's a picture-perfect harbour and several scenic walking paths for a gentle pick-me-up.

Mollösunds Hembygdsmuseum (☎ 214 69; admission free; ☺ 4-6pm late Jun–mid-Aug, ring to visit at other times) is in an old fisherfolk's house near the water and has exhibits about local life.

Slightly inland from the harbour, **Prästgårdens Pension** (☎ 210 58; www.prastgardens.se; Kyrkvägen; d from Skr650; ▣) is the most delightful little spot, with high ceilings, vintage wallpaper, antiques, art and a soothing cottage vibe.

OUR PICK **Vandrarhem, Café & Restaurant Emma**
(☎ 211 75; www.cafeemma.com; sandwiches Skr90-135, salads Skr130, mains around Skr165; ☺ restaurant 11am-midnight Jun–mid-Sep) is an excellent place right on the harbour with a small, welcoming hostel (dorm beds from Skr250) and a cosy cafe-restaurant serving hearty dishes created from local and organic ingredients (the fish soup is exceptional). Out of season, book for the hostel and phone to check restaurant hours.

Mollösunds Wärdshus (☎ 211 08; Kyrkvägen 9; lunch Skr125, mains from Skr155; ☺ restaurant mid-May–Sep, Sat & Sun Apr–mid-May & Oct-Dec) is an upmarket 19th-century inn featuring 10 well-turned-out rooms (available from Easter to December; doubles from Skr1195) and a slinky, sunny-soaked terrace for lazy wining and dining. Enquire here about island-hopping, adrenalin-pumping **RIB Boat Tours** (☎ 217 99; info@oceangroup .se; 2hr tour Skr499), which usually run Wednesday to Saturday in July and August.

There's a supermarket near the harbour.

Bus 375 runs the Uddevalla–Henån–Ellös route around seven times a day from Monday to Friday, continuing to Mollösund on six of these journeys (two buses Saturday and Sunday). The Orustexpressen bus runs several times on weekdays direct from Göteborg to Henån; otherwise change in Stenungsund or Lysekil.

Lysekil & Around
☎ 0523 / pop 14,630

With its air of faded grandeur, the former spa resort of Lysekil feels oddly like an English seaside town. It pampers summer visitors less than other Bohuslän towns, but there's something strangely refreshing about this unfussed attitude.

The **tourist office** (☎ 130 50; info@lysekilsturist.se; Södra Hamngatan 6; ☺ 10am-6pm Mon-Sat, 11am-3pm Sun late Jun–mid-Aug, phone for times mid-Aug–late Jun) offers information on various summer boat tours, including island-hopping swimming trips to fishing jaunts.

The town is amply serviced, with banks and supermarket. The **public library** (☎ 61 33 72; Kungsgatan 18; ☺ noon-8pm Mon-Thu, noon-3pm Fri mid-Jun–mid-Aug, 10am-6pm Mon-Wed, 10am-7pm Thu, 10am-3pm Fri, 10am-1pm Sat mid-Aug–mid-Jun) has free internet access.

SIGHTS & ACTIVITIES
Havets Hus (☎ 66 81 60; www.havetshus.se; Strandvägen 9; adult/5-14yr Skr90/45; ☺ 10am-4pm mid-Feb–Oct, to

6pm mid-Jun–mid-Aug) is an aquarium with sea life from Sweden's only true fjord, which cuts past Lysekil. Wolffish, lumpsuckers, angler-fish…all the cold-water beauties are here.

Lysekil harbours some interesting architecture from its 19th-century spa days: old bathing huts and **Curmans villor**, the wooden seafront houses built in romantic 'Old Norse' style. Carl Curman was the resort's famous physician, who persuaded visitors that Lysekil's sea bathing was a complete cure-all. Crooked street **Gamla Strandgatan** peddles a too-cute collection of painted wooden abodes.

Perched on a hill, the neo-Gothic pink granite **church** (☺ 10am-3pm Mon-Fri, 10am-1pm Sun, closed Sat) has some superb paintings and stained-glass panes honouring local working life.

Out at the tip of the Stångenäs peninsula, the **Stångehuvud Nature Reserve**, crammed with coastal rock slab, is worth a stop for its peaceful bathing spots and wooden lookout tower.

Seal safaris (☎ 66 81 60; adult/under 14yr Skr160/90, combined ticket with Havets Hus Skr220/210; ☺ 1pm & 2.30pm Sun-Fri late Jun–mid-Aug) lasting 1½ hours leave from near Havets Hus: buy tickets at Havets Hus. Recommended three-hour **boat trips** to the picture-perfect island of **Käringön** depart twice weekly in summer; contact the tourist office for details.

Passenger-only ferries cross the Gullmarn fjord roughly hourly to **Fiskebäckskil**, where there are cobbled streets, wood-clad houses and lauded seafood restaurant **Brygghuset** (☎ 222 22). The interior of the **church** recalls an upturned boat, with votive ships and impressive ceiling and wall paintings.

SLEEPING & EATING
The tourist office can book private rooms (singles/doubles from Skr270/550) for a Skr100 fee.

Siviks Camping (☎ 61 15 28; fax 127 27; sites low/high season Skr150/250; ☺ mid-May–mid-Sep) Built on large pink-granite slabs by a sandy beach 2km north of town, Siviks is the best campsite in the area, with ample swimming opportunities. Facilities include shop, restaurant, minigolf, dance floor and laundry.

Strand Vandrarhem & Hotell (☎ 797 51; www .strandflickorna.se; Strandvägen 1; dm Skr300, s/d hostel Skr750/750, hotel Skr935/1120; **P** ☐) The friendly 'beach girls' run a choice of accommodation not far from Havets Hus. The hostel is a typically good SVIF choice, with hotel-style rooms on offer too; some have sea views.

SOUTHWEST SWEDEN

Havshotell (☎ 797 50; Turistaten 13; s/d Sk995/1595; **P** **ꊨ**) Run by the hostel folk, this more upmarket option is based in a sensitively renovated turn-of-the-20th-century house. The atmospheric rooms feature a seafaring/ historical theme.

Café Kungsgatan (☎ 160 01; Kungsgatan 32; lunch Skr80; ⏲ Mon-Sat) Set back from the seafront, this honest cafe serves homemade lunches (pasta, quiche, salads, sandwiches, herring pancakes) washed down with all kinds of tea and coffee.

Pråmen (☎ 143 52; Södra Hamnen; lunch Skr120, mains Skr150-270; ⏲ noon-late Apr-Sep) Crabs, mussels, prawns, halibut, salmon: if it swims, scuttles or sticks to rocks in the sea, this popular floating restaurant-bar will have it on the menu.

There are a few fast-food places on and around Rosviktorg and eateries all along the main street.

GETTING THERE & AWAY
Express bus 840 and 841 run every couple of hours from Göteborg to Lysekil via Uddevalla.

Smögen
☎ 0523
Another seaside star, Smögen sports a buzzing waterside boardwalk, rickety fishermen's houses, and steep steps leading up into a labyrinth of lovingly restored cottages and pretty summer gardens.

The summer-only **tourist office** (☎ 375 44; info@sostenasturism.se; Smögenbryggan; ⏲ 10am-7pm mid-Jun–mid-Aug) sits in a little yellow building just off the boardwalk.

Dubbed **Smögenbryggan**, the boardwalk heaves with bars and shops around the harbour; head in early or out of season if you're seeking solitude. Fishing boats unload their catches of prawns, lobsters and fish at the harbour, where there's a small **fish auction** (www.smogens-fiskauktion.com; Fishhall; ⏲ 8am Mon-Fri, plus 5pm Thu): the big one happens online these days.

Boats (☎ 312 67; return trip Skr70) leave for the nature reserve on the nearby island of **Hållö** up to 16 times daily in summer from Smögen harbour.

The **Kon-Tiki Dykcenter** (☎ 374 74; smogen@ kon-tiki.se; Madenvägen 3) does boat dives, PADI courses and hires out kayaks (Skr250/350 per three hours/day).

our pick **Makrillvikens Vandrarhem** (☎ 315 65; makrillviken@telia.com; Makrillgatan; dm Skr250-300, r from Skr500; **P**), in the former spa bathing house with smashing views of the archipelago, is a sterling, hugely popular budget choice – 500m from the boardwalk crowds, and with an old seaside sauna for guest use. There's a small playground, and canoes for hire. Book ahead!

Hotel Smögens Havsbad (☎ 668 450; www.smogens havsbad.se; Hotellgatan 26; s/d low season Skr1250/1560, high season Skr1550/1950; **P** **ꊨ** **ꊱ**) has a hideous prosthetic extension that is (thankfully for guests) beautiful on the inside, with light Scandi-style rooms, many with sea views. The on-site restaurant celebrates local seafood, with dishes like wolffish with blue mussel froth and sautéed new potatoes.

There's no shortage of appetising cafes, grill-bars and seafood restaurants all along Smögenbryggan.

Anyone pining for an English breakfast will sing hallelujahs at **Coffee Room** (☎ 308 28; Sillgatan 10; breakfast from Skr30, mains Skr90-130; ⏲ 8am-at least 10pm in summer, shorter hours in winter) over the egg, sausage, bacon, tomato and baked beans. There are quick, low-fuss lunchtime snacks (panini, pasta salads, stir-fries), and evening tapas or barbecues in the trendy, laid-back garden.

our pick **Skärets Krog & Konditori** (☎ 323 17; Hamnen 1; mains Skr235-325; ⏲ Sat & Sun May–mid-Jun, daily mid-Jun–mid-Aug), near the Fiskhall, has a ground-floor *konditori* serving light meals and sweet treats and a gourmet upstairs restaurant. Here, the focus is on creative seafood (think mackerel with lavender, dill and smoked bread), cooked by chefs hailing from A-list kitchens including Sydney's Rockpool and New York's Aquavit.

Bus 860 runs regularly from Göteborg to Smögen (around 2½ hours), via Uddevalla, Munkedal, Hunnebostrand and Kungshamn. A couple of the services are direct, otherwise you'll have to change in one of the towns en route.

Fjällbacka
☎ 0525
Film star Ingrid Bergman spent her summer holidays at Fjällbacka (the main square is named after her). Despite the crowds, the tiny town is utterly charming, with its brightly coloured houses squashed between steep cliffs and rolling sea.

SOUTHWEST SWEDEN

NORDENS ARK

Snow leopards, wolves and lynx prowl **Nordens Ark** (☎ 0523-795 90; www.nordensark.se; Åby säteri; adult/5-17yr Skr180/50; ☺ 10am-7pm late Jun–mid-Aug; 10am-5pm late Apr-late Jun & mid-Aug–late Sep; 10am-4pm Jan-late Apr & late Sep-Dec; last entry 2hr before closing time late Apr-late Sep, 1hr before closing time late Sep-late Apr), a fascinating safari park 12km northeast of Smögen. It shows off animals and plants from countries with a similar climate to Sweden's and has breeding programs for endangered species. Guided tours of the park are available daily in peak season and on weekends the rest of the year (included in entry price). Last admission is two hours before closing.

The summer-only **tourist office** (☎ 321 20; Ingrid Bergmanstorg; ☺ 9.30am-6pm mid-Jun–Aug) offers internet access (Skr25 per 15 minutes) and can advise on boat trips to the popular, rocky island of **Väderöarna** (adult/under 13yr return trip Skr300/150).

After pottering about, eating ice cream and browsing the trinket shops, walk up the **Vetteberget** cliff for unforgettable 360-degree views and mesmerising sunsets. From July to mid-August, 1½-hour **island boat trips** (☎ 321 25; info@halsanifjallbacka.se; adult/child Skr150/75; ☺ 3pm) and two-hour **seal safaris** (adult/child Skr150/75; ☺ 7pm Tue & Thu) depart from the harbour.

On a teeny little island just off the harbour, **Badholmens Vandrarhem** (☎ 321 50, 0703-28 79 55; per person Skr200) is a low-fuss hostel reached by a causeway. Four plain bunk-bedded huts look out to sea, and there's a cafe, laundry and free sauna for guests nearby.

ourpick Stora Hotellet (☎ 310 03; www.stora hotellet-fjallbacka.se; Galärbacken; s/d/ste Jun-Aug from Skr1325/1750/2350, Sep-May from Skr1125/1450/1990; 🖳) is a whimsical hotel offering a trip 'around the world in 23 rooms'. It was originally owned by a ship's captain who decorated it with exotic souvenirs. He named each room after his favourite ports and explorers (and girls!), and each tells its own story. Extras include a restaurant, as well as lobster-fishing packages (from Skr2595 per person) from late September to November.

With its killer waterside location and top-notch grub, laid-back **Bryggan Fjällbacka** (☎ 310 60; info@brygganfjallbacka.se; Ingrid Bergmanstorg; d with shared/private bathroom Skr1290/1490, apt Skr2300; meals Skr90-275; ☺ accommodation Easter-Dec, by prior arrangement Jan-Easter; restaurant late May-Aug, Sat & Sun Apr-late May & Sep-Jan) is a massive summer hit. Opt for fantastic pub and cafe fare or posh-nosh options like grilled scallops served with coconut and lemongrass-flavoured mussel soup and mushroom spring-roll. There's an upstairs piano bar and boutique accommodation to boot.

The best way to reach Fjällbacka from Göteborg is to take a Strömstad-bound train to Dingle station, then bus 875 to Fjällbacka. The entire journey should take about two hours and 20 minutes, although it's always best to use the Travel Planner option at www.vast traffik.se to avoid long connection times.

UDDEVALLA

☎ 0522 / pop 50,920

You might find yourself in Bohuslän's capital, Uddevalla, while waiting for transport connections. If so, pop into the museum or take a dip in the old spa area at Gustafsberg. Otherwise, it's a mostly modern, industrial place, giving little reason to linger long. The **tourist office** (☎ 997 20; info@uddevalla.com; Kungstorget 4; ☺ 8am-6pm Mon-Fri, 9am-3pm Sat & Sun mid-Jun–Aug, 10am-4pm Mon-Fri, to 6pm Thu Sep–mid-Jun) can help with information.

Bohusläns Museum (☎ 65 65 00; www.bohuslans museum.se; Museigatan 1; admission free; ☺ 10am-8pm Mon-Thu, 10am-4pm Fri-Sun May-Aug, closed Mon Sep-Apr), near the bus station, tells the history of the area from the Stone Age onwards, with displays on traditional stone, boat-building and fish-preserving industries. There's also an art gallery and restaurant.

Based in an old bathing house, **STF Vandrarhem Gustafsberg/Uddevalla** (☎ 152 00; info@ gustafsberg.se; dm Skr225; ☺ Jun-Aug) enjoys a wonderful waterside location at the old spa of Gustafsberg, 4km from the centre. There are recreation areas and a cafe down this way, too. The area can be reached by boat (Skr25), five times daily from the jetty across the river from the museum, or by local bus.

Regional buses and trains run daily to Strömstad (1¼ hours) and Göteborg (1¼ hours). **Swebus Express** (☎ 0771-21 82 18; www .swebusexpress.com) runs to Oslo (Skr170, three hours) up to six times daily. Buses drop off and pick up from the bus station on the E6 motorway, rather than in the town centre.

STRÖMSTAD
☎ 0526 / pop 11,560

A sparky resort, fishing harbour and spa town, Strömstad is laced with ornate wooden buildings echoing nearby Norway. Indeed, Norwegians head here en masse in summer to take advantage of Sweden's cheaper prices, lending a particularly lively air to the town's picturesque streets and bars.

There are several fantastic Iron Age remains in the area, and some fine **sandy beaches** at Capri and Seläter. Boat trips run to the Koster islands, the most westerly in Sweden and popular for cycling.

The **tourist office** (☎ 623 30; www.stromstadtourist .se; Gamla Tullhuset, Ångbåtskajen 2; ☺ 9am-8pm Mon-Sat, 10am-7pm Sun Jun-Aug, shorter hours Sep-May), between the two harbours on the main square, offers internet access (Skr20 per 15 minutes). Alternatively, log on at the **library** (☎ 193 16; Karlsgatan 17; ☺ 11am-7pm Mon & Tue, 11am-5pm Wed-Fri, closed Sat & Sun).

Sights & Activities

In town, **Strömstads Museum** (☎ 102 75; stromstads .museum@telia.com; Södra Hamngatan 26; admission free; ☺ 11am-4pm Mon-Fri, 11am-2pm Sat) looks at local themes. One of Sweden's largest, most magnificent **stone ship settings** (admission free; ☺ 24hr) lies 6km northeast of Strömstad. Resting in a field full of wildflowers, its lack of visitors makes it a more personal experience than Ales Stenar (p188). There are 49 stones in total, with the stem and stern stones reaching over 3m in height; the site has been dated to AD 400 to 600. Across the road is a huge site containing approximately 40 **Iron Age graves**. Ask at the tourist office or bus station for information on buses out there. Alternatively, there's a gorgeous walking path from the north of town.

Open by appointment only (contact the tourist office), the Romanesque stone **Skee Kyrka** is about 6km east of Strömstad and has a 10th-century nave. There's also a painted wooden ceiling and an unusual 17th-century reredos with 24 sculptured figures. Nearby lie **Iron Age graves**, a curious **bell tower** and a mid-Neolithic **passage tomb** (c 3000 BC).

Boat trips (adult/child return trip Skr120/65) run from Strömstad's north harbour to the beautiful **Koster islands** (www.kosteroarna.com) roughly every 30 minutes from July to mid-August and less frequently at other times. North Koster is hilly and has good beaches. South Koster is flatter and better for cycling.

Inquire at the tourist office about summer **seal safaris**.

Sleeping & Eating

Strömstad Camping (☎ 611 21; info@stromstadcamping .se; Uddevallavägen; sites low/high season Skr160/210, 2-bed cabins Skr490-550; ☺ May-Sep) In a lovely, large park at the southern edge of town, the campsite also has 36 shady cabins for rent.

Crusellska Hemmet (☎ 101 93; www@crusellska.com; Norra Kyrkogatan 12; dm/s/d Skr180/320/440; ☺ Mar-early Dec; ℗ ☐) No, it's not a Disney villain; it's an exceptional STF hostel. Drifting white curtains, pale decor and wicker lounges lend the place a boutique vibe. The kitchen is seriously spacious and there's a peaceful garden for alfresco contemplation, as well as a range of pampering spa treatments. Book ahead.

Hotell Krabban (☎ 142 00; www.hotellkrabban.se; Bergsgatan 15; s/d Skr790/990; ☐) 'The Crab' is a small and personal place in the centre of town. Rooms, based in an old wooden building, have nautical undertones. There are cheaper alternatives (around Skr100 less) if you're happy to share a corridor bathroom.

Laholmens Fisk (☎ 102 40; Torget) Moreish seafood baguettes (from Skr40) are sold along with fish fresh off the boats, just off the main square, next door to Restaurang Bryggan.

Restaurang Bryggan (☎ 600 65; Ångbåtskajen 6; lunch Skr130, mains Skr150-325; ☺ 11am-11pm Mon-Thu, 11am-midnight Fri, noon-midnight Sat, 1-11pm Sun) In a wonderful place for ocean-gazing, this cosy restaurant is tucked along the little harbour lane behind the tourist office. Dishes are fish- and meat-based, with one veggie option, and you can sip'n'sup alfresco in the summer.

Restaurang Trädgården (☎ 127 24; Östra Klevgatan 4; lunch buffet Skr160-175, mains Skr190-295; ☺ lunch year-round, dinner Jun-Aug) Chinking glasses and upbeat alfresco supping lure you to this convivial restaurant. In summer, the grilled seafood and meat lunch buffet is a particular hit, while the immaculate à la carte menu sparkles with culinary marvels.

The **ICA supermarket** (Södra Hamngatan 8) is central, and **Systembolaget** (Oslovägen 7) is a couple of minutes' walk away.

Getting There & Around

Buses and trains both use the train station near the southern harbour. The **Swebus Express** (☎ 0771-21 82 18; www.swebusexpress.com) service from Göteborg to Oslo calls here once or twice daily and Västtrafik runs buses to Göteborg (Skr200) up to five times daily. Strömstad is the northern terminus of the Bohuståg train system, with around six trains daily to/from Göteborg (Skr200).

Ferries run from Strömstad to Sandefjord in Norway (see p336).

For a taxi, call **Strömstads Taxi** (☎ 122 00). For car hire, contact **Statoil** (☎ 121 92; Oslovägen 42). At the time of research, there were no bike-rental facilities in town: contact the tourist office for updates.

DALSLAND

Northern Dalsland is an introspective mix of long lakes, still forests and silent towns, and the perfect spot to escape the hordes. You can paddle through the wilderness all the way to Norway from sleepy **Dals-Ed** (also known as 'Ed'); contact **Canodal** (☎ 618 03; www.canodal.com; Gamla Edsvägen 4, Dals-Ed; 2-person canoes per day/week Skr180/900) for details. The company also supplies equipment for wilderness camping.

The eastern half of Dalsland is equally watery and peaceful, but with more things to see. The scenic **Dalsland Canal** crosses the region and gets especially interesting (we promise) at Håverud. The canal itself is only 10km long, but it links a series of narrow lakes between Vänern and Stora Le, providing a route 250km long. Not everyone wants to relax on these waterways: a new endurance race, the **Dalsland Kanot Maraton** (www.kanotmaraton.se), sees competitors racing their canoes over a gruelling 55km course here in mid-August.

HÅVERUD
☎ 0530
An intriguing triple transport pile-up occurs at tiny Håverud, where a 32m **aqueduct** carries the Dalsland Canal over the river, and a road bridge crosses above them both.

The well-stocked **tourist office** (☎ 189 90; turist@dalsland.se; Dalslands Center; ☼ 10am-7pm Jul, 10am-6pm Jun & Aug, 10am-4pm May & Sep) offers internet access (Skr15 per 15 minutes). The Dalslands Center is the main venue for **Bokdagar i Dalsland** (www.bokdagaridalsland.se, in Swedish), a three-day literature festival held annually in late July or early August, with readings, seminars and book launches focusing on Nordic writers.

The area around the aqueduct is a chilled-out spot, filled with ambling visitors and the crashing noise of water. Pleasures are simple: visit the Tardis-like **Kanalmuséet** (☎ 306 24; adult/under 15yr Skr30/free; ☼ 10am-6pm Jun-Aug) where the history of the canal is told through imaginative displays; sit with a beer and watch boats negotiating the **lock**; or hop on a vessel yourself for various **boat tours** along the canal, including combined boat and scenic-railway trips to Bengtsfors (Skr300 return) and Långbron (from Skr150 return). These mainly run from late June to late August, and can be booked at the tourist office. **Steamboat trips** (adult/under 12yr Skr30/20) to Upperud are also available.

The dinky **STF hostel** (☎ 302 75; Museivägen 3; dm Skr200; [P]) overlooks the canal. Its attic-like rooms are pleasant but can get warm in summer. Outside May to August, book ahead.

Post-industrial **Håfveruds Brasseri** (☎ 351 31; Dalslands Center; mains Skr95-300; ☼ daily Jun-Aug, Sat & Sun May & Aug), based in an old paper mill (chains still hang from the ceiling), and with shaded lockside tables, serves everything from sandwiches to hearty elk sausages. There's a delicatessen for self-caterers.

For transport details, see opposite.

AROUND HÅVERUD
About 3km south of the aqueduct is **Upperud**, home to the savvy **Dalslands Museum & Konsthall** (☎ 0530-300 98; www.dalslandsmuseum.se; admission free; ☼ noon-8pm Tue-Sun Jul & Aug; noon-5pm Wed-Sun mid-Mar–Jun & Sep; noon-5pm Sat & Sun Oct–mid-Dec). Pop in for a compact collection of local art, furniture, ceramics, ironware and Åmål silverware, as well as clued-up temporary exhibitions. The small sculpture park in the grounds features some whimsical installations, including an anarchic wooden tower by eccentric artist Lars Vilks. The on-site **Café Bonaparte** (so-called because Napoleon's niece Christine once lived there) combines yummy coffee and snacks with soothing lake views.

Another few kilometres south at **Skållerud** is a beautiful, shiny-red, 17th-century wooden **church** (☎ 0530-300 14; ☼ 8am-4pm May-Oct, during services Nov-Apr), with well-preserved paintings and biblical sculptures.

Atmospheric **Högsbyn Nature Reserve**, about 8km north of Håverud near Tisselskog, has woodland walks and a shallow bathing spot. Best of all are its impressive Bronze Age **rock carvings** (hällristningar): 50 overgrown slabs feature animals, boats, labyrinths, sun signs, and hand and foot marks. You can get here from Håverud on a **boat trip** (☎ 0530-310 97,

0530-304 00; adult/7-14yr Skr160/65; 🕑 1pm Jul–mid-Aug) that gives you 45 minutes at the carvings.

Baldersnäs Herrgård (☎ 0531-412 13; admission free), 10km further north past the village of Dals Långed, is a beautiful manor house and grounds, complete with English garden, swimming spots, restaurant and cafe, handicraft stalls and a small Naturum. Quality **accommodation** (s/d Skr995/1390) is offered here too.

Getting There & Away

Mellerud is on the main Göteborg–Karlstad train line, and Swebus Express buses between Göteborg and Karlstad stop here once daily (except Saturday) in either direction. Local bus 720 runs a circular route to/from Mellerud via Upperud, Håverud and Skållerud.

VÄSTERGÖTLAND

VÄNERSBORG

☎ 0521 / pop 36,940

Vänersborg, at the southern outlet of lake Vänern, was once known as 'Little Paris', though it's hard to see why today. The scenic nature reserve and royal hunting grounds outside town are its main attraction, although families may get a kick out of Skräcklen park, with its playgrounds, waffles and splash-happy bathing spots.

The **tourist office** (☎ 135 09; www.visittrollhattan vanersborg.se; 🕑 9am-6pm Mon-Fri, 10am-4pm Sat & Sun Jul & Aug, 8am-5pm Mon-Fri Sep-Jun) is at the train station, and banks and other facilities are mostly along Edsgatan.

Vänersborgs Museum (☎ 600 62; Östra Plantaget; admission free; 🕑 noon-4pm Tue, Thu, Sat & Sun year-round, plus noon-4pm Wed Jun-Aug) is the country's oldest provincial museum and has a remarkable southwest African bird collection along with local exhibits and the odd ancient Egyptian artefact.

Described by Linnaeus (see boxed text, p246) as an 'earthly paradise', the **Hunneberg & Hanneberg Nature Reserve** covers two dramatic, craggy plateaus 8km east of town. There are 50km of **walking trails** here that are certainly worth exploring. The deep ravines and primeval forest also make great hiding places for wild elk, and this area has been a favourite royal hunting ground for over 100 years. Three-hour **elk-spotting safaris** (adult/

5-16yr Skr250/175; 🕑 6.30pm Mon & Thu Jul & Aug) leave from the train station: book tickets at the tourist office.

Kungajaktmuseet Älgens Berg (☎ 27 79 91; www .algensberg.com; adult/child Skr60/30; 🕑 10am-6pm Jun-Aug; 11am-4pm Tue-Sun Sep–early Nov & mid-Feb–May; 11am-4pm Tue-Fri early Nov–late Feb), the royal hunting museum, is at Hunneberg and tells you everything you could ever wish to know about elk. There's a great cafe on the grounds, as well as a handicrafts shop. Transport links are tedious – your best bet is to catch the frequent bus 62 from the town square to Vägporten, then walk 2km uphill.

Sleeping & Eating

Hunnebergs Vandrarhem & Kursgård (☎ 22 03 40; Bergagårdsvägen 9B, Vargön; sites from Skr100, dm Skr200; P) In a big old manor house near the cliffs of Hunneberg (7km east of the centre), this is a large, well-equipped SVIF hostel. Camping is permitted in the grounds, and there are bikes for rent. Take bus 62 from the town square to Vägporten, then walk 500m.

Hotell 46:an (☎ /fax 71 15 61; Kyrkogatan 46; s/d Skr595/750) This small, family-run place, on a quiet residential street near Skräcklen park, offers seven bright and homey rooms. Reception service is limited, so phone ahead.

Ronnums Herrgård (☎ 26 00 00; www.ronnums.se; Vargön; s/d/ste Skr1250/1450/1995, summer & weekends Skr1050/1285/1995; P 🖳) Good enough for Nicole Kidman, this luxe mansion is set in gorgeous grounds, out towards Hunneberg. Rooms are seriously elegant, and the oak-floored suites are particularly special. The hotel frequently has special rates and packages: contact them for details. If you feel like a gastronomic treat, the restaurant is one of the region's best.

Ristorante Italia (☎ 612 20; Edsgatan 7; lunch Skr70; mains Skr85-110; 🕑 11.30am-10pm Mon-Thu, 11.30am-11pm Fri, noon-11pm Sat, noon-9pm Sun) Back in town, this is one of your best bests for a decent feed. Reasonably priced Med favourites like pasta and pizza share the menu with home-grown staples, and there's outdoor seating for fine-weather munching.

Getting There & Away

Trollhättan-Vänersborgs airport (☎ 825 00; info@ fyrstadsflyget.se) lies midway between the two towns of Trollhättan and Vänersborgs. There are around five to seven direct flights Monday to Friday (one to two Sunday) to/

from Stockholm. Taxis are the only way to access the airport: **Taxi Trollhättan** (☎ 820 00) charges around Skr150 for the trip from Trollhättan, and Skr200 from Vänersborg. **Taxi Vänersborg** (☎ 666 00) now charges Skr300 (day) and Skr350 (night) for the trip between the airport and Vänersborg.

Local buses run from Torget, while long-distance services stop at the train station. Local bus 61, 62 and 65 run roughly half-hourly between Vänersborg and Trollhättan. Express bus 600 runs several times daily to Trollhättan, continuing to Göteborg.

Säfflebussen (☎ 0771-15 15 15; www.safflebussen.se) has a Göteborg–Trollhättan–Vänersborg–Stockholm service that stops three times daily in Vänersborg. **Swebus Express** (☎ 0771-21 82 18; www.swebusexpress.com) runs once daily (except Saturday) to Göteborg (Skr98, 1½ hours) via Trollhättan, and also north to Karlstad (Skr192, 2½ hours).

SJ trains to Göteborg (Skr82, 1½ hours) run about every hour (some require a change at Oxnered).

TROLLHÄTTAN

☎ 0520 / pop 54,300

'Trollywood', as it's colloquially known, is home to Sweden's film industry. A number of local and foreign flicks have been shot in and around the town, including Lebanese-Swedish director Josef Fares' Oscar-nominated *Jalla! Jalla!* (2000) and Danish director Lars von Trier's *Dancer in the Dark* (1999), *Dogville* (2002) and *Manderlay* (2005). Trollhättan itself has the air of a surreal film set: looming warehouses, foggy canals, crashing waterfalls and a futuristic cable car all give it a bizarre and thrilling edge. The town has made the most of its industrial heritage, with red-brick warehouses housing everything from crowd-pleasing museums to the odd art installation. The pièce de résistance is **Waterfall Days** (www.fallensdagar.se), a thumping three-day celebration held in mid-July with live bands, fireworks and some impressive waterworks.

SOUTHWEST SWEDEN

Information

The **tourist office** (☎ 135 09; www.visittrollhattanvasterborg.se; Åkerssjövägen 10; 10am-6pm mid-Jun–mid-Aug, 10am-4pm Mon-Fri mid-Aug–mid-Jun) is about 1.5km south of the town centre, near the Innovatum. If you want to visit all the attractions, ask for the two-day **Sommarkortet** (1/2 people Skr130/200, under 19yr free on adult ticket), available from late June to late August, which includes cable-car trips and museum admissions. The tourist office also sells a handy *Guidebook to Trollhättan's Falls & Locks*, which details walking routes in the mazelike industrial areas.

For internet access, visit the **library** (☎ 49 76 50; Kungsgatan 25; 10am-7pm Mon-Thu, 10am-6pm Fri, 10am-3pm Sat).

Sights & Activities

Saab Bilmuseum (☎ 843 44; www.saab.com; Åkerssjövägen 10; adult/7-17yr Skr60/30; 9am-5pm mid-Jun–mid-Aug, 11am-4pm mid-Aug–mid-Jun) is a must for car fanatics and Swedish design buffs. Saab car models span the first (a sensational 1947 prototype) to the futuristic (experimental designs running on biofuel that know if you're drunk!). Electronic handsets (40-minutes' playing time) guide you through the goods.

Innovatum Science Center (☎ 28 94 00; www.innovatum.se; adult/7-19yr/family Skr60/40/130; 9am-5pm mid-Jun–Aug, 11am-4pm Tue-Sun Sep–mid-Jun), next door to the Saab Bilmuseum, is a fantastic science centre with interactive experiments aimed mainly at children. But don't let that put you off: push the little blighters out of the way and revel in the gyroscopes and whirlpool machines. Why wasn't physics fun like this when we were kids?

Innovatum also manages **Galleri Nohab Smedja** (☎ 28 94 00; admission varies; 9am-5pm Mon-Fri Jun-Aug during exhibitions), an old smithy's workshop now used for temporary art exhibitions. The gallery is opposite the museum, just behind the tourist office.

In four minutes, the **Innovatum Linbana** (cable car; ☎ 28 94 00; adult/1-19yr Skr40/20; 9am-5pm mid-Jun–Aug, phone for May & Sep times) will sweep you over the canal to the hydroelectricity area. Once you're on the far side of the canal, follow the stairs down to the river, where you'll find one of Sweden's most unusual industrial buildings, the potent-looking **Olidan power station**, which supplied much of the country's electricity in the early 20th century. There are three 30-minute tours daily in summer (ask the tourist office for details).

Take a wander southwest to **Slussområde**, a lovely waterside area of parkland and ancient lock systems. Here you'll find cafes and the **Kanalmuseet** (☎ 47 22 51; Åkersberg; adult/child Skr20/free; 11am-7pm mid-Jun–mid-Aug; noon-5pm Sat & Sun May–mid-Jun & rest of Aug), which runs through the history of the canal as well as exhibiting over 50 model ships.

Northeast near the Hojum power station, be wowed by spectacular cascades when the **waterfall** (☯ 3pm daily Jul & Aug, 3pm Sat May, Jun & Sep) is unleashed. Normally the water is diverted through the power stations, but at set times the sluice gates are opened and 300,000L per second thunders through. For an even more magnificent sight, wait for the night-time **illuminated waterfall** (☯ 11pm) during the Waterfall Days festival held mid-July.

There are also two- to three-hour **canal tours** (per person from Skr195) in summer; enquire at the tourist office for times.

Sleeping & Eating

Gula Villan (☎ 129 60; trollhattansvandrarhem@telia.com; Tingvallavägen 12; dm Skr150; P) The cheery STF hostel, in a pretty old yellow villa, is about 200m from the train station. Breakfast and bikes are available.

Hotell Bele (☎ 125 30; www.hotellbele.se; Kungsgatan 37; s/d Skr995/1095; P ▣) Central, no-frills Bele sits on a pedestrianised street in the heart of town. Accommodation is basic but comfortable, and there's a sauna and solarium for pamper-seeking guests.

Strandgatan (☎ 837 17; Strandgatan; panini Skr70, mains Skr90-100) This trendy bistro is one of the best, busiest and cheapest spots in town for a casual feed and chill. In a fantastic location, with canalside seating in summer, it peddles everything from fresh panini, salads and juices to quiche, fish and chips, plump muffins…and Persian tea!

Albert Hotell (☎ 129 90; info@alberthotell.se; Strömsberg; mains Skr200-400; ☯ dinner Mon-Sat Jun–mid-Aug, lunch & dinner mid-Aug–May; P ▣) This marvellous restaurant-hotel combo is based in a splendid 19th-century wooden villa, overlooking the town from a verdant slope just across the river. Superb, mod-Nordic dishes might include chocolate and cognac sorbet with a nougat-flavoured chocolate tart and a sesame-and poppy-seed biscuit. The hotel itself offers 27 contemporary rooms (singles/doubles Skr1100/1350) in a neighbouring modernist building (request a river-view room), as well as a vintage suite in the main building for hopeless romantics. The place is an easy 10-minute walk across the river from central Trollhättan or a five-minute taxi ride.

Getting There & Around

See p231 for transport details. To reach the attractions in Trollhättan from the train station or the Drottningtorget bus station, walk south along Drottninggatan, then turn right into Åkerssjövägen, or take town bus 21 – it runs most of the way.

You can rent bikes from the Innovatum Science Center (opposite) for Skr40/20/80 per adult/child/tandem for three hours, or Skr75/40/140 per day.

LIDKÖPING
☎ 0510 / pop 37,770

It might be short on wow-factor, but cheery Lidköping – set on Vänern lake – is deeply likeable. Its handsome main square, Nya Stadens Torg, is dominated by the curious, squat **old courthouse** and its tower (it's actually a replica – the original burnt down in 1960). A previous fire in 1849 destroyed most of the town, but the cute 17th-century houses around **Limtorget** still stand.

Ironically, many of Lidköping's finest attractions (like the enchanting castle, Läckö Slott) lie some distance out of town.

The **tourist office** (☎ 200 20; www.lackokinnekulle .se; Nya Stadens Torg; ☯ 10am-7pm Mon-Fri, 10am-6pm Sat, noon-6pm Sun mid-Jun–early Aug; 10am-5pm Mon-Fri, 10am-1pm Sat May–mid-Jun & early Aug–Sep; 10am-5pm Mon-Fri Oct-Dec; noon-5pm Mon-Fri Jan-Apr) is situated in the old courthouse, and the **library** (☎ 77 00 15; Nya Stadens Torg 5; ☯ 10am-8pm Mon, 10am-7pm Tue-Thu, 10am-6pm Fri, 9am-1pm Sat) has free internet access.

Sights & Activities

IN TOWN

Rörstrand Fabriksbod (☎ 823 46; Fiskaregatan 4; ☯ 10am-7pm Mon-Fri, 10am-4pm Sat, noon-4pm Sun) is the second-oldest porcelain factory (still in operation) in Europe. There's a vast shop selling discounted seconds and end-of-line goods, and you can even buy copies of the porcelain used at the Nobel banquets in Stockholm. The small **museum** (admission free) contains everything from 18th-century faience to contemporary creations.

Vänermuseet (☎ 77 00 65; Framnäsvägen 2; adult/7-18yr Skr40/20; ☯ 10am-5pm Tue-Fri, noon-5pm Sat & Sun) has geological exhibits, including an ancient meteorite and displays on Vänern (the third-largest lake in Europe at 5650 sq km). The most curious item is a 3m-long glass boat.

LÄCKÖ SLOTT

An extraordinary example of 17th-century Swedish baroque architecture, with cupolas, towers, paintings and ornate plasterwork, **Läckö Slott** (☎ 103 20; www.lackoslott.se; adult Skr80 early Jun-late Aug, Skr50 May-early Jun & late Aug-Sep, under 26yr free; ◷ May-Sep) lies 23km north of Lidköping near Vänern. The first castle on the site was constructed in 1298, but it was improved enormously by Count Magnus Gabriel de la Gardie after he acquired it in 1615. Admission includes a guided tour.

The lakeside castle now boasts 240 rooms, with the most impressive being the **King's Hall**, with 13 angels hanging from the ceiling and nine epic paintings depicting the Thirty Years War.

Guided tours (◷ 11am-5pm May-Aug, 11am-2pm Sep) run on the hour and last 45 minutes, giving you access to the most interesting rooms, including the representative apartments, the Count's private chambers and the King's Hall; there's an English tour at 3.30pm daily. Otherwise you're free to bumble about in the kitchen, dungeon, armour chamber, chapel and castle gardens. The lower floors also contain shops and the atmospheric castle restaurant, **Fataburen** (lunch Skr125; ◷ noon-3pm & 6-9pm mid-Jun–mid-Aug), which uses vegetables and herbs from the castle garden.

In the castle grounds, there's a **cafe** (lunch Skr85; ◷ 10am-6pm May-Aug) serving snacks and a **rental kiosk** (☎ 207 57; bengtsson@kajakfritid.se; ◷ 9-11am & 1-6pm Jun–mid-Aug) where you can hire swan-shaped boats (Skr180 per hour) or canoes (from Skr130 per half day) for exploring the lake.

Classical music and opera events are held in the courtyard several times weekly in July (tickets around Skr350); enquire at Lidköping tourist office.

From mid-June to mid-August, bus 132 runs four to nine times a day from Lidköping to the castle. Car parking costs Skr30.

HUSABY KYRKA & ST SIGFRID'S WELL

Husaby (around 15km east of Lidköping) is inextricably linked to Sweden's history. King Olof Skötkonung, the country's first Christian king, was converted and baptised here by the English missionary Sigfrid in 1008. Olof's royal dunking took place at **St Sigfrid's Well**, near **Husaby Kyrka** (◷ 9am-4pm Apr, 8am-8pm Mon-Fri, 9am-8pm Sat & Sun May-Aug, 8am-6pm Mon-Fri, 9am-6pm Sat & Sun Sep).

The church dates from the 12th century, but the base of the unusual three-steeple tower may well be that of an earlier wooden

structure. Lurking inside are medieval paintings, as well as a 13th-century font and triumphal cross.

There's a small, seasonal **kiosk** (☎ 34 32 60; Pilgrimsgården; ◷ noon-6pm mid-Jun–mid-Aug) near the church with snacks, tourist brochures and maps. Bus 106 runs to Husaby, but very infrequently.

KINNEKULLE

The 'flowering mountain' **Kinnekulle** (306m), 18km northeast of Lidköping, is a natural wonderland, with unusually diverse geology and plant life, including mighty ancient oaks. It's also home to rare creatures, including the greater crested newt and short-horned grasshopper. There are numerous short nature trails, or you could explore it on the 45km-long **Kinnekulle vandringsled** (walking trail), which runs past remainders of the old limestone workings. The tourist office provides a map and the informative *Welcome to Götene and Kinnekulle* brochure. Local trains run to Källby, Råbäck and Hällekis, with access to the trail.

Sleeping & Eating

STF Vandrarhem Lidköping (☎ 664 30; info@lidkopings vandrarhem.com; Gamla Stadens Torg 4; dm/d Skr140/460) Just a couple of minutes' walk from the train station, this hostel is in a pretty spot in the old town. Standards are high, and the staff are helpful.

Krono Camping (☎ 268 04; www.kronocamping.com; Läckögatan; sites Skr180-230, 2-person cabins Skr395-475; ▣) This is a huge, family-oriented lakeside camping ground, 1.5km northwest of town beside the road to Läckö Slott, where kids can run wild. There's everything you could possibly need: shop, restaurant, laundry, minigolf, boules, Jacuzzi, sauna, playground and boat hire.

Hotel Läckö (☎ 230 00; kontakt@hotellacko.se; Gamla Stadens Torg 5; s/d incl breakfast Skr690/890) Our favourite in town is this old-school, family-run charmer. The spacious rooms boast high ceilings, solid wooden furniture and crisp linen, while breakfast is served on dainty antique porcelain. There's a cosy little reading room with comfy leather armchairs, and quirky touches like whimsical hanging millinery.

Café Limtorget (☎ 251 45; Mjölnagården, Limtorget 1; ◷ Mon-Sat) With its rose-filled garden, this cute old wooden cottage is well worth seeking out. It serves sandwiches and ciabatta for around

Skr40, plus pastries, waffles (in the spring) and other temptations.

Café O Bar (☎ 270 27; Nya Stadens Torg 4; lunch Skr70, mains Skr180-210) This sleek bolt hole, on the main square, is a fashionable restaurant-bar with a soulful selection of meals like soothing fish soup with saffron and aioli.

our pick **Restaurang Sjöboden** (☎ 104 08; restaurang@sjoboden.se; Spikens Fiskehamn; mains Skr145-275; ☼ noon-10pm May-Aug) Six kilometres south of Läckö Slott, the tiny village of Spiken is home to this unmissable harbourside restaurant where outstanding seasonal creations like local roe with horseradish cheesecake keep the foodies swooning. Take bus 132.

Sibling restaurant–wine bar **Pirum** (☎ 615 20; Skaragatan 7; mains Skr245; ☼ from 5pm Mon-Sat) awaits in central Lidköping.

Getting There & Around

Town and regional buses stop on Nya Stadens Torg. Buses 1 and 5 run roughly hourly on weekdays (four Saturday and Sunday) between Trollhättan, Lidköping and Skara. Västtrafik trains from Lidköping to Hallsberg or Herrljunga connect with Stockholm and Göteborg services respectively.

KARLSBORG

☎ 0505 / pop 6850

A quiet little town s-t-r-e-t-c-h-e-d alongside Vättern lake, Karlsborg is some 80km east of Lidköping. Amazingly, this peaceful backwater was once intended to be Sweden's capital in times of war, thanks to its beast of a bastion, Karlsborgs Fästning.

The **tourist office** (☎ 173 50; info@karlsborgsturism.se; Ankarvägen 2; ☼ 9.30am-6pm Jul–mid-Aug, 10am-4pm Mon-Fri mid-Aug–Jun) is in an octagonal wooden house between the fort's main entrance and the lake.

Karlsborgs Fästning was one of Europe's largest construction projects. With a circumference of around 5km, this fortress is so huge that it took from 1820 to 1909 to complete; it was out of date even before it was finished and mothballed immediately. Most of the 30-odd buildings inside are original: there's a **military museum** (☎ 45 18 26; adult/child/family Skr40/10/90; ☼ 10am-4pm mid-May–late Jun; 10am-6pm late Jun–early Aug; 10am-5pm rest of Aug; 10am-3pm Mon-Fri Sep–mid-May) and a **church**, which has an extraordinary candelabra made from 276 bayonets.

The fortress area is always open. If you're after gun smoke, cannon roar and scuttling

rats, though, you'll have to book a special-effect **guided tour** (adult/7-12yr Skr80/40; ☼ noon daily early Jun–mid-Jun & mid-Aug–late Aug; more frequently late Jun–mid-Aug) at the tourist office; from early July to August, there are up to 11 tours every day. The **Lilla Blå tourist train** (adult/7-12yr Skr80/40; ☼ 2.30pm mid-Jun–mid-Aug) also zips round the centre of the fortress.

Karlsborg is the start/end of the western section of the **Göta Canal** (see p140 for details).

Right on the fortress's doorstep, **STF Vandrarhem Karlsborg** (☎ 446 00; Ankarvägen 2; dm/d from Skr160/340; P □) is used as military accommodation for most of the year. A good option is to stay here and self-cater (the nearby town centre has supermarkets), although there are more sleeping and eating options in town, especially beside the Göta Canal about 2km northwest of the fortress (follow the main road).

A bus runs every hour or two to Skövde, connecting with SJ trains to Göteborg or Stockholm.

HALLAND

HALMSTAD

☎ 035 / pop 89,730

After roasting themselves on the 6km-long Blue Flag **beach** at Tylösand (8km west of town), many visitors hit Halmstad's heaving bars and clubs to crank up the party vibe.

Danish until 1645, Halmstad served as an important fortified border town. Its street plan was laid out by the Danish king Christian IV after a huge fire wiped out most of the buildings in 1619. He also awarded Halmstad its coat of arms: you'll see the three crowns and three hearts motif dotted all over the place.

The **tourist office** (☎ 13 23 20; www.halmstad.se/turist; ☼ 9am-7pm Mon-Sat, 11am-6pm Sun late Jun–mid-Aug; 9am-6pm Mon-Fri, 10am-3pm Sat rest of Aug; 10am-12.30pm & 1.30-5pm Mon-Fri Sep-Apr; 9am-5pm Mon-Fri, 10am-1pm Sat May) is inside Halmstads Slott (the castle). For banks and supermarkets, hit Stora Torg and Storgatan. For free internet access, head to the strikingly contemporary **library** (☎ 13 71 81; stadsbiblioteket@halmstad.se; Axel Olsonsgata 1; ☼ 10am-8pm Mon-Thu, 10am-6pm Fri, 10am-4pm Sat May-Aug; 10am-8pm Mon-Fri, 10am-4pm Sat, noon-4pm Sun Sep-Apr).

Sights & Activities

For a small county gallery, **Halmstads Museum** (☎ 16 23 00; Tollsgatan; adult/under 19yr Skr40/free;

SOUTHWEST SWEDEN

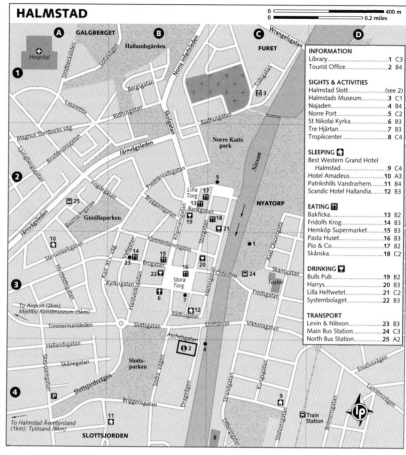

HALMSTAD

SOUTHWEST SWEDEN

noon-4pm Tue-Sun, to 8pm Wed) churns out some impressive art and design exhibitions. Its modest collection of local treasures is ingeniously displayed, with silver hoards and Viking swords set in cases in the floor for that 'just discovered' feeling.

Halmstad Äventyrsland (☎ 10 84 60; Gamla Tylösandsvägen 1; admission Skr180; ☺ 10am-8pm Jul & early–mid Aug, 10am-6pm Jun & mid–late Aug), lying just out of town, is a theme park for littlish kids featuring pirates, fairy-tale characters, dinosaurs, a miniature village, rides and waterslides.

Another family-friendly option, across the river and downstream from the tourist office, **Tropikcenter** (☎ 12 33 33; Strandgatan 19; adult/child Skr70/40; ☺ 10am-6pm Jul, 10am-5pm Aug-Jun) is in

the old customs house and shows off tropical birds, fish and reptiles. At both places, kids under 1m tall get in for free.

The museum ship **Najaden** (voluntary donation appreciated; ☺ 11am-3pm Sat early Jun–early Sep, also 6-8pm Tue & Thu late Jun–early Aug), berthed just outside the castle and built in 1897, was a training ship for the Swedish Royal Navy.

Christian IV built **Halmstad Slott** (open twice yearly for guided tours in early summer: contact lansstyrelsen@n.lst.se for details) and the town walls. The latter were demolished in the 18th century, although fragments like the north gate **Norre Port** remain. Other medieval attractions include the lovely 14th-century church **St Nikolai Kyrka** (☺ 8.30am-6pm Jun-Aug, 8.30am-3pm Sep-May), and the half-timbered

Tre Hjärtan (Three Hearts) building on Stora Torg. In the main square is Carl Milles' sculptural fountain *Europa and the Bull*; Picasso's *(Woman's Head)* is down by the river.

Mjellby Konstmuseum (☎ 13 71 95; adult/under 20yr Skr50/free; ☿ noon-5pm Tue-Sun) is 5km from town but worth a trip if you're into modern art – the museum includes the permanent Halmstad Group exhibition of surrealist and cubist art (labelled in Swedish). Take the irregular bus 330 from the North Bus Station.

Sleeping

IN TOWN

The tourist office can arrange private rooms in town from Skr160 per person (plus booking fee). It's a popular town, with a solid smattering of the large hotel chains.

Patrikshills Vandrarhem (☎ 18 66 66; info@patrikshill .se; Neptunigatan 3; dm Skr175, r Skr350-700; ☿ mid-Jun–mid-Aug; P ☐) Located 500m southwest of St Nikolai Kyrka, this stock-standard hostel has handy extras such as laundry facilities and an outdoor patio with barbecue facilities. Add Skr200 to all prices during the four-day Midsummer holiday period in late June.

Hotel Amadeus (☎ 16 60 00; www.amadeus.nu; Hvitfeldtsgatan 20; s/d Skr850/975, discounted to Skr640/845; P ☐) At 65 rooms this isn't a tiny hotel, yet it manages to retain a personal and welcoming air. Rooms are comfortably mid-market, with new beds recently added. There are budget alternatives (up to Skr200 less) for the kronor-conscious.

There's little difference in price or standards at the following two upmarket places, both with sauna, solarium, bar, restaurant and so on:

Best Western Grand Hotel Halmstad (☎ 280 81 00; www.grandhotel.nu; Stationsgatan 44; s/d Skr1350/1650; P ☐) Handy for the train station with rooms decorated in a traditional style with the odd modern touch.

Scandic Hotel Hallandia (☎ 295 86 00; hallandia@ scandichotels.com; Rådhusgatan 4; r/ste Skr1320/1800; ☐) On the main square with more modern Scandi-style accommodation; some rooms have balconies overlooking the river.

IN TYLÖSAND

First Camp Tylösand (☎ 305 10; www.firstcamp.se/ty losand; Kungsvägen 3; sites Skr130-280, cabins from Skr525) A huge and bustling camping ground near the beach, with loads of family-friendly facilities. Avoid holidays such as midsummer, when prices go stratospheric.

Tylebäck (☎ 19 18 00; info@tyleback.com; Kungsvägen 1; sites Skr230, hostel 1-/2-/3-/4-bed r Skr295/430/600/800, hotel s/d Skr895/1095) Accommodation to suit all travellers – camping, hostel, hotel – is offered at Tylebäck, in a stylishly rustic setting.

Hotel Tylösand (☎ 305 00; info@tylosand.se; Tylöhusvägen; s/d Skr1695/1895, discounted to Skr1245/1395) Check-in here if you're into beaches, clubbing, spa treatments and/or Roxette (it's part-owned by Per Gessle, one half of the Swedish pop duo). It's a large, upmarket complex on the beach, with top-notch sipping and supping options, a shiny spa centre and summer entertainment gigs; check out the glam foyer full of art, and Leifs Lounge nightclub. This is one of the few Swedish hotels where prices go *up* at weekends, although packages are available.

Eating & Drinking

Halmstad is jam-packed with dining spots, pubs and bars, mostly around pedestrianised Storgatan. Alternatively, on summer nights head to the after-beach parties at Tylösand.

Skånska (☎ 21 24 07; Storgatan 40; ☿ Mon-Sat) This is a good old-fashioned bakery with cafe attached. Sandwiches cost around Skr50, and there's a tempting stock of chocolates and cakes to crank up the calories.

Fridolfs Krog (☎ 21 16 66; Brogatan 26; meals Skr75-270; ☿ from 6pm) Loaded with a wide menu, this is another pleasant spot for fine supping. There are low-priced pasta options, or more expensive, well-prepared meat and fish dishes like chilli-marinated swordfish.

Bakficka (Lilla Torg; mains Skr90-170) Behind Pio & Co is this place, which literally means 'back pocket'. It's a more casual spot with outdoor seating and a decent bar menu.

Pio & Co (☎ 21 06 69; Storgatan 37; mains Skr190-290; ☿ from 6pm) Award-winning Pio is an upmarket brasserie with an extensive menu of both Swedish and continental favourites – think Halland pork with roasted garlic and potatoes au gratin, and heavenly cannelloni.

Lilla Helfwetet (☎ 21 04 20; Hamngatan 37; ☿ Mon-Sat) With its funky dancing devil symbol, you can half guess what awaits you in this great converted warehouse near the river. The super-cool restaurant, bar and cocktail lounge transforms into a nightclub on Friday and Saturday nights, when it's party time until 3am.

For something quick, try the **Pasta Huset** (pasta from Skr30) van on Stora Torg. There's a

Hemköp supermarket and a Systembolaget just off Stora Torg.

On the northern part of Storgatan and nearby Lilla Torg are some seriously swinging slosh spots, including pub-style **Harrys** (☎ 10 55 95; Storgatan 22), complete with a great alfresco terrace, and the equally popular **Bulls Pub** (☎ 14 09 21; Lilla Torg), in a former fire station.

Getting There & Away

The **airport** (☎ 12 80 70) is only 2km west of the town centre. Skyways has regular connections to Stockholm's Arlanda airport.

The train station is in the southeastern corner of the town centre, and the main bus station is a few blocks away at Österbro. The North Bus Station, located in the northwestern corner of central Halmstad, mainly services local buses.

Swebus Express (☎ 0771-21 82 18; www.swebusexpress.com) runs buses at least four to five times daily to Malmö (Skr166, 2¼ hours), Helsingborg (Skr98, one hour), Göteborg (Skr119, 1¾ hours) and Lund. Swebus Express also has a direct twice-weekly service to Jönköping (Skr237, 2¾ hours).

Regular trains between Göteborg (Skr145, 1¼ hours) and Malmö (Skr160, two hours) stop in Halmstad and call in at Helsingborg (Skr99, one hour) and Varberg (Skr82, 35 minutes).

Getting Around

Local bus 10 runs half-hourly (hourly in the evenings) to the clubs and beaches at Tylösand (adult/child Skr23/14).

Try **Taxi Halmstad** (☎ 21 80 00) for a taxi or hire a bike from **Levin & Nilsson** (☎ 21 01 17; Brogatan 30; per 24hr/3 days/week Skr100/250/450; ⏱ 10am-6pm Mon-Fri, 10am-1pm Sat).

VARBERG

☎ 0340 / pop 56, 110

Good-looking Varberg lies by the side of a 60km stretch of beautiful white-sand beaches: its population triples in the summer months. The town's darker side includes its fortress, once used as a prison and now home to an impressively preserved bog body.

The **tourist office** (☎ 868 00; www.turist.varberg.se; Brunnsparken; ⏱ 9.30am-7pm Mon-Sat, 1-6pm Sun late Jun-early Aug; 10am-6pm Mon-Fri, 10am-3pm Sat Apr-late Jun & mid-Aug–Sep; 10am-5pm Mon-Fri Oct-Mar) is located in the centre of town; most facilities are nearby.

Sights & Activities

The **medieval fortress** (☎ 828 30; adult/under 20yr Skr50/free; ⏱ 10am-5pm mid-Jun–mid-Aug; 10am-4pm Mon-Fri, noon-4pm Sat & Sun mid-Aug–mid-Jun), with its superb museum, is Varberg's star attraction. In-house oddities include the poor old Bocksten Man, dug out of a peat bog at Åkulle in 1936. His 14th-century costume is the most perfectly preserved medieval clothing in Europe.

Brave the Nordic weather with a dip at **Kallbadhuset** (☎ 173 96; adult/under 15yr Skr55/30; ⏱ mid-Jun–mid-Aug, 1-8pm Wed, 9am-5pm Sat & Sun mid-Aug–mid-Jun), a Moorish-style outdoor bathhouse built on stilts above the sea just north of the fort.

Getterön Nature Reserve is just 2km north of the town and has excellent bird life (mostly waders and geese). The reserve has a **Naturum** (visitors centre; ☎ 875 10; Lassavägen 1; ⏱ 10am-5pm May-Aug; 10am-4pm Mar, Apr, Sep & Oct; 10am-4pm Fri-Sun Oct-Feb) with interesting exhibitions.

On the Unesco World Heritage List, **Varberg Radio Station** (☎ 67 41 90; www.alexander.n.se; Grimeton) lies about 10km east of Varberg. Once part of the interwar transatlantic communication network, it's now the world's only surviving long-wave radio station. Admission is by **guided tour** (adult/child Skr50/free; ⏱ on the hour 10am-3pm daily late Jun–mid-Aug; 11am, 12.30pm & 2pm Sat & Sun only mid-May–mid-Jun & late Aug–mid-Sep). Phone ahead if you'd like an English tour.

Apelviken, 2km south of Varberg, is Sweden's best spot for **windsurfing** and **kitesurfing**. Bring your own kit or rent from **Surfer's Paradise** (☎ 67 70 55; info@surfersparadise.nu; per hr/day from Skr80/300; ⏱ Feb-Nov), which also offers courses from June to August: contact them for details.

Sleeping & Eating

Getteröns Camping (☎ 168 85; www.getteronscamping.se; sites low/high season from Skr180/265, cabins & chalets from Skr200/290; ⏱ May–mid-Sep) On a sandy beach on the Getterön peninsula, this well-equipped place has plenty of tent spaces, though it does get busy in high season.

Fästningens Vandrarhem (☎ 868 28; vandrarhem@turist.varberg.se; dm/s/d from Skr220/330/515) Within the fortress, this SVIF hostel is one of Sweden's finest. Old prison cells make up the single rooms, with larger rooms in surrounding buildings.

our pick **Hotell Gästis** (☎ 180 50; gastis@hotellgastis.nu; Borgmästaregatan 1; s/d Skr1150/1495) Behind a deceptively humdrum exterior awaits a one-of-a-kind hotel. Quirky details (there are many!)

include an elevator shaft covered in pulp fiction covers and a glimmering basement bathhouse (Skr100) modelled on a vintage Russian version and complete with a giant candlelit Jacuzzi. Individually styled rooms are cosy, with sparkling bathrooms and nooks full of books. Room prices also include a decent dinner buffet. Best of all, nonguests can also use the bathhouse, but call ahead first.

Most cheap restaurants line pedestrianised Kungsgatan. **Café Fästnings Terrassen** (☎ 105 81; ⏰ 11.30am-10pm Jun-Aug, weather permitting), at the fortress, offers the best sea views in town, delicious shrimp sandwiches, waffles and pastries, as well as live waltz tunes from 7pm on Wednesday, Saturday and Sunday in summer.

Head to **Grappa** (☎ 179 20; Brunnsparken; mains Skr160-300; ⏰ Mon-Sat), next to the tourist office, for slinky interiors, fine Swedish and Italian nosh, and a civilised sip.

Getting There & Around

Buses depart from outside the train station; local buses run to Falkenberg, but regular trains are your best bet for Halmstad, Göteborg and Malmö.

Stena Line ferries operate between Varberg and the Danish town of Grenå (see p335); the ferry dock is next to the town centre.

Bike hire from **Erlan Cykel** (☎ 144 55; Västra Vallgatan 41) costs from Skr80/350 per day/week. For a taxi try **Varbergs Taxi** (☎ 165 00).

Central Sweden

A compact wonderland of painted wooden horses marching across green hills dotted with little red cabins, central Sweden is such a perfect distillation of all the Swedish highlights that it could almost be one of those Las Vegas theme parks. It's an easily explored area right in the middle of the country, which means that even travellers on a tight schedule can see a lot of what makes Sweden so Swedish.

The area around Lake Siljan – all idyllic wooden villages and evergreen forest – represents the country's heartland, as mellow as it is adorable. Moving further north, the landscape gets wilder and more rugged, a teaser offering hints of Lappland and the far north.

The main cities in the central region – especially Uppsala and Örebro – are lively and youthful cultural centres with plenty of well-preserved historical buildings and some great museum collections, dining, shopping and nightlife. Active travellers and outdoorsy types will have plenty to do, too, as the region is rich with opportunities for cycling, mountain biking, dogsledding, horse-riding, birdwatching, hiking, skiing, rock climbing and canoeing.

Several defining episodes in Swedish history also happened here: there's an important pre-Viking burial ground and more than one castle whose stone walls enclosed royal murders and gruesome betrayals. Ancient rune stones pop out of the grass all over the place. In short, this area makes an ideal destination for anyone seeking to delve into most any aspect of Sweden's cultural heritage and traditions, from wooden horses to decapitated kings.

HIGHLIGHTS

- Explore some of Sweden's formative myths in a beautiful setting at **Gamla Uppsala** (p244)
- Take a hike to the 'troll church' at **Tiveden National Park** (p261)
- Discover the Swedish underground – via silver mines at **Sala** (p256) and copper mines at **Falun** (p266)
- Sleep on a train, then ride a museum railway in the cute wooden town of **Nora** (p257)
- Pick up some tips on domestic bliss at **Carl Larsson's house** (p267) in Sundborn
- Get a taste of the remote and rugged north in **Idre** (p275)

■ AREA: 80,843 SQ KM	■ POPULATION: 3,469,486	■ HIGHEST ELEVATION: STORVÄTTESHÅGNA (1204m)

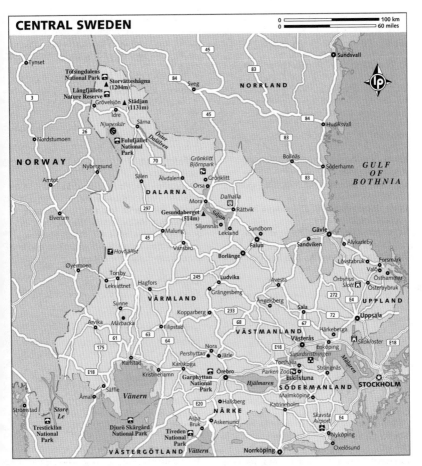

CENTRAL SWEDEN

Orientation

Central Sweden (Svealand) consists of six *landskap* (provinces). In the east are Uppland and Södermanland (also known as Sörmland), in the middle there's Västmanland and Närke, and the west has Värmland and Dalarna.

The attractions of Stockholms län (Stockholm County) are covered in a separate chapter (see p67).

Information

Visitors can contact the following regional tourist offices for more detailed information on the area:

Destination Örebro (☎ 019-21 21 21; destination@ orebro.se; Box 328 00, Slottet, 70135 Örebro)

Discover Västmanland (www.vastmanland.se)

Sörmlands Turism (☎ 0155-22 27 70; www.sorm landsturism.se; Västra Kvarngatan 62, 61132 Nyköping) The office for Södermanland (aka Sörmland).

Turistinformation Dalarna (☎ 023-640 04; www .dalarna.se; Trotzgatan 10-12, 79183 Falun)

Uppsala Tourism (☎ 018-727 48 00; www.uppland .nu; Fyristorg 8, 75310 Uppsala)

Visit Värmland (☎ 054-701 10 00; www.varmland .org, visit@varmland.se; Box 1022, Lagergrensgata 2, 65115 Karlstad)

Getting Around

Driving, though expensive, is one of the best ways to see the hidden corners of the region. Car-hire companies with offices at Stockholm Arlanda airport are listed on p338.

Express buses connect major towns in southern areas. For the west and north of the region, you'll need to use *länstrafiken* (regional network) services.

The following companies provide regional transport links. For longer trips, it's worth enquiring about discount cards, monthly passes or a *sommarkort*, offering cheaper travel in the peak summer period (late June to mid-August).

Dalatrafik (☎ 0771-95 95 95; www.dalatrafik.se, in Swedish)

Länstrafiken Örebro (☎ 0771-22 40 00; www.lanstrafiken.se/orebro)

Länstrafiken Sörmland (☎ 0771-22 40 00; www.lanstrafiken.se/sormland)

Upplands Lokaltrafik (☎ 0771-14 14 14; www.upplandslokaltrafik.se/en)

Värmlandstrafik (☎ 0771-32 32 00; www.kollplatsen.com, in Swedish)

Västmanlands Lokaltrafik (☎ 0774-41 04 10; www.vl.se)

SJ (☎ 0771-75 75 75; www.sj.se) trains run along both sides of Mälaren lake. Hallsberg is a major junction and trains continue west to Karlstad and Oslo, Norway. There are good services from Stockholm to Uppsala, Mora and other destinations.

UPPLAND

UPPSALA
☎ 018 / pop 182,000

Drenched in history but never stifled by the past, Uppsala has the party vibe of a university town to balance out its large number of important buildings and general

---

WORKS THAT NO LONGER WORK

Central Sweden's industrial past is well preserved in these evocative attractions:

- Engelsberg Bruk (p257)
- Falu Kopparbergsgruva (p266)
- Österbybruk (p249)
- Lövstabruk (p249)
- Forsmark (p250)
- Sala Silvergruva (p256)
- Rademachersmedjorna (p252)

---

atmosphere of weighty cultural significance. It's a terrific combination, and one that makes the town both fun and functional, not to mention very rewarding for the interested traveller.

On the edge of the city is Gamla (Old) Uppsala, the original site of the town, once a flourishing 6th-century religious centre where humans made sacrifices to the Norse gods and home to an ancient burial ground.

Information
BOOKSHOPS
Akademibokhandeln Lundequistska (☎ 13 98 30; Forumgallerian, Dragarbrunnsgatan 43-45; ⏰ 10am-7pm Mon-Fri, 10am-5pm Sat, noon-4pm Sun) Large English-language book selection, upstairs in the shopping centre.

Pressbyrån (Sankt Persgatan 10) Newsstand carrying international publications; there's another branch inside the train station, plus other locations.

EMERGENCY
Police (☎ 114 14; www.polisen.se/english; Svartbäcksgatan 49)

INTERNET ACCESS
Library (☎ 727 17 00; Svartbäcksgatan 17; ⏰ noon-6pm Mon-Fri, 11am-2pm Sat late Jun–mid-Aug, 9am-8pm Mon-Thu, 9-6pm Fri, 11am-4pm Sat & Sun mid-Aug–late Jun) Free internet access; bring ID and expect longish waits.

Sidewalk Express (per hr from Skr29) Inside the train station. To log on, buy vouchers from the coin-operated machines.

LEFT LUGGAGE
Train station (small/medium/large lockers per 24hr Skr25/30/35)

MEDICAL SERVICES
Apoteket Kronan (Svartbäcksgatan 8; ⏰ 10am-7pm Mon-Fri, 10am-3pm Sat) Pharmacy chain; one of five city centre locations.

Uppsala University Hospital (Akademiska sjukhuset; ☎ 611 22 97; Uppsala Care, Entrance 61, Sjukhusvägen) Has an urgent-care facility for foreign visitors, as well as an after-hours pharmacy.

MONEY
Head to Stora Torget for banks and ATMs. Next door to the tourist information office is a **Forex** (☎ 10 30 00; Fyristorg 8; ⏰ 9am-7pm Mon-Fri, 9am-3pm Sat) office that offers currency-exchange services.

UPPSALA

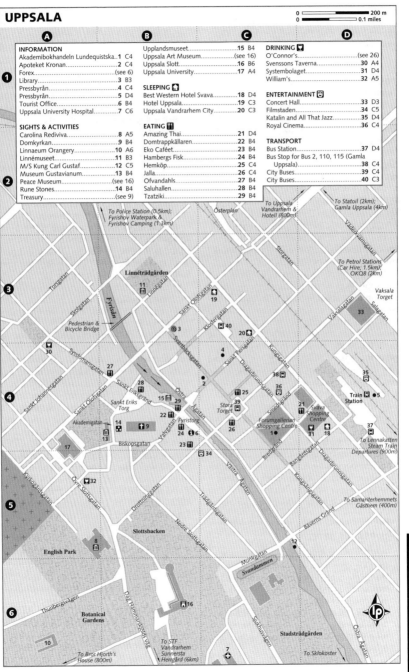

0 ———— 200 m
0 ———— 0.1 miles

INFORMATION
Akademibokhandeln Lundequistska..**1** C4
Apoteket Kronan............................**2** C4
Forex..(see 6)
Library..**3** B3
Pressbyrån...................................**4** C4
Pressbyrån...................................**5** D4
Tourist Office...............................**6** B4
Uppsala University Hospital............**7** C6

SIGHTS & ACTIVITIES
Carolina Rediviva..........................**8** A5
Domkyrkan...................................**9** B4
Linnaeum Orangery.......................**10** A6
Linnémuseet.................................**11** B3
M/S Kung Carl Gustaf....................**12** C5
Museum Gustavianum....................**13** B4
Peace Museum.............................(see 16)
Rune Stones................................**14** B4
Treasury.....................................(see 9)

SLEEPING
Upplandsmuseet...........................**15** B4
Uppsala Art Museum...................(see 16)
Uppsala Slott...............................**16** B6
Uppsala University.......................**17** A4

SLEEPING
Best Western Hotel Svava..............**18** D4
Hotel Uppsala..............................**19** C3
Uppsala Vandrarhem City..............**20** C3

EATING
Amazing Thai...............................**21** D4
Domtrappkällaren.........................**22** B4
Eko Caféet..................................**23** B4
Hambergs Fisk.............................**24** B4
Hemköp.......................................**25** C4
Jalla...**26** C4
Ofvandahls.................................**27** B4
Saluhallen...................................**28** B4
Tzatziki......................................**29** B4

DRINKING
O'Connor's.................................(see 26)
Svenssons Taverna.......................**30** A4
Systembolaget.............................**31** D4
William's.....................................**32** A5

ENTERTAINMENT
Concert Hall................................**33** D3
Filmstaden..................................**34** C5
Katalin and All That Jazz................**35** D4
Royal Cinema...............................**36** C4

TRANSPORT
Bus Station.................................**37** D4
Bus Stop for Bus 2, 110, 115 (Gamla
  Uppsala)...................................**38** C4
City Buses...................................**39** C4
City Buses...................................**40** C3

CENTRAL SWEDEN

POST

You can buy stamps at the tourist office, most supermarkets and Pressbyrån shops. There are mailboxes at Stora Torget and Uppsala Central Station.

TOURIST INFORMATION

Tourist office (☎ 727 48 00; www.uppsalatourism.se; Fyristorg 8; ❧ 10am-6pm Mon-Fri, 10am-3pm Sat year-round, plus noon-4pm Sun mid-Jun–mid-Aug) Pick up the *Walking Tour of Uppsala* leaflet, and *What's On Uppsala* for event listings.

Sights

GAMLA UPPSALA

The seat of Western culture, according to Olof Rudbeck's 1679 book *Atlantica*, was Sweden: specifically, Gamla Uppsala. Rudbeck (1630–1702), a scientist, writer and all-around colourful character, amassed copious evidence proving that Gamla Uppsala was, in fact, the mythical lost city of Atlantis.

In retrospect, this seems unlikely. But the spot, 4km north of the modern city, is a fascinating attraction nevertheless. One of Sweden's largest and most important burial sites, Gamla Uppsala contains around 300 mounds from the 6th to 12th centuries. The earliest and most impressive are three huge **grave mounds** (admission free; ❧ 24hr). Legend has it they contain the pre-Viking kings Aun, Egil and Adils, who appear in *Beowulf* and Icelandic historian Snorre Sturlason's *Ynglingsaga*. More recent evidence, however, suggests that the occupant of Östhögen (East Mound) was a woman, probably a female regent in her twenties or thirties.

Speculation has surrounded the burial site from the beginning. Early press reports included medieval chronicler Adam of Bremen – who was never actually here – describing a vast golden temple in Gamla Uppsala in the 10th century. Allegedly, animal and human sacrifices were strung up in a sacred grove outside.

When Christianity arrived in 1090, Thor, Odin and the other Viking gods faded (see boxed text, opposite). From 1164, the archbishop of Uppsala had his seat in a cathedral on the site of the present **church** (☎ 0708-56 33 22; admission free; ❧ 9am-6pm Apr-Sep, 9am-4pm Oct-Mar).

Gamla Uppsala Museum (☎ 23 93 00; www.raa.se /gamlauppsala; adult/child/under 6yr Skr50/30/free; ❧ 11am-5pm May-Aug, noon-3pm Wed, Sat & Sun Sep–mid-Dec & Jan-Apr) contains finds from the cremation mounds, a poignant mix of charred and melted beads, bones and buckles. More intact pieces come from various **boat graves** in and around the site. The museum is arranged as a timeline – useful for recreating the history of the area.

Follow signs from the grave mounds to **Disagården** (☎ 16 91 80; admission free; guided tours adult/child Skr30/free; ❧ 10am-5pm mid-May–Aug, tours 1pm & 2pm weekdays, 11am Sat & Sun, evening tours 7.30pm Wed 25 Jun-30 Jul), a 19th-century farming village turned open-air museum consisting of 26 timber buildings and a platform stage that serves as the focal point for Uppsala's Midsummer celebrations.

Next to the unexcavated flat-topped mound, Tingshögen (Court Mound), is **Odinsborg** (☎ 32 35 25; buffet Skr165; ❧ noon-6pm), a restaurant known for its horns of mead and Viking feasts (although daintier refreshments are offered at the summer cafe downstairs).

If you feel like a wander, **Eriksleden** is a 6km 'pilgrims path' between the cathedral in Uppsala and the church in Gamla Uppsala. Its namesake, Erik the Holy, was king of Sweden from around 1150 until the Danes beheaded him 10 years later. The story is that his head rolled down the hill, and where it stopped a spring came up. The main trail also provides access to a ridged wilderness area called **Tunåsen**, with a panoramic viewpoint (follow signs along Eriksleden just south of Gamla Uppsala to 'utsiktsleden').

Buses 2, 110 and 115 run to Gamla Uppsala daily and are very frequent (between them there's one every 10 minutes Monday to Friday, and every 40 minutes at weekends).

UPPSALA SLOTT

Pink and ponderous, **Uppsala Slott** (☎ 54 48 11; www.uppsalaslott.se; admission by guided tour only, adult/child Skr70/20; ❧ tours in English 1pm & 3pm Tue-Sun Jun-Aug) was built by Gustav Vasa in the

---

UPPSALA KORTET

This handy little three-day discount card (Skr125) gives free or discounted admission to many of the town's attractions, plus free local bus travel and parking. There are also discounts at participating hotels, restaurants and shops. The card is valid from June to August, and can be bought from the tourist office. It covers one adult and up to two children.

EVERYDAY GODS

Some of the greatest gods of the Nordic world – Tyr, Odin, Thor and Frigg – live on in the English language as the days of the week: Tuesday, Wednesday, Thursday and Friday, respectively.

Tyr was the god of justice, a deity who lost his hand to a giant wolf. The gods tried to trick the wolf, Fenrir, into captivity by challenging him to break an indestructible chain. The wolf was suspicious, but accepted the challenge on condition that one of the gods place a hand in his mouth. Tyr agreed and the gods succeeded in fettering Fenrir, but the furious wolf retaliated by biting off Tyr's right hand.

The most eminent of the Nordic gods was one-eyed Odin, whose eight-legged flying horse, Sleipnir, had runes etched on its teeth. Odin gave up his eye in exchange for wisdom; he also gleaned information from his two ravens Hugin and Munin, who flew daily across the worlds in search of knowledge. As the god of war, Odin sent his 12 Valkyries (battle maidens) to select heroes killed in battle to join him at the palace of Valhalla.

Frigg, Odin's wife, was a fertility goddess and the goddess of marriage.

The thunder god, Thor, protected humankind from the malevolent ice giants with his magic hammer, Mjolnir (Thor's-hammer talismans are frequently found in Viking graves). Immensely strong, he would hurl Mjolnir into the clouds to create vast thunderstorms before the hammer came boomeranging back again.

1550s. It contains the state hall where kings were enthroned, and where Queen Kristina abdicated (see p33). It was also the scene of a brutal murder in 1567, when crazy King Erik XIV and his guards killed Nils Sture and his two sons, Erik and Svante, after accusing them of high treason. The castle burned down in 1702, but was rebuilt and took on its present form in 1757.

In the dungeon below the castle's south tower is the **Peace Museum** (☎ 50 00 08; www .fredsmuseum.se; adult/under 19yr Skr40/free; ☼ 2-6pm Wed, noon-4pm Sat & Sun), with displays on various world conflicts and atrocities, as well as Sweden's long record of neutrality and the achievements of former UN secretary general Dag Hammarskjöld.

At the castle entrance marked E, the **Uppsala Art Museum** (☎ 727 24 82; www.uppsala.se/konstmuseum; adult/under 20yr Skr40/free; ☼ noon-4pm Tue-Fri, 11am-5pm Sat & Sun) displays Swedish and international contemporary art and ceramics as well as the art-study collection of Uppsala University.

DOMKYRKAN

The Gothic **Domkyrka** (Cathedral; ☎ 18 72 01; www .uppsaladomkyrka.se; admission free; ☼ 8am-6pm May-Sep, 10am-6pm Sat Oct-Apr) dominates the city, just as some of those buried here, including St Erik, Gustav Vasa and the scientist Carl von Linné (p246) dominated their country.

Gustav's funerary sword, silver crown and shiny golden buttons are kept in the **treasury** (☎ 18 72 01; adult/child Skr30/free; ☼ 10am-5pm Mon-Sat, 12.30-5pm Sun May-Sep, limited hours Oct-Apr) in the cathedral's north tower, along with a great display of medieval textiles. Particularly fine are the clothes worn by the three noblemen who were murdered in the castle (see opposite): they're the only example of 16th-century Swedish high fashion still in existence.

BOTANICAL GARDENS

The **Botanical Gardens** (☎ 471 28 38; www.botan.uu.se; Villavägen 6-8; admission free; ☼ 7am-9pm May-Sep, 7am-7pm Oct-Apr), below the castle hill, show off more than 10,000 different species and are pleasant to wander through. Attractions include the 200-year-old **Linnaeum Orangery** (☼ 9am-3pm Mon-Fri May-Sep, 9am-2pm Mon-Fri Oct-Apr) and a tropical **greenhouse** (Skr40).

MUSEUMS

A wondercabinet of wondercabinets, the **Museum Gustavianum** (☎ 471 75 71; www.gustav ianum.uu.se; Akademigatan 3; adult/under 12yr Skr40/free; ☼ 11am-4pm Tue-Sun) rewards appreciation of the weird and well organised. The shelves in the pleasantly musty building hold case after case of obsolete tools and preserved oddities, like Joseph Cornell shadowboxes gone wrong: stuffed birds, astrolabes, alligator mummies, exotic stones and dried sea creatures. Holding wider appeal is the 17th-century **Augsburg Art Cabinet** and its thousand ingenious trinkets. Don't miss Olof Rudbeck's vertiginous **anatomical theatre**, where executed criminals were dissected.

CARL VON LINNÉ

He may sound eccentric – a syphilis doctor who kept monkeys in his back garden – but Carl von Linné (1707–78), better known by his earlier name of Carolus Linnaeus, was a scientific genius. Known as the 'Father of Taxonomy', Linné invented a precise method for ranking minerals, plants and animals. Described in his work *Systema Naturae*, the basis of his system is still used today.

Von Linné believed that by studying the natural world, man could fathom God's plans. His minute observations led him to devise a classification system of plants (based on their sexual organs) in which one Latin name indicates the genus, and one the species. Some contemporary scientists were appalled at the system's sexual explicitness, but Von Linné obviously had a sense of humour about it: he named a small and insignificant weed after one of his most vocal critics.

As an inspirational professor at Uppsala University, he packed his pupils off around the globe to bring back samples; two of them even joined Captain Cook's expedition to Australia. Among his other achievements, Linné took Celsius' temperature scale and turned it upside down, giving us 0°C for freezing point and 100°C for boiling point, rather than the other way around.

Rare-book fiends should go directly to **Carolina Rediviva** (☎ 471 39 00; Dag Hammarskjölds väg 1; adult/under 12yr Skr20/free; ☻ 9am-5pm Mon-Fri, 10am-5pm Sat, 11am-4pm Sun mid-Jun–mid-Aug; 9am-8pm Mon-Fri, 10am-5pm Sat mid-Aug–mid-Jun), the university library. In a small, dark display room, glass cases hold precious maps and manuscripts, including some illuminated Ethiopian texts and the first book ever printed in Sweden. Occupying its own glowing VIP nook is the surviving half-of the *Codex Argentus* (AD 520), aka the Silver Bible, written in gold and silver ink on purple vellum; aside from being pretty, it's also linguistically important as the most complete existing document written in the Gothic language.

Upplandsmuseet (☎ 16 91 00; www.upplands museet.se, in Swedish; Sankt Eriks Torg 10; admission free; ☻ noon-5pm Tue-Sun), in an 18th-century watermill, houses county collections on folk art, music and the history of Uppsala from the Middle Ages onwards, as well as more modern displays. (A recent installation presented photographs from the life of author Astrid Lindgren.) Kids particularly will find the inventive dioramas and reconstructions engrossing.

No matter how many times the brochures refer to Linné's 'sexual system' of classification (see boxed text, above), the excitement to be had at **Linnémuseet** (☎ 13 65 40; www .linnaeus.se, in Swedish; Svartbäcksgatan 27; adult/under 16yr Skr50/free; ☻ 11am-5pm Tue-Sep) is primarily intellectual; still, botanists and vegetarians will enjoy a visit to the pioneering scientist's home and workshop. The adjoining **Linnéträdgården** (☎ 471 25 76; admission free with Linnémuseet ticket; ☻ shop & exhibit 11am-5pm Tue-Sun

May-Sep, park 11am-8pm Tue-Sun May-Sep) is a reconstructed version of Sweden's oldest botanical garden – Linné's playground – with more than 1300 species arranged according to the system he invented.

Bror Hjorth's House (☎ 56 70 30; www.brorh jorthshus.se; Norbyvägen 26; adult/under 19yr Skr30/free, Fri free; ☻ noon-4pm Thu-Sun, also Tue-Wed in summer), the studio of beloved local artist Bror Hjorth (1894–1968), is jam-packed with Hjorth's charming paintings and sculpture, and hosts temporary exhibitions.

OTHER SIGHTS

On the lawn between Domkyrkan and the main Uppsala University building are nine typical Uppland **rune stones**.

On 30 April, students dressed in white gather to celebrate the **Walpurgis Festival**. Traditionally, this includes a student boat race on the river at 10am and a run down Carolinabacken at 3pm, as well as various processions and singing.

Activities

You can ride the narrow-gauge steam train **Lennakatten** (☎ 13 05 00; www.lennakatten.se; all-day ticket adult/child Skr160/75; ☻ Thu, Sat & Sun Jul-Aug, Sun Sep) 33km into the Uppland countryside. Schedules vary, so check online for updates. The trains depart from the Uppsala Östra museum station, in Bergsbrunnaparken, about 1km east of Uppsala Central Station.

Slow the pace with a boat cruise to the baroque castle of Skokloster. **M/S Kung Carl Gustaf** (☎ 14 48 00; www.kungcarlgustaf.se), a 19th-century ex-steamship, sails Tuesday to Sunday from mid-May to mid-August. Tours (adult/child

Skr200/100) leave Islandsbron at 11am and return at 4.15pm, allowing about two hours at Skokloster. There are also evening river cruises at 7pm Tuesday to Saturday from mid-May to mid-September; the cruise plus buffet and entertainment costs Skr350 per person.

Families with water-loving children should head for **Fyrishov** (☎ 727 49 50; www.fyrishov.se; Idrottsgatan 2; adult/child Skr75/60; ⏱ 9am-9pm, times vary for each section), one of Sweden's largest water parks with the full complement of slides, Jacuzzis, waterfalls and wave machines.

Sleeping

Fyrishov Camping (☎ 727 49 60; www.fyrishov.se; Idrottsgatan 2; sites Skr130, 4-bed cabins from Skr695) This campsite, 2km north of the city, is great for families with water babies: it's attached to one of Sweden's largest water parks, with discounted swim-and-stay packages (from Skr795 for cabins). Take bus 1 from Dragarbrunnsgatan.

Uppsala Vandrarhem & Hotell (☎ 24 20 08; www .uppsalavandrarhem.se; Kvarntorget 3; dm Skr170-200, s/d hostel Skr400/500, s/d hotel weekdays Skr795/895, weekends Skr650/800; P) This new hotel-hostel combo, located in a sort of mini-mall, is removed from the action but easily walkable from the train station. Hostel rooms are upstairs; hotel rooms on two levels have an enclosed courtyard that works as a breakfast room. (Late sleepers should ask for an upstairs room.) Access to the kitchen and a grocery store on the corner make self-catering convenient. Breakfast is included in the hotel prices and Skr75 extra for hostellers.

STF Vandrarhem Sunnersta Herrgård (☎ 32 42 20; www.sunnerstaherrgard.se; Sunnerstavägen 24; dm Skr200, s/d from Skr340/380; ⏱ Jan–mid-Dec; P ▢) This hostel in a historic manor house about 6km south of the city centre has a parklike setting at water's edge and a good restaurant on site. You can rent bikes (Skr50/200 per day/week) or borrow a boat and there's free wi-fi. Hotel-standard rooms are available (single/double Skr605/710). Take bus 20.

Uppsala Vandrarhem City (☎ 10 00 08; www .uppsalavandrarhem.se; Sankt Persgatan 16; dm/s/d from Skr220/400/500; ▢) Vandrarhem City is recommended for its sheer convenience – you really can't stay anywhere more central for these prices. Rooms, all named after famous Uppsala landmarks, are small but decent (although dorms suffer from traffic and

level-crossing noise). There's wi-fi access in parts of the hostel. No breakfast is served, but a kitchen is available.

Samariterhemmets Gästhem (☎ 10 34 00; fax 10 83 75; Samaritergränd 2; s/d incl breakfast from Skr500/760) Run by the Swedish church, this clean, central and inviting guesthouse shares a building with a church. Old-style rooms with separate bathrooms are decorated in cool creams and antique furniture.

Hotel Uppsala (☎ 480 50 00; hoteluppsala@profilho tels.se; Kungsgatan 27; s/d from Skr1350/1550, discounted to Skr750/800; P ▢) Uppsala's largest hotel, and one of its nicest, Hotel Uppsala has all the standard business-hotel amenities plus Hästens beds, birchwood floors, and microwaves and fridges in many rooms. There's also a new Scottish-style pub attached to the hotel.

Best Western Hotel Svava (☎ 13 00 30; www.best western.se; Bangårdsgatan 24; s/d Skr1375/1625, discounted to Skr675/800; P ✿) Named after one of Odin's Valkyrie maidens, Hotel Svava, right opposite the train station, is a very comfortable top-end business-style hotel with weekend discounts that make it a smashing deal.

Eating

RESTAURANTS & CAFES

Ofvandahls (☎ 13 42 04; Sysslomansgatan 3-5; cakes & snacks around Skr40) Something of an Uppsala institution, this classy *konditori* (bakery-cafe) dates back to the 19th century and is a cut above your average coffee-and-bun shop. It's endorsed by no less a personage than the king, and radiates old-world charm; somehow those faded red-striped awnings just get cuter every year.

Eko Caféet (☎ 12 18 45; Drottninggatan 5; snacks Skr50-70) This funky little place with retro and mismatched furniture serves some of the best coffee in town. It does Italian-style whole food, turns into a tapas bar on Wednesday to Saturday evenings, and frequently hosts live jazz and folk, as well as changing art exhibits and general studenty goings-on. Things quieten down somewhat in the summer, when it just opens for lunch Monday to Friday.

Amazing Thai (☎ 15 30 10; Bredgränd 14; starters Skr50, mains Skr110-140; ⏱ lunch & dinner) This small, family-friendly spot is popular for lunch thanks to its great-value buffet (from Skr65). The evening menu features a good selection of fragrant stir-fries, noodle dishes and curries, as well as a set menu (Skr139).

Tzatziki (☎ 15 03 33; Fyristorg 4; starters Skr50-70, mains Skr110-170) Tzatziki will supply all your moussaka and souvlaki needs. There's cosy seating in the 16th-century interior, and in summer the outside tables by the riverside thrum with diners. Service is fast, the food tasty and there are several veggie options.

our pick **Hambergs Fisk** (☎ 71 00 50; Fyristorg 8; lunch from Skr80, dinner mains Skr150-240; ☿ Tue-Sat) No need to ask at the tourist office about where to eat: if you're there, you'll be close enough to smell the aromas of dill and seafood tempting you into this excellent fish restaurant. Self-caterers should check out the fresh fish counter inside.

Domtrappkällaren (☎ 13 09 55; info@domtrappkal laren.se; Sankt Eriksgränd 15; lunch from Skr85, dinner mains Skr200-290; ☿ Mon-Sat) Once a prison, this is now a top-notch restaurant set in an atmospheric cellar (lunch is served upstairs) at the foot of the cathedral. It specialises in gamey dishes and Swedish cooking, such as venison, reindeer and cloudberry soufflé.

QUICK EATS & SELF-CATERING

Jalla (Stora Torget 1; meals Skr50-85; ☿ 10am until late) Get your fix of cheap and (relatively) healthful felafel, kebabs and meze platters at this efficient fast-food joint right on the main square; it's packed with young people at all hours.

Saluhallen (Sankt Eriks Torg; ☿ 10am-6pm Mon-Fri, 10am-2pm Sat) Stock up on meat, fresh fish, cheeses and fancy chocolates at this indoor market, or hit one of the restaurant corners for a bite; a couple stay open late for dinner, with pleasant terrace bars available in summer.

Find groceries at the central **Hemköp supermarket** (Stora Torget; ☿ to 10pm). For alcohol, **Systembolaget** (Dragarbrunnsgatan 50) is inside the Svava shopping centre.

Drinking & Entertainment

In the evenings, local students converge on the university bars on Sankt Olofsgatan (hard to get into if you're not an Uppsala student, but worth a go). Just follow the crowds to find out which ones are currently primo.

Concert Hall (☎ 727 90 00; Vaksala Torget 1; ☿ 5-8pm Tue-Sat & during evening events) For a cool view over the city, head to the 6th-floor bar inside the huge, blocky Concert Hall.

Katalin and All That Jazz (☎ 14 06 80; Godsmagasinet, Östra Station) Katalin, in a former warehouse behind the train station, hosts regular live jazz and blues, with occasional rock and pop bands. There's a good restaurant too, and in summer the sun-splashed back patio is jammed with great-looking people acting like they're not checking each other out.

O'Connor's (☎ 14 40 10; Stora Torget 1) Upstairs from Jalla is this friendly Irish pub and restaurant with live music six nights a week and a selection of over 70 beers from around the world.

Svenssons Taverna (☎ 10 09 08; Sysslomansgatan 14) This cool taverna has a winning combination of vaguely mariner-themed interior and shady outdoor seating area.

William's (☎ 14 09 20; Övre Slottsgatan 7) In the university quarter, William's is a cosy English-style pub that also serves cheap food, including a lunch buffet (11am to 2pm, Skr79).

Hollywood blockbusters play at the **Royal Cinema** (☎ 13 50 07; Dragarbrunnsgatan 44) and **Filmstaden** (☎ 08 56 26 00 00; www.sf.se, in Swedish; Drottninggatan 3).

Getting There & Away

The Flygbuss (bus 801) departs at least twice an hour around the clock for nearby Arlanda airport (45 minutes, adult/child Skr100/60); it leaves from outside the Uppsala train station.

Swebus Express (☎ 0200-21 82 18; www.swe busexpress.se) runs regular direct services to Stockholm (Skr54, one hour, at least hourly), Gävle (Skr82, 1½ hours, two daily), Västerås (Skr157, 3½ hours, six daily), Örebro (Skr220, 4½ hours, four to seven daily) and Falun (Skr296, 5½ hours, one daily).

There are frequent SJ trains to/from Stockholm (Skr39 to Skr69, 40 minutes one way). SJ trains to/from Gävle (Skr135, 50 minutes, at least seven daily), Östersund (Skr764, five hours, at least two daily) and Mora (Skr224 to Skr572, 3¼ hours, two daily) also stop in Uppsala.

For car hire, seek out **Statoil** (☎ 20 91 00; Gamla Uppsalagatan 48), next to the Scandic Uppsala Nord. There are three petrol stations for car hire, 1.5km along Vaksalagatan: **OKQ8** (☎ 29 04 96; Årstagatan 5-7) often has some good deals.

Getting Around

Upplands Lokaltrafik (☎ 0771-14 14 14; www .ul.se, in Swedish) runs traffic within the city and county. City buses leave from Stora Torget and the nearby streets. Tickets for unlimited travel for 90 minutes cost from Skr20.

NORTHERN UPPLAND

Once a centre of industry, this region is now mainly a series of picturesque relics ideal for picnicking, lazing on the grass, taking photos and generally idling about. The landscape consists of buttery green hills dotted with small red cottages and postcard villages linked by winding roads, loads of birch trees and ultra-lush vegetation. The main sights of interest are the centuries-old ironworks and mines scattered around the countryside. From vast gorges ripped into the ground to spic-and-span forge workers' cottages, they make fascinating visual history lessons.

The word *'bruk'*, which is part of many local place names, means an industrial village that processed raw materials, such as iron ore. Most appeared in the 17th century and were owned, run and staffed by Dutch and Walloon (Belgian) immigrants. The profits were used to build fine mansions, surrounded by humble workers' homes.

For more about the area's industrial heritage, ask at tourist offices for the free booklet *Vallonbruk in Uppland*, or check out www.vallonbruken.nu.

Österbybruk
☎ 0295

You'd never guess from its placid air, but Österbybruk and its ironworks were founded solely to make munitions for Gustav Vasa's interminable wars. Today the village is a sleepy place, but it does contain most basic facilities (bank, bakery, supermarket, pizzerias etc) and a summer **tourist office** (☎ 214 92; ☙ 11am-5pm Jun-Aug) amid the ironworks milieu.

The pleasant ironworks area includes the mansion **Österbybruk Herrgård**, which has **summer art exhibitions** (☙ noon-4pm Sat & Sun May-Sep, daily noon-4pm Jun-Aug), **workers' homes** and the world's best-preserved 17th-century **Walloon forge**. The forge here mainly produced bar iron that was exported to Sheffield: it bore a stamp of two linked Os. In winter, the stacks of iron were taken to the port by sled. Tours of the grounds take place daily in summer (mid-June to mid-August; adult/child Skr40/free).

The impressive 15th-century castle **Örbyhus Slott** (☎ 214 06; www.orbyhus-slott.com; admission by tour only, adult/12-16yr Skr50/15; ☙ 1pm daily Mar, 1pm & 3pm daily Jul, 1pm Sat & Sun mid-May–mid-Sep), 10km further west, is where mad King Erik XIV was imprisoned by his brother Johann. Erik was then murdered with a bowl of pea soup laced with arsenic.

A diminutive hostel with 20 beds, **Dannemora Vandrarhem** (☎ 215 70; Storrymningsvägen 4; dm Skr175; ☙ May-Oct; P) is near the Dannemora mine and based in old mineworkers' houses. Reception is only open from 5.30pm to 7pm, so be sure to plan ahead.

Part of the ironworks estate, **Wärdshuset Gammel Tammen** (☎ 212 00; info@gammeltammen.se; annex Skr895, discounted to Skr645, s/d Skr995/1350, discounted to Skr745/1095) is a lovely old inn in one wing of Österbybruk Herrgård. Its 26 rooms are cosy and peaceful – some have views over the duck pond – and there's a good restaurant (snacks Skr70, mains Skr150). An annex holds 10 simpler, single rooms.

Just uphill from the Gammel Tammen, in a former stable, **Karins Stallcafé** (☎ 401 48; coffee Skr15, snacks from Skr30; ☙ 11am-5pm May-Jul, 11am-4pm Aug) is a summer cafe and twee crafts shop that serves lunches and snacks, set off by chunks of homemade bread, on outdoor picnic tables.

Bus 823 runs from Uppsala to Österbybruk (Skr75, one hour, at least 10 daily).

Lövstabruk
☎ 0294

Tiny Lövstabruk (Leufsta Bruk), 24km due north of Österbybruk, is a great example of a mansion with associated factories. In 1627 the Dutchman Louis de Geer came to Lövstabruk, and the mansion was built for his grandson, Charles de Geer, around 1700. The house and its factories were destroyed by a Russian attack in 1719, but everything was rebuilt and iron production continued until 1926.

The **tourist office** (☎ 310 70; tours Skr50; ☙ 11am-5pm mid-Jun–mid-Aug, 11am-2pm Sat & Sun mid-Aug–mid-Jun) has moved into the Stora Magasinet building, next to the Wärdshus. Buy tickets here for various one-hour guided tours: the mansion (1pm and 4pm), the mansion and park (2.30pm) and the factory (11.30am). There's also a themed tour, the subject of which changes every year. Tours run daily from mid-June to August, and on Saturdays and Sundays from mid-May to mid-June.

B&B Läkarvillan (☎ 310 04; www.bedandbreakfast.lovstabruk.se; s/d Skr650/900) is a well-preserved house on the ironworks grounds that has whitewashed rooms decorated with pretty antiques. There's also a fine restaurant (mains Skr165 to Skr185) serving everything from coffee and cakes to a full à la carte menu.

To reach Lövstabruk, take bus 811 from Uppsala to Östhammar (1¼ hours, every 30 minutes Monday to Friday, hourly at weekends), then change to bus 832 (45 minutes, four to eight daily). The total cost of the journey is Skr80.

Forsmark
☎ 0173

The surroundings of the **Forsmarksbruk** ironworks are ideal for photographers; its bone-white church, manor house, workshops and English gardens, set around a central pond, are starkly beautiful. The **statue of Neptune** in the middle of the pond dates from 1792. The seasonal **tourist office** (☎ 500 15; ☼ 9am-4pm Jul–mid-Aug) is staffed until 4pm, but open until 9pm for brochures. These days the main employer in the area is the nearby nuclear power station, which is infamous for leaking radio-active waste into the Baltic Sea in June 2005.

The **bruksmuseum** (adult/child Skr20/free; ☼ 11am-4pm Sat & Sun May, 11am-4pm daily mid-Jun–mid-Aug), full of old carriages, rusty tools, sleeping quarters and a factory office, is definitely worth a look, although its opening times are erratic. **Eldorado** (admission free; ☼ 9am-4pm Mon-Fri, 11.30am-4pm Sat & Sun mid-Jun–mid-Aug), a tiny experiment station for kids, has a fantastic rolling-ball machine guaranteed to hypnotise.

Friendly staff at **Forsmark Wärdshus** (☎ 501 00; www.forsmarkswardshus.se, in Swedish) cope admirably with the hungry coach parties at this lovely old inn. As well as devouring lunch (Skr75), you can stay in one of the charming rooms (single/double including breakfast Skr550/750) overlooking the English park, and rent bicycles (Skr100 per day).

To reach Forsmark, take bus 811 from Uppsala to Östhammar (1¼ hours, every 30 minutes Monday to Friday, hourly at weekends), then change to bus 832 (45 minutes, four to eight daily). The total cost of the journey is Skr80.

SÖDERMANLAND

NYKÖPING
☎ 0155 / pop 50,000

Once the setting for one of Swedish royalty's greatest feuds, Nyköping these days is a mellow, pretty town where the big activities include strolling along the river and sitting by the harbour. There's a **tourist office** (☎ 24 82 00; turism@nykoping.se; Stadshuset, Stora Torget; ☼ 8am-6pm Mon-Fri, 9am-1pm Sat mid-Jun–mid-Aug, 8am-5pm Mon, Tue & Thu, 8am-6pm Wed, 8am-4pm Fri mid-Aug–mid-Jun) inside the town hall on the main square. Banks, supermarkets and other services can be found on Västra Storgatan, running west from Stora Torget.

Sights & Activities

The ruined castle **Nyköpingshus** (admission free; ☼ 24hr) hosted some violent times in the Swedish monarchy. The bickering among King Birger and his two brothers, Erik and Valdemar, peaked in 1317, when Birger invited his brothers to a 'peace banquet'. When they arrived at the castle, he hurled them into the dungeon and threw the keys in the river, letting them starve to death. (It didn't do Birger much good, as he was driven to exile in Denmark the following year.) This cheerful episode is recreated each summer as *The Nyköping Banquet*, a traditional play; ask for a schedule at Sörmlands Museum.

Inside the castle grounds, **Sörmlands Museum** (☎ 24 57 20; admission free; ☼ 10am-5pm mid-Jun–mid-Aug, 11am-5pm Tue-Sun mid-Aug–mid-Jun) includes **Kungstornet** (King's Tower), a whitewashed four-storey castle tower; **Gamla Residenset**, the old governor's residence; and the neighbouring **Konsthallen**, with interesting art exhibitions and a collection of 19th-century boathouses. Free guided tours of Kungstornet take place in English at 2pm Saturday and Sunday all year and daily in summer.

By Stora Torget, there's the old **rådhus** (town hall) and **St Nicolai Kyrka**, with a splendid pulpit. Two **rune stones** and 700 Bronze Age **rock carvings** decorate Släbroparken, about 2.5km northwest of town.

Take a walk along the river: 'Sweden's longest museum' – or so the publicity goes. For longer hikes, the 1000km-long **Sörmlandsleden** (☎ 355 64; www.sormlandsleden.se) passes through town on its way around the county. In summer you can also explore the nearby **archipelago**; enquire at the tourist office.

Sleeping & Eating

Strandstuviken Camping (☎ 978 10; strandstuviken@ hotmail.com; sites Skr150, 4-/5-bed cabins Skr375/425; ☼ May-Sep) The nearest camping ground is this family beachside place, with sauna, minigolf, and canoe and bicycle hire. It's a good 8km southeast of town, though, with no public transport.

Nyköpings Vandrarhem (☎ 21 18 10; Brunnsgatan 2; dm Skr160; **P**) So close to the castle that you'd feel threatened if there were a siege, this SVIF hostel is homely and casual. The kitchen is great, there are picnic tables in the yard, and the folks in charge are accommodating and helpful. Its inches-from-the-riverside location is hard to beat.

Clarion Hotel Kompaniet (☎ 28 80 20; cc.kompaniet@ choice.se; Folkungavägen 1; s/d Skr1295/1595, discounted to Skr875/1125; **P** 🖳 🛱) This enormous building near the harbour features stylish modern rooms – not huge, but intelligently arranged, and many with nice views – in a riverside building that was once home to a furniture factory. Prices vary by time of year, but all include breakfast and a dinner buffet (or a sandwich for those who arrive late).

Café Hellmans (☎ 21 05 25; Västra Trädgårdsgatan 24; buffet breakfast/lunch Skr55/65; 🕑 9am-6pm Mon-Fri, 9am-4pm Sat, 11am-2pm Sun) A charming cafe with a boutique shop attached, Hellman's is a nice spot for lunch, with expansive buffets as well as bagels and subs from Skr35, good coffee and excellent cakes to enjoy in the summer courtyard.

Lotsen (☎ 21 21 03; Skeppsbron; meals Skr80-160; 🕑 to 2am Wed, Fri & Sat) Lotsen is one of several casual bar-restaurants along the harbour; the crowds shift from one terrace to the other according to time of day and availability of live music. Lotsen is the simplest in the line-up, with basic meals like pizza, meatballs and burgers, and huge steins of beer at happy hour.

Getting There & Around

Nyköping's **Skavsta airport** (☎ 28 04 00; www .skavsta-air.se), 8km northwest of town, has flights to/from the UK and the European continent with Ryanair (see p330). Airport buses meet most flights and run to/from Stockholm (Skr150, 80 minutes). Local buses run every 10 minutes from Nyköping to Skavsta (Skr20, 20 minutes); alternatively, a **taxi** (☎ 21 75 00) costs about Skr150.

The bus and train stations are roughly 800m apart on the western side of the central grid. Nyköping is on the regular **Swebus Express** (☎ 0200-21 82 18; www.swebusexpress.se) routes, including Stockholm–Norrköping–Jönköping–Göteborg/Malmö, and Stockholm–Norrköping–Kalmar. To get to Eskilstuna, take local bus 701 or 801. SJ trains run every hour or two to Norrköping (Skr72, 40 minutes), Linköping (Skr143, 1¼ hours) and

Stockholm (Skr101, one hour). Most X2000 services don't stop in Nyköping.

The tourist office has bikes for rent (Skr40/200 per day/week).

ESKILSTUNA
☎ 016 / pop 93,000

Although its suburban ordinariness doesn't exactly scream 'tourist destination', Eskilstuna has a couple of family-friendly sights, primarily its famous zoo. It also has an interesting history as the one-time murder capital of Sweden. The small old town is now an attractive shopping district. And just northeast of town is one of the most extraordinary rock carvings in Sweden.

The **tourist office** (☎ 710 23 75; www.eskilstuna .se; Nygatan 15; 🕑 10am-6pm Mon-Fri, 10am-2pm Sat year-round, plus 10am-2pm Sun May-Aug) dispenses helpful information. You'll find most services around Fristadstorget and the pedestrianised part of Kungsgatan. The central **public library** (☎ 10 13 51; Kriebsensgatan 4; 🕑 9am-8pm Mon-Thu, 9am-6pm Fri, 10am-3pm Sat) has free internet access.

Sights & Activities
PARKEN ZOO

One of central Sweden's most popular family attractions is the zoo and amusement park **Parken Zoo** (☎ 10 01 01; www.parkenzoo.se; adult/3-16yr Skr150/110; 🕑 10am-6pm daily Jul–mid-Aug, 10am-4pm Mon-Fri, 10am-6pm Sat & Sun May-Jun & mid-Aug–early Sep). Animals on show include monkeys, komodo dragons and some beautiful white tigers who were successfully bred here. It's not a cheap day out though: additional charges are levied for **parking** (Skr40); the **amusement park** (day ticket Skr135; 🕑 as for the zoo but opens at noon), which has kiddies' rides and some larger whizzy things; and the **swimming pool** (adult/7-14yr Skr40/30; 🕑 10am-7pm or 8pm Jun-Aug).

Parken Zoo is 1.5km west of the town centre. Bus 1 (Skr21, 25 minutes) leaves frequently from the train and bus stations.

SIGURD CARVING

The vivid, 3m-long Viking Age rock carving **Sigurdsristningen** (admission free; 🕑 24hr) illustrates the story of Sigurd the Dragon Slayer, a hero whose adventures are described in *Beowulf* and the Icelandic sagas. The story inspired Wagner's *Ring Cycle,* and *The Hobbit* and *Lord of the Rings* also borrow from it.

Carved into the bedrock around AD 1000, the carving shows Sigurd roasting the heart of the dragon Fafnir over a fire. Sigurd's stepfather Regin has persuaded him to kill Fafnir for the dragon's golden treasure. Sigurd touches the heart to see if it's cooked, then sucks his finger, and voila – he tastes the dragon's blood and suddenly understands the language of birds. They warn him that Regin is plotting to kill him and keep the treasure, so Sigurd attacks first, chopping off his stepfather's head; the unfortunate fellow is shown in the left corner of the carving, among his scattered tools. Also depicted is Sigurd's horse Grani, a gift from Odin, tied to the tree where the birds perch.

The runes in the dragon's body, unrelated to the legend, explain that a woman named Sigrid raised a nearby bridge (the abutments can still be seen) in memory of her husband Holmger. A walking path along the river starts from the parking lot; ask at the tourist office about raft trips.

The carving is situated near Sundbyholms Slott and Mälaren lake, 12km northeast of Eskilstuna. To get there, take bus 225.

OTHER SIGHTS

The **Rademachersmedjorna** (Rademacher Forges; ☎ 710 13 71; Rademachergatan; admission free; ⊙ 10am-4pm Mon-Fri year-round, plus some weekends in summer) contain the carefully preserved 17th-century remnants of Eskilstuna's ironworking past. Visitors can see workshops where the tradition continues: iron-, silver- and goldsmiths all still work here. Stay alert for sightings of 'Sundin of the Gab', a local craftsman who produced masterworks despite his convention-flouting lifestyle.

Faktoriet (☎ 10 23 75; admission free; ⊙ 11am-4pm Tue-Sun), on the island Strömsholmen, tells the story of Eskilstuna's industrial and cultural heritage; it was closed for renovations at time of research, and due to reopen in 2009, so check with the tourist office for details.

Eskilstuna Konstmuseum (☎ 710 13 69; Portgatan 2, Munktellstaden; admission free; ⊙ 11am-4pm Tue, Wed & Fri, 11am-8pm Thu, noon-4pm Sat & Sun) has an ambitious and very cool art collection in a beautiful space in the Munktell area. A chic little restaurant is attached.

In **Torshälla**, 6km north of the town centre, **Brandt Contemporary Glass** (☎ 35 52 30; brandtglass .com; Klockberget; admission Skr30; ⊙ 11am-4pm Fri & Sat), just behind the church, is a workshop and gallery exhibiting vases and sculptures. **Ebelingmuseet** (☎ 10 73 05; Eskilstunavägen 5; admission free; ⊙ noon-4pm Wed-Sun) has bizarre steel sculptures by Allan Ebeling and paintings by his daughter Marianne, plus various temporary exhibitions. The old wooden houses and pretty riverside areas in Torshälla are also worth a look. Take bus 2 or 15 from Eskilstuna to Torshälla (Skr21, 40 minutes).

Sleeping & Eating

STF Hostel Eskilstuna (☎ 51 30 80; www.vilstasport hotell.nu; dm Skr160, s/d hostel from Skr300/420, hotel from Skr695/890; P) Lying in the Vilsta nature reserve 2km south of town, this hostel is well provided for – all rooms have en-suite bathrooms and TV. It's part of the Vilsta sport complex, so there are gym, Jacuzzi and sports facilities on hand. Hotel rooms are also available; room rates include breakfast. Take bus 12 from Fristadstorget.

City Hotell Eskilstuna (☎ 10 88 50; www.cityhotell .se; Järnvägsplan 1; s/d/tr/q from Skr975/1470/1833/2080, discounted to Skr645/920/1140/1388) Right opposite the train station, this is among the better hotels. Rooms are spacious and comfortable, and some have balconies or cylindrical Swedish stoves, giving them a hint of the 19th century.

Sundbyholms Slott (☎ 016-42 84 00; www.sundby holms-slott.se; weekend packages from Skr1295; P ⌨) Luxury suites, perfect for a romantic weekend, are available in the tasteful mansion here, 12km northeast of Eskilstuna on the road toward the Sigurd carvings (catch bus 225). The castle, by Mälaren lake, also houses a top-quality restaurant, and there's a popular beach and walking trails nearby.

Café Kaka (☎ 13 10 94; Kyrkogatan 6; meals Skr50-75) Kaka is a funky, upbeat cafe and meeting place, serving sandwiches, pasta and salads, with the occasional live DJ.

Restaurang Tingsgården (☎ 51 66 20; Rådhustorget 2; starters Skr70-115, mains Skr150-220; ⊙ 11.30am-2pm & 6-9pm Mon-Fri, 1-9pm Sat, 1-8pm Sun) This intimate restaurant, inside a wonderful wooden 18th-century house in the old town, is a treat. Its menu is heavy on the meat and fish, from lamb and goose to mountain trout, with a dessert menu of Swedish favourites. The set 'Sverigemenu' (Skr425) includes two types of herring, Västerbotten cheese, warm cloudberry dessert and other specialities. In summer, you can sit out on a large deck overlooking the twinkling river.

Getting There & Around

The bus station is located 500m east of the train station, beside the river. Local bus 701 goes roughly hourly to Nyköping (Skr96, 1¾ hours). **Swebus Express** (☎ 0200-21 82 18; www .swebusexpress.se) operates up to six buses daily on its Stockholm–Eskilstuna–Örebro route, but trains are best for destinations such as Örebro (Skr102, one hour, every two hours), Västerås (Skr41, 30 minutes, hourly) and Stockholm (Skr94, one hour, hourly).

VÄSTMANLAND

VÄSTERÅS

☎ 021 / pop 131,000

With its cobbled streets, higgledy-piggledy houses and flourishing flower gardens, Västerås' old town is an utter delight. Sweden's sixth-largest city is a place of two halves: head southeast and you'll find modern shopping centres, large industries and sprawling suburbs that bear no resemblance to the teeny lanes and crafts shops you've left behind.

Västerås is also a handy base for exploring Mälaren lake and important pagan sites nearby.

Information

The **tourist office** (☎ 39 01 00; www.vasterasmalarsta den.se; Kopparbergsvägen 8; ⊙ 10am-6pm Mon-Fri, 10am-3pm Sat) can help with visitor enquiries for the town and region.

There's a **Forex** (☎ 18 00 80; Stora Gatan 18; ⊙ 9am-7pm Mon-Fri, 9am-3pm Sat) currency-exchange office, banks, ATMs and most other services visitors will require along Stora Gatan. The **library** (☎ 39 46 00; Biskopsgatan 2; ⊙ 10am-7pm Mon-Thu, 10am-6pm Fri, 10am-2pm Sat) is opposite the cathedral and offers free internet access. There's also internet access inside **Mailboxes Etc** (Munkgatan 18; per hr Skr35; ⊙ 9am-5pm Mon-Fri).

Sights

MUSEUMS

The **Konstmuseum** (☎ 16 13 00; Fiskartorget 2; admisson free; ⊙ 11am-4pm Tue-Fri, noon-4pm Sat & Sun Jun-Aug, 10am-5pm Tue-Fri, noon-5pm Sat & Sun Sep-May), based in the stately town hall, devotes its energies to exhibiting contemporary Swedish painters. The permanent collections, with works by artists such as Ivan Aguéli and Bror Hjorth, also get an occasional airing.

Vallby Friluftsmuseum (☎ 39 80 70; www.vall byfriluftsmuseum.se; admission free; ⊙ 10am-5pm), off Vallbyleden near the E18 interchange, 2km northwest of the city, is home to an extensive

open-air collection. Among the 40-odd buildings, there's an interesting farmyard and craft workshops. Take bus 10 or 12.

Västmanlands Länsmuseum (☎ 15 61 00; www .vastmanlandslansmuseum.se; Slottsgatan; admission free; ⊙ noon-4pm Thu-Sun), inside Västerås Slottet, is a cultural centre that stages exhibitions of contemporary art, photography and sculpture, as well as hosting speakers and presentations; look for a current schedule of events at the tourist office or online.

OTHER SIGHTS

The fine brick-built **Domkyrka** (Cathedral; Biskops-gatan; ⊙ 8am-5pm Mon-Fri, 9.30am-5pm Sat & Sun) was begun in the 12th century, although most of what you see today is late-14th-century work. It contains carved floor slabs, six altar pieces and the marble sarcophagus of crazy King Erik XIV.

Behind the cathedral is the quaint old-town area **Kyrkbacken**. Once the student district and now a well-preserved portion of pre-18th-century Västerås, it's studded with artisans' workshops.

The city is surrounded by ancient pre-Christian sites. The most interesting and extensive is **Anundshög** (admission free; ⊙ 24hr), the biggest tumulus in Sweden, 6km northeast of the city. It has a full complement of prehistoric curiosities, such as mounds, stone ship settings and a large 11th-century rune stone. The two main stone ship settings date from around the 1st century. The area is part of the Badelunda Ridge, which includes the 13th-century **Badelunda Church** (1km north) and the 16m-wide **Tibble Labyrinth** (1km south). Ask the tourist office for the handy map Badelunda Forntids Bygd. Take bus 12 to the Bjurhovda terminus, then walk 2km east.

Sleeping

Västerås Mälarcamping (☎ 14 02 79; Johannisbergsvägen; sites/cabins from Skr80/400; 🖳) The closest camp site is this place, 5km southwest of the city near Mälaren lake. It has recently been renovated and renamed (from Johannisbergs Camping), with up-to-date facilities including wireless internet access. To get there, take bus 25.

STF Vandrarhem Västerås/Quality Hotel (☎ 30 38 00; info.vasteras@quality.choicehotels.se; Svalgången 1, Vallby; dm/s/d Skr205/390/520; P 🖳) A couple of kilometres out of town, this hotel offers hostel accommodation through STF in about a dozen of its regular hotel rooms. The building

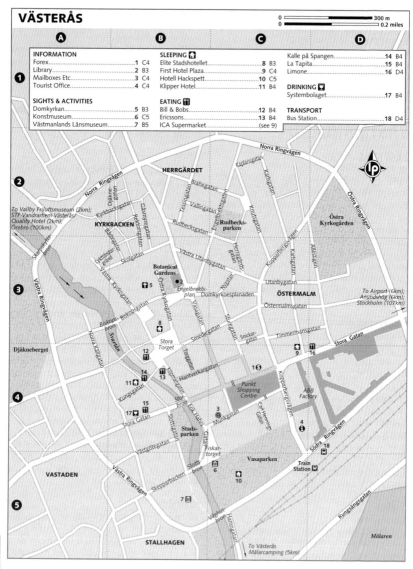

VÄSTERÅS

0 ———— 300 m
0 ———— 0.2 miles

is a crazy suburban-industrial colossus with its exterior and common areas painted entirely in varying shades of white. Glass roofs over some of the rooms let in the long summer nights (if you want them to).

There's a bar and restaurant in the lobby, as well as a pool table, a sauna and a swimming pool.

Klipper Hotel (☎ 41 00 00; www.klipperhotel.com; Kungsgatan 4; budget r Skr395, s/d incl breakfast & dinner from Skr595/1190; P) The attractive, family-run Klipper has one of the best locations in the city, near the river in the old town and 700m from the bus and train stations. The comfortable (if smallish) rooms are simple and fresh. Parking costs Skr50.

ARTY ALTERNATIVE LODGINGS

In addition to Västerås' normal, run-of-the-mill hotels, there are two unique accommodation possibilities in and around town. Both created by local artist Mikael Genberg, they are well worth investigating if you like your lodgings with a twist.

The **Hotell Hackspett** (Woodpecker Hotel) is a fabulous tree house in the middle of Vasaparken, behind the Konstmuseum. The cabin is 13m above the ground in an old oak tree; guests (and breakfast) are hoisted up and down in a basket. The second of Genberg's fascinating creations is the **Utter Inn**, a small, red, floating cabin in the middle of Mälaren lake, only accessible by boat. The bedroom is downstairs – 3m below the surface – and is complete with glass viewing panels to watch the marine life outside. There's room for two people, and a canoe is provided.

Accommodation in the tree house or lake cabin costs Skr1000 per person per night if you bring your own food and bed linen; the 'deluxe package' (when linen is supplied and you will be delivered food in the evening and breakfast in the morning) is Skr1500 per person. Both places can be booked through the Västerås tourist office (p253). Genberg also has a website (www.mi kaelgenberg.com); it's in Swedish, but the photographs will give you an idea of his creations.

First Hotel Plaza (☎ 10 10 10; reservations.plaza@ firsthotels.se; Karlsgatan 9A; s/d from Skr850/1250, discounted to Skr650/850; P ⊠ ⌨) Bang in the centre of the modern city, this 25-storey skyscraper was built for gravity-defying lounge lizards: it boasts the highest cocktail bar in Sweden! Some rooms have views over Mälaren lake, and there's a spa with masseurs, a sauna, a gym and a Mediterranean-inspired restaurant.

Elite Stadshotellet (☎ 10 28 00; info@vasteras.elite.se; Stora Torget; s/d from Skr1250/1500, discounted to Skr550/795; P ⌨) Many of the rooms at the Elite, in a lovely art-nouveau building, have prime views over the main square – request one if you like people-watching. The decor is tasteful (pale walls, leafy bedspreads and mahogany timber), the staff are obliging and there's a highly regarded restaurant and English-style pub attached.

Eating & Drinking

La Tapita (☎ 448 03 33; Stora Gatan 46; tapas Skr25-55, mains Skr70-185; ☺ 11am-11pm Mon-Fri, 5-11pm Sat) This Spanish-themed tapas bar and restaurant has a mellow atmosphere, enhanced by Latin music and piles of southern Mediterranean grub. Nibble an array of tapas, tuck into pasta, fish and meat mains, or share a *paella Valenciana* with a friend.

Bill & Bobs (☎ 41 99 21; Stora Torget 5; bar snacks from Skr65, meals Skr80-200) A diverse crowd settles down at this casual spot to drink and chatter at the outdoor tables on the square. Thai chicken and hamburger with bacon bits are a couple of Bill & Bobs' popular 'classic' dishes.

Kalle på Spangen (☎ 12 91 29; Kungsgatan 2; mains around Skr75) This great cafe, right by the river

in the old part of town, has several cosy, creaky-floored rooms filled with mismatched furniture and gilt-edged grandfather clocks. Lunch specials such as lasagne are hefty and include salad, beverage, bread and coffee.

Limone (☎ 41 75 60; Stora Gatan 4; starters Skr75-110, pastas half/full Skr90/120, dinner mains Skr205-245; ☺ 11am-1.30pm & 5.30-10pm Mon-Fri, 5.30-10pm Sat) Limone is an elegant, upmarket Italian restaurant with stylish decor and impressive menu items such as linguine with mussels and lobster sauce, or grilled veal wrapped in Parma ham.

There's an ICA supermarket around the corner from the First Hotel Plaza (left). **Ericssons** (☎ 13 55 12; Stora Torget 3) is an excellent delicatessen for stocking up on picnic supplies. For alcohol, visit **Systembolaget** (Stora Gatan 48).

Getting There & Around

The **airport** (☎ 80 56 00; www.vasterasflygplats.se) is 6km east of the city centre, and is connected by bus L941. Budget carrier Ryanair flies here daily from the UK, and other budget airlines reach a variety of destinations, including Crete and Turkey (weekly). Check the airport website for an updated schedule.

The bus and train stations are adjacent, on the southern edge of Västerås. Regional buses 65 and 69 run to Sala (Skr64, 45 minutes, up to eight weekdays, two Saturday and Sunday) as do trains (Skr41, 25 minutes, three daily). **Swebus Express** (☎ 0200-21 82 18; www.swebusexpress .se) runs to Uppsala (Skr157, three hours, five daily), Stockholm (Skr103, 1½ hours, six daily) and Örebro (Skr103, 1¼ hours, eight daily).

Västerås is accessible by hourly trains from Stockholm (Skr113, one hour). Trains to Örebro (Skr98, one hour), Uppsala (Skr113, 1½ hours) and Eskilstuna (Skr62, 30 minutes) are also frequent.

For taxis, call **Taxi Västerås** (☎ 18 50 00).

SALA

☎ 0224 / pop 21,560

The source of tiny Sala's parklike charm is distinctly unfrivolous. The local silver mine made Sweden rich in the 16th and 17th centuries, and its creation changed the face of the town centre: those small rivers, ponds and canals that weave so prettily through and around the town were built to power the mines.

The **tourist office** (☎ 552 02; www.sala.se/turism; Stora Torget; 8am-5pm Mon-Fri year-round, plus 10am-2pm Sat May-Sep) inside the town hall faces the main square; it doesn't always stick to posted hours, but brochures are also available at the **library** (☎ 555 01; Norra Esplanaden 5). Free internet access is available at both the tourist office and library. The free town map is useful if you want to use the walking paths.

Sights & Activities

Even if you're reluctant to take the plunge, the above-ground parts of **Sala Silvergruva** (☎ 67 72 50; www.salasilvergruva.se; 10am-5pm May-Sep, 11am-4pm Oct-Apr), a mine about 2km south of the town centre, are nice to walk around. Bring a camera – the weird landscape of mysterious, purpose-built structures occasionally sprouts chimneys or falls away into deep holes. The mine closed in 1908. The 30-odd listed buildings in the **museum village** contain artists' workshops, a cafe, a **mine museum** and a small Swedish-only **police museum** (adult/child Skr20/10; noon-4pm Jun-Aug), full of rusty knuckledusters.

Beneath the surface are 20km of galleries, caverns and shafts, which you can explore on one of two mine tours. The more frequent tour is the informative one-hour **60 Metersturen** (adult/child Skr100/50). The 90-minute tour, **150 Metersturen** (Skr200), goes down to 150m. Tours aren't scheduled in advance; they're given depending on when enough people show up and how deep most of them want to go. To be sure of catching a tour in English, book ahead.

Both village and mine are off the Västerås road. It's a pretty walk along the **Gröna Gången** (Green Walk), which takes you southwest via the parks and the **Mellandammen** pond at Sofielund. Public transport connections

aren't good; take the Silverlinjen bus from the train station to Styrars, then walk the remaining 500m.

In the main park in town is **Väsby Kungsgård** (☎ 106 37; www.vasbykungsgard.se; Museuigatan 2; adult/child Skr25/free; 1-4pm Mon-Fri), a 16th-century royal farm where Gustav II Adolf (possibly) met his mistress. Excitement for the traveller is confined to the beautifully preserved interiors and 17th-century weapons collection.

Aguélimuseet (☎ 138 20; www.sala.se/turism/ague limuseet; Vasagatan 17; admission free; 11am-4pm Wed-Sun) exhibits the largest display of oils and watercolours by local artist Ivan Aguéli (1869–1917) in Sweden, as well as work by some of his contemporaries. In summer there are also temporary exhibitions, including a recent display of Bertil Vallien glasswork. Entry is via the town library.

The houses and courtyard called **Norrmanska Gården** (Norrbygatan) were built in 1736; the area is now home to shops and a cafe.

Sleeping & Eating

STF Vandrarhem & Camping Sala (☎ 127 30; sites from Skr50, dm Skr140, s/d from Skr210/280) This haven of tranquillity is in the woods near the Mellandammen pond, 2km southwest of the centre. It's a pet-friendly complex with camping, minigolf and a homely cafe (open June to August). Walk along Gröna Gången from the bus station, or take the Silverlinjen bus to the water tower and walk the rest of the way. Reservations are necessary from September to mid-May.

Hotell Svea (☎ 105 10; www.hotellsvea.com; Väsby gatan 19; s/d Skr595/695, discounted to Skr495/595) Friendly 10-roomed Svea puts the emphasis on its personal service. Rooms are old-fashioned but clean and comfortable, and it's exceptionally handy for the train and bus station.

Norrmanska Kök & Bar (☎ 174 73; Brunnsgatan 26; lunch from Skr65, dinner mains Skr85-150; 11am-2pm Mon & Tue, 11am-10pm Wed & Thu, noon-1am Fri & Sat) This restaurant, in a rustic 18th-century wooden courtyard, has a great outdoor patio and includes a cute pub. Lunch meals include pasta, panini, baked potatoes and salads. It's a popular evening spot, too, with a decent dinner menu.

Värdshuset Gruvcaféet (☎ 195 45; mains Skr80-150; 11am-5pm May-Aug) If you're out sightseeing at the mine, this charming cafe, in a wooden building (dating from 1810), does good cakes, sandwiches and hot dishes.

Getting There & Around

For transport to and from Västerås, see p255. Going to or from Uppsala, take regional bus 848 (1¼ hours, hourly Monday to Friday, nine buses Saturday and Sunday). Sala is on the main Stockholm–Mora rail line (via Uppsala), with daily trains roughly every two hours (Skr143, 1¾ hours).

Ask about bike hire at the tourist office.

ÄNGELSBERG
☎ 0223

Looking more like a collection of gingerbread houses than an industrial relic, **Engelsberg Bruk**, a Unesco World Heritage site in the tiny village of Ängelsberg, was one of the most important early-industrial ironworks in Europe. During the 17th and 18th centuries, its rare timber-clad **blast furnace** and **forge** (still in working order) were state-of-the-art technology, and a whole town sprang up around them. Today you can wander the perfectly preserved estate, made up of a mansion and park, workers' homes and industrial buildings. Guided tours (Skr50) run daily from mid-June to mid-August, and less frequently from May to mid-June and mid-August to mid-September; call ☎ 131 00 for details or pop into the tourist information hut near the parking area.

Nya Servering (☎ 300 18; ☷ 11am-8pm) is not far from Ängelsberg train station and serves fast food, coffee and simple sandwiches. There's a good view from here across to the island Barrön on Åmänningen lake, where the world's oldest-surviving **oil refinery** is located; it was opened in 1875 and closed in 1902.

Ängelsberg is around 60km northwest of Västerås, from where regional trains run every hour or two (Skr84, 45 minutes); from Ängelsberg train station it's a 1.5km walk north to the Engelsberg Bruk site. If you have your own wheels, it's a gorgeous drive from pretty much any direction.

NORA
☎ 0587 / pop 10,530

One of Sweden's most seductive old wooden towns, Nora sits snugly on the shores of a little lake, clearly confident in its ability to charm the pants off anyone. Slow your pace and succumb to its cobbled streets, steam trains, mellow boat rides and decadent ice cream.

At the train station by the lake, the **tourist office** (☎ 811 20; Stationshuset; ☷ 10am-6pm Mon-Sat, 10.30am-4pm Sun Jun & Aug; 9am-7pm Mon-Sat, 10.30am-4pm Sun Jul; 9am-noon & 1-4pm Mon-Fri Sep-May) books various guided tours (from June to August), including a **town walk** (adult/7-14yr Skr60/30) available in English. Alternatively, buy a brochure (Skr10) for self-guided walks.

Sights & Activities

Trips on the **museum railway** (return/one way Skr90/60; ☷ mid-Jun–mid-Aug) take you 10km southeast to Järle or 2.5km southwest to the excellent old mining village at **Pershyttan**, where there's a guided tour at 3pm daily from July to August, and 3pm Saturday and Sunday from May to June and September). The train operates to a complex timetable that also includes regular weekend trips from Midsummer to mid-August.

The manor house, **Göthlinska Gården**, just off the main square, was built in 1739 and is now a museum featuring furniture, decor and accoutrements from the 17th century onward; join a summer-only **guided tour** (adult/child Skr60/free; ☷ 1pm Jul-Aug).

Though it's technically a youngsters' activity, you don't need to be a child to appreciate the goofball storyteller who entertains groups on boat trips to **Alntorps island** (☎ 070-216 65 24; adult/child return Skr15/5; ☷ 10am-6pm Jul & Aug, 10am-6pm Sat & Sun mid-May–Jun & early Sep). Boats depart roughly every half hour from the little jetty near the STF hostel. A walk around the island takes about an hour, and there are swimming spots and a cafe.

Sleeping & Eating

our pick STF Nora Tåghem (☎ 146 76; info@norataghem .se; dm Skr120; ☷ May–mid-Sep) Outdoing its home town in the cuteness department, this hostel lets you sleep in the tiny but adorable antique bunks of 1930s railway carriages. All compartments have great views over the lake, and there's a cafe that does breakfast, and sandwiches and snacks in summer.

Trängbo Camping (☎ 123 61; www.trangbocamp ing.se; sites Skr135, cabins from Skr300; ☷ May-Sep) This small camp site is by the lake 1.5km north of Nora (there's a lakeshore path for walkers starting from the train station/tourist office). Amenities are fine if basic, but there's a swimming place and the beach volleyball is popular. Guests can hire boats and canoes (Skr30/175 per hour/day).

Lilla Hotellet (☎ 154 00; www.lillahotelletnora .com, in Swedish; Rådstugatan 14; s/d from Skr500/800)

CENTRAL SWEDEN

The charming 'Little Hotel' has a warm and homely feel, with large rooms (some with shared facilities) decorated in 1940s style. There's a good level of service, and the place exudes heart and soul.

Nora Stadshotell (☎ 31 14 35; www.norastadshotell.se; Rådstugugatan 21; s/d Skr850/1150, discounted to Skr690/990) You can't miss this elegant building, planted smack on the main square, although the white-furnitured rooms don't quite live up to the exterior's promise. However, there are good-value lunch deals (Skr85) at the restaurant, which can be eaten on the airy summer terrace, along with à la carte evening mains from Skr150 and a pub menu of meals around Skr70.

ourpick Nora Glass (☎ 123 32; Storgatan 11; ice creams Skr20-65; ☒ 10.30am-6.30pm May-Aug) Nora is renowned for its incredible ice cream, made here for more than 80 years. You never know what flavours will be available – as three or four different ones are churned out freshly each day – but you do know that they're worth queuing for.

Strandstugan (☎ 137 22; Storgatan 1; snacks Skr40-50; ☒ summer only) Down by the lake is this delightful red wooden house, set in a flower-filled garden, where you can get coffee, sandwiches, cakes and other home-baked goodies.

Self-caterers will find supermarkets on Prästgatan and near Nora Glass at the end of Storgatan.

Getting There & Around

Länstrafiken Örebro buses run every hour or two to Örebro (Skr52, 40 minutes) and other regional destinations.

Ask at the tourist office about bike rental.

NÄRKE

ÖREBRO

☎ 019 / pop 126,990

A substantial, culturally rich city, Örebro buzzes around its central feature, the huge and romantic castle surrounded by a moat filled with water lilies. The city originally grew as a product of the textile industry, but it's now decidedly a university town – students on bicycles fill the streets, and relaxed-looking people gather on restaurant patios and in parks. It's an ideal spot to indulge in standard holiday activities like nursing a beer in a terrace cafe or shopping unhurriedly along a cobbled street.

Information

The **tourist office** (☎ 21 21 21; www.orebro.se/turism; ☒ 10am-6pm Mon-Fri, 10am-2pm Sat & Sun Sep-May, 10am-6pm Mon-Fri, 10am-4pm Sat & Sun Jun-Aug) is inside the castle.

Banks can be found along Drottninggatan, south of the castle. The **library** (☎ 21 10 00; Näbbtorgsgatan) has internet access.

Sights & Activities

The magnificent **Slottet** (☎ 21 21 21; www.orebroslott.se; guided tours adult/6-15yr Skr65/25; ☒ Jun-Aug) now serves as the county governor's headquarters. While the castle was originally constructed in the late 13th century, most of what you see today is from 300 years later. The outside is far more dramatic than the interior (where the castle's conference business is all too evident). Parts of the interior are open for exhibits, but to really explore you'll need to take a tour; there's a historical one at 4.30pm (in Swedish or English, depending on numbers) or 'Secrets of the Vasa Fortress' at 2.30pm (in English), which is a slightly toe-curling piece of costumed clowning around. Book either one through the tourist office. The northwest tower holds a small **history exhibition** (admission free; ☒ 10am-5pm daily May-Aug, noon-4pm Tue-Sun Sep-Apr).

East of the castle, Örebro is blessed with the **Stadsträdgården**, an idyllic and kid-friendly park once voted Sweden's most beautiful. It stretches alongside Svartån (the Black River) and merges into the **Wadköping** museum village. The village contains craft workshops, a bakery and period buildings – including Kungsstugan (the King's Lodgings; a medieval house with 16th-century ceiling paintings) and Cajsa Warg's house (home of an 18th-century celebrity chef). You can wander round the village at any time, but the shops, cafe, displays and museums are open roughly 11am to 4pm (sometimes 5pm) Tuesday to Sunday year-round; there are guided tours at 1pm and 3pm June to August (Skr20).

The **Länsmuseum & Konsthall** (☎ 602 87 00; info@orebrolansmuseum.se; Engelbrektsgatan 3; admission free; ☒ 11am-5pm Tue-Sun, until 9pm Wed) has temporary exhibits, a permanent collection of artwork grouped by theme, and historical displays about the region (mostly in Swedish).

Many Swedish schools once had private natural history collections, but most were binned in the 1960s. Örebro's **Biologiska Museet** (☎ 21 65 04; Fredsgatan; adult/under 16yr Skr25/10; ☒ 11am-2pm Mon-Fri mid-Jun–mid-Aug), in Karolinska Skolan, is

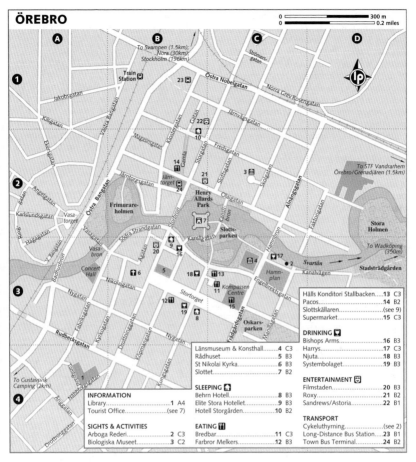

ÖREBRO

0 | 300 m
0 | 0.2 miles

INFORMATION
Library..**1** A4
Tourist Office.........................(see 7)

SIGHTS & ACTIVITIES
Arboga Rederi..............................**2** C3
Biologiska Museet........................**3** C2

Länsmuseum & Konsthall..........**4** C3
Rådhuset......................................**5** B3
St Nikolai Kyrka...........................**6** B3
Slottet..**7** B2

SLEEPING
Behrn Hotell.................................**8** B3
Elite Stora Hotellet......................**9** B3
Hotell Storgården.......................**10** B2

EATING
Bredbar..**11** C3
Farbror Melkers..........................**12** B3

Hälls Konditori Stallbacken.....**13** C3
Pacos..**14** B2
Slottskällaren.......................(see 9)
Supermarket..............................**15** C3

DRINKING
Bishops Arms..............................**16** B3
Harrys...**17** C3
Njuta..**18** B3
Systembolaget...........................**19** B3

ENTERTAINMENT
Filmstaden..................................**20** B3
Roxy..**21** B3
Sandrews/Astoria.......................**22** B1

TRANSPORT
Cykeluthyrning.....................(see 2)
Long-Distance Bus Station........**23** B1
Town Bus Terminal....................**24** B2

a survivor, and is worth a glance for its tier upon tier of stuffed birds.

The 13th-century church **St Nikolai Kyrka** (Storgatan 27; 10am-5pm Mon-Fri, 11am-3pm Sat) has some historical interest: it's where Jean Baptiste Bernadotte (Napoleon's marshal) was chosen to take the Swedish throne. Just opposite, on Drottninggatan, is **Rådhuset** (town hall); if you're around at the right time, stop to hear the **chimes** (12.05pm & 6.05pm year-round, plus 9pm Jun-Sep), when sculptures representing the city's past, present and future come wheeling out of a high arched window.

The first of Sweden's modern 'mushroom' water towers, **Svampen** (611 37 35; www.svampen .nu; Dalbygatan 4; admission free; 10am-6pm, until 9pm Wed) was built in 1958 and now functions as a lookout tower. There are good views of lake Hjälmaren and a cafe at the top (daily specials Skr95). Take bus 11.

Arboga Rederi (10 71 91; info@lagerbjelke.com) offers a number of cruises. Their evening trips on Hjälmaren (Skr250; 7pm Wednesday to Friday mid-May to September, plus Saturday in July) include an onboard shrimp supper.

Sleeping

Gustavsvik Camping (19 69 50; www.gustavsvik .se; Sommarrovägen; sites/cabins from Skr150/575; mid-Apr–early Nov;) This camping facility is 2km south of the city centre. It's huge and family-oriented, with pools, minigolf, a cafe, a gym, a restaurant and bike rental (Skr60 per day). Take bus 11.

CENTRAL SWEDEN

STF Vandrarhem Örebro/Grenadjären (☎ 31 02 40; www.grenadjaren.se; Kaptensgatan 1; dm/s/d without bathroom Skr160/330/360, with bathroom Skr220/370/460, flats from Skr550; P) This large hostel in a former military building 1.6km northeast of the train station has bright, sunny rooms, a spacious kitchen and good, modern facilities. There are also well-equipped flats for up to four people in the apartment complex next door. Bicycle hire is available and encouraged (Skr70/300 per day/week). Take bus 16 or 31.

Hotell Storgården (☎ 12 02 00; www.hotellstorgarden.se; Fredsgatan 11; s/d from Skr650/790, discounted to Skr500/595) It could do with a lick of paint, but this 1st-floor budget hotel is handily central. Rooms, with shuttered windows, are large and airy – all have TVs and most have private facilities.

Behrn Hotell (☎ 12 00 95; www.behrnhotell.se; Stortorget 12; s/d Skr1095/1395, discounted to Skr645/845; P ⊠ 💻) Excellently situated on the main square, the Behrn Hotell goes the extra mile, with homely rooms individually decorated, ranging from strictly business to farmhouse to edgy modern Scandinavian. Do it right and get a room with a balcony or a suite with old wooden beams, chandeliers and a Jacuzzi. There's also a spa, and a restaurant that serves dinner Tuesday to Friday.

Elite Stora Hotellet (☎ 15 69 00; info.orebro@elite.se; Drottninggatan 1; s/d from Skr1200/1500, discounted to Skr600/795; P 💻) This is the pick of the town's hotels. Many of the sumptuous, Scandinavian-luxury rooms have stunning views of the castle, and all offer the mod cons you'd expect from an upmarket chain. It also has a fine-dining restaurant, Slottskällaren (right).

Eating

Hälls Konditori Stallbacken (☎ 611 07 66; Engelbrektsgatan 12; light meals & snacks Skr35-65) One of two locations of this bakery-cafe (the other's in Järntorget), Hälls is a classic old-style *konditori*. Go for salads, quiche, sandwiches and teetering piles of creamy cakes and pastries.

Farbror Melkers (☎ 611 81 99; Stortorget 6; meals around Skr60) If you're the modern sort, head for this stylish place, with good light meals (sandwiches, baked potatoes), plus a large window so you can stare onto the square.

Bredbar (☎ 31 50 20; Kungsgatan 1; salads from Skr60; 🕙 10am-8pm Mon-Thu, 10am-7pm Fri, 11am-5pm Sat & Sun) In summer, Bredbar is an ultrapopular place for lunch, thanks to its outdoor courtyard seats. A constant dance of customers swirls in and out for ciabattas, huge bowls of salad and pasta, or hotplate dishes.

Pacos (☎ 10 10 46; Olaigatan 13A; lunch from Skr65, dinner mains Skr80-150; 🕙 11am-11pm Mon-Thu, 11am-midnight Fri & Sat, noon-5pm Sun) OK, maybe Tex-Mex isn't exactly what you expected to be eating in the middle of Sweden, but the fun decor and chirpy music at Pacos make for a nice change of pace, especially the lunch specials are good value, especially the pizza-pasta-salad buffet (Skr79).

Slottskällaren (☎ 15 69 60; Drottninggatan 1; mains Skr190-225; 🕙 lunch Mon-Fri Sep-Jun, dinner from 5pm Tue-Sat year-round) The restaurant at the equally posh Elite Stora Hotellet (left) offers fine dining and a good wine cellar in the atmospheric 14th-century vaults, or head out on the terrace where you can drink in the glorious castle views.

Cheap eat options such as pizza and kebabs abound. For self-caterers there's a supermarket in the Kompassen centre on Stortorget.

Drinking & Entertainment

Njuta (☎ 10 19 00; Kungsgatan 4; 🕙 11am-10pm Mon-Thu, 11am-1am Fri & Sat, noon-midnight Sun) Formerly the ubertrendy Babar, this sleek hang-out is still fashionable with young, hip students; the menu gets more attention these days and includes tapas and Asian fusion dishes (lunch from Skr69; dinner mains Skr130 to Skr170).

Bishops Arms (☎ 15 69 20; 🕙 until at least midnight) Whether or not you're convinced by the 'authentic English pub' schtick, the bar's outdoor drinking area, with super castle views, is a swinging spot on a summer evening. There are also pub meals available for under Skr100.

Harrys (☎ 10 89 89; Hamnplan; 🕙 from 5pm) Though it's part of a sort of blah chain, Harrys is in a good location down by the river. It's popular and has a comprehensive menu of pub meals (Skr80 to Skr180), live music on a Thursday, and a nightclub on Friday and Saturday.

For alcohol go to **Systembolaget** (Stortorget 10).

Cinemas in Örebro showing mainstream films include **Filmstaden** (☎ 611 84 00; www.sf.se; Drottninggatan 6), the **Roxy** (☎ 12 31 44; Olaigatan 19) and **Sandrews/Astoria** (☎ 10 44 24; www.sandrewmetronome.se; Storgatan 19). Tickets cost about Skr85.

Getting There & Away

Long-distance buses leave from opposite the train station and run almost everywhere in southern Sweden. **Swebus Express** (☎ 0200-21

82 18; www.swebusexpress.se) has connections to Norrköping, Karlstad and Oslo (Norway); Mariestad and Göteborg; Västerås and Uppsala; and Eskilstuna and Stockholm.

Train connections are also good. Direct SJ trains run to/from Stockholm (Skr209, two hours) every hour with some via Västerås (Skr98, one hour); and Göteborg (Skr256, 2¾ hours). Other trains run daily to Gävle (Skr286, three to four hours) and Borlänge (Skr182, 2¼ hours), where you can change for Falun and Mora.

Getting Around

Town buses leave from Järntorget and cost Skr20/10 per adult/child. **Cykeluthyrning** (☎ 21 19 09), at the Hamnplan boat terminal, rents bikes from May to September from Skr90 per day.

For a cab, call **Taxi Kurir** (☎ 12 30 30).

ASKERSUND & AROUND
☎ 0583 / pop 11,480

There's not much to Askersund beyond a cute harbour and cobblestone square (which doubles as a parking lot), but it's a nice place to relax or to stock up for a visit to the nearby Tiveden National Park. It's also one of Närke's oldest inhabited places; Vikings started a burial ground here around AD 900.

The **tourist office** (☎ 810 88; turistbyran@askersund .se; Lilla Bergsgatan 12A; ☒ 10am-7pm mid-Jun–mid-Aug, 10am-12.30pm & 1-4pm Mon-Fri mid-Aug–mid-Jun) is on the main square. Ask for information on walking and cycling routes around the lake, as well as canoe and kayak rental (Skr75/250 per hour/day). There's an **internet cafe** (☎ 141 21; Stöökagatan 10; per hr Skr20; ☒ 10am-9pm Mon-Fri, 10am-2pm Sat) in a computer shop off the main square.

Sights
TIVEDEN NATIONAL PARK

Carved by glaciers, this trolls' home and former highwaymen's haunt about 33km south of Askersund makes for wonderful wild walking. The park is noted for its ancient virgin forests, which are very rare in southern Sweden, and has lots of dramatic bare bedrock, extensive boulderfields and a scattering of lakes.

Several self-guided walks, including the 6km Trollkyrka ('troll church') trail, start from the **National Park visitors centre** (☒ 10am-4pm May-Sep, 11am-4pm Sat & Sun Apr & Oct) in the southeastern part of the park, 5km north of Rd 49 (turn-off at Bocksjö). You can pick up brochures and maps here, and there's a small shop.

A few kilometres north along Rd 49 is the turn-off to **Fagertärn**, a pretty lake that fills with blood-red water lilies in July. Legend says a fisherman called Fager traded his daughter to the fearsome water spirit Näcken in exchange for a good catch. On their wedding day, the daughter rowed out onto the lake alone and drove a knife into her heart, and the lilies have been stained red ever since.

The park is a bit out of the way, and there's no public transport, but if you have your own wheels it's worth a stop, especially for hikers.

The area is also good for **cycling** (Sverigeleden passes nearby), **canoeing** (☎ information 0584-47 40 83), **fishing**, **cross-country skiing** and **horse riding** (☎ information 070-654 91 59). The tourist office in Askersund can help make arrangements.

OTHER SIGHTS

Home to Prince Gustav, 'the Singing Prince', in the 1850s, **Stjernsund Manor** (☎ 100 04; admission by tour only, adult/under 12yr Skr50/free; ☒ 11am, noon, 2pm, 3pm & 4pm mid-May–Aug) contains one of the best-preserved 19th-century interiors in Sweden, with elegant furniture and gilt, glass and velvet fixtures and fittings. There's also an appealing cafe in the nearby estate-manager's old house. The manor is 5km south of Askersund; the best way to get there is via a day cruise on the M/S *Wettervik*.

In July and early August, the **M/S Wettervik** (☎ 0709-77 02 63; www.wettervik.se) makes various trips from the harbour, including an excursion to **Stjernsund Manor** (adult/12-15yr/under 12yr Skr160/80/ free), which departs Askersund at 1.15pm and returns at 4.30pm. The price includes boat tour, castle tour and light refreshments. Book at the tourist office or online.

Hembygdsgård (Hagavägen; admission free; ☒ noon-3pm Mon-Fri mid-Jun–mid-Aug) has a collection of old wooden farm buildings, and a children's zoo with rabbits, sheep and ducks.

Sleeping & Eating
Husabergsudde Camping (☎ 71 14 35; www.husaberg sudde.se; sites low/high season Skr140/160, cabins from Skr330; ☒ May-Aug) This is a large, lakeside camping ground with top amenities, 1.5km south of town on highway 50. You can rent canoes and rowing boats (Skr35/180 per hour/day) and bicycles (Skr15/75 per hour/day). There's no

public transport to the site, and the reception closes at 3pm on Sundays.

Tivedstorp (☎ 0584-47 20 90; www.tivedstorp.se; dm Skr160, s/d from Skr290/380; ☻ Mar-Oct) Newly added to the STF network, this complex has hostel accommodation in cute red grass-roofed cabins, plus a cafe (open 10am to 7pm daily June to August, and 10am to 4pm Saturday and Sunday May and September) and activity centre. It's about 3km north of the Tiveden National Park information centre; you'll need your own transport to get here.

ourpick Café Garvaregården (☎ 104 45; www.cafe garvaregarden.com; Sundsgatan; r summer Skr700, s/d winter Skr500/600) This desperately lovely B&B in the centre of town is a real find. It offers simple but charming accommodation in an 18th-century house, around a flower-filled courtyard. There's an inviting cafe downstairs (open 10am to 5pm; weekends only in winter).

Aspa Herrgård (☎ 502 10; www.aspaherrgard.se; s/d from Skr1330/1990, discounted to Skr795/1590; P 🖵) For a true treat, try this luxurious boutique hotel, based in a 17th-century manor house in a comely country setting (17km south of town on Rd 49). With its draped beds, flowery cushions and graceful Greek statues, it's the perfect place for a romantic weekend. There's also an exclusive restaurant (nonguests should reserve) and a tiny Bellman museum.

Café Tutingen (☎ 141 39; Storgatan; pastries Skr35, sandwiches Skr40-65) Built in 1784, this charming cafe across the square from the tourist office has low ceilings, warped old floorboards and mismatched but shapely seating, and does good sandwiches and excellent pastries, baked on the premises. Best of all is the garden, filled with roses and daisies, and containing the perfect balance of sun and shade.

Wärdshuset Sundsgården (☎ 100 88; Sundsbrogatan 1; lunch Skr65, meals Skr75-180) For dining, the pick of the pile is this fetching old inn. It has a riverside deck so you can sit in the sun and watch the boats sail by, and a selection of good-value light meals (baked potatoes, pasta, salads) for under Skr100.

Getting There & Around

Länstrafiken buses 708 and 841 each run four times on weekdays to Örebro (841 doesn't run in July). Bus 704 runs frequently to the mainline train station at Hallsberg.

Husabergsudde Camping does bike and boat hire (see p261).

VÄRMLAND

KARLSTAD
☎ 054 / pop 81,770

A pleasant and compact town centre wrapped in layers of perpetually snarled traffic, Karlstad makes itself useful as a base for travellers pursuing outdoor activities in Värmland. There are several sights worth seeing in town, and a large student population means it has a decent restaurant and bar scene.

Sharing the same building as the library at the edge of the town centre, the **tourist office** (☎ 29 84 00; www.karlstad.se; Bibliotekshuset, Västra Torggatan 26; ☻ 9am-7pm Mon-Fri, 10am-6pm Sat, 10am-3pm Sun mid-Jun–late Aug; 9am-6pm Mon-Thu, 9am-5pm Fri, 10am-3pm Sat late Aug–mid-Jun) has lots of info on both town and county (including fresh-air escapes in the region's forests) and its rivers and lakes. Internet access is available in the library. Banks and ATMs line Storgatan.

Sights & Activities

The award-winning and imaginative **Värmlands Museum** (☎ 14 31 00; www.varmlandsmuseum .se; adult/under 20yr Skr40/free; ☻ 10am-5pm) is on Sandgrundsudden near the library. Its sensory displays cover local history and culture from the Stone Age to current times, including music, the river, forests and textiles. Some components of the museum are open-air, activity-based displays about local industry and working life, including a log-driving museum and a mineral mine, just outside of town; pick up brochures at the museum or tourist office.

For green spaces and picnic spots, seek out **Mariebergsskogen** (☎ 29 69 90; www.mariebergsskogen .se; Stadspark; admission free; ☻ 7am-10pm), a leisure park/open-air museum/animal park in the southwestern part of town (about 1km from the centre). Take bus 1 or 31.

It's worth peeking into the 18th-century **domkyrka** (☻ 10am-7pm Mon-Fri, 10am-4pm Sat, 10am-6pm Sun Jun-Aug, 10am-4pm Sep-May), a soothing space with chandeliers and votive ships. You can visit the small and creepy **old town prison** (Karlbergsgatan 3; admission free; ☻ 10am-5pm) in the basement of Clarion Hotel Bilan (opposite), with original cells and prisoners' letters. On the eastern river branch, find **Gamla Stenbron**, Sweden's longest stone bridge at 168m.

From Tuesday to Saturday late June to mid-August, there are regular two-hour **boat cruises** (☎ 21 99 43; adult/child Skr80/50) on Vänern lake, leaving from the harbour behind the train station. A cheaper option (Tuesday to Sunday, summer only) is the 'boat bus' – city 'bus' 92 circles Karlstad on the water, and you can use your regular city bus ticket (Skr19).

Sleeping

Skutbergets Camping (☎ 53 51 20; www.camping.se/s10; sites low/high season Skr150/205, cabins from Skr575) This big friendly lakeside campground, 7km west of town off the E18 motorway, is part of a large sports recreation area, with beach volleyball, a driving range, minigolf, exercise tracks and a mountain-bike course. There are also sandy and rocky beaches nearby. Take bus 18.

Hotell Freden (☎ 21 65 82; www.fredenhotel.com; Fredsgatan 1; dm Skr175, s/d Skr510/610, discounted to Skr400/440) One of a number of central hotels opposite the train station, Freden is a simple budget hotel with comfortable single, double and dorm rooms with shared bathrooms.

STF Vandrarhem Karlstad (☎ 56 68 40; karlstad.vandrarhem@swipnet.se; dm Skr195, s/d from Skr320/540; **P**) The hostel, a newly renovated military building, is off the E18 at Kasernhöjden, 1km southwest of Karlstad's centre, and has good facilities. Take bus 100.

Clarion Hotel Bilan (☎ 10 03 00; cc.bilan@choice.se; Karlbergsgatan 3; s/d from Skr1320/1630, discounted to Skr990/1190; **P**) The town's old jail cells have been converted into large, bright and cleverly decorated rooms with exposed-wood ceiling beams and funky shapes – and a display in the basement letting you in on the building's history. Prices include an evening buffet.

Eating & Drinking

Make tracks to the main square, Stora Torget, and its surrounds for good eating and drinking options – most have outdoor summer seating.

Valfrids Krog (☎ 18 30 40; Östra Torggatan; snacks Skr45, mains Skr150-220) This is a relaxed spot for a drink or meal, with light, tapas-style snacks (such as mini-chorizo, chicken drumsticks and asparagus), and good Swedish and international mains catering to most tastes.

Kebab House (☎ 15 08 15; Västra Torggatan 9; meals from Skr50) Don't be fooled by the name – the Kebab House is a cut above regular fast-food places and serves good-value pizza, kebabs, pasta and salads. In summer, battle your way to one of the popular outdoor tables, in the middle of the busy pedestrianised street.

Källaren Munken (☎ 18 51 50; restaurang@munken.nu; Västra Torggatan 17; lunch Skr65, mains Skr195-255; closed Sun & mid-Jun–mid-Aug) Inspired gourmet meals, like pistachio-baked lamb with artichoke butter, are served up in this elegant but cosy 17th-century vaulted cellar.

The **Hemköp supermarket** (☎ 15 22 00; Fredsgatan 4) is inside Åhléns, and **Systembolaget** (☎ 15 56 00; Drottninggatan 26) is nearby.

The huge **Ankdammen** (☎ 18 11 10; Magasin 1, Inre Hamn; Jun-Aug), on a floating jetty at the harbour, is Sweden's largest open-air cafe and a very popular summer drinking (and eating) spot.

Getting There & Around

Karlstad is the major transport hub for western central Sweden. The long-distance bus terminal is at Drottninggatan 43, 600m west of the train station.

Swebus Express (☎ 0200-21 82 18; www.swebusexpress.se) has daily services on a number of routes, including Karlstad–Falun–Gävle, Karlstad–Göteborg, Stockholm–Örebro–Karlstad–Oslo and Karlstad–Mariestad–Jönköping.

Intercity trains to Stockholm (Skr365, 3¼ hours) run frequently. There are also several daily services to Göteborg (Sk209, three to four hours) and express services to Oslo (Skr272, three hours).

Värmlandstrafik (☎ 020-22 55 80) runs regional buses. Bus 302 travels to Sunne (Skr79, 1¼ hours, one to five daily) and Torsby (Skr96, two hours, one to three daily). Local trains also operate on this route – prices are the same as for buses.

Free bikes are available from the city's two **Solacykeln booths** Stora Torget (☎ 29 50 29; 7.30am-7pm Mon-Fri, 10am-3.30pm Sat May-Sep); outer harbour (9.30am-5.30pm Mon-Fri, 10am-3.30pm Sat Jun-Aug). All you need is a valid ID.

SUNNE

☎ 0565 / pop 13,600

Sunne is the largest ski resort in southern Sweden. In summer, it's a quiet spot with a number of cultural attractions in the vicinity. It also has a proud literary heritage, as the hometown of both Selma Lagerlöf and Göran Tunström.

The **tourist office** (☎ 164 00; www.sunne.info; Kolsnäsvägen 4; 9am-5pm Mon-Fri mid-Sep–mid-Jun; 9am-9.30pm daily mid-Jun–mid-Aug; 9am-5pm Mon-Fri, 9am-2pm Sat & Sun mid-Aug–mid-Sep) is at the camp site reception building (see p264) and offers internet access (Skr10 for 15 minutes). Banks, supermarkets and most other tourist facilities are on Storgatan.

Sights & Activities

The most interesting place in the area is the house at **Mårbacka** (☎ 310 27; www.marbacka.s.se; adult/child Skr70/35; ✆ 10am-4pm mid-May–Aug; until 5pm Jul; 11am-2pm Sat & Sun Sep; open for guided tours only 2pm Sat Oct-mid-May), where Swedish novelist Selma Lagerlöf (1858–1940) was born. She was the first woman to receive the Nobel Prize for Literature, and many of her tales are based in the local area. Admission is by guided tour only (45 minutes), which leave on the hour – a tour in English is given daily in July at 2pm. Mårbacka is 9km southeast of Sunne; enquire at the tourist office about buses.

Sundsbergs Gård (☎ 103 63; adult/child Skr40/free; ✆ noon-4pm Tue-Thu, Sat & Sun late Jun–mid-Aug), opposite the tourist office, featured in Lagerlöf's *Gösta Berling's Saga* and now contains a forestry museum, furniture and textiles collection, art exhibition, cafe and manor house.

Known as 'Ekeby' in *Gösta Berling's Saga*, **Rottneros Park** (☎ 602 95; iwww.rottnerospark.se; adult/4-15yr Skr100/50; ✆ 10am-4pm mid-May–mid-Sep, until 6pm mid-Jun–mid-Aug), 6km south of Sunne, soothes travel-weary adults with flower gardens, a tropical greenhouse and an arboretum. There's lots for kids, including the rope-swinging delights of Sweden's largest climbing forest. Motorheads should see the attached museum of vintage motorcycles. Rottneros has its own train station. Take bus 302.

The steamship **Freya af Fryken** (☎ 415 90; angbatfreja.nu; short tours adult/child Skr100/50, with fika Skr190/100) sank in 1896, but it was raised and lovingly restored in 1994. Now you can sail along the lakes north and south of Sunne; departures are several times weekly from July to mid-August. Lunch and dinner cruises are also on the program.

Ski Sunne (☎ 602 80; www.skisunne.se), the town's ski resort, has 10 different descents, a snowboarding area and a cross-country skiing stadium. In summer the resort becomes a mountain-bike park.

Sleeping & Eating

Sunne SweCamp Kolsnäs (☎ 164 00; kolsnas@sunne.se; sites low/high season Skr150/200, 2-bed cabins Skr365, 4-bed cabins Skr465; ✆) This is a large, family-oriented camping ground at the southern edge of town, with minigolf, a restaurant, a beach and assorted summer activities, plus bikes, boats and canoes for rent. There's a good restaurant attached.

STF Vandrarhem Sunne (☎ 107 88; www.sunnevandrarhem.se; Hembygdsvägen 7; dm Skr170) Part of a little homestead museum just north of town, this well-equipped hostel has beds in sunny wooden cabins. There's a futuristic kitchen, antique dining room and outside tables and chairs for alfresco meals. Breakfast is available (Skr50) and bikes can be rented (Skr50 per day).

Länsmansgården (☎ 140 10; info@lansman.com; Ulfsby; s/d from Skr895/1190) This historic 'sheriff's house' also features in Lagerlöf's *Gösta Berling's Saga*. It's a picturesque place for a fine lunch or restful evening in one of the romantic bedrooms, named after the books' characters. The restaurant (*dagens* lunch Skr85; evening buffet Skr150) specialises in Swedish cuisine, made using fresh local ingredients including pike, salmon, beef, reindeer and lamb. The mansion is 4km north of Sunne centre, by Rd 45 (toward Torsby).

ourpick Saffran & Vitlök (☎ 120 09; Storgatan 27; lunch Skr35-70; ✆ 11am-6pm Mon-Fri, 10am-3pm Sat) A haven of calm beside a busy intersection, this cafe serves giant bowls of hefty salads to take away or dine in, as well as excellent coffee, sandwiches, pastries and hot dishes. It lives up to the name (*vitlök* is garlic), so just follow your nose and you'll find it.

Strandcaféet (☎ 104 88; Strandpromenaden; mains Skr80-130; ✆ summer) In the park is this appealing beach cafe, with outdoor seating over the water and live music on some summer evenings.

Getting There & Around

Bus 302 runs to Torsby (Skr56, 45 minutes, one to three daily) and Karlstad (Skr79, 1¼ hours, one to five daily). Regional trains to Torsby and Karlstad (one to three daily) are faster than the bus, but cost the same.

TORSBY

☎ 0560 / pop 13,085

Sleepy Torsby, deep in the forests of Värmland, is only 38km from Norway. It's the home town of Sven-Göran Eriksson, the former manager of England's national football team. The area's history and sights are linked to emigrants from Finland, who settled in western parts of Sweden in the mid-16th century and built their own distinctive farms and villages in the forests.

The **tourist office** (☎ 105 50; www.torsby.se, in Swedish; Gräsmarksvägen 12; 9am-6pm Mon-Fri, 10am-3pm Sat & Sun mid-Jun–Aug; 9am-4pm Mon-Fri Sep–mid-Jun) is in the large Torsby Infocenter a couple of kilometres west of town, on Rd 45.

Sights

Torsby Finnkulturcentrum (☎ 162 93; www.finnkulturcentrum.com; Rd 45; admission Skr20; 11am-5pm mid-Jun–mid-Aug; 10am-4pm Tue-Fri, 10am-2pm Sat mid-Aug–mid-Jun) is just beyond the Infocenter towards town, and has displays describing the 17th-century Finnish settlement of the area, covering smoke-houses, hunting, music and witchcraft. There's also a terrace cafe, with seats overlooking a lulling lake.

Next door, the **Fordonsmuseum** (☎ 712 10; Gräsmarksvägen 8; adult/under 15yr Skr40/free; noon-5pm daily mid-May–Aug, weekdays only in Sep) will appeal to gearheads, with its collection of vintage cars, motorcycles and fire engines.

Hembygdsgården Kollsberg (☎ 718 61; Levgrensvägen 36; adult/child Skr20/free; guided tours Skr40; noon-5pm Jun-Aug), down beside Fryken lake, is a dinky homestead museum with several old houses, including a Finnish cabin. A cafe serves coffee and waffles (Skr40) and the traditional local dish *motti med fläsk* (oat porridge with pork, Skr80).

Known for its characteristic smokehouse, **Ritamäki Finngård** (☎ 501 76; admission free; 11am-6pm Jun-Aug), 25km west of Torsby and 5km from Lekvattnet, is one of the best-preserved Finnish homesteads in the area. It was probably built in the late 17th century and was inhabited until 1964, making it the last permanently inhabited Finnish homestead in Sweden. It's surrounded by a nature reserve. Bus 310 goes to Lekvattnet but there is no public transport to Ritamäki.

Activities

There are a number of summer activities and tours in the area, including fishing, canoeing, white-water rafting, rock climbing, mountain biking, and beaver and elk safaris. Contact the tourist office for information.

Finnskogleden is an easy and well-marked long-distance path that roughly follows the Norwegian border for 240km – from near Charlottenberg to Søre Osen (in Norway); it passes the old Finnish homestead Ritamäki Finngård (left). A guide book (available from tourist offices, Skr125) has text in Swedish only but all the topographical maps you'll

need. The best section, Øyermoen to Röjden (or vice versa), requires one or two overnight stops. Bus 311 runs from Torsby to near the border at Röjdåfors (twice daily on weekdays), and bus 310 runs to Vittjärn (twice daily on weekdays), 6km from the border on Rd 239.

You can catch boat trips on the Freya af Fryken (opposite) from Torsby.

Looking like something you might use to smash atoms, the world's longest ski tunnel (1.3km) is Torsby's **Fortum Ski Tunnel** (☎ 270 00; www.fortumskitunneltorsby.se; Vaserudsvägen 11, Valberget; adult/child rental packet Skr290/150, 3hr pass Skr180/120; noon-7pm Tue-Fri, 10am-5pm Sat & Sun Jun-Jul & Dec–mid-Jan; 9am-8pm Mon-Sat, 9am-5pm Sun Aug-Nov; 3-7pm Thu-Fri, 10am-3pm Sat & Sun mid-Jan–Feb). The arena also contains the world's only indoor biathlon shooting range.

Skiing outdoors is possible from December through early April, 20km north of Torsby at **Hovfjället** (☎ 313 00; www.hovfjallet.se). There are several ski lifts and a variety of runs. Day passes start at Skr245/200 per adult/child. Alpine **ski hire** (☎ 312 55) per day costs Skr230/190 per adult/child. The resort also offers dogsledding on weekends, plus other activities such as snowshoeing, mountain biking and wolf-viewing trips.

Sleeping & Eating

Torsby Camping (☎ 710 95; www.torsbycamping.se; Bredviken; sites Skr150, cabins from Skr350; May–mid-Sep) With its child-friendly beach, playgrounds and minigolf, this large, well-equipped lakeside campground (5km south of town along Rd 45) is a popular family spot. There's a variety of huts and chalets for rent, including a cool 'studio' cottage with a lake-facing picture window (Skr950).

Vägsjöfors Herrgård (☎ 313 30; info@vagsjoforsherrgard.com; dm Skr200, B&B per person from Skr350) Twenty kilometres north of Torsby, by a stunning lake, is this large manor house. B&B rooms are individually decorated so it's hard to say what you'll get, but the decor is genteel, and there are hostel beds too. Lunch is also served (Skr70, noon to 3pm).

Hotell Örnen (☎ 146 64; hotell-ornen@telia.com; Östmarksvägen 4; s/d Skr740/890, 1-/2-/3-/4-bed apt Skr890/1100/1310/1520) Cosy Örnen is a pretty lemon-coloured place set behind a white picket fence smack-bang in the town centre. Bright white Swedish-style rooms practically vibrate with wholesomeness and folky charm. There are also similar flatlets with private kitchens.

Heidruns Bok- & Bildcafé (☎ 421 26; www.heidruns .se; Fensbol 39; fika from Skr28; ☺ noon-5pm mid-Jun–Aug) In summer there's live music, poetry and other entertainment at this charming cafe, run by local poet Bengt Berg; Sundays are the big day for entertainment. You can feast on books and artwork, or on excellent home-baked cakes. Heidruns is 10km north of Torsby, at Fensbol on Rd 45.

Faktoriet (☎ 149 80; Båthamnen; meals around Skr80; ☺ 11.30am-10pm Mon-Thu, noon-2am Fri & Sat, noon-8pm Sun) By far the most appealing eatery in Torsby is down at the harbour (at the far end of Sjögatan). With a patio deck over the water, this is a cool restaurant with light meals (pasta, baked potatoes, fajitas) and a popular bar.

Getting There & Around

See p264 for travel information. There are a few buses that run north of Torsby, but generally on weekdays only.

DALARNA

FALUN

☎ 023 / pop 55,000

An unlikely combination of industrial and adorable, Falun is home to the region's most important copper mine and, as a consequence, the source of the deep-red paint that renders Swedish country houses so uniformly cute. It's the main city of Dalarna, putting it within easy striking distance of some of Sweden's best attractions, and the town itself is a pretty place to roam. Falu Kopparbergsgruva (Copper Mountain mine) is unique enough to appear on Unesco's World Heritage List. Even more compelling is the home of painter Carl Larsson, a work of art in itself and absolutely unmissable.

Information

The **tourist office** (☎ 830 50; www.visitfalun.se; Trotzgatan 10-12; ☺ 9am-7pm Mon-Fri, 9am-5pm Sat, 11am-4pm Sun mid-Jun–mid-Aug; 10am-6pm Mon-Fri, 10am-2pm Sat mid-Aug–mid-Jun) can help with visitor information.

Most services (banks, supermarkets etc) are on or just off Stora Torget. There's free internet access at the **public library** (☎ 833 35; Kristinegatan 15; ☺ 10am-7pm Mon-Thu, 10am-6pm Fri, 11am-3pm Sat).

Sights & Activities
FALU KOPPARBERGSGRUVA

Falun's copper mine was the world's most important by the 17th century and drove many of Sweden's international aspirations during that period. Today it's on Unesco's World Heritage List and makes for a fascinating day out.

Tradition says a goat called Kåre first drew attention to the copper reserves, when he rolled in the earth and pranced back to the village with red horns. The first historical mention is in a document from 1288, when the Bishop of Västerås bought shares in the company. As a by-product, the mine produced the red paint that became a characteristic of Swedish houses – Falu Red is still used today. The mine finally closed in 1992.

The **mining complex** (☎ 78 20 30; www.kopparber get.com; ☺ daily), to the west of town at the top end of Gruvgatan, contains various sights. Most dramatic is the **Stora Stöten** (Great Pit), a vast hole caused by a major mine collapse in the 17th century. By a miracle, the miners were on holiday that day and no one was harmed. There are lookouts around the crater edge, and numerous **mine buildings** including a 15m waterwheel and shaft-head machinery. Opening hours are complicated – check the website for details. Take bus 709.

The **mine museum** (adult/under 15yr Skr50/free; ☺ 10am-6pm) contains everything you could possibly want to know about the history, administration, engineering, geology and copper production of the mine, as well as the sad story of Fat Mats the miner (see boxed text, opposite).

You can go on a one-hour tour of the **disused mine** (adult/child Skr150/50) – bring warm clothing. Prices include museum entry and in high season you shouldn't have to wait more than an hour for an English tour. Between October and April, tours must be booked in advance.

If you're getting peckish, the pretty cafe **Gjuthuset** (☎ 132 12), serving coffee, sandwiches and cake, teeters on the edge of the Great Pit. Opposite the main reception is **Geschwornergården Värdshus** (☎ 78 26 16; lunch Skr75), which is a more stately affair and does excellent hot lunch specials.

CARL LARSSON-GÅRDEN

Whatever you do, don't miss **Carl Larsson-gården** (☎ 600 53; www.carllarsson.se; Sundborn; admission by guided tour only, adult/child Skr100/50; ☺ 10am-5pm May-Sep, 11am-Fri Oct-Apr), home of artist Carl Larsson and his wife, Karin, in the picturesque village of Sundborn. After the couple's deaths, their early-20th-century home was preserved in its entirety by their children, but it's no gloomy memorial. Lilla Hyttnäs is a work of art, full of brightness, humour and love.

Superb colour schemes and furniture fill the house: Carl's portraits of his wife and children are everywhere, and Karin's tapestries and embroidery reveal she was as skilled an artist as her husband. Even today, the modern styles throughout the house (especially the dining room) will inspire interior decorators, and the way the family lived, suffused in art and learning, will inspire practically everyone.

Tours (45 minutes) run hourly; call in advance for times of English tours (alternatively, follow a Swedish tour with an English handbook, Skr20).

If you like Larsson's work, you can see more at the **Carl Larssons Porträttsamling** (☎ 600 53; Kyrkvägen 18, Sundborn; adult/under 12yr Skr25/free, free with ticket stub from Carl Larsson-gården; ☺ 11am-5pm mid-Jun–mid-Aug), where there are 12 portraits of local worthies.

Bus 64 (Skr34) runs from Falun to Sundborn village (13km).

OTHER SIGHTS

The Unesco World Heritage listing actually encompasses a much larger area than just the Kopparbergsgruva. The free brochure *Discover the Falun World Heritage Site* places Falun in historical context and pinpoints all the smelteries, slag heaps and mine estates within a 10km radius of the town.

Dalarnas Museum (☎ 76 55 00; www.dalarnasmuseum.se; Stigaregatan 2-4; admission free; ☺ 10am-5pm Tue-Fri, noon-5pm Sat & Sun) is a super introduction to Swedish folk art, music and costumes. Selma Lagerlöf's study is preserved here, and there are ever-changing art and craft exhibitions.

A sea of baroque blue-and-gold hits you at **Kristine Kyrka** (☎ 545 70; Stora Torget; ☺ 10am-6pm Jun-Aug, 10am-4pm Sep-May), which shows off the riches brought to town by the 17th-century copper trade.

Falun's oldest building is **Stora Kopparbergs Kyrka** (☎ 546 00; Kyrkbacksvägen 8; ☺ 10am-6pm Mon-Fri, 10am-6pm Sat, 9am-6pm Sun), dating from the late

---

FAT MATS

At Falun's cathedral, Stora Kopparbergs Kyrka, look on the southern side of the churchyard for the grave of 'Fat Mats', aka Mats Israelsson. Mats was a miner whose well-preserved corpse was found in 1719, when the mine that had collapsed on him 50 years earlier was drained. Sulfates in the water had essentially pickled him. His corpse looked so healthy that when it was put on display, his former fiancée (by then an old woman) recognized him and fainted. He was displayed for about 30 years, until the preservative effects wore off and he was buried properly in 1749.

14th century, with brick vaulting and folk-art flowers running round the walls.

Hopptornen (☎ 835 61; ☺ 10am-6pm Sun-Thu, 10am-11pm Fri & Sat mid-May–mid-Aug), the tower and ski jump in the hills behind the town, has great views; you can either walk or take a lift to the top (Skr20).

Sleeping

Lugnets Camping & Stugby (☎ 835 63; lugnet-anl@falun.se; sites Skr190, simple 2-bed huts from Skr210, cabins Skr700; ☒) This long, thin camp site is 2km northeast of town, in the ski and sports area. Amenities are good: crazy golf, boules and a nearby open-air swimming pool will keep kids amused. Take bus 705 or 713.

Falu Fängelse Vandrarhem (☎ 79 55 75; info@falufangelse.se; Villavägen 17; dm/s Skr210/300; ☐) The SVIF hostel really feels like what it is – a former prison. Dorm beds are in cells, with heavy iron doors and thick walls, concrete floors, steel lockers for closets etc. The place is extremely friendly, though, and common areas are spacious and full of well-worn, den-like furniture. There's a back deck in summer. The shower and toilet facilities are somewhat limited, so it's worth asking for a room with bathroom if available.

Hotel Falun (☎ 291 80; Trotzgatan 16; s/d with shared shower Skr520/620, with private shower Skr620/720; P ☐) There are some good hotel choices near the tourist office, including this place, which has comfortable modern rooms (cheaper rooms have private toilet and shared shower).

Scandic Hotel Lugnet Falun (☎ 669 22 00; falun@scandic-hotels.com; Svärdsjögatan 51; s/d from Skr1220/1440, discounted to Skr640/840; P ☐ ☒) This large, modern building stands out a mile with its ski-jump design. It has heaps of facilities, including a restaurant, a bar and even a bowling hall in the basement! The hotel is just east of the centre on Rd 80, close to Lugnet.

Eating & Drinking

Bryggcaféet (☎ 233 30; Fisktorget; fika Skr35; ☒ 10am-6pm) This fab cafe is in a dinky little building that was once the fire station. It serves good coffee and cakes, and has a large deck by the river.

ourpick Kopparhattan Café & Restaurang (☎ 191 69; Stigaregatan 2-4; lunch buffet Skr80, mains Skr75-150) An excellent choice is this funky, arty cafe-restaurant, attached to Dalarnas Museum. Choose from sandwiches, soup or a good vegetarian buffet for lunch; and light veggie, fish and meat evening mains. There's an outside terrace overlooking the river, and live music on Friday nights in summer.

Rådhus Källaren (☎ 254 00; Stora Torget; dagens lunch Skr90-110, mains Skr255-275; ☒ lunch & dinner Mon-Sat) The town hall's atmospheric 17th-century cellars are another good spot for upmarket dining – better yet is the garden upstairs, open for dining in summer. Dishes are a Swedish-world fusion, focusing on meaty mains. The bar next door is the place to be seen, and stays open until 2am on Friday and Saturday.

Banken Bar & Brasserie (☎ 71 19 11; Åsgatan 41; basic mains Skr110-145, à la carte mains Skr130-200; ☒ lunch & dinner Mon-Sat, until 1am Fri & Sat) Based in a former bank, classy Banken has a splendid interior and matching service. The menu includes a *gott & enkelt* ('good and simple') category – featuring the likes of burgers and pasta – plus more upmarket 'world cuisine' options.

As ever, kebab shops and pizza joints abound. For self-caterers, there's a centrally located **ICA supermarket** (Falugatan 1) as well as a **Systembolaget** (Åsgatan 19).

Getting There & Around

Falun isn't on the main train lines – change at Borlänge when coming from Stockholm or Mora – but there are direct trains to and from Gävle (Skr129, 1¼ hours, roughly every two hours), or regional buses (Skr97, two hours) equally often.

Swebus Express (☎ 0200-21 82 18; www.swebus press.se) has buses on the Göteborg–Karlstad–

Falun–Gävle route, and connections to buses on the Stockholm–Borlänge–Mora route.

Regional transport is run by **Dalatrafik** (☎ 0771-95 95 95; www.dalatrafik.se, in Swedish), which covers all corners of the county of Dalarna. Tickets cost Skr20 for trips within a zone, and Skr15 extra for each new zone. A 31-day *länskort* (county pass) costs Skr1000 and allows you to travel throughout the county; cards in smaller increments are also available. Regional bus 70 goes approximately hourly to Rättvik (Skr50, one hour) and Mora (Skr80, 1¾ hours).

LAKE SILJAN REGION

Typically, when you ask Swedes where in Sweden they would most like to go on holiday, they get melty-eyed and talk about Lake Siljan. It's understandable – the area combines lush green landscapes, outdoor activities, a rich tradition of arts and crafts, and some of the prettiest villages in the country.

It's the picture of tranquillity now, but 360 million years ago, Lake Siljan felt Europe's largest meteoric impact. Crashing through the Earth's atmosphere, the giant lump of rock hit with the force of 500 million atomic bombs, obliterating all life and creating a 75km ring-shaped crater.

The area is a very popular summer destination, with numerous outdoor festivals and attractions. Maps of **Siljansleden**, an excellent network of walking and cycling paths extending for more than 300km around Lake Siljan, are available from tourist offices for Skr20. Another way to enjoy the lake is by boat: in summer, **M/S Gustaf Wasa** (☎ 070-542 10 25; www .wasanet.nu; Skr80-275) runs a complex range of lunch, dinner and sightseeing cruises from the towns of Mora, Rättvik and Leksand. Ask at any tourist office or go online for a schedule.

The big midsummer festival **Musik vid Siljan** (www.musikvidsiljan.se) is held in venues around the lakeside towns in early July; look for schedules at tourist offices.

Check out the Siljan area website (www .siljan.se) for lots of good information.

Leksand

☎ 0247 / pop 15,500

Leksand's main claim to fame is its **Midsummer Festival**, the most popular in Sweden, in which around 20,000 spectators fill the bowl-shaped green park on the first Friday evening after

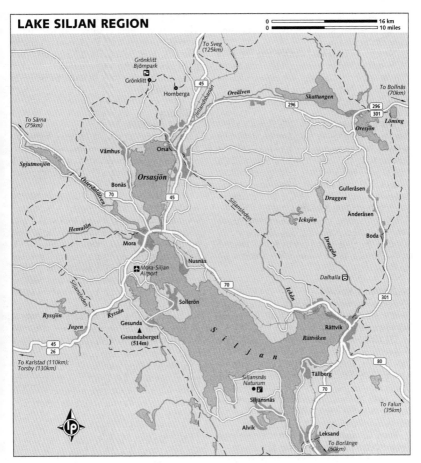

LAKE SILJAN REGION

21 June to sing songs and watch costumed dancers circle the maypole.

The **tourist office** (☎ 79 61 30; leksand@siljan.se; Norsgatan 40; 9am-7pm Mon-Fri, 10am-5pm Sat & Sun mid-Jun–mid-Aug; 10am-5pm Mon-Fri mid-Aug–mid-Jun) is on the main drag through town; banks and supermarkets line Sparbankgatan. The **library** (☎ 802 45; Kulturhuset, Kyrkallén), across the street from the tourist office, has internet access (including wireless), regional information and art exhibitions.

SIGHTS & ACTIVITIES
Built by Axel Munthe (1857–1949), who served as the Swedish royal physician and wrote the best-selling memoir *The Story of San Michele*, **Munthe's Hildasholm** (☎ 100 62; www.hildasholm.org; Klockaregatan 5; admission by guided tour only, adult/12-16yr Skr90/30; 11am-5pm Mon-Sat, 1-5pm Sun Jun–mid-Sep) is a sumptuously decorated National Romantic-style mansion, set in beautiful gardens by the lake. Munthe built it for his second wife, an English aristocrat, in 1910–11; Munthe himself rarely visited the mansion as he spent most of his time attending to the Swedish Queen Victoria on the island of Capri. Tours run on the hour; phone ahead for tours in English.

Leksands Kyrka (☎ 807 00; Kyrkallén; 10am-6pm Jun–mid-Aug, 9.30am-3.30pm mid-Aug–Jun), with its distinctive onion dome, dates from the early 13th century, but has been extensively renovated and enlarged. The church contains extravagant baroque furnishings; check the posted schedules for guided tours and evening concerts in summer.

Nearby is **Leksands Konstmuseum** (☎ 79 79 74; www.leksandskonstmuseum.se; Kyrkallén 8; adult/under 18yr Skr50/free; ☖ 11am-4pm May-Aug), which is fairly small but hosts strong collections of work by both young and well-established regional artists.

Siljansnäs Naturum (☎ 221 05; Siljansnäs; admission free; ☖ 10am-6pm May-Aug; 9am-5pm Wed, Fri, Sat & Sun Sep-Apr), 14km northwest of Leksand, has information about the meteor and local flora and fauna, with a slightly moth-eaten collection of 50 stuffed animals. Two-hour English-language guided tours of the nature reserve take place at 11am Mondays and Fridays. The highlight is the 22m-high **viewing tower**, from where you get stunning 360-degree views around the lake. Bus 84 runs from Leksand to Siljansnäs, from where it's a 300m walk to Naturum.

SLEEPING & EATING

Quick eats surround the main square, where you'll also find branches of all the main supermarket chains.

STF Vandrarhem Leksand (☎ 152 50; info@vandrarhemleksand.se; Parkgården, Källberet; dm Skr150; ☐) It's a little out of the way (2km south of town), but this is a lovely wee hostel and Dalarna's oldest, with ultracute wooden huts built around a flowery courtyard. Bikes are available for rent (Skr70 per day). Reserve early, as it's popular with groups.

Hotell Leksand (☎ 145 70; www.hotelleksand.com; Leksandsvägen 7; s/d from Skr800/900; ☐) This is a small, modern and conveniently situated hotel in the heart of town. The rooms are mostly nondescript, but the people here are friendly and it's not a bad place to lay your head. Phone ahead, as the reception keeps short hours.

Siljans Konditori (☎ 150 70; Sparbanksgatan 5; sandwiches Skr35-65, buffet Skr60-80; ☖ 9am-7pm Mon-Fri, 11am-5pm Sat & Sun) This large and inviting bakery-cafe serves good sandwiches on its own fresh bread from a busy corner of Stora Torget.

Bygatan 16 (☎ 155 05; Bygatan 16; lunch Skr90, mains Skr125-200; ☖ Mon-Sat) Bygatan is a smart place with a menu of light and main meals, including creative pasta, beef and fish dishes. The restaurant is closely linked to the local hockey team, and has a special 'hockey menu' during the playing season.

GETTING THERE & AROUND

There are a couple of direct intercity trains every day running from Stockholm to Leksand (Skr240, three hours). Bus 58 regularly connects Leksand with Tällberg (Skr35, 20 minutes), and bus 258 goes to Rättvik (Skr50, 20 to 50 minutes).

Tällberg
☎ 0247 / pop 200

The main reason to visit Tällberg is that it's adorable: a whole village of precious little gingerbread houses, mostly painted Falu Red, sprinkled over a green hillside sloping toward a lake.

It knows it's cute, too – the town of 200 residents supports eight upmarket hotels and several chic boutiques. It's a tourist hot spot and an appealing place for lunch and a walk, but unless you're after a romantic countryside escape, it's perhaps better to stay in Rättvik or Leksand and visit for the afternoon.

The town has its own website (www.infotallberg.nu). It's in Swedish, but has links to all the hotels.

Charm personified, **Klockargården** (☎ 502 60; www.klockargarden.com; Siljansvägen 6; s/d/ste from Skr635/1270/2070; ☐) is a collection of old timber buildings set around a grassy green courtyard, plus a newer wing built in 2004. Each unique room is decorated in a tasteful country style, all the suites have Jacuzzis, and several rooms have balconies. Frequent summer craft fairs and folk concerts take place on the grounds. The restaurant has a daily lunch buffet for around Skr100; à la carte mains cost Skr145 to Skr245. Weekend and holiday packages are available.

Tällberg's oldest hotel, **Åkerblads** (☎ 508 00; www.akerblads.se; Sjögattu 2; s/d from Skr850/1430, discounted to Skr745/995; ☐ ☖) is an elegant affair, arranged inside a beautiful collection of buildings dating from the 15th century onwards. There's a relaxation suite and a whole menu of spa treatments, garden tennis and ping-pong for entertainment, and a restaurant that's considered one of the region's finest, with a lunch buffet and à la carte main courses nightly (*dagens* lunch Skr125, fish buffet Skr165 and mains Skr195 to Skr345).

Bus 58 between Rättvik and Leksand stops in the village regularly (two to six times daily). Tällberg is also on the train line that travels around Lake Siljan; the train station is about 2km below the village proper.

THE DALA HORSE

What do Bill Clinton, Elvis Presley and Bob Hope have in common? They've all received a Swedish Dalahäst as a gift. These iconic, carved wooden horses, painted in bright colours and decorated with folk-art flowers, represent to many people the essence of Sweden.

The first written reference to a Dalahäst comes from the 17th century, when the bishop of Västerås denounced such horrors as 'decks of cards, dice, flutes, dolls, wooden horses, lovers' ballads, impudent paintings', but it's quite likely they were being carved much earlier. Sitting by the fireside and whittling wood was a common pastime, and the horse was a natural subject – a workmate, friend and symbol of strength. The painted form that is so common today appeared at the World Exhibition in New York in 1939 and has been a favourite souvenir for travellers to Sweden ever since.

The best-known Dala horses come from Nusnäs, about10km southeast of Mora. The two biggest workshops are **Nils Olsson Hemslöjd** (☎ 372 00; www.nohemslojd.se; ☺ 8am-6pm Mon-Fri, 9am-5pm Sat & Sun mid-Jun–mid-Aug; 8am-5pm Mon-Fri, 10am-2pm Sat mid-Aug–mid-Jun) and **Grannas A Olsson Hemslöjd** (☎ 372 50; www.grannas.com; ☺ 9am-6pm Mon-Fri, 9am-4pm Sat & Sun mid-Jun–mid-Aug; 9am-4pm Mon-Fri, 10am-1pm Sat mid-Aug–mid-Jun), where you can watch the carving and painting, then buy up big at the souvenir outlets. Wooden horse sizes stretch from 3cm high (Skr70) to 50cm high (Skr3338).

Public transport to Nusnäs isn't great: there are three buses from Mora, running Monday to Friday only.

Rättvik

☎ 0248 / pop 10,900

Rättvik is a totally unpretentious town in an area that sometimes borders on the precious. Nonetheess, it's a very pretty place, stretching up a hillside and along the shores of Lake Siljan. There are things to do year-round, for kids and adults alike, whether you like skiing, cycling, hiking or lolling on beaches.

A full program of special events in summer includes a **folklore festival** (www.folklore.se) in late July and **Classic Car Week** (www.classiccarweek.com, in Swedish) in late July or early August.

The **tourist office** (☎ 79 72 10; rattvik@siljan .se; Riksvägen 40; ☺ 10am-7pm Mon-Fri, 9am-5pm Sat & Sun mid-Jun–mid-Aug; 10am-5pm Mon-Fri mid-Aug–mid-Jun) is at the train station. Rättvik's facilities include banks and supermarkets on Storgatan and a **library** (☎ 701 95; Storgatan 2) with internet access.

SIGHTS & ACTIVITIES

The 725m-long **SommarRodel** (☎ 513 00; info@ rattviksbacken.nu; 1/3 rides Skr50/125; ☺ 11am-6pm or 7pm Jun-Aug, closed when raining), a sort of snow-less bobsled chute, is lots of fun. You hurtle downhill at 56km/h, which feels fairly fast so close to the ground.

An enterprising 17-year-old built **Vidablick Utsiktstorn** (adult/child Skr30/5; ☺ 10am-7pm mid-Jun–mid-Aug), a viewing tower about 5km southeast of town, from where there are great panoramas of the lake, a good cafe and a summer-only youth hostel (dorm beds Skr125 to Skr150). On your way up the tower, check out the miniature reconstruction of the village at the turn of the century, done by a local carpenter in the 1930s.

Scandinavia's longest wooden pier, the impressive 628m **Långbryggan**, runs out into the lake from just behind the train station. The 13th-century church has 87 well-preserved **church stables**, the oldest dating from 1470. The pseudo-rune **memorial** beside the church commemorates the 1520s uprising of Gustav Vasa's band against the Danes – the rebellion that created modern Sweden.

You can get your open-air-museum fix at **Hembygdsgård Gammelgård** (☎ 514 45; admission free; ☺ 11am-5pm mid-Jun–mid-Aug), 500m north of the church – it's a 1909 collection of buildings that were moved here during the '20s from villages around Rättvik parish. There's a good collection of furniture painted in the local style. The grounds are always open for exploring, but the cafe and building interiors are open summer-only.

Central **Kulturhuset** (☎ 701 95; Storgatan 2; admission free; ☺ 11am-7pm Mon-Thu, 11am-3pm Fri, 11am-2pm Sat, 1-5pm Sun) houses the public library, art exhibitions and a display describing the Siljan meteor impact. The helpful staff go above and beyond to answer any questions you might have about the area.

The easy **ski slopes** (www.rattviksbacken.nu; day pass adult/child Skr215/170) are excellent; there are four lifts.

Dalhalla (☎ 79 79 50; www.dalhalla.se), an old limestone quarry 7km north of Rättvik, is used as an open-air theatre and concert venue in summer; the acoustics are incredible and the setting is stunning.

SLEEPING

Summer accommodation in Rättvik disappears fast, so it's worth booking ahead – even for camp sites. Central places to stay are few and far between.

Rättviksparken (☎ 561 10; rattviksparken@rattviks -parken.fh.se; Furudalsvägen 1; campsites low/high season Skr130/170, cabins from Skr425) A large, bustling camp site by the river off Centralgatan (1km from the train station), behind the STF hostel, this area includes a *fäbod* (summer livestock farm) and is built to echo the traditional, rustic look of old farmhouse buildings. Siljansleden (p268) passes through the site.

Siljansbadet Camping (☎ 516 91; www.siljansbadet .com; sites low/high season Skr130/200, 4-bed cabins from Skr450; ☺ May-Oct) Near the train station, this quiet, woodsy camp site is on the lake shore and boasts its own Blue Flag beach.

ourpick **STF Vandrarhem** (☎ 105 66; Centralgatan; dm Skr150; ☺ reception 8-10am & 5-6pm; P ☐) A comfortable hostel with dorm rooms in three wooden buildings clustered round a grassy courtyard, this quiet place has good facilities including a nice kitchen with a large dining/ TV room in the main building, and picnic tables on the lawn for alfresco dining.

Stiftsgården Rättvik (☎ 510 20; www.stiftsgarden .org; Kyrkvägen 2; s with shared bathroom Skr380, s with/without shower Skr640/525, d with/without shower Skr1020/760) This picturesque, church-run place is by the lake, away from the hustle and bustle of town but within easy walking distance and near footpaths and outdoor activities. Rooms are simple but pleasant; breakfast is included, and lunch (Skr80) and dinner (Skr95) are available. Canoes and cycles can be hired.

Hotell Vidablick (☎ 302 50; vidablick@hantverksbyn .se; Faluvägen; s/d from Skr650/1050, discounted to Skr600/850) Vidablick is an excellent choice, with rustic hotel accommodation in grass-roofed huts, some with lake views. The hotel is behind the OKQ8 petrol station on the road to Leksand, about 3km south of town. The attached restaurant (open May to August; *dagens* lunch Skr78; coffee and cakes Skr32) has free wi-fi, a

great view from its outdoor tables, and dance nights on Thursday.

Jöns-Andersgården (☎ 130 15; www.jons-andersgar den.se; Bygatan 4; d with shared/private bathroom Skr750/1150, ste from Skr1300; ☺ mid-Apr–mid-Oct; P) Beds here are in traditional wooden huts dating from the 15th century, way up on the hill with superb views. Rooms are all in tip-top shape with modern interiors, and there's one suite that has its own sauna. If you don't have transport, the owners will pick you up from the train station by arrangement, and breakfast is included in the price. Take bus 74.

EATING & DRINKING

Fricks Konditori (☎ 133 36; Stora Torget; fika Skr26, sandwiches from Skr35) An old-fashioned bakery-cafe with a casual, neighbourhoody feel, Fricks offers sandwiches, quiches and salads but specialises in decadent cakes and pastries. It's opposite the train station and is a local gossip hang-out.

Restaurang Anna (☎ 126 81; Vasagatan 3; dishes Skr75-100; ☺ noon-9pm Tue-Sun, until 10pm Fri & Sat) Now a Thai and Chinese restaurant, Anna has a nice outdoor patio next to its cute red building. It offers fixed-price menus (Skr100 to Skr110) and takeaway as well.

Jöns-Andersgården (☎ 130 15; www.jons-anders garden.se; Bygatan 4; mains Skr135-295; ☺ Thu-Sun May-Sep) If you can stir your stumps and make it up the hill, you'll find this rather sweet restaurant tucked at the top. Dishes such as lemony chicken with gremolata potatoes, and tagliatelle with truffle oil, bring a taste of Italy to this very Swedish establishment. Take bus 74.

There's a **Systembolaget** (Storgatan), with supermarkets on the same street.

GETTING THERE & AROUND

Buses depart from outside the train station. Dalatrafik's bus 70 runs regularly between Falun, Rättvik and Mora. A couple of direct intercity trains per day from Stockholm (Skr263, 3½ hours) stop at Rättvik (otherwise you have to change at Borlänge). There are local trains every couple of hours between Rättvik and Mora (Skr53, 25 minutes).

Mora
☎ 0250 / pop 20,100
Mora is spliced with Sweden's historic soul. Legend has it that in 1520 Gustav Vasa arrived here in a last-ditch attempt to start a rebellion

against the Danish regime. The people of Mora weren't interested, and Gustav was forced to put on his skis and flee for the border. After he left, the town reconsidered and two yeomen, Engelbrekt and Lars, volunteered to follow Gustav's tracks, finally overtaking him in Sälen and changing Swedish history.

Today the world's biggest cross-country ski race, **Vasaloppet**, which ends in Mora, commemorates this epic chase, and involves 90km of gruelling Nordic skiing. Around 15,000 people take part in the first Sunday in March. In summer, you can walk the route on the 90km **Vasaloppsleden**.

The **tourist office** (☎ 59 20 20; mora@siljan.se; ⊙ 10am-5pm Mon-Fri, 10am-2pm Sat year-round, closed Mon mid-Sep–mid-Nov) is at the train station. Banks, supermarkets and other facilities line Kyrkogatan. The **library** (☎ 267 79; Köpmangatan) has free internet access.

SIGHTS & ACTIVITIES

Even if you have no interest in skiing, you may be pleasantly surprised by the excellent **Vasaloppsmuseet** (☎ 392 25; www.vasaloppet.se; Vasagatan; adult/child Skr30/10; ⊙ 10am-5pm mid-Jun–mid-Sep, 10am-5pm Mon-Fri mid-Sep–mid-Jun), which really communicates the passion behind the world's largest cross-country skiing event. There's some fantastic crackly black-and-white film of the first race, a display about nine-times winner and hardy old boy Nils 'Mora-Nisse' Karlsson, and an exhibit of prizes. Outside the museum is the race **finish line**, a favourite place for holiday snaps.

Zornmuseet (☎ 59 23 10; www.zorn.se; Vasagatan 36; adult/up to 15yr Skr50/free; ⊙ 9am-5pm Mon-Sat, 11am-5pm Sun mid-May–mid-Sep; noon-5pm Mon-Sat, 1-5pm Sun mid-Sep–mid-May) displays many of the best-loved portraits and characteristic nudes of the Mora painter Anders Zorn (1860–1920), one of Sweden's most renowned artists. His naturalistic depictions of Swedish life and the countryside are on display, as well as the Zorn family silver collection.

Next door, the Zorn family house **Zorngården** (☎ 59 23 10; Vasagatan 36; admission by guided tour adult/7-15yr Skr60/20; ⊙ 10am-4pm Mon-Sat, 11am-4pm Sun mid-May–mid-Sep; noon-3pm Mon-Sat, 1-4pm Sun mid-Sep–mid-May) is an excellent example of a wealthy artist's house and reflects Zorn's National Romantic aspirations (check out the Viking-influenced hall and entryway). Access to the house is by guided tour (every 15 minutes in summer; phone ahead for English tours).

SLEEPING

Moraparken (☎ 276 00; moraparken@mora.se; tent & car Skr160, 2-/4-bed cabins from Skr270/400, hotel s/d Skr995/1295, discounted to Skr730/830; P ⬜) This camp site and hotel are combined in a great waterside spot, 400m northwest of the church, and both have solid facilities. The hotel rooms (all ground floor) have wooden floors and a sleek modern look. The Vasaloppet track and Siljansleden pass through the grounds, and you can hire canoes to splash about on the pond.

our pick **Målkull Ann's Restaurang, B&B & Vandrarhem** (☎ 381 96; www.maalkullann.se; Vasagatan 19; hostel dm Skr170, s/d Skr320/500, B&B s/d Skr600/960, pensionat r from Skr720; P ⬜) Housed in several buildings near the Vasaloppsmuseet, this comfortable place has a good range of options. There are cosy B&B rooms with cheerful countrified decor (tariffs include breakfast) and there's the STF youth hostel (at Fredsgatan 6) for just the basics. There's also one suite with a view over the finish line of the Vasaloppet path (Skr960). Guests can book time in the sauna; there are bikes for hire (Skr70 per day); and there's a computer with internet access (Skr20). Reservations are recommended.

Mora Hotell & Spa (☎ 59 26 50; www.morahotell .se; Strandgatan 12; s/d from Skr1170/1350, discounted to Skr748/948; P ⬜ 🏊) There's been a hotel here since 1830, although the current version is as modern as it gets, with all the facilities you'd expect from a big chain – plus personality. Rooms combine clean lines, wooden floors and earthy tones with bright folk-art accents. Head to the spa for steam rooms, Jacuzzis, massage and body treatments.

EATING

Mora Kaffestuga (☎ 100 82; Kyrkogatan 8; meals Skr35-75) For a quick lunch – your basic salads, quiches and sandwiches – this coffeeshop has a restful grassy garden out back.

Helmers Konditori (☎ 100 11; Kyrkogatan 10; meals Skr35-75) Next door is another good cafe-bakery, with homemade bread, sandwiches and cakes.

Claras Restaurang (☎ 158 98; Vasagatan 38; lunch Skr75, mains Skr110-190) In the picturesque old town, near the Zorn museum, you'll find convivial Claras, with excellent service and a menu of filling staples. Try the wonderful dessert of deep-fried camembert with warm cloudberries.

Målkull Ann's (☎ 381 90; Vasagatan; mains Skr145-185; ⓨ 11am-8pm Sun-Thu, 11am-10pm Fri & Sat) Run by the same folks who keep the hostel and Målkull Ann's B&B, this cosy restaurant and cafe occupies a cute wooden 19th-century building opposite Vasaloppsmuseet.

GETTING THERE & AROUND

The Mora-Siljan airport is 6km southwest of town on the Malung road. **Nextjet** (www .nextjet.se) has two to three flights to Stockholm Arlanda on weekdays and one on Sunday (50 minutes).

All Dalatrafik buses use the bus station at Moragatan 23. Bus 70 runs to Rättvik and Falun, and buses 103, 104, 105 and 245 run to Orsa. Once or twice daily, bus 170 goes to Älvdalen, Särna, Idre and Grövelsjön, near the Norwegian border.

Mora is the terminus for **SJ** (☎ 0771-75 75 75; www.sj.se) trains and the southern terminus of Inlandsbanan (Inland Railway), which runs north to Gällivare (mid-June to mid-August). The main train station is about 1km east of town. The more central Mora Strand is a platform station in town, but not all trains stop there, so check the timetable. When travelling to Östersund, you can choose between Inlandsbanan (Skr395, 6¼ hours, one daily, mid-June to August only) or bus 45 (Skr250, 5¼ hours, four daily). For more information on the Inlandsbanan, see p280.

Hire a car in Mora to see the best of the region, especially northwest Dalarna; for smaller budget models try **OKQ8** (☎ 139 58; Vasagatan 1). You can rent bikes at **Intersport** (☎ 59 39 39; Kyrkogatan 7).

Orsa & Grönklitt
☎ 0250 / pop 7,030

Orsa, 16km north of Mora, is a natural stopping point on the way to the area's biggest attraction, the humongous bear park further north in Grönklitt.

There's a **tourist office** (☎ 55 25 50; orsa@siljan .se; Dalagatan 1; ⓨ 10am-4pm Mon-Fri, 10am-2pm Sat mid-Jun–mid-Aug; 10am-5pm Mon-Fri mid-Aug–mid-Jun) in Orsa, with a bank about three blocks down Dalagatan and a grocery and Systembolaget both nearby.

Fat-bottomed roly-poly bear cubs are the star attraction at **Grönklitt Björnpark** (☎ 462 00; www.orsagronklitt.se; family/adult/6-15yr Skr380/140/100; ⓨ 10am-6pm mid-Jun–Aug, 10am-3pm Sep–mid-Jun), a wildlife reserve 16km from Orsa. Even if

there are no cubs around during your visit, there's plenty to see: lynx, wolves, red foxes and wolverines. The animals have a lot of space and natural surroundings, which is ideal for them, but means there's plenty of room to hide, so you may not see the more skittish creatures. For the closest views, follow the posted feeding schedule. Summer activities such as fishing, canoeing, and elk or beaver safaris can also be booked at the park, and on certain mornings you can do yoga on 'tiger hill' (check online for schedules). Plans are underway to expand the park to nearly twice its current size. Bus 118 runs from Mora to Grönklitt, via Orsa (twice daily weekdays, once on Sunday).

In winter there's a **ski area** (day ski pass adult/child Skr240/195; ⓨ Dec-Mar) at Grönklitt.

Orsa Camping (☎ 462 00; www.orsagronklitt.se; Orsa; sites low/high season Skr120/195, cabins per week from Skr5400; ⚑) is a big camp site beautifully situated on the shores of the lake in Orsa. It's particularly suitable for families, with several playgrounds, a waterslide, canoe hire, crazy golf and a beach to keep the kids happy.

Run by the Björnpark folks, **Björnlängan Hostel** (☎ 462 00; Grönklitt; 2-/4-bed r Skr560/1500; Ⓟ) is a private hostel by the park entrance. There's no 10-to-a-cubbyhole here: rooms are for two or four people. There's also a sauna for guests. The hostel is frequently occupied by large groups, so book early.

Buses 103 and 104 run regularly between Mora and Orsa.

SÄLEN & AROUND
☎ 0280 / pop 400

A split-personality village, Sälen transforms itself completely from a quiet fishing paradise in summer into Sweden's largest and poshest ski resort in winter. It's a tiny spot in the wilds of Dalarna, and in addition to its seven ski areas it's a good base for all kinds of outdoor activities, including canoeing, horse riding and wildlife safaris (ask at the tourist office).

Head first to the Centrumhuset complex, where you'll find a bank, doctor, pharmacy, Systembolaget and most other facilities, including the **tourist office** (☎ 187 00; info@salen.se; Centrumhuset; ⓨ 9am-6pm Mon-Fri, 9am-3pm Sat & Sun Jun-Aug & Dec-Apr; 9am-6pm Mon-Fri, 10am-2pm Sat May & Sep-Nov). Opposite the complex are supermarkets and stores where you can rent ski gear in winter, and inline skates, boats and canoes in summer.

Activities

The **ski areas**, with chalets, pubs and night-clubs, are strung out for 20km along the road running through the steep-flanked mountains west of Sälen. There are over 100 lifts, pistes of all degrees and guaranteed snow from 15 November to mid-April. For details visit www.skistar.com. About 45km north of Sälen, cheaper and quieter skiing is available at **Näsfjället**.

In summer, the ski hills convert to **mountain-bike parks**; the ski area at **Lindvallen** (☎ 0771-84 00 00) has a whole summer season built around the sport, and you can rent helmets and gear at the lift or via the tourist office. The bike park is open Thursday to Sunday from mid-June through August.

There's some good **hiking** in the area in summer, mainly north of the road. A map of the southern section of Kungsleden (p60) costs Skr20 at the tourist office.

Sleeping & Eating

Winter visitors should contact their travel agent or the tourist office for accommodation, or contact **SkiStar** (☎ 0771-84 00 00; www.skistar.com) for packages. The village's most visible hotel-restaurant, **Sälens Gästgiveri**, was closed and up for sale at the time of research, but the tourist office can recommend other accommodations in the area.

STF Vandrarhem Sälens (☎ 820 40; info@salensvan drarhem.se; Gräsheden; dm Skr150-170, s & d from Skr300) Perhaps slightly less 'away from it all' as it used to be, thanks to a new development of houses going up across the road, this rustic little hostel 27km north of Sälen is nevertheless a fantastic hideaway. It's based in a peaceful nature reserve at Gräsheden (near Näsfjället), with some great walks nearby and the southern section of Kungsleden (p60) passing 2km from the hostel. Breakfast is available for Skr55.

Inside Centrumhuset there's a bakery and a delicatessen selling fresh local produce.

Getting There & Around

Bus 95 runs from the ski area to Mora via Sälen, once daily in the ski season (otherwise you have to change buses at Lima). A ski bus tours around the ski area in winter.

IDRE & GRÖVELSJÖN
☎ 0253

Though it's still part of the Swedish heartland, Idre and its surrounding wilderness feel utterly remote – the rugged landscape looks nothing like the rest of Dalarna. The skiing and hiking here are excellent.

The **tourist office** (☎ 200 00; info@idreturism .se; Framgårdsvägen 1; ☺ 10am-7pm Mon-Fri, noon-6pm Sat & Sun Jun-Aug, 8am-5pm Mon-Fri Sep-May; ☐) has brochures, hiking advice and internet access. Staff can book accommodation and arrange activities such as dogsledding, skiing, hiking, canyoning, rock climbing, boat trips, elk and beaver safaris, horse riding, rafting and canoeing.

Idre Fjäll ski centre (☎ 410 00; www.idrefjall.se; ☺ Nov-Apr), 9km east, has three chairlifts, 29 ski-tows and 42 downhill runs – including 11 black runs. Day lift passes are Skr290 for adults and Skr235 for kids. There's also 60km of prepared cross-country tracks.

Grövelsjön, 38km northwest of Idre and close to the Norwegian border, lies on the edge of the wild 690-sq-km **Långfjällets Nature Reserve**, which is noted for its lichen-covered heaths, moraine heaps and ancient forests. Reindeer from Sweden's southernmost Sami community near Idre wander throughout the area.

Sörälvens Fiske Camping (☎ 201 17; www.sor alven-camping.com; sites/cabins Skr150/495) has rather shadeless camping areas but good cabins, and is popular with the fishing crowd. The camp site is just out of Idre, 2.5km towards Grövelsjön.

The excellent **STF Fjällstation Grövelsjön** (☎ 59 68 80; grovelsjon@stfturist.se; dm/s from Skr270/330; ☺ Feb-Apr & mid-Jun–Sep) mountain lodge in Grövelsjön has a wide array of facilities, including a kitchen, spa, shop and outdoor gear hire. The restaurant serves breakfast, lunch and dinner; enquire about half-board and full-board arrangements.

Idre has a supermarket and several grills and pizzerias.

Dalatrafik bus 170 travels on a route between Mora, Idre and Grövelsjön (2¼ hours from Mora to Idre; 3¾ hours to Grövelsjön). There are three services to Grövelsjön on weekdays, and one or two on weekends.

Northern Sweden

You won't find mobs of people up here, but the odds of encountering wildlife are high – everything from moose to mosquitos thrives in northern Sweden. Herds of reindeer clomp around like cattle, occasionally trotting out onto roads to frighten drivers. Birds of every description can be seen, and the lakes and streams are popular with fishermen. Arctic foxes are less visible, but you may get lucky and spot one. Just stay alert: 'We have a lot of bears in this area,' warns a guide at Rogen Nature Reserve, near Funäsdalen. (It's safe to say only the very lucky few will catch a glimpse of Storsjöodjuret, the sea monster that haunts Östersund's waters.)

The human population of northern Sweden is concentrated in the major towns and cities on the Bothnian coast and in central Jämtland around the Storsjön lake. Here you'll find tiny fishing villages, many of which are still functioning, as well as some excellent museums on the history and culture of the area.

The region is more accessible than Lappland, but no less spectacular. It includes the World Heritage–listed Höga Kusten, a mind-blowingly pretty stretch of coastline in Ångermanland. Most of the landscape is coniferous forest dotted with summer cottages. Rivers tend to be slow-moving and wide; away from the coast, long, narrow lakes are common. The coastal islands here are small and often part of an archipelago. In summer, sandy beaches, long days and relatively warm coastal waters make the seaside a big draw. And there's great skiing and downhill mountain biking in the chic mountain village of Åre.

HIGHLIGHTS

- Hire a canoe and paddle to Norway from **Rogen Nature Reserve** (p295)

- Hit the slopes on skis or mountain bikes in **Åre** (p293)

- Wander the footbridge across Östersund's big lake to **Frösön** (p291), keeping an eye out for the sea monster, Storsjöodjuret

- Explore some of the pretty **fishing villages** (p285) around Sundsvall

- Catch your breath as you survey the dizzying height of the **Höga Kusten suspension bridge** (p288)

- Dig into local history and liquorice at Gävle's absorbing **Länsmuseet Gävleborg** (p279)

| ▓ AREA: 76,193 SQ KM | ▓ POPULATION: 667,049 | ▓ HIGHEST ELEVATION: HELAGSFJÄLLET (1797M) |

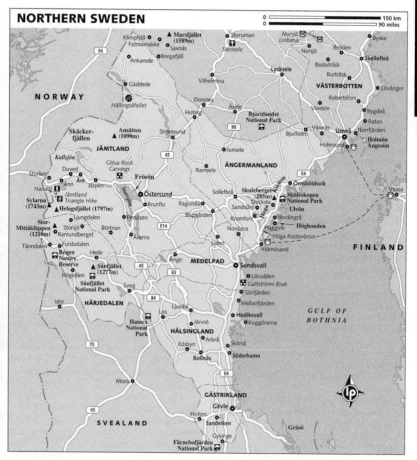

NORTHERN SWEDEN

Orientation

This chapter covers four regions (landskap) along the Bothnian coast (Gästrikland, Hälsingland, Medelpad and Ångermanland) and two along the Norwegian border (Härjedalen and Jämtland).

Just to make things complicated, each region is part of a larger county (län) but the borders don't always match up: Gästrikland and Hälsingland form Gävleborgs län. Medelpad with most of Ångermanland forms Västernorrlands län.

Härjedalen and Jämtland form Jämtlands län.

And don't worry – there won't be a quiz. People generally use the region name, not the län.

Information

Visitors can contact the following agencies for more detailed information on the area:

Gästrikland Turism (☎ 026-66 00 26; www .gastrikland.com) The regional tourist office serving Gastrikland.

Hälsingland Turism (☎ 0278-62 40 08; www.halsin gland.com; Collinigatan 12, 82143 Bollnäs) At this tourist office's website, you can download information about the region in English, plus watch a short film online.

Jämtland Härjedalen Turism (☎ 063-14 40 22; www.jamtland.info; Rådhusgatan 44, 83182 Östersund) This office covers the Jämtland and Härjedalen regions.

Mitt Sverige Turism (☎ 0611-55 77 50; www.upplev mittsverige.nu; Norra Kyrkogatan 15, 87132 Härnösand) This office covers Ångermanland and Medelpad.

Getting Around

BUS

The following companies provide regional transport links, and if you're planning to spend much time in any of these counties, it's worth asking about monthly passes or a *sommarkort* for discount travel from Midsummer to mid-August. Websites have information on routes, schedules, fares and passes; they're often in Swedish, but if you call the telephone numbers listed you'll reach someone who can help you in English.

Länstrafiken i Jämtlands Län (☎ 063-16 84 00; www.lanstrafiken-z.se, in Swedish)

Länstrafiken i Västernorrland (☎ 020-51 15 13; www.dintur.se, in Swedish) Also commonly known as Din Tur.

X-Trafik i Gävleborgs Län (☎ 0270-741 00; www.x-trafik.se, in Swedish)

Ybuss (☎ 0771-33 44 44; www.ybuss.se, in Swedish) Express buses daily between Stockholm and Sundsvall, Östersund and Umeå.

Regional services link destinations in this chapter with those further north. Handy routes include Länstrafiken i Västerbotten bus 100, which runs several times daily between Sundsvall and Luleå (Skr423, 8½ hours) via the major towns along the E4 motorway; and bus 45, which runs daily between Östersund and Gällivare (Skr465, 11 hours).

Länstrafiken i Jämtland bus 45 runs twice daily between Mora (Dalarna) and Östersund (five hours).

TRAIN

A historic railway, **Inlandsbanan** (☎ 0771-53 53 53; www.inlandsbanan.se), runs for 1300km through Sweden's interior from Kristinehamn to Gällivare via Mora and Östersund, Storuman, Arvidsjaur and Jokkmokk (see boxed text, p280). Today the route is covered by a combination of *rälsbuss* (railcar) and steam train, but only from late June (just after midsummer) to mid-August. Travel on the line is slow as the average speed is 50km/h – it takes six hours from Mora to Östersund (Skr395) and 12 hours from Östersund to Gällivare (Skr795), including stops – but you can break your journey in any of the small towns en route. Prices are based on a rate of Skr1.23 per kilometre. You can buy tickets for certain legs of the journey or a card that will allow you two weeks' unlimited travel on

the route (Skr1395). ScanRail, Interrail and Eurail passes all apply. Up to two children aged 15 years and under can ride free with a paying adult. Those aged between 16 and 19 years, and students with valid ID, get a 25% discount.

Statens Järnväg (Swedish Railways; SJ; ☎ 0771-75 75 75; www.sj.se) trains run as far north as Härnösand; beyond there the line darts inland to connect to places further north and on to Finland and Norway, mostly via night train. Länstrafiken buses (bookable through the SJ website) fill some of the route gaps.

Due to be completed in 2010 or 2011, the Skr13.2-billion, 190km **Botniabanan** (www.botniabanan.se), a single-track railway being laid from the bridge over Ångermanälven north of Kramfors via Örnsköldsvik to Umeå, will speed travellers along at up to 250km/h.

GÄSTRIKLAND

GÄVLE

☎ 026 / pop 92,000

Infamous among certain naughty youngsters because its name sounds a lot like a Swedish curse word, Gävle is a lively industrial centre and university town with several things to see and do. It's situated about 175km north of Stockholm, along the newly improved E4 motorway.

The university has some 13,500 students, and this fact may account for the city's affection for cheesy theme bars like Church Street Saloon (p281), but it also adds a certain energy to the parks and street life. Gävle is home to an important regional museum, which (perhaps because of the city's large student population) is extra hip. The city seems to have a sense of humour about itself, judging by the oft-repeated legend of the Julbock (Christmas Goat); ask for details at the tourist office or look for signboards around town retelling the story.

Information

The **tourist office** (☎ 14 74 30; www.gastrikland.com; Gallerian 9:an, Drottninggatan 9; ☺ 10am-7pm Mon-Fri, 10am-4pm Sat, noon-4pm Sun) is inside a shopping centre on a pedestrianised street.

Banks and services line Drottninggatan and Stortorget. The public **library** (Slottstorget 1; ☺ 9am-7pm Mon-Thu, 9am-6pm Fri, 10am-3pm Sat & Sun), near the bridge Rådmansbron, is a cool

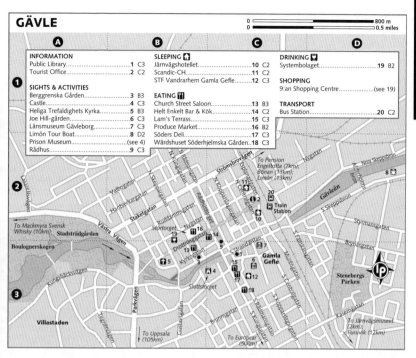

GÄVLE

0 — 800 m
0 — 0.5 miles

INFORMATION	
Public Library	1 C3
Tourist Office	2 C2

SIGHTS & ACTIVITIES	
Berggrenska Gården	3 B3
Castle	4 C3
Heliga Trefaldighets Kyrka	5 B3
Joe Hill-gården	6 C3
Länsmuseum Gävleborg	7 C3
Limön Tour Boat	8 D2
Prison Museum	(see 4)
Rådhus	9 C3

SLEEPING	
Järnvägshotellet	10 C2
Scandic-CH	11 C2
STF Vandrarhem Gamla Gefle	12 C3

EATING	
Church Street Saloon	13 B3
Helt Enkelt Bar & Kök	14 C2
Lam's Terrass	15 C3
Produce Market	16 B2
Söders Deli	17 C3
Wärdshuset Söderhjelmska Gården	18 C3

DRINKING	
Systembolaget	19 B2

SHOPPING	
9:an Shopping Centre	(see 19)

TRANSPORT	
Bus Station	20 C2

hang-out, with an internet cafe and a regular cafe as well as local information (and books).

Sights & Activities

Founded in 1446, Gävle is officially Norrland's oldest town, but not much of its original incarnation remains. A fire in 1869 wiped out most of the old wooden buildings that formed the town's core. Today the little cluster that survived the fire is preserved in the rickety jumble that is **Gamla Gefle**, just south of the city centre. It's fun to wander through and surprisingly easy to get lost in, considering its tiny size. One of the houses is now **Joe Hill-gården** (☎ 61 34 25; Nedre Bergsgatan 28; admission free; ☺ 10am-3pm Jun-Aug), a museum marking the birthplace of the US labour-union organiser. Hill was wrongly convicted of a murder and executed in Utah in 1915. Some of his poetry forms part of the memorial here.

The county museum, **Länsmuseum Gävleborg** (☎ 65 56 00; www.lansmuseet.se; Södra Strandgatan 20; adult/child Skr50/free, admission free Wed; ☺ 10am-4pm Tue-Fri, 10am-9pm Wed, noon-4pm Sat & Sun), has beautifully designed exhibitions on regional culture

through the ages, from the 'golden era' (mid-19th century) to modern times, with recreated sitting rooms and shopfronts, the life stories of key figures in Gävle's history, and multimedia augmentation (a speaker plays recordings of a Swedish ship trader's love letters; a video screen shows old advertisements for Läkerol pastilles starring Björn Borg). Gävle's porcelain factory played a huge role in local industrial development, and you can see some of its finer specimens here. Temporary

---

OUTDOOR ACTIVITIES

- **Åre** (p293) for hiking, biking and skiing
- **Höga Kustenleden** (p288) for hiking
- **Jämtland Triangle** (p294) for hiking and fishing
- **Skuleskogen National Park** (p288) for hiking and fishing
- **Rogen Nature Reserve** (p295) for canoeing
- **Helagsfjället** (p295) for hiking

NORTHERN SWEDEN

INLANDSBANAN

Until the early 20th century, Norrland's rich natural resources had been left largely unexploited. The Inlandsbanan (Inland Railway) was intended to change this by opening up the northern forests and mountains for colonisation and development.

Digging ditches, excavating gravel, blasting mountains and laying sleepers and rails in an area where there were no roads was no mean feat. For over 30 years, the sleepers continued their inexorable progress northwards, from Kristinehamn in the south to Gällivare in the north: a distance of over 1300km. The Inlandsbanan was the last major undertaking of the Swedish navvies; construction began in 1907 and was completed in 1937.

By the time the Inlandsbanan was inaugurated, however, a serious competitor to the train – the car – was already making an impact on Sweden. Railway lines soon closed in many parts of the country. Proposals to close even larger stretches of the Inlandsbanan led to strong protests, not only from the regions directly affected but from all over Sweden. The Inlandsbanan north of Mora is still operating today largely as a result of the popular support it received in the face of closure.

If you'd like to know more about the history of the Inlandsbanan and the people who made it happen, visit the Inlandsbanan Museum (p314) in Sorsele or the railway museum in Jamtli (p291) in Östersund.

---

exhibits are more cutting-edge; a recent one spotlighted graffiti.

Berggrenska gården (☎ 10 50 10; Kyrkogatan 14) is the only remaining early-19th-century commercial courtyard in Gävle. It's now home to artists' studios and galleries, which are open to the public (Thursday to Saturday), and a central bakery and coffeeshop. The nearby **rådhus** (town hall) wasn't so lucky – its present appearance is post-1869, but a town hall has stood on the site since 1628.

The oldest of the churches in Gävle is the **Heliga Trefaldighets kyrka** at the western end of Drottninggatan; it has an 11th-century **rune stone** inside. The buildings of the **castle** on the southern bank of Gävleån are now in administrative use, but there are temporary **art exhibitions** here and a small **prison museum** (☎ 65 44 30; ⌚ noon-4pm Wed-Sun, daily Jul-Aug, tours by appointment).

From mid-June to mid-August daily **boat tours** (adult/child Skr40/25 each way) run from Södra Skeppsbron to the island of **Limön**, part of the surrounding archipelago. The island has a **nature trail**, **mass grave** and **memorial** to the sailors of a ship that was lost here in the early 1800s.

Bönan, 13km northeast of town, is a pretty waterside settlement that's also worth a look; attractions include a fish smokehouse and restaurant. Bus 95 runs out here (Skr35, one hour).

The national rail museum, **Järnvägsmuseet** (☎ 14 46 15; Rälsgatan; adult/child Skr40/free; ⌚ 10am-4pm

Tue-Sun, daily Jun-Aug), has old steam trains and carriages you can climb onto and pretend to drive. It's 2km south of the town centre, off Österbågen.

There's been a circus on the site of **Furuvik** (☎ 17 73 00; www.furuvik.se; adult/child Skr155/125, ride coupons Skr15, armband Skr175; ⌚ 31 May–mid-Aug) for aeons. This entertainment zone, which now incorporates a leisure park and zoo about 12km southeast of Gävle, aims to provide a little of everything; you can act like a monkey on the amusement rides and then see the real thing at the ape enclosure. From the train station, take the frequent bus 838.

For grown-ups, there's whisky-tasting (three types Skr125) at **Mackmyra Svensk Whisky** (☎ 13 29 79; www.mackmyra.se, in Swedish; Bruksgatan 4, Valbo; ⌚ tours 1.30pm Wed-Sun Jun-Aug), established in 1999 as the first Scandinavian malt whisky distillery. It's set in a historic *bruk* (works) about 10km west of Gävle; tours (Skr125) must be booked in advance, via the website, or ask for help at the tourist office.

Sleeping

STF Vandrarhem Gamla Gefle (☎ 62 17 45; stf.van drarhem@telia.com; Södra Rådmansgatan 1; dm from Skr160, s/d Skr305/400; ⌚ reception 8-10am & 4.30-7pm summer, 8-10am & 5-7pm winter) Set in one of Gamla Gefle's old-style wooden buildings around a pleasant courtyard, this place is very quiet but a mere block from the busy street Södra Kungsgatan. Bike hire is available, as is breakfast, and there's a good kitchen.

Pension Engeltofta (☎ 996 60; engeltofta@swipnet .se; Bönavägen 118; r from Skr550; ⏳ Jun-Aug; **P**) This historic building, once an STF hostel, has freshly renovated guesthouse rooms with shared bathrooms in a lovely park setting by the sea, about 6km northeast of the city (take bus 95). Golf and fishing weekend packages are good bargains (from Skr650 per person).

Järnvägshotellet (☎ 12 09 90; s with/without bathroom Skr720/435, d Skr875/675; **P**) Just across a public square from the train station, this small family-run hotel in a historic building has 18 individually decorated rooms; breakfast is included. For longer stays, two furnished apartments are available (Skr3500 per week). The reception isn't open all day, so call to make reservations and get the building code. Next door is a handy Asian grocery and cafe.

Scandic-CH (☎ 495 84 00; Nygatan 45; s/d from Skr1300/1380, discounted to Skr920/1220; **P** 🐕) Near the train station is this business-friendly hotel, which overcomes chaininess with cheery staff and small perks like bicycles for guests to borrow. Rooms are typical of Scandic: Ikea-style furniture and bedding, flat-screen TVs, ecoconscious wall art and clever rubbish bins that help you sort your recycling.

Eating & Drinking

Södra Kungsgatan is a good foraging street. Drinking options include a nameless summer-only pub in the centre of the park in front of Rådhuset, a couple of Irish pubs, and some at-your-own-risk theme bars.

Söders Deli (Södra Kungsgatan 11; lunches Skr50-75) If you're not paying attention, you might walk right past this tiny shopfront, but you'd miss out on really good coffee, salads, pastas and salami sandwiches made on Italian *ciabatta*.

Lam's Terrass (☎ 60 07 30; Slottstorget 3; mains from Skr75; ⏳ lunch & dinner) A Thai joint with a primo location, Lam's serves good food either inside at stylish restaurant booths or on its namesake terrace, with a view over what must be Gävle's ultimate cruising street; all the cool cars and bikes roll past this riverside spot to show off.

Wärdshuset Söderhjelmska Gården (☎ 61 33 93; Södra Kungsgatan 2B; set lunches Skr85-125) Set back a bit from the busy road, this garden cafe manages to be an oasis of calm. The wooden house dates from 1773, but the outdoor seating is where you want to be. The set lunch is usually a typical Swedish dish and a lighter option; à la

carte meals ranging from snacks to traditional Swedish dishes are also available.

Church Street Saloon (☎ 12 62 11; Kyrkogatan 11; mains from Skr100; ⏳ from 5pm Mon-Fri, noon-2am Sat, closed Sun) Fun and popular despite being silly, this Wild West–theme saloon is encrusted with cowboy kitsch: antique saddles, Confederate flags and barrels of hooch. Locals stampede the place, which means there's often a long wait to be seated, and another before food arrives. The menu is heavy on the Tex-Mex.

Helt Enkelt Bar & Kök (☎ 12 06 04; Norra Kungsgatan 3; starters Skr45-75, mains Skr98-175, children's menu Skr50; ⏳ 4pm-midnight Mon-Thu, 4pm-1am Fri, noon-1pm Sat, 5-10pm Sun) At the edge of the main square, Helt Enkelt hasn't lost its hold over locals despite upping prices and feeling a bit samey over the years. Its decor is Scandinavian chic, elegant and unfussy, and the menu matches: fish, meat and potatoes in creamy sauces dominate.

Self-caterers should visit the daily **produce market** (Stortorget). The 9:an shopping centre houses a Systembolaget.

Getting There & Away

Numerous long-distance bus services leave from behind the train station (connected by underpass). **Ybuss** (☎ 0200-33 44 44) runs daily to Sundsvall (Skr240, 3½ hours, five daily), Umeå (Skr375, seven hours, three daily) and Östersund (Skr300, 5½ hours, once daily); for all three, you have to take a 'Busstaxi' (Skr50, paid when you book your ticket) from the train station to connect in Gävlebro. **SGS Bussen** (☎ 13 30 30) has three to five daily services to Stockholm (Skr130, about two hours). **Swebus Express** (☎ 0200-21 82 18; www.swebusexpress .se) runs to both Uppsala (Skr90, 1½ hours) and Stockholm (Skr104, 2½ hours) once or twice daily.

SJ (☎ 0771-75 75 75) offers X2000 train service several times daily between Stockholm and Gavle (Skr390, one hour 25 minutes).

GYSINGE
☎ 0291

Gysinge, 55km south of Gävle and on the border with Uppland, is known for the fine **Gysinge Bruk** ironworks that operated from 1668 to the early 20th century. It's also the gateway to Färnebofjärden National Park (p282) and an excellent fishing area.

There's a small **tourist office** (☎ 210 00; turist .gysinge@sandviken.se; Granövägen 6; ⏳ 10am-5pm May-Sep, 10am-5pm Mon-Fri Oct-Apr) where you can rent boats and canoes. Pick up the free self-guided tour pamphlet for a walk around the site.

Try your hand at forging at **Krokiga Smedjan** (Crooked Forge; admission free; ☺ 10am-6pm Jun-Aug, noon-5pm Tue-Sun Sep-May), which began operations in 1764; there's also a good **handicraft exhibition** and **craft shop** (☺ noon-5pm Tue-Sun). The traditional **Bagarstugan** still bakes unleavened bread and is a good place for a coffee and sandwich. In **Smedsbostaden** (Smith's Cottage; admission free; ☺ noon-5pm May-Sep) you can see what local living conditions were like in the late 19th century. And the **Flottningsmuseum** (Museum of River Driving; adult/child Skr30/20; ☺ noon-5pm mid-Jun—mid-Aug) covers the once crucial, but now defunct, occupation of guiding logs downstream to the sawmills.

Gysinge Wärdshus (☎ 212 00; www.gysinge.com; r from Skr1000, 4-bed cottages Skr800), in the middle of the ironworks area at Gysinge, has plush antique-furnished rooms and an excellent **restaurant** (mains Skr130-190, dagens rätt Skr92) that's big on the Swedish traditionals, especially salmon and herring dishes.

Bus 49 runs four to six times daily from Gävle to Gysinge.

FÄRNEBOFJÄRDEN NATIONAL PARK

About half water, Färnebofjärden occupies 260 sq km south of Gysinge, bisected by the river Dalälven. It has excellent fishing and enough sandy beaches to please those nature-lovers who prefer the type of wildlife typically seen on Swedish beaches in the summer. But primarily the park is known as a birdwatcher's paradise, with ospreys, sea eagles, seven types of woodpecker, Ural owls and capercaillie.

Get information and maps at the **Naturum visitor centre** (☎ 47 10 40; Gysinge Bruk; admission free; ☺ 10am-5pm Apr-Sep, noon-5pm Wed, Sat & Sun Oct-Mar), which also has a small exhibition about the local wildlife and ecology.

In thick, shady woods at the water's edge, **Östa Stugby** (☎ 0292-430 04; osta@stugby.com; tent sites Skr150, 6-bed chalets per week Skr5550; ☺ year-round) is about 30km south of Gysinge near the national park. Aside from camping, there are luxurious six-bed chalets with private beach access, and canoe and boat hire is available (Skr250/850 per day/week). There's a sign-posted 'free beach' nearby – be prepared, however, because what it's free of is clothing.

There's no public transport to the park. Västmanlands Lokaltrafik bus 71 runs one to six times daily from Heby (connections from Sala) to Tärnsjö (8km from Östa).

HÄLSINGLAND

SÖDERHAMN & AROUND
☎ 0270 / pop 26,750

Söderhamn is like that vaguely boring friend everyone has – the one you only call when you need someone to help you move furniture. There's nothing wrong with the town, it just isn't terribly charming or handsome. But it's an important bus-transit hub and a good base for exploring the area's small islands (which *are* both charming and handsome). It's also close to one of the prettiest fishing villages on this part of the coast.

Information
The **tourist office** (☎ 753 53; info@turism.soderhamn .se; ☺ 8.30am-6pm Mon-Fri, 10am-2pm Sat & Sun) is at the bus station, just off the E4 motorway and 1.5km west of the town centre. In the town centre, which is concentrated along Köpmangatan, you'll find banks, supermarkets and a couple of desolate shopping centres.

Sights
Söderhamns Museum (☎ 157 91; Oxtorgsgatan 5; adult/ child Skr25/free; ☺ noon-5pm Tue-Sun mid-Jun—mid-Aug) covers the town's history. Just south of the town centre sits Östraberget, capped with the odd 23m-high tower **Oscarsborg** (admission free; ☺ 11am-5pm Jun-Aug); there's a summer-only cafe on top. Reach the tower via the stairs behind the railroad tracks. Keep a close eye on the clock – a sign on the door says anyone left inside when the tower is closed will be locked in!

The strikingly red **Ulrika Eleonora Kyrka** (☺ 8am-4pm Mon-Fri), just north of the town hall, was designed by Nicodemus Tessin the Younger and completed in 1693. **Söderhamns F15 Flygmuseum** (☎ 142 84; adult/child Skr40/20; ☺ 10am-3pm Jun-Aug, 11am-3pm Sun Sep-May), by the airfield, 5km southeast of town, has a collection of old military aircraft, model planes and a reconstructed command centre. Take bus 59.

Skärså, an ideal cycling destination 12km north of Söderhamn, is one of the most beautiful fishing villages in the area. The picturesque red-painted buildings include old boat sheds, summer houses, a **museum** (☺ 10am-9pm Jun-Aug) and a good cafe, Albertina (opposite). There's also a takeaway fish shop. Bus 65 goes to Skärså (four daily, weekdays only).

The granite walls of **Trönö Gamla Kyrka** (☺ May-Sep), about 15km northwest of town on

Rd 50, have been left virtually untouched over the years – it's just been added onto, so the oldest part of the church, dating from the 13th century, is still intact. There's a free-standing wooden bell tower and a well-preserved wooden roofed wall surrounding the church. Take bus 67 (Skr35, several daily).

Sleeping & Eating

Kalles Gatukök, opposite Mousquet, is one of about a zillion handy fast-food outlets; diners are ever fickle, and at the time of research the mirror-image *gatukök* (literally 'street kitchen') at the opposite end of Köpmangatan was getting steadier crowds. Follow your nose.

Mohed Natura Camping (☎ 42 52 33; www.moheds camping.se; Mohedsvägen 59; sites Skr100, dm from Skr130, cabins Skr250-575; **P**) This very busy lakeside spot, 11km west of Söderhamn, is a well-equipped camping ground that cohabits with the spotless STF Vandrarhem in what looks like an antique school building. You can rent bikes and boats here. Bus 63 and 100 run frequently to Mohed from Söderhamn.

First Hotel Statt (☎ 735 70; Oxtorgsgatan 17; r/tr from Skr1070/1350; **P** **X** **Q**) All the rooms at this elegant hotel have a view, either on the back garden or facing the town hall square; there's a piano museum inside the hotel, and spa packages are available. Ask about the occasional 'stay free – *if you dare*' deals on one room that's supposedly haunted by an 1880s barman.

our pick **Albertina** (☎ 320 10; mains Skr75-150; lunch & dinner until 10pm) Perched over the water in Skärså, with harbour views, this is the nicest place to eat in the area. The menu includes lots of herring and salmon, plus meals for those who aren't fish-lovers. There's a tiny fishing museum attached.

Getting There & Away

Buses and trains leave from Resecentrum, at the train station. Ybuss runs daily to Östersund (Skr235, 4½ hours, twice daily), Stockholm (Skr235, three to four hours, several daily), Umeå (Skr320, five hours, three daily) and Uppsala (Skr235, two to three hours, several daily).

SJ trains run daily to Hudiksvall (Skr95, 30 minutes, twice daily), Sundsvall (Skr116, one to two hours, four daily), Härnösand (Skr173, two hours, once daily), Gävle (Skr68, one hour, three to five daily) and Stockholm (Skr573, two to three hours, several daily).

JÄRVSÖ & AROUND

☎ 0651 / pop 1900

As if arranged specifically to show off the pretty wooden houses of Hälsingland, Järvsö and its surrounding homesteads may leave photographers (and those travelling with them) a little crazed. The sleepy village sits at the northern end of a string of lakes that extends from the Bothnian coast at Ljusne, just south of Söderhamn. The lovely buildings scattered up and down the river valley are worth going out of your way to see.

There's a **tourist office** (☎ 403 06; Turistvägen 29; 10am-6pm Mon-Fri, 10am-4pm Sat mid-Jun–mid-Aug, 9am-4.30pm Mon-Fri rest of year) on the appropriately named main road through town, as well as banks, cafes and supermarkets.

Sights

A 3km boardwalk guides visitors through **Järvzoo** (☎ 411 25; adult/child/under 5yr Skr160/90/free; 10am-5pm Jun-Aug, 10am-3pm rest of year), a well-stocked zoo full of birds and animals from Hälsingland in relatively natural environments – you'll see bears, lynxes, honey buzzards, snowy owls and wolverines, among others.

Completed in 1838, **Järvsö Kyrka** (9am-4pm) is one of the largest rural churches in Sweden and it has an impressive location on an island in the river. Most of the island is a wooded nature reserve.

Öjeberget, the hill just west of the village, has great views – there's a **restaurant** (11am-6pm) on top, plus a little gift shop, and you can ski down in winter.

Just across the bridge from the church (on the eastern bank of the river), **Stenegård** (☎ 76 73 00; 10am-4pm May-Sep, Sat & Sun Oct-Apr) is an old manor and farm with handicraft stalls, a cafe, a restaurant and a theatre in an old barn. Even if you don't go in, the strikingly pretty manor house is worth going by for a quick look.

Sleeping & Eating

Gästgivars (☎ 416 90; Jon Persvägen 7; dm/s Skr170/220; **P**) Ubercasual and friendly, this beautifully situated, comfortable red house has a handful of hostel beds and double rooms (with shared bath). Doubles have French doors opening onto a deck with views of the river. It's near the bridge (follow the signs). Breakfast is available (Skr40) and there's a nice guest kitchen for self-caterers.

Condis (☎ 410 80; Stenevägen 1B; dagens lunch Skr60, mains Skr89-139; lunch & dinner until 11pm, midnight Fri

& Sat) At the corner of Turistvägen, this small cafe has good-value salads, pastas and baked potatoes, as well as coffee and pastries, and a pretty yard with outdoor seating in summer.

Järvsöbaden (☎ 404 00; www.jarvsobaden.se; lunch/dinner mains from Skr95/280; **P**) This friendly hotel was founded as a health farm in 1905, and is on a charming old spread in pretty grounds that include a nine-hole golf course. It has a variety of rooms (singles/doubles from Skr590/800), some with shared facilities. The restaurant here has a superb lunch smörgåsbord that has to be seen to be believed.

Getting There & Away

Bus 51 runs regularly between Bollnäs and Ljusdal, via Arbrå and Järvsö. Trains run north from Järvsö to Östersund, and south to Gävle and Stockholm.

HUDIKSVALL & AROUND

☎ 0650 / pop 37,050

Hudiksvall (aka 'Glada Hudik' or 'Happy Hudik') has a cute harbour surrounded by old wooden houses (Möljen), and it's within easy reach of several historic chapels and fishing villages, including some that are still in operation. Located picturesquely between a lake and a fjord, it's a charming little place to spend a few hours.

The **tourist office** (☎ 191 00; www.hudiksvall.se; Storgatan 33; ☉ 10am-4.30pm Mon-Fri) is at Möljen, by the harbour, and has internet access. In town, you'll find banks and other services on Storgatan and Drottninggatan.

Sights & Activities

The **Hälsinglands Museum** (☎ 196 00; Storgatan 31; admission free; ☉ noon-4pm Mon, 9am-4pm Tue-Fri, 11am-3pm Sat) covers local history, culture and art, including a recreated cottage interior with traditional painted furniture and costumes from the region. Just southwest of the centre, **Jakobs kyrka** dates from 1672. Parts of **Hälsingtuna Church**, 4km north, were built around 1150, but more extraordinary is the 15th-century **Bergöns Kapell**, 18km northeast, a fishermen's church thought to be the oldest in the district.

Attractive **Kuggörarna** is about 30km east of Hudiksvall and is an excellent example of a fishing village; take bus 37 (twice daily). The coast is a good place to witness the raised beaches caused by postglacial uplift (still going on) and forests that are growing in

boulder fields. **Mellanfjärden**, 30km north of Hudiksvall, is one of the few fishing villages that's still operating. It has hotels, a gallery displaying local crafts, a summer theatre, a good restaurant and several nearby nature reserves. **Sörfjärden**, 10km north of Mellanfjärden, has an unusual harbour in the river Gnarpsån, and a good sandy beach nearby.

For those with their own wheels, a lovely driving or cycling route goes through the fields and farmsteads between lakes **Norrdellen** and **Sördellen**, just west of Hudiksvall. Around the neoclassical **Norrbo Kyrka** there are nine Iron Age graves, church stables from the 1920s and a mid-18th-century bell tower.

Sleeping & Eating

Hudiksvall keeps things casual; there are gatukök and kebab stands aplenty, but anything more formal is tough to find. Sleeping options provide a better range.

Malnbadens Camping & STF Hudiksvall (☎ 132 60; www.malnbadenscamping.com; sites low/high season Skr125/175, dm Skr175; **P**) Four kilometres east of the centre of Hudiksvall, this is a large wooded camping ground that's also home to the pleasant STF hostel, open year-round. Bus 5 runs out here in summer.

First Hotell Statt (☎ 150 60; Storgatan 36; s/d from Skr1075/1795; **P** ✗ ✉) Looking ever so slightly down its nose at the rest of the town, this upmarket hotel has a nautical theme; service is on the stiff side, but the digs are plush. A disco and restaurant are attached; the nightclub, Kalas, is apparently the place to be on weekends.

Möljens Gatukök (☎ 163 30; Möljen) Follow the crowds to this take-away counter at the end of the row of red wooden buildings in the historic town core. Rather than yet another grillad korv (hot dog), try a herring sampler (three kinds for Skr20) or a strömmingrulle (fried herring in a wrap; Skr50).

Dackås Konditori (☎ 123 29; Storgatan 34, sandwiches from Skr50) Though it's beginning to look slightly seedy, with its neon sign gathering dust, this bakery still churns out good sandwiches, cakes and pastries, served at a couple of tables out front or upstairs in the main dining room.

Getting There & Away

Ybuss travels to Gävle (Skr220, 1½ hours, several daily), Östersund (Skr225, 3½ hours, twice daily), Stockholm (Skr265, 3½ hours, several daily) and Umeå (Skr300, five hours, twice daily). The bus station is next to the main train station, by the harbour.

SJ trains run to Sundsvall (Skr120 to Skr160, 50 minutes, several daily), Gävle (Skr166, one hour, twice daily), Söderhamn (Skr95, 30 minutes, twice daily) and Stockholm (Skr500 to Skr700, 2½ hours, twice daily).

MEDELPAD

SUNDSVALL
☎ 060 / pop 93,300

When Sundsvall burned to the ground in 1888, civic leaders made a decision that left behind the city's small-town feel and gave it a new sense of weight and significance: the old wooden houses were rebuilt in stone. This forced poorer residents to the city's outskirts while wealth and power collected in the centre, but it also meant that modern Sundsvall, which might have been just another architecturally bland coastal city, is today not only historically significant but also quite pretty.

Information
Library (Kulturmagasinet, Sjögatan) Has free internet access.

Tourist office (☎ 61 04 50; www.sundsvallturism .com; Stora Torget; 🕒 10am-5pm Mon-Fri, also 10am-3pm Sat Jul-Aug) Has information on activities, including summer boat tours.

Sights & Activities
Kulturmagasinet, on Sjögatan down near the harbour, is a magnificent restoration of some old warehouses. The buildings now contain the library and **Sundsvall Museum** (☎ 19 18 03; adult/child Skr20/free; 🕒 10am-7pm Mon-Thu, 10am-6pm Fri, 11am-4pm Sat & Sun), which has exhibits of local art, natural history, Iron Age archaeology and geology. The tiny **cafe** (🕒 10am-4pm) serves a buffet lunch (Skr65).

There's a viewing tower on the hill **Norra Stadsberget** (150m). The southern hill, **Södra Stadsberget** (250m), has an extensive plateau that is good for hiking, with trails up to 12km long. Buses run to either hill once every two hours in summer.

The large island just east of Sundsvall, **Alnö**, has the magnificent **Alnö Gamla Kyrka** (admission free; 🕒 noon-7pm mid-Jun–mid-Aug), 2km north of the bridge (at Vi). The old church, below the

road, is a mixture of 12th- and 15th-century styles. Whitewashing damaged the lower parts of the wall paintings in the 18th century, but the upper wall and ceiling paintings are nearly perfect. The painting was probably done by one of Albertus Pictor's pupils. Even better is the late 11th-century carved wooden **font** in the new church across the road; the upper part combines Christian and Viking symbolism, while the lower part shows beasts that embody evil. Catch bus 1 to Vi (two or three hourly), then take a Plus bus to the churches (every one or two hours).

For a pleasant excursion, head to **Lörudden**, a picturesque fishing village about 30km southeast of town, with a tiny cafe and fish smoke-house. There's a beach of flat rocks here, which is perfect for warming up in the sun after a dive into the sea. Take bus 20 south to Njurundabommen, then bus 126.

Liden, by the ribbon lake on Indalsälven, is about 46km northwest of Sundsvall on Rd 86. **Liden Gamla Kyrka**, completed in 1510, has a lovely location and contains excellent medieval sculptures from the 13th, 15th and 16th centuries. There are faded wall paintings from 1561 and a 13th-century crucifix. The view from the **Vättberget**, reached by a 3km unsurfaced road from Liden, is one of the finest in Sweden, showing the ribbon lake to its best advantage. To reach Liden, take bus 30.

Sleeping
STF Vandrarhem Sundsvall (☎ 61 21 19; www.gaffel byn.se; Gaffelbyvägen; dm Skr160-220, s/d from Skr275/320) The STF hostel is above the town on Norra Stadsberget, and has both older rooms and more expensive modern rooms with private bathroom. The 20-minute walk to the hostel from the city centre is pleasant, but not much fun with heavy bags – a bus runs up here in summer from the train and bus stations.

Lilla Hotellet (☎ 61 35 87; Rådhusgatan 15; s/d Skr595/795) In a stone building designated a historical monument, this small family-run hotel has a great location and a friendly vibe. Rooms have interesting architectural details, many including ceramic tile stoves.

Best Western Hotel Baltic (☎ 14 04 40; www.baltic hotell.com; Sjögatan 5; s/d from Skr1179/1339, discounted to Skr659/769; 🅿) Toward the upper end of the accommodation scale is the attractive Baltic, at the water's edge near Kulturmagasinet and the bus station. Discounted rates make its bright, modern rooms a good deal.

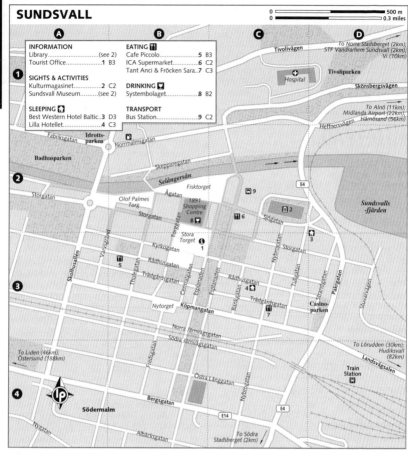

SUNDSVALL

INFORMATION	
Library	(see 2)
Tourist Office	1 B3

SIGHTS & ACTIVITIES	
Kulturmagasinet	2 C2
Sundsvall Museum	(see 2)

SLEEPING	
Best Western Hotel Baltic	3 D3
Lilla Hotellet	4 C3

EATING	
Cafe Piccolo	5 B3
ICA Supermarket	6 C2
Tant Anci & Fröcken Sara	7 C3

DRINKING	
Systembolaget	8 B2

TRANSPORT	
Bus Station	9 C2

Eating

There's a huge selection of casual restaurants along Storgatan, plus the usual number of pizzerias and burger joints.

OUR PICK Tant Anci & Fröcken Sara (☎ 785 57 00; Trädgårdsgatan 14; sandwiches/soup Skr50/65; ☺ 10am-9pm Mon-Fri, 11am-6pm Sat, noon-9pm Sun) Humongous bowls of soup or salad are the speciality at this adorable organic cafe, where you can also get hearty sandwiches, giant bowls of pasta and pastries. There are only a few tables, but takeaway is available; part of the space is devoted to a small health-food shop for organic tea and coffee, chocolate, snacks and cooking supplies.

Cafe Piccolo (☎ 12 10 84; Rådhusgatan 37; mains Skr65-75; ☺ 10am-7pm Mon-Thu, 10am-midnight Fri, Sun winter)

This bright and spacious cafe-coffeeshop has a massive, tempting lunch buffet, plus – even better – an ice-cream buffet (Skr50).

There's a central **ICA supermarket** (Esplanaden 5) along with a **Systembolaget** (1891 shopping centre, Storgatan).

Getting There & Away

Midlanda Airport (☎ 19 76 00) is 22km north of Sundsvall; buses run from the bus station three to nine times daily (Skr80) to connect with SAS and Skyways flights to Göteborg, Luleå and Stockholm.

Buses depart from the Sundsvall bus station, near Kulturmagasinet. Ybuss runs daily to Östersund (Skr190, 2½ hours, twice daily), Gävle (Skr240, 3½ hours, four daily) and Stockholm (Skr275, six hours, four to five daily). Länstrafiken Västerbotten bus 100 runs several times daily to Umeå (Skr285, 3¾ hours), Luleå (Skr423, eight hours) and most other coastal towns.

Trains run west to Östersund and south to Söderhamn, Gävle and Stockholm. The station is just east of the town centre on Landsvagsalen, which is a continuation of Köpmangatan.

ÅNGERMANLAND

HÄRNÖSAND

☎ 0611 / pop 25,280

Grown from a pre-Viking trading post on the island of Härnön, Härnösand was burned to the ground three times in the 1700s: once by accident, once by schoolboy pranksters, and once when Russian Cossacks flattened the town in 1721, destroying all but three buildings. Then in 1877, just when everyone had begun to relax, it burned again. These days it's a small, subdued place without much going on, but it has a pretty harbour and makes an excellent base for exploring the coast.

The **tourist office** (☎ 881 40; www.harnosand .se; Stora Torget 2; ☺ 9am-6pm Mon-Fri, 10am-3pm Sat & Sun Jun-Aug, weekdays only Sep-May) is on the main square; there's a tiny gallery upstairs with displays of local artwork and occasional cultural speakers and events.

Sights & Activities

Länsmuseet Västernorrland (☎ 886 00; www.murber get.se; Murberget; admission free; ☺ 11am-5pm Tue-Sun) is an excellent regional museum dedicated to the culture and history of Ångermanland. In addition to the permanent exhibitions, which include furniture, historic photographs and Sami handicraft, the museum hosts temporary displays of more recent art and sculpture. A self-guided tour on tape (in English) costs Skr20. The open-air museum, **Friluftsmuseet Murberget** (admission free; ☺ 11am-5pm mid-Jun–mid-Aug), adjacent to Länsmuseet Västernorrland, includes a 19th-century shop, church and school in the style typical of this part of Norrland. Take bus 2 or 52.

Boat trips taking in the impressive coastal scenery are available in summer, with some routes journeying up to the dramatic Höga Kusten bridge – enquire at the tourist office for details.

The regional library, **Härnosand Sambibliotek** (☺ Mon-Sat Aug-Jun), hosts rotating art exhibits in a cool, cutting-edge building; the stylish cafe inside offers a cheap lunch buffet with vegetarian options (from Skr70).

A shop that doubles as a handicraft museum, the classy **Svensk Slöjd** (☎ 51 13 27; Storgatan 25; ☺ 10am-6pm Mon-Fri, 10am-3pm Sat), across from Hemköp supermarket, is a good place to find souvenirs; they're not cheap but the quality is top-notch, as the shop is an outlet of the official Swedish handicraft organisation, Svensk Slöjd.

Sleeping & Eating

STF Mitti Härnösand (☎ 243 00; mitti@telia.com; Franzengatan 14; dm/s/d Skr150/225/300; ☺ reception 3-5pm; ℗) Directly across the street from the cathedral in a restored building that dates from 1844, this cosy, friendly place has good facilities and a handy location.

First Hotell Stadt (☎ 55 44 40; Skeppsbron 9; s/d from Skr1222/1422, discounted to Skr650/850; ℗ 🐾 🖳) This huge, grim-looking building that looms at the edge of the harbour is at the other extreme. Rooms are spacious and pleasant, with Scandinavian-modern decor and all the usual amenities; most have views over the marina. There's a bar in the lobby that serves snacks.

Kanalkafeet (☎ 106 66; Storgatan 18; snacks Skr35-50, meals from Skr75) In a pretty yellow building at one end of the pedestrianised shopping street, old-style Kanalkafeet serves big salads, light meals, cakes and coffee.

Hamnkrog (☎ 219 11; mains Skr75-125) The best bet for dinner is this bar-restaurant, attached to the guest harbour just across the bridge from the town centre. It has a deck with great views over the water in summer.

Getting There & Around

Länstrafiken Västerbotten bus 100 runs several times daily to Sundsvall (Skr86, one hour), Luleå (Skr423, eight hours) and points in between. Ybuss runs daily to Gävle (Skr260, 4½ hours, twice daily) and Stockholm (Skr310, six to seven hours, several daily). Local buses service Sundsvall for train connections to Gävle and Stockholm.

HÖGA KUSTEN

☎ 0613

Some of the most dramatic scenery on the Swedish coastline is found here, on the Höga Kusten (meaning 'High Coast'). The secret to its spectacular beauty is elevation; nowhere else on the coast do you find such a mountainous landscape, with sheer rocky cliffs plunging straight down to the sea, as well as lakes, fjords and islands. The region was recently recognised as a geographically unique area and listed as a Unesco World Heritage site.

The combined processes of glaciation, glacial retreat and land rising from the sea (which continues today at a rate of 90cm per century) are the combined forces that led to this stunning scenery. It's a wonderful area for scenic drives, although the narrow twisty roads can make it difficult for whoever's stuck behind the wheel.

Höga Kusten stretches from north of Härnösand to Örnsköldsvik, and either place makes a handy base for exploration. The regional **tourist office** (☎ 504 80; www.hogakusten.com) can help you with information on exploring the region by bus, car or on an organised tour; it's located inside Hotell Höga Kusten, just north of **Höga Kustenbron**, the spectacular E4 suspension bridge over Storfjärden. Here you can pick up information on attractions and accommodation options in the tiny villages along the coast, as well as a detailed map of the scenic byway.

The information area is full of brochures and open all year, and the desk is staffed from 10am to 6pm June to August. There's also useful information on the internet at www.hogak usten.com.

Unfortunately, there's little public transport in the area. Buses cruise along the E4, but don't make it into the villages, and as a result this area is virtually impossible to explore thoroughly without your own set of wheels. That's unless, of course, you wish to walk the **Höga Kustenleden**, a 127km hiking trail stretching from Höga Kustenbron to Örnsköldsvik, with shelters and cabins situated along its length.

Ask the tourist office for the map and guide book (Skr80). It's also very easy to walk smaller sections of the trail as day or half-day trips.

In addition to the striking landscapes, the other major attractions of the region are the many well-preserved **fishing villages** – the pick of them being Barsta, Bönhamn and Norrfällsviken – and the lovely offshore **islands**, especially Högbonden and Ulvön; for transport information see opposite.

Ulvön is worth a visit for the view from the hill, **Lotsberget** (100m), though in peak summer season the main village can be spoiled by the large tour groups that line up to see the tiny, 17th-century **chapel**.

Also worth checking out are **Hembygds-gården**, a 19th-century house with furnishings, and **Sandviken**, a 17th-century village at the northern end of the island.

Norrfällsviken is a picture-perfect half circle of red and white fishing huts around a narrow inlet. There's a hilltop chapel from 1649 (the key is kept next to the door), and the friendly **Fiskar Fänget** (☎ 0613-211 42; fish plates Skr70-120; ☺ late Apr–mid-Sep) sells smoked fish to take away, as well as more substantial meals in its cosy wood-panelled restaurant-pub. Next door is a tiny **fishing museum** (☺ 11am-4pm) where you can learn the history of *surströmming*, the fermented herring that's famously an acquired taste, including how (and more to the point *why*) it's made.

Skuleberget Naturum (☎ 401 71; admission free; ☺ 9am-7pm May-Sep, 10am-5pm Wed-Sun Oct-Apr), by the E4 north of Docksta, has exhibitions and lots of information on the area. The steep mountain, **Skuleberget** (285m), soars above the Naturum, where you can ask about hiking routes, the cable car on the other side, and rock-climbing routes (grades 2 to 3).

Skuleskogen National Park, a few kilometres northeast, contains varied and magnificent scenery, including **Slåtterdalskrevan**, a 200m-deep canyon. It was once a hideout for bandits; a film on view at Naturum tells the story. The park is signposted from the E4, and the Höga Kustenleden walking trail passes through it.

Sleeping & Eating

STF Vandrarhem Docksta (☎ 130 64; dm Skr130-200, s/d from Skr170/260; ℗ ☙) This attractive and busy hostel is 3km south of Docksta at Skoved, right along the Höga Kustenleden (High Coast Trail). It has a party atmosphere and good facilities, including a restaurant and an outdoor stage for summer concerts. Camping sites (Skr130) are available; reservations recommended.

Vandrarhem Högbonden (☎ 230 05, 420 49; dm from Skr200; ☺ May-Oct) This is a relaxing getaway on the little island of Högbonden, reached by boat from Barsta (also from Bönhamn in high season; see opposite). There's a kitchen here, and a cafe open in summer. Book well in advance.

Hotell Höga Kusten (☎ 72 22 70; s/d Skr895/1095, discounted to Skr600/845) You'll wake up on top of the world if you stay at this place, the large hotel just off the E4, next to the bridge. Rooms are simple, square-ish and art-themed. A cafe here serves coffee and snacks, and the attached restaurant serves basic meals from Skr85.

Kustgårdens Vandrarhem (☎ 212 55; dm Skr160), in Norrfällsviken, operated by the nearby **Brittas Restaurang** (☎ 212 55; d/f from Skr695/1095; P ♨), is a popular summer complex consisting of a restaurant and pub, hotel and hostel, plus family-friendly activities like minigolf and fishing.

Norrfällsviken has a very good **camping ground** (☎ 213 82; sites Skr135, cabins from Skr400). There are supermarkets in Ullanger, Nordingrå, Docksta and Mjällom.

Getting There & Around

Bus 217 runs one to six times daily between Nordingrå, the bridge and Kramfors. Länstrafiken Västerbotten bus 100 runs along the E4.

Ferries to Högbonden (☎ 0613-230 05, winter 231 00; adult/child return Skr150/50) depart Barsta from mid-May to mid-June and from mid-August to October (noon Friday to Sunday), and leave both Barsta and Bönhamn in peak summer – from mid-June to mid-August. During this period boats leave from Barsta at 9.30am, 11.30am, 2.30pm and 5.30pm, and from Bönhamn at 10am, noon, 3pm and 6pm.

Ferries to Ulvön (☎ 070-651 92 65; adult/child return Skr150/50; ☽ Jun-Aug) leave year-round from Köpmanholmen (twice daily) and mid-June to August from Ullånger (9.30am) and Docksta (10.15am).

ÖRNSKÖLDSVIK

☎ 0660 / pop 29,000

Famous within Sweden for producing the handsome ice-hockey star Peter 'Foppa' Forsberg and the artist Hans Hedberg, Örnsköldsvik is a fine base for exploring the Höga Kusten and has a couple of interesting things to see and do.

The **tourist office** (☎ 881 00; www.ornskoldsvik.se; Strandgatan 24; ☽ 10am-6pm Mon-Fri, 10am-2pm Sat & Sun Jul-Aug, 10am-6pm Mon-Fri & 10am-2pm Sat Sep-Jun) is inside Paradisbadet. Banks surround Storatorget, and the **library** (Lasarettsgatan 5) offers internet access.

Walk up **Varvsberget** (80m) for a good view of the town; some 275 steps lead up from Modovägen. There's a cafe and minigolf course at the top.

The impressive **Örnsköldsviks Museum & Konsthall** (☎ 886 01; Läroverksgatan 1; adult/child Skr20/free, special exhibits Skr150/100; ☽ 10am-7pm) covers 9000 years of local history and includes a section on the Sami. It also hosts temporary exhibitions of art and culture, including a recent *Star Wars*–themed blockbuster, portraits of Astrid Lindgren and work by up-and-coming photographers.

Sculptor Hans Hedberg (1917–2007) was born just south of Örnsköldsvik, and you can see some of his work – including his signature huge sculptures of fruit and eggs – at the **Hans Hedberg Museum** (☎ 785 00; Arken; admission free; ☽ 8am-5pm Mon-Fri; guided tours Skr20), in the shiny modern building by the harbour.

About 5km south of the centre is **Gene Fornby** (☎ 537 10; adult/child Skr65/35; ☽ noon-5pm Jul–mid-Aug), an interesting reconstruction of an Iron Age farm, complete with actors and a wide range of activities, from baking to iron working. Guided tours run at 12.30pm, 2pm and 3.30pm. Take bus 21 to Geneåsvägen, then walk to the farm, or ask at the tourist office about the regular direct bus service from town.

Sleeping & Eating

STF Vandrarhem (☎ 702 44; Högsnäsgården, Högsnäs 99; dm Skr160, s/d from Skr250/420; P) This tiny place, open year-round, is in a lovely waterside setting 8km west of town, just off the E4. Take bus 40 or 412. The hostel can also arrange canoe rentals.

First Hotel Statt (☎ 26 55 90; Lasarettsgatan 2; s/d from Skr1439/1639, discounted to Skr719/919; P ♨) The First Hotel Statt is a landmark hotel in a pretty, pinkish building by the harbour, with a terrace bar and a weekend nightclub. Some rooms have great views of the bay.

Café Galleri M (☎ 168 60; Storgatan 8; lunch from Skr65; ☽ lunch Mon-Sat, dinner Mon-Fri) A pleasant little cafe inside an art gallery, this is a good spot for lunch.

Getting There & Away

Länstrafiken Västerbotten runs bus 100 along the E4 several times daily – south to Sundsvall (2½ hours), north to Umeå (three hours) and Luleå (six hours).

NORTHERN SWEDEN

JÄMTLAND

ÖSTERSUND

☎ 063 / pop 58,000

The best way to appreciate Östersund is to take the footbridge across to the adjacent island of Frösön and gaze back at the city in profile, ideally around sunset. Seen in that light, this fun-loving town is hard to resist. Dedicated sightseers will stay busy, but what Östersund really encourages is relaxation: in summer, people flock to the terrace bars and cafes at the water's edge (often hopping in for a quick dip) or idly wander the pedestrianised shopping streets, stopping here and there for a beer or an ice cream. In winter, they burn off all the beer and ice-cream with a variety of outdoor activities. With its stroll-friendly centre, numerous parks and easy access to hill or beach, the city seems designed for leisure.

A gigantic annual three-day music festival, **Storsjöyran** (Great Lake Festival; www.storsjoyran.se), is held in the town centre in late July/early August and features a range of international artists, from Blondie to Motorhead. Some 55,000 people attend, so note that beds are scarce and expensive around then.

Information

The **tourist office** (☎ 14 40 01; www.turist.ostersund.se; Rådhusgatan 44; ⏲ 9am-5pm Mon-Thu, 10am-3pm Fri-Sun) is opposite the town hall, and has free internet

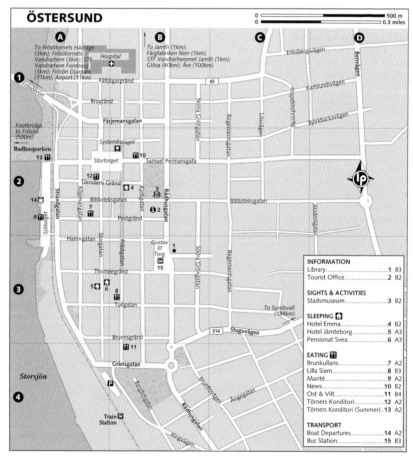

ÖSTERSUND

access. Ask about the **Östersund Card** (adult/child Skr270/120), which gives discounts or free entry to many local attractions and in winter includes a free day pass (worth Skr90/55) to Gustavsbergsbacken ski hill.

Östersund's **library** (☎ 14 30 50; Rådhusgatan 25-27; ⏰ 10am-7pm Mon-Thu, 10am-6pm Fri, 11am-3pm Sat Jun-Aug; 10am-8pm Mon-Thu, 10am-6pm Fri, 11am-3pm Sat Sep-May) has free internet access.

Sights & Activities

Don't miss **Jamtli** (☎ 15 01 00; www.jamtli.com; adult/child mid-Jun–Aug Skr110/free, Sep–mid-Jun Skr60/free; ⏰ 11am-5pm daily Jun-Aug, closed Mon Sep-May), 1km north of the town centre. It combines an open-air museum park (à la Skansen in Stockholm) with a first-rate regional culture museum. In the outdoor section, guides wearing period costumes explain the traditions of the area. A perpetual stroller convention goes on at Hackåsgården, the large section of the park set aside for the tiniest tots. Indoors, the regional museum exhibits the **Överhogdal Tapestry**, a Christian Viking relic from around 1100 that features animals, people, ships and buildings (including churches). It's one of the oldest of its kind in Europe and may even predate the famous Bayeux tapestry.

Guided tours in English leave from the Östersund 1895 square just inside the entrance at 2pm daily mid-June through August.

An offshoot of Färgfabriken in Stockholm, the newly opened **Färgfabriken Norr** (☎ 390 00 00; www.fargfabriken.se; Byggnad 33, Infanterigatan 30; admission free; ⏰ noon-5pm Thu-Fri, noon-4pm Sat & Sun) is a huge new art space across the E14 motorway from Jamtli (take bus 14 or 8). It's a cavernous room with an ambitious curatorial scope; the initial exhibition included work by some 80 artists, including David Lynch and JG Thirlwell, representing pretty much all forms, from painting, sculpture and video to installations using broken glass, body hair and lightning.

The **Stadsmuseum** (☎ 12 13 24; adult/child Skr30/free; ⏰ 10am-4pm Mon-Fri, 1-4pm Sat & Sun mid-Jun–Aug, noon-3pm Sat Sep–mid-Jun), near the tourist office, contains items of local historical, cultural and topographical interest.

Activities include **lake cruises** (adult/child Skr80/40, Lake Storsjön tour Skr90/40; ⏰ tours Tue-Sun, Jun-early Sep) on the old S/S *Thomée* steamship, including themed tours, dinner tours and trips to the small castle-capped island of Verkön (Skr110/40). Book through the **tourist office**

(☎ 14 40 01); the schedule's complicated, but it's posted on a sign by the boat at the harbour. A handful of rush tickets are usually available at the harbour before each trip.

An increasingly fashionable activity is **Icelandic horse riding** (☎ 212 77; Sörbygården, Brunflo). Prices (from Skr300) include helmets and a snack; book through the tourist office. The riding school is 5km south of Östersund.

FRÖSÖN

The nicest way to explore this island is to walk across the footbridge from the middle of Östersund (it starts at Badhusparken), then catch a bus up the hill. (Buses 5 and 9 also go to the island from outside the tourist office.)

Just across the footbridge, outside Landstingshuset and near the Konsum supermarket, is Sweden's northernmost **rune stone**, which commemorates the arrival of Christianity in 1050.

Also on the island are the animals at **Frösöns Djurpark** (☎ 51 47 43; www.frosozoo.se; adult/child/family Skr180/90/500; ⏰ 10am-4pm mid–late Jun & Aug, 10am-6pm Jul) and the restored, late-12th-century **Frösöns kyrka** (⏰ 8am-8pm summer, Mon-Fri rest of year), with its distinctive separate bell tower. Buses 5 and 3, respectively, will get you to these sights. If you are a skier there are both slalom and nordic ski runs on the island at Östberget, where there is also a **viewing tower** (adult/child Skr10/5; ⏰ 11am-6pm mid-May–mid-Sep, 9am-9pm mid-Jun–mid-Aug) and a cafe.

GLÖSA ROCK CARVINGS

Glösa, 40km northwest of Östersund and by the Alsensjön lake, has some of Sweden's finest **Stone Age rock carvings** (admission free; ⏰ 24hr, souvenir shop & guided tours 11am-4pm Tue-Sun Jul & Aug). The carvings, on rock slabs beside a stream, feature large numbers of elk and date from 4000 BC. There's also an excellent reconstruction of a **Stone Age hut** and replicas of skis, snowshoes, a sledge and an elk-skin boat.

Nearby are some displays about elk hunting using traps (prohibited since 1864) and more modern methods. There are roughly 13,000 *fångstgropar* (pit traps) in Jämtland, set in lines across migration routes; a short walk through the woods (follow the sign saying *Fornminne*) will take you to four of them.

Take bus 533 from Östersund (two or three daily), then follow the sign from the public road (a 500m walk).

Sleeping

ourpick STF Vandrarhem Jamtli (☎ 12 20 60; vandrar hemmet@jamtli.com; Museiplan; dm Skr140-160, s/d from Skr235/280; ℗) Inside the gates of Jamtli museum park is this comfortable hostel, housed in a low, barnlike wooden building with a huge kitchen. There are two- to five-bed dorms, and facilities are all top-notch. Reservations are recommended. Take bus 2 to get here.

STF Vandrarhem Fornborgen (☎ 13 91 00; micke2@ algonet.se; Fornborgsvägen 15; dm Skr140-170, s/d from Skr230/280; ℗) Out on the island of Frösön, this large hostel in a beige apartment block won't be winning the Charming Building Awards any time soon, but it has plenty of room and top-notch facilities, and it's super handy if you want to explore the island. Cycle hire is available. Reservations are recommended October through May.

Frösötornets Vandrarhem (☎ 51 57 67; www.froso tornet.se; Utsiktsvägen 10; dm per adult/child Skr150/75; ℗) This quiet hostel in the trees next to the Frösön viewing tower has dorm beds in small, cabinlike grass-roof huts.

Hotel Jämteborg (☎ 51 01 01; www.jamteborg.se; Storgatan 54; hostel d/tr Skr440/660, hotel s/d from Skr520/690; ℗) This place offers accommodation in just about every possible form – hostel beds, B&B or hotel – in several centrally located buildings. The hotel section has cheerful rooms in bright colours that defy Sweden's 'earth tones only' rule; all hotel rooms include private bathrooms and breakfast. Rooms across the street in Pensionat Svea have shared shower and bath but include breakfast; the summer-only hostel rooms don't include breakfast.

ourpick Hotel Emma (☎ 51 78 40; www.hotel emma.com; Prästgatan 31; s/d from Skr895/995, discounted to Skr650/750; ℗) Emma couldn't be better located: it's on the main pedestrian shopping street, right above a whisky bar. The hotel has all the comforts of a fancy chain but with personality: its rooms are nestled into crooked hallways on two floors, with homey touches like squishy armchairs and imposing ceramic stoves; some rooms have French doors facing the courtyard and buttery wood floors. Parking costs Skr35 per overnight stay.

Eating & Drinking

You'll be tripping over kebab and pizza joints. For street snacks, try the food carts at Stortorget; recently a Thai cart's noodle plates (Skr30 to Skr55) were drawing crowds.

Ost & Vilt (☎ 51 01 12; Prästgatan 19; ☻ 10am-6pm Mon-Fri, 10am-3pm Sat) As much a gift shop as a self-caterer's delight, this tiny gourmet outlet sells handmade jams, cheeses, sausages and other special delicacies from Jämtland.

Törners Konditori (☎ 12 96 60; Badhusparken; snacks Skr23-50; ☻ 8am-6pm May-Sep) This cute cafe at the water's edge serves coffee, cakes and ice cream in a summery park setting between the miniature golf course and a swimming hole. It's only open in summer, but there's another branch (☎ 51 87 60; Storgatan 24) that's open all year.

News (☎ 10 11 31; Samuel Permansgata 9; lunch buffets Skr70) You can't miss this buzzing hangout on a busy corner, with its deck full of fashionable diners. The menu was recently revamped and now includes a vast Lebanese lunch buffet from 11am to 2pm weekdays. The restaurant gradually shifts toward nightclub as the evening progresses.

Lilla Siam (☎ 51 20 30; Prästgatan 54A; mains Skr75-105; ☻ 11am-9pm Mon-Thu, 11am-10pm Fri, noon-10pm Sat, 2-8pm Sun) An affordable Thai restaurant in an atmospheric dining room, this new place has a good lunch buffet and a classy dinner menu full of Thai staples, including plenty of vegetarian dishes.

Marité (☎ 12 42 26; www.marite.nu; Sjötorget 3; mains Skr99-129; ☻ lunch & dinner until late) Down by the harbour is this bar-restaurant that gets hopping on summer afternoons, with locals cramming onto the patio for live music and queuing up for cold beer.

Brunkullans (☎ 10 14 54; Postgränd 5; mains Skr115-149; ☻ 11am-2pm Mon-Fri, from 5pm Tue-Sat, from 4pm Fri) A local favourite for its outdoor patio, Brunkullans also has a wonderfully atmospheric, candlelit 19th-century interior space. The menu features Swedish classics and upscale versions of basic bar food, like a decadent bacon-cheese burger or a quesadilla made with crème fraiche.

Getting There & Around

The **airport** (☎ 19 30 00) is on Frösön, 11km west of the town centre, and the airport bus leaves regularly from the bus terminal (adult/child Skr70/20). SAS flies several times daily to Stockholm; Fly Nordic and Nordic Regional serve Luleå and Umeå.

The train station is a short walk south from the town centre, but the main regional bus station is central on Gustav III

Torg; local buses usually run to both. Local buses 1, 3, 4, 5 and 9 go to Frösön (Skr20). Most city buses stop in front of the tourist office.

Länstrafiken bus 45 runs to Mora (5½ hours, two to four daily). Bus 155 runs west to Åre (1½ hours), while bus 63 runs northeast to Umeå (six hours, two to four daily).

SJ trains run from Stockholm (Skr923, six hours) via Gävle, and some continue to Storlien (from where you can catch trains to Trondheim, Norway). You can also catch a train east to Sundsvall (Skr164, 2½ hours). In summer the Inlandsbanan train runs once daily, to Gällivare (Skr918) or Mora (Skr395).

In summer, bikes and inline skates can be hired from the tourist office (half-/full day Skr50/100, week Skr300).

ARÅDALEN & PERSÅSEN

This seldom-visited part of Jämtland is a favourite spot for trekkers. Its lonely landscapes make you feel like you're really in the middle of absolutely nowhere – and pretty happy to be there.

In spring, keep your eyes trained on the marshy ground for signs of reddish-yellow cloudberries *(hjortron)* – the rest of the year your only company may be reindeer and a few wild birds.

The rustic, 18-bed **STF Vandrarhem Arådalen** (☎ 0687-140 54; dm/s/d Skr130/150/300; ☼ mid-Jun–Aug; ℗) is an excellent hiking base and probably the best place in the area to get regional information. Ask the helpful staff about a 5km walk to **Östra Arådalens fäbod**, a well-preserved Sami farm that once produced cheese and is still in use for part of the year.

The 'barely there' village of Persåsen is now essentially confined to the large and modern museum-shop-hotel-restaurant complex that is the **Persåsen Hotell & STF Vandrarhem** (☎ 0643-44 55 50; www.persasen.se; Persåsen 3370, Oviken; dm Skr130-350, cabins from Skr500, hotel s/d from Skr795/1190; ℗ ✕ ▢). It was the home of inventor John Ericsson (1803–89) for several years while he served in the military. Ericsson invented the caloric engine and the propeller while residing here, and the museum displays an intriguingly conflicted exhibit about his life. The shop is almost a handicraft museum, with an astounding array of fine woodwork and textiles from across the region.

ÅRE & AROUND

☎ 0647 / pop 9,700

A fun, outdoorsy place to hang out in during the low season, Åre is beautifully situated in a mountain valley, but it gets uncomfortably crowded in winter, thanks to its famed **ski area** (www.skistar.com/are). The place has 45 ski lifts, 100 pistes and 1000 vertical metres of skiable slopes, including a 6.5km downhill run. The skiing season is from November to mid-May, but conditions are best from February, when daylight hours increase.

Åre's **tourist office** (☎ 177 20; www.visitare.se) is above the train station and has free internet access; next door is the public library and an STF information desk. The same building also contains **luggage lockers** (small/large per day Skr30/70), internet **kiosks** (per hr Skr29), a sporting-goods store and an ICA supermarket.

Counterbalancing all those healthy outdoor activities is **Åre Chokladfabrik** (☎ 155 80; Björnänge; ☼ 10am-5pm Mon-Sat), where you can stop in and sample the inventive new flavours. It's 3km east of Åre on the E14.

There are excellent cross-country tracks in the area, plus other winter activities, such as dogsledding, snowmobile safaris and sleigh rides (horse- or reindeer-drawn!). Åre also offers great summer outdoor recreation, including hiking, kayaking, golf, rafting and fishing, as well as good mountain biking (see boxed text, p64). The area west of Åre is popular among fell walkers, and there's a network of STF wilderness huts and lodges here for enthusiasts.

Sleeping & Eating

Note that accommodation fill up quickly in winter, so plan well ahead. Not all hotels stay open in summer, but those that do offer great bargains.

our pick STF Vandrarhem Åre (☎ 301 38; www.bratlandsgarden.se; dm Skr140, s/d from Skr180/280; ℗ ▢) is a lovely spot on an old farmstead with dorm rooms tucked into red wooden buildings and a huge living room-dining area. A good kitchen and laundry are available, and wireless internet (Skr30 per hour). Several nice walks pass by the hostel, and there are Icelandic ponies grazing on the hillside – ask at reception about arranging day rides. The place is 8km east of Åre, in Brattland; a daily bus connects it to town, although service is spotty.

Hotel Åre Torg (☎ 515 90; www.hotellaretorg.se; Kabinbanevägen 22; dm Skr180-390) This newish place has hostel beds in four- and five-bed dorms with sleek new black-and-white furnishings. Some rooms have sun decks, and there's a restaurant onsite that serves a *dagens rätt* (daily lunch special; Skr75).

Fjällgården (☎ 145 00; www.fjallgarden.se; s/d from Skr495/990; **P**) Up on the hillside, this is as much an activity centre as a hotel. It offers fishing, mountain biking, golf, horse riding, paddling and a chance to try the zipline, which lets you fly across the valley on a tiny string. Rooms are large and decorated in faux-rustic, après-ski style.

ourpick **Åre Bageri** (☎ 523 20; Årevägen 55; sandwiches Skr50-60; ⏰ 7am-3.30pm) A sprawling organic cafe and stone-oven bakery with a comfy, shabby-chic atmosphere, this place lends itself to lingering. In addition to great coffee, pastries and huge sandwiches, it does an enormous all-you-can-eat breakfast spread for Skr79 (7am to 10am).

Werséns (☎ 505 05; lunch mains Skr85, pizzas from Skr99, mains Skr139-269; ⏰ 3-10pm Sun-Fri, noon-11pm Sat Jun-Aug, from noon daily Sep-May) is a white-tablecloth brasserie and pizzeria, with take-away options and half-portions available. There's a bar and a cluster of outside tables in good weather.

Getting There & Away

Regional bus 157 runs from Östersund and connects Åre to the nearby winter-sports centre of Duved (Skr20, 15 minutes, several daily). Bus 571 connects Duved to Storlien (Skr80, one hour). Regular trains between Stockholm and Storlien, via Östersund, stop at Åre (Skr724, seven hours).

STORLIEN & AROUND
☎ 0647

A microvillage near the Norwegian border, Storlien is home to a lot of Swedish holiday cabins (the Swedish king himself has a winter chalet here) and a downhill skiing area. The **tourist office** (☎ 704 00; turistinformation@storlien.se; ⏰ 9-11.30am & 4.30-7.30pm mid-Jun–Aug) is near the train station.

Ask at the tourist office for information about fell-walking in the area west of Åre, especially around Sylarna, one of Sweden's finest mountains for trekking and climbing. Look for the free STF Jämtland mountains trail map, which outlines good hiking routes in what's known as the **Jämtland Triangle** and describes the network of STF wilderness huts and lodges along trails. (The huts don't take

reservations, but you're guaranteed a spot to sleep, even if it's the floor.)

STF Vandrarhem Storvallen/Storlien (☎ 700 50; dm Skr175, s/d from Skr265/700), 600m off the E14 about 4.5km east of Storlien, provides top-quality accommodation in simple dorm rooms with warm, wood-panelled common areas, a good restaurant (there's also a guest kitchen) and good hiking advice. It's also an ideal place from which to launch a hut-to-hut hiking trip.

Le Ski (dagens lunch Skr74, mains around Skr125), at Hotel Storlien, is a friendly pub with bar food and a great patio for summer dining. Try the 'Bullfighterribs'. There's a **supermarket** (⏰ 9am-6pm Mon-Sat, noon-6pm Sun) with attached cafe as you enter the village, next to a weird little shop that sells trolls.

Storlien is the terminus for SJ trains – change here for Norwegian trains to Hell and Trondheim.

HÄRJEDALEN

This is the least populated of Sweden's counties, but that just means fewer people to get in the way of its spectacular views. Härjedalen is a wilderness of forest, lake and mountain in the west, and forest, lake and marsh in the east. The rugged mountain scenery in the far northwest is breathtaking. The lack of substantial population centres in the region means it's best to organise your visit by activity rather than by town.

FUNÄSDALEN & AROUND
☎ 0684 / pop 2000

Funäsdalen is a small, narrow village arranged along a single road – because that's the only place flat enough to be accessible when the area is buried in snow for half the year. Dominated by the impressive peak **Funäsdalsberget**, the village and surrounding area are popular with hikers, skiers and other outdoor sports enthusiasts – understandably, as the landscape is vast and varied.

The **tourist office** (☎ 155 80; Rörosvägen 30; ⏰ 9am-5pm Mon-Fri May–mid-Jun; 9am-6pm Mon-Fri & 10am-6pm Sat & Sun mid-Jun–Sep; 9am-5pm Mon-Fri & 10am-2pm Sat Oct-Nov), inside the Fjällmuseum, will book accommodation in the area if you're stuck (Skr50 fee). A supermarket, petrol station, cafes and lodgings are on Rörosvägen, the main road through town.

Sights & Activities

Härjedalens Fjällmuseum (☎ 164 10; adult/child Skr80/free) has displays covering the Sami, local farmers and miners, and includes the Fornminnesparken outdoor section.

Forestry agency **Naturum** (☎ 242 00; ☷ 9am-9pm mid-Jun–Aug, 9am-4pm Mon-Fri Dec-Apr) has an office and information centre 15km south at Tännäs Fiskecentrum. It sits at the edge of the **Rogen Nature Reserve**, and has brochures about the geology of the area (including moraine ridges) and the local musk ox. Naturum also sells maps and all kinds of outdoor sporting equipment, from fishing lures to bug spray. A pamphlet mapping several easy local walks costs Skr10. Boat hire (Skr100 to Skr200 per day) is available.

A short drive from the Naturum office, the landscape transforms into a series of linked pools and lakes, and you can **canoe** across the border into Norway. Canoes can be rented in Käringsjön village, but be sure to pick up maps and information and double-check your list of supplies at Naturum first. The office also sells **fishing** licences. Excellent **hiking** can be found in the reserve, but it's better accessed from Grövelsjön in Dalarna.

There's a **golf course** in **Ljusnedal**, just east of town.

For **skiing**, head to **Ramundberget** (20km north of Funäsdalen) and **Tänndalen** (12km west), which offer both downhill and nordic sections. Between them, they comprise 24 ski lifts and 75 runs, and the 300km of cross-country trails constitute the longest ski system in the world.

If you have your own transport, it's worth the haul to the village of **Ljungdalen** (www .ljungdalen.com), about 40km north of Funäsdalen along an unimproved, mostly gravel road. It's slow going, but the scenery is spectacular; it looks like a glacier passed through here five minutes ago. Along the road are some Sami huts and a shop (with erratic hours, but open most days June to August) that sells dried or smoked reindeer meat. This is also one of the few areas in Scandinavia where the nearly extinct **arctic foxes** thrive. There's a small **tourist office** (☎ 0687-200 79) here.

Ljungdalen is close to **Helagsfjället** (1797m), the highest peak in the area, where you'll find good hiking and skiing. The 12km one-way hike from Kläppen (north of Ljungdalen) to the STF cabin at Helags goes via some old summer farms and is reasonably easy.

Sleeping & Eating

Both the **STF Hostel Ljungdalen** (☎ 0687-202 85; Dunsjögården; dm Skr170) and the **STF Tännäs** (☎ 240 67; www.tannasgarden.se; Bygatan 51; dm Skr150) are open year-round.

ourpick STF Tänndalen/Skarvruets Fjällhotel (☎ 221 11; www.skarvruet.com; dm Skr165-190, s/d Skr215/ 350) This great hostel in Tänndalen is 7km west of Funäsdalen along Rd 84, on a steep hillside with well-equipped rooms (kitchens, full baths, sturdy wooden bunks) in several red cottages with awesome views of the mountains across the valley. Hikes and nordic ski tracks start from the parking lot. Take bus 623 (reservations ☎ 020-85 00 85) from Funäsdalen.

Hotel Funäsdalen (☎ 214 30; www.hotell-funasdalen .se; dm summer/winter Skr195/225, B&B per person from Skr345, hotel r from Skr1165; ⓅⓈ) This is the go-to accommodation in Funäsdalen: a large, modern hotel with everything from hostels to hotel rooms in two levels of fanciness. It's open all year and has a good restaurant (whose daily lunch draws in lots of locals) and a pool.

Wärdshuset Gyllene Bocken (☎ 210 90; www .gyllenebocken.se; main house s/d Skr715/1050) This is a lovely old inn opposite the golf course in Ljusnedal, with a good restaurant attached (mains Skr86 to Skr205). Rooms in the 'bruk' are slightly cheaper than those in the main house. The hotel is open for ski season (November to April) and golf season (mid-June to mid-October).

ourpick Villan 1951 (☎ 215 60; Rörosvägen 10; espresso Skr20; ☷ 8am-9pm Mon-Fri, 10am-6pm Sat & Sun) On the main road through town, this tiny, industrial-chic cafe takes its espresso seriously, which is a rarity in Sweden, so it's a real find. There are also tempting pastries and, in the evenings, inventive cocktails.

Getting There & Away

Härjedalingen (www.harjedalingen.se, in Swedish) runs buses between Stockholm and Funäsdalen (Skr420), via Gävle and Järvsö, several days a week; on Saturday buses also connect with Tänndalen and Ramundberget (Skr440). See the tourist office for info and bookings.

Local bus 622 and 623 run from Funäsdalen to Ramundberget and Tänndalen, respectively; there are also daily ski buses in winter. There is not a direct connection with Ljungdalen; take the daily bus 613 from Åsarna (which has an Inlandsbanan train station), about 100km east. Bus 164 runs from Funäsdalen via Åsarna to Östersund once or twice daily.

Lappland & the Far North

Travelling in Lappland and the far north of Sweden can draw you into an unusual rhythm. The long, lonely stretches between towns are epic and often completely deserted – you're almost guaranteed to see more reindeer than fellow travellers on the roads up here. It takes a long time to get from anywhere to anywhere else, regardless of what kind of transport you're using. Consequently, people who live in these parts take things slowly; even their manner of speaking is more ponderous and deliberate than elsewhere in Sweden. At first it may be disorienting to travel through: you might take six hours to reach a town and then discover when you arrive that absolutely nothing is going on, the museum is closed and there's only one restaurant – and it only serves dinner on Tuesday. After a while you'll get used to this; stay a little longer and you'll fall in love with the unhurried pace. It makes you take deep breaths and look at the places in between the usual points of interest. And so you should: one must slow down to properly see Lappland.

When you do, what you'll find is unparalleled natural beauty: impenetrable dark forests, icy mountain ranges, silent stretches of wide-open tundra, wide slow-moving rivers and, of course, herds of reindeer, often nonchalantly strolling right down the middle of the road you're on. (They're in on it, too – you can't rush them.) The far north is also home to most of Sweden's Sami population and is the best place to gain an appreciation for their traditional nomadic culture.

HIGHLIGHTS

- Get a close-up view of Lapporten, the gateway to Lappland, at **Abisko National Park** (p309)
- Hike up to the Sami holy mountain of **Atoklimpen** (p315)
- Chug along up the middle of the country on the historic train line, **Inlandsbanan** (p280)
- Delve into Sami culture at the best museum on the topic, **Ájtte Museum** (p312) in Jokkmokk
- Visit the fantastically well-preserved church village of **Gammelstad** (p302)

- AREA: 151, 466 SQ KM
- POPULATION: 644,376
- HIGHEST ELEVATION: KEBNEKAISE (2111M)

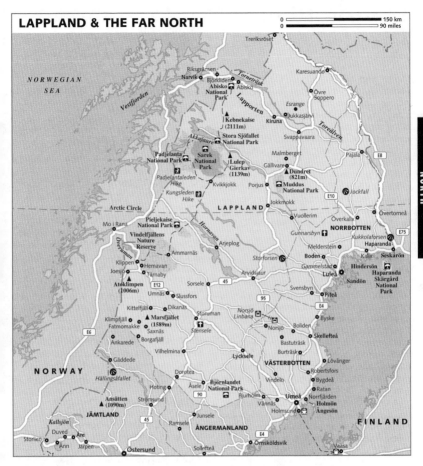

LAPPLAND & THE FAR NORTH

Orientation

The three regions (landskap) of Norrbotten, Västerbotten and Lappland make up the territory covered in this chapter. These correspond roughly, but not exactly, with the counties (län) of Norrbotten and Västerbotten. Landskap designations are historical and cultural, rather than administrative, and especially in the northern part of Sweden they're more likely than the official counties to shape a visitor's experience.

Information

As well as the tourist offices listed throughout the chapter, visitors can contact the following agencies for more information on the area:
Swedish Lapland (www.swedishlapland.com)

Västerbottens Turism (☎ 090-785 71 76; www .vasterbotten.net; Västra Norrlandsgatan 13, Umeå)

Getting Around

BUS

The following companies provide regional transport links, and if you're planning to spend much time in the area, it's worth asking about monthly passes or a sommarkort for discount travel from Midsummer to mid-August. Websites have information on routes, schedules, fares and passes; they're often in Swedish only, but if you call the telephone numbers listed you'll usually reach someone who can help you in English.
Länstrafiken i Norrbotten (☎ 020-47 00 47; www .ltnbd.se)

Länstrafiken i Västerbotten (☎ 0771-10 01 10;
www.tabussen.nu, in Swedish)
Ybuss (☎ 0771-33 44 44; www.ybuss.se, in Swedish)
Express buses daily between Stockholm and Umeå.

Handy regional bus service routes include
Länstrafiken i Västerbotten bus 100, which
runs several times daily between Sundsvall and
Luleå (Skr423, 8½ hours) via the major towns
along the E4 motorway; bus 45, which runs
daily between Östersund and Gällivare (Skr465,
11 hours); and bus 300, which connects Umeå
and Mo i Rana (Norway, eight hours) once
daily via Storuman and Tärnaby.

Länstrafiken i Norrbotten runs two daily
buses connecting Luleå and Kiruna (Skr293,
five hours). Its bus network covers 100,000
sq km (a quarter of Sweden) and it will carry
bikes for Skr50 extra.

TRAIN

The historic **Inlandsbanan** (☎ 0771-53 53 53; www
.inlandsbanan.se) runs from Kristinehamn to
Gällivare via Mora and Östersund, Storuman,
Arvidsjaur and Jokkmokk from late June (just
after Midsummer) to mid-August (see boxed
text, p280). Travel on the line is slow (the
average speed is 50km/h), but you can break
your journey in any of the small towns en
route. Prices are based on a rate of Skr1.23
per kilometre. You can buy tickets for certain legs of the journey or a card that will
allow you two weeks' unlimited travel on
the route (Skr1395). ScanRail, Interrail and
Eurail passes all apply. Up to two children
aged 15 years and under can ride free with
a paying adult. Those aged between 16 and

FOR TAKING IN SAMI CULTURE

- Explore Ájtte Museum (p312) in
  Jokkmokk

- Pet a reindeer at Gárdi (p307) in
  Jukkasjärvi

- Stroll around Samegården (p307) in
  Kiruna

- Shop for crafts at Fatmomakke (p316)

- Wander around the huts at Lappstaden
  (p314)

- Hike to Atoklimpen (p315) from Tärnaby

- Hike the Paddus trail (p309) from
  Abisko

---

19 years, and students with valid ID, get a
25% discount.

Statens Järnväg (Swedish Railways; SJ; ☎ 0771-
75 75 75; www.sj.se) trains go from Stockholm,
Göteborg and Västerås to Umeå, Luleå,
Kiruna and Abisko.

Veolia Transport (☎ 0771-26 00 00; www.connex
.se) runs overnight trains from Stockholm to
Luleå and Abisko.

VÄSTERBOTTEN

UMEÅ

☎ 090 / pop 112,000

With the vibrant feel of a college town (it
has around 30,000 students), Umeå is a
welcome outpost of urbanity in the barren
north. It's one of the fastest-growing towns
in Sweden and an agreeable place in which
to hang out, wind down or stock up for an
outdoor adventure.

Umeå is also widely considered the most
'metal' town in Sweden, thanks to its thriving metal and straight-edge music scene.
Legendary hardcore band Refused started
here, and an annual music festival, **House of
Metal** (www.houseofmetal.se, in Swedish), takes place
at Folkets Hus in early February – the darkest
time of the year, of course.

Information

Forex (Renmarkstorget) Near the tourist office.
Library (Rådhusesplanaden 6A; ☻ 11am-7pm Mon-Thu,
11am-5pm Fri, 11am-3pm Sat) Internet access.
Naturkompaniet (Rådhusesplanaden 7) Sells outdoor
gear.
Tourist office (☎ 16 16 16; www.visitumea.se;
Renmarkstorget 15; ☻ 8.30am-7pm Mon-Fri, 10am-4pm
Sat, noon-4pm Sun Jun–mid-Aug; 10am-6pm Mon-Fri,
10am-2pm Sat mid-Aug–Sep; 10am-5pm Mon-Fri Oct-Apr)
Located on a central square.

Sights & Activities

Don't miss **Gammlia** (☎ 17 18 00; admission free;
☻ 10am-5pm mid-Jun–mid-Aug; 10am-4pm Tue-Fri,
noon-4pm Sat, noon-5pm Sun rest of year), a cluster of
museums 1km east of the town centre. They
include cultural and historical exhibits and
Sami collections at the regional **Västerbottens
Museum**; the modern art museum, **Bildmuseet**;
and the **Maritime Museum**. These are surrounded by **Friluftsmuseet**, an open-air historic village where staff wear period clothes
and describe traditional homestead life.

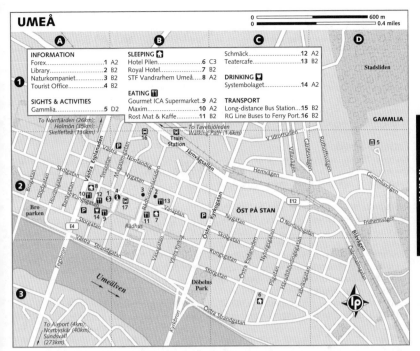

UMEÅ

0 — 600 m
0 — 0.4 miles

INFORMATION	
Forex	1 A2
Library	2 B2
Naturkompaniet	3 B2
Tourist Office	4 B2

SIGHTS & ACTIVITIES	
Gammlia	5 D2

SLEEPING	
Hotel Pilen	6 C3
Royal Hotel	7 B2
STF Vandrarhem Umeå	8 A2

EATING	
Gourmet ICA Supermarket	9 A2
Maxim	10 B2
Rost Mat & Kaffe	11 B2

Schmäck	12 A2
Teatercafe	13 B2

DRINKING	
Systembolaget	14 A2

TRANSPORT	
Long-distance Bus Station	15 B2
RG Line Buses to Ferry Port	16 B2

LAPPLAND & THE FAR NORTH

The walking path **Tavelsjöleden** stretches 39km from Umeå north to Torrberget, through all kinds of terrain and with some stunning views. The trail begins at Regementet, north of Umeå city centre. The first 5km segment to Hamptjärnsberget ends at an excellent viewpoint with a picnic area, but if you have transport it's nicer to start here, avoiding the urbanised first bit of the hike and starting with the 10km walk to Hissjö. The trail mostly parallels Rd 363, so on–off points are frequent, and Länstrafiken bus 16 navigates Rd 363 several times daily.

Ask for maps at Umeå tourist office or call **Umeå Fritid** (☎ 16 16 00). Walkers and paddlers should pick up the useful pamphlet *Paddling & Hiking in the Umeå Region* at the tourist office.

Holmön, known as the sunniest place in Sweden, is a 15km-long offshore island with a **boat museum** (☎ 552 20; adult/child Skr20/free; ⊙ mid-Jun–mid-Aug) and a collection of traditional craft, plus a good quayside restaurant and swimming beaches. In July there's a row-boat race to Finland, which is only 36km away. **Ferries** (www.holmon.com) depart two to three times daily

from Norrfjärden (check the website for timetables), 26km northeast of Umeå; take bus 118 or 119 (Skr45). If the sea freezes in winter, you can take a snowmobile or hydrocopter across the ice.

The island of **Norrbyskär**, 40km south of Umeå, is another worthwhile destination. A sawmill community was built up here from nothing in less than 10 years, only to disappear just as suddenly 10 years later. A museum describes the life of the sawmill workers. Buses run to and from Umeå to Norrbyn, to connect with ferries – enquire at the tourist office for times.

Sleeping

STF Vandrarhem Umeå (☎ 77 16 50; info@umeavandrarhem.com; Västra Esplanaden 10; dm Skr140, s/d from Skr240/280; Ⓟ) Rooms are tiny but comfortable at this busy and efficient youth hostel, one of the few in the region that's actually occupied by youth. It's in a great location: a residential neighbourhood at the edge of the town centre.

Hotel Pilen (☎ 14 14 60; Pilgatan 5; s Skr650-750, d Skr850) This small boutique hotel has comfy, unfussy rooms in a quiet area some 600m from the town centre and close to the river. There's a good restaurant attached.

Royal Hotel (☎ 10 07 30; www.royalhotelumea.com; Skolgatan 62; s/d Skr1240/1440, discounted to Skr650/850) The Royal Hotel has its own cinema, a fancy sauna and a popular restaurant, Greta's, right in the heart of town. Staff will serve you breakfast (on request) in your spacious, clean-lined, Scandi-chic room.

Eating & Drinking

No fewer than three lively pubs – with competing music and outdoor seating in summer – surround Renmarkstorget, the square near the tourist office.

Schmäck (☎ 19 68 48; Kungsgatan 49; ☝ 10am-5pm Mon-Sat Jun-Aug, Wed-Sat Sep-May) Next to Maxim is this funky, laid-back coffeeshop-chocolaterie, where you can sample the latest chocolate decadence, sip fair-trade coffee and browse the little design boutique adjoining the cafe.

Rost Mat & Kaffe (☎ 135 800; Rådhusesplanaden 4B; soup Skr65; ☝ 11am-6pm Mon-Fri, 11am-4pm Sat) This teeny industrial-chic coffeeshop is covered in tiles and doles out good espresso and light meals.

Maxim (☎ 13 82 83; Kungsgatan 47; dinner specials Skr59-89) This popular and fashionable pub-restaurant specialises in pizza and beer package deals, but it also does upmarket pub grub. It's handily located near the STF hostel.

Teatercafe (☎ 15 63 21; Vasaplan; light meals Skr95, dinner mains Skr125-165; ☝ 11am-midnight Mon-Thu, 11am-2am Fri, noon-2am Sat) Part of the Folkets Hus performance hall, across from the Royal Hotel, is this upmarket garden-party restaurant and terrace bar, where classy-looking people linger in a fenced-off patio over salads and chic reinventions of traditional Swedish food.

Self-caterers should try the **Gourmet ICA supermarket** (Renmarkstorget 5A; ☝ 8am-8pm); for alcohol there's **Systembolaget** (Kungsgatan 50A).

Getting There & Away

AIR

The **airport** (☎ 71 61 00) is 4km south of the city centre. SAS and Malmö Aviation each fly to Stockholm up to seven times daily; there are also direct flights to Luleå, Göteborg and Örebro.

BOAT

RG Line (☎ 090-18 52 00;; www.rgline.com) operates ferries between Umeå and Vaasa (Finland)

once or twice daily (Sunday to Friday). A bus to the port leaves from near the tourist office an hour before RG Line's departures.

BUS

The long-distance bus station is directly opposite the train station. Ybuss runs services south up to three times daily to Gävle (Skr375, seven hours) and Stockholm (Skr415, nine hours), via the coastal towns of Sundsvall, Örnsköldsvik, Härnösand, Hudiksvall and Söderhamn.

Umeå is the main centre for **Länstrafiken i Västerbotten** (☎ 020-91 00 19; www.ltnbd.se), the regional bus network. Direct buses to Mo i Rana (Norway) run once daily (bus 300, eight hours), but buses going as far as Tärnaby (Skr233, 5½ hours) run up to four times a day. Other destinations include Östersund (Skr326, 6½ hours, three daily), Skellefteå (Skr148, two hours, several daily) and Luleå (Skr285, four hours 40 minutes, several daily).

TRAIN

Tågkompaniet trains leave daily from Umeå, to connect at Vännäs with the north–south trains between Stockholm (Skr831, 7½ hours, four daily) and Luleå (Skr262, 5½ hours, once daily); northbound trains stop in Boden, from where there are connections to Kiruna (Skr498, nine hours, twice daily) and Narvik (Norway).

Getting Around

Local buses leave from Vasaplan on Skolgatan. The **Flygbuss** (☎ 16 22 50) leaves the airport for the city centre 10 minutes after every flight from Stockholm (Skr35, 20 minutes); transfers to other city buses are free for two hours. Or call **Umeå Taxi** (☎ 77 00 00); it's about Skr150 to the airport.

SKELLEFTEÅ & AROUND

☎ 0910 / pop 73,000

Strewn along the river like a temptress on a chaise longue, and playing up its attractions by setting them in parks along the water, Skellefteå seduces and rewards the unhurried. It's like one long, lovely open-air museum designed for idle meandering – with the bonus of a pedestrianised town centre nearby.

The **tourist office** (☎ 73 60 20; www.skelleftea.se; Trädgårdsgatan 7; ☝ 10am-6pm Mon-Fri, 10am-3pm Sat, noon-3pm Sun mid-Jun–Aug, Mon-Fri Sep–mid-Jun) is in the town centre, on the corner of the pedestrianised

Nygatan and the central square. It has a computer with internet access (Skr20 for 15 minutes) and helps arrange accommodation for a fee. Banks are along Nygatan.

The huge, industrial-chic **Stadsbibliotek** (☎ 73 61 00; Viktoriaplatsen; ☻ Mon-Fri), in the eastern part of the town centre (follow Kanalgatan east), has free internet access and a gallery-cafe where you can sample Västerbotten cheese for Skr10.

Sights & Activities

A pleasant walk along the river west of the town centre takes you to **Nordanå park**, a well-preserved historic precinct that's home to the cultural and historical collections of the **Skellefteå Museum** (☎ 73 55 10; www.skelleftea museum.se; admission free; ☻ noon-4pm Tue-Sun) and several old houses, some of which contain handicraft shops. The path continues as a pleasant 10km loop that crosses the river before returning to the town centre – great for joggers and cyclists.

Just west of Nordanå is **Bonnstan**, a church village with 392 wooden houses built between 1830 and 1940, many of them still inhabited in summer.

Continuing west, you reach a footbridge to the small island of **Kyrkholmen**, and the nearby early-16th-century **Skellefteå Landsförsamling Kyrka** (☎ 78 79 00; www.svenskakyrkan.se/skelleftelands; ☻ 10am-4pm Mon-Fri). The neoclassical church in its current incarnation dates from 1800, but its sacristy is from 1507 and inside is a 13th-century wooden **Madonna**. An adjacent tithe storehouse dates from 1674. Jumping off the footbridge in hot weather is not strictly endorsed, but it's certainly not unheard of.

Continue west and you'll come to the pretty **Lejonströmsbron**, Sweden's longest wooden bridge, built during the year 1737. Crossing it is a fun experiment in vehicle-pedestrian compromise.

About 35km west of Skellefteå is a gold-mine museum, **Bergrum Boliden** (☎ 58 00 60; adult/child Skr20/10; ☻ 10am-4pm Jun-Aug), with interesting multimedia displays covering geology and mining. Take bus 204 or 205 to get here.

Lövånger, 50km south of the town by the E4, has a pretty medieval **church** with separate bell tower, and a well-preserved **church village** that now houses an excellent STF hostel. Some houses have doors big enough to admit a horse and carriage, as well as the church-goers. Buses run roughly hourly from Skellefteå.

Sleeping

Skellefteå Camping & Stugby (☎ 188 55; sites low/high season Skr100/170, 2-bed chalets Skr550/625) At the foot of the Vitberg ski hill, this large camping ground has all manner of huts, cabins, tent sites, RV spots and so on; it's great for families. There's free internet access and a small shop at reception.

ourpick Stiftsgården (☎ 72 57 00; www.stiftsgarden .se; Brännavägen 25; dm Skr230, s from Skr280, hotel-standard s/d from Skr750/1100) Behind Landsförsamling church on Brännavägen, this church-run place spread across green fields near a cemetery is home to a hotel and, in an annex, Skellefteå's STF hostel. The cute whitewashed rooms are simple and comfortable. In the hotel they include full bathrooms, desks and TVs. Reception keeps short hours, especially in summer, so book ahead and call to make arrangements if you'll be arriving after 4pm.

Hotel & Café Viktoria (☎ 174 70; Trädgårdsgatan 8; s/d Skr840/1030, discounted to Skr550/695; ⓟ) Across the street from the tourist office, this place offers simple but more than adequate rooms in a small hotel above a cafe. Steep summer discounts add to the appeal. Parking costs Skr50 overnight.

Eating & Drinking

There's no shortage of grill-bars and cafes along Nygatan and around the main square, as well as on the busier Kanalgatan.

ourpick Kyrkholmen Cafe (☎ 78 79 35; waffles Skr35; ☻ 11am-8pm Mon-Fri, 11am-4pm Sat & Sun mid-Jun–mid-Aug) Across the footbridge to the small island Kyrkholmen is a tiny summer cafe in a nicely preserved old building; coffee and waffles are the speciality but there are also sandwiches and other snacks.

Café Lilla Mari (☎ 391 92; Nygatan 33) This sweet cafe in a small, leafy courtyard offers sandwiches from Skr35, hot lunches from Skr60 and an array of desserts.

Käffeln (☎ 777 540; Tjärhovsgatan 14; daily specials Skr98; ☻ 11am-late Mon-Sat, 11am-4pm Sun) This modern, arty place has cool design, great-value specials – usually a hearty dish of pasta with a beer – and live music some nights.

Getting There & Away

Bus 100 departs every two hours on the Sundsvall–Umeå–Skellefteå–Luleå route (some buses continue as far north as Haparanda). Skellefteå's nearest train station is Bastuträsk; bus 27 connects there three times daily.

NORRBOTTEN

LULEÅ

☎ 0920 / pop 45,050

Luleå is a pretty town with several parks and a sparkling bay with a marina. There's a compact pedestrian thoroughfare full of shops and restaurants. It's the capital of Norrbotten, chartered in 1621; the town centre moved to its present location in 1649 because of the falling sea level (9mm per year), due to postglacial uplift of the land. An extensive offshore archipelago contains some 1700 large and small islands, many decorated with classic red-and-white Swedish summer cottages and easy to visit from the town centre.

The **tourist office** (☎ 45 70 00; www.lulea.se; Kulturens Hus; ☼ 10am-7pm Mon-Fri, 10am-4pm Sat & Sun) is inside Kulturens Hus, along with the **library** (☼ closed Sun), with free internet access.

Boat tours of the archipelago depart from Södra Hamn daily between June and August; typical prices are from around Skr300 to Skr400 for adults, and Skr150 for children. Evening cruises are also popular; pick up a brochure at the tourist office.

Sights & Activities

If you just can't get enough of those little red Swedish cottages with the white trim and lace curtains, head for the mother lode: the Unesco World Heritage–listed **Gammelstad** (Old Town; ☎ 45 70 10; www.lulea.se/gammelstad; admission

LAPPLAND & THE FAR NORTH

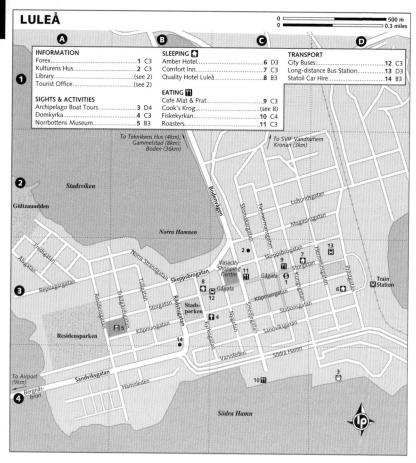

LULEÅ

0 — 500 m
0 — 0.3 miles

INFORMATION
Forex.................................1 C3
Kulturens Hus....................2 C3
Library...........................(see 2)
Tourist Office..................(see 2)

SIGHTS & ACTIVITIES
Archipelago Boat Tours.........3 D4
Domkyrka.........................4 C3
Norrbottens Museum.............5 B3

SLEEPING
Amber Hotel......................6 D3
Comfort Inn......................7 C3
Quality Hotel Luleå.............8 B3

EATING
Cafe Mat & Prat..................9 C3
Cook's Krog...................(see 8)
Fiskekyrkan....................10 C4
Roasters........................11 C3

TRANSPORT
City Buses......................12 C3
Long-distance Bus Station.......13 D3
Statoil Car Hire................14 B3

To Teknikens Hus (4km);
Gammelstad (8km);
Boden (36km)

To SVIF Vandrarhem
Kronan (3km)

Stadsviken

Gültzauudden

Norra Hamnen

Lulsundsgatan

Magasinsgatan

Skeppsbrogatan

Vasacity Shopping Centre

Residensparken

Stadsparken

Köpmangatan

Sandviksgatan

Södra Hamn

Hamnleden

To Airport (9km)

Bergnäsbron

Train Station

Södra Hamn

free; 24hr). This little settlement – row after zigzaggy row of cute little red-and-white cottages – was the medieval centre of northern Sweden. The stone church (from 1492), 424 wooden houses (where the pioneers stayed overnight on their weekend pilgrimages) and six church stables remain. Many of the buildings are still in use, but some are open to the public and the site is lovely to walk around.

Guided tours (Skr30) leave from the Gammelstad **tourist office** (25 43 10; worldherit age.gammelstad@lulea.se; 9am-6pm mid-Jun–mid-Aug, 10am-4pm Tue-Thu rest of year) every hour on the hour between 10am and 4pm from mid-June to mid-August. (Tours are given in the language of whoever booked first, so you may have to wait an hour for one in English.) Bus 32 runs hourly from Luleå.

Adjoining the church village is an open-air museum, **Hägnan**, which houses a gift shop, 'olde tyme' candy store and petting zoo.

Back in Luleå, **Norrbottens Museum** (24 35 02; Storgatan 2; admission free; 10am-4pm Tue-Fri, noon-4pm Sat & Sun) is worth a visit just for the Sami section, but there are also exhibits about the Swedish settlers, plus films and musical performances, an outdoor maze and a kids playground. In summer it's also open on Mondays.

The neo-Gothic **Domkyrka** (cathedral; Mon-Fri summer) dates from 1893 and has an unusual altarpiece.

Kids will love the gigantic, educational playground that is **Teknikens Hus** (492201; adult/child Skr50/30; 10am-4pm daily mid-Jun–Aug, Tue-Sun rest of year), within the university campus 4km north. The museum has hands-on exhibitions about everything from hot-air balloons to the aurora borealis (northern lights), plus a planetarium (take bus 17 or 35).

Boden, some 36km northwest of Luleå, is Sweden's largest military town. Built in defence against Russia, it's surrounded by forts and has several good museums. **Rödbergsfortet** (0921-48 30 60; tours adult/child Skr100/75; tours 11am-3pm late Jun–mid-Aug), one of the five forts defending Boden, is open for guided tours hourly in summer and by appointment the rest of the year. The **Defence Museum** (0921-506 70; www.forsvaarsmuseum.se; Granatvägen 2; adult/child Skr60/30; 11am-4pm Wed-Sun) covers the history of the Swedish military from the 1800s to the present. Outdoors are examples of military vehicles.

Sleeping

SVIF Vandrarhem Kronan (43 40 50; www.vandrar hemmetkronan.se; Kronan H7; dm/s Skr170/250; P) About 3km from the centre, this year-round hostel is the best budget option in the area, with good facilities set in a forested location. To get here, take any bus heading toward Kronanområdet.

our pick Amber Hotel (102 00; www.amber hotell.nu; Stationsgatan 67; s/d Skr790/980, discounted to Skr500/690; P) The pick of the city-centre hotels is this small wooden guesthouse; its spacious rooms have all the modern touches, such as flat-screen TV, but still feel homey. It's just a few steps from the train station.

Strenuously mod in its decor, the designy **Quality Hotel Luleå** (20 10 00; lulea@quality.choice hotels.se; Storgatan 17; s/d from Skr1095/1195, discounted to Skr695/795; P) has a nightclub and several restaurants, a pool, and top of the line facilities in its rooms. A cheaper and more casual option is its sister hotel at the opposite end of Storgatan, the **Comfort Hotel** (220 220; Storgatan 59; s/d from Skr895/1095, discounted to Skr695/795; P), which transcends its worn state with charming staff and a faded-library theme – old books in each room, plus a book-lined reading room in the lobby. Guests at either hotel get free admission to the Cleo Nightclub inside the Quality (Thursday to Saturday evenings). Parking at either costs Skr125.

Eating & Drinking

Cafe Mat & Prat (28 11 90; Storgatan 51; mains Skr56-71; 10am-6pm Mon-Fri, 10am-4pm Sat) Sure, it's inside a shopping mall, but this is a pleasant, homely cafe serving real espresso as well as pastas, focaccia, sandwiches, salads and a good Thai curry.

Fiskekyrkan (22 02 01; Södra Hamnen; meals Skr65-175) In an old warehouse at the south harbour, Fiskekyrkan has live music Wednesday to Saturday, plus an affordable lunch buffet (around Skr70) and a range of meals on offer, from fast food (kebabs and pizzas) to more 'gourmet' offerings. This is a very popular late-night drinking spot.

Cook's Krog (21 18 00; Storgatan 17; meals Skr85-250) At the Quality Hotel, this is an upmarket but comfortable place serving Norrbotten regional specialities. Attached is Invit, a more casual bar-cafe, open Monday to Saturday until 9pm.

Roasters (888 40; Storgatan 43; mains Skr80-125) With a prime location for people-watching,

LAPPLAND & THE FAR NORTH

especially in nice weather when outdoor tables open in the middle of the street, this cafe serves coffee and a varied lunch menu and segues toward after-work drinks hang-out as the day progresses.

Getting There & Around

AIR

The **airport** (☎ 24 49 00) is 9km southwest of the town centre. SAS, Direktflyg and Nordic Airways fly regularly to Stockholm, Sundsvall and Umeå. Other airlines serve smaller destinations, including Pajala. Take the **airport bus** (☎ 122 00) from outside the Comfort Hotel on Storgatan (Skr45).

BUS

Bus 100 runs between Haparanda, Luleå, Skellefteå, Umeå and Sundsvall at least four times daily. Buses run frequently to Boden (Skr49, one hour), Arvidsjaur (Skr162, three hours, via Boden and Älvsbyn), and Jokkmokk (Skr179, three hours) and on to Gällivare (via Boden and Vuollerim).

TRAIN

Direct Tågkompaniet trains from Stock-holm and Göteborg run at night only. Most trains from Narvik and Kiruna via Boden terminate at Luleå.

PITEÅ

☎ 0911 / pop 22,500

Calling itself the 'Riviera of the North', Piteå has a compact, sweetly pastel town centre with a made-for-summer vibe and warm coastal waters that draw sun-worshiping visitors.

Piteå has all the usual services and a **tourist office** (☎ 933 90; www.pitea.se; Bryggargatan 14; 9am-7pm Mon-Sat, 10am-4pm Sun mid-May–Aug; 8am-5pm Mon-Fri Sep–mid-May) in a pretty yellow building next to a hopping beer garden, by the bus station. You can rent bikes here (Skr30 per day).

Sights & Activities

Piteå church (www.piteastadsforsamlin.nu; Sundsgatan; admission free), built in 1686, is among the oldest wooden churches in Norrland. It escaped being burned by the Russians in 1721 because they were using it as their headquarters.

There are several interesting wooden buildings on Storgatan, including the **rådhuset** (town hall), built in 1829 in a Finnish-Russian style imported from across the Baltic. The square it anchors is unique in

that its corners are closed. Rådhuset now houses displays about the area's cultural history in the **Piteå Museum** (☎ 126 15; www .piteamuseum.nu; Rådhustorget; admission free; 9am-4pm Tue-Fri, 11am-3pm Sat).

In nearby **Öjebyn**, 6km north of town, there is an interesting early 15th-century church with a clock tower thought to be the oldest building in Norrbotten. Around the church are cottages where parishioners from afar would stay overnight when visiting the church or the market. The town of Piteå originally sprouted up here, around the church, but was later moved closer to the sea. The church village has a **museum** (www .pitealandsforsamling.nu; admission free; 10am-4pm Mon-Fri Jun-Aug) and an attached cafe.

Piteå's **archipelago** has about 70 islands: Transport and cottages (from Skr350 per person) can be booked through the tourist office year-round.

Sleeping & Eating

STF Vandrarhem Piteå (☎ 158 80; pitevandrarhem.fh@ telia.com; Storgatan 3; dm Skr200) The STF hostel, with a nice location in Badhusparken, the city's main park/playground, can arrange visits to the church at Öjeby.

Pite Havsbadet (☎ 327 00; www.pite-havsbad.se; sites Skr230, cabins from Skr490, hotel s/d from Skr1040/1390;) This beachside area, about 10km south of Piteå and connected by the frequent bus 1, is the summer destination of choice for many holidaymakers. It's huge and has a restaurant, a cafe, various pools, minigolf, a children's playground, 'Dinosaurieland' and other family-focused activities, plus summer concerts and events.

Piteå Stadshotell (☎ 23 40 00; www.piteastadshotell .com; Olof Palmesgata 1; s/d from Skr1195/1425, discounted to Skr850/990) This elegant old hotel has good facilities, top-notch service and contains Statt Nightclub, a two-storey bar and dance club, plus a casino, a spa and multiple dining options. Rooms are small but nicely arranged, and more spacious suites (Skr2280) are available.

ourpick Krokodil (☎ 191 94; www.krokodil.nu; Storgatan 39; snacks from Skr35; 10am-4pm Mon-Sat plus evenings for events) A public living room, this 'culture cafe' has live music, readings, performances, art exhibits, coffee and pastries in a retro lounge.

Röda Rummet (☎ 23 40 00; dinner mains Skr125-235; lunch & dinner) At Piteå Stadshotell, this aptly named restaurant (the Red Room) serves traditional Swedish lunches (pancakes and lingonberries on Thursday!) from 11am to 1.30pm. The attached pub has a more casual atmosphere and menu to match.

Getting There & Around

Regional buses go frequently to Luleå (Skr70, 50 minutes), Haparanda (Skr187, three to four hours), Umeå (Skr220, 3½ hours) and other points. Buses connect Piteå to Älvsbyn, from where SJ night trains run to Stockholm (Skr770, 14 hours). **City buses** (☎ 917 00; www .citybuss.se) stop near the tourist office; tickets are Skr18.

HAPARANDA

☎ 0922 / pop 10,300

Bargain-hunter's alert! Haparanda has become a full-scale shopper's paradise, thanks to a 2005 decision to build an Ikea store in this tiny town nestled up against Finland. The furniture giant's arrival rescued the town's economy and encouraged other businesses (mainly big-box retail stores) to invest as well. This means great deals and hectic parking lots, but the move makes some historical sense, in a way: Haparanda was founded in 1821 as a trading centre to replace Sweden's loss of Torino (now in Finland) to Russia.

Haparanda's main **tourist office** (☎ 120 10; www.haparandatornio.com; Green Line; ⏰ 8am-8pm Mon-Fri, 10am-6pm Sat & Sun) is shared with Tornio on the 'green line'.

Sights & Activities

Haparanda's primary attraction, other than shopping, is its unique golf course. The **Green Zone Golf Course** (☎ 106 60) lies right on the border with Finland, and during a full round of golf the border is crossed four times. Around Midsummer you can play under the midnight sun; book in advance.

Full-day **boat tours** (☎ 120 10; www.bosmina.se) of the archipelago sail in July (adult/child Monday and Friday Skr450/400; Tuesday, Wednesday and Thursday Skr550/450) and include a visit to **Sandskär**, the largest island in Haparanda Skärgård National Park. It's possible to hire a cabin on the island (Skr400 per day). Book both through the tourist office.

The tourist office can also help to arrange white-water rafting trips on the scenic **Kukkolaforsen rapids**, which are on the

Torneälv 15km north of Haparanda and speed past at three million litres per second. In summer, you can watch locals hunting for whitefish using medieval dip nets. There's an excellent tourist village here, which includes a **camping ground and cabins** (☎ 310 00; sites Skr190, 4-bed cabins from Skr590), plus a restaurant, a cafe, a fish smoke-house, saunas and a museum.

Sleeping & Eating

Vandrarhem Haparanda (☎ 611 71; info@haparanda vandrarhem.com; Strandgatan 26; dm/s/d from Skr180/ 250/470; ⏰ reception 4-7pm year-round) This comfy, waterfront hostel is at the edge of a park and close to the town centre.

Stadshotellet (☎ 614 90; Torget 7; s/d from Skr820/ 1020, dm mid-May–Aug Skr300) This large, dignified hotel is the architectural focus of the town, and has two upmarket, ultra-atmospheric restaurants along with a more casual but still pretty pub-restaurant, Gulasch Baronen, with a great range of meals.

Getting There & Around

Tapanis Buss (☎ 129 55; www.tapanis.se) runs express coaches from Stockholm to Haparanda two to three times a week (Skr600, 15 hours). Regional buses reach Luleå (Skr134, 2½ hours, three daily) and towns further south. Daily bus 53 travels north along the border via the scenic Kukkolaforsen rapids, Övertorneå (Skr88, one to 1½ hours, three daily) and Pajala (Skr187, 3½ to 4½ hours, three daily), then continues west to Kiruna (Skr298, six hours, three daily).

PAJALA

☎ 0978 / pop 7300

Pajala makes a handy stopping point along this section of the Sweden-Finland border. It has a tiny town centre with most facilities, and a nice riverside pathway.

The **tourist office** (☎ 100 15; www.pajalaturism .bd.se; ⏰ 9am-7pm Jul & Aug, 8am-4pm Mon-Fri Sep-Jun) is near the bus station. Nearby is the world's largest **circular sundial**. Toward the river is **Laestadius pörtet** (☎ 120 55; Laestadiusvägen 36; ⏰ Jun-Aug), the mid-19th-century home of Lars Levi Laestadius, a local vicar and founder of a religious movement.

The new **Snickarbacken Lägenhetshotell** (☎ 100 70; Kirunavägen; huts Skr175, apt per person from Skr270) has impeccable apartment-style suites for up to eight people, as well as single and double rooms with kitchens, and tiny 'sleep huts' with TV, microwave, minirefrigerator, and a shared bathroom and sauna.

The **STF hostel** (☎ 741 80; Torneälvens strand; sites/dm Skr90/145, cabins Skr320-510) is integrated with the camping ground, near the river. Beds are in small cabins; it's a picturesque setting, but make sure you have bug spray, as the waterside location is a mosquito's paradise.

Bus 55 runs from Luleå to Pajala via Överkalix (Skr211, 3½ hours, twice daily), while bus 53 runs between Haparanda and Kiruna (Skr298, six hours, twice daily) via Övertorneå and Pajala.

From Pajala, you can press on southwest to Gällivare on bus 46 (Skr153, two hours, three daily), or northwest to Vittangi on bus 51 or 53 (Skr117, two hours, twice daily). From Vittangi you can journey through the wilderness: north to Karesuando on bus 50 (Skr117, 1½ hours) or west to Kiruna on bus 50, 51 or 53 (Skr88, one hour, three daily).

LAPPLAND

KARESUANDO
☎ 0981 / pop 350

If your visions of Lappland (Gárrasavvon) involve acres and acres of open tundra uninterrupted except for the odd lost reindeer or dilapidated hut, this is your town. Karesuando, across the bridge from the Finnish town of Kaaresuvanto, is the northernmost church village in Sweden, and it feels that way: utterly remote and exquisitely lonely. The area revels in the romance of extremes: the midnight sun shines here from late May to mid-July, but in winter the temperature hits -50°C.

There's a **tourist office** (☎ 202 05; www.karesuando.com) on the bridge to Finland, with regional information, souvenirs and a coffeeshop. There are no banks in the village, but there is a convenience shop and fuel station; eating options are very limited.

Karesuando boasts the northernmost **church** (☉ 7am-4pm) in Sweden, built in 1816; the wooden altar was made by Swedish artist Bror Hjorth. There's also **Vita Huset** (☎ 201 70; guided tours Skr20; ☉ 9am-5pm Mon-Tue & Fri, noon-8pm Wed), a folk museum in a former policemen's residence with mainly Norwegian items from WWII; a simple **log cabin** (☉ 24hr) that was home to preacher-botanist Lars Levi Laestadius; and **Sámiid Viessu**, a Sami art and handicraft exhibition and museum.

Treriksröset, 100km northwest of the village, marks the point where Norway, Sweden and Finland meet; it's about 10m out into lake Goldajärvi. Ask the tourist office about boats leaving from the Finnish village Kilpisjärvi (three daily mid-June to mid-August) to visit this hard-to-access area. You can also reach it via a hiking trail through Malla National Park, or by snowmobile in winter.

Karesuando has a small **STF Vandrarhem** (☎ 203 30; dm Skr140; ☉ Apr–mid-Sep), about a kilometre before you reach the bridge and tourist office. It's operated jointly with the **Hotel Karesuando** (☎ 203 30; s/d Skr600/700), across the road.

KIRUNA
☎ 0980 / pop 23,407

The citizens of Kiruna (Giron) live up to their nickname – 'the No-problem People' – by remaining unperturbed at the news that their city is on the verge of collapsing into a mine pit. A few years back, it became clear that years of iron-ore extraction was sucking the stability out of the bedrock underneath the town. In 2007 the town voted to shift itself a couple of miles northwest; plans are to move the railway and about 450 homes by 2013, with the rest of the town centre to follow gradually.

It's probably worth the trouble: Kiruna is home to the world's largest iron-ore deposit, going 4km deep. The government-run mining company LKAB originally mined via open pits, but switched in the 1960s to tunnelling underground; the action now happens 914m below the surface.

The **tourist office** (☎ 188 80; www.lappland.se; Folkets Hus, Lars Janssonsgatan 17; ☉ 8.30am-9pm Mon-Fri, 8.30am-6pm Sat & Sun Jun-Aug, Mon-Sat Sep-May), on the main square, has internet access and can book mine tours and accommodation as well as various activities, including rafting, dogsledding and snow-scooter trips. There's a cafe upstairs.

Held in the last week of January, the **Kiruna Snow Festival** (www.kiruna.com/snowfestival) is based around a snow-sculpting competition. The tradition started in 1985 as a space-themed snow-sculpture contest to celebrate the launching of a rocket (Viking) from nearby space base Esrange (p308).

Sights & Activities
A visit to the depths of the **LKAB iron-ore mine**, 540m underground, is recommended; some

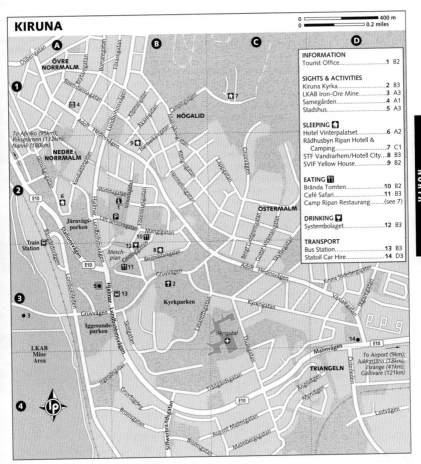

KIRUNA

| 0 | 400 m |
| 0 | 0.2 miles |

INFORMATION
Tourist Office..........................1 B2

SIGHTS & ACTIVITIES
Kiruna Kyrka..........................2 B3
LKAB Iron-Ore Mine.............3 A3
Samegården...........................4 A1
Stadshus................................5 A3

SLEEPING
Hotel Vinterpalatset...............6 A2
Rådhusbyn Ripan Hotell &
    Camping..........................7 C1
STF Vandrarhem/Hotell City...8 B3
SVIF Yellow House...................9 B2

EATING
Brända Tomten....................10 B2
Café Safari.............................11 B3
Camp Ripan Restaurang.......(see 7)

DRINKING
Systembolaget......................12 B3

TRANSPORT
Bus Station...........................13 B3
Statoil Car Hire....................14 D3

of the stats you'll hear on a tour are mind-blowing. Tours leave daily from the tourist office, and more frequently from mid-June to mid-August (adult/student/child Skr280/180/50). Tours in English happen only a few times a week; make bookings through the tourist office.

Kiruna kyrka (Gruvvägen; 10am-9pm summer) looks like a huge Sami *kåta* (hut); it's particularly pretty against a snowy backdrop. Another landmark, at the opposite end of the aesthetics spectrum, is the **Stadshus** (town hall; 705 21; Hjalmar Lundbohmsvägen; 9am-6pm), which, despite its grim facade, is actually very nice inside and has a free slide show on the hour, and free guided tours.

Samegården (170 29; Brytaregatan 14; adult/child Skr20/free; 7am-4pm Mon-Fri Jun-Aug) has displays about Sami culture and a handicrafts shop attached to a hotel-restaurant.

The district surrounding Kiruna includes Sweden's highest peak, **Kebnekaise** (2111m), and some of Sweden's best national parks and hiking routes; see p309 for suggestions on tackling them.

Around Kiruna
JUKKASJÄRVI

As well as the famous Ice Hotel, tiny Jukkasjärvi, 18km east of Kiruna, is home to a **church** (8am-10pm summer), which has a modern Sami painting behind the altar. Near the church is **Gárdi** (adult/child Skr60/30; tours 10am-6pm

THE ICE HOTEL

Every winter at Jukkasjärvi, 18km east of Kiruna, the amazing **Ice Hotel** (www.icehotel.com) is built from hundreds of tonnes of ice taken from the frozen local river. This custom-built 'igloo' has a chapel (popular for weddings – giving new meaning to the expression 'cold feet'!) and a bar – you can drink from a glass made of ice – and ice-sculpture exhibitions. It also has 50 'hotel rooms' outfitted with reindeer skins and sleeping bags guaranteed to keep you warm despite the -5°C temperatures (and in winter that's nothing – outside the hotel it can be as low as -30°C).

Staff can arrange numerous pursuits such as snowmobile safaris, skiing, ice-fishing and dogsledding.

Even after the Ice Hotel has melted away in summer, visitors can still experience a little of the magic. Inside a giant freezer warehouse, called the **Ice Hotel Art Center**, at a temperature of -5°C, there are a few of the Ice Hotel features: a bar, ice sculptures and guest igloos.

Rooms in the ice hotel in winter cost from Skr2600/2700 per single/double room. There are also stylish hotel rooms (heated – and *not* made of ice); three-bed cabins with skylights, enabling you to watch the northern lights in winter; and chalets (with kitchen) sleeping up to four. These are all available year-round – summer prices are quite reasonable (Skr870/1050). See the website for more details and a list of seasonal rates.

mid-Jun–mid-Aug), a reindeer yard that you can tour with a Sami guide to learn about reindeer farming and Sami culture. Regular bus 501 runs between Kiruna and Jukkasjärvi (Skr29, 30 minutes, several daily).

ESRANGE

Some 23km further out is the space base **Esrange**, a facility where scientists research outer space as well as atmospheric phenomena like the northern lights. Detailed four-hour **tours** (adult/child Skr390/200) of the facility are offered to enthusiasts in summer, but must be arranged in advance; enquire at the Kiruna tourist office. There's no public transport; taxi fare should be around Skr500.

Sleeping

Rådhusbyn Ripan Hotell & Camping (☎ 630 00; www.ripan.se; Campingvägen 5; sites Skr125, hotel s/d from Skr1200/1535, discounted to Skr795/920, cabins from Skr995; P 🛒) In the northern part of town, this large and well-equipped camping ground has hotel-standard chalets in addition to its caravan and tent sites. Ask about the organised walk to Samegården, the museum of Sami culture (Skr450, 1pm Friday), and other activities.

SVIF Yellow House (☎ 137 50; www.yellowhouse.nu; Hantverkaregatan 25; dm from Skr150, s/d Skr300/400) The SVIF hostel also has budget hotel rooms; the excellent facilities include a sauna, kitchen and laundry, a TV in each room, and a pretty, quiet enclosed garden.

STF Vandrarhem/Hotell City (☎ hostel 171 95, hotel 666 55; Bergmästaregatan 7; dm/s/d from Skr160/320/400,

hotel s/d Skr650/700) This central hostel has good facilities right next to the wooden church; it's run in conjunction with the new low-budget hotel at the same address.

ourpick **Hotel Vinterpalatset** (☎ 677 70; www.vinterpalatset.se; Järnvägsgatan 18; s/d from Skr720/930, discounted to Skr660/790; P 🖵) Inside this dark-brown wooden building near the train station are pretty, spacious B&B rooms, each with a TV and modern bathroom, plus an upstairs lounge and a breakfast room almost flowery enough to make you think you're in the Cotswolds. The decadent breakfast includes cured salmon and roast game.

Eating & Drinking

Café Safari (☎ 174 60; Geologsgatan 4; meals Skr35-65) This is the nicest cafe in town – a long skinny room with good coffee and cakes, plus light meals such as sandwiches, quiche and baked potatoes.

Brända Tomten (☎ 101 09; Föreningsgatan 6; meals Skr35-65) In the city centre, this casual cafe and fast-food joint serves surprisingly good coffee and filling lunch items – layered sandwiches, salads, pies and so on. Big windows make for fun people-watching.

ourpick **Camp Ripan Restaurang** (Campingvägen; lunch buffets Skr90, meals Skr135-255; ☽ lunch 11am-2pm). This restaurant at the camping ground (of all places) has an interesting and creative menu, which includes vegetarian *pierogi*, reindeer, salmon, elaborate salads and burgers, and an unusually expansive lunch buffet that's heavy on the veggies.

Getting There & Around

The small **airport** (☎ 680 00), 7km east of the town, has two to three daily direct flights to Stockholm with SAS, and to Umeå (weekdays only) with Skyways. The **airport bus** (☎ 156 90) operates during peak summer season.

Regional buses to and from the **bus station** (Hjalmar Lundbohmsvägen), opposite the Stadshus, serve all major settlements around Norrbotten. Bus 10 runs twice daily to Gällivare (Skr134) and Luleå (Skr293), and bus 92 goes two to four times daily to Nikkaluokta (Skr79) for the Kebnekaise trail head. To reach Karesuando and Finland, take bus 50 (Skr179, Sunday to Friday).

Trains between Kiruna and Narvik have earned a reputation as unreliable and often late, so you'll want to plan around a flexible schedule. SJ connects Kiruna with Luleå (Skr269, four hours), Stockholm (Skr854, overnight) and Narvik (Norway; Skr207, three hours). Trains to Narvik call at Abisko (Skr91, 1½ hours) and Riksgränsen.

Contact **Statoil** (☎ 143 65; Växlaregatan 20) for car hire.

ABISKO
☎ 0980

Spectacular scenery, friendly people, a long tradition of Sami culture and extremely easy access to all of these make Abisko (Abeskovvu) one of the highlights of any trip to Lappland. The 75-sq-km **Abisko National Park** spreads out from the southern shore of scenic lake Torneträsk. It's framed by the striking profile of Lapporten, a 'gate' formed by neighbouring hills that serves as the legendary gate to Lappland.

Abisko is less rugged than either Sarek or Padjelanta, and easier to get to by train, bus and the scenic mountain motorway between Kiruna to Narvik. This is also the driest part of Sweden, giving the area a completely distinct landscape – it's wide, open and arid, and consequently has a relatively long (for northern Sweden) hiking season.

Abisko has two train stops – Östra station puts you in the centre of the tiny, tiny village, while Abisko Turiststation is across the highway from the STF lodge.

The **STF Turiststation/Abisko Mountain Lodge** (☎ 402 00; www.abisko.nu; ☼ 8am-9pm 22 Dec–3 Jan, 15 Feb–4 May & 6 Jun–21 Sep) provides information on local hikes; **guides** (☼ 8-9am & 7-8pm) are available for consultation, and several thematic

tours (8.30pm Thu & Sun, Skr150) and **Sami camp tours** (per person Skr290-640; ☼ 8.40am-5pm) leave from here. There's a small shop with supplies, snacks and **equipment rentals** (☼ 8am-8pm Jun, 8am-10pm Jul & Aug), as well as a restaurant and hostel (see p310).

Naturum (☎ 401 77; ☼ 10am-6pm mid-Jun–Sep, until 9pm Wed & Fri) has an office and exhibition space next to STF Abisko Turiststation/ Abisko Mountain Lodge; staff can suggest hikes and answer questions about where to hike and what to bring. Various guided tours are available (Skr50 to Skr75 per person), and a simple map offers suggestions based on the amount of time you might have ('If you have two hours…').

Sights & Activities

Hiking is the big activity here – trails are varied in both distance and terrain, and they're easy to reach. Between the STF Turiststation and Naturum, you'll find all the expertise and equipment you need for everything from a day hike to a month-long trek along the popular Kungsleden.

The **Kungsleden** trail (p60) follows the Abiskojåkka valley, and day trips of 10km to 20km are no problem from Abisko. Kungsleden extends 450km south from Abisko to Hemavan, with STF huts serving most of the trail; the hut at Alesjaure is 15km from the trailhead.

Other hikes include the overnight trip to the STF hut at **Kårsavagge** (west of Abisko, 15km each way); the four-hour return trip to rock formations at **Kärkevagge**, with **Rissájávrre** the 'Sulphur Lake'; and a great four-hour return hike to **Paddus**, a former Sami sacrificial site with awesome views of Lapporten and lake Törnetrask. The staff at Naturum have free basic maps and up-to-date information on trail conditions, weather and such.

There's also a route around **Abisko canyon** and a 39km-long **Navvy Trail** to Riksgränsen, alongside the railway line.

If you can invest the time, there's a highly recommended 100km trek from Abisko to Nikkaluokta that runs via the STF lodge Kebnekaise Fjällstation (p310).

For hikes in this area, employ the map *Fjällkartan BD6* (Skr110 to Skr120, available at the STF lodge, Naturum and most sporting-goods stores). For more information on the Kungsleden trail see p60.

Across the highway from the STF Turiststation, a **chair lift** (one way/return daytime Skr140/175, late night Skr175/220; ☑ 9.30am-4pm, also 10pm-1am Tue, Thu & Sat mid-Jun–mid-Jul) takes you up the neighbouring Mt Nuolja (1169m), where those without vertigo can enjoy epic views from the deck of the **Panorama Café** (☑ 9.30am-4pm). In summer this is a prime spot from which to see the midnight sun. Tickets are sold at the STF reception desk.

In Björkliden, 8km northwest of Abisko, you will find **Hotell Fjället** (☎ 641 00; www.bjorkli den.com; s/d from Skr750/1100), which offers various summer and winter activities, including hiking and caving (spelunking). There's a welltrodden walking path from behind Abisko tourist station to Björkliden.

The unique and highly rated **Björklidens golf course** (☎ 0980-641 00; info@bjorkliden.com; ☑ 8am-4.30pm Apr-Sep) is the world's northernmost golf course – and as a result has a fairly short season (it is covered in snow for most of the year).

Sleeping & Eating

our pick Abisko Fjällturer (☎ 401 03; www.abisko .net; dm Skr175) Just behind the town, this is a backpacker's delight. The small hostel has basic comfortable accommodation and a wonderful wooden sauna, but the treat is in the reasonably priced activities on offer, especially during the winter. Brothers Tomas and Andreas keep a large team of sledge dogs; one package on offer includes a night's accommodation plus the chance to drive your own sled, pulled by dogs, for about 10km. There are also very popular week-long sled trips (around Skr8000), which include all of your meals and accommodation – you will need to book very early for these. During summer you can take mountain walks with the dogs. To find the place, follow signs from Abisko Östra to the 'Dog Hostel'.

STF Abisko Turiststation/Abisko Mountain Lodge (☎ 402 00; www.abisko.nu; dm Skr210, hotel s/d from Skr690/1190, hostel s/d from Skr450/680; ☑ 8am-9pm 22 Dec–3 Jan, 15 Feb–4 May, 6 Jun–21 Sep) This huge place, which also serves as a local information centre, has 300 beds in various configurations, kept to the usual high STF standards. In winter, when the lake freezes, the Turiststation opens its new Abisko Ark Hotel, which consists of fishing hut–style cabins and a sauna built directly on the ice – popular for those hoping to glimpse the northern lights (book in advance). Trekking

gear can be hired here, and there's a variety of guided tours each day. There's also a shop with basic groceries. Breakfast/lunch/dinner (Skr80/80/290) is available (lunch from noon to 2pm, dinner from 6pm to 8pm and à la carte from 8pm to 9pm).

STF huts (bed Skr215-260, nonmembers additional Skr50-100) These self-service huts along the Kungsleden trail are spread at 10km to 20km intervals between Abisko and Kvikkjokk; you'll need your own sleeping bag. Campers are charged Skr40.

Kebnekaise Fjällstation (☎ 0980-550 00; kebnekaise@stfturist.se; dm Skr310, s/d from Skr810/1080; ☑ Mar-Apr & mid-Jun–mid-Sep) Meals are available here, and guided tours to the summit of Kebnekaise are offered. Buses go to Nikkaluokta, a 19km hike away.

Lapporten Stormarknad (☑ 9am-8pm Mon-Fri, shorter hours Sat & Sun) In Abisko village this grocery store also carries a range of outdoor supplies, such as batteries, candles, insect spray and basic camping gear.

Getting There & Away

In addition to trains (stations at Abisko Östra and Abisko Turiststation) between Luleå and Narvik, bus 91 runs from Kiruna to Abisko (Skr107, one hour 20 minutes).

RIKSGRÄNSEN

☎ 0980

A tiny ski-resort town tucked just inside the border with Norway (Riksgränsen translates as 'National Border'), this town is the place to be if you have a hankering to ski into Norway and back at midnight in May.

The historical **Navvy Trail** walkway follows the railway line and takes you to Abisko (39km) or Rombaksbotn (Norway; 15km).

Rental of downhill ski gear costs from Skr250 per day, and day lift-passes start at around Skr300.

Katterjokk Turiststation (☎ 431 08; www.kat terjokk.se; dm summer/winter Skr250/310; ☑ Feb-Sep) is a well-run hostel 2km east of Riksgränsen. Three-hour to whole-day guided walks can be arranged (Skr200 to Skr550), as well as fishing, hunting, mountain biking etc.

Dominating the hillside, **Riksgränsen** (☎ 400 80; info@riksgransen.nu; s/d from Skr1200/1800) is a large resort that's popular with skiers in winter and converts to an 'alpine spa' retreat in summer. Rooms in the comfy little annex, Meteorologen, are homier and cheaper.

Getting There & Away

From Kiruna, bus 91 (Skr144, two hours, two or three daily) goes to Riksgränsen, via Abisko. Riksgränsen is the last train station in Sweden before the train rushes through tunnels and mountain scenery back to sea level at Narvik in Norway; three daily trains run on the Luleå–Kiruna–Narvik route, although reportedly not always on schedule.

GÄLLIVARE

☎ 0970 / pop 19,500

Gällivare (Váhtjer) and its northern twin, Malmberget, are surrounded by forest and dwarfed by the bald Dundret hill. After Kiruna, Malmberget (Ore Mountain) is the second-largest iron-ore mine in Sweden; the town belongs to government-owned mining company LKAB. And like Kiruna, the area's sustaining industry is simultaneously threatening the town with collapse: all that digging around below the surface has weakened the foundations beneath Malmberget, so buildings are gradually being shifted to sturdier ground. The populace seems unfazed.

The **tourist office** (☎ 166 60; turistinfo@gellivare.se; Centralplan 3; ⊙ 8am-6pm daily mid-Jun–mid-Aug, Mon-Fri rest of year) is near the train station in the town's centre, and staff can organise a number of activities and wilderness excursions. The town has banks and supermarkets on Storgatan. The **library** (Hantverkargatan) has free internet access.

Sights & Activities

The **Gällivare Museum** (☎ 186 92; Storgatan 16; admission free; ⊙ 11am-3.30pm daily mid-Jun–Aug) has exhibitions on railway workers, Sami culture and early settlers, plus a collection of local artefacts and the famous Mosquito Museum, relocated from a nearby bog.

The squat white 'new' **church** (Lasarettsgatan 10; ⊙ summer), from 1882, is worth a look, as is the diminutive **old church** (⊙ summer), nicknamed the 'one-penny church' because that's the amount each household had to contribute to get it built back in 1755. It's near the train station.

The **hembygdsområde** (historic community centre; admission free; ⊙ mid-Jun–Aug), by the camping ground, has pioneer and Sami huts in a small open-air museum.

Dundret (821m) is a nature reserve with excellent views, and you can see the midnight sun here from 2 June to 12 July. In winter there are four nordic courses and 10 ski runs

of varying difficulty, and the mountaintop resort rents out gear and organises numerous activities. If you have your own car, it's a rather hair-raising drive to the top.

In Malmberget, 5km north of Gällivare, **Kåkstan** (admission free) is a historical 'shanty town' museum village, dating from the 1888 iron-ore rush. Contact the Gällivare tourist office for details of the **LKAB iron-ore mine tour** (Skr250; ⊙ tours 9.30am-1pm mid-Jun–mid-Aug, by appointment in winter), which takes you down on a bus.

And if you like that, you will simply love the **Gruvmuseum** (Puoitakvägen; adult/child Skr40/free; ⊙ 2-6pm Tue-Thu mid-Jul–late Aug, by appointment other times), covering 250 years of mining. Bus 1 to Malmberget departs from directly opposite the Gällivare church; outside of summer hours, contact the Gällivare tourist office to arrange a visit.

AROUND GÄLLIVARE

Stora Sjöfallet National Park is a wild area of mountains and lakes that lies over 115km west of Gällivare, but transport links are good in summer. At the eastern end of the park, you can cross the Stora Lulevatten lake on the STF ferry to Saltoluokta lodge, and climb **Lulep Gierkav** (1139m) for the best views.

There's an interesting **Sami church** and **handicraft outlet** at Saltoluokta, and the Kungsleden trail (p309) runs north and south from here. **Stora Sjöfallet** is now dry, due to the hydroelectric schemes, and many of the local lakes have artificial shorelines. Take the bus to the end of the road at the Sami village **Ritsem**, where there's an STF lodge, and you can cross by ferry to the northern end of the **Padjelantaleden** (p62). Ask for details, maps and road conditions at the tourist office, or at any STF in the area.

Sleeping & Eating

Gällivare Camping (☎ 100 10; info@gellivarecamping .com; Hembygdsområdet; sites Skr130, 2-/4-bed cabins from Skr300/450) This camping ground, now open year-round, shares a lovely riverside spot with the *hembygdsområde* (see left). Cabins are set up more like apartments, with excellent, modern facilities, and reception can organise activities including trips up Dundret to eat waffles under the midnight sun (Skr300 per person) or day hikes with reindeer as pack animals (Skr780).

Grand Hotel Lapland (☎ 77 22 90; www.grandho tellapland.com; Lasarettsgatan 1; s/d Skr1295/1675) This modern hotel opposite the train station has comfortable rooms, and its 2nd-floor dining room is apparently *the* place to meet for *dagens* lunch (Skr78). The ground-level pub is dark and cosy, with covered outdoor seating for summer.

Restaurang Husmans (☎ 170 30; Malmbergsvägen 1; mains from Skr55; ☒ 9am-9pm Mon-Fri, 11am-8pm Sat & Sun), close to the tourist office and behind Hotel Lapland, serves kebabs and salads, and in the evenings has a small dining nook where you can get Arabic food.

Getting There & Away

Regional buses depart from the train station. Bus 45 runs daily to Östersund (Skr465, 11 hours) via Jokkmokk and Arvidsjaur; bus 93 serves Ritsem (Skr204, three hours) and Kungsleden in Stora Sjöfallet National Park (mid-June to mid-September only); buses 10 and 52 go to Kiruna (Skr134, two hours); and bus 44 runs to Jokkmokk and Luleå (Skr234, three hours).

Tågkompaniet (☎ 0771-44 41 11; www.tagkompaniet .se in Swedish) trains come from Luleå and Stockholm (sometimes changing at Boden), and from Narvik in Norway. More exotic is the **Inlandsbanan** (☎ 0771-53 53 53; www.inlandsbanan .se), which terminates at Gällivare.

JOKKMOKK

☎ 0971 / pop 5,600

An important town in Sami culture, Jokkmokk (Dálvvadis) has not only the definitive Sami museum but is also the site of a huge annual market gathering. Just north of the Arctic Circle, it's a quiet little town that makes a good base for visitors to **Laponia World Heritage site** (see Map p55); ask for information about the site at the tourist office or at the Ájtte museum's information desk.

Started as a Sami market and mission, Jokkmokk has been home since 1605 to the **Sami winter fair** – a three-day event that attracts some 30,000 people and starts on the first Thursday in February – during which you can shop seriously for Sami *duodji* (handicraft).

The **tourist office** (☎ 121 40; www.turism.jokkmokk .se; Stortorget 4; ☒ 9am-7pm Mon-Fri, 10am-6pm Sat & Sun mid-Jun–Aug; 8.30am-noon & 1-4pm Mon-Fri rest of year) can help with information and has internet access. There are banks and supermarkets in the town centre.

About 7km south of Jokkmokk you will cross the **Arctic Circle** on Rd 45. There is a cafe

and camping ground at the site that sells cute but corny certificates to those interested in having proof that they have travelled this far north.

For daily weather reports and forecasts, call ☎ 0980-113 50.

Sights & Activities

The welcoming and illuminating **Ájtte Museum** (☎ 170 70; Kyrkogatan 3; adult/child Skr50/free; ☒ 9am-6pm mid-Jun–mid-Aug, 10am-4pm Mon-Fri rest of year) is the highlight of a visit to Jokkmokk; it's Sweden's most thorough introduction to Sami culture, including traditional costume, silverware and some 400-year-old magical painted shamans' drums. Look for replicas of sacrificial sites and a diagram explaining the uses and significance of various reindeer entrails. One section details the widespread practice of harnessing the rivers in Lappland for hydroelectric power and the consequences this has had for the Sami people and their territory. There are extensive notes in English. The museum also has a very practical section, with information on Lappland's mountain areas, including detailed maps, slides, videos and a reference library.

Stop by **Sami Duodji** (☎ 128 94; Porjusvägen 4; ☒ 9am-3pm) to browse and shop for authentic Sami handicraft.

The squat red **wooden church** (Storgatan; ☒ Jun-Aug) is worth a visit; it's from 1976 but was built in the style of its predecessor of 1607. The colour scheme is inspired by Sami clothing.

Jokkmokks Fjällträdgård (adult/child Skr25/free), by the lake, introduces mountain trees and other local flora, and there's a **homestead museum** just across the road. A marked path around the lake features information boards about local wildlife.

The tourist office has a brochure about outdoor adventure tours available in the area, from fly-fishing to berry picking.

AROUND JOKKMOKK

Tiny **Kvikkjokk** (Huhttán), around 100km west of Jokkmokk, is on the Kungsleden (p60) and Padjelantaleden (see p62). Several fantastic day walks start from the village, including climbs to the mountain **Snjerak** (809m; three hours return) and a steeper ascent of **Prinskullen** (749m; three hours return). Follow signs to a car park at the top of the hill to catch the trail; if you instead continue straight ahead until the road ends, you'll find another car park

---

SAMI CULTURE & TRADITIONS

Sami life was originally based on hunting and fishing, but at some point during the 16th century the majority of reindeer were domesticated and the hunting economy transformed into a nomadic herding economy. While reindeer still figure prominently in Sami life, only about 16% of the Sami people are still directly involved in reindeer herding and transport by reindeer sled, and only a handful of traditionalists continue to lead a truly nomadic lifestyle.

A major identifying element of Sami culture is the *joik* (or *yoik*). This is a rhythmic poem composed for a specific person to describe their innate nature, and is considered to be owned by the person it describes. Other traditional elements of the culture include the use of folk medicine, shamanism, artistic pursuits (especially woodcarving and silversmithing) and striving for ecological harmony.

The Sami national dress is the only genuine folk dress that's still in casual use in Sweden, and you'll readily see it on the streets of Jokkmokk, especially during the winter fair. Each district has its own distinct fashion, many of which are displayed at Jokkmokk's Ájtte Museum (opposite).

---

and the **STF Fjällstation** (☺ late Jun-Aug), where you can get information and brochures.

The best hiking in this area, at least for experienced and well-kitted trekkers, is in **Sarek National Park** (☎ 0920-962 00). Full of sharp peaks and huge glaciers, its largest valley, Rapadalen, is lush with birch and willow trees. The Kungsleden trail dips briefly into Sarek, at the southeastern corner of the park. Trekking here is certainly not for the casual walker, and hikers must be prepared for very rugged conditions. Major trails are often washed out or in poor repair, and the extremes of terrain make for volatile weather conditions. There are no tourist facilities within the park, so be sure to check with an STF lodge or the National Park office before setting out. For more information on hiking in these regions see p58.

Sleeping & Eating

STF Vandrarhem Åsgård (☎ 559 77; asgard@jokkmokk-hostel.com; Åsgatan 20; dm Skr125-160; ☺ reception 8-10am & 5-8pm; [P]) The STF hostel has a lovely setting among green lawns and trees, right near the tourist office; it's a comfortable place with numerous bunk beds, a kitchen, a TV lounge, showers in the basement and a computer with internet access (Skr10 per 15 minutes, when reception is open). Cycle hire is available (half/full day Skr40/75).

Hotell Gästis (☎ 100 12; www.hotell-gastis.com; Herrevägen 1; s/d from Skr850/1095; [P]) This place has pleasant rooms in a small grey building. There's also a good restaurant here, with lunch specials and à la carte dinners.

Café Glasskas (Porjusvägen 7; mains Skr35-75) A coffeeshop, bar and internet cafe, Glasskas has a great, wide patio for warm-weather dining,

casual but filling meals (salads, quiches, sandwiches etc) and friendly service.

our pick Ájtte Museum restaurant (mains Skr75-90; ☺ noon-4pm) At the museum cafe, it's possible to enhance what you've learned about the local wildlife by sampling some of them as a lunch special.

There are supermarkets along Storgatan.

Getting There & Away

Buses arrive and leave from the bus station on Klockarvägen. Buses 44 and 45 run twice daily to and from Gällivare (Skr107, one to three hours), and bus 45 goes to and from Arvidsjaur once a day (Skr162, two to three hours). Bus 94 runs to Kvikkjokk (Skr134, two hours) twice daily.

In summer, Inlandsbanan trains stop in Jokkmokk. For main-line trains, take bus 94 to Murjek via Vuollerim (Skr68, one hour, up to six times daily) or bus 44 bus to Boden and Luleå (Skr163, two to three hours).

ARVIDSJAUR

☎ 0960 / pop 6948

The small settlement of Arvidsjaur, on the Inlandsbanan rail line, was established as a Sami marketplace, but it's most famous now as a testing ground for fast machines. Local companies specialise in setting up test tracks on the frozen lakes in the area, then putting vehicles through their paces. At the time of research, construction workers were busily remaking the main street, a long-term project that should keep traffic interesting for some time.

Just off Storgatan, the town's main road, is the **tourist office** (☎ 175 00; www.arvidsjaur.se/turism;

Östra Skolgatan 18C; ☼ 9.30am-6pm Mon-Fri, noon-4.30 Sat & Sun Jun-Aug, 8.30am-4.30pm Mon-Fri Sep-May). Storgatan is also where you'll also find banks, two supermarkets, pizza joints and petrol stations. The **library** (Medborgarhuset, Storgatan; ☼ Mon-Fri) has free internet access.

Sights & Activities

The first church was built in Arvidsjaur in 1607, in the hope of introducing the Sami to Christianity. Church attendance laws imposed a certain amount of pew time upon the nomadic Sami, so to make their church visits more manageable they built small cottages (*gåhties*) for overnighting. Some 80 of these are preserved now in **Lappstaden** (admission free, tours Skr30; ☼ 10am-7pm, tours 5pm Jun-Aug), just across Storgatan from the modern church. The buildings are owned by the forest Sami and are still in use. In the last week of August, Lappstaden is home to **Storstämning**, an annual feast, party and Sami association meeting.

From early July to early August, an old **steam train** (☎ 136 58; adult/child Skr190/free, Inlandsbanan travellers Skr120) makes return evening trips to Slagnäs on Friday and Saturday, departing at 5.45pm and returning around 10pm, with a stop along the way for a beach barbecue and swim.

Also in summer is the opportunity for **white-water rafting** (☎ 070-253 05 83; adult/child Skr445/295) on the nearby Piteälven.

For a more mellow diversion, follow the winding Kyrkstigen path from the church to the **hembygdsomradet** (☼ 10am-4pm), an open-air homestead museum.

Sleeping & Eating

Fast food restaurants and tiny cafes line the main drag through town; for something fancier, try the restaurant-bar in **Hotell Laponia** (☎ 555 00; www.hotell-laponia.se; ☼ 3-10pm).

Lappugglans Turistviste (☎ 124 13; lappugglan@ hem.utfors.se; Västra Skolgatan 9; dm per adult Skr130-145, per child Skr65; P) A hostel with a likable hippie vibe, Lappugglan is close to the train station and as endearing as it is handy, with a small museum and a resident chain-saw sculptor (he made the elk standing in front of the library on Storgatan). One sleeping option is a four-bed Lappish hut.

Lapland Lodge (☎ 137 20, 0768-47 57 17; www.laplandlodge.eu; Östra Kyrkogatan 18; s/d Skr550/700, f Skr750-1050; P ▯) A new B&B next to the church, this friendly place offers a range of room

configurations in a pretty yellow house with contemporary comforts (spa bathtubs, flat-screen TVs, free wi-fi) amid antique style (it's decorated with old wooden skis, antlers and snowshoes). Family rooms are huge. An outdoor Jacuzzi and sauna are available.

Getting There & Around

Arvidsjaur Airport (☎ 0960-173 80; www.ajr.nu) is 11km east of the centre and has frequent connections to Stockholm-Arlanda (three daily Monday to Friday, one or two Saturday and Sunday, two hours). At the time of research, there was talk of adding a direct connection between Arvidsjaur and Hemavan airports.

Länstrafiken Norrbotten bus 45 goes daily between Gällivare and Östersund, stopping at the bus station on Storgatan. Bus 200 runs daily between Skellefteå and Bodø (Norway) via Arvidsjaur. In summer the Inlandsbanan train can take you north to Gällivare (Skr336) via Jokkmokk, or south to Mora via Östersund (Skr582).

SORSELE

☎ 0952 / pop 3,000

Sleepy Sorsele, on Inlandsbanan, has the small but sincere **Inlandsbanemuseet** (www.grandnordic .se; adult/child Skr20/free; ☼ summer) at the train station. The adjoining **tourist office** (☎ 140 90; turist@ vindelalven.se; ☼ 9am-5pm Mon-Fri, noon-5pm Sat & Sun) can arrange activities including fishing and canoe tours. Sorsele has all facilities, including a bank, supermarket and public library (with internet access).

Pensionat Holmen (☎ 536 40; www.pensionatholmen.se; Strandvägen 33; s/d Skr475/680) has five simple rooms in a house on a residential street. The owners can arrange fishing excursions (Skr550 per day).

The Inlandsbanan train stops here, and bus 45 runs daily on the Gällivare–Jokkmokk–Arvidsjaur–Sorsele–Storuman–Östersund route.

TÄRNABY & AROUND

☎ 0954

There's a lot to see and do around Tärnaby, especially if you have your own transport. However, even if you don't, the cycling is great and the bus coverage decent. Plant yourself here and spend some time skiing, hiking, fishing, stalking wildlife, checking out Sami villages and traditional holy sights, exploring caves, paddling canoes or just driving around and admiring the view, depending on your interests and the mood of the weather gods.

The **tourist office** (☎ 104 50; www.tarnaby.se; 🕐 8.30am-7pm Mon-Fri, 10am-6pm Sat & Sun mid-Jun–mid-Aug, 9am-5pm Mon-Fri rest of year) is on the main highway through the village, the 'Blue Road' (Blå vägen). It has free internet access, coffee and helpful staff. You can buy maps, fish licences and snow-scooter licences here, as well as arrange tours and activities.

Sights & Activities

A good way to start your visit is to hike to the top of **Laxfjället** (820m) for perspective-shifting views of the surrounding lakes and mountain ranges. The best approach, if you have wheels, is to drive up to a car park (follow signs to Laxfjället off E12 on the south end of town; it's the turn-off for the camping ground) and hike the remaining 1km to the top. Otherwise, there are a number of approaches, the most direct being a straight line underneath the ski lift up the hill.

For a longer hike, try the **Laisaleden trail**, which starts out along Drottningsleden. To catch the trail, follow signs to a turn-off 15km north of the Tärnaby tourist office along the main road; there's a parking lot with signposts to the trail at the top of the hill.

For anyone interested in Sami culture, it's worth going out of your way to visit **Atoklimpen** (☎ information 0954-104 50), a holy mountain that has been the object of worship from the nomadic society's early days. Evidence of sacrifices, camping and reindeer herding are scattered across the area; a 3km trail leads up to the top. Near the car park (off Rd 1116) is a peat hut and a small cottage. A Sami couple built the hut in 1920 and the cottage in 1925, at a time when the Sami were forbidden to build permanent structures; the ensuing debate over the cottage helped to change the law. The surrounding area still serves as a reindeer breeding ground.

Mountain biking is a warm-weather activity growing in popularity in the region – it's a way to use the popular **ski area** year-round. Many of Sweden's champion skiers hail from the area, notably Ingemar Stenmark.

Hemavan, 18km north of Tärnaby, has a larger **ski area** and basic facilities.

The southern entry to **Kungsleden** (Sweden's finest hiking route; see p60) is in Hemavan. To reach it, head up the hill toward the ugly

golden dome in Fjällparken; the ground floor of the building houses **Naturum** (☎ 380 23, 070-393 80 23; www.vindelfjallen.se; 🕐 9am-4.30pm Mon-Fri May–mid-Jun, 9am-6pm daily mid-Jun–Aug), where there's an exhibit on the local flora and fauna (including a section that explains what kind of droppings you'll step on along the trail). Staff can arrange tours and provide information about trekking in the area.

Sleeping & Eating

STF Vandrarhem Tärnaby/Åkerlundska gården (☎ 300 02; dm Skr170-220, s/d from Skr330/340; 🕐 Mar-May & mid-Jun–Sep) The newly renovated hostel, perched on the hillside, has awesome views across the valley, comfortable bunks in cosy rustic rooms, modern facilities and a homey atmosphere. There's a restaurant on the ground floor that serves meals, including a vast breakfast buffet (around Skr70). Reservations are required.

our pick **Tärnaby Lapland B&B** (☎ 107 00; www .tarnabylapland.com; Blå vägen 18; dm Skr190, s/d from Skr450/550; 🖳) The most fun place to stay in town is this one, run by the thoroughly entertaining Matt and Lindy, an Australian-Swedish couple who go out of their way to make sure you enjoy the area. Spotless rooms with water views hold comfortable dorm or double beds. There's a guest kitchen, a lounge area, a sauna, a new high-tech shower, free use of bicycles and canoes, and wi-fi. A separate building houses a warm wood-lined cafe-pub and tiny bookshop; the cafe serves lunch year-round and is open late in summer.

Hotell Sånninggården (☎ 330 00; www.sanninggar den.com; B&B/full board per person from Skr395/725) About 6km north of Hemavan, this hotel has good-value accommodation in a simple red barnlike building, and a **restaurant** (starters Skr59-115, dinner mains Skr155-295) that is not kidding around. If you're out this way, it's well worth stopping in for a unique meal – try, for example, roe deer in chantarelle sauce, whole fried mountain trout, or ripa (ptarmigan) with lingonberries and Västerbotten cheese potato gratin. There are vegetarian options for those uncomfortable with consuming the local wildlife, and the magnificent desserts will please everyone. If you overindulge, there are hiking and skiing trails right across the street.

There's an ICA **supermarket** (🕐 daily) in Hemavan, and Tärnaby has a Coop Konsum, with a **Systembolaget** (☎ 148 80; 🕐 9am-6pm Mon-Sat, noon-6pm Sun) inside.

STORUMAN

☎ 0951 / pop 6595

Though it sounds like a villain from *Lord of the Rings*, Storuman is perfectly harmless; in fact it can be a very useful stop on the way to exploring the remote areas nearby, and excellent walking trails surround it.

The **tourist office** (☎ 333 70; entrelappland@swipnet .se; Järnvägsgatan 13; ☒ 9am-5pm Mon-Fri, 10am-2pm Sat & Sun Jun-Aug; Mon-Fri only Sep-May) is at Hotell Luspen, near the train station. The town has all the basic facilities. For internet access, head to the **library** (☒ noon-5pm Mon-Fri), attached to the huge activity centre on the main drag.

The very scenic **Strandvägen** road links the centre with a series of islands, including **Luspholmen**, with a small outdoor museum. Follow the road Utsiktsvägen (across the E12 from the train station) for 1.5km to the viewpoint at **Utsikten**; sunsets over the lake are magnificent.

Sweden's largest **wooden church** is at **Stensele**, about 3km from Storuman towards Umeå on the E12.

Hotell Luspen (☎ 333 80; luspenhotell@swipnet.se; hostel s/d from Skr300/400, hotel s/d incl breakfast Skr600/700) is a friendly place by the train station, offering rooms to suit most budgets. Hostel rooms have private bathrooms; breakfast can be had for Skr40 and cycle hire is Skr60 per day.

There's a pub-grill in the same building as the bus station waiting room, next door to Hotell Luspen. Across the street is the cosier **Kita's Krog Piccolo** (mains from Skr65; ☒ lunch & dinner Mon-Sat), a homey cafe with an unlikely combination of Thai and Italian dishes.

Bus 45 runs every day on the Gällivare–Jokkmokk–Arvidsjaur–Sorsele–Storuman–Östersund route. Buses between Mo i Rana (Norway) and Umeå also run daily, via Storuman and Tärnaby, and the **Lapplandspilen** (☎ 333 70; www.lapplandspilen.se) buses run overnight three times weekly from Hemavan to Stockholm, via Storuman (Skr640). In summer, Inlandsbanan trains stop here.

SAXNÄS & AROUND

Saxnäs is a small village set in a scenic spot between lakes, and considered a paradise for fishing folk. Just outside the village, in Kultsjon, is **Trappstegsforsen** (☎ 0940-152 70), an impressive waterfall. Not far away, the late-18th-century Sami church village at **Fatmomakke** has an exhibition, *kåta* and other old buildings. Silver shamanistic Sami jewellery was found here in 1981.

The southern areas of Lappland have some of the finest mountain scenery in Sweden, particularly around the mountain **Marsfjället** (1590m); you can hike up and back from Fatmomakke, but it's a long day (28km, 10 hours). The trek through the mountains to the village of **Kittelfjäll** (where the scenery is even more impressive), via the wilderness cabin **Blerikstugan**, is best over two days (32km).

The small **STF Hostel Kultsjögården** (☎ 0940-700 44; www.kultsjogarden.se; dm/s/d Skr145/220/290) at Saxnas has comfortable rooms above a restaurant-pub (the only place in the area to eat outside of peak season), plus a few small cabins. The staff can answer questions about fishing, hiking and cycling in the area.

Directory

CONTENTS

ACCOMMODATION

Accommodation in Sweden is generally of a high standard; you'd have to be unlucky to stay in a dump. Sleeping reviews are organised by budget, with least expensive options appearing first. Budget options cost under Skr800, midrange costs from Skr800 to Skr1600, and top-end places come in at over Skr1600.

BOOK YOUR STAY ONLINE

For more accommodation reviews and recommendations by Lonely Planet authors, check out the online booking service at www.lonelyplanet.com/hotels. You'll find the true, insider low-down on the best places to stay. Reviews are thorough and independent. Best of all, you can book online.

Cabins & Chalets

Swedes are all for the outdoors, and cabins and chalets *(stugor)* are everywhere, either at campsites or scattered liberally through the countryside. Most contain four beds, with two- and six-person cabins sometimes on offer, too. They're particularly good value for small groups and families, costing between Skr350 and Skr800 per night. In peak summer season, many are rented out by the week (generally for between Skr800 and Skr5000).

The cheapest cabins are simple, with bunk beds and little else (you share the bathroom and kitchen facilities with campers or other cabin users). Chalets are generally fully equipped with their own kitchen, bathroom and even living room with TV. Bring your own linen and clean up yourself to save cleaning fees of around Skr500.

Pick up the brochure *Campsites & Cottages in Sweden: Greater Freedom* from any tourist office, or check out the website www.stuga.nu.

Camping

Camping is wildly popular in Sweden, and there are hundreds of camping grounds all over the country. Most open between May and August only. The majority are extremely busy family holiday spots with fantastic facilities, like shops, restaurants, pools, playgrounds, canoe or bike rentals, minigolf, kitchens and laundry facilities. Most also have cabins or chalets.

Camping prices vary (according to the season and facilities) from around Skr120 for a small site at a basic ground to Skr250 for a large site at a more luxurious camping ground. Slightly cheaper rates may be available if you're a solo hiker or cyclist. If you're on the move, look out for grounds offering a Quick Stop reduction: where you get a discount if you arrive after 9pm and leave by 9am the following day.

You must have a Camping Card Scandinavia to stay at most Swedish campsites. Apply for one in advance by writing to **Sveriges Camping & Stugföretagares Riksorganisation** (www.camping .se) or fill in the form on the website; otherwise pick up a temporary card at any Swedish

---

PRACTICALITIES

- Use the metric system for weights and measures.

- Watch out for the Swedish word *mil*, which Swedes may translate into English as 'mile' – a Swedish *mil* is actually 10km.

- Some shops quote prices followed by '/hg', which means per 100g.

- Use the PAL system for video recorders and players.

- Plug appliances into the round, continental-style two-pin sockets for (220V, 50Hz AC) power supply.

- Domestic newspapers (including the Göteborg and Stockholm dailies and evening tabloids) are in Swedish only. A good selection of English-language imports is sold at major transport terminals, Press Stop, Pressbyrån and tobacconists – even in small towns.

- On the internet, **Sweden Globe** (www.swedentimes.com) has English-language articles about Sweden.

- **Radio Sweden International** (www.sr.se/international) broadcasts programs nationally and to Europe on 1179kHz (89.6FM in Stockholm): check the website for a full list of frequencies and schedules.

- Try National Swedish Radio (variable stations around the country, see www.sr.se for a directory) for classical music and opera, pop and rock.

- National TV channels TV1 and TV2 broadcast mainly about local issues, in Swedish only. TV3, TV4 and TV5 have lots of shows and films in English.

---

campsite. The card costs Skr125 a year. One card covers the whole family.

Primus and Sievert supply propane gas for camping stoves, and containers are available at petrol stations. *T-sprit Röd* (methylated spirit; denatured alcohol) for Trangia stoves can be bought at petrol stations, and *Fotogen* (paraffin; kerosene) is sold at paint shops such as Fargtema and Spektrum.

See boxed text (p59) for information on free camping in Sweden.

Hostels

Sweden has well over 450 hostels *(vandrarhem)*, usually with excellent facilities. Outside major cities, hostels aren't backpacker hangouts but are used as holiday accommodation by Swedish families, couples or retired people. A related oddity is the frequent absence of dormitories, meaning you often have to rent out a room rather than a bed. Some hostels also have singles and doubles with en suite bathrooms that are almost of hotel quality, for very reasonable rates. About 50% of hostels open year-round; many others open from May to September, while some open only from mid-June to mid-August.

Be warned, Swedish hostels are virtually impossible to enter outside reception opening times, and these hours are frustratingly short (except in Stockholm and Göteborg): generally between 5pm and 7pm, and occasionally also between 8am and 10am. The secret is to prebook by telephone – reservations are highly recommended in any case, as hostels fill up fast.

Sleeping bags are usually allowed if you have a sheet and pillowcase; bring your own, or hire them (Skr50 to Skr65). Breakfast is sometimes available (Skr50 to Skr75). Before leaving, you must clean up after yourself; cleaning materials are provided. Most hostels are affiliated with STF or SVIF (see below), but there are other unaffiliated hostels also with high standards of accommodation.

STF

Some 315 hostels are affiliated with **Svenska Turistföreningen** (STF; ☎ 08-463 21 00; www.svenskaturistforeningen.se), part of Hostelling International (HI). STF produces a free detailed guide to its hostels, but the text is in Swedish only (the symbols and maps are easy to understand). Hostel details on its website are in English.

Holders of HI membership cards pay the same rates as STF members. Nonmembers can pay Skr50 extra (Skr100 at some mountain lodges) or join up at hostels (see p322 for membership costs). In this book we quote prices at STF hostels for members. Children under 16 pay about half the adult price.

All STF hostels have kitchens.

SVIF

Around 190 hostels belong to STF's 'rival', **Sveriges Vandrarhem i Förening** (SVIF; ☎ 0413-55 34 50; www.svif.se). No membership is required and rates are similar to those of STF hostels. Most SVIF hostels have kitchens, but you sometimes need your own utensils. Pick up the free guide at tourist offices or SVIF hostels.

Hotels

Private, family-owned hotels with individuality are few and far between: the big hotel chains – with comfortable but often rather bland rooms – tend to monopolise hotel accommodation options.

Sweden is unusual in that hotel prices tend to *fall* at weekends and in summer (except in touristy coastal towns), sometimes by as much as 40% or 50%. In this book, we've listed the standard rates first, followed by weekend and summer discount rates. Many hotel chains are now also offering flex rates, which let you change your reservation details until the last minute, and lower rates for early booking online. Hotel prices include a breakfast buffet unless noted in individual reviews. Ask at tourist offices for the free booklet *Hotels in Sweden* or visit the website www.hotelsinsweden.net.

Travellers on a budget should investigate the two cheapest hotel chains, both with flat rates for rooms. **Formule 1** (www.hotelformule1 .com) has four hotels (Göteborg, Jönköping, Malmö and Stockholm); the small but functional rooms (Skr390) have shared facilities and can sleep up to three people. **Ibis** (www .ibishotel.com) hotels offer simple rooms (Skr495 to Skr700) with private facilities. Breakfast is additional at both chains (Skr40 and Skr70, respectively).

The following hotels are the most common midrange and top-end chains:

Best Western (www.bestwestern.se)
Choice (www.choicehotels.se)
Countryside (www.countrysidehotels.se)
Ditt Hotell (www.ditthotell.se)
Elite (www.elite.se)
First (www.firsthotels.com)
Radisson SAS (www.radisson.com)
Scandic (www.scandic-hotels.com)
Sweden Hotels (www.swedenhotels.se, in Swedish)

Radisson SAS and Elite are the most luxurious. Scandic is known for being environmentally friendly. The top-end Countryside chain has the most characterful rooms, in castles, mansions, monasteries and spas.

Mountain Huts & Lodges

Most mountain huts (*fjällstugor*) and lodges (*fjällstationer*) in Sweden are owned by STF. There are about 45 huts and nine mountain lodges, usually spaced at 15km to 25km intervals, primarily in the Lappland region. Reception hours are quite long as staff members are always on site. Basic provisions are sold at many huts and all lodges, and many lodges have hiking equipment for hire.

STF huts have cooking and toilet facilities (none have showers, but some offer saunas). Bring your own sleeping bag. Huts are staffed during March and April and also from late June to early or mid-September. You can't book a bed in advance, but no one is turned away (although in the peak of summer this may mean you sleep on a mattress on the floor). Charges for STF or HI members vary depending on the season, and range from Skr190 to Skr300 (children pay about Skr75), with the highest charges on northern Kungsleden. Nonmembers pay Skr100 extra. You can also pitch a tent in the mountains, but if you camp near STF huts you are requested to pay a service charge (Skr60/80 for members/nonmembers), which gives you access to any services the hut may offer (such as kitchen and bathroom facilities).

At the excellent STF mountain lodges, accommodation standards range from hostel (with cooking facilities) to hotel (with full- or half-board options), and overnight prices range from Skr200 to around Skr800. There are often guided activities on offer for guests, plus they usually have a restaurant and shop.

Private Rooms, B&Bs & Farmhouses

Many tourist offices have lists of rooms in private houses, which is a great way of finding well-priced accommodation and getting to meet Swedish people. Singles/doubles average Skr300/400.

Along the motorways (primarily in the south), you may see 'Rum' or 'Rum & frukost' signs, indicating informal accommodation (*frukost* means 'breakfast') from around Skr250 to Skr350 per person. Kitchen facilities are often available, and those who bring

DIRECTORY

their own sheets or sleeping bags may get a discount.

The organisation **Bo på Lantgård** (☎ 035-12 78 70; www.bopalantgard.org) publishes a free annual booklet on farmhouse accommodation (B&B and self-catering), available from any tourist office. B&B prices average about Skr300 per person in a double room. Prices for self-caterers range from Skr300 to Skr850 per night, depending on the time of year, facilities and number of beds.

BUSINESS HOURS

General opening hours are listed here, but there are variations (particularly in the largest cities where opening hours may be longer). Hours are listed in individual reviews where they differ substantially from these.

Banks Open 9.30am to 3pm Mon-Fri; some city branches open 9am to 5pm or 6pm.

Bars & pubs Open 11am or noon to 1am or 2am.

Department stores Open 10am to 7pm Monday to Saturday (sometimes later) and noon to 4pm Sunday.

Government offices Open 9am to 5pm Monday to Friday.

Museums Generally museums have short opening hours, even in July and August; see individual museums for more details.

Restaurants Open for lunch from 11.30am to 2pm, and dinner between 5pm and 10pm; often closed on Sunday and/or Monday.

Shops Open 9am to 6pm Monday to Friday and 10am to 4pm Saturday.

Supermarkets Open 8am or 9am to 7pm or 9pm.

Systembolaget Open 10am to 6pm Monday to Friday and 10am to 2pm (often until 5pm) Saturday, sometimes with extended hours on Thursday and Friday evenings.

Tourist offices Usually open daily Midsummer to mid-August, 9am to 5pm Monday to Friday mid-August to Midsummer; see individual destinations for specific hours.

CHILDREN

If you've got kids, you're guaranteed an easy ride in Sweden as it's very family-centric. In general, get the kids involved in your travel plans: if they've helped to work out where you're going, the chances are they'll still be interested when you arrive! Remember, don't try to cram too much in. Lonely Planet's *Travel with Children,* by Cathy Lanigan, is a useful source of information.

Practicalities

Hotels and other accommodation options often have 'family rooms' that sleep up to two adults and two children for little more

than the price of a regular double. Campsites have excellent facilities and are overrun with ecstatic, energetic children. They get very busy in summer, so book tent sites or cabins well in advance.

High chairs and cots (cribs) are standard in most restaurants and hotels. Swedish supermarkets offer a relatively wide choice of baby food, infant formulas, soy and cow's milk, disposable nappies (diapers) etc. There are nappy-changing facilities in most toilets (men's and women's) and breastfeeding in public is not an issue.

Car-rental companies will hire out children's safety seats at a nominal cost, but it's essential that you book them in advance. Long-distance ferries and trains, hotels and some restaurants may even have play areas for children.

Sights & Activities

Swedes treat children very well, and domestic tourism is largely organised around children's interests. Many museums have a kids' section with toys, hands-on displays and activities, and there are numerous public parks for kids, plus theme parks, water parks and so on. Most attractions allow free admission for young children – up to about seven years of age – and half-price (or substantially discounted) admission for those up to about 16. Family tickets are often available.

Liseberg amusement park (p210) in Göteborg is Sweden's largest; other major places for kids include Junibacken, Skansen and Gröna Lund Tivoli, all found in Stockholm's Djurgården (p78); Göteborg's Universeum (p210); and Astrid Lindgrens Värld (p152) in Vimmerby.

CLIMATE CHARTS

Sweden has a mostly cool temperate climate, but the southern quarter of the country is warmer than the rest. Norway's mountain ranges act as a rain break, so yearly rainfall is moderate.

Swedish summers are generally fairly sunny with only occasional rainfall, but August can be wet. The average maximum temperature for July is 18°C in the south and around 14°C in the north. Long hot periods in summer aren't unusual, with temperatures soaring to over 30°C.

The harsh Lappland winter starts in October and ends in April, and temperatures

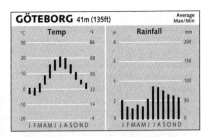

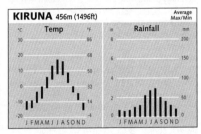

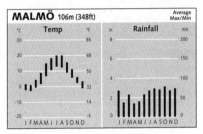

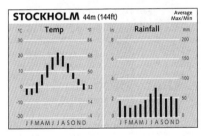

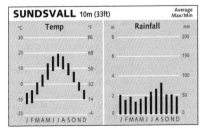

can plummet as low as -50°C. Snow can accumulate to depths of several metres in the north, making for superb skiing, but snow depths in the south average only 20cm to 40cm. It usually rains in winter in the far south (Skåne).

The west coast is warmer than the east, thanks to the warming waters of the Gulf Stream. For more information on when to go, see p16.

CUSTOMS

Duty-free goods can only be brought into Sweden from non-EU countries and Åland. Tobacco products and alcoholic drinks can only be brought into Sweden duty-free by those over 18 and 20, respectively.

Duty-free alcohol allowances for travellers from outside the EU are 1L of spirits, 2L of fortified wine, 2L of wine and a quantity of beer that must be included within the Skr1700 limit. The tobacco allowance is 200 cigarettes, 50 cigars or 250g of smoking tobacco.

The limits on goods brought into Sweden with 'tax paid for personal use' from within the EU are more generous: 10L of spirits, 20L of fortified wine, 90L of wine (but no more than 60L of sparkling wine) and 110L of beer. The tobacco allowance is 800 cigarettes, 400 cheroots, 200 cigars or 1kg of tobacco.

Going through customs rarely involves any hassles, but rules on illegal drugs are strictly enforced; you may be searched on arrival, especially if you're travelling from Denmark. Live plants and animal products (meat, dairy etc) from outside the EU, and all animals, syringes and weapons must be declared to customs on arrival. For the latest regulations, contact **Swedish Customs** (☎ 0771-23 23 23; www.tullverket.se).

DANGERS & ANNOYANCES
Opening Hours & Queuing

Dangers are few, but certain quirks of Swedish society can register as annoyances. It's difficult for foreigners to understand why some tourist offices aren't open at weekends, for example, or why museums open at 11am and close by 4pm (even in July), and hostels (and some hotels) only have reception for two or three hours in the afternoon. Don't even think of going to a liquor store in the evening or for most of the weekend – it will be closed.

Queuing by number is a national pastime in Sweden: hunt down the ticket machine as soon as you enter shops, post offices, liquor stores, offices, police stations etc. Don't miss your turn, or you'll have to go back to the end of the queue.

Road Hazards

Motorists should be awake to the risks posed by elk and reindeer; see p338.

Theft

Sweden is fairly safe, but petty crime may be of concern. In Stockholm, Göteborg, Malmö and Linköping, ask locally for advice on areas to avoid before wandering around at night. Beware of pickpockets and bag-snatchers in crowded public places.

DISCOUNT CARDS
City Summer Cards

Göteborg, Malmö, Stockholm and Uppsala have worthwhile tourist cards that get you into their major attractions and offer parking, travel on public transport and discounts at participating hotels, restaurants and shops; see the individual city in the destination chapters for details.

Hostel & Student Cards

A Hostelling International (HI) card means cheaper beds in STF hostels, mountain stations and cabins. You can join the STF at hostels and many tourist offices while in Sweden (membership costs Skr295 for adults, Skr125 for those aged between 16 and 25, Skr25 for six-to 15-year-olds and Skr430 for families). The most useful student card is the International Student Identity Card (ISIC), which offers discounts on many forms of transport (including some airlines, international ferries and local public transport) and on admission to museums, sights, theatres and cinemas.

Seniors

Seniors normally get discounts on entry to museums and other sights, cinema and theatre tickets, air tickets and other transport. No special card is required, but show your passport if asked for proof of age (the minimum qualifying age is generally 60 or 65).

EMBASSIES & CONSULATES

The diplomatic missions listed here are in Stockholm; some neighbouring countries have additional consulates in Göteborg, Malmö and Helsingborg.

Australia (Map p82; ☎ 08-613 29 00; www.sweden
.embassy.gov.au; 11th fl, Sergels Torg 12)
Canada (Map p82; ☎ 08-453 30 00; www.canadaemb
.se; Tegelbacken 4)
Denmark (Map p82; ☎ 08-406 75 00; www.ambstock
holm.um.dk, in Danish; Jakobs Torg 1)
Finland (Map pp70-1; ☎ 08-676 67 00; www.finland
.se/fi, in Finnish & Swedish; Gärdesgatan 9-11)
France (Map p82; ☎ 08-459 53 00; www.ambafrance
-se.org, in French & Swedish; Kommendörsgatan 13)
Germany (Map pp70-1; ☎ 08-670 15 00; www.stock
holm.diplo.de, in German & Swedish; Artillerigatan 64)
Ireland (Map pp70-1; ☎ 08-661 80 05; irish.em
bassy@swipnet.se; Östermalmsgatan 97)
Netherlands (Map p82; ☎ 08-55 69 33 00; www
.netherlands-embassy.se; Götgatan 16A)
New Zealand (☎ 070-346 93 24; nzemb@xs4all.nl;
Carnegielaan 10; 2517 KH The Hague) No representation in
Sweden: closest embassy is in the Netherlands.
Norway (Map pp70-1; ☎ 08-665 63 40; emb.stock
holm@mfa.no; Skarpögatan 4)
UK (Map pp70-1; ☎ 08-671 30 00; www.british
embassy.se; Skarpögatan 6-8)
USA (Map pp70-1; ☎ 08-783 53 00; http://stockholm
.usembassy.gov; Dag Hammarskjöldsväg 31)

FOOD

Eating reviews are categorised by price, with least expensive options listed first. Budget meals cost Skr75 or under, midrange between Skr75 and Skr185, and top-end places come in at over Skr185. For in-depth information on Swedish cuisine, see Food & Drink, p45.

GAY & LESBIAN TRAVELLERS

Sweden is a famously liberal country and allows gay and lesbian couples to form 'registered partnerships' that grant general marriage rights, with a few exceptions (such as not permitting access to church weddings). In 2002 the Swedish parliament voted in favour of allowing gay couples to adopt.

The national organisation for gay and lesbian rights is **Riksförbundet för Sexuellt Likaberättigande** (RFSL; Map pp70-1; ☎ 08-457 13 00; Sveavägen 57-59), with an attached bookshop, restaurant and nightclub. Gay bars and nightclubs in the big cities are mentioned in this book, but ask local RFSL societies or your home organisation for up-to-date information. The *Spartacus International Gay Guide,* published by Bruno Gmünder Verlag (Berlin), is an excellent international directory of gay entertainment venues, but it's best used in conjunction with more up-to-date listings in local papers; as elsewhere, gay venues in the region can change with the speed of summer.

Another good source of local information is the free monthly magazine *QX*. You can pick it up at many clubs, shops and restaurants in Stockholm, Göteborg, Malmö and Copenhagen (Denmark). The magazine's website www.qx.se has excellent information and recommendations in English.

One of the capital's biggest parties is the annual **Stockholm Pride** (www.stockholmpride.org), a five-day festival celebrating gay culture, held between late July and early August. The extensive program covers art, debate, health, literature, music, spirituality and sport.

HOLIDAYS

There's a concentration of public holidays in spring and early summer. In particular, Midsummer brings life almost to a halt for three days: transport and other services are reduced, and most shops and smaller tourist offices close, as do some attractions. Some hotels close between Christmas and New Year, and it's not uncommon for restaurants in larger cities to close during July and early August (when their owners join the holidaying throngs at beach or lakeside areas).

School holidays vary from school to school, but in general the kids will be at large for Sweden's one-week sports holiday (February/March), the one-week Easter break, Christmas, and from June to August.

Many businesses close early the day before and all day after official public holidays, including the following:

Nyårsdag (New Year's Day) 1 January
Trettondedag Jul (Epiphany) 6 January
Långfredag, Påsk, Annandag Påsk (Good Friday, Easter Sunday & Monday) March/April
Första Maj (Labour Day) 1 May
Kristi Himmelsfärds dag (Ascension Day) May/June
Pingst, Annandag Pingst (Whit Sunday & Monday) Late May or early June
Midsommardag (Midsummer's Day) First Saturday after 21 June
Alla Helgons dag (All Saints' Day) Saturday, late October or early November
Juldag (Christmas Day) 25 December
Annandag Jul (Boxing Day) 26 December

Note also that Midsommarafton (Midsummer's Eve), Julafton (Christmas Eve; 24 December) and Nyårsafton (New Year's Eve; 31 December) are not official holidays, but

are generally nonworking days for most of the population.

INSURANCE

Depending on the type of policy you choose, insurance can cover you for everything from medical expenses and luggage loss to cancellations or delays in your travel arrangements.

In Sweden, EU citizens pay a fee for all medical treatment (including emergency admissions), but showing an EHIC form will make matters much easier. Enquire about the EHIC well in advance at your social security office, travel agent or local post office. Travel insurance is still advisable, however, as it allows treatment flexibility and will also cover ambulance and repatriation costs.

If you do need health insurance, remember that some policies offer 'lower' and 'higher' medical-expense options, but the higher one is chiefly for countries that have extremely high medical costs, such as the USA. Everyone should be covered for the worst possible case, such as an accident requiring an ambulance, hospital treatment or an emergency flight home. You may prefer a policy that pays health-care providers directly, rather than you having to pay on the spot and claim later.

See p341 for information on medical insurance.

INTERNET ACCESS

If you plan to carry your notebook or palmtop computer with you, remember that the power-supply voltage in Sweden may vary from that at home. To avoid frying your electronics, use a universal AC adaptor (many laptop adaptors already include this; check the label on your power cord) and a plug adaptor, which will enable you to plug in anywhere. Also worth purchasing is a 'global' or 'world' modem, as your PC-card modem may not work outside your home country.

For comprehensive advice on travelling with portable computers, visit the website of **World Wide Phone Guide** (www.kropla.com). **Teleadapt** (www.teleadapt.com) sells all the gizmos you'll need. Most hotels have wireless LAN connections, and some even have laptops you can borrow.

Nearly all public libraries offer free internet access, but often the half-hour or hour slots are fully booked for days in advance by locals, and facilities may occasionally be blocked. Many tourist offices also offer a computer terminal for visitor use (sometimes free of charge).

Internet cafes are rare outside big cities, as most Swedes have internet access at home. Where internet cafes do exist, they're full of teenage lads playing computer games. They typically charge around Skr1 per online minute, or Skr50 per hour. Wireless internet at coffeeshops, train stations and hotels is on the increase, although in many cases you have to pay a fee for access.

See p18 for a list of suggested internet resources.

LEGAL MATTERS

If arrested, you have the right to contact your country's embassy, which can usually provide you with a list of local lawyers. There is no provision for bail in Sweden. Sweden has some of the most draconian drug laws in Western Europe, with fines and possible long prison sentences for possession and consumption.

MAPS

Tourist offices, libraries and hotels usually stock free local town plans.

The best maps of Sweden are published and updated regularly by Kartförlaget, the sales branch of the national mapping agency, **Lantmäteriet** (☎ 026-63 30 00; www.lantmateriet.se). Maps can be bought at most tourist offices, bookshops and some youth hostels, service stations and general stores.

Motorists planning an extensive tour should get *Motormännens Sverige Vägatlas* produced by Kartförlaget (around Skr280 at most shops), with town plans and detailed coverage at 1:250,000 as far north as Sundsvall, then 1:400,000 for the remainder.

The best tourist road maps are those of Kartförlaget's *Vägkartan* series, at a scale of 1:100,000 and available from larger bookshops. Also useful, especially for hikers, is the *Fjällkartan* mountain series (1:100,000, with 20m contour interval); these are usually priced around Skr120 apiece and are available at larger bookshops, outdoor equipment stores and mountain stations operated by **Svenska Turistföreningen** (STF; ☎ 08-463 21 00; www.svenskaturistforeningen.se).

To purchase maps before you arrive, try online at Lantmäteriet's website, which has a good mail-order service, or at **Kartbutiken** (Map p82; ☎ 08-20 23 03; www.kartbutiken.se; Kungsgatan 74, Stockholm).

MONEY

Sweden uses the krona (plural kronor) as currency. One krona is divided into 100 öre. See the Inside Front Cover for exchange rates, and p16 for typical costs.

Cash & ATMs

The simplest way to get money in Sweden is by accessing your account using an ATM card from your home bank. 'Bankomat' ATMs are found adjacent to many banks and around busy public places such as shopping centres. They accept major credit cards as well as Plus and Cirrus cards. Note that many ATMs in Sweden will not accept PINs of more than four digits; if your PIN is longer than this, just enter the first four and you should be able to access your account. Also be aware that ATMs in busy locations often have extremely long queues and can actually run out of money on Friday and Saturday nights.

Credit Cards

Visa, MasterCard, American Express and Diners Club cards are widely accepted. You're better off using a credit card because exchange rates are better and most transaction fees are avoided. Credit cards can be used to buy train tickets but are not accepted on domestic ferries, apart from sailings to Gotland. Electronic debit cards can be used in most shops.

If your card is lost or stolen in Sweden, report it to one of the following appropriate agencies.

American Express (☎ 336-393 1111)
Diners Club (☎ 08-14 68 78)
MasterCard (☎ 020-79 13 24)
Visa (☎ 020-79 56 75)

Moneychangers & Travellers Cheques

Banks around the country exchange major foreign currencies and accept international brands of travellers cheques. They may, however, charge up to Skr60 per travellers cheque, so shop around and compare service fees and exchange rates before handing over your money.

Forex (☎ 0200-22 22 20; www.forex.se) is the biggest foreign money exchange company in Sweden, with good rates and branches in major airports, ferry terminals and town and city centres; these are noted where appropriate in the destination chapters. They charge a service fee of Skr15 per travellers cheque exchanged.

Tipping

Service charges and tips are usually included in restaurant bills; a common practice is to round up a restaurant bill to the nearest Skr10. There's certainly no problem if you want to reward good service with an extra tip. It's also customary to round up the taxi fare, particularly if there's luggage.

PHOTOGRAPHY & VIDEO

Print and slide film are readily available, but prices (including developing costs) are fairly high. It's better to bring your own film and develop your photos or slides back home. Expert, a chain of electrical goods shops, sells a wide range of film, and camera equipment can be bought or repaired there.

It's particularly important to ask permission before taking photos of people in Sami areas, where you may meet resistance. Photography and video is prohibited at many tourist sites, mainly to protect fragile artwork. Photographing military establishments is forbidden, and although it may seem hilarious to take photos of signs banning photography around military establishments, we don't recommend doing so.

The clear northern light and glare from water, ice and snow may require use of a UV filter (or skylight filter) and a lens shade. ISO 100 film is sufficient for most purposes. In winter, most cameras don't work below -20°C. Lonely Planet's *Travel Photography*, by Richard I'Anson, contains some handy hints.

POST

Since 2002, the Swedish postal service **Posten** (☎ 020-23 22 21; www.posten.se) has been radically reorganised: in a cost-cutting bid, it closed its regular post offices and instead opened up a network of around 3000 counter services in shops, petrol stations and supermarkets across the country. Look for the yellow post symbol on a pale blue background, which indicates that postal facilities are offered.

Most Swedes now buy their stamps and post letters while going about their grocery shopping. If your postal requirements are more complicated (such as posting a heavy parcel), ask at the local tourist office – package services are offered at certain office-supply stores, as well as places like Mailboxes Etc.

Postal Rates

Mailing letters or postcards weighing up to 20g within Sweden costs Skr5.50; it's Skr11 to elsewhere in Europe and beyond. The *ekonomibrev* (economy post) option for within Sweden takes longer to reach its destination and costs marginally less (Skr5). Airmail will take a week to reach most parts of North America, perhaps a little longer to Australia and New Zealand.

At the time of writing, a package weighing 2kg costs Skr282.50 by airmail within Europe and Skr305 outside Europe.

SHOPPING

In Sweden, there's no shortage of the gorgeous furniture and interior design for which the country is famous. Head to **DesignTorget** (www.designtorget.se), which showcases the work (usually quite affordable) of established and new designers. There are branches in Stockholm, Täby, Göteborg and Malmö.

Souvenirs, handicrafts and quality Swedish products in glass, wood, amber, pewter or silver are relatively expensive, but tend to be a lot cheaper when bought directly from the manufacturer; some places will organise shipping for you. The best souvenirs include glassware (such as bowls, jugs, vases and ornaments) from Glasriket (p147), Swedish painted wooden horses from Dalarna (see boxed text, p271), wooden toys, and jewellery made from amber and silver. Some foodstuffs, such as *hjortronsylt* (cloudberry jam) and *sill* (pickled herring), are also well worth taking home. Sale prices in shops are advertised with the word *rea;* for discounts or special offers look for *lågpris, extrapris, rabatt* or *fynd.*

Handicrafts carrying the round token *Svensk slöjd*, or the hammer and shuttle emblem, are endorsed by Svenska Hemslöjdsföreningarnas Riksförbund, the national handicrafts organisation whose symbol is found on affiliated handicraft shops. Look out for signs reading *hemslöjd*, indicating handicraft sales outlets.

If you're interested in Sami handicrafts, look for the *Duodji* label (a round, coloured, authenticity token) and, if possible, go to a Sami village and make your purchase there.

DIRECTORY

FLATPACK FURNITURE TAKES OVER THE WORLD

If you're a few billion dollars poorer than you'd like to be, the Ikea success story is one that you should study closely. From humble beginnings selling pens, watches and nylon stockings from a shed in Älmhult, Småland, Ikea's creator-god Ingvar Kamprad has turned himself into one of the world's richest men. He was No 7 in *Forbes* magazine's 2008 list of the world's billionaires, with a personal fortune of around US$31 billion (although Ikea's business structure is notoriously secretive).

The Ikea name (a combination of Kamprad's initials and those of the farm and village he grew up in) was officially registered in 1943. Furniture was added to the company's products four years later, gradually evolving into the Ikea-designed flatpack creations so familiar today. There was almost an early end to the Ikea empire when the first Stockholm shop and all its stock burned down in 1970. But, besides his devotion to work and obsession with cost-cutting, Kamprad also seems to thrive on adversity: Ikea bounced back.

The company sells a look and lifestyle that seems to be craved universally; shoppers are offered clean, cleverly designed Scandinavian style at prices that sometimes seem too cheap to be real. It's estimated that 10% of Europeans were conceived in an Ikea bed!

Ikea is a mine of paradoxes, however, and is worshipped and criticised in equal measures. The clean-cut company was rocked in 1994 by revelations that Kamprad once had links with a pro-Nazi party in Sweden (he later offered a public apology, and expressed much regret for this time of his life). Ikea also seems to induce mass hysteria: a stampede in Jeddah left three people dead; and UK readers may recall the fighting crowds, evacuation of wounded people and cars abandoned on the North Circular when the Edmonton shop opened in London. Cheap and innovative designs are great, but what does it say about the value of individuality when every house in the land has Billy bookshelves and a Klippan sofa?

Still, like it or loathe it, Ikea is here to stay. Kamprad has taken a back seat, with control over his empire now divvied up among his three children, and more new stores are planned. Today Ikea has stores in 40 countries; branches first opened in Australia in 1975, Saudi Arabia in 1983, the US in 1985, Britain in 1987, China in 1998 and Russia in 2000.

Be careful of some town shops that may have fakes on the shelves. Some typical Sami handcrafts include ornately carved sheath knives, cups, bowls, textiles and jewellery. Reindeer bone, wood (birch), reindeer hide and tin are commonly used materials.

Tax-Free Shopping

At shops that display the 'Tax Free Shopping' sign, non-EU citizens making single purchases of goods exceeding Skr200 are eligible for a VAT refund of up to 17.5% of the purchase price. Show your passport and ask the shop for a 'Global Refund Cheque', which should be presented along with your unopened purchases (within three months) at your departure point from the country (before you check in), to get export validation. You can then cash your cheque at any of the refund points, which are found at international airports and harbours. The free *Tax Free Shopping Guide to Sweden* is available from tourist offices or call ☎ 020-74 17 41 for more information.

Bargaining

Bargaining isn't customary, but you can get 'walk-in' prices at some hotels and *stugby* (chalet parks).

SOLO TRAVELLERS

Travelling in Sweden poses no particular problems for lone travellers, though it can be trickier than most other countries to meet people. Hostel dormitories aren't common, except in cities, and quite often you'll end up stuck in a room on your own, surrounded by families. Female solo travellers should obviously take care at night in the cities, and check with locals about any dodgy areas to avoid.

TELEPHONE & FAX

Swedish phone numbers have area codes followed by a varying number of digits. Look for business numbers in the **Yellow Pages** (www.gulasidorna.se, in Swedish). The state-owned telephone company, Telia, also has phone books, which include green pages (for community services) and blue pages (for regional services, including health and medical care).

Public telephones are usually to be found at train stations or in the main town square. They accept phonecards or credit cards (although the latter are expensive). It's not possible to receive return international calls on public phones.

For international calls dial ☎ 00, followed by the country code and then the local area code. Calls to Sweden from abroad require the country code ☎ 46 followed by the area code, and telephone number (omitting the first zero in the area code).

Mobile phone codes start with ☎ 010, ☎ 070, ☎ 073 and ☎ 0730. Toll-free codes include ☎ 020 and ☎ 0200 (but can't be called from public telephones or abroad).

Directory assistance (☎ 118 119) International.
Directory assistance (☎ 118 118) Within Sweden.
Emergency services (☎ 112) Toll-free.

Fax

Fax is not a common form of communication in Sweden and is difficult for on-the-road travellers to access. Many post offices used to offer a fax service but don't any longer, so your best bet is to ask at the local tourist office or your place of accommodation. Faxes can still be received at most hotels for free and you can often send a fax for a moderate charge.

Mobile Phones

It's worth considering bringing your mobile phone from your home country and buying a Swedish SIM card, which gives you a Swedish mobile number. Vodafone, for example, sells a local SIM card for Skr95, which you then need to load with at least Skr100 worth of credit. You can then purchase top-ups at many stores, including petrol stations and Pressbyrå shops. Your mobile may be locked onto your local network in your home country, so ask your home network for advice before going abroad.

Phonecards

Telia phonecards (*telefonkort*) for public phones cost Skr50 and Skr120 (for 50 and 120 units, respectively) and can be bought from Telia phone shops and newsagents.

You can make international telephone calls with these phonecards, but they won't last long! For international calls, it's better to buy (from tobacconists) one of a wide range of phonecards, such as a Star phonecard, which give cheap rates for calls abroad. These are generally used in public phone boxes in conjunction with a Telia card: so you might have to put the Telia card into the phone, dial the telephone number shown on the back of your cheap international phonecard, then follow the instructions given. International collect calls cannot be made from pay phones.

TIME

Sweden is one hour ahead of GMT/UTC and is in the same time zone as Norway and Denmark as well as most of Western Europe. When it's noon in Sweden, it's 11am in London, 1pm in Helsinki, 6am in New York and Toronto, 3am in Los Angeles, 9pm in Sydney and 11pm in Auckland. Sweden also has daylight-saving time: the clocks go forward an hour on the last Sunday in March and back an hour on the last Sunday in October.

Timetables and business hours are quoted using the 24-hour clock, and dates are often given by week number (1 to 52).

TOILETS

Public toilets in parks, shopping malls, libraries, and bus or train stations are rarely free in Sweden; some churches and most museums and tourist offices have free toilets. Except at larger train stations (where there's an attendant), pay toilets are coin operated and usually cost Skr5. Be sure to keep a Skr5 coin on hand, as that's all the toilets accept and it can be difficult to persuade anyone to give you change.

TOURIST INFORMATION
Local Tourist Offices

Most towns in Sweden have centrally located tourist offices (*turistbyrå*) that provide free street plans and information on accommodation, attractions, activities and transport. Brochures for other areas in Sweden are often available. Ask for the handy booklet that lists addresses and phone numbers for most tourist offices in the country; the website of **Swedish Tourism Associated** (www.turism.se) also has this information. See the Information section in each destination chapter for contact details of regional tourist offices.

Most tourist offices are open long hours daily in summer; from mid-August to mid-June a few close down, while others have shorter opening hours – they may close by 4pm, and not open at all at weekends. Public libraries or large hotels are good alternative sources of information.

Tourist Offices Abroad

The official website for the **Swedish Travel and Tourism Council** (www.visit-sweden.com) contains loads of excellent information in many languages, and you can request to have brochures and information packs sent to you.

The following tourist offices can assist with enquiries and provide tourist promotional material by phone, email or post (most don't have a walk-in service). In countries without a designated tourist office, a good starting point for information is the nearest Swedish embassy.

France (☎ 01-70 70 84 58; servinfo@suede-tourisme.fr; Office Suédois du Tourisme et des Voyages, 11 rue Payenne, F-75003 Paris)

Germany (☎ 069-22 22 34 96; info@swetourism.de; Schweden-Werbung für Reisen und Touristik, Michaelisstrasse 22, DE-20459 Hamburg)

UK (☎ 020-7108 6168; info@swetourism.org.uk; Swedish Travel & Tourism Council, 5 Upper Montagu St, London W1H 2AG)

USA (☎ 212-885 9700; usa@visit-sweden.com; Swedish Travel & Tourism Council, PO Box 4649, Grand Central Station, New York NY 10163-4649)

TRAVELLERS WITH DISABILITIES

Sweden is one of the easiest countries to travel around in a wheelchair. People with disabilities will find transport services with adapted facilities, ranging from trains to taxis, but contact the operator in advance for the best service.

Public toilets and some hotel rooms have facilities for disabled people; **Hotels in Sweden** (www.hotelsinsweden.net) indicates whether hotels have adapted rooms. Some street crossings have ramps for wheelchairs and audio signals for visually impaired people, and some grocery stores are wheelchair accessible.

For further information about Sweden, contact **De Handikappades Riksförbund** (☎ 08-685 80 00; www.dhr.se), the national association for the disabled.

Also, contact the travel officer at your national support organisation; they may be able to put you in touch with tour companies that specialise in disabled travel. The disability-friendly website www.allgohere.com has an airline directory that provides information on the facilities offered by various airlines.

VISAS

Citizens of EU countries can enter Sweden with a passport or a national identification card (passports are recommended) and stay up to three months. Nationals of Nordic countries (Denmark, Norway, Finland and Iceland) can stay and work indefinitely, but nationals of other countries require residence permits *(uppehållstillstånd)* for stays of between three months and five years; there is no fee for this permit for EU citizens.

Non-EU passport holders from Australia, New Zealand, Canada and the US can enter and stay in Sweden without a visa for up to three months. Australian and New Zealand passport-holders aged between 18 and 30 can qualify for a one-year working-holiday visa (see below).

Citizens of South Africa and many other African, Asian and some Eastern European countries require tourist visas for entry. These are only available in advance from Swedish embassies (allow two months); there's a non-refundable application fee of Skr550 for most applicants. Visas last up to three months, and extensions aren't easily obtainable.

Non-EU citizens can also obtain residence permits, but these must be applied for before entering Sweden. An interview by consular officials at your nearest Swedish embassy is required – allow up to eight months for this process. Foreign students are granted residence permits if they can prove acceptance by a Swedish educational institution and are able to guarantee that they can support themselves financially.

Migrationsverket (☎ 011-15 60 00; www.migrationsverket.se) is the Swedish migration board and it handles all applications for visas and work or residency permits.

WORK

Non-EU citizens require an offer of paid employment prior to their arrival in Sweden. They need to apply for a work permit (and residence permit for stays over three months), enclosing confirmation of the job offer, completed forms (available from Swedish diplomatic posts or over the internet), two passport photos and their passport. Processing takes six to eight weeks, and there's a nonrefundable application fee of Skr1000.

EU citizens only need to apply for a residence permit (free) within three months of arrival if they find work, then they can remain in Sweden for the duration of their employment (or up to five years).

Australians and New Zealanders aged 18 to 30 years can qualify for a one-year working holiday visa. Full application details are available online through **Migrationsverket** (www .migrationsverket.se).

Work permits are only granted if there's a shortage of Swedish workers (or citizens from EU countries) with certain in-demand skills; speaking Swedish may be essential for the job. Students enrolled in Sweden can take summer jobs, but these can be hard to find and such work isn't offered to travelling students. No seasonal work permits were granted in 2006 or 2007 and none were expected to be issued for several years.

Plenty of helpful information can be found online from the **Arbetsförmedlinga** (AMV; Swedish National Labour Market Administration; www .ams.se).

Transport

CONTENTS

GETTING THERE & AWAY

Sweden is mostly hassle-free when it comes to getting to/from the country or moving within its borders. For visa requirements, see p328.

AIR

Airports & Airlines

The main airport is Stockholm-Arlanda, which links Sweden with major European and North American cities. Göteborg Landvetter is Sweden's second-biggest international airport. Stockholm Skavsta (actually 100km south of Stockholm, near Nyköping) and Göteborg City both act as airports for the budget airline Ryanair.

THINGS CHANGE...

The information in this chapter is particularly vulnerable to change. Check directly with the airline or a travel agent to make sure you understand how a fare (and ticket you may buy) works and be aware of the security requirements for international travel. Shop carefully. The details given in this chapter should be regarded as pointers and are not a substitute for your own careful, up-to-date research.

Göteborg City (code GSE; ☎ 031-92 60 60; www .goteborgcityairport.se)
Göteborg Landvetter (code GOT; ☎ 031-94 10 00; www.lfv.se)
Stockholm-Arlanda (code ARN; ☎ 08-797 60 00; www.arlanda.se)
Stockholm Skavsta (code NYO; ☎ 0155-28 04 00; www.skavsta-air.se)

For travelling between international airports and city centres, see the Getting Around sections in the relevant chapters.

Scandinavian Airlines System (SAS) is the regional carrier with a good safety record.

AIRLINES FLYING TO & FROM SWEDEN
Most of the usual airlines fly into Sweden including the following:
Air France (airline code AF; ☎ 08-51 99 99 90; www .airfrance.com) Hub: Charles de Gaulle, Paris.
Blue1 (airline code KF; ☎ 0900-102 58 31; www.blue1 .com) Hub: Helsinki-Vantaa, Finland.
British Airways (airline code BA; ☎ 0200-77 00 98; www.britishairways.com) Hub: Heathrow Airport, London.
City Airline (airline code CF; ☎ 0200-25 05 00; www .cityairline.com) Hub: Göteborg.
Finnair (airline code AY; ☎ 0771-78 11 00; www.finnair .com) Hub: Helsinki-Vantaa, Finland.
Icelandair (airline code FI; ☎ 08-690 98 00, ext 2; www.icelandair.net) Hub: Keflavík, Iceland.
Lufthansa (airline code LH; ☎ 08-611 59 30; www .lufthansa.com) Hub: Frankfurt, Germany.
Ryanair (airline code FR; ☎ 0900-202 02 40; www .ryanair.com) Hub: Dublin, Ireland.
SAS (airline code SK; ☎ 0770-72 77 27; www.scandina vian.net) Hub: Stockholm-Arlanda.
Skyways (airline code JZ; ☎ 0771-95 95 00; www .skyways.se) Hub: Stockholm-Arlanda.

Tickets

Most airline websites list special offers, and there are good online ticket agencies, such as www.travelocity.co.uk and www.deckchair .com, that will compare prices for you.

Dealing direct with a travel agent, however, can give you extra details, like which airlines have the best facilities for children, or which travel insurance is most suitable for you.

If you're planning on visiting the south, flights to Copenhagen airport, which is just across the Öresund bridge from Sweden, may be cheaper than flights to Malmö.

Departure tax is included in the ticket price.

Continental Europe

SAS offers numerous direct services between Stockholm and European capitals including Amsterdam, Berlin, Brussels, Dublin, Geneva, Helsinki, Moscow, Oslo, Paris and Prague. Many services are routed via Copenhagen or Frankfurt. It also has routes from Göteborg to Copenhagen and Frankfurt.

Finnair has direct flights from Helsinki (which Swedes call Helsingfors) to Stockholm (around 15 daily) and Göteborg (up to four services daily). Blue1 has regular daily flights from Stockholm to Helsinki, Oulu, Tampere, Turku (known as Åbo in Swedish) and Vaasa, and from Göteborg to Helsinki.

Skyways has several flights daily from Copenhagen to Swedish regional centres such as Karlstad, Linköping, Norrköping and Örebro.

The budget airline Ryanair has frequent flights from Stockholm Skavsta to Barcelona, Brussels, Düsseldorf, Frankfurt, Hamburg, Milan, Paris, Riga and Rome.

The following sources may be useful for making arrangements.

UK & Ireland

Budget airline Ryanair flies from London Stansted to Stockholm Skavsta, Göteborg City and Malmö Sturup; Glasgow Prestwick to Stockholm Skavsta and Göteborg City; London Luton to Västerås; and Shannon to Stockholm Skavsta.

Between London (Heathrow) and Stockholm Arlanda, several commercial airlines have regular daily flights, including SAS, British Airways and bmi. Prices start at around UK£150.

SAS flies at least four times daily from Stockholm Arlanda to Manchester and Dublin via London or Copenhagen. SAS also flies daily between London (Heathrow) and Göteborg.

City Airline has two flights weekly from Göteborg (Landvetter) to Birmingham and Manchester.

USA

Thanks to the large ethnic Swedish population in Minnesota, North Dakota and Wisconsin, you may find small local agencies in those areas specialising in travel to Scandinavia and offering good-value charter flights.

Icelandair has services from Baltimore-Washington, Boston, New York, Minneapolis and Orlando via Reykjavík to many European destinations, including Stockholm. Twice per week, between mid-May and mid-October, you can also fly from/to San Francisco.

If you're planning on flying within Scandinavia, SAS offers a Visit Scandinavia/Europe Air Pass to its transatlantic passengers. SAS's North American hub is New York City's Newark Airport, with direct daily flights to/from Stockholm.

LAND
Border Crossings

Customs and immigration posts on border crossings between Sweden and Denmark, Finland or Norway are usually deserted, so passports are rarely checked. There are many minor roads between Sweden and Norway that don't have any border formalities at all.

Services across Swedish borders are operated by the following:

Eurolines (☎ 08-762 5960; www.eurolines.com) See also the boxed text, p334.

Säfflebussen (☎ 0771-15 15 15; www.safflebussen .se, in Swedish, Norwegian & Danish) Long-distance buses within Sweden and to Oslo (Norway) and Copenhagen (Denmark).

Sveriges Järnväg (SJ; ☎ 0771-75 75 99; www.sj.se) Train lines in the southern part of the country, with services to Copenhagen (Denmark).

Swebus Express (☎ 0200-21 82 18; www.swebus express.se) Long-distance buses within Sweden and to Oslo (Norway) and Copenhagen (Denmark).

Tågkompaniet (☎ 0771-44 41 11; www.tagkom paniet.se, in Swedish) Trains in the north of the country, with services to Narvik (Norway).

Denmark
BUS

Apart from Eurolines (see boxed text, p334), Swebus Express has five buses daily from Copenhagen to Göteborg (Skr356, four hours), as does Säfflebusen (Skr315).

TRANSPORT

CAR & MOTORCYCLE

You can drive from Copenhagen to Malmö across the Öresund bridge on the E20 motorway. Tolls are paid at Lernacken, on the Swedish side, in either Danish (single crossing per car Dkr260) or Swedish (Skr325) currency, or by credit or debit card.

TRAIN

Öresund trains operated by **Skånetrafiken** (www.skanetrafiken.se) run every 20 minutes from 6am to midnight (and once an hour thereafter) between Copenhagen and Malmö (return trip Skr140, 35 minutes each way) via the bridge. The trains usually stop at Copenhagen Airport.

From Copenhagen, it's necessary to change in Malmö for Stockholm-bound trains. Six or seven services operate directly between Copenhagen and Göteborg (Skr327, four hours). Trains every hour or two connect Copenhagen, Kristianstad and Karlskrona. X2000 high-speed trains are more expensive.

Germany
BUS

For information on getting to/from Sweden by bus, see boxed text, p334.

TRAIN

Hamburg is the central European gateway for Scandinavia, with direct trains daily to Copenhagen and a few on to Stockholm.

There are direct overnight trains running every day between Berlin and Malmö via the Trelleborg–Sassnitz ferry. The journey takes nine hours and a couchette/bed costs €88/125. See www.berlin-night-express.com for details.

Finland
BUS

Frequent bus services run from Haparanda to Tornio (Skr10, 10 minutes). **Tapanis Buss** (☎ 0922-129 55; www.tapanis.se, in Swedish) runs express coaches from Stockholm to Tornio via Haparanda twice a week (Skr570, 15 hours).

Länstrafiken i Norrbotten (☎ 020-47 00 47; www .ltnbd.se) operates buses as far as Karesuando, from where it's only a few minutes' walk across the bridge to Kaaresuvanto (Finland). There are also regular regional services from Haparanda to Övertorneå (some continue to Pello, Pajala and Kiruna). You can walk across the border at Övertorneå or Pello and pick up a Finnish bus to Muonio, with onward connections from there to Kaaresuvanto and Tromsø (Norway).

CAR & MOTORCYCLE

The main routes between Sweden and Finland are the E4 from Umeå to Kemi and Rd 45 from Gällivare to Kaaresuvanto; five other minor roads also cross the border.

Norway
BUS

Säfflebussen runs from Stockholm to Oslo (Skr425, 7½ hours, fives times daily) via Karlstad, and from Göteborg to Oslo (Skr265, four hours, seven daily).

Swebus Express has the same routes with similar prices.

In the north, buses run once daily from Umeå to Mo i Rana (eight hours) and from Skellefteå to Bodø (nine hours, daily except Saturday); for details, contact **Länstrafiken i Västerbotten** (☎ 0771-10 01 10; www.tabussen.nu) and **Länstrafiken i Norrbotten** (☎ 0771-10 01 10; www.ltnbd.se), respectively.

CAR & MOTORCYCLE

The main roads between Sweden and Norway are the E6 from Göteborg to Oslo, the E18 from Stockholm to Oslo, the E14 from Sundsvall to Trondheim, the E12 from Umeå to Mo i Rana, and the E10 from Kiruna to Bjerkvik. Many secondary roads also cross the border.

TRAIN

The main rail links run from Stockholm to Oslo, from Göteborg to Oslo, from Stockholm to Östersund and Storlien (Norwegian trains continue to Trondheim), and from Luleå to Kiruna and Narvik.

Trains run daily between Stockholm and Oslo (Skr500 to Skr706, six to seven hours), and there's a night train from Stockholm to Narvik (Skr811, about 20 hours). You can also travel from Helsingborg to Oslo (Skr750, seven hours), via Göteborg. X2000 high-speed trains are more expensive.

UK
BUS

For information on getting to/from Sweden by bus, see boxed text, p334.

RAILWAYS & FERRIES

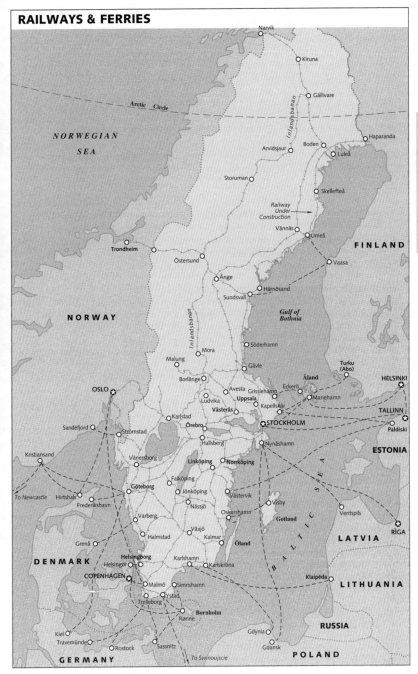

TRANSPORT

TRAVELLING TO SWEDEN BY EUROLINES

Eurolines (www.eurolines.com) is an association of companies forming Europe's largest international bus network. It links Swedish cities such as Stockholm, Göteborg and Malmö directly to Denmark, Germany and Norway, and indirectly to cities all over Western and Central Europe. Advance ticket purchases are compulsory. Most buses operate daily in summer and several times per week in winter.

The Eurolines Pass allows unlimited travel to 35 cities across Europe. From mid-June to mid-September, and around late December, a 15-/30-day pass costs €329/439 (€279/359 for those under 26 years or over 60; it's cheaper outside these months). Some popular routes include the following:

■ Denmark (Copenhagen) to/from Stockholm (without pass Dkr280, nine hours, at least three per week) and Göteborg (Dkr200, 4½ hours, daily).

■ Germany (Berlin) to/from Stockholm (Skr710, 17 hours, three weekly), Göteborg (Skr649, 12 hours, daily) via Copenhagen, and Malmö (Skr439, 8½ hours, daily) via Copenhagen.

■ Germany (Hamburg) to/from Stockholm (Skr769, 14 hours, four weekly), Göteborg (Skr679, 11 hours, two daily) and Malmö (Skr469, seven hours, two daily) all via Copenhagen.

■ UK (London) to/from Stockholm (Skr1250, 30 hours, one to four times weekly) via Amsterdam and Hamburg – if you're booking online you'll need to book each leg of the journey separately, and you may have to change buses three or four times.

Eurolines Representatives in Northern Europe

Bayern Express (☎ 030-8609 62 11; www.berlinlinienbus.de, in German; Mannheimer Str 33/34, 10713 Berlin)
Deutsche Touring/Eurolines (☎ 040-280 45 38; www.deutsche-touring.com; Am Römerhof 17, 60486 Frankfurt am Main)
Eurolines Scandinavia (☎ 031 10 02 40; Nils Ericson platsen 17, 41103 Göteborg)
Eurolines Scandinavia (☎ 033 88 70 00; Reventlowsgade 8, 1651 Copenhagen V; temporary office at Vesterbrogade 20, 4th fl, First Hotel)
Eurolines Scandinavia (☎ 08 762 59 60; www.eurolinestravel.com; Klarabergsviadukten 72, Cityterminalen, 11164 Stockholm)
Eurolines UK (☎ 0207 259 9285; www.eurolines.co.uk; 4 Vicarage Rd, Edgbaston, Birmingham B15 3ES)
Norway Bussekspress (☎ 022 17 20 00; www.nor-way.no; Karl Johans gate 2, NO-0154 Oslo)

TRAIN

Connections from the UK go through the Channel Tunnel to Continental Europe. From Brussels, you can connect to Hamburg, a main gateway to Scandinavia. To book these tickets online, however, you usually have to reserve each section separately.

From London, a 2nd-class single ticket (including couchette) costs around UK£250 to Stockholm. For reservations and tickets, contact **Deutsche Bahn UK** (☎ 08702 435 363; www.bahn.co.uk).

SEA
Ferry

Ferry connections between Sweden and its neighbours are frequent and straightforward. Most lines offer substantial discounts for seniors, students and children,

and many rail-pass holders also get reduced fares. Most prices quoted in this section are for single journeys at peak times (weekend travel, overnight crossings, mid-June to mid-August); at other times, fares may be up to 30% lower.

DENMARK
Göteborg–Fredrikshavn

Stena Line (☎ 031-704 00 00; www.stenaline.se) Three-hour crossing. Up to six ferries daily. Pedestrian/car with five passengers/bicycle Skr185/1525/225.

Stena Line (Express) Two-hour crossing. Up to three ferries daily. Pedestrian/car with five passengers/bicycle Skr285/1795/275.

Helsingør–Helsingborg

This is the quickest route and has frequent ferries (crossing time around 20 minutes).

ACE Link (☎ 042-38 58 80; www.acelink.se, in Swedish)
Regular passenger-only ferries to Helsingør from around
7am to 8pm daily. Pedestrian/bicycle Skr48/16.

HH-Ferries (☎ 042-19 80 00; www.hhferries.se) A
24-hour service. Pedestrian/car with up to nine passengers
Skr24/300.

Scandlines (☎ 042-18 63 00; www.scandlines.se)
Similar service and prices.

Varberg–Grenå

Stena Line (☎ 031-704 00 00; www.stenaline.se) Four-
hour crossing. Three or four daily. Pedestrian/car with five
passengers/bicycle Skr285/1595/280.

Ystad–Rønne

BornholmsTrafikken (☎ 0411-55 87 00; www.born
holmstrafikken.dk) Conventional (1½ hours) and fast (80
minutes) services, two to nine times daily. Pedestrian/car
with five passengers/bicycle from €23/133/25.

EASTERN EUROPE

To/from Estonia, **Tallink** (☎ 08-666 60 01; www
.tallink.ee, in Estonian) runs the Stockholm–Tallinn
and Kapellskär–Paldiski routes.

Scandlines (☎ 08-5206 02 90; www.scandlines.dk) operates Ventspils–Nynäshamn ferries around
five times per week.

To/from Lithuania, **Lisco Line** (☎ 0454-33680;
www.lisco.lt) runs daily between Karlshamn
and Klaipėda.

To/from Poland, **Polferries** (☎ 040-121700; www
.polferries.se) and **Unity Line** (☎ 0411-556900; www.unit
yline.pl) have daily Ystad–Swinoujscie crossings.
Polferries also runs the Nynäshamn–Gdańsk
route. **Stena Line** (☎ 031-704 00 00; www.stenaline.se)
sails from Karlskrona to Gdynia.

FINLAND

Helsinki is called Helsingfors in Swedish, and
Turku is Åbo.

Stockholm–Helsinki and Stockholm–Turku
ferries run daily throughout the year via the
Åland islands (exempt from the abolition of
duty-free within the EU, making them a popular outing for Swedes). These ferries have minimum age limits; check before you travel.

Stockholm–Åland Islands (Mariehamn)

Besides the Silja Line and Viking Line routes
above, two companies offer foot passenger-
only overnight cruises. Prices quoted are for
return trips.

Birka Cruises (☎ 08-702 72 00; www.birkacruises
.com) A 22-hour round-trip. One or two daily. Berths from
Skr350. Prices include supper and breakfast.

Eckerö Linjen (☎ 0175-258 00; www.eckerolinjen.fi)
Runs to the Åland Islands from Grisslehamn.

Ånedin-Linjen (☎ 08-456 22 00; www.anedinlinjen
.com, in Swedish) Six hours, daily. Couchettes cost Skr75,
berths start at Skr250.

Stockholm–Helsinki

Silja Line (☎ 08-22 21 40; www.silja.com) Around 15
hours. Ticket and cabin berth from €122.

Viking Line (☎ 08-452 40 00; www.vikingline.fi) Operates the same routes with slightly cheaper prices.

Stockholm–Turku

Silja Line (☎ 08-22 21 40; www.silja.com) Eleven
hours. Deck place €11, cabins from €49; prices are
higher for evening trips. From September to early May,
ferries also depart from Kapellskär (90km northeast of
Stockholm): connecting buses operated by Silja Line are
included in the full-price fare.

Viking Line (☎ 08-452 40 00; www.vikingline.fi)
Operates the same routes with slightly cheaper prices. In
high season it offers passage from both Stockholm and
Kapellskär.

RG Line (☎ 090-18 52 00; www.rgline.com) runs the
Umeå–Vaasa and Sundsvall–Vaasa routes.

GERMANY
Göteborg–Kiel

Stena Line (☎ 031-704 00 00; www.stenaline.se)
Fourteen hours. One crossing nightly. Pedestrian/car with
up to five passengers from Skr495/1760. Rates are flexible
depending on how early you book and which cabin level
you choose.

Trelleborg–Rostock

Scandlines (☎ 042-18 61 00; www.scandlines.se)
Six hours (night crossing 7½ hours). Two or three daily.
Pedestrian/car with up to nine passengers Skr195/1025.
Passenger with bicycle Skr225. A fuel surcharge of
between Skr50 and Skr80 may be added.

TT-Line (☎ 0410-562 00; www.ttline.com) Operates the
same as Scandlines, with similar prices.

Trelleborg–Sassnitz

Scandlines (☎ 042-18 61 00; www.scandlines.se) A
3¾-hour trip. Two to five times daily. Pedestrian/car with
up to nine passengers Skr125/925. Passenger with bicycle
Skr195. A fuel surcharge of Skr50 to Skr80 may be added.

Trelleborg–Travemünde

TT-Line (☎ 0410-562 00; www.ttline.com) Seven
hours. Two to five daily. Pedestrian/car with up to five
passengers from Skr290/1045. Passenger with bicycle from
Skr390. Berths are compulsory on night crossings.

TRANSPORT

NORWAY

There's a daily overnight **DFDS Seaways** (☎ 031-65 06 80; www.dfdsseaways.com) ferry between Copenhagen and Oslo, via Helsingborg. Passenger fares between Helsingborg and Oslo (14 hours) cost from Skr1100, and cars Skr475, but the journey can't be booked on-line; you'll need to call. DFDS also sails from Göteborg to Kristiansand (Norway), three days a week (from seven hours); contact them for prices. A **Color Line** (☎ 0526-620 00; www.colorline.com) ferry between Strömstad (Sweden) and Sandefjord (Norway) makes the trip two to six times daily (2½ hours) year-round. Tickets start from Nkr175 (rail passes get 50% discount).

UK

DFDS Seaways (www.dfdsseaways.com; ☎ Göteborg 031-65 06 50, UK 08705-333 000) has two crossings per week between Göteborg and Newcastle via Kristiansand (Norway). The trip takes 25 hours. Fares start from around £35 per person including economy berth; cars cost £75 and bicycles are free. Again, though, booking these trips online is somewhat maddening; it's best to call instead.

GETTING AROUND

Public transport is heavily subsidised and well organised. It's divided into 24 regional networks (länstrafik), but with an overarching **Resplus** (www.samtrafiken.se) system, where one ticket is valid on trains and buses. Timetables are available online, with local versions available free of charge or for a nominal fee from tourist offices or the operators.

Holders of International Student Identification Cards (ISIC) will get discounts with some operators – it pays to ask.

AIR
Airlines in Sweden

Domestic airlines in Sweden tend to use **Stockholm-Arlanda** (code ARN; ☎ 08-797 60 00; www.lfv.se) as a hub, but there are 30-odd regional airports. Flying domestic is expensive on full-price tickets (usually between Skr1000 and Skr3000 for a single ticket), but substantial discounts are available on internet bookings, student and youth fares, off-peak travel, return tickets booked at least seven days in advance or low-price tickets for accompanying

family members and seniors. It's worth asking about stand-by fares. The following is a selection of Sweden's internal flight operators and the destinations they cover.

Malmö Aviation (airline code TF; ☎ 040-660 29 00; www.malmoaviation.se) Hub: Stockholm Bromma. Covers Göteborg, Stockholm and Umeå.

Scandinavian Airlines System (SAS; airline code SK; ☎ 0770-72 77 27; www.flysas.com) Hub: Stockholm-Arlanda. Covers Arvidsjaur, Borlänge, Gällivare, Göteborg, Halmstad, Ängelholm-Helsingborg, Hemavan, Hultsfred, Jönköping, Kalmar, Karlstad, Kiruna, Kramfors, Kristianstad, Linköping, Luleå, Lycksele, Norrköping, Malmö, Mora, Örnsköldsvik, Oskarshamn, Oskersund, Skellefteå, Stockholm, Storuman, Sundsvall, Sveg, Torsby, Trollhättan, Umeå, Vilhelmina, Visby, Västerås and Örebro.

Skyways (airline code JZ; ☎ 0771 95 95 00; www.skyways.se) Hub: Stockholm-Arlanda. Covers Arvidsjaur, Borlänge, Göteborg, Halmstad, Hemavan, Jönköping, Karlstad, Kramfors, Kristianstad, Linköping, Lycksele, Norrköping, Mora, Skellefteå, Stockholm, Storuman, Sundsvall, Trollhättan, Vilhelmina, Visby and Örebro.

Air Passes

Visitors who fly SAS to Sweden from Continental Europe, North America or Asia can buy tickets on a Visit Scandinavia Air Pass, allowing one-way travel on direct flights between any two Scandinavian cities serviced by SAS, Skyways and other operators. When you buy your international ticket, you buy up to eight coupons, each of which can be used on one domestic flight and is valid for three months. A coupon for use within Sweden costs €69 (except the Stockholm–Kiruna, which is €122); international flights between Sweden, Denmark, Norway and Finland cost €80. They can be purchased after arriving in Sweden if you have a return SAS international ticket. For the latest information, call SAS or check their website.

BICYCLE

Cycling is an excellent way to see Sweden and a very common mode of transport for Swedes. Most towns have separate lanes and traffic signals for cyclists. For more information see p63.

BOAT
Canal Boat

The canals provide cross-country routes linking the main lakes. The longest cruises, on the Göta Canal from Söderköping (south of Stockholm) to Göteborg, run from mid-May to mid-September, take at least four days and include the lakes in between. **Rederiaktiebolaget Göta Kanal** (☎ 031-15 83 11; www.gotacanal.se) operates three ships over the whole distance with fares from ranging from Skr9425 to Skr17,825 for a four-day cruise, including full board and guided excursions. For shorter, cheaper trips on the canal, contact tourist offices in the area.

Ferry

An extensive boat network and the 16-day Båtluffarkortet boat passes (Skr340, plus a Skr40 supplement for first-time buyers) open up the attractive Stockholm archipelago (see p119). Gotland is served by regular ferries (see p164) from Nynäshamn and Oskarshamn, and the quaint fishing villages off the west coast can normally be reached by boat with a regional transport pass – enquire at the Göteborg tourist offices (p207).

BUS

You can travel by bus in Sweden on any of the 24 good-value and extensive *länstrafik* networks (contact details are given at the beginning of each chapter) or on national long-distance routes.

Express Buses

Swebus Express (☎ 0200-21 82 18; www.swebusexpress .se) has the largest network of express buses, but they only serve the southern half of the country (as far north as Mora in Dalarna). **Svenska Buss** (☎ 0771-67 67 67; www.svenskabuss.se, in Swedish) and **Säfflebussen** (☎ 0771-15 15 15; www.safflebussen .se, in Swedish, Danish & Norwegian) also connect many southern towns and cities with Stockholm; prices are often slightly cheaper than Swebus Express, but services are less frequent.

North of Gävle, regular connections with Stockholm are provided by several smaller operators, including **Ybuss** (☎ 0771-33 44 44; www.ybuss.se, in Swedish), which has services to Sundsvall, Östersund and Umeå.

You don't have to reserve a seat on Swebus Express services. Generally, tickets for travel between Monday and Thursday are cheaper, or if they're purchased over the internet or more than 24 hours before departure. If you're a student or senior, it's worth asking

ROAD DISTANCE (KM)

	Gävle	Göteborg	Helsingborg	Jönköping	Kalmar	Karlstad	Kiruna	Linköping	Luleå	Malmö	Skellefteå	Stockholm	Sundsvall	Umeå	Uppsala	Örebro
Göteborg	520															
Helsingborg	690	220														
Jönköping	450	150	240													
Kalmar	560	350	290	215												
Karlstad	325	250	470	245	455											
Kiruna	1090	1645	1785	1540	1660	1420										
Linköping	365	280	365	130	235	230	1440									
Luleå	755	1300	1440	1210	1310	1080	342	1116								
Malmö	740	280	65	290	290	530	1835	415	1500							
Skellefteå	620	1185	1310	1075	1175	950	470	970	135	1360						
Stockholm	175	480	565	330	415	305	1265	205	930	620	795					
Sundsvall	215	765	890	670	770	540	875	575	540	955	405	390				
Umeå	485	1010	1140	935	1040	810	605	850	270	1230	135	660	270			
Uppsala	110	485	615	380	460	285	1195	250	860	665	725	70	320	590		
Örebro	235	285	450	200	350	115	1340	115	970	495	840	200	445	705	170	
Östersund	385	795	990	790	950	560	815	680	595	1075	470	560	185	370	490	590

TRANSPORT

TRANSPORT

about fare discounts; however, most bus companies will only give student prices to holders of Swedish student cards (the exception is Swebus Express, where you can get an ISIC discount).

Regional Networks
The *länstrafik* bus networks are well integrated with the regional train system, with one ticket valid on any local or regional bus or train. Rules vary but transfers are usually free if they are within one to four hours. Fares on local buses and trains are often identical.

In remote areas, taxis may have an arrangement with the county council to provide a reduced-fare taxi trip to your final destination. These fares are only valid when arranged in advance (they cannot be bought from the taxi departure point). Ask the regional bus company for details.

Bus Passes
Good-value daily or weekly passes are usually available from local and regional transport offices, and many regions have 30-day passes for longer stays, or a special card for peak-season summer travel.

CAR & MOTORCYCLE
Sweden has good roads, and the excellent E-class motorways rarely have traffic jams.

Automobile Associations
The Swedish national motoring association is **Motormännens Riksförbund** (☎ 020-21 11 11; www .motormannen.se).

Bring Your Own Vehicle
If bringing your own car, you'll need your vehicle registration documents, unlimited third-party liability insurance and a valid driving licence. A right-hand-drive vehicle brought from the UK or Ireland should have deflectors fitted to the headlights to avoid dazzling oncoming traffic. You must carry a reflective warning breakdown triangle.

Driving Licence
An international driving permit isn't necessary; your domestic licence will do.

Hire
To hire a car you have to be at least 20 (sometimes 25) years of age, with a recognised licence and a credit card.

Fly-drive packages may save you money. International rental chains (such as Avis, Hertz and Europcar) are more expensive but convenient; all have desks at Stockholm-Arlanda and Göteborg Landvetter Airports and offices in most major cities. The best car hire rates are generally from larger petrol stations (like Statoil and OK-Q8) – look out for signs saying *biluthyrning* or *hyrbilar*.

Avis (☎ 0770-82 00 82; www.avisworld.com)

Europcar (☎ 020-78 11 80; www.europcar.com)

Hertz (☎ 0771-21 12 12; www.hertz-europe.com)

Mabi Hyrbilar (☎ 08-612 60 90; www.mabirent.se) National company with competitive rates.

OK-Q8 (☎ 020-85 08 50; www.okq8.se, in Swedish) Click on *hyrbilar* in the website menu to see car-hire pages.

Statoil (☎ 08-429 63 00; www.statoil.se/biluthyrning, in Swedish) Click on *uthyrningsstationer* to see branches with car hire, and on *priser* for prices.

Road Hazards
In the north, elk (moose, to Americans) and reindeer are serious road hazards, particularly around dawn and dusk; around 40 people die in collisions every year. Look out for the signs saying *viltstängsel upphör,* which means that elk may cross the road, and for black plastic bags tied to roadside trees or poles – this means Sami have reindeer herds grazing in the area. Report all incidents to police – failure to do so is an offence.

In Göteborg and Norrköping, be aware of trams, which have priority; overtake on the right.

Road Rules
In Sweden, you drive on and give way to the right. Headlights (at least dipped) must be on at all times when driving. Use of seat belts is compulsory, and children under seven years old should be in the appropriate harness or child seat.

The blood-alcohol limit is 0.02% – one drink will put you over. The maximum speed on motorways (signposted in green and called E1, E4 etc) is 110km/h, highways 90km/h, narrow rural roads 70km/h and built-up areas 50km/h. The speed limit for cars towing caravans is 80km/h. Police using hand-held radar speed detectors can impose on-the-spot fines of up to Skr1200.

On many major roads broken lines define wide-paved edges, and a vehicle being overtaken is expected to move into this area to allow faster traffic to pass safely.

EXPLORING THE WILDERNESS

Vildmark i Värmland (☎ 140 40; www.vildmark.se) organises outdoor activities in the pristine wilderness of Värmland in summer, including canoe trips (one to six days), beaver-spotting safaris, rock climbing and rafting.

For a real get-away-from-it-all, back-to-nature experience, try one of their raft trips on the Klarälven. With help, you actually make your own six-person craft from cut logs and lengths of rope. Prices start at Skr690 for a day trip, and rise to Skr2460 for a full week (eight days, seven nights). The longer trips let you sleep on board the moored raft, or climb ashore and camp for the night (equipment can be hired at additional cost). You can while away your days fishing, swimming, spotting wildlife and enjoying the serenity. Check out the website for more information.

HITCHING

Hitching is never entirely safe in any country, and we don't recommend it. Travellers who decide to hitch should understand that they are taking a small but potentially serious risk; consider travelling in pairs and let someone know where you're planning to go.

Hitching isn't popular in Sweden and very long waits are the norm. It's prohibited to hitch on motorways.

LOCAL TRANSPORT

In Sweden, local transport is always linked with regional transport (*länstrafik*). Regional passes are valid both in the city and on the rural routes. Town and city bus fares are around Skr20, but it usually works out cheaper to get a day card or other travel pass.

Swedish and Danish trains and buses around the Öresund area form an integrated transport system, so buying tickets to Copenhagen from any station in the region is as easy as buying tickets for Swedish journeys.

Stockholm has an extensive underground metro system, and Göteborg and Norrköping run tram networks. Göteborg also has a city ferry service.

Beware of getting ripped off in taxis. IAgree to a fare before the trip. In Stockholm, flag fall is around Skr32, then Skr7 per km; most taxis in the capital will take you to Arlanda airport for between Skr400 and Skr450, although taxis working as part of the Flygbussarna system are cheaper. **Airport Cab** (☎ 08-25 25 25; www.airport cab.se) goes from Stockholm to Arlanda for a flat fee of Skr350, and the opposite direction for Skr430.

TOURS

Recommended tours appear throughout this book and include those run by the following companies:

Svenska Turistföreningen (STF; Swedish Touring Association; ☎ 08-463 21 00; www.svenskaturistforenin gen.se) Offers scores of events and tours, mostly based on outdoor activities (eg kayaking and hiking).
Sweden Booking (☎ 0498-20 33 80; www.sweden booking.com) Can organise rail tickets as well as package trips, like Christmas in Dalarna or canoeing in Värmland.

TRAIN

Sweden has an extensive and reliable railway network, and trains are certainly faster than buses. Many destinations in the northern half of the country, however, cannot be reached by train alone. The following are the two main train operators in the country:

Sveriges Järnväg (SJ; ☎ 0771-75 75 75; www.sj.se) National network covering most main lines, especially in the southern part of the country. Its X2000 fast trains run at speeds of up to 200km/h.

Tågkompaniet (☎ 0771-44 41 11; www.tagkom paniet.se, in Swedish) Operates excellent overnight trains from Göteborg and Stockholm north to Boden, Kiruna, Luleå and Narvik, and the lines north of Härnösand.

There are smaller regional train companies, but they tend to cooperate closely with SJ.

In summer, some tourist trains offer special rail experiences. The best is **Inlandsbanan** (☎ 0771-53 53 53; www.inlandsbanan.se), the slow, scenic 1300km Kristinehamn–Gällivare route, one of the great rail journeys in Scandinavia. Several southern sections have to be travelled by bus, but the all-train route starts at Mora. It takes seven hours from Mora to Östersund (Skr395) and 15 hours from Östersund to Gällivare (Skr918). A pass allows two weeks' unlimited travel for Skr1450.

Costs

Travel on the super-fast X2000 services is much pricier than on 'normal' trains. Full-price 2nd-class tickets for longer journeys are expensive (around twice the price of equivalent bus trips), but there are various discounts available, especially for booking a week or so in advance *(förköpsbiljet)*, or at the last minute (for youth and pensioner fares). Students with a Swedish CSN (Centrala stud-iestödsnämnden) or SFS (Sveriges förenade studentkårer; Swedish National Students Union) card if aged over 26, and people aged under 26 get a 30% discount on the standard adult fare.

X2000 tickets include a seat reservation. All SJ ticket prices are reduced in summer, from late June to mid-August. Most SJ trains don't allow bicycles to be taken onto trains (they have to be sent as freight), but those in southern Sweden (especially Skåne) do; check when you book your ticket. Station luggage lockers cost Skr30 to Skr50 for 24 hours.

Train Passes

ScanRail no longer exists, but several other passes offer similar benefits. The Sweden Rail Pass, Eurodomino tickets and interna-tional passes, such as Inter-Rail and Eurail, are accepted on SJ services and most regional trains.

The **Eurail Scandinavia Pass** (www.eurail.com) en-titles you to unlimited rail travel in Denmark, Finland, Norway and Sweden; it is valid in second class only and is allows four, five, six, eight or 10 days of travel in a two-month pe-riod (prices start from US$255/335 per youth/ adult). It also provides free travel on Scandlines' Helsingør–Helsingborg route, and 20% to 50% discounts on the following ship routes:

Route	Operator
Frederikshavn-Göteborg	Stena Line
Grenå-Varberg	Stena Line
Stockholm-Helsinki	Viking or Silja Line
Stockholm-Turku	Viking or Silja Line

X2000 trains require all rail-pass holders to pay a supplement of Skr65 (including the obligatory seat reservation).

Health

CONTENTS

You're unlikely to encounter serious health problems in Sweden. Travel health depends on your predeparture preparations, your daily health care while travelling, and how you handle any problem that does develop.

BEFORE YOU GO

Before departure, obtain travel insurance with good medical coverage. If you wear glasses or contact lenses, take a spare set and a copy of your optical prescription. If you require a particular medication, carry a legible copy of your prescription from your doctor. Most medications are available in Sweden, but brand names may be different, so you'll need the generic name.

RECOMMENDED VACCINATIONS

Immunisations aren't necessary for travel to Sweden, unless you've been travelling somewhere where yellow fever is prevalent. Ensure that your normal childhood vaccines (against measles, mumps, rubella, diphtheria, tetanus and polio) are up to date.

IN SWEDEN

AVAILABILITY & COST OF HEALTH CARE

Sweden's medical system is state run, so instead of visiting a private general practitioner for emergencies, go to a local medical centre (*vårdcentral*) or a hospital (*sjukhus*), where duty doctors are standing by. There are centres in all districts and main towns, listed by area under municipality (*kommun*)

in the local telephone directory. Be prepared to show your passport.

Pharmacies (*apotek*) sell nonprescription (and prescription) medicines and give advice on how to deal with everyday ailments and conditions.

For EU citizens with an European Health Insurance Card (EHIC), a doctor visit costs from Skr100 to Skr150; those under 20 are treated free of charge. At hospitals, in-patient treatment is generally free with a nonrefundable, standard fee of Skr80 per day. Out-patient treatment charges vary. Seeing a specialist costs from Skr200 to Skr300.

Non-EU citizens should have adequate travel insurance or be prepared to face high costs, although some countries (such as Australia) have reciprocal health-care agreements with Sweden.

The rate scheme for dentists (*tandläkare*) changed in July 2008; initial visits cost Skr615 (free for children). Costs for other services vary (fillings cost between Skr585 and Skr1050). Most of these charges are not reimbursed, even for EU citizens.

For general emergencies and ambulance service, call ☎ 112.

TRAVELLER'S DIARRHOEA

Simple things such as a change of water, food or climate can cause mild diarrhoea, and a few rushed toilet trips with no other symptoms do not indicate a major problem. Stomach upsets are as possible in Sweden as anywhere else. Occasionally, cooked meats displayed on buffet tables may cause problems. Also, take care with shellfish (cooked mussels that haven't opened properly aren't safe to eat), and unidentified berries and mushrooms.

Dehydration is the main danger with any diarrhoea, particularly in children or the elderly. Under all circumstances fluid replacement (at least equal to the volume being lost) is the most important thing to remember. With severe diarrhoea a rehydrating solution to replace lost minerals and salts is preferable. Commercially available oral rehydration salts can be added to boiled or bottled water. In an emergency, add a solution of six teaspoons of sugar and a half teaspoon of salt to a litre of boiled water.

Gut-paralysing drugs such as loperamide or diphenoxylate can be used to bring relief from the symptoms, although they do not cure the problem. Use these drugs only if you do not have access to toilets, eg if you *must* travel. Do not use these drugs for children under 12 or if the person has a high fever or is severely dehydrated.

Giardiasis

Stomach cramps, nausea, a bloated stomach, watery foul-smelling diarrhoea and frequent gas are all symptoms of giardiasis, which can occur several weeks after you have been exposed to the parasite (usually through drinking water from rivers and lakes in the wild). The symptoms may disappear for a few days and then return; this can go on for several weeks.

ENVIRONMENTAL HAZARDS
Hypothermia

This condition occurs when the body loses heat faster than it can produce it and the core temperature of the body falls. It's surprisingly easy to progress from very cold to dangerously cold due to a combination of wind, wet clothing, fatigue and hunger, even if the air temperature is above freezing. It's best to dress in layers; silk, wool and some of the new artificial fibres are all good insulating materials. A warm hat and a strong, waterproof outer layer (and a space blanket for emergencies) are essential in remote areas. Carry basic supplies, including food containing simple sugars to generate heat quickly, and fluid to drink.

The symptoms of hypothermia are exhaustion, numb skin, shivering, slurred speech, irrational or violent behaviour, lethargy, stumbling, dizzy spells, muscle cramps and violent bursts of energy. Irrationality may take the form of sufferers claiming they are warm and trying to take off their clothes.

To treat mild hypothermia, first get the person out of the wind and/or rain, remove their clothing if it's wet and replace it with dry, warm clothing. Give them hot liquids (not alcohol) and some high-calorie, easily digestible food. Do not rub victims; instead, allow them to slowly warm themselves. This should be enough to treat the early stages of hypothermia. Early treatment of mild hypothermia is the only way to prevent severe hypothermia, which is a critical condition.

Insect Bites & Stings

Mosquitoes, blackflies and deerflies are common from mid-June to the end of July, and fly swarms in northern areas are horrific. To avoid bites, completely cover yourself with clothes and a mosquito head net. Any exposed areas of skin, including lower legs (and even underneath trousers), should be treated with a powerful insect repellent containing DEET (although frequent application of DEET isn't recommended). Calamine lotion, a sting relief spray or ice packs will reduce the pain and swelling of bites.

Sunburn

In high northern latitudes you can get sunburnt surprisingly quickly, even through clouds, and especially when there's complete snow cover. Use sunscreen, a hat, and a barrier cream for your nose and lips. Calamine lotion or commercial after-sun preparations are good for mild sunburn. Protect your eyes with good quality sunglasses, particularly if you'll be near water, sand or snow.

Water

Tap water is safe to drink in Sweden, but drinking from streams may be unwise due to the presence of farms, old mine workings and wild animals. The clearest-looking stream water may contain giardia and other parasites, and despite the assurances of wildlife guides and rangers, it's best to be cautious.

If you don't have a filter and can't boil water, it should be treated chemically: iodine is effective and is available in both liquid and tablet form.

Language

The national language of Sweden is Swedish, a Germanic language belonging to the Nordic branch that is spoken throughout Sweden and in parts of Finland. Swedes, Danes and Norwegians can make themselves mutually understood, and most Swedes speak English as a second language.

Since they share common roots, and the Old Norse language left sprinklings of words in Anglo-Saxon, you'll find many similarities between English and Swedish – albeit with different pronunciations. There are three letters at the end of the Swedish alphabet that don't exist in the English version, namely **å**, **ä** and **ö**.

Swedish verbs are the same regardless of person or number: 'I am, you are' etc are, in Swedish, *jag är, du är* and so on. There are two genders, common (non-neuter) and neuter. Gender is reflected in the articles *en* and *ett* (a/an). The definite article (the) is added to the ends of nouns, eg *ett hus* (a house), *huset* (the house). Unfortunately there are no set rules for determining gender – it's something that has to be learnt word by word.

PRONUNCIATION

Sweden is a large country with considerable dialectal variety. There are sounds in Swedish that don't exist in English, so in the following pronunciation guides we've tried to give the closest English equivalents. In terms of dialect, we've gone with the version you'll hear in Stockholm. If you follow the pronunciation guides and listen to the way the Swedes themselves speak the language, you'll soon start getting the hang of it. The first thing you'll need to master is the songful rise and fall that is so characteristic of Swedish and Norwegian.

ACCOMMODATION

hotel
  hotell   ho·*tel*
guesthouse
  gästhus   *yest*·hoos
youth hostel
  vandrarhem   vaan·dra·*hem*
camping ground
  campingplats   kam·ping·*plats*

Where is a cheap/good hotel?
  Var är ett billigt/bra hotell?
  vaa air et *bil*·ligt/braa ho·*tel*?
What's the address?
  Vilken adress är det?
  vil·ken aa·dres air det?
Could you write the address, please?
  Kan du skriva ner adressen?
  kan doo *skree*·va neer a·*dre*·sen?
Do you have any rooms available?
  Finns det några lediga rum?
  fins de *nor*·gra *le*·di·ga room?
How much is it per person/night?
  Hur mycket kostar det per person/natt?
  her *moo*·ket *ko*·sta det per per·*soon*/nat?

I'd like ...
  Jag skulle vilja ...   ya skool·le *vil*·ya ...
  a single room
    ha ett enkelrum   haa et en·kel·*room*
  a double room
    ha ett dubbelrum   haa et *doo*·bel·*room*
  a room with a bathroom
    ha ett rum med bad   haa et room med baad
  to share a dorm
    bo i sovsal   boo ee *soov*·sal

for one night
  en natt   en nat
for two nights
  två nätter   tvo·a *ne*·te
Does it include breakfast?
  Inkluderas frukost?   in·kloo·*dair*·ras froo·kost?

LANGUAGE

May I see the room?
Kan jag får se rummet?   kan ya for *se*·ya *room*·met?
Where is the bathroom?
Var är badrummet?   vaa air baad·*room*·met?

CONVERSATION & ESSENTIALS
Hello.
  Hej.   hay
Goodbye.
  Adjö/Hej då.   ai·yer/hay·dor
Yes.
  Ja.   yaa
No.
  Nej.   nay
Please.
  Snälla.   snel·la
Thank you.
  Tack.   tak
That's fine.
  Det är bra.   de air braa
You're welcome.
  Varsågod.   var·sha·good
Excuse me.
  Ursäkta mig.   ur·*shek*·ta may
I'm sorry. (forgive me)
  Förlåt.   for·*lort*
May I/Do you mind?
  Får jag/Gör det något?   for yaa/yer de *nor*·got?
What's your name?
  Vad heter du?   vaa *he*·te doo?
My name is ...
  Jag heter ...   ya *he*·te ...
Where are you from?
  Varifrån kommer du?   vaa·re·fron *ko*·mer du?
I'm from ...
  Jag kommer från ...   ya *ko*·mer fron ...

DIRECTIONS
Where is ...?
  Var är ...?   vaa air ...?
Can you show me on the map?
  Kan du visa mig på   kan du *vee*·sa may poor
  kartan?   *kar*·tan?
Go straight ahead.
  Gå rakt fram.   gor *rakt* fraam
Turn left.
  Sväng till vänster.   sveng til *ven*·sta
Turn right.
  Sväng till höger.   sveng til *her*·ga
near
  nära   *nair*·a
far
  långt   lorngt

beach
  strand   strand

SIGNS	
Ingång	Entrance
Utgång	Exit
Information	Information
Öppen	Open
Stängd	Closed
Förbjuden	Prohibited
Polisstation	Police Station
Lediga Rum	Rooms Available
Toalett	Toilets
Herrer	Men
Damer	Women

castle
  slott   slot
cathedral
  domkyrka   dom·*sher*·ka
church
  kyrka   *sher*·ka
main square
  huvudtorg   hoo·vood·*toy*
monastery
  kloster   *kloo*·sta
old city
  gamla stad   *gam*·la staad
palace
  palats   pa·*lats*

HEALTH
Where is the ...?
Var är ...?   vaa air ...?
  chemist/pharmacy
  apoteket   a·poo·*te*·ket
  dentist
  tandläkaren   tan·*lair*·ka·*ren*
  doctor
  läkaren   *lair*·ka·ren
  hospital
  sjukhus   *shoo*·koos

I'm ill.
  Jag är sjuk.   ya air shook
My friend is ill.
  Min vän är sjuk. (m/f)   min ven air shook
I need medication for ...
  Jag behöver ett medel   ya bee·her·ver et me·del
  mot ...   moot ...
I have a toothache.
  Jag har tandvärk.   ya haar tand·*vairk*
I'm pregnant.
  Jag är gravid.   ya air gra·*veed*
antiseptic
  antiseptisk   an·tee·*sep*·tisk

EMERGENCIES

Help!
Hjälp! | yelp!
Call a doctor!
Ring efter en doktor! | ring *ef*·ter en dok·*toor!*
Call the police!
Ring polisen! | ring poo·*lee*·sen!
Call an ambulance!
Ring efter en | ring *ef*·ter en
    ambulans! | am·boo·*lants!*
Go away!
Försvinn! | fer·*shvin!*
I'm lost.
Jag har gått vilse. | ya har got vil·*se*

condoms
kondomer | kon·*do*·mer
diarrhoea
diarré | dee·a·re·a
medicine
medicin | me·de·*seen*
nausea
illamående | il·la·*mo*·en·de
stomachache
ont i magen | oont e *maa*·gen
sanitary napkins
dambindor | dam·bin·dor
tampons
tamponger | tam·*pong*·er

I'm ...
Jag är ... | ya air ...
    asthmatic
    astmatiker | ast·ma·*tee*·kair
    diabetic
    diabetiker | de·a·*be*·tee·ker

I'm allergic to antibiotics/penicillin.
Jag är allergisk mot antibiotika/penicillin.
yaa air a·ler·*gisk* moot an·tee·bee·*yo*·tee·ker/pen·ne·see·*len*

LANGUAGE DIFFICULTIES

Do you speak English?
Talar du engelska? | *ta*·la du en·gel·ska?
Does anyone here speak English?
Finns det någon här | fins de non hair
    som talar engelska? | som *ta*·la en·gel·ska?
I (don't) understand.
Jag förstår (inte). | ya fer·*stor* (in·te)
Could you speak more slowly, please?
Kan du vara snäll och | kan du *va*·ra snel ok
    tala lite långsammare? | *ta*·la *lee*·te *long*·sa·ma·rer?

SAMI LANGUAGES

Sami languages are related to Finnish and other Finno-Ugric languages. Five of the nine main dialects of the Sami language are spoken in Sweden, with speakers of each varying in number from 500 to 5000.

Most Sami speakers can communicate in Swedish, but relatively few speak English. Knowing some Sami words and phrases will give you a chance to access the unique Sami culture.

FELL (NORTHERN) SAMI

The most common of the Sami languages, Fell Sami is considered the standard variety of the language. It's spoken in Sweden's far north around Karesuando and Jukkasjärvi.

Written Fell Sami includes several accented letters, but it still doesn't accurately represent the spoken language – even some Sami people find the written language difficult to learn. For example, *giitu* (thanks) is pronounced 'geech-too', but the strongly aspirated 'h' isn't written.

Hello. | *Buorre beaivi.*
Hello. (reply) | *Ipmel atti.*
Goodbye.
    (to person leaving) | *Mana dearvan.*
    (to person staying) | *Báze dearvan.*
Thank you. | *Giitu.*
You're welcome. | *Leage buorre.*
Yes. | *De lea.*
No. | *Li.*
How are you? | *Mot manna?*
I'm fine. | *Buorre dat manna.*

1	*okta*
2	*guokte*
3	*golbma*
4	*njeallje*
5	*vihta*
6	*guhta*
7	*cieza*
8	*gávcci*
9	*ovcci*
10	*logi*

NUMBERS

0	*noll*	nol
1	*ett*	et
2	*två*	tvo·a
3	*tre*	tree
4	*fyra*	few·ra

LANGUAGE

5	*fem*	fem
6	*sex*	sex
7	*sju*	shoo
8	*åtta*	ot·*ta*
9	*nio*	*nee*·ye
10	*tio*	*tee*·ye
11	*elva*	*el*·va
12	*tolv*	tolv
13	*tretton*	*tre*·ton
14	*fjorton*	*fyoo*·ton
15	*femton*	*fem*·ton
16	*sexton*	*sex*·ton
17	*sjutton*	*shoo*·ton
18	*arton*	*ar*·ton
19	*nitton*	*nee*·ton
20	*tjugo*	*shoo*·go
21	*tjugoett*	*shoo*·go·et
30	*trettio*	*tre*·tee
40	*fyrtio*	*fyor*·tee
50	*femtio*	*fem*·tee
60	*sextio*	*sex*·tee
70	*sjuttio*	*shoo*·tee
80	*åttio*	*ot*·tee
90	*nittio*	*nee*·tee
100	*ett hundra*	et *hoon*·dra
1000	*ett tusen*	et *too*·sen
1,000,000	*en miljon*	en mil·*yoon*

SHOPPING & SERVICES

I'm looking for ...
Jag letar efter ...   yaa *lee*·ta ef·ta
 a bank
 en bank   en bank
 the city centre
 centrum   sent·*room*
 the ... embassy
 ... ambassaden   ... am·ba·*sa*·den
 the market
 marknaden   mark·*naa*·den
 the museum
 muséet   moo·*zee*·et
 the post office
 posten   *pos*·ten
 a public telephone
 en offentlig telefon   en o·*fent*·lig tel·le·*foon*
 a public toilet
 en toalettkiosk   en toa·*let*·she·osk
 the tourist office
 turistinformationen   too·*rist*·in·for·ma·*shoo*·nen

What time does it open/close?
Hur dags (öppnar/   hur daags (*erp*·na/
stänger) de?   *steng*·er) det?

Could I please have ...?
Kan jag få ...?   kan ya for ...?
How much is it?
Hur mycket kostar den?   her *mi*·ke *kos*·ta den?

bookshop
 bokhandel   *book*·han·del
camera shop
 fotoaffär   fo·*to*·a·*fair*
clothing store
 modebutik   *mood*·boo·*teek*
delicatessen
 delikatessaffär   del·li·*kaats*·a·*fair*
laundry
 tvätt   tvet
newsagency
 pressbyrå/tabaksaffär   pres·*bew*·ro/ta·*bak*·sa·*fair*
souvenir shop
 souveniraffär   soov·ven·*nee*·ra·*fair*
stationers
 pappershandel   pa·pairs·*haan*·del

TIME & DATE
What time is it?
 Vad är klockan?   vaa air *klo*·kan?
today
 idag   ee·dag
tonight
 i kväll   ee kvel
tomorrow
 imorgon   ee·mor·*ron*
yesterday
 igår   ee·*gor*
morning
 morgonen   moo·ron·*nen*
afternoon
 efter middagen   ef·ter mid·da·gen
night
 natt   nat

Monday
 måndag   *mon*·dag
Tuesday
 tisdag   *tees*·dag
Wednesday
 onsdag   *ons*·dag
Thursday
 torsdag   *torsh*·dag
Friday
 fredag   *fre*·dag
Saturday
 lördag   *ler*·dag
Sunday
 söndag   *sern*·dag

LANGUAGE

January
januari   yan·u·*aa*·ree
February
februari   fe·broo·*aa*·ree
March
mars   mars
April
april   a·*preel*
May
maj   may
June
juni   yoo·nee
July
juli   yoo·lee
August
augusti   o·*goos*·tee
September
september   sep·*tem*·ber
October
oktober   ok·*too*·ber
November
november   no·*vem*·ber
December
december   de·*sem*·ber

TRANSPORT
Where is the ...?
Var är ...?   vaa air ...?
  bus stop
  busshållplatsen   boos·hol·*plat*·sen
  train station
  tågstationen   torg·sta·*shoo*·nen

tramstop
  spårvagnshållplatsen   spor·vaags·hol·*plat*·sen

What time does the ... leave/arrive?
När avgår/kommer ...?   nair av·gor/ko·mer ...?
  boat
  båten   bor·ten
  bus
  bussen   boos·sen
  tram
  spårvagnen   spor·*vaagn*
  train
  tåget   tor·get

I'd like ...
Jag skulle vilja ha ...   ya skoo·le vil·ya haa ...
  a one-way ticket
  en enkelbiljett   en en·*kel*·bil·yet
  a return ticket
  en returbiljett   en re·*toor*·bil·yet

1st class
  första klass   *fer*·shta klas
2nd class
  andra klass   an·dra klas
left luggage
  effektförvaring   e·*fekt*·fur·*vaa*·ring
timetable
  tidtabell   tee·ta·*bel*

Where can I hire a car/bicycle?
Var kan jag hyra en   vaa kan ya hee·ra
bil/cykel?   en beel/en see·*kel*?

Also available from Lonely Planet:
Western Europe Phrasebook

Glossary

You may encounter some of the following terms and abbreviations during your travels in Sweden. See also the Language chapter (p343) and the glossary in the Food & Drink chapter (p49).

Note that the letters **å**, **ä** and **ö** fall at the end of the Swedish alphabet, and the letters **v** and **w** are often used interchangeably (you will see the small town of Vaxholm also referred to as Waxholm, and an inn can be known as a *värdshus* or *wärdshus*). In directories like telephone books they usually fall under one category (eg *wa* is listed before *vu*).

aktie bolaget (AB) – company
allemansrätt – literally 'every person's right'; a tradition allowing universal access to private property (with some restrictions), public land and wilderness areas
ank – arrives, arrivals (abbreviation for *ankommer*)
apotek – pharmacy
aquavit – a potent, vodka-like spirit
ateljé – gallery, studio
avg – departs, departures (abbreviation for *avgång*)
avgift – payment, fee (seen on parking signs)
avhämtning – takeaway

bad – swimming pool, bathing place or bathroom
bakfickan – literally 'back pocket'; a low-profile eatery usually associated with a gourmet restaurant
bankautomat – cash machine, ATM
barn – child
bastu – sauna
bensin – petrol, gas
berg – mountain
bibliotek – library
bil – car
biljet – ticket
biljetautomat – ticket machines (eg for street parking)
biluthyrning – car hire
bio, biograf – cinema
björn – bear
bokhandel – bookshop
bro – bridge
bruk – factory, mill, works
bryggeri – brewery
buss – bus
busshållplats – bus stop
butik – shop
båt – boat

campingplats – camping ground
centrum – town centre
cykel – bicycle

dag – day
dagens rätt – daily special, usually on lunchtime menus
dal – valley
diskotek – disco
domkyrka – cathedral
drottning – queen
dubbelrum – double room
duodji – Sami handicraft
dusch – shower
dygn – a 24-hour period
dygnet runt – around the clock
dygnskort – a daily transport pass, valid for 24 hours

ej – not
enkelrum – single room
exkl – excluded (abbreviation)
expedition – office

fabrik – factory
fest – party, festival
fika – coffee and cake
fjäll – mountain
fjällstation – mountain lodge
fjällstugor – mountain huts
fjärd – fjord, drowned glacial valley
flod – large river
flyg – aeroplane
flygbuss – airport bus
flygplats – airport
folkdräkt – folk dress
folkhemmet – welfare state
fr o m – from and including (abbreviation used in timetables)
friluft – open-air
frukost – breakfast
fyr – lighthouse
fågel – bird
färja – ferry
färjeläge – ferry quay
fästning – fort, fortress
förbjuden – forbidden, prohibited
förbund – union, association
förening – organisation, association
förlag – company

galleri, galleria – shopping mall
gamla staden, gamla stan – the 'old town', the historical part of a city or town
gammal, gamla – old
gatan – street (often abbreviated to 'g')
gatukök – literally 'street kitchen'; kiosk, stall or grill selling fast food
glaciär – glacier
grotta – grotto, cave
grundskolan – comprehensive school
gruva – mine
gräns – border
gymnasieskolan – upper secondary school
gård – yard, farm, estate
gästgiveri – guesthouse
gästhamn – 'guest harbour', where visiting yachts can berth
gästhem, gästhus – guesthouse

hamn – harbour
hav – sea
hembygdsgård – open-air museum, usually old farmhouse buildings
hemslöjd – handicraft
hiss – lift, elevator
hittegods – lost property
hotell – hotel
hund – dog
hus – house
husmanskost – homely Swedish fare; what you would expect cooked at home when you were a (Swedish) child
hytt – cabin (especially on a boat)
hällristningar – rock carvings
hälsocentral – health clinic
höst – autumn

i – in
i morgon – tomorrow
idrottsplats – sports venue, stadium
inkl – included (abbreviation of *inklusive*)
inte – not
is – ice
ishall – ice hockey stadium

joik – see *yoik*
jul – Christmas
järnvägsstation – train station

kaj – quay
kanot – canoe
kanotuthyrning – canoe hire
karta – map
Kartförlaget – State Mapping Agency (sales division)
klockan – o'clock, the time

klocktorn – bell tower
kloster – monastery
kommun – municipality
konditori – baker and confectioner (often with an attached cafe)
konst – art
kontor – office
kort – card
kreditkort – credit card
krog – pub, restaurant (or both)
krona (kronor) – the Swedish currency unit
kulle (kullar) – hill (hills)
kung – king
kust – coast
kväll – evening
kyrka – church
kyrkogård – graveyard
kåta – tepee-shaped Sami hut
källare – cellar, vault
kök – kitchen

lagom – sufficient, just right
landskap – province, landscape
lavin – avalanche
lilla – lesser, little
linbana – chairlift
lo – lynx
loppis – secondhand goods (eg as found at flea markets)
län – county
Länstrafiken – public transport network of a *län*

magasin – store (usually a department store), warehouse
mat – food
medlem – member
Midsommardag – Midsummer's Day; first Saturday after 21 June (the main celebrations take place on Midsummer's Eve)
miljö – environment, atmosphere
MOMS – value added tax (sales tax)
morgon – morning (but *i morgon* means tomorrow)
museet, museum – museum
mynt – coins
mynt tvätt – coin-operated laundry
målning – painting, artwork

natt – night
nattklubb – nightclub
naturcamping – camping site with a pleasant environment
naturistcamping – nudist colony
naturreservat – nature reserve
Naturum – visitor centre at national park or nature reserve

Naturvårdsverket – Swedish Environmental Protection Agency (National Parks Authority)
nedre – lower
norr – north
norrsken – aurora borealis (northern lights)
ny – new
nyheter – news

obs! – take note, important
och – and
ordning och reda – orderliness

palats – palace
pendeltåg – commuter train
pensionat – pension, guesthouse
P-hus – multistorey car park
polarcirkeln – Arctic Circle, latitude N66°32′
polis – police
pris, prislista – price, price list
på – on, in
påsk – Easter

raukar – limestone formations
ren – reindeer
resebyrå – travel agent
restaurang – restaurant
RFSL – Riksförbundet för Sexuellt Likaberättigande (national gay organisation)
riksdag – parliament
rum – room
rådhus – town hall
rökning förbjuden – no smoking

SAS – Scandinavian Airlines Systems
Schlager – Catchy, camp, highly melodic pop tunes that are big on sentimentality, and commonly featured at the Eurovision Song Contest
simhall – swimming pool
sjukhus – hospital
självservering – self-service
sjö – lake, sea
skog – forest
skål! – cheers!
skärgård – archipelago
slott – castle, manor house
smörgås – sandwich
smörgåsbord – Swedish buffet
snabbtvätt – quick wash (at laundrette)
snaps – distilled alcoholic beverage drunk as a shot
snö – snow
sommar – summer
sovsal – dormitory
spårvagn – tram
stark – strong

statsminister – prime minister
STF – Svenska Turistföreningen (Swedish Touring Association)
stor, stora – big or large
stortorget – main square
strand – beach
stuga (sg), stugor/na (pl) – cabin
stugby – chalet park; small village of cabins
städning – room cleaning
sund – sound
svensk – Swedish
Sverige – Sweden
SVIF – Sveriges Vandrarhem i Förening; hostelling association
Systembolaget – state-owned liquor store
säng – bed
söder – south

t o m – until and including (till och med)
tandläkare – dentist
teater – theatre
telefon kort – telephone card
tid – time
tidtabell – timetable
toalett – toilet
tomte – mythical gnomelike creature; often associated with Christmas
torg, torget – town square
torn – tower
trappe – stairs
trädgård – garden open to the public
tull – customs
tunnelbana, T-bana – underground railway, metro
turistbyrå – tourist office
tåg – train
tågplus – combined train and bus ticket
tält – tent

uteservering – outdoor eating area
uthyrningsfirma – hire company

vandrarhem – hostel
vattenfall – waterfall (also the name of a Swedish power company)
vecka – week
vik – bay, inlet
vinter – winter
vuxen – adult
vår – spring
vårdcentral – hospital
väg – road
vänthall, väntrum, väntsal – waiting room
värdekort, värdebevis – value card; a refillable travel pass
värdshus – inn, restaurant

väst – west (abbreviated to 'v')
västra – western
växel – switchboard, money exchange

wärdshus – inn

yoik – a type of traditional Sami singing (also *joik*)

å – stream, creek, river
år – year

älg – elk
älv – river

ö – island
öl – beer
öppettider – opening hours
öst – east (abbreviated to 'ö')
östra – eastern
övre – upper

The Authors

BECKY OHLSEN
Coordinating Author, Central Sweden, Northern Sweden, Lappland & the Far North

Becky grew up with a thick book of Swedish fairy tales illustrated by John Bauer, so the deep, black forests of Norrland hold a particular fascination for her. When hiking through them, she's constantly on the lookout for *tomtes* and changelings, green-haired witches and moss-covered trolls (which, to the untrained eye, look just like enormous rocks). Though raised in Colorado, Becky has been a frequent explorer of Sweden since childhood, while visiting her grandparents in Stockholm and her great-aunt in Härnösand. She loves the music of the Swedish language, although she can't really dance to it. She loves herring and gravlax, Swedish potatoes and *aquavit*. But mostly she loves getting lost in those forests, among the trolls and *tomtes*.

CRISTIAN BONETTO
Stockholm, Southeast Sweden, Southern Sweden, Southwest Sweden

Considering his soft spot for blondes, it's not surprising that Cristian Bonetto calls Sweden his 'Nordic nirvana'. Despite his many returns, the crush is yet to mellow; nor is his fondness for *glögg* and Swedish pop. Born and bred in Australia, the reformed TV-soap scribe is smitten with Sweden's sense of space, its enlightened attitudes and its fascination with the new. Cristian's musings on Sweden have appeared in both Australian and UK magazines and he is also the author of *Stockholm Encounter*. When he's not scouring Nordic streets for the next big thing, you might find Cristian in his home town of Melbourne, listening to his first ever album, ABBA's *Arrival*. Cristian also wrote the Culture and Food & Drink chapters in this guide.

Behind the Scenes

THIS BOOK

This 4th edition of *Sweden* was written and updated by Becky Ohlsen and Cristian Bonetto. Becky Ohlsen and Fran Parnell worked on the previous edition, which was based on the 2nd edition written by Carolyn Bain and Graeme Cornwallis. This guidebook was commissioned in Lonely Planet's London office, and produced by the following:

Commissioning Editors Jo Potts, Fiona Buchan, Emma Gilmour

Coordinating Editors Victoria Harrison, Pete Cruttenden

Coordinating Cartographer Tony Fankhauser

Coordinating Layout Designer Pablo Gastar

Senior Editors Helen Christinis, Katie Lynch

Managing Cartographers Mark Griffiths, Shahara Ahmed

Managing Layout Designer Laura Jane

Assisting Editor Gabbi Stefanos

Assisting Cartographers Barbara Benson, Fatima Basic

Cover Designer Mary Nelson Parker

Project Managers Chris Girdler, Craig Kilburn

Language Content Coordinator Quentin Frayne

Thanks to Lucy Birchley, Daniel Corbett, Sally Darmody, Adriana Mammarella, Trent Paton, Andy Rojas, Wibowo Rusli, Jacqui Saunders, Herman So

THANKS
BECKY OHLSEN

Thanks to co-author Cristian Bonetto and to Fran Parnell, co-author of the previous edition; Lonely Planet commissioning editors Emma Gilmour, Fiona Buchan and Jo Potts; my frequent co-explorers Joel and Christina Ohlsen and Karl, Natalie and Clara Ohlsen; Mormor Elisabeth Odeen, Kristina Björholm and Captain Joe Eriksson; Matt and Lindy in Tärnaby; Jannike Åhlund in Fårö; the awesome librarians in Rättvik who helped me find out more about the Mörksuggan; the commander of the paint-ball war in Härnösand who rescued us from certain discomfort; the bartender in Gävle who let me watch the Moto GP race on TV; and the cyclist who shared his breakfast at Björkvatten youth hostel.

CRISTIAN BONETTO

Thanks to co-author Becky Ohlsen, and Fran Parnell, co-author of the previous edition. In-house, a big thanks to Emma Gilmour, Fiona Buchan, Jo Potts, Victoria Harrison, Gabbi Stefanos, Mark Griffiths and his cartography crew. On the road, *tack så mycket* to Penny Christodoulides, Anders Cato, Ann-Charlotte Jönsson, Ulrika Palmblad,

---

THE LONELY PLANET STORY

Fresh from an epic journey across Europe, Asia and Australia in 1972, Tony and Maureen Wheeler sat at their kitchen table stapling together notes. The first Lonely Planet guidebook, *Across Asia on the Cheap*, was born.

Travellers snapped up the guides. Inspired by their success, the Wheelers began publishing books to Southeast Asia, India and beyond. Demand was prodigious, and the Wheelers expanded the business rapidly to keep up. Over the years, Lonely Planet extended its coverage to every country and into the virtual world via lonelyplanet.com and the Thorn Tree message board.

As Lonely Planet became a globally loved brand, Tony and Maureen received several offers for the company. But it wasn't until 2007 that they found a partner whom they trusted to remain true to the company's principles of travelling widely, treading lightly and giving sustainably. In October of that year, BBC Worldwide acquired a 75% share in the company, pledging to uphold Lonely Planet's commitment to independent travel, trustworthy advice and editorial independence.

Today, Lonely Planet has offices in Melbourne, London and Oakland, with over 500 staff members and 300 authors. Tony and Maureen are still actively involved with Lonely Planet. They're travelling more often than ever, and they're devoting their spare time to charitable projects. And the company is still driven by the philosophy of *Across Asia on the Cheap*: 'All you've got to do is decide to go and the hardest part is over. So go!'

Petter Lundgren, Madelaine Possman, Tia Lindström, Tove Råberg, Malin Persson, Daniel Eriksson, Karin Stenmar, Annika Axelsson, Anna Reimegård, Maria Hanseblad, Matilda Lindvall, Carolina Falkholt (aka Blue), Alexandra Pascalidou, Anna Lindahl, Mathias Dahlgren, Ragnar Olofsson, Camilla Bäckman, Neil Stewart, Andreas Jemn, the team at Röda Sten in Göteborg, Theodore Bergström and family, Jan Erkinantti, Hulya Baysal, Linda Kante, Eleisha Mullane, Lia Sandberg, Cameron Macintosh, the wonderful tourist office staff who helped out, and the many Swedes who spoilt me with their insight and hospitality. Last, but never least, a huge *puss och kram* to my very patient family and friends.

OUR READERS

Many thanks to the travellers who used the last edition and wrote to us with helpful hints, useful advice and interesting anecdotes:

John Adolfsson, Johan Ahlström, Jee Sung Ahn, Shannon Andrus, Christel Bockting, Sarah Burston, Caroline Coombes, Petra Cyganski, Niklas Damm, Edwin Deventer, Lars Doyer, Stian Eriksen, Robert Gerzon, Not Given, Stéphane Henriod, Lisanne Imhof, Adrian Jones, Esther Jones, Anne Juhl, Alex Kim, Vlastimil Koncel, Pepijn Lemmens, Ulf Lowhagen, Barbro Lowhangen, Luke Lundmark, Shad Magno, Ruth Mair, Ellen Mattisson, Bill Mcginn, Asa Melander, Jo Middleton, Kris Oreskov, Alan Pearson, Julia Roberts, Fee Romein, Ankie Rutgersson, Nathan Slowinski, Jenny Sundqvist, Annemieke Van Den Dool, Lisette Van Eijk, Harry Van Kints, Anton Van Veen, Lukas Wampfler, James Welsh, Johan Wikland, Redmar Woudstra.

ACKNOWLEDGMENTS

Many thanks to the following for the use of their content:

Globe on title page ©Mountain High Maps 1993 Digital Wisdom, Inc.

Internal photographs Pixonnet.com/Alamy p98 (#1); Bryan & Cherry Alexander/Alamy p100 (#1). All other photographs by Lonely PlanetImages, and by Anders Blomqvist p93 (#1), p94 (#1), p99 (#2); Graeme Cornwallis p95 (#2); Jonathan Smith p96 (#1); Dennis Johnson p97 (#2); Holger Leue p97 (#3); Christian Aslund p100 (#2).

All images are the copyright of the photographers unless otherwise indicated. Many of the images in this guide are available for licensing from Lonely Planet Images: www.lonelyplanetimages.com.

SEND US YOUR FEEDBACK

We love to hear from travellers – your comments keep us on our toes and help make our books better. Our well-travelled team reads every word on what you loved or loathed about this book. Although we cannot reply individually to postal submissions, we always guarantee that your feedback goes straight to the appropriate authors, in time for the next edition. Each person who sends us information is thanked in the next edition – and the most useful submissions are rewarded with a free book.

To send us your updates – and find out about Lonely Planet events, newsletters and travel news – visit our award-winning website: **lonelyplanet.com/contact**.

Note: we may edit, reproduce and incorporate your comments in Lonely Planet products such as guidebooks, websites and digital products, so let us know if you don't want your comments reproduced or your name acknowledged. For a copy of our privacy policy visit lonelyplanet.com/privacy.

Index

000 Map pages
000 Photograph pages

NOTE

The Swedish letters å, ä and ö
fall at the end of the alphabet.

INDEX

INDEX

> **NOTE**
> The Swedish letters å, ä and ö fall at the end of the alphabet.

NOTE
The Swedish letters å, ä and ö fall at the end of the alphabet.

INDEX

INDEX

INDEX

NOTE

The Swedish letters å, ä and ö
fall at the end of the alphabet.

INDEX

NOTE
The Swedish letters å, ä and ö
fall at the end of the alphabet.

GreenDex

Researching this guidebook we discovered many hostels, mountain lodges and hotels, cafes, restaurants and attractions demonstrating a commitment to sustainability, and we take great pleasure in highlighting some of them here. We've selected places to eat that support local producers or champion organic foods. We've focused on sights and attractions that encourage a respectful attitude toward nature and that value the country's indigenous history. We've listed accommodation deemed to be environmentally friendly, demonstrating, for example, a commitment to recycling or energy conservation (and they've got to be a great place to stay, too). And Sweden's rich natural landscape means there are a variety of 'green' attractions and activities to choose from. If you want to learn more about how it all works and what makes something 'green', see the Getting Started chapter (p17). To do your part, check out www.lonelyplanet.com/responsibletravel for some ideas. And if you want to add to the list, or if you disagree with our choices, email talk2us@lonelyplanet.com.au and set us straight for next time.

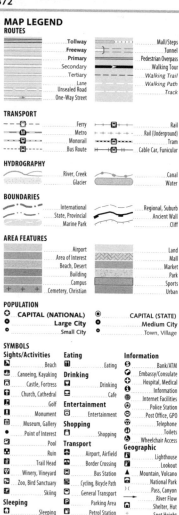

MAP LEGEND
ROUTES
Tollway
Freeway
Primary
Secondary
Tertiary
Lane
Unsealed Road
One-Way Street
Mall/Steps
Tunnel
Pedestrian Overpass
Walking Tour
Walking Trail
Walking Path
Track

TRANSPORT
Ferry
Metro
Monorail
Bus Route
Rail
Rail (Underground)
Tram
Cable Car, Funicular

HYDROGRAPHY
River, Creek
Glacier
Canal
Water

BOUNDARIES
International
State, Provincial
Marine Park
Regional, Suburb
Ancient Wall
Cliff

AREA FEATURES
Airport
Area of Interest
Beach, Desert
Building
Campus
Cemetery, Christian
Land
Mall
Market
Park
Sports
Urban

POPULATION
CAPITAL (NATIONAL)
Large City
Small City
CAPITAL (STATE)
Medium City
Town, Village

SYMBOLS
Sights/Activities
Beach
Canoeing, Kayaking
Castle, Fortress
Church, Cathedral
Golf
Monument
Museum, Gallery
Point of Interest
Pool
Ruin
Trail Head
Winery, Vineyard
Zoo, Bird Sanctuary
Skiing

Sleeping
Sleeping
Camping

Eating
Eating

Drinking
Drinking
Cafe

Entertainment
Entertainment

Shopping
Shopping

Transport
Airport, Airfield
Border Crossing
Bus Station
Cycling, Bicycle Path
General Transport
Parking Area
Petrol Station
Taxi Rank

Information
Bank/ATM
Embassy/Consulate
Hospital, Medical
Information
Internet Facilities
Police Station
Post Office, GPO
Telephone
Toilets
Wheelchair Access

Geographic
Lighthouse
Lookout
Mountain, Volcano
National Park
Pass, Canyon
River Flow
Shelter, Hut
Spot Height
Waterfall

LONELY PLANET OFFICES

Australia
Head Office
Locked Bag 1, Footscray, Victoria 3011
☎ 03 8379 8000, fax 03 8379 8111
talk2us@lonelyplanet.com.au

USA
150 Linden St, Oakland, CA 94607
☎ 510 250 6400, toll free 800 275 8555
fax 510 893 8572
info@lonelyplanet.com

UK
2nd fl, 186 City Rd,
London EC1V 2NT
☎ 020 7106 2100, fax 020 7106 2101
go@lonelyplanet.co.uk

Published by Lonely Planet Publications Pty Ltd
ABN 36 005 607 983

© Lonely Planet Publications Pty Ltd 2009

© photographers as indicated 2009

Cover photograph: Fishing village, Bohuslän coast, Sweden, Jeppe Wikstrom/Getty Images. Many of the images in this guide are available for licensing from Lonely Planet Images: www.lonelyplanetimages.com.

Printed through Colorcraft Ltd, Hong Kong.
Printed in China.

Lonely Planet and the Lonely Planet logo are trademarks of Lonely Planet and are registered in the US Patent and Trademark Office and in other countries.

Lonely Planet does not allow its name or logo to be appropriated by commercial establishments, such as retailers, restaurants or hotels. Please let us know of any misuses: www.lonelyplanet.com/ip.

Although the authors and Lonely Planet have taken all reasonable care in preparing this book, we make no warranty about the accuracy or completeness of its content and, to the maximum extent permitted, disclaim all liability arising from its use.

MIX
Paper from responsible sources
FSC™ C021741
www.fsc.org